Records of Clarke County Georgia

1801-1892

In the Georgia Department of Archives & History

Compiled by:

Robert Scott Davis

Southern Historical Press, Inc.
Greenville, South Carolina

Please direct all correspondence and orders to:

www.southernhistoricalpress.com
or
SOUTHERN HISTORICAL PRESS, Inc.
PO BOX 1267
375 West Broad Street
Greenville, SC 29601
southernhistoricalpress@gmail.com

ISBN #0-89308-485-9

Printed in the United States of America

Dedicated To:

Mary Bondurant Warren

for her many valuable contributions to American Genealogy

Athens, Ga. in the painting "View From Carr's Hill" by George Cooke. Used courtesey of the Hargrett Rare Book Manuscripts Library, which owns the original.

TABLE OF CONTENTS

Page

Introduction: Clarke County, Georgia

PART I: LOOSE ORIGINAL RECORDS (RECORD GROUP 129)

I. Inventory of Original Estate Records, 1801-1923 5

II. List of Court Case Files of the Interior Court, 1805-1895 23

III. Description of the Miscellaneous Files, 1800-1925 65

PART II: ABSTRACTS FROM THE MISCELLANEOUS FILES (RG 129-2-4)

IV. Records in Miscellaneous Box 1 71

V. Records in Miscellaneous Box 2 79

VI. Civil War Era Records in Miscellaneous Box 2 83

VII. Militia Records, 1804-1830's, in Miscellaneous Box 2 103

VIII. Records in Miscellaneous Box 3 131

IX. Poor School Records, 1823 & 1837 133

PART III: ORIGINAL MARRIAGE RECORDS (RG 129-2-1)

X. 1804-1850's 137

PART IV: MICROFILMED RECORDS

XI. Inventory of County Records on Microfilm at the Georgia Archives 189

XII. Militia Records from Duke University, 1804-1820's 201

APPENDIX A: A missing Page from the 1840 Census of Clarke County 213

APPENDIX B: Land Court Minutes, 1803-1832 213

APPENDIX C: Some Clarke County Deaths, 1834-1877 219

INTRODUCTION: CLARKE COUNTY, GEORGIA

Clarke County, named for General Elijah Clarke (1742-1799) of Georgia, was created by Act of December 5, 1801 from Jackson County, which was itself created from Franklin County by Act of February 11, 1796 and Franklin County was created from newly ceded Indian lands by Act of February 24, 1784. A map of the original boundary between Jackson and Clarke counties, dated December 24, 1801, is in the Georgia Surveyor General Department on page 0 of the "County Line Disputes". This area was officially settled by whites and blacks beginning in 1783 through Georgia's headright and bounty land grant system although settlement had taken place there illegally much earlier. Records of Georgia headright and bounty grants are in the Georgia Surveyor General Department, 330 Capitol Ave SE, Atlanta, GA. 30334. See Index to Headright and Bounty Grants of Georgia, 1756-1909 (1968) and E. Merton Coulter, "The Birth of a University, a Town, and a County," 46 (1962): 113-50, Georgia Historical Quarterly.

By acts of December 1, 1802 and December 9, 1807 additional territory was added to the south end of original Clarke County. Madison County was created from Clarke, Oglethorpe, Jackson, Franklin, and Elbert counties by Act of December 5, 1811. Minor boundary changes between Clarke County and Oglethorpe, Madison, Walton, and Jackson counties, usually only involving individual residences, have taken place over the years.

By Act of February 25, 1875, Oconee County was created from Clarke County, leaving Clarke County the smallest county in land area in Georgia. Watkinsville, which had been the county seat of Clarke County, then became the county seat of Oconee County and Athens, home of the University of Georgia, became the new county seat of Clarke County. See E. Merton Coulter, "The Politics of Dividing a Georgia County: Oconee from Clarke," Georgia Historical Quarterly 57 (1973): 475-92.

A file of the boundary changes of Clarke County is in the Georgia Surveyor General Department.

Books useful in Clarke County Research: For a more extensive bibliography see James E. Dorsey, Georgia Genealogy and Local History: a Bibliography (Spartanburg: Reprint Co., 1983).

Robert P. Brooks, A Brief History of the 1st Methodist Church, Athens, Ga. (Athens: the author, 1924).

Emanuel Church, 100 Years of Life (Athens, the author, 1943).

1st Presbyterian Church, The Exercises Commemorating the Centennial of the 1st Presbyterian Church of Athens (Athens: the author, 1920).

Ga. Chapters, DAR Historical Collections 5 vols. (1926; rep. ed. Easley, SC.: Southern Historical Press, 1968). (Vol. 1, pp. 15-26, includes lists of names in the minutes of superior court, lists of jurors, wills, & marriages.)

Walter B. Hill, Rural Survey of Clarke Co., Ga., With Special Reference to the Negroes (Athens: Univ. of Ga. Press, 1916).

Augustus L. Hull, Annals of Athens, Ga., 1801-1901 (1879; rep. ed. Danielsville: Heritage Papers, 1966).

Ernest C. Hynds, Antebellum Athens & Clarke Co., GA. (Athens: Univ. of Ga. Press, 1974).

Elsa A. Johnson, History of the Tuckston Methodist Church, Athens, Ga. (Athens: the author, 1960).

Frances T. Long, The Negroes of Clarke Co., Ga., During the Great War (Athens: Univ. of Ga. Press, 1919).

Silas E. Lucas, Some Ga. County Records 3 vols. (Easley, S.C.:

Southern Historical Press, 1977). (Vol. 2, pp.1-41, includes wills, 1803-1842; administrators & Guardians bonds, 1801-1825; & marriages, 1807-1821.)

Charlotte T. Marshall, *Oconee Hill Cemetery: Tombstone Inscriptions* (Athens: Athens Historical Society, 1971).

Edward B. Mell, *A Short History of the Athens Baptist Church, Now the 1st Baptist Church of Athens, 1830-1953* (Athens: the author, 1954).

Sylvanus Morris et al., *History of Athens & Clarke Co.* (Athens: H.J. Rowe Pub. Co., 1923).

Frances W. Reid & Mary B. Warren, *Mars Hill Baptist Church* (constituted 1799) *Clarke-Oconee Co., Ga.* (Athens: Heritage Papers, 1966).

Peter E. Schinkel, "The Negro in Athens & Clarke Co., 1872-1900," (Masters Thesis, Univ. of Ga., 1971).

John F. Stegemen, *These Men She Gave: Civil War Diary of Athens, Ga.* (Athens: Univ. of Ga. Press, 1964).

Charles M. Straham, *Clarke Co., Ga., & the City of Athens* (Atlanta: Chas. P. Bird, 1893).

R. J. Taylor, Jr. Foundation, *Index to Georgia Tax Digests, 1789-1817* (5 vols. 1986).

Mary Warren, *Marriage Book A* (*1805-1821*) *Clarke Co., Ga. Including Previously Unrecorded Marr. Licenses Found in the Office of the Ordinary* (Danielsville: Heritage Papers, 1966).

Mary Warren, *Jackson Street Cemetery, Original City Cemetery of Athens, Ga.: Tombstone Inscriptions & Obituaries* (Athens: Heritage Papers, 1966).

Mary Warren, *Marriages & Deaths From Extant Georgia Newspapers* (2 vols.) Danielsville: Heritage Papers, 1968 and 1972. Covers 1763-1829.

The Athens Historical Society publishes papers on Athens history in their series *Papers of the Athens Historical Society*. Archives has "History of Clarke Co. by Its People" on microfilm reel 18-80, 18-59, 76-50, 18-71, and 18-72.

PART 1: LOOSE ORIGINAL RECORDS (RECORD GROUP 129)

1. Estate Records, 1801-1923 (Record Group 129-2-6)

This series consists of miscellaneous unbound arranged estate records filed with the Clarke County Court of Ordinary (now Probate Court). These papers were submitted by administrators or executors of estates as required by law to document the settling of the estates of deceased citizens.

The most commonly found documents are administrator's bonds, inventories and appraisements of estates and sale bills. Also included in some cases are guardian's bonds, letters of administration, orders of dismission of administrators, orders to sell lands, returns of widow's support, probated wills (no originals) and receipts taken by an administrator or executor when he made payments in settling an estate.

The word "ward" beside an individual's name indicated that person was a minor or an adult in need of guardianship.

The records are arranged alphabetically by the surname of the deceased or individual to whom a guardianship was issued. Please see the following shelf list for names of the deceased or individuals to whom a guardianship was issued and the inclusive dates of the documents.

Aaron, Lodie B., (formerly Bradley), (ward)	1916
Aaron, Samuel T.	1866
Aaron, W.M., (children of)	1904-05
Abbott, D.Q.	1907
Abney, Martin J., (children of)	1909-10
Adair, Joseph M.	1859-61
Adams, Florida V.	1885-1890
Adams, John	1824-35
Adams, John Maxie	1877
Adams, Mrs. Mary M.	1877
Adams, Nolie G.H. (ward) (see John Maxie Adams)	1877
Adams, Samuel J.	1907
Adams, Mrs. Susan	1902
Adams, William A.	1842
Adams, William C.	1843
Adams, W.B.P.	1835
Adams, William C.	1826-27
Aiken-Betsey	1853
Aiken, Frances	1845
Aiken-Henry M. (children of)	1876-82
Aiken-Polly	1845-46
Aiken-Rhoda	1857
Aiken-Tabitha	1858-59
Akin-James	1817-18
Akridge-Calvin Walker (ward)	1860-71
Akridge-Ezekiel	1843-47
Akridge-Troup	1909-10
Akridge, Virgil W.	1850-59
Albitz, Nancy J.	1898-99
Alexander, John	1828
Alexander, John (ward)	1833
Alexander, Joseph	1892-97
Alexander, Mary E. (children of)	1894
Alexander, Samuel P. (ward)	1841
Alexander, W.S. (children of)	1890
Allen, James (children of)	1817-19
Allen, Margaret	1912
Allen, Mose	1916
Allen, William M.	1909
Allgood, James (children of)	1901
Allgood, James F.	1911-12
Alliston, Charles (ward)	1865-66
Alred, Jonathan	1823-26
Amis, J.W.	1905-06
Amis, J.W. (children of)	1905
Anderson, Albert Elmers (ward)	1854
Anderson, Amanda	1917
Anderson, Charles E.H. (ward)	1851
Anderson, Emery F. (ward)	1843
Anderson, Frances E.	1849-61
Anderson, J.H.	1908
Anderson, James	1816
Anderson, James C.	1837-39
Anderson, William W.	1849
Anderson, William W. (ward)	1843
Anesley, Madison (ward)	1841
Anthony, Cicero H. (children of)	1875
Anthony, Robert (ward)	1906
Appling, Otho H.	1816
Appling, Walter A. (children of)	1843-45
Appling, William	1818
Archer, Cicero S.	1894-96
Archer, George A.	1865
Archer, Nina N.	1904-09
Arnold, Charles W.	1886-87
Arnold, Clarence B. (ward)	1905-06
Arnold, Daniel	1878-79
Arnold, Mary V.	1886-89
Arthur, Caleb	1845-46

Arthur, Mary (ward)	1907-10
Arze, Barnardo J.	1860-63
Ash, John E.	1891-92
Ash, Millie M. (ward)	1892
Ash, W.C. (children of)	1903
Ashford, William H.	1871-84
Ashford, William H. (children of)	1871-73
Askew, Josiah F.	1848-49
Aspy, Joseph	1862
Atkinson, Arthur C.	1828
Atkisson, Fannie A.H.	1890
Artree, Alexander Jr.	1906
Autry, Mary Cleo	1905
Aycock, Isaac P.	1845
Aycock, James	1803-10
Aycock, James (orphans of)	1804-09
Bacon, Robert	1888
Bailey, George Albon	1915
Bailey, Lula K.	1915
Bailey, William (children of)	1872-84
Bailey, William W.	1908
Bailey, William W. (children of)	1908
Bailey, Wesley E. (children of)	1873-74
Baker, Chas (children of)	1908
Baker, John T.	1847-51
Baldwin, James J.	1884-87
Ball, William	1847
Bancroft, Edward (children of)	1896
Bancroft, George L.	1878
Bankston, Henry	1811-19
Bankston, Henry (children of)	1816
Bankston, Peter	1804-09
Bankston, William	1809-19
Barber, Arnie L. (ward)	1898
Barber, Greensby W.	1883-85
Barber, James	1847-49
Barber, R.C.	1920
Barber, Robert	1853-54
Barber, Sarah	1853-54
Barefield, Jemimah	1851
Barfield, Brown	1912
Barnard, Annis L.	1879
Barnard, Mollie (ward)	1883
Barnes, Henry Marshall	1863
Barnett, Caroline	1842
Barnett, Claborn	1879
Barnett, John	1811-16
Barnett, Lewis	1824-30
Barnett, Margaret Ann (ward)	1849
Barnett, Nathan	1827
Barnett, Zilla A. (ward)	1858-63
Barnhard, Frances Elizabeth	1869-80
Barrett, Benjamin H.	1825-29
Barrett, Joseph S. (ward)	1836
Barrett, William G.	1876
Barrett, William B. (children of)	1852-69
Barrow, Clara E.	1880
Barrow, David C. Sr.	1899
Barry, Frank	1897
Barry, Joseph M.	1895-1918
Barton, Caleb J.	1857
Barton, Gincy (ward)	1830
Barton, Rebecca	1867-71
Barwick, Stancil	1890-99
Bass, William F.	1863-66
Bass, William F. (children of)	1867
Battle, Milton A.	1852-54
Baxter, Eli L.	1862-70
Baxter, Mary	1869
Baxter, R.B. Jr.	1907
Baxter, Thomas W.	1844
Baynard, Ephraim M.	1866-79
Beal, Zephariah	1831-40
Beard, Moses	1837
Beard, Moses	1860-1911
Bearden, Aaron	1847
Bearden, Aaron	1890-92
Bearden, Richard	1831-33
Beasley, John A.	1845
Beasley, Marqarett (ward)	1856
Bedell, Pendleton	1842
Bedell, Robert (ward)	1848
Bell, Daniel C.	1840
Bellah, Moses	1809
Benedict, John A.	1899
Benedict, Jno A. (children of)	1903
Benedict, Mary Louise	1908
Benedict, S.R.	1914
Bennett, Nancy	1883
Bentley, M.A.	1911
Benton, Emma Dora (ward)	1890
Benton, Lloyd S.	1883-84
Benton, Mary C.	1901
Benton, William L.	1878
Benton, William M.	1888
Benard, (children of)	1899
Berrian, Martha P. (ward)	1838
Berry, John (children of)	1837
Bertling, Jane E.	1886-90
Bertling, Marie Louise	1890-92
Bertling, Robert	1886
Betts, Z.H. (children of)	1895-1901
Biddle, Pendleton T. (children of)	1838
Biggers, Lucy E.	1883-84
Biggers, Mary	1879-80
Biggers, Nathan	1879-81
Biggs, Aaron	1815-34
Biggs, James P.	1863
Biggs, Joel	1809
Biggs, Willis J.	1858-63
Biggs, Willis J. (children of)	1860-71
Blair, Green	1889
Billups, Edward S.	1840-46
Billups, John	1864-72
Billups, Lucy Jane	1840
Billups, Robert R.	1836-43
Billups, William	1818
Binyon, Burton	1892
Bishop, Edward P.	1881-93

Bishop, Joseph 1884
Bishop, Mary C. 1885
Bishop, Thomas 1866
Blackmon, Mrs. E.M. 1912
Blair, J.C. (children of) 1908
Blair, Nathan P. 1891
Blair, Thomas 1893-94
Blakley, Samuel 1868-71
Blakinship, William 1810-14
Bloomfield, R.K. (children of) 1885
Bloomfield, Robert K. 1882-90
Boggs, Aaron 1855-56
Boggs, Harriet 1885
Boggs, John M. 1853-61
Boggs, Sarah Caroline (ward) 1857
Bohannan, Duncan (ward) 1818
Bohannan, Isaiah W.D. (ward) 1816
Bohannan, Wiley (children of) 1828-44
Bohannan, William 1815
Bohannan, William (ward) 1821
Boling, Samuel 1806-20
Bondurant, Mary J. 1897
Bone, Mildred 1884
Bonner, Allen 1827-33
Bonner, Allen (ward) 1835
Bonner, Frances E. (ward) 1833
Bonner, Junsha (ward) 1829
Bonner, Melvin 1883-84
Bonner, Thomas 1804-07
Bonner, William H. 1842-47
Booth, Mary F. 1885-1910
Booth, Walton H. (ward) 1838
Boram, George W. 1837
Borne, Daniell 1820
Bostick, Rebekah 1834-45
Bowen, Mary Jane (ward) 1844
Bowen, Uriah N. 1838
Bowling, Thomas 1810-16
Bowls, Thomas 1841
Boyd, Robert Jr. (ward) 1907
Boylston, Dubose (ward) 1909
Bradberry, Christopher C. 1868
Bradberry, Rutha 1868
Bradem, Lewis R. (ward) 1890
Bradford, Anna L. 1876-82
Bradley, Minnie (children of) 1911-17
Branch, Charity 1884
Branch, Dicey 1851-53
Branch, James C. 1869
Branch, William S. 1838-45
Brand, Malaciah (ward) 1811
Bray, Benjamin A. (children of) 1877-88
Brewer, Hundley 1822
Brewer, William (children of) 1818-29
Bridges, Arminda 1910
Bridges, Elizabeth 1884
Brightwell, Andrew J. (ward) 1835
Brightwell, Frances A. 1845
Brightwell, John 1835-44
Brightwell, John M. (ward) 1842
Brisco, John (children of) 1822
Brisco, Sallie (ward) 1897
Britt, Agnes (children of) 1837
Brittain, John 1891
Brittain, Thomas 1810-16
Broach, James 1809-16
Broadnax, William (children of) 1833
Brooks, Georgia 1914-15
Brooks, Lucile (ward) 1920
Brown, Bedford 1819-29
Brown, Betsy Ann 1811-18
Brown, Carter 1891-92
Brown, Dolly 1877
Brown, Earnest Stewart 1905
Brown, Elijah 1852-54
Brown, Frances (ward) 1855
Brown, Gary (children of) no date
Brown, George 1901
Brown, Hattie Lou (ward) 1887
Brown, Henry 1890
Brown, Jeremiah 1805-11
Brown, Jeremiah (children of) 1809
Brown, John B.J. (ward) 1855
Brown, Margaret (ward) 1887
Brown, Minor W. 1907-10
Brown, Minta 1914
Brown, Nellie 1913
Brown, Thomas 1805-23
Brown, Viny 1903-06
Browne, William M. 1882-86
Brownfield, Jincey (ward) 1806
Browndielf, John 1810-11
Browning, Francis H. & James H. 1848
Browning, John 1838-45
Browning, John (children of) 1839
Browning, Joshua 1807-47
Browning, Josiah 1882
Browning, Lucy Ann Susan (ward) 1841
Browning, Margaret 1840-45
Brumby, Ephraim R. (children of) 1884
Brumby, John W. (children of) 1887
Brumby, Lucy Lee (ward) 1890
Brumby, Richard T. 1875-83
Brunely, Trapier 1876
Brydie, Camilla (children of) 1909
Brydie, Eugene W. (children of) 1889
Buchannan, Charles J. 1866
Buchannan, Frances E. 1877-79
Buckhannan, Catherine 1905-06
Bugg, Sarah A. 1848
Bullock, Eliza S. 1899-01
Bullock, W.S. 1900-01
Burbank, E.L. 1897
Burger, Daniel N. (children of) 1853
Burger, John A. 1863

Name	Date
Burgess, Jonathan (children of)	1839
Burgess, Linton S. (ward)	1861-77
Burke, Theophilus	1823-27
Burke, Thomas A.	1878-85
Burke, Thomas (children of)	1880
Burnett, Bedford	1865-67
Burnett, Jeremiah	1822-24
Burnett, Margaret Ann (ward)	1849-53
Burroughs, B.W.N.	1892-1907
Burton, James M. (ward)	1844
Burton, Robert E. (ward)	1832
Butler, Cynthia D.	1863
Butler, E.L.	1860
Butler, John W. (children of)	1906
Butler, Lucy (ward)	1909
Bynum, Alfred	1839
Cabbell, Robert J.	1823-36
Cabbell, Robert W. (ward)	1836
Caffin, Patience	1866
Camak, Annie T. (ward)	1874-75
Camak, James	1847-75
Camak, James W.	1893-94
Camak, Lewis (ward)	1893-94
Camak, Margaret Ann (ward)	1850
Camak, Thomas (ward)	1850
Campbell, Charles D.	1892-93
Campbell, C.D. (ward)	1892
Campbell, Duncan G.	1829-31
Campbell, Jesse I. (ward)	1892
Camron, John Jr.	1816-17
Cannon, William (?)	no date
Carithers, Edy H.	1881-82
Carithers, Johnnie L. (ward)	1881-85
Carithers, Martha F.	1892-99
Carlton, Dr. J.B.	1881-82
Carnes, Thomas P.	1822-28
Carr, Elijah W.	1873
Caruthers, Edy H.	1881
Cary, Margaret	1905
Cary, Orlando	1816
Cash, Floyd	1890
Castleberry, Henry	1807-18
Cauterbury, Phillip	1834
Center, George W.	1876-78
Center, William M. (ward)	1878-81
Chaffin, Patience	1866-71
Chaffin, Lemuel (children of)	1838-46
Chancey, John	1861-83
Chancey, Saul J.	1895
Chandler, C.H.	1909
Chappell, Robert	1898
Chase, Alban	1867
Cheatham, Anthony R.	1832-41
Cheatham, Anthony R. (children of)	1832
Cheatham, C.L.	1909-10
Cheatham, Clifford W.	1873
Cheatham, E.S.	1910
Cheatham, John S.	1840
Cheatham, Laura	1853-65
Cheney, F.W. (children of)	1885-86
Cheney, Frances (children of)	1905
Cheney, Franklin W.	1892
Cheney, Lucas	1893
Cheney, Mary Louisa	1885-89
Cheney, Paul	1887-88
Cherry, William	1846
Chissom, Appleton (ward)	1832
Christy, Ida Laura (ward)	1904
Christy, John H.	1877
Church, Alonzo	1861-63
Clark, John M.	1855
Clark, Lucy (children of)	1809
Clark, William (children of)?	1814
Clayton, Augustin S.	1839-73
Clement, John	1816-18
Clifton, George	1840
Clifton, Young B.	1889
Clinch, Robert T.	1883-89
Clower, (children of)	1890
Coats, John G.	no date
Cobb, A.P.	1872
Cobb, Edwin Newton (ward)	1898
Cobb, Howell	1868-92
Cobb, Howell (children of)	1884
Cobb, Howell	1909-10
Cobb, Lamar	1907
Cobb, Lucy B.	1880
Cobb, Marion Thomas (ward)	1871-81
Cobb, Mary Ann	1869-1902
Cobb, Thomas R.R.	1860
Cock, Jack F.	1816-33
Cohn, Herman	1898-1901
Coile, James N.	1882
Coile, James N. (children of)	1883-89
Colbert, W.C.	1875
Colbert, William C. (children of)	1883
Colclough, John	1869
Colclough, John (children of)	1868-81
Cole, Josiah	1829-30
Cole, Sarissa B.	1900
Cole, Sarah	1857
Coleman, Clementine (ward)	1838
Coleman, Mary A. (children of)	1895
Collier, Thomas	1860-73
Collier, William	1849
Collins, Ellen, Mrs.	1902
Colly, George W.	1882
Colly, John	1848
Colt, John H.	1881-89
Compton, Lora A. (ward)	1885
Compton, Thomas M.	1889-92
Conger, Abijah	1866-68

Conger, Hedges T.	1836	Daniel, Jesse	1892-1903
Connell, Elizabeth	1909	Daniell, Asa B.	1848-56
Connor, Bolin (children of)	no date	Daniell, Francis M.	1865
Cook, Arthur (ward)	1892-93	Daniell, Henrietta	1863
Cook, F.W.C.	1865	Daniell, Jeremiah	1852
Cook, Hartwell	1813-73	Daniell, Josiah	1845-52
Cook, James W.	1858	Daniell, Josiah	1869-73
Cook, James W. (children of)	1858	Daniel, Josiah (children of)	1851-61
Cook, John W.	1857	Daniell, Josiah (ward)	1845
Cook, Kelin	1857	Daniell, Sarah	1868
Cook, Susan	1897	Daniell, Thomas M.	1876-79
Cook, William M. (children of)	1866-72	Daniell, William	1835-42
Cooper, Amelia	1860	Daniell, William B.	1864
Cosby, James R. (children of)	1867-79	Danielly, Elizabeth	1850
Couey, Lizzie A. (children of)	1890	Darby, James W.	1820
Cousons, John	1857-64	Darby, James W. (children of)	1821
Coussons, Thoams	1882-89	Darby, Julius G.	1903
Covington, Henry	1897-1902	Davenport, Mary D. (ward)	1866-69
Cox, Elizabeth M.	1860-64	Davenport, Nancy	1863
Cox, Richard	1837	Davis, Angeline	1884
Cox, Richard	1863-69	Davis, Emery (ward)	1897
Craft, Daniel. Sr.	1845-46	Davis, Emma M. (ward)	1885
Craft, Elijah	1869	Davis, Emmie (ward)	1878
Craig, Lewis S.	1852-56	Davis, Fuller	1890
Craig, Rebecca	1851	Davis, Madison	1902-04
Craig, Sally C.	1856-63	Davis, Marion T. (ward)	1885-87
Craig, William	1851	Davis, Milley Ann	1878-82
Crane, Charles A. (ward)	1866	Davis, Nancy A.	1878
Crane, Fanny T. (children of)	1892	Davis, Prior L.	1890
Crane, James R.	1912	Davis, William	1853
Crane, John R.	1887	Dawson, George M.	1853-59
Crane, Ross	1866-85	Dawson, Lucien W.	1866
Crawford, Frances Ann Dunkling	1820	Dawson, Sarah D.J. (ward)	1854
Crawford, H.H.	1896-97	Dean, John	1868-75
Crawford, John	1897-1903	Dean, Westly	1909
Crawford, John A.	1879	Dearing, Albin D.	1885
Crawford, John R.	1908-09	Dearing, Eugenia	1887
Crawford, Julia F.	1874-81	Dearing, Marcella	1867
Crawford, Susan	1871-75	Dearing, Margaret (ward)	1841
Crawford, Thomas	1871-85	Dearing, Thomas H.	1891-95
Crawford, Thomas (children of)	1877-87	Dearing, William	1887-95
Crenshaw, Daniel	1845-46	Deas, John (children of)	1894
Crenshaw, Zadock F.	1862-63	DeLacy, Henry M.	1870
Crews, John	1826-27	Delay, Josi-Ann	1921
Crow, Aarow	1866-70	Deloney, Rosa E.	1897-99
Crow, Margaret	1834-37	Deloney, William G.	1864
Crow, Stephen	1834-67	Delph, Natalie	1898
Croxton, James	1834-37	Demore, Nancy	1885
Culbertson, Jeremiah	1808-10	Demore, William R.	1879
Culbreath, Nancy	1809-16	Derricoate, Mike	1904
Culp, Henry T. (ward)	1882-1901	Deupree, Francina (ward)	1871-72
Culp, Peter	1892-1900	Deupree, Lucy D. (ward)	1872-73
Cumming, Elizabeth	1878	Deupree, Lucy Y.	1871-84
Cunningham, (children of)	1928	Dicken, Catherine (ward)	1874
		Dicken, Richard B.	1856-68
Dale, John M. (ward)	1889-1902	Dicken, Richard B. (children of)	1865
Dalton, Lewis O.	1835-36	Dicken, William	1861
Damron, Peter	1906	Dickerson, John N.	1847
Daniel, Duke A. (children of)	1894	Dixon, Floyd	1892
		Dixon/Dickson, Isaac	1880
		Dixon, Thomas	1819-22

Dobbins, William J.	1907
Dodson, Daniel	1841
Doggett, Chattin	1817
Doggett, Chattin, Jr.	1820
Doggett, George	1844-52
Doggett, Richard	1848
Doran, Anderson	1834-36
Dorsey, F.S.	1857
Dorsey, James P.	1875-90
Dorsey, William H.	1867
Doster, Francis M.	1864-71
Doublehead, Bird	1817
Dougherty, Charles (children of)	1815
Dougherty, Charles	1811-18
Dougherty, Charles	1854-58
Dougherty, Elizabeth	1858
Dougherty, Rebekah	1827
Douglas, Thomas	1807-10
Doyle, Patrick H.	1871
Dudley, Benjamin	1840
Duerden, P.H.	1935
Duke, Beverly A.	1833-34
Dunn, Leah	1892
Dunnahoo, James	1856-59
Durham, Abraham	1826-27
Durham, Cornelia	1874
Durham, Henry (children of)	1832
Durham, John	1814-15
Durham, Lindsey, Jr.	1858-59
Durham, Napoleon B.	1867-70
Durham, Samuel D.	1829
Durham, Samuel D.	1871-81
Durley, (children of)	1908
Ealy, Gad	1803
Early, Jacob	1828
Early, Sarah G.	1868-83
Easley, Roderick	1814-37
East, Silas	1868
Eberhart, Ann E.	1882-83
Eberhart, Edward P.	1905-07
Eberhart, John	1887-89
Echols, Emeline	1890
Echols, George	1892
Echols, Hannah	1873-74
Echols, Ida (ward)	1873-83
Echols, James	1825-26
Echols, Obadiah T.	1880-83
Echols, Obadiah T. (children of)	1881-88
Echols, Silas	1892
Edge, Frank G.	1890
Edge, Sarah	1898
Edge, Warren	1894
Edwards, Henry L.	1867-69
Edwards, Richard J.	1879
Edwards, Robert H.	1875
Edwards, Soloman	1844-54
Edwards, Susan E. (ward)	1846
Eidsen, Lewis	1871-93
Eidsen, Margaret (children of)	1894
Eidsen, John T.	1859-65
Elder, Asbury B.	1863-64
Elder, David, Sr.	1853-54
Elder, David G.	1862-63
Elder, David M.	1863
Elder, Edmonds	1875
Elder, Hartwell	1845-46
Elder, Henderson	1885
Elder, Howell	1840
Elder, John	1812-16
Elder, John (children of)	1812
Elder, Joseph M.	1852
Elder, Joseph M. (children of)	1844
Elder, Joshua Sr.	1850
Elder, Martha	1887
Elder, Philip T.	1854
Elder, Sterling	1825-32
Elder, Sterling	1850
Elder, Thomas P.	1858-61
Elder, Thomas P. (children of)	1864-72
Elder, William Y.	1858
Elliott, Sarah	1807-12
Epps, J. Milten	1894
Epps, Josephine	1893-94
Epps, Thoams N.	1854
Epps, Thomas N.	1863
Epps, William	1865-73
Espy, John	1846
Evans, Benjamin J.	1851-58
Evans, John	1869-86
Evans, Lucius P. (ward)	1863-64
Evans, Sallie E. (ward)	1862-63
Everett, Sherod	1841-58
Ewing, James D.	1826-30
Ewing, Samuel	1807-12
Fambrough, Anderson	1815-23
Fambrough, Anderson (children of)	1815-27
Fambrough, James M. (ward)	1857
Fambrough, James (children of)	1861
Fambrough, John R.	1868
Fambrough, William A.	1854-68
Fellows, Almira C. (ward)	1897
Fellows, Mary Ann	1879-82
Fellows, George P.	1875-76
Felton, R.J.	1916
Few, Hill	1880-82
Few, Martha A.	1898
Few, Martha (children of)	1898
Finch, William	1812
Flippin, Mary	1816
Flournoy, (children of)	1864
Flournoy, Mary M.	1830
Flournoy, Robert	1827
Flournoy, Robert (children of)	1830-38
Floyd, Benjamin (children of)	1854
Floyd, Wilhilmind H.	1869-70
Foster, Emily (ward)	1840
Foster, John	1826-32
Foster, John (children of)	1832
Fowler, Cody	1852-70
Fowler, Ida	1879
Fowler, Marvin	1893
Frederick, Felix	1874
Frederick, Felis (children of)	1874

Freeman, Calthriss	1837
Freeman, John	1840
Freeman, Samuel	1875-77
Freeman, Samuel (children of)	1876-78
Fulcher, James	1885-86
Fulcher, Samuel	1890-95
Fullwood, Robert	1822
Fulton, Margarett J. (ward)	1832
Galloway, James	1900
Gamble, William	1815
Gann, Alex	1896
Gann, Ann (ward)	1818
Gann, David	1899
Gann, John Sr.	1856-59
Gann, Mrs. Malenda	1911
Gann, William Sr.	1852
Gannet, Jeff	1912
Gantt, Frances L.	1878
Garfield, Thomas B.	1928
Garner, Elijah	1827-28
Garner, Eliza (ward)	1834
Garner, Jael	1832-34
Garner, Presley	1827
Garner, Pressley (ward)	1837-51
Garret, John	1811
Garrett, Riley	1884-94
Garrison, J.D.	1911
Gates, Lucy	1915
Gauraine, Mary Antoinette	1819
Gean, Anna	1899
Gean, Nancy B.	1890-91
Gentry, Elisha	1804-12
George, Bailey	1816-27
George, Bailey (children of)	1819-27
George, Maria	1915
George, Travis	1807-14
Gerarden, Adelaide V.	1864-69
Gerardin, John	1838-46
Gerdine, John	1903-04
Gerdine, Linton (ward)	1903
Gerdine, Marion C. (ward)	1903
Gerdine, Mary E. (ward)	1906
Gerdine, Sarah H. (ward)	1903-08
Gerdine, Susan G.	1923
Giles, Maj (ward)	1891
Gilleland, Henderson	1868-70
Gilleland, Mary F.	1896
Gilleland, William	1868
Gilleland, William A.	1891
Glascom, Daniel	1891
Glassin, Henry (ward)	1813
Glenn, Nicholas Jr.	1866-73
Glenn, Robt. L. (ward)	1902
Gober, Wesley B.	1862-63
Gober, William H.	1874
Goff, Nancy J.	1866-69
Golding, Hunter	1878-87
Golding, John R.	1826-27
Golding, John R. (ward)	1827
Golding, Susan	1875-81
Golding, Thomas (children of)	1876
Goodwin, Elizabeth	1837

Goolsby, John	1891-1892
Goolsby, Lucy	1911-1912
Gordon, Robert J. (children of)	1833
Gordon, Robert S.	1830
Gorley, Jonathan	1833
Gorley, Mary	1862-64
Gould, Mary E.	1899-1907
Gould, Russell	1900-03
Grady, William S.	1864-69
Grady, William S. (children of)	1868-72
Graham, Abner	1862-63
Graham, Andrew	1829-35
Graham, Doctor R.	1862-63
Graham, George (children of)	1853
Grant, James R.	1891
Gray, Anna	1822
Gray, George	1811-17
Gray, Jeremiah G. Sr.	1880
Gray, Martha (ward)	1856
Gray, Martha M.	1854
Gray, Phebe (ward)	1854
Green, John R. (children of)	1817
Green, John R.	1814
Green, Thomas F. Jr.	1877-82
Greene, Ethel	1884
Greer, Asel	1828-37
Greer, Cynthia W.	1850
Greer, James	1825-34
Greer, John C.	1860
Greer, Richard C.	1889-91
Greer, Thomas	1843-50
Gregory, James L.	1874
Gresham, Davis	1819
Gresham, Robert (ward)	1917
Gresham, Young	1820-25
Griffith, Charles R.A. (ward)	1870-76
Griffith, John L.	1871-79
Griffith, Michael R.	1869-70
Grimes, George (children of)	1897
Gunnison, John Jr.	1854
Gunter, Mrs. Ila Hall	1930
Haygood, John	1829
Haygood, Varena (ward)	1849
Haygood, William	1849-50
Hagins, Edward	1805-10
Hagins, James	1814-15
Hailes, Joel, Jr.	1820-28
Hailes, John	1823
Hale, Frances	1863-64
Hale, Gussie	1910
Hale, John A.	1863-1903
Hale, Josiah W.	1865-1881
Hale, Mary A.	1902
Hale, Mary G.	1896-97
Hale, Miss M.E.	1907-09
Hale, Moab	1858-61
Hale, Noah	1859
Hale, Robert W.	1901
Hale, S.C.	1905
Hale, Wiley	1863
Hale, William	1885-87
Hale, William B.	1882
Hale, William J.	1909-10
Hall, George W.	1912

Name	Date
Hall, James P.	1884
Hall, W.A.S.	1925-30
Hamilton, Barton	1828-34
Hamilton, Drury I.	1854
Hamilton, Duke	1887-1901
Hamilton, Henry	1805-06
Hamilton, James S.H.	1888
Hamilton, Mary E.	1914-16
Hamilton, Sarah S.	1876-77
Hammondtree, Sarah S.	1909-11
Hampton, Eliza	1883-85
Hampton, Jonathan	1883-86
Hancock, A.C.	1928
Hancock, James	1904
Hancock, Thomas	1853-57
Hancock, W.J.	1937
Hannah, Thomas	1808
Hansford, Mary Ella (ward)	1903
Hanson, Nancy	1896
Hardeman, Mary E.	1885-87
Hardeman, Mary E. (children of)	1887
Hardeman, Nancy S.	1910-11
Hardeman, William J.	1885
Hardiman, Benjamin	1872-75
Harden, (children of)	1892
Harden, Martha W.	1863
Harden, Mary E.G.	1887-93
Harden, Robert R.	1843-45
Harden, Robert R. (children of)(ward)	1845
Harden, William P.	1848
Harden, William R.	1822
Harper, Daisy (ward)	1903
Harper, Henry	1923
Harper, John W.	1836
Harper, Young W.	1845
Harris, Baker (ward)	1819
Harris, Care Y.	1907
Harris, Charlotte (ward)	1809
Harris, (children of)	1827
Harris, Cordelia	1875
Harris, Hugh N.	1897-98
Harris, J. Otis	1907
Harris, James M.	1879-81
Harris, Jeremiah	1823-32
Harris, John	1870-82
Harris, Josh (ward)	1896
Harris, Judith	1827
Harris, Lavinia R.	1905
Harris, Martha	1881-83
Harris, Mary S. (ward)	1823
Harris, Myrtis	1881-87
Harris, Myrtis (children of)	1885
Harris, Paulina T.	1882-83
Harris, Rebecca	1818-19
Harris, Samuel Baker	1806
Harris, Samuel B. (children of)	1810
Harris, Sarah H.	1870
Harris, Thomas (ward)	1808-10
Harris, Turner	1873-79
Harris, Walton	1820-34
Harris, William	1823
Harris, Young L.G.	1894-99
Harrison, Alonzo T.	1860-68
Harrison, James J.	1868-69
Harrison, Mentoria B.	1866
Hart, Angeligue (ward)	1910
Harvey, John	1823
Harvie, William	1814-26
Hathorn, Hugh	1804-14
Hawks, Sherman B.	1911-12
Hawthorn, Hugh	1804
Hayes, Edmond	1815-17
Hayes, Hiram	1857-58
Hayes, John R.	1856-58
Hayes, John E. (children of)	1858
Hayes, M.T.	1907-08
Hayes, Peter W.	1862-63
Hayes, Richard	no date
Haynes, Franklin B. (ward)	1838
Hays, Robert	1863
Head, Carrie	1885-88
Head, Jesse J.	1885-86
Heard, George E.	1891
Heard, Mrs. M.E.	1923
Hedges, Joseph Sr.	1882-83
Hemphill, Sarah A.	1920
Hemphill, W.S.	1874
Hemrick, Julia	1928-32
Henderson, Julia	1911
Henderson, Mathew H.	1881-84
Henderson, Robert	1859-66
Hendon, Elijah (ward)	1812-13
Hendon, James	1845-57
Hendon, Lorena	1860
Hendon, Sarah E. (ward)	1845-47
Henley, Albert P.	1896
Henning, Margaret	1816
Henze, D.N. (ward)	1863
Herndon, George	1816
Herrins, Ann R.	1906
Herring, Eleanor C.M. (ward)	1875
Herring, Stephen W.	1873-74
Herring, William	1813-29
Herring, William (children of)	1819
Hester, Charles	1821-27
Hester, Elizabeth	1831
Hester, Robert	1825-27
Hester, Samuel	1839
Hester, Stephen	1824-33
Hester, Stephen	1857-63
Hester, Stephen C.	1837-39
Hester, Stephen C. (children of)	1839
Hester, William (children of)	1864
Hewell, Catherine	1874-79
Hewell, John T.	1857
Hewell, Nathaniel N. (children of)	1877
Hicks, Daniel	1822
Hicks, Mary (ward)	1822
Hightower,	1827
Hill, Althea (ward)	1890
Hill, Ann	1809-16
Hill, Baker	1907-09
Hill, Baker (children of)	1908
Hill, Blanton A.	1857-87
Hill, Elizabeth Ann	1894
Hill, Isaac	1833-56
Hill, J.B.	1909-10

Hill, Nancy	1850-52	Howard, Patrick	1894
Hill, Thomas	1822	Hoyt, Nathan	1863
Hilliard, C.M. (children of)	1921	Hubbard, Charles Lews	1910
Hinesly, Irvin	1863	Hubert, Gabriel	1811-14
Hinsly, Martha	1841	Hubert, James (ward)	1812
Hinson, Armistead	1850-1910	Hudson, George W.	1863-72
Hinton, John	1800's early	Hudson, Katie	1884
Hinton, Susan Tallulah	1898-1902	Hudson, Katie (children of)	1884
Hinton, Thomas	1827-32	Hudson, May Belle & Charles L. (ward)	1899
Hinton, William H.	1868-69	Huff, Elizabeth (ward)	1845-61
Hitchcock, Murry S. (children of)	1881	Huff, Elizabeth	1847
Hodge, G.J.	1896	Huff, George	1901
Hodge, John	1819-20	Huff, Greene	1865
Hodge, Louisa J. (ward)	1834-43	Huff, Greene (children of)	1852-63
Hodgson, Annie	1935	Huff, Henry	1864
Hodgson, Asbury H. Sr.	1919	Huff, Rachael (ward)	1881
Hodgson, E.R., Sr.	1920	Huggins, Mrs. J.H. Sr.	1902
Hodgson, Edward R. Sr.	1874-79	Hughes, Harrisden S.	1883
Hodgson, Julia (children of)	1902	Hughes, Harrisden S.	1883
Hodgson, Robert B.	1875-79	Hull, Asbury (ward)	1883-87
Hodgson, Robert P.	1905	Hull, Elmira	1909
Hodgson, William V.P.	1877-82	Hull, Lula M.	1881-83
Hoff, Rachael (ward)	1881	Humphries, Uriah	1818-32
Hogg, Sarah (ward)	1851	Humphries, Uriah (children of)	1817
Hogue, Jacob	1817	Hunnicutt, James Bernard	1903
Holbrook, Nathan	1863-66	Hunnicutt, Rosa May	1903
Holder, John	1823-41	Hunnicutt, W.L.C.	1910
Holder, John H.	1854	Hunter, Alfred (ward)	1896-1900
Holder, Tapley	1859-61	Hunter, Henry (ward)	1817-25
Hollbrook, Martha	1906	Hunter, Sarah Ann (ward)	1816-25
Holleway, Ruth	1806	Hunter, S.M. (children of)	1897-99
Holliman, B.L.	1905	Hunter, Starkie	1861
Hollowell, Asa	1804-07	Hunter, John	1812-15
Holmes, James	1806-07	Hurley, Langston	1906
Holmes, John	1811-18	Hutcheson, Peter W.	1880
Holmes, John (children of)	1811	Hutcheson, Peter W. (children of)	1880-82
Holsey, Albon	1914	Hutson, Coly	1822
Holsey, Sally	1909	Hutson, Shadrack (children of)	1816-20
Holt, Cicero	1833-36		
Holt, Edgar (ward)	1900	Irby, Sarah	1822
Hood, Beulah V.	1912	Iverson, Frances E.	1852
Hood, Beulah (children of)	1912	Iverson, Robert	1851-68
Hoover, Lawson P.	1874	Iverson, Robert (ward)	1866
Hopkins, Eleanor H.	1949		
Hopkins, Emily (ward)	1821	Jack, James K.P.	1814-15
Hopkins, Eusabens (children of)	1858-63	Jack, Col. Samuel	1814-18
Hopkins, Hannah	1857	Jack, Col. Samuel (children of)	1814
Hopkins, Joseph (ward)	1804-06	Jack, Samuel	1821-24
Hopkins, Joseph	1810	Jacks, Greene B.	1859
Hopkins, Lambeth	1806-12	Jackson, (children of)	1830
Hopkins, Moses	1809-14	Jackson, Camilla (ward)	1911
Hopkins, William (ward)	1821	Jackson, Daniel	1814-16
Hopping, Ephraim S.	1853-56	Jackson, David W.	1903-04
Horton, Alfonzo	1905	Jackson, Drury	1823
Horton, Daniel T. (ward)	1890-91	Jackson, Francis	1848-55
Horton, T.A.	1910	Jackson, Francis (children of)	1853
House, Rebecca Ann (ward)	1851-55	Jackson, Harriet	1889-91
Houze, Angeline (ward)	1838-39	Jackson, Hartwell, Sr.	1859-71
Houze, Darius	1840	Jackson, Henry	1840
Houze, Joseph (children of)	1863-64	Jackson, Hillman	1874
Howard, Hiram	1831	Jackson, Jane	1864-71

Name	Date
Jackson, John Sr.	1849-54
Jackson, John W.	1865-83
Jackson, Luticia	1862
Jackson, Lottie B. (ward)	1896
Jackson, Maggie (ward)	1908
Jackson, Margaret	1865-71
Jackson, Ruth M. (ward)	1900
Jackson, Stephen	1865-80
Jackson, W.A.	1900
Jackson, William (children of)	1874
Jacobson, Rosa C.	1897
James, Henry	1829-35
Jarrell, George A.	1866-73
Jarrell, James S.	1836-57
Jarrell, Martin	1857
Jarrell, Mike	1877
Jarrell, Mike	1885
Jefferson, Robert (children of)	1901-09
Jeffries,	1849
Jeffries, Joseph A. (children of)	1869
Jemisison, Ella	1910-11
Jenkins, John (ward)	1852
Jenkins, Peter	1893
Jennings, Giles	1863
Jennings, Henry	1862
Jennings, Henry (children of)	1863
Jennings, James	1845-48
Jennings, James (children of)	1843-45
Jennings, James (children of)	1845-65
Jennings, Joseph B.	1862
Jennings, Mary T.	1891
Jennings, Robert	1888-93
Jennings, Robert H.	1899
Johns, Lillie Angelina	1870
Johnson, Allen R.	1889-1907
Johnson, David H.	1886-88
Johnson, Frankey	1859
Johnson, George T.	1898
Johnson, Joe	1893
Johnson, J.T.	1909
Johnson, L.G.	1904-05
Johnson, Letitia (ward)	1818
Johnson, Lousia	1897
Johnson, Tunes	1897-80
Johnson, William D.	1909
Johnson, William D. (children of)	1909
Jones, Adaline	1906-07
Jones, Andrews S. (children of)	1880
Jones, E.E. (children of)	1896-1901
Jones, Elijah	1800's early
Jones, Frank	1888
Jones, James D.	1862-64
Jones, John	1876-77
Jones, John T.	1897
Jones, Joseph S.	1863-73
Jones, Mary	1911
Jones, Lena	1888-89
Jones, Letty	1880
Jones, Lydia	1856-64
Jones, Nannie Lou (ward)	1911
Jones, P. Calvin	1907-08
Jones, Robert A. (children of)	1850
Jones, Wiley A. (children of)	1864-73
Jones, William	1848-1911
Joseph, Helen	1890
Keese, John S.	1927
Kellum, Lavonia	1896
Kellum, W.E.	1911
Kemp, William C.	1884
Kennard, Annabel (ward)	1907-11
Kennard, Joel S.	1909-1911
Kennedy, Thomas (children of)	1875-81
Kenney, Clifford A. (ward)	1908
Kenney, D.M.	1905-06
Kenney, George	1903-10
Kenney, Isaac M.	1885
Kenney, Isaac (children of)	1884
Kenney, James S.	1856-63
Kenney, John S.H.	1862
Kenney, Joseph A.	1886
Kenney, Louisa A.	1907-09
Kenney, Louisa	1863
Kenney, Samuel	1848
Kenney, Sarah Sophia (ward)	1849
Kent, Soloman P.	1844-48
Kettle, William	1874-77
Kidd, Gabriel	1907
Kidd, Theodore H.	1854
Kigny, W. Beatty	1821
Kilgore, Peter	1815-16
King, Agnes B.	1860
King, Caroline	1894-95
King, Emily	1864-72
King, Francina E.	1885
King, John G.	1827
Kinley, James	1902-07
Kinnebrew, B.T.	1908
Kinney, Alford	1883
Kinney, Jane	1822
Kirk, Hampton	1907
Kirkpatrick, John	1876-79
Kirkwood, James	1806
Kittle, Elizabeth	1929-31
Kittle, James (ward)	1881-82
Kittle, John	1881-85
Kittle, John H. (ward)	1910
Kittle, Margaret	1883-84
Kittle, Rufus C. (ward)	1910
Kittle, William	1874-83
Kittle, Willis	1907-10
Klutts, Jacob	1865-80
Klutts, Samuel	1834-43
Kroner, Frank H. (ward)	1891
Lamar, Andrew J. (ward)	1836-46
Lamar, Andrew J. (children of)	1855
Lamar, Zachariah	1835-36
Lambert, John H.	1907-08
Lambert, Thomas	1827
Lamkin, R.W.	1917
Lampkin, Cobb (children of)	1908
Lampkin, Lewis J.	1885

Lampkin, Mattie	1903
Lampkin, Robert H. (children of)	1872
Lampkin, Washington	1876
Lampkin, William H.	1902
Lampkin, Winnie	1914
Land, Elizabeth	1816
Landrum, Ardella	1905-06
Lane, Jesse	1813-14
Lane, Richard (children of)	1804-16
Langford, James	1832-34
Langford, Joseph B.	1873-76
Lanier, George M.	1854
Lasseter, Mary	1848
Launins, Mrs. S.A.	1908
Lavender, Nancy E.	1888-89
Lawles, Peter (ward)	1845
Lawless, Permelia	1881-84
Lawrence, Camilla	1883
Lawrence, Richard	1815
Lawson, Lizzie (children of)	1895
Leak, James (ward)	1808
Lee, John	1837
Lee, John W.	1847-57
Lee, Johnathan	1843
Lee, Judith	1866-67
Lee, Sandford	1880
Lester, A.N. (children of)	1909-11
Lester, Elijah R. (children of)	1873
Lester, Emily	1879
Lester, Lewis	1869-86
Lester, Ned	no date
Lester, Patman (ward)	1847
Lester, William P. (children of)	1896
Lewis, Judith A.	1859-71
Ligon, Cesar	1880
Ligon, James	1822
Ligon, Joseph Sr.	1822
Ligon, Robert	1837
Ligon, Robert (children of)	1842-48
Lilly, Edward	1889-91
Lilly, Sarah A.	1893
Linton, A.B.	1839-42
Linton, Lucy Ann	1880-1907
Linton, John Sr. (children of)	1881-87
Lloyd, Rebecca Francis (ward)	1819
Lloyd, Sarah A.	1818-21
Lombard, Charles B.	1862-75
Long, Crawford W.	1878
Long, Elizabeth	1857
Long, Susan J.	1894-95
Long, Willie Julian (ward)	1880-84
Lord, Archibald	1841-46
Lord, Ebenezer	1839-40
Lord, Elizabeth	1806-12
Lord, Elizabeth	1853
Lord, Benjamin B.	1840
Lord, Margaret	1807-10
Lord, William	1846-47
Loving, Sanford (children of)	1850-60
Lowe, Joe B.	1907-08
Lowe, John H.	1863-1903
Lowe, Sarah	1852
Lowe, Walter H. (ward)	1893
Loyal, Francis	1800-17
Lucas, Martha S.	1908-09
Lumpkin, Charles M.	1872-73
Lumpkin, Edward P.	1873-75
Lumpkin, Edwin King (ward)	1863
Lumpkin, Frank	1876-90
Lumpkin, George R.	1859
Lumpkin, George R.	1876
Lumpkin, George W.	1832
Lumpkin, George (children of)	1874-79
Lumpkin, Joseph Henry	1867-79
Lumpkin, Mary Bryant	1877
Lumpkin, Minnie	1879
Lumpkin, Robert C.	1876-77
Lumpkin, Samuel P.	1863-76
Lumpkin, Wilson	1873-78
Lyle, Fannie C.	1906-07
Lyle, James Sr.	1834
Lyndon, A.O. (children of)	1890
Lyndon, Oscar	1911
Lyons, C.H.	1894-95
Lyons, C.H. (children of)	1895
Mack, Daniel	1838-39
Macon, (children of)	1897
Macon, Alethia	1861
Maddox, J.A.	1912
Maddox, John C.	1890-93
Maddox, Joseph	1836-45
Magbee, Hiram	1819
Malcomb, Edna (ward)	1893-1907
Mallory, Henry	1910
Malon, Martin H.	1885
Malone, Isaac	1902-1904
Malone, John	1808-09
Malone, Phoebe	1880
Malone, Robert (children of)	1838-39
Malone, William	1826
Man, Milly	1863
Mandeville, Eliza	1873
Mangum, T.B.	1908
Mann, Jonathan (children of)	1835
Manuel, Millie	1908
Mapp, Littleton	1814-15
Marable, Augustine W.	1851-55
Marable, Augustine W. (children of)	1854-57
Marable, John	1817-19
Marable, John (children of)	1818
Marable, Minnie S. (children of)	1911
Marable, Robert (children of)	1860
Marable, Robert	1858-73
Marable, William A.	1874-88
Marbury, Leonard	1830
Marks, Myer	1899
Marks, Simon	1888-91
Marsh, Alex R.	1813
Marshall, Clarence	1933
Marshall, Francis	1854-58

Martin, Dicy E. 1901
Martin, George 1828
Martin, George W. 1865
Martin, Jacob 1805-12
Martin, John A. 1854-55
Martin, John A. (children of) 1855-58
Martin, Mary (ward) 1851
Martin, Mary 1870-72
Martin, Robert 1827-28
Martin, Robert (ward) 1871
Martin, Miss S.C. 1909
Martin, William (children of) 1878-80
Mary Ann (A free person of color) 1850
Mash, Henrietta 1813
Mason, Henry Lamar (ward) 1890
Mason, William 1890
Mathews, Willie L. 1884-85
Mathews, B.J. 1887
Matthews, James D. 1886-95
Matthews, James D. (children of) 1879
Matthews, Jennie B. 1907
Matthews, Jesse 1863
Matthews, John R. 1882
Matthews, John R. (children of) 1885
Matthews, Lucy O. (ward) 1858-60
Matthews, Martha E. 1881
Matthews, Mary 1866-69
Matthews, Mary E. 1874-79
Matthews, Robert D. 1889-93
Matthews, R.D. (children of) 1904
Matthews, Mrs. W.H. 1911
Matthews, William 1858-60
Matthews, William F. 1878-89
Matthews, William F. (children of) 1879-83
Maupin, LaFayette 1877-79
Maxey, Albert J. 1872-74
Maxey, Booz 1872-74
Maxey, E.E. Mc P.B. (ward) 1833
Maxey, Edward H. 1833
Maxey, Elizabeth 1871
Maxey, Henry 1868-70
Maxey, John 1811-26
Maxey, John (children of) 1812-15
Maxey, Joseph 1856-58
Maxey, Joseph (children of) 1860-65
Maxey, Josiah 1858-59
Maxwell, Sarah H. 1863-64
Mayfield, Thomas 1833
Mayne, James P. (children of) 1859-73
Mayne, Geo. S. (children of) 1910
Mayne, John A. 1846-83
Mayne, John W. 1863-64
Mays, Levi 1832-34
Mays, Lucy Ann 1886-88
Meads, Allen (children of) 1882
Meeker, Christopher C. 1862-66
Mell, Patrick H. 1888
Melton, Jonathan 1815-35
Melton, Jonathan (children of) 1835
Memno, Elvira Lee (ward) 1869
Merritt, Berryman G. 1836
Merritt, Celia 1868-69
Merritt, W.D. 1910
Meriwether, David 1822-29
Meriwether, George Ann (ward) 1833-36
Meriwether, James 1907
Meriwether, James (children of) 1833
Meriwether, Martha M. 1859
Meriwether, Richard 1832
Meriwether, William 1826-37
Meriwether, William (children of) 1837
Michael, Thomas (children of) 1866
Middlebrooks, Anderson C. 1871-83
Middlebrooks, Mattie Bell (ward) 1909
Middlebrooks, Thos. E. (children of) 1904
Middlebrooks, Zack B. 1869
Miles, Martha 1878-79
Miller, Jesse 1817
Mills, Alford 1907
Mitchell, Albert L. 1905-06
Mitchell, Giles 1869-74
Mitchell, Henderson (ward) 1848
Mitchell, John (ward) 1908
Mitchell, S.D. (children of) 1881
Mitchell, Thomas 1852-79
Mitchell, William Jr. 1808-33
Mitchell, William L. 1882
Mitchell, Maj. William L. 1862-71
Montgomery, Absalom 1837-51
Montgomery, Absalom (children of) 1836-37
Montgomery, Calista A. 1883-85
Moon, Collin 1909
Moon, Eva (ward) 1898
Moon, John W. 1859
Moon, Susan 1904
Moon, Isaac S. 1877-80
Moon, William 1842
Moore, Alsa 1843-44
Moore, Eleanor 1878
Moore, Emma 1903-05
Moore, Francis 1833
Moore, Francis 1865-74
Moore, Henrietta (ward) 1844
Moore, J.W. 1910
Moore, John 1859
Moore, Lizzie A. 1872
Moore, Martha H. 1873
Moore, Mary H. (ward) 1899-1901
Moore, Richard D. 1874-83
Moore, Robertus (ward) 1835
Moore, Robert 1834-56
Moore, Stephen E. (ward) 1874
Moore, Thomas 1870-74
Moore, Thomas Cobb (ward) 1876-81

Moore, William	1835-52
Moore, William C.	1903-04
Moore, Willie C. (ward)	1899
Morgan, Ruby (ward)	1909
Morris, Casper	1890
Morris, Cassie	1891
Morris, Charles	1893
Morris, Israel	1891-92
Morris, Mrs. M.M.	1914
Morris, Rosa	1892-97
Morris, Soloman A. (children of)	1876-82
Morton, Frederick S.	1909
Morton, Joel	1839-50
Morton, John (ward)	1819
Morton, John	1856
Morton, Joseph F.	1877-80
Morton, Josiah	1803-20
Morton, Judith	1849
Morton, Lizzie	1907
Morton, M.B.	1890
Morton, Mrs. M.E.	1895-96
Morton, Margaret J. (ward)	1819
Morton, Robert	1815
Moseley, Thomas (children of)	1844
Moss, Daisy	1904
Moss, Emma	1885
Moss, John (children of)	1817
Moss, John D.	1864-66
Moss, Salley (ward)	1820
Mose, Thomas	1882-94
Moss, Willis	1823-27
Moynihan, Thomas	1822-27
Murden, Dora	1927-28
Murray, William H.	1861
Murrell, Catherine C. (ward)	1892
Murrell, Clinton H. (ward)	1931-40
Myers, Moses	1896-1903
Mygatt, George	1877

McAllister, Joseph L.	1869-1905
McAlpin, Dr. R.T.	1889
McAlpin, Robert	1804
McBee, James	1815-17
McCarty, Hannah	1808-15
McCleskey, David M.	1886-88
McCleskey, Georgia Bell	1882-83
McCleskey, Greene L. (children of)	1881-83
McCleskey, William W.	1885
McCombs, Nelson (ward)	1891
McCommon, James	1810
McCord, James	1816-29
McCowen, George Francis (ward)	1837
McCoy, Henry	1809-38
McCree, Jourdan	1900
McCullough, William	1833
McCurdy, James G.	1876-78
McCurdy, James (children of)	1887
McDowell, William A.	1900
McDowell, Willie (ward)	1910-12
McGee, James	1809-16
McGee, James (children of)	1821
McGinty, Henry C.	1911
McKee, Samuel	1811
McKie, John S. (children of)	1898
McKie, Mary E.	1894-98
McKigney, Beaty	1810-25
McKinney, Mollie	1911
McKinney, R.W.	1911
McKinney, Zora (ward)	1911-12
McLeroy, Cornelia (children of)	1898
McLeroy, Needham	1856-60
McLeroy, Stephen J.	1869
McLester, James G.	1890
McMillian, John B.	1850
McNeill, Clay King (ward)	1909
McRee, Benjamin	1837
McRee, Benjamin	1856-57
McRee, Isabella	1855
McRee, James M.	1859
McRee, John	1833
McRee, John	1855-59
McRee, John (children of)	1874
McRee, Rowan	1867-69
McRee, Rowan (children of)	1868-72
McRee, William	1830-35
McSparn, John	1819-20
McSparn, John (children of)	1819
McWhorter, Cassandra	1883-87
McWhorter, Lizzie	1906-09
McWhorter, Lizzie (children of)	1899
McWhorter, Moses E.	1869-71
McWhorter, William	1889

Nabers, William	1886-90
Nail, Elisha	1819-40
Nall, Richard	1818
Nance, John	1862-64
Nance, Reuben	1825
Nash, Abner (ward)	1822
Neal, Mayo	1910
Neal, W.N.	1909-10
Neisler, Hugh	1862
Nesbit, James	1832-33
Nesbit, Penelope	1833-36
Nesbitt, Martha D.	1832-47
Nesbitt, Mary W.	1884-87
Nevitt, John W.	1888
Nevitt, Harry M.	1887
Newton, Catherine	1846-49
Newton, Charlotte	1883-84
Newton, Clary	1828
Newton, E.L.	1906-07
Newton, Elizue L.	1882-83
Newton, James	1889
Newton, John H.	1909
Newton, Walter J.	1814
Nichols, Emma	1878
Nichols, Henry M. (ward)	1881
Nichols, James C.	1865
Nichols, John R.	1894-95
Nichols, Lilly (ward)	1892
Nichols, Mary A. (children of)	1896
Nichols, Ransome	1856-60
Nichols, Roberta	1909

Nicholson, H.B.	1887
Nicholson, James M.	1897-98
Nicholson, John W.	1886
Nicholson, Martha M.	1893
Nixon, Henry	1870
Nixon, John	1821
Nixon, Rhoda (children of)	1909
Noell, Carlton (ward)	1898
Noell, James R. (children of)	1899-1904
Noell, Thomas	1838
Noell, Upson C.	1897-99
Norris, John Q.A.	1869-70
Norris, William J.	1860
North, John R. (ward)	1856
North, Thomas	1817
Norton, William	1827-41
Nunnally, J.C.	1904
Nunnally, John	1826-52
Nunnally, M.S.D.	1901
Nutt, William	1818-21
Oates, James S.	1828-29
O'Farrell, Charles (ward)	1902
Ogden, Joseph H.	1824-25
Oglesby, Anna (ward)	1907
Oldham, W.D.	1907
Oliver, Francis H. (children of)	no date
Oliver, Joseph	1811-16
Onar, Benj (children of)	1853-58
Osborn, Francis	1853-58
Osborn, J.N.	1892
Osborn, John	1835-36
Osborn, John	1860-62
Osborn, Nancy	1836-52
Osborn, Nicholas	1841-52
Osborn, Sallie C.	1905-07
Overby, James L.	1836-38
Overby, Thomas	1837-49
Paine, Edward	1843-52
Paine, Edward C.	1856-58
Paine, Floyd	1874
Paine, George D.	1848
Paine, Seaborn	1875
Palmer, Edmond	1863-75
Parker, William H.	1845-55
Parks, Willis	1885
Parr, B.J.	1889
Parr, John C.	1823
Parrish, Charles	1837-39
Patman, Thomas H.	1869-82
Patman, William	1883
Patman, William A.	1859-60
Patton, Jane	1814-16
Paullett, David	1819
Perkins, Robert	1821-27
Perkins, Sarah B.	1827-34
Perry, Alonzo (ward)	1882
Perry, John C.	1850
Perry, Peter	1820-34
Pettiford, Lows	1863-69
Pettis, Alford	1893
Phillips, Joel	1836
Phinizy, Fredinand	1889-93
Phinizy, Ferdinand Bowdle	1877-88
Phinizy, Harry Hall	1890-91
Phinizy, Jacob	1853-56
Phinizy, Jacob	1890
Phinizy, Marco	1816-22
Pinson, Joseph	1832-33
Pinson, Thomas	1825-28
Pitner, John C.	1889-90
Pittard, America	1890
Pittard, Humphrey	1866-73
Pittard, James D.	1884-85
Pittard, William	1884-1906
Plat, George	1811
Ponder, John	1805-18
Pool, Jackson	1883-84
Pope, Burwell	1849-51
Pope, Eliza S.	1866-68
Pope, Mary	1843
Pope, Sarah K.	1877
Pounds, Richard	1807-20
Pounds, William Sr.	1810-13
Powell, Dempsey	1815
Powell, Henry	1814
Powers, Will	1919
Pressley, Rev. Samuel P.	1836-39
Preston, Thomas	1836-41
Price, Elizabeth	1846
Price, James	1839
Price, William	1834-36
Prince, Oliver H.	1838-40
Pringle, George	1850
Puryear, John	1827-38
Puryear, Judith M.	1884
Puryear, Peter	1827-35
Puryear, Peter	1844-45
Puryear, William	1797-1812
Puryear, William H.	1859-69
Puryear, William H.	1870-72
Quarterman, Minnie (ward)	1902
Radford, Henry	1805-14
Radford, Silas (ward)	1817
Ramey, Elizabeth (ward)	1816
Ramey, William	1812-16
Ramey, Talitha E.	1867
Randolph, Carvey M.	1890
Randolph, James H.L. (ward)	1892
Randolph, Peter	1816
Ranson, Reuben	1831-50
Ray, Margaret	1889-90
Ray, Mary	1910
Ray, William (ward)	1906-07
Reaves, Anna E.	1887-89
Reaves, Edward A.	1868-71
Reaves, Ethel (ward)	1902-05
Reaves, John W.	1862
Reaves, John (children of)	1865
Reese, Charles S.	1881-84
Reese, Charles S. (ward)	1865
Reese, Charles M.	1862
Reese, Elizabeth W.G.	1853
Reese, Sidney C.	1882-83
Reid, Adline	1904-05
Reynolds, M.W.	1892-93
Reynolds, W.N.	1904-05

Rhodes, James	1855-60
Rice, Benjamin	1803-07
Rice, Benjamin (children of)	1808
Richard, Bessie M.	1907-08
Richards, Richard	1910
Richardson, Alford	1872
Richardson, David	1828-34
Richardson, David	1875-76
Richardson, James	1842-43
Richardson, James M. (ward)	1847
Richardson, Jane G.	1875-77
Richardson, Hillery A. (ward)	1852-72
Richardson, Orlando F.	1856-76
Richardson, Richard	1839
Riddle, John	1815
Ridgeway, Nelson	1855-90
Ridling, Alsa F.	1924
Riviere, Georges A. (children of)	1911
Roberts, Anna	1903-05
Roberts, D.A.	1856
Roberts, Deasey Ann	1846-53
Roberts, John	1814-26
Roberts, Thomas	1814-15
Roberts, William (children of)	1837
Robertson, Dock (ward)	1884
Robertson, Fredinand (ward)	1814-15
Robertson, Fryar	1837-39
Robertson, James A.	1862
Robertson, Jesse M.	1822-27
Robertson, John L.M.	1820-25
Robertson, Dr. W.V.	1910
Robinson, Gertrude	1910-11
Robinson, John	1815-34
Robinson, Lousia Jane (ward)	1819
Robinson, Sally	1826-32
Robinson, Senith	1821-33
Robinson, William	1802-20
Robinson, William (ward)	1827-28
Robison, Eliza Ann	1840-45
Robison, James (children of)	1828-44
Rockford, George	1821
Rodgers, Lily S. (ward)	1914
Rosenberg, H.	1907-08
Rosett, Nelson	1893
Rosseter, White	1828
Roman, Abraham	1863
Rowland, William W.	1877
Royal, Frances (children of)	1894
Royal, J.H.	1893
Royal, James M.	1862-63
Royal, John E.	1880
Royster, John (ward)	1871
Royster, Robert	1816-22
Royston, Robertus (ward)	1816-18
Rucker, Oliver	1877
Rucker, Tinsley W. (children of)	no date
Runnells, Annis	1843
Runnells, Dudley	1808
Runnells, Patrick M.	1834
Russell, Edward B.	1877
Russell, Hariette	1903-04
Rutledge, John	1814-16
Rutledge, John (children of)	1821
Sage, Martha J.	1886
Sage, William P.	1854
Sailors, Jeffie (ward)	1911
Salter, Caswell A.	1836
Salter, James S.	1853-54
Salter, Thomas W.	1863
Sansen, (children of)	1876
Sanson, Delilah P.	1855
Sanson, James T.	1868-69
Sanson, James T. (children of)	1871
Sanson, John	1806-11
Sanson, Robert	1887-88
Sanson, Thomas	1852-60
Sanson, Virginia	1855
Sapp, Edward (children of)	1884
Sapp, Edward	1884-85
Savage, Susan B.	1869-70
Sawtelle, John W.	1841-47
Saye, James W.	1881-86
Schackelford, H.T.	1901
Schell, Jessie B. (ward)	1902
Sears, Marcus A.	1873-78
Selman, John W. (continued)	1847-49
Selman, Josiah S.	1857
Settlemoir, Able	1846
Sharp, Lewis	1816
Shaw, Margaret	1886-87
Shaw, William	1809-14
Shaw, William (children of)	1810
Sheats, John L. (children of)	1861-73
Sheats, Joseph	1887-88
Sheats, Nicholas	1835-48
Sheats, Nicholas (children of)	1847
Sheats, Squire	1907
Shed, William	1910-11
Shepard, Augusta (ward)	1898
Shewell, George S.	1897
Shewell, George S. (children of)	1908
Sibbald, Jane	1834
Sikes, John R.	1885
Sikes, Prudence	1863
Sikes, Zachariah	1879-1912
Silvey, (children of)	1898
Silvey, G.F.	1911
Simmons, John	1816
Simmons, Sarah	1872-76
Simonton, Jean	1812
Simonton, Theophilus	1821-35
Simonton, Tehophilus (children of)	1821
Sims, Charly	1841
Sims, Hattie P.	1883-84
Sims, Robert	1840-59
Sims, Robert	1930
Sims, William Isaih	1904
Sissons, Rodman	1839
Sizer, R.W.	1931

Slater, L.D. 1909-10
Sledge, James A.
(children of) 1882
Sledge, Mary E. 1881-83
Smith, Ammos Young 1909
Smith, Araminta 1890-91
Smith, Arthur (ward) 1904
Smith, Billy (ward) 1813
Smith, Elizabeth Mariah 1883
Smith, Francis Alice
(ward) 1906
Smith, Frank 1892
Smith, H.L. 1899
Smith, Harknus 1889
Smith, Henry M. 1910-11
Smith, Herman 1913
Smith, Herman
(children of) 1914
Smith, Horace G. 1914
Smith, John W.
(children of) 1838
Smith, John W. 1838-1906
Smith, Joseph Sr. 1839
Smith, L.J. 1922
Smith, L.K.
(children of) 1906
Smith, Levin 1851
Smith, Lucy 1902
Smith, Lula V. 1949
Smith, Martin L. 1866-1915
Smith, Mary 1845
Smith, Mary Ann Arabella 1880-83
Smith, Mary B. 1894-97
Smith, Mary
(children of) 1804
Smith, Mary W. 1834
Smith, Nancy 1824
Smith, Nellie (ward) 1892-97
Smith, Patrick 1886-87
Smith, Peter 1885
Smith, Polly 1840
Smith, Robert M. 1879
Smith, Robert M. 1879
Smith, Rosanna J. 1892
Smith, Ruby (children
of) 1941
Smith, Sally 1824-26
Smith, Samuel H.
(children of) 1868
Smith, Sarah 1884
Smith, Sarah E. 1884-85
Smith, Sarah E.
(children of) 1869
Smith, Sarah Francis
(ward) 1912
Smith, Wales 1870-71
Smith, William (ward) 1816
Smith, Willie Burch 1914
Snead, Morgan J. 1872
Snead, Roy N. (ward) 1892-99
Sorrell, Nancy 1852
Sorrells, James (ward) 1906
Sparks, Thomas H. 1866
Sparks, Thomas H. 1895
Spalding, Frank E. 1884-87
Spears, George C. 1907-11
Spears, John 1818
Speer, Annie E. 1911
Speer, John 1808-09
Spencer, Paul
(children of) 1820
Spencer, Sallie C. 1894-96
Spinks, Charles B. 1925-27
Spinks, Enoch
(children of) 1847
Sprauldìng, Frank 1884
Spullock, Drury 1815-16
Spullock, James 1806-16
Spullock, James
(children of) 1808
Spullock, Morning (ward) 1808-13
Spullock, Owen 1816-27
Spullock, Winiford 1813-16
Spurlock, Elizabeth 1857
Stafford, Epsy 1887-89
Stafford, Malcolm 1881-82
Stanley, H.D. 1889
Stanley, H.D.
(children of) 1889-91
Stanley, Julia P. 1894
Starks, Jones
(children of) 1827-30
Starnes, William P. 1818
Statham, (children of) 1894
Stephens, David 1837-60
Stephens, David
(children of) 1837-41
Stephens, John 1822-25
Stephens, John W.H.
(ward) 1833
Stephens, Prince 1887
Stephens, Thomas H.
(ward) 1840
Stephens, Young John
William (ward) 1837
Stephenson, Martha J. 1870-76
Stephenson, Thomas W. 1868-71
Stern, Charles 1910-11
Stevens, Mary Emma 1914
Stevens, Oliver 1881
Stewart, ? (children of) 1837-45
Stewart, Charles 1810-22
Stewart, Frederick
(children of) 1840
Stewart, Isaac 1820-27
Stewart, Richard 1815-30
Stone, James 1808
Stone, John W.N. 1882
Stone, Uriah 1847
Story, (children of) 1890
Stovall, B.A. 1892
Stovall, Harvey G.
(ward) 1892
Stovall, John
(children of) 1851-52
Stovall, Maria 1850
Stovall, Pleasant 1864
Strachan, Alexander 1816
Streckfuss, C.F.
(children of) 1898-09
Streckfuss, C.F. 1897-98
Streckfuss, John F. 1877-78
Strickland, John A. 1833
Strickland, John J.
(children of) 1906-09
Stringer, James 1848-53
Strong, Elijah 1814
Strong, Harriet 1817-26
Strong, Isham 1799-15
Strong, James M. 1828
Strong, John Sr. 1815-19
Strong, John 1823-29

Strong, Montford 1827
Strong, Peggy 1819
Strong, Sherwood 1825-29
Strong, Sherwood (children of) 1826-29
Strong, William 1810-32
Strong, William (children of) 1813-27
Strong, William J. 1828-29
Stroud, John 1806-15
Stroud, Mark 1870-72
Stroud, Martha 1845
Stroud, William 1870-73
Stroud, William Sr. 1828
Sturdivant, Jesse 1809
Sturgis, Andrew 1835
Sturgis, Henry (children of) 1836-43
Suber, E.M. 1902
Swann, Lemuel 1888

Talmadge, C.G. 1896
Talmadge, William K. 1886-87
Talmadge, William P. 1877-87
Talmage, John 1849
Tappan, John H. 1869
Tappan, Theodore 1867-71
Tarpley, Augustine (children of) 1856-68
Tarpley, Jennett L. 1859
Tarpley, Joel (children of) 1830
Tarpley, Joseph 1826-40
Tarpley, Joseph (children of) 1832-34
Tarpley, Richard 1859
Tate, Caroline 1890
Taylor, Richard D.B. 1864-69
Taylor, Richard D.B. (children of) 1864-76
Taylor, Robert G.T. 1857-69
Taylor, Sarah Ann (ward) 1836-40
Thomas, John J. 1888-89
Thomas, William 1860-69
Thomas, William Sr. 1849-51
Thompson, John N. 1861
Thornton, Isaac N. 1865
Thrasher, Barton (ward) 1861
Thrasher, Barton 1867
Thrasher, Herbert (ward) 1816
Thrasher, Harbert 1820
Thrasher, Isaac 1816-17
Thrasher, Isaac (children of) 1816
Thrasher, Jackson M. 1847
Thrasher, John F. 1862-69
Thrasher, Joseph C. 1803
Thrasher, Josephine V. (ward) 1861
Threlkeld, Thomas D. 1870-72
Threlkeld, William B. (ward) 1871-82
Thurman, Anne 1811
Thurman, Evaline S. 1854
Thurman, Harris 1848
Thurman, Harris (children of) 1848-55
Thurman, John F. 1862-63
Thurman, John F. (children of) 1863
Thurman, Mary 1823-27
Thurman, William 1811
Thurmand, John 1841-42
Thurmon, Oliver N. 1908
Thurmond, Benjamin 1817
Thurmond, Benjamin (children of) 1817-18
Thurmond, Elizabeth A. 1897
Thurmond, Sallie 1889
Thweatt, Daniel 1804-06
Tigner, Philip 1819-60
Tigner, Philip (children of) 1819
Tiller, Elisha 1863
Tindall, Laurana 1870
Tindall, William (children of) 1836
Todd, Mrs. M.L. (children of) 1910
Todd, T.B.F. 1910
Towns, Alfred (ward) 1903
Towns, Elizabeth D. (ward) 1825
Trammell, Daniel 1815-18
Trammell, Daniel (children of) 1815
Trammell, Robert 1835
Trammell, Robert (children of) 1836
Traylor, Francis 1826
Traywick, Burrwell 1815
Traywick, Lunsford 1809
Traywick, Lunsford (children of) 1810-13
Treadwell, Isaac 1840-60
Tribble, Mary E. 1872
Troutman, M.L. 1912-19
Turnell, John 1850
Turnell, Robert (children of) 1857
Turnell, Salena Scott 1856
Tweedy, J.K. 1887-88
Tweedy, J.K. (children of) 1882-86

Upshaw, Ben 1890

Vickers, Absalum 1867

Waddell, Charles 1829-30
Waddell, William Henry 1879
Wade, Thomas B. 1866-73
Waggonman, Susannah 1804
Walker, Edwin A. 1842-45
Walker, Joseph 1825
Wallace, Sarah 1889
Wansley, Mrs. T.A. 1907
Ward, Elam 1839-49
Ward, Ithamer 1817-20
Ward, James A. 1869
Ward, James A. (children of) 1865
Ward, John 1852
Ward, Matthus A. 1863-69
Ware, Brittain 1876-77
Ware, Edward R. 1873-87
Ware, Margaret E. 1874-87
Ware, Sally 1874
Waters, J.P. 1918
Watkins, Lizzie 1891
Watkins, Robert J. 1865

Name	Date
Watson, Miss L.J.	1884
Watson, Thomas L. (ward)	1870-80
Webster, Robert	1822
Weil, Peter	1899
Welch, Louisa A.	1880
Welch, Narcissa L.	1884
Welch, W.P.	1896
Wells, Mary	1878
Wells, Thomas	1821-32
Wharton, Benjamin	1873
Wheeler, James	1863
Wheeler, William Augustus	1880-84
White, Cary	1857-59
White, Charles F.	1853
White, I.R.	1857
White, John	1802
White, John	1874-95
White, John	1881
White, John R.	1857-61
White, Rebecca B.	1885
White, Samuel L. (children of)	1837-42
White, William N.	1867-68
White, Mrs. William N.	1885-86
Whitehead, Arron	1863
Whitehead, Elizabeth	1811
Whitehead, John P.	1862
Whitehead, Reason	1862-63
Whitehead, Richard	1821-30
Whitehead, William S.	1863
Whitfield, Thomas	1808-09
Whiting, Benjamin C.	1867-72
Whitton, Elizabeth	1822
Whitton, James	1847
Whitton, John	1825
Whitton, John	1848
Whitton, John Sr.	1837-40
Whitton, John (children of)	1831-33
Whitton, William	1822-23
Wier, John Sr.	1816-17
Wier, Nathan Hoyt	1888-89
Wier, Samuel	1848-63
Wier, Sarah J.	1887-88
Wier, William C.	1865-71
Wilkerson, Isaac	1897-82
Willcoxon, Samuel J.	1862
Williams, Ann J.	1883-87
Williams, Austin	1884
Williams, George (children of)	1875-81
Williams, James	1841
Williams, Jane	1838-41
Williams, Joel	1837
Williams, Joe (children of)	1837-50
Williams, John Sr.	1857-59
Williams, John	1859-80
Williams, Lewis (ward)	1837-38
Williams, Mary	1872
Williams, Robert G. (children of)	1880-84
Williams, Wiley	1848-78
Williams, Wiley (ward)	1849-74
Williams, William	1811-29
Williams, William	1843-69
Williams, William Leonidas (ward)	1845-50
Williamson, Ann E.	1833
Willingham, Henderson	1873-83
Willoughby, Elijah	1822-34
Willoughby, Ellis (children of)	1844-57
Willoughby, Robert	1834-39
Willoughby, William B.	1827-38
Willoughby, William D. (ward)	1878
Willoughby, William R.	1834-36
Willoughby, William R. (children of)	1865-67
Wills, Edward	1822-29
Wilson, J.S.	1889-1900
Wilson, Richard	1856-57
Wilson, Robert C.	1856
Winter, Henry A.	1908
Wise, Patterson	1833-36
Wise, Walden	1862-63
Wise, Williamson P.	1861
Witherspoon, Cicero V.	1846
Witherspoon, Elizabeth	1877
Witherspoon, James A.	1885
Witherspoon, Robert L.	1895
Wood, Faith	1872
Wood, Richard	1803-17
Wood, William	1870-75
Wood, William P.	1857-58
Woodley, Agustus	1819
Woods, B.F. (children of)	1890
Woods, Josiah	1850
Woods, Oliver P.	1891
Woods, S.F.	1904-05
Woods, Sarah C.	1864
Woodson, Alexander	1867-73
Wozencraft, Thomas	1852-53
Wray, Thomas	1863-84
Wright, Alfred W.	1821
Wright, John Sr.	1833
Wright, John G.	1841
Wright, William	1821-28
Wright, Winfield J.	1823-27
Yancy, Goodloe H. (children of)	1893-1912
Yancey, Lucy D. (ward)	1873-75
Yancey, Lucy Grattan	1893
Yancey, Sarah P.	1878-91
Yarborough, John	1866-68
Yarborough, Lannie Allie	1893
Yates, William (ward)	1884
Yerby, Burwell	1862-74
Yerby, Everett	1873-77
Yerby, Everett (children of)	1875-80
Yerby, Mary J.	1911-12
Yerby, Mary Opheliz (ward)	1862
Yerby, Sarah H.	1893-94
Young, Agnes	1898-1902
Young, Daniel	1920
Young, Jane D.	1874-78
Young, Ophelia	1916-17
Young, Thomas H.	1857-71
Youngblood, John W.	1885
Youngkin, E.H.	1923-24
Youngkin, Jesse (children of)	1867-74

2. Court Case Files of the Inferior and County Courts, 1805-1895 (Record Group 129-2-2)

This series contains original, unbound papers which formed portions of civil case files including but not limited to:

(1) Debts
(2) Summonses
(3) *Fi Fas*
(4) Complaints
(5) Distress Warrants
(6) Bail Bonds
(7) Attachments
(8) Promissory Notes
(9) Affidavits
(10) Assumsits

The records have been flattened, cleaned, and placed in folders. They are grouped alphabetically by the surname of the plaintiff(s). Where the plaintiff's name appears more than once, the records are grouped chronologically by date. The records are dated 1800 to 1895.

A small number of miscellaneous records also are included, listed chronologically by date.

Acock, Isaac P. vs Cogburn, Moses H. 1840
Adams, Edmond B. vs Stephens, Harris 1837
Adams, Edward vs Stuart, James 1802
Adams, John; Parmelle, Albert G.; Webster, Hosea vs Billups, James; Shackelford, Edwin 1834
Adams, John M.; Parmelee, Alberto; Webster, Hosea vs Walker, William F.; Flemming, Abel 1831
Adams, Richard for use of Strong, Charles vs Newton, Josiah; Newton, Elizer L. 1826
Adams, William vs Reynolds, John 1841
Akeridge, Ezekiel vs Akeridge, David 1843
Akin, James vs Trawick, Lunsford 1802
Akins, James vs Trawick, Lunsford 1803
Akins, James S. vs Barber, William 1827
Akridge, Ezekiel vs Akeridge, David 1842
Alein, William vs Alein, James J. 1835
Alexander, Aaron vs Dicken, Richard 1845
Alexander, Aaron vs Dicken, Richard 1847
Allen, Ben for the use of Strong, William vs Runnels, Preston 1806
Allen, Benjamin for use of Benge, William vs Runnels, Preston; Strong, John 1804
Allen, Benjamin for use of Strong, William vs Runnels, Preston 1805
Allen, Henry J. vs Turner, William P. 1856
Allen, James vs Fleteher, James 1806
Allen, James vs King, Sarah 1837
Allen, James vs Ramey, Absalom 1811
Allen, Woodson for use of Jones, Rupel vs Earley, Richard 1807
Allen, Woodson for use of Jones, Russell vs Easley, Richard; Miller, Caleb 1808
Allison, Robert vs Barnette, John 1811
Allison, Robert vs Jones, Thomas, Jr. 1810
Anderson, J. H. vs Walker, Susan V.; Richardson, John M. 1847
Anderson, James for use of John Adams vs Barcley, John 1806
Anderson, James for use of Adams, James vs Barcley, John; Rosseter, White 1810
Anderson, James vs Maxey, Edward H.; Jackson, John 1827
Anderson, James C. vs Foster, John F. 1833
Anderson, James B. vs Anderson, Robert 1846
Anderson, John T. vs Robinson, Jesse 1839
Apperson, Thomas vs Dean, Nathaniel 1808
Appling, Thomas vs Dean, Nathaniel 1809
Appling, Walter A. vs Dickin, Richard 1844
Appling, William vs Fielding, William 1836
Appling, William vs Vickers, Martin 1838
Arnold, Elijah B. vs Barnett, Nathan C.; Arnold, Jesse H. 1834
Arnold, Fielding W. vs Treadway, Elijah 1837
Arnold, Fields W. vs Love, David H.; Oliver, Francis H. 1831
Arnold, Fields W. vs Love, David H.; Oliver, Francis H.; Garrett, John H. 1831
Arnold, Jesse H. vs Selmon, James J. 1847

Arnold, Park E. vs Tinsley, James 1838
Arthur, Barney vs Scroggin, Chattin; Arthur Talbot 1803
Arthur, Talbot vs Barney, John 1819
Athens, Gas Light Co. vs Whitfield, Jim 1880
Atkinson, Fannie vs Mayfield, Charles; Mayfield, Malinda 1879
Atkinson, Thomas P.; Atkinson, Wash. G.; Exect. of Atkinson, A. C. vs Bouchelle, Jesse C. 1829
Atkinson, Thomas P.; Washington G. Atkinson vs Bouchelle, Jesse C. 1829
Augusta Insurance and Banking Company vs Cobb, John A. 1840
Autrey, William vs Benge, Micajah; Garnishee of Carreway, John 1803
Autrey, William vs Caraway, John 1803
Baggett, Stephen vs Boaders, John H. 1828
Bailey, Richard vs McCrue, William 1812
Bailey, William; Barber, George vs Easley, Roderick 1811
Baker, Alfred vs Taylor, James Jones 1841
Baker, John vs Appling, Thomas 1812
Baker, Jordan vs McDonnell, Alexander 1810
Baker, Jordan vs M. A. Qauvain 1809
Baker, Joshua Sr. vs Taylor, Roland 1810-11
Baker, Obed vs Smith, Radford 1817
Baldwin, Catherine W. vs Sledge, Charles M. & Towns, Benjamin 1830
Baldwin, Cyrus G. & Sears, Jason G. vs Moore, Alsa 1833
Baldwin, Damacis C. vs Hedge, Charles M. & Dunn, John T. No date
Baldwin, Damavis C. vs Likins, Thoams M. 1830
Baldwin, Damarius vs Likens, Thomason 1834
Baldwin, Damaris vs Shaw, George W. as bail for Likens, Thomas M. 1831
Baldwin, Elijah vs Newton, Josiah 1826
Baldwin, James G. vs Luckie, James 1817
Baldwin, Joseph B. vs Newton, Josiah 1826
Baldwin, Loami & Henderson, Elijah vs Shaw, George W. 1833
Banefield, Loyd K. vs Vickers, Young 1852
Bank of Augusta vs Hopkins, Eusebeus A. 1838
Bank of Milledgeville vs Oliver, Francis H. 1839
Bank of the State of Ga. vs Brown, William 1842
Bank of the State of Ga. vs Cobb, Howell 1840
Bank of the State of Ga. vs Cobb, Howell 1840
Bank of the State of Ga. vs Cobb, Howell 1840
Bank of the State of Ga. vs Cobb, Howell 1841
Bank of the State of Ga. vs Cobb, Howell 1842
Bank of the State of Ga. vs Cobb, John A. 1840
Bank of the State of Ga. vs Cobb, John A. 1840
Bank of the State of Ga. vs Cobb, John A. 1840
Bank of the State of Ga. vs Cobb, John A. 1840
Bank of the State of Ga. vs Cole, Sarah 1842
Bank of the State of Ga. vs Elliott, Benjamin 1840
Bank of the State of Ga. vs Hancock, Thomas 1842
Bank of the State of Ga. vs Hancock, Thomas 1842
Bank of the State of Ga. vs Harden, Edward R. 1842
Bank of the State of Ga. vs Hearns, Jeptha & Clayton, William W. 1851
Bank of the State of Ga. vs Hull, Henry 1842
Bank of the State of Ga. vs McKinley, Charles G. 1841
Bank of the State of Ga. vs Mitchel, Thomas 1840
Bank of the State of Ga. vs Newton, Elizer L. 1842
Bank of Ga.; Cashier Porter, Anthony vs St. John, Isaac R. & St. John, David W. 1837
Bank of the State of Ga. vs Robinson, Jesse 1840
Bank of the State of Ga. vs Robinson, Jesse 1840
Bank of the State of Ga. vs Winter, John G. 1807
Bank of the State of Ga. vs Jennings, Jefferson & Jeinings, Henry 1883
Banks, Linton vs Johnson, Fanny 1879
Banks, Linton vs Marks, S. 1879
Banks, Linton vs Marks, S. 1879
Bankston, Abner vs Echols, Milner 1805
Bankston, Abner vs Echols, Obediah no date
Bankston, Sarah; Melton, Jonathan; Executor's of Bankston, William vs Taylor, Roland no date
Bailey, Eliza vs Baily, Green 1878
Baker, John vs Culp, B. F. 1879
Banner, Polly for use of Jesse McCristion vs Humphreys, William 1828
Barber, Allen Attorney for Shackleford, Lloyd vs Albritton, J.M. 1840

Barber, William for use of David Meriwether vs Dunn, John T. 1828
Barker, William vs Paine, Edward C. & Dicken, William 1845
Barnet, Nathaniel B. vs Hightower, Thomas; Starn, William; Harris, David; Harris, Tyre; Harris, Isham 1807
Barnett, John F. vs Cocke, Jack & Moore, John 1815
Barnett, John F. vs Strong, Elijah & Cocke, Jack F. 1815
Barnett, John H. vs Wood, Thomas, Jr. NID
Barnett, Nathan C. vs Hanson, Jesse & Sims, James 1839
Barnett, Nathan C. vs Sansom, James 1843
Barnett, Nathan E.; Brightwell, William B.; Paulett, Jesse C. vs Harden, Robert R. 1841
Barnett, Nathaniel B. vs Hightower, Thomas; Starn, William; Harris, David; Harris, Tyre; Harris, Isham 1808
Barnett, Uriah vs Lee, Johathan 1808
Barnett, William B. for use of Sears, Albert vs Knott, James & Williams, Joel 1829
Barr, Michael J. vs Dauenbaum & Florshein 1878
Barret, James M. vs Akindige, William 1852
Barrett, James & Barrett, Mary Ann vs Thomas Sansom 1842
Barrett & Sims vs Carnes, Thomas P. & Gresham, Young 1813
Barrett, Thomas & Sims, Benjamin vs Carrey, Thomas P. & Dooly, John M. 1878
Barry, J. M. vs Crawford, W. S. 1878
Barry, J. M. vs Dericot, Anthony 1879
Barry, J. M. vs Mills, Edward 1879
Barry, J. M. vs Patat, J. A. 1879
Barry, Patrick vs Royal, James & Hodgeson, Edward R. 1852
Baswell, W. P. vs Kemp, W. C. 1877
Bates, John R.; Bales, Stephen; Ellison, Henry G.; Ellison, Hannah & Bates, Mary vs Crafts, David 1846
Baxter, Andrew vs Harper, George 1802
Baxter, Andrew vs Moore, R. D. no date
Baxter, Thomas W. vs Hemphill, William S. 1841
Baxter, Andrew & Baxter, Thomas W. vs Wright, John L. 1848
Baxter, Thomas W. vs Wooldridge, Isma W.; Thomas, James L.; Hancock, Thomas 1842
Baymon, Watkins vs Flourney, Howell C. 1839
Baymon, Watkins vs Kirkpatrick, John & Newton, Ebenezer 1838
Baymon, Watkins & Cherry, William vs Rogers, Right 1834
Bazell, James vs Hayes, Missouri & Echols, Ester 1879
Bazzell, James vs Thomas Henry 1879
Beal, C. W. vs Spencer, William 1879
Beal, Nathan H.; Executor of Bostwick, Rebecca vs Sledge, Wiley 1836
Beall, E. B. vs Whaly, James 1833
Beall, Egbert B. vs Barnett, Nathan C. 1841
Beall, Elias & Theophelus vs Rakestraw, Gainham 1819
Beall, Elias & Beall, Theophelus vs Rakestraw, Gainhain L. 1820
Bearden, Aaron vs Francis Marshall 1842
Beardin, Richard for use of Hammock, Benjamin & Bearden, John 1828
Beavers, John F. vs Harvey, Edward G. 1829
Beck, Thomas J. vs Jennings, Calab 1843
Bedell, Benjamin for use of Watts, Jacobus vs Meriwether, James 1815
Beecher, Samuel T. & Brown, John H. vs Fleming, Abel 1836
Beers, William P.; Sturgis, Josiah; Thurman, Ansan vs Brown, Samuel & Mitchell, Thomas 1823
Bell, James for use of McElhannon, Christopher vs Williamson, Peter 1812
Belton, Soloman vs Lane, Johathan 1816
Bennet, Edward & Milliken, William vs Billips, Joseph & Shakelford, Edmund 1833
Bessman, John W. for use of Goodrick, William H. vs Hendrick, Manvel T. 1853
Bethune, William M. vs Freeman, Allen 1826
Beusse, J. H. D. vs Williams, William D. 1879
Biggars, Nathan vs Vickers, Martin 1838
Biggers, John F. vs Jackson, William H. 1844
Biggs, Aaron vs Strong, William 1807
Biggs, Aaron Adm. of Cocke, Jack F. for use of Stokes, William M. & Strong, Sherwood vs Brown, Joseph & Ward, Leonard 1817
Biggs, Aaron Adm. of Cocke, Jack F. for use of Stokes, William & Strong, Sherwood vs Brown, Joseph & Ward, Leonard no date

Biggs, Aaron Adm. of Cocke, Jack F. vs Strong, Elijah 1820
Billups, John vs Cabell, Robert S. 1812
Billups, John vs Cabell, Robert J. 1813
Billups, John vs Cabell, Robert J. 1813
Billups, John vs Espy, John 1826
Billups, John vs Herring, Cyril 1814
Billups, John R. vs Erwin, Leander A. 1819
Billups, John & Bowen, Christopher vs Brmord, John 1812
Billups, John & Bowen, Christopher vs Cabell, Robert J. 1812
Billups, John & Bowen, Christopher vs Garlington, Christopher 1812
Billups, John & Bowen, Christopher vs Ormond, James 1812
Billups, John; Cook, James C.; Billups, Robert vs Billups, John; Bowen, Christopher; Temple, Lee 1812
Billups, John; Cook, James C.; Billups, Robert vs Marable, John 1812
Billups, John for use of Cunningham, Thomas & Cunningham, John vs Sims, Zachariah & Ramon 1826
Billups, John for use of Scott, Thomas W. vs Cherry, Aquilla & Middlebrooks, Isaac 1810
Billups, Joseph for use of Cunningham, Thomas & Cunningham, John vs Barnett, John F. 1826
Billups, Joseph for use of Cunningham, Thomas & Cunningham, John vs Harden, Robert 1826
Billups, Joseph for use of Cunningham, Tho. & Cunningham, Jno. vs Sims, Zachariah & Nichols, Ranson 1827
Billups, Richard, Jr. vs Cabell, Robert J. 1812
Billups, Robert T. vs Burton, Larry M. 1821
Billups, Robert R. vs Moore, John O. no date
Billups, Robert for use of Billups, John vs Garrar, George Y. 1812
Billups, Robert R. vs Tyson, Eugene H. 1819
Bishop, Brice H. vs Davenport, Thomas 1840
Bishop, Thomas vs Moore, Richard D. 1849
Bishop, Thomas vs Waddel, James P. 1845
Bishop, Thomas vs Wooldridge, Isma W. & Sims, Arthur L. 1841
Blackbourn, Nancy by her guardian Cameron, Ambros vs Jones, John 1805
Blair, John; Blair, Dickson; Blair, William M. vs Fuller, William 1827
Blake, William for use of Gaston, Thomas vs Tidwell, Roderick 1806
Blanton, Benjamin; Hill, Miles; Taylor, Benjamin; Pope, Robert; Executors of Pope, Henry vs Tye, John & Tye, James 1810
Blanton, James A. vs Biscoe, Phillip 1827
Bledsoe, Robert vs Watkins, Robert 1809
Boggs, Aaron vs Wallace, James; Whitehead, Richard; Whitehead, Rachel 1811
Boggs, Archibald vs Leftweek, John T. & Parr, Daniel W. 1833
Boggs, Archibald vs Parr, Daniel W. 1833
Boggs, Joseph A. vs Espy, James W. & Espy, Thomas 1836
Boggs, Joseph A. vs Sneed, Meridith & McGuive, Thompson 1835
Bones, John & Bones, Samuel vs Brightwell, William B. & Paulette, Jesse C. 1841
Bones, John & Bones, Samuel vs Sheats, Benejah S. & Sheats, Marshall M. 1841
Bonner, Jordon vs Miers, Nathan 1802
Bonner, Jordon vs Miers, Nathan 1804
Bonner, Jorden vs Miers, Nathan 1905
Bonner, Jordan vs Hubert, Gabriel 1808
Boggs, Archibald vs Wright, Thomas A. 1829
Booth, G. M. vs Harris, S. 1879
Booth, George J. vs Hancock, Thor 1849
Booth, Thomas vs Davidson, James M. 1830
Booth, Thomas vs Martin, Robert 1809
Booth, Thomas & Co. vs Jinkins, Moore & Co. 1883
Booth, Thomas vs Pryer, Allen 1810-11
Borders, Michael A. vs Moore, Memory J. D. 1838
Bostwick, William vs Davis, William 1839-1840
Bowdre, Albert vs Durham, Brightwell no date
Bowdre, Hays vs Rich, William C. & Stovall, William L. 1851
Bowen, Christopher vs Biggs, Aaron 1819
Bowen, Christopher vs Fambrough, William 1825
Bowen, Christopher vs Haynie, Samuel 1830
Bowen, Christopher Adm. of Strong, Sherwood vs Strong, Elizabeth & Strong William 1829
Bowen, Christopher Adm. of Strong, Eherwood vs Strong, Elizabeth 1829

Bowen, Christopher Adm. of Strong, Sherwood vs Strong, William E. 1829
Bowen, Christopher Guardian of Strong, Washington vs Gordon, Robert S. & Biggs, Freeman 1829
Bowen, Christopher Surviving Copartner of Billups, John & Co. vs Lea, Temple & Lea, Green 1813
Bowes, John & Carmichael, Robert D. vs Stephens, David; Barnett, Nathan C.; Brightwell, William B. & Paullett, Jesse C. 1840
Bowie, James; Barker, William; Bowie, Langders vs Sams, Joseph; Nunally, Aaron F.; Moore, Robert H.; Moore, Thomas 1843
Boyd, George as agent for Totty, John & Hay, John W. vs Vickers, Martin 1838
Boyer, Elias vs Hargrove, John R. 1823
Brackenridge, William A. vs Speer, Emory 1879
Bradley, Elijah & Knappen, Thomas vs Rosseter, White 1805
Braswell, Samuel for use of McNeed, William vs Herndon, Elisha 1822
Breedlove, John A. vs Selman, James J. 1847
Brewer, Hundley vs Chisolm, John 1812
Brewer, Hundley vs Chislom, John 1812
Brewer, Hunley vs Braswell, Allen 1806
Brewer, L. R. vs Ninson, Obadiah no date
Brewer, Littleton R. vs Akin, James S. 1830
Brewer, Littleton R. vs Davenport, Jonett 1826
Brewer, Littleton R. vs Dunson, Obadiah 1826
Brewer, Littleton R. vs Hodges, William 1830
Brewer, Littleton R. vs Langford, James 1828
Brewer, Littleton R. vs Moffett, Gabriela 1834
Brewer, Littleton R. vs Sears, Marcus A. 1830
Brewer, Littleton R. vs Wheeler, Thomas 1827
Brewer, William vs Echols, Robert 1805
Brewer, William vs Nichols, Obediah 1805
Brewer, William vs Ramey, John 1819
Bridges & Gibson vs Edwards, Sage D. 1834
Bridges & Gibson vs Winston, Joseph B. & Ruso, Thadeus B. 1835
Bridges, John W. vs Taylor, John H. 1834
Bridges, John W. & Gibson, Lewis vs Crenshaw, James J. 1834
Bridges, John W. & Gibson, Lewis vs Oliver, John & Oliver, Francis H. 1832
Bridges, John W. & Gibson, Lewis vs Winston, Joseph B. 1833
Bridges, Killis C. vs Cavender, Eleanir; Lane, Theophilus; Lane, Jonathan 1821
Brightwell, John vs Moore, George W. 1828
Brightwell, Samuel for use of Pye, William vs Andrews, John & Davenport, William 1824
Brightwell, William B. & Paulett, Jesse C. vs Harden, Robert R. 1814
Briscoe, Nathan vs Barnett, John H. 1830
Brooks, Oliver C.; Parsons, Rock; Brooks, George G. vs Nixson, James 1820
Brown, B & W vs Braswell, Allen 1806
Brown, Bedford vs Hopkins, Dennis 1806
Brown, Bedford vs Ramey, John & Ramey, Absalom 1813
Brown, Bedford Executors vs Shackleford, Rich D. 1820
Brown, Bedford vs Shackleford, Richard 1823
Brown, Bedford vs Taylor, Roland; Freeman, Allen; Taylor, John 1814
Brown, Bedford & Elder, Sterling vs Jackson, Samuel 1811
Brown, David vs Laurence, Joseph 1806
Brown, David vs Laurance, Joseph 1807
Brown, James vs Herbert, Gabriel 1813
Brown, James vs Redd, Charles A. 1812
Brown, Joseph vs Clark, Lucy 1812
Brown, Joseph vs Taylor, Edward W. & Sims, James 1817
Brown, Littleton R. vs Thomas, William R. & Reynolds, Thomas 1833
Brown & Mitchell vs Erwin, Leander A. 1820
Brown, Murphy & Co. vs Cabell, Robert J. 1812
Brown, Samuel vs Brown, Joseph 1812
Brown, Samuel vs Brown, Joseph 1812
Brown, Samuel vs Sims, Zachariah 1820
Brown, Wes vs Mitchell, Florence 1879
Brown, William vs Nichols, Milner 1805
Brown, William & Reynolds, John vs Jackson, John 1838
Brown, William & Reynolds, John vs Kirkpatrick, John 1838
Browning, Margaret vs Neisler, Hugh 1833
Browning, Margaret vs Steadley, William 1839-1840

Browning, William vs Caraway, John 1803
Bruce, John for use of Ligon, Joseph vs Stephens, Joshua 1820
Brux & Pope vs Gauvain, Michael 1809
Bryan, Eli vs Suttle, Jesse 1811
Bryan, Felix vs Love, Robert 1827
Bryan, Filix vs Knott, James 1829
Bryan, Isaac vs Carr, William A. 1828
Bryan, Isaac vs Simms, Arthur L. 1829
Bryant, Archer for use of Thomas, Stevens vs Prince, Noah F. 1827
Brydie, A. vs Gilleland, Coil no date
Brydie, Archibald vs Moore, Benjamin P. 1840
Brydie, Archibald vs Bouchelle, Jesse C. 1832
Brydie, Archibald vs Weatherly, William S. 1838
Brydie, Archibald vs Wells, William B. 1840
Bryson, William vs Owen, Jeremiah 1830
Bryson, William & Bryson, Harper vs Jones, Job 1832
Bucher & Brown vs Paine, Sidney 1814
Bucher, Samuel T. & Brown, John H. vs Clark, Ely K. 1836
Buckley, James K. vs Garner, Elijah 1823
Buckly, James K. vs Gauvain, Rosalia 1823
Buesse, H. vs Lowe, Abram 1879
Brunson, Isaac W. vs Thrasher, William H. 1840
Burbank, E. L. vs Noble, William G. & Noble, Augustus Hill 1879
Burch, Charles C. vs Taylor, William B. 1826
Burch, William R.; Weller, John; Robbins, Allen vs Brydie, Archibald 1834
Burke, Richard E. vs Hendon, Isham 1821
Burpee, A. L. vs Royal, E. D. 1879
Burke, William B. for use of Shepherd, Carter vs Dunnel, John T. 1830
Burnett, Jeremiah vs Dickinson, Joel 1810
Burnett, Jeremiah vs Dickinson, Joel 1810
Burnett, Jeremiah vs Sansom, James & Sansom, William 1820
Burnett, Jeremiah vs Sansom, William & Roberts, William 1810
Burnett, Nathan C. vs Steadley, William 1839
Burney, William V. vs Dunams, David & Dunams, Jacob 1846
Burton, James & Williamson, William vs Lowe, Thomas 1833
Bustin, Edward vs Jackson, William 1845
Bustin, Edward vs Jones, James W. 1838
Bustin, Edward vs Tate, James C. 1838
Bustin, Musgrove vs Shaw, Geo. W. 1834
Butler, Moses vs Gresham, Albert Y. & Brown, William T. 1829
Butler, Richard vs Stratham, Anderson & Stratham, Nelson 1833
Buzzell, James vs Echols, Ester 1879
Bynton, Hollis vs Cheatham, Thomas H. 1842
Byrum, John W. & Farrer, John vs Thomas, Leuis W. & Farrer, Thomas J. ND
Callan, Thomas for use of Andrews, Garrell vs Dimaurt, David 1846
Camak, James & Ragland, Thomas vs Harden, Robert R. 1831
Camp, Abner Admin. of Camp, Edmond vs Braswell, Samuel & Haile, William 1828
Canny, Thomas P. vs McDonald, Alexander 1815
Carhart & Bros vs Hood, Wiley F. 1879
Carmichael, Andrew W. & Carmichael, William P. vs Lyle, David J. 1852
Carmichael, John C. vs Lyle, David J. 1851
Carnes, Thomas P. vs Ligon, James 1819
Carnes, Thomas Petters vs Rice, Nancy & Hall, Martin 1806
Carnes, William W. vs Fitzsimmons, Henry 1823
Carnes, William W. for use of Meriwether, David vs Hunt, William H. 1822
Carr, Thomas vs Meriwether, David 1816
Carr, William A. vs Byrd, John A. 1832
Carr, William A. vs Clarke, Eli & Young, Benjamin 1832
Carroll, David vs Arthur, Caleb 1824
Carter, Christopher A. vs Barber, James 1808
Carter, Hawkins & Sloan vs Schevenell, Leonard & Yancey, Goodloe H. 1877
Cary, Lucy Exec of Cary, Dudley vs Hays, William 1808
Case, Leonard E. vs Vandeford, Richard 1835
Casey, John A. vs Gauvain, Michael A. 1812
Cash, Benjamin W. vs Nichols, Ransom 1853
Cater, Charles & Davies, John vs Jones, Robert A. 1834
Cebra, John Y. & Cuming, Thomas B. vs Totty, John 1842
Central Bank of Ga. vs Billups, Joseph; More, Thomas; Hull, Asbury 1835

Central Bank of Ga. vs Davenport, Robert; Hester, Joseph; Davenport, Thomas; Totty, John 1841
Central Bank of Ga. vs Davenport, Thomas; Davenport, Heney; Knott, John 1843
Central Bank of Ga. vs Davenport, Thomas; Davenport, Robert; Davenport, Henry; Davenport, Henry, Jr.; Totty, John 1841
Central Bank of Ga. vs Hay, John W.; Totty, John; Branch, James C.; Davenport, Thomas 1841
Central Bank of Ga. vs Hester, Joseph; Davenport, Robert; Davenport, Thomas; Totty, John 1841
Central Bank of Ga. vs Sansom, Thomas; Adm. of Lord, Ebenezer & Lord, Benjamin B.; Tenney, Shubael; Hancock, Thomas 1841
Central Bank of Ga. vs Shaw, George E.; Shaw, Oliver P.; Billups, Joseph 1836
Central Bank of Ga. vs Totty, John; Hay, John W.; Hester, Joseph 1841
Chatham, Mary W. vs Cobb, John A. (Prin.) & Cobb, Howell (security) 1840
Cheatham, Thomas for use of Meriwether, Francis H. vs Jackson, William H. 1828
Cherry, William L. & Dodson, Daniel vs Adams, Nathaniel A. 1844
Cherry, William L. vs Donnald, Robert 1840
Cherry, William L. vs Hartley, John B. 1845
Chester, Elisha W. vs Ward, Leonard 1823
Chislom, John vs Pounds, Richard 1802
Chislom, John vs Sanders, Julius 1802
Chislom, John vs Saunders, Julius 1802
Choice, John; Choice, Cyrus; Choice, Tully for use of Baxter, Thomas W. vs Towns, Benjamin 1839-40
Church, Alenzo vs Bacon, William 1843
Clark, Eli K. vs Sherrod, Frederic O. A. 1836
Clark, Elijah vs Williamson, Peter 1809
Clark, F. & Clark, H. vs Brydie, Archibald 1833
Clark, Francis; Clark, Horace; Rackett, George vs Barnett, Mathan C. & Paulett, Jesse C. 1841
Clark, Jeremiah H. & Holland, Neal vs Frost, Samuel 1839
Clark, John vs Harden, Robert R. no date
Clark, Samuel vs Hendricks & Johnson 1842
Clark, Samuel vs Johnston, Benjamin F. & Hendricks, John 1843
Clark, William Sr. vs Elder, David 1826
Clark, William Sr. vs Elder, Harrison W. 1826
Clarke, Absalom vs Ramey, John 1809
Clarke County vs Elias Busby (Principal); Jackson, William; Jackson, Stephen; Wooldridge, Isma W.; Hopkins, Eusibas A. 1840
Clarke Inferior Court vs Bransford, James; Strong, William; Strong, Johnson 1806
Clarke Co. Inferior Ct. vs Echols, Obediah; Echols, Milner; Taylor, Roland; Bond, Edward no date
Clarke Inferior Ct. vs Smith, John 1812-17
Clarke, Ely K. vs Sherrod, Frederic A. 1836
Clarke, Frederick A.; Booram, Thomas L.; Rathbone, Jacob B. vs Taylor, James Jones & Jones, James W. 1839-40
Clarke, Julia vs Hunter, Benj. F. 1875
Clarke, William vs Clarke, Lucy & Brown, Joseph no date
Clarke, William Sr. vs Elder, Harrison W. 1826
Clayton, A. J. vs Wisdom, Jesse 1834
Clayton, Augustin S. vs Wisdom, Jesey 1834
Clayton, Augustine S. vs Erwin, Leander A. 1820
Clayton, Augustine S. vs Meigs, Josiah 1812
Clayton, Augustine S. vs Meige, Josiah 1813
Clayton, Augustus S. vs Cobb, John A. as guardian of McKinzie, Alexander 1833
Clayton, William W. & Clayton, Edward P. vs Yarborough, John 1842
Clement, James vs Clement, John & Mathews, Gabriel T. 1812
Clement, James vs Clement, William & Epps, William 1812
Clements, Charles for use of Sparks, Martin T. vs Stewart, Samuel 1810
Cliff, William vs Suttles, Isaac 1812
Clifton, George vs Hawkins, John B. & Thomas, James L. 1826
Clifton, George Jr. vs Oqilby, Peter F. 1822
Clinard, A. D. vs Downing, R. H. 1879
Cline, William vs Gray, Hezekiah & Borders, John H. 1829
Clock, Darius; Cunningham, John; Cunningham, Thomas vs Flournoy, Howell C. 1839

Clock, Darius; Cunningham, John; Cunningham, Thomas; Morrison, William A. vs Baldwin, Francis G. 1841
Clock, Darius; Cunningham, Thomas; Cunningham, John vs Baldwin, Damaris C. 1841
Clock, Darius; Morrison, William A.; Cunningham, John; Cunningham, Thomas vs Harden, Edward R. 1839
Clock, Darius; Morrison, William A.; Cunningham, Thomas; Cunningham, John vs Taylor, James Jones 1841
Clock, Darius; Morrison, William A.; Cunningham, Thomas; Cunningham, John vs Yarbrough, Thomas H. 1840
Clute, John D. & Meade, Henry M. vs Jones, James W. 1838
Cobb, John B. & Crawford, Thomas vs Sims, James & Hendon, James no date
Cobb, Lamar agent for Evans, Arthur vs Morrison, George 1879
Cobb, Lamar trus. Cobb, Lucy vs Bain, W. A. 1877
Cobb, Thomas W. vs Shaw, William 1809
Cobb, Thomas W. for use of Meriweather, William vs Ward, Leonard & Brown, Samuel 1825
Cobell, Robert J. vs Richard Billups, Jr. 1813
Clock, Jack F. vs Strong, Elijah 1823
Cocke, Jack F. vs Farrar, George Y. 1815
Cocke, Jack F. vs Ramey, Sanford L. 1809
Cocke, Jack F. vs Ramey, Sanford L. 1817
Coe, Ann A. vs Rogers, Right & Frost, Samuel 1837
Coffin, Lee & Co. vs Collins, J. W. 1877
Cohen, J. vs Macon, Thomas G. 1875
Coil, W. M. Adm for Offices of Court vs Pass, Thomas W. & Pass, Dicy A. 1882
Cole, Samuel vs Paulett, Richard 1812
Cole, Samuel vs Paulett, Richard; Paulett, Lewis; Paulett, Henry; McMichael, William 1812
Cole, Sarah vs Cobb, John A. 1840
Coleman, Andrew vs East & Cox 1879
Coleman, John vs Kinney, John 1809
Collier, Cuthbert Indorsee of Colquit, John T. vs Ramey, John 1806
Collins, Bryon W. vs Taylor, James J. 1845
Collins, Robert vs Barnett, Nathan C. 1841
Collins, Samuel vs Campbell, Thomas 1827
Combs & Mason for use of Combs, George D. vs Wood, Thomas 1838
Combs, Sterling vs Appling, Thomas & Freeman, Nicholas 1808-11
Conally, George A. vs DeTrobraind, Rosalie Gauvain; Newton, Josiah ND
Condict, Steven H.; Norton, John A.; Jennings, David; Tomlinson, Robert vs Hunter, David Van & Barrett, Michaels S. 1852
Conger, Abijab vs Towns, Daniel 1847
Conger, Thomas for Talmage, John vs Greene, William P. & Judd, George B. 1826
Connally, George A. vs Hodges, Joseph 1840
Connally, George A. & Newton, Elizar L. vs Frost, Samuel 1839
Connally, George A. & Newton, Elizar L. vs Jones, James W. 1838
Connally, George A. & Newton, Elizar L. vs King, Sarah & King, Agness B. 1838
Connally, George A. & Newton, Elizar L. vs Yarborough, Thomas H. 1826
Conner, Daniel vs Glass, James & Wood, Tabitha 1809
Conner, Edward vs Yarborough, John 1832
Conway, P. C. vs Clarke Co. Bldg. Loan & Improvement Co. 1895
Cook, Henry H. & Cook, James vs Love, Robert 1827
Cook, J. S. vs Rammy, Sanford L. 1810
Cook, James C. vs Moore, George W. 1810
Cook, William B. vs Sims, John H. 1832
Cook, William M. vs Delay, Hiram R. & Vanderford, William ND
Cook, William M. vs Cade, Thomas L. & Wallis, Nicholas ND
Cook, Zadock vs (?) 1814
Cook, Zadock vs Moore, George W. 1810
Cook, Zadock vs Moore, George W. 1811
Cook, Zadock vs Stringer, James 1810
Cook, Zadock & others vs Watts, James 1807
Cooke, Eugene D. vs Barrfield, Lloyd K. 1838
Cooper, Willis vs Yarborough, John 1842
Corbett, James vs Trammill, Daniel 1812
Cord, John M. vs Winn, Hinchey 1819
Conger, Thomas & Talmage, John vs Greene, William P. & Judd, George B. 1826

Cousins, Fanny vs Wright, William G. 1820
Cowen, James vs Hudson, Shaderick 1802
Cowen, James vs Hutson, Shadrick 1804
Cox, Edwin F. agent for Poullain, Thomas N. & Poullain, Antoine vs Wilkerson, Robert B. 1840
Cox, John J. vs Hickman, John 1819
Coy, Thomas W. vs Martin and Duke 1807
Craft, Hannah vs Jackson, Stephen 1846
Craft, Rebecca vs Jackson, Stephen 1840
Crain, Thomas vs Davis, Edward 1806
Crane, Benjamin F. & Morrison, William A. vs Howell, Cobb 1842
Crane, Benjamin F. & Morrison, William A. vs Yarborough, Thomas H. 1840
Crane, J. R. vs Booth, G. M.; Booth, J. N.; Booth, J. M. ND
Crane, J. R. vs Edwards, Jim 1879
Crane, John W. vs Walker, Taylor 1879
Crane, Ross Admr. of Sawtell, John W. vs Yarborough, Job & Conger, Abijah 1842
Cravin, William M. vs Henden, James W. 1852
Crawford, Archibald vs Thurman, Benjamin 1813
Crawford, Archibald vs Trammell, Daniel 1811
Crawford, Joseph for use of Billips, John vs Sims, John H. 1828
Crawford, William H. vs Deans, Charles 1809
Crews, John vs Reynolds, Reuben 1817
Crews, John vs Reynolds, Reuben 1817
Crocker, William vs Bankston, John; Bankston, Levi; Dyson, William 1806
Crow, Abner vs Bankston, Henry 1811-13
Crow, Jocob vs Borders, John H. 1827
Crow, Steven vs Kelly, Jacob 1807
Crowley, Charly vs Pryer, Obadiah 1815
Cullen & Newman vs Collins, J. W. 1877
Cullum, Francis for use of Billups, John vs Bickerstaff, Johnston; Marable, John; Cox, Richard 1812
Cullum, Francis for use of Billups, John; Hendon, Norris; Martin, Robert 1812
Cuningham, Andrew vs Ramey, William 1804
Cuningham, Thomas & Cuningham, John vs Harden, Edward 1838
Cunningham, William R. vs Cobb, John A.; Cobb, Howell; Robinson, Jepe 1840
Cunningham, William R. vs Poore, Benjamin P. 1840
Curry, James W. vs Baldwin, Benjamin C. 1836
Daneill, Joseph vs King, Sarah 1837
Danforth, Jacob vs Rosseter, White 1806
Danforth, Jacob vs Rosseter, White 1807
Daniel (?) vs Christopher, William J. 1845
Daniel, Allen vs Sims, Zachariah 1826
Daniel, Amos vs Curry, John 1802
Daniel, Ezekiel vs Henderson, James 1819
Daniel, Josiah vs Melton, Stroud; Melton, Tabitha; Harper, Anselmn L. 1831
Daniel, Josiah vs Parr, Benjamin J. 1834-36
Daniell, Jesse vs Gann, John 1837
Daniell, Robert vs Shaw, William 1851
Dannell, Nathaniel vs Shaw, William ND
Danniel, Russell C. vs Yorkum, Washington C. 1847
Darnald, Nicholas H. for use of Nance, Reuben vs Cutchen, Lemuel R. 1825
Darnald, Nicholas H. for use of Nance, Reuben vs Cutchens, Lemuel 1825
Darnel, Nicholas H. for use of Nance, Reuben vs Cutchens, Lemuel R. 1826
Davenport, John A. vs Taylor, James H. 1830
Davenport, Thomas vs Fleming, Able; Stovall, Litteberry 1839
David, Martha C. for Officers of Court vs David, Robert 1877
Davidson, John J. vs Humprey, Benjamin 1808
Davidson, John J. vs Humphrey, Benjamin 1810
Davis, & Barber for use of Crawford, Henry vs Maxey, Josiah 1838
Davis, & Barber for use of Crawford, Henry vs Maxey, Josiah & his Daughters; Maxey, Harriett 1839
Davis, John vs Runnells, Preston & Braswell, Allen 1803
Davis, John; Runnels, Preston; Braswell, Allen 1803
Davis, Thomas vs Harper, George 1804
Davis, Thomas vs Harper, George 1804
Davison, Harris vs Talmadge, John 1839

Davison, John & Bryson, Harper C. vs Byrnes, Thomas & Levins, James 1837
Dawson, Elijah vs Bone, William 1809
Dawson, Henry T. for use of Hungerford, J. & Hungerford, W. S. vs Byrdie, John A. 1834
Dear vs Durham; Wiley ND
Dean, Henry G. vs Durham; Wiley 1863
Dearing, William vs Brown, William 1842
Dearing, William vs Clower, Daniel M. 1847
Dearing, William vs Cole, Sarah 1843
Dearing, William vs Haggard, French; Starks, Benton; Security of Riden, John S. 1841
Dearings, William vs Harden, Robert R. 1841
Dearing, William vs Shepherd, Thomson 1826
Dearing, William vs Witherspoon, Elizabeth 1843
Dearing, William vs Witherspoon, Elizabeth & Witherspoon, Cicero N. 1843
DeAufignac, William D. & Turpin, William H. vs Harden, Robert R. 1837
DeButts, Joshua for use of Scott, William & Radcliffe, John vs Shaw, William 1809
DeButts, Joshua for use of Scott & Radcliffe vs Shaw, Margaret; Randolph, Peter; Adm. of Shaw, William 1811
Demond, W. A. & Co. vs Binyon, George 1879
Demond, W. R. vs Carrithers, Lucy 1879
Demond, W. R. & Co. vs Childers, Henry 1879
Demond, W. R. & Co. vs Davis, Mrs. Rebecca 1879
Demond, W. R. vs Eberhart, Thomas 1879
Demond, W. R. & Co. vs Galloway, Mrs. Arura Alias Galloway, Mrs. James; Galloway, James 1879
Demond, W. R. & Co. vs Harris, Myrtus 1879
Demond, W. R. & Co. vs Herring, Macy 1879
Demond, W. R. & Co. vs Merriweather, W. S. 1879
Demond, W. R. & Co. vs Nations, William Jasper 1879
Demond, W. R. & Co. vs Parker, J. W. 1879
Demond, W. R. & Co. vs Royal, Ed. 1879
Demond, W. R. & Co. vs Sprawling, Frank 1879
Demond, W. R. & Co. vs Whitfield, James 1879
Demond, W. R. & Co. vs Williams, Dawson 1879
Demond, W. R. & Co. vs Williams, Laura 1879
Demond, W. R. & Co. vs Barnard, Nathaniel L. 1879
Demond, W. R. & Co. vs Harris, Myrtus 1879
Demond, W. R. & Co. vs Whitehead, Thomas 1879
Demond, William R. & Co. vs Reynolds, Mrs. Mary C. 1879
Demond, W. R. & Co. vs Suirling, John 1879
Demond, William R. & Co. vs Black, J. W. 1879
Demond, William R. & Co. vs Carrithers, Mrs. E. H. ND
Demond, Wm. R. & Co. vs Flanigan, Mrs. Eliza 1879
Demond, Wm. R. & Co. vs William Tolbert 1874
Dent, George vs Ashley, Peter G. & Bailey, William 1833
Dent, George vs Cobb, John B.; Robinson, Jesse; Cobb, Howell 1840
Dent, George vs Galliher, Samuel & Newton, E. L. 1834
Dent, George vs Hawkins, John B.; Wright, John C.; Oliver, Francis H. 1838
Dent, George vs Hodges, William & Harper, John W. 1830
Dent, George vs Sledge, Charles M.; Dunn, John T.; Newton, Elizar Z. 1829
Denton, John vs Byrd, John A. 1828
Denton, John B. vs Witter, James 1835
Dicken, Richard vs Bell, Joseph 1836
Dicken, Richard vs Clarkson, Joseph 1807
Dicken, Richard vs Echols, Robert E. 1810
Dicken, Richard vs Echols, Robert E. 1809
Dicken, William vs Baldwin, Larkin L. 1829
Dicken, William vs Bird, Henry 1843
Dicken, William vs Richard Adams; Ball, John P. 1840
Dicken, William vs Love, Robert; Love, David H. 1832
Dicken, Richard vs Hodges, Joseph 1842
Dickers, Richard vs Appling, Walter A. 1852
Dickin, Thomas vs Dickin, Joseph 1810
Dickin, William vs Brightwell, William B.; Paulett, Jesse C.; Barnett, Nathan C. 1841
Dickin, William vs Wozencraft, Thomas ND

Dickins, Richard vs Hodges, Joseph 1832
Dinkins, Samuel H. & Sadler, Stanhope vs Hemphill, William S. 1840
Dickson, Richard for use of Ga. R. R. Banking Co. vs Christopher, Wm. G. 1843
Dickson, Richard for use of Ga. R. R. Banking Co. vs Hopkins, Eusibusa 1843
Dobbs, S. C. vs Ga. Railroad 1879
Dobbs, S. C. vs Ga. R. R. & Banking Co. 1879
Doggett, Thomas; Higganbotham, Oliver; Adm. of Estate of Doggett, Chattin vs McCallam, William; Campbell, Thomas 1818
Dooly, John M. vs Jackson, Samuel 1821
Dorman, John vs Lee, Wiat 1829
Dorsett, Charles L. vs Cooper, James A. 1840
Dortic, German I.; Lafette, Augustus vs Jackson, John ; Hicks, Burton 1834
Dougherty, Charles Att. for Williams, Ebenezer; Mash. Moricai; Stilwell, Richard vs Colt, Joseph C. 1840
Dougherty, Charles Executor of Holt, Cicero vs Moffett, Gabriel A. ND
Dougherty, Charles vs Murdock, Bartlett W. 1841
Dougherty, Rebecca Adminx. vs Clark, Lucy 1812
Dougherty, William vs Taylor, William B. 1826
Dougherty, William; Puryear, John Admin. of Puryear, Peter vs Arthur, Lewis & Bailey, John A. 1829
Dowell, Thomas vs Adams, Nathaniel A. 1828
Drake, William A. & Murrell, George M. vs Sims, William 1832
Duke, Macy vs Clifton, Clement 1828
Duken, Richard vs Echols, Robert E. 1808
Dukin, Richard vs Clarkson, Joseph 1807
Dula, Thomas vs Beegles, William 1802
Dula, Thomas vs Beegles, William 1803
Duncan, Robert B.; Duncan, Terry E.; Sloan, Alexander vs Ross, Rice F. 1824
Dunlap, John C. vs Wooldridge, Isma W. 1840
Dunn, John for use of David Meriwether vs Jackson, William 1828
Dunn, John T. vs Seisler, Hugh 1828
Dunnaghy, Samuel vs Harper, George 1807
Dupree, William for use of Wright, Wingfield Jett vs Lane, Philip 1823
Dupree, William for Wright, Winfield J. vs Lane, Philip 1823
Durhan, Joseph vs Carson, Sampson 1834
Durhan, Joseph vs Carson, Sampson 1834
Easley, Roderick vs Merewether, David 1812
Easley, Roderick vs Spillas, Warrington 1809
Echols, Absalom vs Brown, Joseph 1819
Echols, James vs Armsted, Miller 1807
Echols, Milner vs Brewer, William 1808
Echols, Milner Guardian of Harris, Robert L. vs Hopkins, Samuel; Hopkins, Anselmn L. 1826
Echols, Obediah vs Brewer, William 1807
Echols, Reuben vs Hunton, James 1820
Echols, Reuben & Smith, George L. vs Hunton, James 1821
Echols, Robert vs Brewer, William 1808
Echols, Robert E. vs Leak, Robert & Runnels, Preston 1807
Ector, John vs Riggs, Aaron 1816
Ector, Joseph vs Walker, William F. & Fleming, Abel 1831
Edgar, Mathias & Edgar, William Jr. vs Jones, James W. 1828
Edge, Ezekiel for officers of the Court vs Hunt, D. J. 1884
Edge, Ezekiel S. for Officers of Court vs Word, T. J. ND
Edward Williams & Co. vs Callwell, William 1819
Edward Williams & Co. vs Caldwell, William 1819
Edwards, Albert H. Adm. of Hughes, Richard vs Elder, William Y. 1866
Edwards, Gage D. vs Jackson, William H. 1833
Edwards, Joseph vs Hambey, Joseph 1836
Elder, David for use of Fambrough, William vs Silvey, Abraham 1823
Elder, Harrison vs Maxey, Edward H. 1829
Elder, Howell vs Brown, Samuel 1820-22
Elder, Jordan vs Rockfort, George 1819
Elder, Joseph vs Williams, Clark T.; Ector, Joseph; Elder, Howard 1828
Elder, Sterling vs Anderson, Thomas 1813
Elder, Sterling vs Brown, Lemuel 1821
Elder, Sterling vs Burton, James M. 1818
Elder, Sterling vs Crews, John 1820

Elder, Sterling vs Crews, John 1820
Elder, Sterling vs Hendon, Isham 1821
Elder, Sterling vs Strong, Elijah 1817
Elliott, Benjamin vs Welch, James 1837
Elliott, Benjamin vs Zebenne, Joseph D. 1840
Elliott, Benjamin vs Zebenne, Joseph B.; Macurvin, Anthony; Truelle, John; Bacon, William 1840
Ellis & Gregg vs Ford, A. J. 1879
Ellis, Thomas for use of Easley, Wosham vs Laurence, Joseph 1812
Newton, Elizur L. vs Jackson, William H. 1842
Embry, Joel; Johnson, Isaac; Executors of Estate of Embry, William vs Brown, Samuel 1832
Emerson, Walter vs DeGaffenreid, Boswell B. 1829
Epps, William vs Vinson, Obediah 1826
Erwin, Francis; Graham, Abner Adm. of Graham, Andrew vs Bouchells, Jesse C.; Loyd, James H.; Jackson, William H. 1831
Erwin, L. A. vs Clark, Michael N. ND
Erwin, Leander A. vs Clark, Michael N. 1825
Erwin, Leander A. vs Hinton, Rachel 1829
Eskridge, John vs Richey, James F. 1820
Eskridge, John vs Winfield, Joel ND
Eskridge, John vs Winfield, Joel 1821
Espy, Thomas vs Espy, Robert 1829
Eustis, William F.; Callender, Benjamin vs Alexander, Aaron; Reid, Samuel 1849
Evans, Charles vs Cobb, John A. 1839
Evans, Charles vs Harden, Edward 1839
Evans, Charles vs Jackson, James; Cobb, Howell; Nisbet, John 1840
Evans, Charles vs Jackson, William H. & Nisbet, John ND
Evans, Charles vs King, George W.; Cobb, Howell; Wilkins, Joseph C. 1839
Evans, Charles vs Sarah King 1839
Evans, Charles vs Morrow, Thomas & Nisbet, John 1839
Evans, Henry W. vs Watts, James 1809
Evans, Jacks vs Scott, Jim 1879
Evans, Jehue Indorsee vs Marabel, William & Marabel, John 1805-06
Evans, Parke & Co. vs Collins, J. W. 1877
Ewings, Arthur vs Wright, John L. & Sims, John H. 1829
Execution for Tax vs Brown, Joseph 1819
Fambro, John N. vs Selman, James J.; Selman, Susan; Jacks, Green B. 1849
Fambrough, John A. vs Selman, James J.; Selman, Simon; Jacks, Green B. ND
Fambrough, John A. vs Walker, William F. & Branch, Armsted 1838
Fambrough, John E. & Hollaway, James vs Burton, James M.; Davenport, Thomas; Totty, John; Smith, Anderson V.; Trustees of Salem Academy ND
Fambrough, John A. vs Walker, William F. & Branch, Armstead 1838
Fann, William vs Beasley, John 1811
Farrar, Francis vs Davenport, Moses N. & Davenport, Martin S. 1840
Farrow, George W. for use of Gibson, Lewis vs Wright, Thomas A. 1832
Felker, Stephen vs Thrasher, William H. 1854
Felker, Stephen vs Woddail, Thomas; Woddail, John C.; Blasingham, John 1843
Fellows, George P. vs Weathersby, William S. 1836
Fellows, Ella M. vs Bazell, Isham 1879
Fellows, James; Wadsworth, Francis; Campbell, Isaac vs Jones, James W. 1839
Ferry, Ebenezer L. & Ferry, George W. vs Elder, Joshua P. 1852
Ferry, George W. & Ferry, Ebenezer vs Elder, Joshua P. 1852
Ferry, George W. & Ferry, Ebenezer L. vs Yoakin, Washington C. 1852
Few, Seaborn for use of Sheats, Marshall M. vs Burton, Robert E.; Tarpley, Augustine 1845
Field, William G. vs Moffett, Gabriel A. 1830
Field, William G. vs Moffett, Gabriel A. & Barnett, John F. 1830
Fields, Henry H. & Co. vs Kissellburg, Henry J. & Holbrook, Nathan 1833
Fields, Henry H. vs Sledge, Isham; Burks, Rheea H. H.; Burke, Betsey Ann 1831
Finch, T. Charles vs Herring, Benjamin 1837
Findley, John B. vs Herring, Richard 1816
Findley, Mathew vs Ormond, James & Ormond, John 1812
Findley, Thomas vs Billips, Richard 1811
Fitch & Chatterton vs Schevenell, Leonard & Yancey, Goodloe H. 1877
Fitzsimmons, Henry vs Fitzpatrick, Patrick 1826
Fleming, Daniel F. vs Hunt, Josiah M. 1848

Fleming, Miller vs Sturdivant, J. Jesse 1810
Fleming, Robert vs Akridge, David 1824
Fleming, Robert vs Akridge, David 1837
Fleming, Mary & Fleming, John vs Wright, William 1812
Flippin, William vs Garlington, Christopher 1820
Flournoy, Howell C. vs Frierson, James D. 1839-40
Flournoy, John G. vs Cobb, John A. & Schley, George 1837
Floyd, John vs Bell, George 1808
Floyd, Stewart Adm of Cherry, Valentine J. vs Booth, George J. & Booth, Robert 1846
Fluker, Robert vs Fullwood, Robert 1812
Force, Benjamin W. vs Hunt, Josiah M. 1848
Force, Lewis M.; Force, John P.; Force, Benjamin W.; Couley, Benjamin vs Johnston, Benjamin F. 1842
Ford, John for use of Lewis, Gilley vs Flippen, Jesse 1806
Foster, Adam G. vs Paine, Edward 1843
Foster, Adam G. vs Paine, Edward C. 1843
Foster, Samuel H.; Easton, George L. vs Wooldridge, Isma W. 1840
Fowler, Drury vs Sikes, Mathew 1841
Fraser, Hugh A. & Hastie, William S. vs King, Sarah & King, Agnes B. 1838
Frazier, Julian vs Turner, James 1827
Freeman, Catherine vs Reynolds, John 1833
Freeman, Hugh vs Freeman, Robert 1805
Freeman, James vs Arthur, Talbot 1802
Freeman, James vs Arthur, Talbot 1803
Freeman, James Clerk for Freeman, Robert vs Close, Elijah 1810
Freeman, John vs Kelbourn, Daniel 1807
Freeman, John vs Kilbourn, Daniel 1807
Freeman, Robert vs Booth, John 1819
Freeman, Robert vs Gauvain, Michael A. 1811
Freeman, Robert vs Jones, Thomas Jr. 1810-11
Freeman, Robert vs Oliver, James 1811
Freeman, Robert vs Taylor, Rowland 1810-11
Freeman, Robert vs Thurman, William 1810
Frierson, James D. & his wife Frieson, Margarette formerly Bostick, Margarette vs Beal, Nathan Executor of Bostick, Rebecca 1845
Fullwood, Jane W. vs Richardson, Richard; Vincent, Isaac L. Adms. of Ligon, Robert 1844
Fullwood, Robert vs Caddy, David & Dean, Burket 1808
Fullwood, Robert vs Lang, John 1806
Fullwood, Robert vs Garretson, Soloman 1816
Gage, Mathew for Murphy, Paschal vs Farrar, George Y. & Redd, Charles A. 1812
Gahagan, Lawrence vs Conger, Thomas 1825
Gaily, Joseph vs Davis, Edward 1807
Gaithright, William M. vs Newton, Josiah 1826
Gaithur, Greenberry vs Paulette, Richard 1826
Galphin, Thomas for use of Heard, George vs Bostick, Floyd Executor of Bostick, William 1806
Gamel, Anthony vs Watson, Columbus 1842
Gantley, Daniel W. vs Jones, James M. 1839
Garner, Charles vs Moffett, Gabriel A. 1826
Gates, James vs Gann, Samuel 1832
Gates, James for use of Chauncey, John vs Gann, Samuel 1832
Gathright, Ausborne M. vs Parr, Charles & Sisson, Rodman 1828
Gathright, Ausburn M. vs McKinley, William 1831
Gathright, William M. vs Newton, Josiah 1829
Gentry, Elyah vs Stringer, James 1807
George, William & George, Bailey vs Ramey, John, Jr. & Brown, Joseph 1812
Georgia Insurance & Trust Co. vs Jones, James M. 1838
Georgia R. R. & Banking Company vs Appling, William 1840
Ga. R. R. & Banking Co. vs Cobb, Howell 1840
Ga. R. R. Banking Co. vs Cobb, John A. 1840
Ga. R. R. Banking Co. vs Cole, Sarah 1842
Ga. R. R. Banking Co. vs Conner, Bowlin 1840
Ga. R. R. Banking Co. vs Hunt, James M. 1847
Ga. R. R. Banking Co. vs McKinley, Charles G. 1840
Ga. R. R. Banking Co. vs Newton, Elizia L. 1842
Ga. R. R. Banking Co. for officers of Court vs Sims, Augustus F. 1877

Ga. R. R. Banking Co. vs Stephens, Harris 1840
Ga. R. R. Banking Co. vs Wooldridge, Isma W. & Thomas, James L. 1840
Gerrald, Isaac vs Gaydon, John 1823
Gerrald, Isaac F. vs Gayton, John 1823
Gibson, Andrew vs Stringer, Leonard 1804
Gibson, Lewis & McLaughlin, Gerard vs Wood, William B. 1839
Gibson, Lewis vs Yarborough, William 1832
Gibson, Francis vs Jackson, John 1841
Gibson, Francis vs Wilson, Moses & Wilson, James 1836
Gilbert, Felix & Gilbert, William vs Decken, Richard 1808
Gilbert, William vs Laurence, Thomas 1811
Gilbert, William H. & Gilbert, Felix vs Dicken, Richard 1807
Gilbert, William & Gilbert, Felix H. vs Jones, Thomas 1807
Gilbert, William & Gilbert, Felix vs Jones, Thomas 1808
Gilberts & Hay vs Davis, Edward 1806
Gilliland, William H.; Gilliland, William D.; Howell, Sidney S. vs Butler, Littleton R. & Butler, Henry S. 1845
Gilman, Sanders vs Craft, Edward 1830
Glass, Thomas for use of Barber, James vs Oligsby, Allen 1804
Glass, Thomas for use of Barber, James vs Rigsby, Allen 1808
Glenn, Joshua N. vs Barber, Allen & Epps, Thomas M. 1840
Glover, John H. vs Windsworth, Archibald H. 1856
Goin, Drury vs Blalock, William 1810
Goldberg, Robert vs Lighfield, Manried & Nordham, Alexander 1851
Golding, John R. for use of Moore, Thomas vs Paulett, Richard & McMichael, William 1823
Golding, Sarah vs Lasiter, James 1841
Golding, Sophanisba for use of Daniel, Josiah vs Lloyd, James W. & Harden, Edward 1832
Goodman, Robert H. vs Saye, Richard W. 1852
Goodman, Robert H. vs Saye, Richard M. 1854
Goolsby, Isaiah vs Gardner, Robert 1810
Gordon, James F. vs Crenshaw, James J. & Moore, Thomas 1827
Gorham, Mfg. Co. vs L. Schenenell & Co. 1877
Grady, William S. vs Farrell, John 1853
Graham, William P. vs Burton, James M. 1838
Grannis, George; White, Edward; White, Frederick vs Davenport, Moses N. 1838
Grannis & White vs Davenport, M. N. & Barnett, Nathan C. ND
Grant, Aura vs Smith, Iverson & Smith, Synthia 1879
Grant, Orra vs Smith, Iverson 1879
Graves, John W. for use of Nisbet, John vs Anderson, James C. 1829
Graves, John W. vs Perry, Burwell 1836
Graves, John W. vs Perry, Burwell 1838
Greenwood, Thomas; Greenwood, Polly Adms. for Greenwood, William vs Turner, James 1812
Greenwood, William Adms. vs Turner, James 1813
Greer, John C. vs Wallis, William B. 1820
Greer, John C. vs Wallis, William B. A. 1821
Greer, Mary Ann vs James, John 1833
Gresham, Davis C. & Harper, Nathaniel vs Booth, Thomas 1836
Griffith, Morgan vs Wright, William G. 1812
Grimes, Thomas W. vs Arthur, Talbot 1801
Grimes, Thomas W. vs Arthur, Talbot 1803
Grimmit, William vs Braswell, Allen 1806
Habersham, Robert vs Jackson, William H. 1832
Hagood, John vs James, Samuel & James, Enoch 1819
Haines, William vs Swinney, Marke E. 1848
Hale, John vs Jackson, William H. 1841
Hale, Moab vs Baldwin, Benj. C. 1836
Hale, Obed vs Hailes, Wiley, Jr. & Hailes, Wiley, Sr. 1843
Hall, Henry vs Andrews, John & Bankston, Henry 1806
Hall, Henry vs Andrews, John & Bankston, Henry 1807
Hall, Thomas vs Magowen, Robert 1807
Hambleton, John vs Niesler, Hugh 1812
Hamilton, Eleazar vs Nixon, William 1829
Hamilton, Thomas N. vs Clayton, Philip; Clayton, William; Clayton, Edward P. 1848
Hammock, Benjamin & Beardin, Sarah (Adams) vs Beardin, Richard 1828
Hampton, John Executor of Malone, John vs Ramey, William 1810

Hancock. Richardson vs Thurmond, John 1841
Hancock, Thomas vs Welch, James 1837
Hand, Daniel & Barton, Benjamin vs Wright, Thomas R. 1829
Hand, David vs Wood, Thomas 1839
Hanland, Risley & Co. vs Turner, William P. & Turner, John C. 1856
Hannin, Abraham vs Jackson, James 1832
Hansen, Thomas vs Taylor, William B. 1826
Harden, Edward vs Thurmond, John & Yarborough. John 1841
Harden, John vs Redd, Charles A. & Farrar, George Y. 1812
Harden, Robert R. vs Burke, Richard E. 1826
Harden, Robert R. & Johnson, John Calvin vs Dicken, Richard 1832
Harden, Robert R. & Johnson, John C. vs Gann, John 1832
Harden, Robert R. vs Harris, Walton B. 1827
Harden, Robert R. vs Harris, Walton B. 1838
Harden, Robert R. & Morgan, William W. vs Hester, Francis 1834
Harden, Robert R. vs Jones, Joseph 1827
Harden, Robert R. & Johnson, John C. vs Kirkpatrick. John 1832
Harden, Robert R. vs Moore, George W. 1828
Harden, Robert R. vs Ridgeway, Drury 1828
Harden, Robert R. vs Wright, John L. 1828
Harden, Thomas H.; Dearing, William for use of Evans, Charles vs Harden, Edward 1839
Hardin, Aleck vs Long, Berry 1879
Hargraves, George vs Oliver, Francis H.; Oliver, John L.; Oliver, John, Sr.; Fleming, Abel; Anderson, James C.; Wright, Thomas A. 1831
Hargraves, George vs Wright, John C.; Oliver, John L.; Oliver, Francis H.; Oliver, John Sr. 1831
Hargraves, George vs Wright, Thomas A.; Knott, James; Oliver, Francis H.; Akridge, Ezekiel 1831
Hargraves, George Sr. vs Wright, John C.; Oliver, Francis H.; Oliver, John L.; Oliver, John, Sr. 1831
Haviland, James C.; Haviland, Robert B.; Kesse, Theodon; Risley, Hubbell W.; Harral, James; Allen, Samuel L. vs Conner, Bowlin 1840
Haviland, James C.; Haviland, Robert B.; Kesse, Theodore; Risley, Hubbell W.; Harrell, James; Allen, Samuel L. vs Taylor, James Jones 1843
Harmony, John Frederick for Smith, Howard vs Martindale, John 1816
Harme, John H. for use of Smith, Howard vs Martindale, John ND
Harnage, Ambrose for use of Kellogg, Freeman vs Brown, William T. 1829
Harper, Anselmn; Shaw, William Adim. vs Daniel Robert & Huck, Thomas A. ND
Harper, Anselmn L.; Shaw, William Adm. of Harper, John W. vs Carr, William A. 1843
Harper, Anelmn L.; Shaw, William Admin. of Harper, John W. vs Cooper, Willis & Moore, Thomas 1840
Harper, Amselmn L. vs Herndon, Isham 1821
Harper, Anselmn L.; Admin. of Harper, John W. vs Hughes, Richard; Nunnally, John A.; Nunnally, Aaron F. 1842
Harper, Anselmn L. vs Melton, Stroud & Melton, Tabitha 1840
Harper, Anselmn L. vs Shaw, James & Stephens, Joshua 1831
Harper, George vs Dixon, Joseph 1803
Harper, George vs Dixon, Joseph 1803
Harper, George vs Dixon, Joseph 1806
Harper, George vs Donaghey, Samuel & Lee, Temple 1806
Harper, George vs Dunnaghy, Samuel 1806
Harper, George for use of Barber, James vs Echols, Absalom 1810
Harper, George vs Lea, Jonathan 1811
Harper, James & Brown, Joseph vs Ligon, Joseph 1809
Harper, John W. vs Summers, Duel & Tuck, Thomas A. 1834
Harraw, Joseph for use of Johnson, Thomas vs Hay, John W. & Totty, John 1841
Harris, Buckner vs Hubert, Gabriel 1804
Harris, Gabriel & Low, John H. vs Runnels, Preston 1807
Harris, Jesse vs Stewart, John 1807
Harris, John W. vs Elder, William Y. & Robison, John S. 1866
Harris & Lowe vs Bell, George 1812
Harris & Lowe vs Runnels, Preston 1809-1812
Harris, Sampson W. vs Appling, William; Vincent, Isaac S.; Dicken, William 1839
Harris, Sampson W. vs Cobb. John A. & Cobb, Howell 1839
Harris, Thomas W. vs McKinley, Charles G. 1840

Harris, Tyre vs Barnett, John F. 1826
Harris, Tyre vs Wood, William & Wood, Oliver 1835
Harris, William L. vs Edwards, James C.; Lord, Benjamin B.; Hancock, Thomas 1835
Harris, Young L. G. vs Dicken, Richard 1845
Harris, Young L. G. vs Dicken, Richard & Wood, John L. 1843
Harrison, Averton vs Moore, George W. 1824
Harrison, Richard vs Sweeny, Miles 1824
Harrison, Richard vs Moffett, Gabriel A. 1826
Harriss, Hendley vs Granade, Banjamin M. 1825
Hart, James B. vs Lyle, David L. 1852
Haseltine, William H. vs Wooldridge, Isma W. & Thomas, James L. 1841
Hathorn, Benjamin; Indorsee of Brown, David vs Laurance, Joseph & Parr, Banjamin 1808
Haviland, James C.; Haviland, Robert; Kesse, Theodon; Risley, Hubbell W.; Allen, Samuel L. vs Wooldridge, Isma W. 1840
Haviland, R. B. Z. Co. vs Brown & Brown 1828
Hawkins, Nicholas vs Ims, John Alias John Iams 1807
Hawkins, Nicholas vs James, John 1807
Hawkins, Stephen vs Duke, Stephen & Duke, Abraham 1811
Hawkins, William vs Dukes, Stephen & Dukes, Abram 1810
Hawthorne, Benjamin; Endorsee of Brown, David vs Lawrence, Joseph 1807
Haygood, Green B. vs Hodges, Joseph 1841
Haygood, William; Haygood, Polly Admin. of Haygood, John vs James, Samuel & James, Enoch 1820
Hayes, George vs Pass, John J. 1826
Haynes, Parmenas vs Clifton, John 1837
Haynie, Wilkins vs Davis, William 1844
Hays, William vs Cary, Lucy Executor Cary, Dudly 1807
Head, Samuel B. vs Rogers, Edwin G. 1826
Headly, Harvey S. vs Swinney, Mark E. 1849
Healy, Thomas vs Birch, Charles & Birch, John 1828
Heard, Abraham vs Runnels, Preston 1803
Heard, Franklin C. & Cook, Drury H. vs Harden, Edward 1833
Heard, Jesse vs Humpharies, Elijah 1837
Heard, Jesse & Dearing William vs Allen, Hannibal 1835
Heard, Jesse & Dearing, William vs Callier, Charles W. 1835
Heard, Jesse & Dearing, William vs Cobb. John A. 1835
Heard, Jesse & Dearing, William vs Crenshaw, James T. 1835
Heard, Jesse & Dearing, William vs Hicks, Burton 1835
Heard, Jesse & Dearing, William vs Hunt, William H. 1835
Heard, Jesse & Dearing, William vs Jackson, William H. 1835
Heard, Jesse & Dearing, William vs Jones, William E. 1835
Heard, Jesse & Dearing, William vs Owen, Alfred 1835
Heard, Jesse & Dearing, William vs Rogers, Right 1835
Heard, Jesse & Dearing, William vs Witter, James 1835
Heard, Joseph vs Wright, Thomas A. Adm. of Larkin, Clark 1829
Heard, Samuel vs Goodwin, Heard; Goodwin, Elizabeth; Loyd, Thomas 1804
Heard, Samuel vs Goodwynn, Herod; Goodwynn, Elizabeth; Lloyd Thomas 1803
Henderson, James vs Evans, John 1819
Henderson, James by his Atty Holt, Cicero vs Strong, George J. 1828
Henderson, John vs Cocke, Jack F. 1813
Henderson, John vs Cocke, Jack F. 1813
Henderson, John H. vs Wood, Thoams 1828
Henderson, Josiah; Henderson, Elias; Borders, John; Henderson, Isabella Executors of Henderson, Samuel vs Henderson, James ND
Henderson, Samuel vs Gaddy, David 1807
Henderson, Samuel vs Gaddy, David 1808
Hendon, James for use of Edward Quinn & Co. vs Langford, Bazaleel 1828
Hendon, James for use of Edward Quinn & Co. vs Langford, James 1828
Hendon, Norris vs Duke, Thomas 1810
Hendrick, John Adm. of Adkins, Francis vs Beane, Nathaniel; Carleton, Gabriel 1804
Henderson, John vs Lyle, David J. 1857
Hendricks, John vs Selman, James J. 1843
Henry, Jeff vs Crane, J. R. 1879
Herbert, Isaac vs Megs, Josiah 1808
Herbert, Isaac vs Meigs, Josiah 1807
Herrin, Moses vs Ramey, Stanford & Ramey, John 1806
Hester, Francis vs Selman, James J. & his wife Selman, Susan V. ND
Hester, Francis vs Selman, James J. & Selman, Susan V. 1849

Hester, Stephen Adm. of Marable, Augustine W. vs Hughes, Hamden Sidney; Gordon, Edward P.; Hughes, Richard 1852
Hicks, Burton vs Carter, Levi H. 1827
Hightower, John P. vs Hubert, Gabriel 1811
Hightower, William vs Pope, LeRoy & Bibb, Thomas 1807
Hill, Abram S. vs Brydie, Archibald 1834
Hill, Josiah vs Easley, Roderick 1812
Hill, Roderick vs Land, John H. 1852
Hillyer, James vs Welsh, James & Newton, Josiah 1835
Hillyer, Junius vs Clark, Eli K.; Haynes, Pamenas; Newton, Elizer L. 1833
Hillyer, Junius vs Onstead, John & Cobb, John A. 1832
Hillyer, Junius vs Yarbrough, John & Conger, Abijah 1842
Hillyer, Junius vs Yarbrough, John & Nichols, Ransom 1812
Hillyer, Shaler Adm. of Freeman, John vs Hicks, Daniel 1810-11
Hillyear, Shaler Adm. of Freeman, John vs Thurman, Benjamin; Thurman, John 1812
Hiner, Mary; Hiner, John Executrix & Executor of Hiner, Lewis vs Conner, Edward & Stuart, Robert 1831
Hinton, Jacob for Bankston, Abner vs Fullwood, Robert & Taylor, Roland 1811
Hinton, Jacob for Bankston, Abner vs Fallwood, Robert 1811
Hinton, Jason vs Calahan, Moses P. 1823
Hitchcock, William vs Ramey, John 1809
Hitchcock, Williams vs Ramey, John 1810
Hitchcock, William vs Williams, Jacob & Freeman, Heartwell 1805
Hitt, Charles B. & Dill, Robert L. vs Prince, Noah F. 1839-40
Hodges, Joseph vs Wooldridge, Isma W. 1840
Holbrook, Henry M.; Carter, Joseph R.; Holbrook, John F. vs Alexander, Aaron; Reed, Samuel A. 1849
Holbrooks, L. W. vs Matthews, Anderson 1879
Holbrook, L. W. vs Thomas, Miles 1879
Holbrooks, Lorenzo W. vs Thomas, Miles 1879
Holder, Tapley vs Garwood, Johnston & Allen, James 1842
Holloway, Anny vs Niesler, Hugh 1812
Holman, Francis & Wheeler, Joseph vs Elder, Joshua 1852
Holmes, David vs Langford, James 1825
Holt, Cicero Attorney for Harrison, James vs Strong, George J. ND
Hood, C. W. vs Newton, John H. 1877
Hood, W. F. vs Long, Willie 1879
Hood, W. F. vs Brown, Jacob 1879
Hood, W. F. vs Eberhart, S. P. 1879
Hood, W. F. vs Hunter, Sam 1879
Hood, W. F. vs Waggoner, George 1879
Hood, W. F. vs Grant, Aura 1879
Hood, W. F. vs Hill, Charles 1879
Hood, W. F. vs Joiner, J. W. 1879
Hood, Wiley F. vs Moore, Zip Alias Jefferson, Z. P. 1879
Hood, W. F. vs McDermed, P. W. 1879
Hood, Wiley F. vs Bell, John 1879
Hood, Wiley F. vs Burch, J. B. 1879
Hood, Wiley R. vs Williams, James 1879
Hood, W. F. vs Thomas, Randall 1879
Hood, Wiley F. vs Achols, Essie 1878
Hood, Wiley F. vs Allen, George 1879
Hood, Wiley F. vs Beall, C. W. 1879
Hood, Wiley F. vs Bass, William 1879
Hood, Wiley F. vs Burch, J. B. 1879
Hood, Wiley F. vs Gann, W. H. 1879
Hood, Wiley F. vs Harris, Robert 1879
Hood, Wiley F. vs Houston, Cobb 1879
Hood, Wiley F. vs Huggins, James 1879
Hood, Wiley F. vs Jackson, Trump 1879
Hood, Wiley F. vs Johnson, Edwin 1879
Hood, Wiley F. vs King, Ed 1879
Hood, Wiley F. vs McDermond, P. W. 1879
Hood, Wiley F. vs Morrison, George 1879
Hood, Wiley F. vs Newton, James 1879
Hood, Wiley F. vs Sale, F. A. 1879
Hood, Wiley F. vs Scott, James 1879

Hood, Wiley F. vs Smith, David 1877
Hood, Wiley F. vs Strickland, Burton 1879
Hood, Wiley F. vs Thomas, Randall 1879
Hood, Wiley F. vs Thornton, Homer 1879
Hood, Wiley F. vs White, Ben 1879
Hood, Wiley F. vs Whitehead, Thomas 1879
Hood, Wiley F. vs Witherspoon, Isaac 1879
Hopkins, Eusebius A. vs Easterling, Henry 1841
Hopkins, Lambeth; Kolb, Charley; Fann, Joseph A. vs Crawford, Levi M.; Grady, William S. 1852
Hopkin, Laurabeth; Kolb, Charly; Fannin, Joseph A. vs Crawford, Levi M.; Grady, William S.; Nicholson, John W. 1852
Hopkins, Lambeth; Kolb, Charly; Fannin, Joseph A. vs Dicken, Richard; Nicholson, Grady 1852
Hopkins, Lambeth; Kolb, Charly; Fannin, Joseph A. vs Harden, Robert R.; Dicken, Richard; Grady, William S. 1852
Hopkins & Phillips vs Turner, James & Jack, Green B. 1812
Hopkins, Rachel vs Haynes, Parmenas, Jr. 1809
Hopkins, Solomon A. vs Rakestraw, Robert G. 1812
Hoppins, Ephraim L. vs Clifton, William 1824
Howard, John vs Torry, Alexander 1806
Howard, John; Howard, William; Howard, Rhesa vs Carnes, Thomas Pl; Cummings, Thomas; Lowe, William; Clayton Augustus Smith; Executors of Clayton, Phillip 1810
Howell, James vs Wright, William G. & Cocke, Jack F. 1815
Howland, Clavin L. vs Clack, John C. F. 1839
Hubbard, Thomas for use of Irwin, Francis vs Winston, Joseph 1833
Hubbard, William vs Smith, Andrew Adm. of Thompson, Thomas B. 1839
Hubbard, William vs Thompson, Thomas B. 1838
Huff, Elizabeth vs Wooldridge, Isma W. & Thomas, James L. 1841
Huff, Littleberry; Huff, Valentine; Huff, Leroy; Huff, Greene B.; Huff, Elizabeth; Jones, Benjamin F.; his wife Lydia; Durham, Joseph; his wife Lona vs Huff, Elizabeth Widow of Huff, John; Akridge, William 1845
Huggan, Alexander vs Cawson, John 1830
Huggins, James H. vs Bray, B. A. 1879
Huggins, John vs Hailes, Henry J. & Hale, Wiley 1843
Huggins, John J. vs Neisler, Hugh 1843
Huggins, John J. vs Newton, Josiah 1841
Huggins, John J. vs Welch, James 1836
Hughes, George H. vs Crain, William 1811
Hughs, Richard, Adm. of Gordon, Robert vs James, William Adm. of James, Henry 1830
Hughs, Richard & Grodon, Robert vs Lampkin, Edward 1828
Hulings, James vs Davis, Edward 1808
Hulings, James Adm. for use of Executors of Hopkins, Lemuel vs Hopkins, William 1809
Hulings, James vs Stewart, Samuel 1809
Hulings, James Adm. of Hunton, John vs Walton, George Ad, of Walton, John C. 1808
Hull, Asbury vs Irwin, David 1852
Hull, Hope Guardian of Lane, Joel vs Cary, John; Thomas, Jett 1808
Hull, Hope vs Clarke, Lucy 1810
Humphreys, William vs Moffett, Gabriel A. 1832
Humphries, George; Bradley, John Adm. of McDonald, Josiah vs Hopkins, William; Brown, Joseph; Ramey, John Jr. 1812
Humphries, Uriah vs Gauvian, Michael 1811
Humpharies, Uriah vs Runnels, Preston 1807
Humphries, Uriah vs Runnels, Preston 1809
Humphries, Uriah vs Trawick, Spencer 1811
Humphries, Uriah vs Cary, John 1805
Hungerford, John; Hungerford, William S. vs Scott, Archibald H. 1833
Hunt, Thomas vs Strong, Samuel J. 1840
Hunter, Alexander vs Cox, John J. 1822
Hungtinton, G. J. vs Collins, James L. 1938
Husson, Alexander vs Brown, Lemuel 1810-11
Husson, Alexander vs Sturdivant, Jesse 1809 vs The Administrators of Jesse Studivant 1811
Hutson, Thomas vs Moon, George W. 1829
Inferior Court vs Brown, Bedford 1813
Inferior Court vs Humphries, Elijah ND

Inferior Court vs Oates, James; Oates, Richard W.; Edmondson, Thomas 1828
Inferior Court vs Oats, James; Oats, Richard W.; Edmondson, Thomas ND
Inferior Court vs Wood, Pucket & Kinney, James 1828
Irvin, Josephus vs Braswell, Samuel 1821
Irwin, Francis; Graham, Abner; Adms. of Grahsm, Andrew vs Dunn, John T. 1834
Jacks, Isaac vs Thrasher, Pinckney B. 1826
Jackson, Amanda vs Jackson, Ivery 1879
Jackson, Asa M. vs Parnell, Nathan C. 1842
Jackson, Asa M.; Burnett, Nathan C. vs Taylor, John H. ND
Jackson, Asa M. vs Vincent, Isaac S. 1843
Jackson, Hartwell, Sr. vs Brightwell, Andrew 1840
Jackson, Hartwell, Sr. vs Gann, John; Stephens, David 1840
Jackson, Hartwell, Jr. vs Wozencraft, Thomas; Wozencraft, William J. 1842
Jackson, Hartwell, Sr. vs Hughes, William; Vincent, Isaac S. 1840
Jackson, Hartwell, Sr. vs Nunnally, John A.; Davenport, James B.; Nunally, Aaron F. 1841
Jackson, Hartwell, Sr. vs Nunnally, John A.; Deavenport, James B.; Nunnally, Aaron B. 1841
Jackson, Isaac R. vs Rivers, Jones 1813
Jackson, Isaac R. vs Rivers, Jones 1817
Jackson, John vs Barton, James M. ND
Jackson, John vs Jackson, William H. 1831
Jackson, John vs Jackson, William Henry 1830
Jackson, John vs Langford, Bazaleel 1832
Jackson, John; Jackson, Samuel vs Biggs, Aaron 1819
Jackson, John for use of Jackson, John vs Smith, Philip 1819
Jackson, John; Hicks, Barton vs Barrett, John F. 1827
Jackson, Land; Jackson, John vs Hendon, Isham ND
Jackson, Obediah; Doggett, Richard vs Whitehead, Ranson A.; Doggett, George 1849
Jackson, R. M. vs Biggers, James 1878
Jackson, S. J. vs Booth, Thomas ND
Jackson, S. & J. vs Crews, John 1819
Jackson, S. & J. vs Crews, John 1819
Jackson, Samuel; Jackson, John vs Connel, Benjamin 1819
Jackson, Samuel; Jackson, John vs Haile, Joel 1819
Jackson, Samuel vs Harper, Haywood 1811
Jackson, Samuel; Jackson, John vs Hendon, Isham 1821
Jackson, Samuel; Jackson, John vs Mitchell, William 1819
Jackson, Samuel; Jackson, John for use of Jackson, John vs Taylor, Roland 1819
Jackson, Samuel; Jackson, John vs Winfield, Joel 1819
Jackson, S. & T. vs Winfield, Joel 1821
Jackson, Samuel; Sims, James Glen vs Hubert, Gabriel 1807
Jackson & Sims vs Hubert, Gabriel 1808
Jackson, Stephen vs Yarbrough, John 1842
Jackson, Steven vs Harrell, Susannah 1845
Jackson & Thomas vs Fournoy, Martha Ann 1883
Jackson, William E.; Jackson, George J.; O'Neill, Hugh vs Ritch, William C.; Stovall, William W. 1852
Jackson, William H. vs Snead, Meridith 1832
James, Henry vs Gordon, Robert S. 1828
Jarrel, Tilman for Moffett, Gabriel A. vs Trammell, Francis 1826
Jarrell, Isaac F. vs Trammell, John 1826
Jarrell, Stinson S.; Jackson, Stephen vs Hopkins, Eusebias A. 1842
Jarrell, Stinson S. vs Tucker, Richard O. 1840
Jenkins, E. B. vs Vaughn, Reuben 1813
Jenkins, Edmund Booker vs Brewer, William 1807
Jennings, James vs Cox, John J. 1820
Jennings, James vs Gay, Charles H. 1841
Jennings, James vs Gay, Charles H. 1841
Jennings, James vs Turner, James 1823
Jennings, Jefferson vs Brockman, W. H. 1852
Jewell, William vs Barber, Allen; Barber, James 1841
Jimison, John M.; Grimage, Joshua for use of Fleming, Miller vs Moore, George W. 1809
Johns, W. B. vs Hardiman, Susan 1879

Johns, W. B. vs Hardiman, Susan 1880
Johnson, Benjamin F. for use of Burleson Bowie vs Adams, Edmand B. 1843
Johnson, James vs Beasley, John & Williams, Nathaniel 1809
Johnson, John Calvin vs Paine, George M. & Dicken, Richard 1848
Johnson, Nehemiah vs Jackson, William C. & Jackson, Obadiah 1843
Johnson, Thomas vs Paine, George M. 1842
Johnson, William vs Leggett, William 1806
Johnson, William vs Nobles, Jonathan 1807
Johnson, William vs Nobles, Jonathan 1809
Johnston, Benjamin F. vs Harden, Robert R. 1842
Johnston, Benjamin F. vs Yarbrough, John 1842
Joiner, William R. & Co. vs Joiner, J. J. 1879
Jones, Edward for use of Johnson, Isaac W. vs Hayes, Hiram 1842
Jones, Ephraim for Exors. of Strong, William vs Niesler, Hugh 1812
Jones & Gardner for use of Jones, Russell vs Easley, Richard 1808
Jones, Jacob vs Fulcher, Jesse 1834
Jones, James W. vs Poore, Benjamin 1841
Jones, John H. vs Lyle, Lee M. 1877
Jones, John H. & Co. vs Lyle, Lee M. 1877
Jones, Richard vs Runnells, Reuben 1827
Jones, Richard vs Runnells, Reuben 1827
Jones, Russell & Gordon, Samuel vs Earley, Richard 1807
Jones, Seaborn vs Hill, Isaac, Sr. & Hill, Middleton 1829
Jones, & Semmes vs Murdock, Joseph 1807
Jones & Simmes vs Murdock, Joseph 1808
Jones, Walter R. vs Stephens, David; Jackson, Asa M.; Barnett, Nathan C. 1840
Jones, Walter R. vs Stephens, David; Jackson, Asam; Barnett, Nathan 1841
Jones, Walter R. vs Stephens, Brankey; Stephens, Overton; Jackson, Asa M.; Barnett, Nathaniel C. 1840
Jones, William Atty vs Young, Gresham 1820
Keiffer Bros.; H. B. Clayton & Co. vs Harris, M. L. 1884
Kelly, Allen vs Burnett, Jeremiah & Melton, Jonathan 1811
Kelly, Allen vs Burnett, Jeremiah & Melton, Jonathan 1811
Kelly, Francis vs Stephens, Joshua & Gann, Nathan 1828
Kelly, John & Kelly, William vs Manley, William 1832
Kelsey, Charles; Kelsey, George H.; Halsted, Job S. vs Weatherly, Joseph I. 1838
Kelsey, George & Halstead, John vs Tottey, John 1842
Kemp, Joseph vs Booth, Thomas 1809
Kemp, Joseph vs Booth, Thomas; Gresham, Young 1810
Kemp, Stephen vs Bond, Edward 1808
Kemp, Stephen vs Sims, John H. 1810
Kennedy, Charles vs Davies, Edward 1807
Kent, Gilbert vs Kent, William H. 1835
Kent, Gilbert vs Kent, William H. 1836
Kent, Peter vs Simpson, John 1817
Kerr, Andrew; Kerr, John; Graham, Andrew; Hope, John vs Billups, Joseph; Shakleford, Edmund C.; Shakleford, Loyd W. 1834
Kerr, Jesse vs Barnett, John F. 1826
Kerr, William vs Bonner, Zadock 1819
Kidd, James; Freeman, Timothy vs Powell, Seymore R.; Fann, Wiloughby 1807
Kilgore, Benjamin vs Niesler, Hugh 1830
Kilgore, John vs Wooten, John 1819
Kilgore, Willis vs Rushing, Briant 1807
Kilgore, Willis vs Rushing Bryant 1806
King, James vs Jackson, John & Hendon, James 1841
King, Jesse vs Barnett, Nathan C. 1829
King, William vs Waters, R. C. 1879
King, James vs Waters, R. C. 1879
Kinney, James vs Laurence, Joseph 1812
Kirkpatrick, John vs Gloson, Henry 1832
Kirkpatrick, John vs Parr, Benjamin J. 1838
Kirkpatrick, John vs Robinson, Jesse 1837
Kittle, Clarissa vs Kittle, John, Jr. 1883
Knowland, Soloman; Kilburn, John R. vs Harden, Robert R. 1837
Lackey, James vs Ramey, John 1809
Lagre, Nathan C.; Terrell, William Executor of Taylor, Hugh vs Adams, Nathaniel A. 1837

Lamar, Andrew C. vs Flournoy, Howell C. 1846
Lampkin, Edward vs Graves, John W. & Richardson, Richard 1842
Land, Archibald vs Oliver, Francis H. 1837
Landers, Benjamin vs Reaves, James A. 1835
Lane, Isaac vs Thomas, Giles 1809
Lane, Jesse vs Chandler, John B. 1811
Lane, Theo S. & Co. vs Erwin, Leander A. 1820
Lane, Theo S. & Co. vs Thornton, Francis 1819
Land, Wiley vs Brown, William 1842
Langford, James vs Brown, William F. 1830
Langford, John W. vs Vanney, Jasper 1869
Lanier, George for use of Shields, Samuel; Mantey, William vs Harris, Webb 1822
Lanigan, Mary L. vs Pritchard, Mary L. 1851
Lanos, Charles vs Deane, Charles & Deane, Nathaniel 1811
Lanos, Charles vs Peeples, Hanry 1813
Laurence, Richard vs Scott, James, Jr. 1805
Laney, Charles vs Peoples, Harvy 1871
Lazarus, Morris & Co. vs L. Schevenell & Co. 1877
Lea, Green vs Ramey, Sandford 1807
Lea, Green vs Ramey, Sandford 1806
Lea, Green vs Ramey, Sandford & Ramey, John 1807
Lea, Noal vs Runnels, Preston 1807
Lea, Noel vs Runnels, Preston 1816
Lea, Temple vs Gaddy, David 1813
Lea, Temple vs Vickers, Gresham 1809
Lea, Temple & Armstrong, James W. vs Marabel, Robert 1810
Lea, Temple for use of Mosely, Peter; Mosely, Sally vs Trammell, Francis 1819
Leavenworth, Mark vs Wright, Thomas S. 1830
Leben, Joseph B. vs Macuin, Anthony 1840
Ledbetter, William vs Allen, John 1804
Ledbetter, Williamson vs Allen, John 1807
Lee, John for use of Melton, Isaac vs Fenn, Willerby 1806
Lee, Theophilus; Lane, Jonathan; Rakestraw, Gaijham L. vs Thorton, Francis 1819
Lee, William; Bonner, Jordan vs Stringer, James 1806
Lee, William Indorsee of Bonner, Jordan vs Stringer, James 1807
Leeb, Arthur J. vs Taylor, John H.; Whittan, John; Vincent, Isaac S. 1841
Leeper, Allen vs Lanos, Charles 1809
Lemand, Robert F. vs Rutherford, Thacker V.; Harris, James W. 1845
Lenaes, Charles for Baldwin, James G. vs Wright, Richard; Wright, William 1811
Lester, A. L. vs Morris, Carrie M. (formerly) Brown, Carrie M. 1879
Lester, James Trustee of Daniell, William vs Adams, Edmund B. & Macon, Thomas G. 1858
Lewis, Nicholas vs Borman, Henry D. as bail for Earley, Augustus W. 1827
Lewis, Nicholas vs Early, Augustus W. 1826
Ligon, James vs Brown, William W. 1819
Ligon, Joseph Executor of Ligon, James vs Fambrough, Joshua 1822
Ligon, James vs Ligon, Joseph 1810
Ligon, James vs Meriwether, David 1820
Ligon, Joseph for use of Low, George vs Fulwood, Robert 1821
Ligon, Joseph vs Hartsfield, Middleton 1820
Ligon, Joseph vs Hendon, Isham 1821
Ligon, Joseph vs Lasater, Joel 1819
Ligon, Joseph (Liggon) vs Laseter, Joel 1819
Ligon, Joseph vs Winfield, Joel 1821
Ligon, Thomas vs Turner, James 1812
Leonard, Patrick for use of Raymond, Allen H. vs Scott, Archibald H.; Leonard, Patrick 1827
Linten, John S. Executor of Linten, Alexander B. vs Moore, Richard O. 1841
Linten, John S. Executor of Linten, Alexander B. vs Terrey, Shubael; Brydie, Archibald 1841
Lipham, Aaron vs Findley, William 1804
Littlepage, Thomas W. vs Neisler, Hugh 1821
Lockwood, Eleazer & Peck, David vs Schoonmaker, Lodwick 1831
Loften, Samuel vs Britten, James Jr. 1803
Loften, Samuel vs Britten, James 1804

Logan, Charles vs Hardin, Sally 1879
Lord, Benjamin B.; Lord, Ebanazer vs Thomas, James Jr. 1836
Lord, Robinson & Co. vs Collins, I. W. 1877
Love, Hugh for use of Hungerford, Anson; Hungerford, Dana vs Brown, William 1829
Love, Robert vs Meriwether, William 1828
Love, William & Co. vs Robison, William 1804
Love, William & Co. vs Robison, William 1804
Low, George vs Hewell, Susannah 1828
Lowe, John H. vs Fambrough, William 1822
Lowe, John A. Sr. vs Cox, Richard 1856
Lowe, John H. vs Lynch, Lettice Executrix of Lynch, David 1831
Lowe, John H.; Jones, William Executors of Paine, Edward vs Simms, Arthur L. 1843
Lowe, John H., Sr. vs Huff, Leeroy 1845
Lowe, John H. Sr. vs Reynold, Thomas; Major, Paul 1842
Lowe, John H. Sr. vs Thrasher, William H. 1854
Lowe, Robert vs Meriwether, George ND
Lowe, Thomas vs Brightwell, John 1834
Lowe, Thomas vs Fleming, Able 1831
Lowrey, Levi vs Clark, Ely K. 1833
Lucy, Cobb Institute vs Moses, Henry 1879
Luitte, Susan M. vs Adams, N. A. 1845
Luallen, William for use of Evans, Henry vs Fenn, Willerby 1808
Lumpkin, George vs Jones, Thomas, Jr.; Wright, John L. 1811
Lumpkin, Samuel vs Jack, Samuel; Jack, Margaret 1822
Lumpkin, William vs Buckley, James K.; Moss, William 1822
Lumpkin, William vs Harris, West 1824
Lyles, Dilmus vs Dean, Burkett; Lea, Green; Armstrong, Jas. W. 1808
Lyles, William Henry vs Dixon, Henry 1802-03
MacCrerry, William vs Gauvain, Michael C. 1811
Macky, Peter vs Allan, David 1807
Macon, Thomas G. for Officers of Court vs Winter, John 1876
Macuion, Anthony vs Tiberne, Joseph B. 1841
Maddox, James Executor; Norwood, James Execut.; Joseph Maddox vs Robinson, Patrick L. 1841
Maddox, Joseph vs Cocke, Jack F. 1812
Mahony, Dennis vs Pope, John C. 1829
Mahoney, William; Mahoney, Dennis vs Adams, Nathaniel A. 1837
Maine, Alexander vs Hopkins, Benjamin B. 1834
Malone, Robert; Malone, Steven for use of Malone, Madison vs Marable, John 1819
Manley, William; Shields, Samuel vs Dougherty, Charles 1833
Manley, William vs Gresham, Albert Y. 1832
Manley, William Admin. of Waddell, Charles vs Harden, Robert R. 1833
Manly, William vs Lampkin, Edward 1828
Mann, Baker vs Earnest, John B. 1809
Manning & Bibb vs Thompson, Robert 1809
Mapp, Littleton vs Shepherd, John 1807
Marabel, Mathew vs Erwin, Leandr A. 1820
Marshall, W. L.; Marshall, M. R. vs Kenney, John 1828
Marshall, William vs Haile, Moab 1851
Martin, James vs Byrd, John A.; Moore, Finney H. 1833
Martin, John vs Byrd, John A. 1831
Martin, John for use of Martin, James vs Byrd, John A. 1831
Martin, John vs Davis, Edward 1808
Martin, John vs Freeman, Benjamin 1806
Martin, John vs Freeman, Benjamin 1807
Martin, John vs Megs, Josiah 1808
Martin, John vs Meigs, Josiah 1807
Martin, Robert vs Lea, Temple; Lea, Green; Armstrong, James W. 1809
Martin, Robert vs Ramey, John 1809
Martin, Robert vs Starn, William; Ramey, Absalom 1808
Mason, Academy, Trustees vs Shaw, William 1810
Mason, Emily vs Collins, Tom 1879
Mason, John C. vs Wright, James A. 1833
Mathews, Charles L. Admin. vs Freeman, William 1808
Mathews, John R.; Mathews, Leroy C. vs Saye, Richard W. 1852
Mathews, John R.; Gordman, Robert H.; Mathews, Leroy C. vs Saye, Richard M. 1852

Matthews, Charles L. vs Crompton, John; Turner, James; Hutson, Robert 1818
Matthews, Charles L. Admin. vs Freeman, William; McCree, William 1807
Matthews, W. F. Admin. of Crane, J. R. vs Henry, Samuel 1879
Mattox, James G. vs Colt, Joseph C. 1840
Maxey, Boze vs Wooldridge, Isma W.; Connor, Bowlin 1840
Maxey, George W. vs Maxey, Augustus R. 1852
Maxey, George W. vs Maxey, Augustus R. 1854
May, Lewis his wife May, Elizabeth Adm. of Sansom, John vs Sansom, James 1808
Mayer, Son & Co. vs Barry P. & Son 1877
Mays, S. J.; Huggins, John J. vs Welch, James ND
Mays, Seaborn J. vs Allen, James 1838
Mays, Seaborn J.; Clayten, William W. vs Cobb, John A. 1840
Mays, Seaborn T.; Dearing, William vs Jackson, William H. 1832
Mays, Seaborn, J. vs Kirkpatrick, John 1838
Mays, Seaborn J. vs Talmage, John 1839-40
Mays, Seaborn J. vs Weatherly, William S. 1838
Mays, Seaborn J. vs Welch, James 1836
McBoyde, John; McBoyde, James vs Jackson, James 1832
McBurney, William; Hyatt, Edmund; Hyatt, Nathaniel vs Baker, James L.; Baker, John H. 1840
McCartan, Thomas vs Wallace, Joseph; Winfield, Joel 1818
McCarter, James J.; Allen, Thomas P. vs Ralls, James F. 1846
McCay, Thomas vs Harvey, Elijah B. 1829
McClesky, John vs Rakestraw, Gainham 1819
McCollough, John J. by his next Friend Byrd, John A. vs Young, Benjamin; Clark, Eli K. 1832
McCord, James L. vs Burton, James M.; Webster, Joseph; Davenport, Robert; Akridge, Levi 1835
McCree, Alexander vs Cox, Bolling; Brown, Joseph 1810-11
McCree, William vs Thurman, William 1810
McCree, William vs Admin. of Thurman, William 1813
McDaniel, Henry D. for officers of Court vs Lumpkin, Miller G.; Wilkins, James C. 1884
McDill, Newton vs Arther, Lewis 1841
McGee, Adam vs Easley, Roderick 1803
McGee, Adam vs Easley, Roderick 1804
McGovern, John vs Yarborough, John 1835
McGowen, Robert vs Cain, William 1803
McGuire, Lewis L. vs Baldwin, Benj. C. 1836
McGuire, Lewis L. vs Burton, James M. 1836
McIntire, Charles; Kelsey, Charles; Rockwell, Charles W.; Kelsey, George H. vs Manley, William 1832
McKigney, B. vs Findley, William 1805
McKigney, Beattie vs Armstrong, Jonathan 1805
McKigney, Beattie vs Arthur, Talbot 1805
McKigney, Beattie vs Arthur, Talbot; Parks, G. W. 1805
McKigney, Beattie vs Fullwood, Robert 1805
McKigney, Beattie vs Fullwood, Robert 1805
McKigney, William by his next friend Puryeur, John vs Bailey, William; Bailey, John A. 1830
McKinley, Archibald C. Admin. of Upson, Stephen vs Boyers, Henry; Strong, John 1831
McKinly, Archibald C.; Boardman, Elijah in right of his wife Boardman, Hannah C. formerly Upson, Hannah; Boardman, Hannah Admin of Upson, Stephen vs Wood, Thomas 1829
McKinney, Samuel vs Thomas, James L. 1822
McLeroy, Needham vs Ramsey, Seaborn; Wallis, Nicholas 1833
McLester, James vs Crewshaw, David 1852
McNaught & Scutchin vs Beavers, W. R. 1878
McNaught & Scutchin vs Beavers, W. R. 1878
McNeed, William vs Haynes, Parminas; Meriwether, George W. 1822
McNees B. Samuel; Linton, B. vs Holbrook, Nathan 1838
McNees, William Guardian of George, William B. vs Stuart, Robert 1827
McNey, William vs Hundon, Elisha 1823
McWhorter, James H. M. vs Jones, Richard; Arthur, Lewis 1835
Meadows, Enoch vs Simonton, Samuel 1848
Melton, Ethen vs Whittendon, Clavin 1823
Melton, Isaac vs Herndon, Joseph 1806
Melton, Moses vs Stephens, Joshua 1820

Melton, William vs Wooton, Bartley; Wooton, Gilly 1801
Mead, Joseph H.; Strong, Elisha vs Smith, Charles 1820
Mennard, William vs Harden, Robert R. 1835
Mercer, William A. & Officers of Walton Superior Court vs Oglesby, George S. 1849
Merchants Bank vs Robinson, Jesse 1841
Meriwether, David vs Barber, William; Harper, John W. 1830
Meriwether, George W. vs Yarborough, John; Yarbrough, William; Gunn, Nathan 1830
Meriwether, Sarah T. vs Nunnaly, John A.; Meriwether, George W. 1831
Messer, William vs Trawick, Spencer 1807
Messer, William vs Trawick, Spencer 1808
Middlebrooks, A. C. vs Burton, James M.; Jackson, John ND
Middlebrooks, A. C. vs Davenport, Moses N. 1833
Middlebrooks, A. C. vs Weatherly, William 1833
Middlebrooks, Isaac vs Ormond, James 1812
Middleton, John vs Patterson, Gideon 1809
Millandon, Laurent vs Simms, Arthur L. 1842
Miller, Horatis; Ripley, Samuel P.; Miller, George N.; Miller, Ephrain; Chamberlain, Charles V.; Peck, Orin M. vs Selman, James J.; Wilson, James C. 1847
Miller, James & Co. vs Clayton, Philip 1848
Milner vs Kent, William & Boggs 1811
Milsaps, Thomas vs Hubert, Gabriel 1809
Milton, Ethan vs Doggett, Mark (?) 1819
Milton, Hannah E. Executor of Milton, John vs Bryan, Laury 1831
Minton, Jason vs Callahan, Moses P. 1822
Mitchell, John Admin. of Vs Freeman, William; Lane, Joseph 1806
Mitchell, Thomas Admin. of Mitchell, William vs Brent, Kendal C. 1809-10
Mitchell, Thomas vs Weir, John ND
Mitchell, Thomas R. vs Brown, William W. 1819
Mitchell, Thomas R. vs Hendon, Isham 1821
Mitchell, Thomas R. vs Lampkin, Lewis 1816
Mitchell, Thomas R. vs Lampkin, Lewis 1816
Mitchell, Thomas R. vs Winfield, Joel 1821
Mitchell, William L. vs Baker, John; Zwoll, Francis 1839
Mitchell, William L. vs Crenshaw, James J. 1829
Mitchell, William L. vs Mitchell, William 1830
Mitchell, William L. vs Veronee, William 1833
Mitt, David; Cosby, James C. vs Colbert, Thomas 1802
Moffet, Gabriel vs Roberts, White 1825
Moffett, Gabriel A. vs Carter, Levi H. 1826
Moffett, Gabriel A. vs Gathright, Ausban M.; Newton, Elizur L. 1827
Moffett, Gabriel A. vs Sims, Zachariah; Moore, Thomas 1826
Moffett, Gabriel A. vs Sims, Zachariah; Stewart, Alfred 1826
Moffett, Gabriel A. vs Taylor, William B.; Whitter, James 1826
Moffett, Gabriel A. vs Wright, William 1826
Moffett, Henry vs McDonald, Alexander; Gaines, Zenophon J.; Bryant, Samuel 1815
Monsfield, Eli; Burnett, William vs Adams, Nathaniel A. 1837
Montgomery, Nancy vs Appling, William; Sansom, Thomas 1840
Moon, George W. vs Hooker, Richard 1838
Moon, Thomas Executors of Cobell, Robert J. vs Harden, Robert R.; Jones, Richard 1833
Moore, Benning B. vs Mastin, James C. 1838
Moore, Duff vs Bird, Joseph 1879
Moore, Finney H. vs Epps, William 1842
Moore, Finney H. vs Harden, Edward R. 1842
Moore, Finny H. vs Welch, James 1837
Moore, George W. vs Hendon, Isham 1822
Moore, Henry vs Roberson, William 1808
Moore, Henry vs Robison, William 1809
Moore, John; Davis, Joseph vs Totty, John 1842
Moore, John; Gillespie, James vs Barnett, John F. 1822
Moore, John R. vs Clay, William H. 1822
Moore, Joshua G. vs Booth, Benjamin H. 1821
Moore, Joshua G. vs Mitchell, John; Holbrook, Nathan 1834
Moore, Joshua G. vs Weaver, David 1838
Moore, Richard D. vs Holbrook, Nathan 1842
Moore, Richard D. vs Jackson, William H. 1842
Moore, Thomas vs Hadley, Joshua 1852

Moore, Thomas vs Jackson, James 1830
Moore, Thomas Executor of Cabbell, Rob I. vs William H. Jackson ND
Moore, Thomas vs Jackson, William H. 1830
Moore, Thomas; Hampton, James vs Seisler, Hugh 1827
Moore, Thomas; Billups, Robert; Executor of Catbell, Robert L. vs Sims, Zachariah; Newton, Josiah 1828
Moore, William vs Davenport, Jovett; Davenport, William; Davenport, James 1823
Moss, Joseph vs Harden, Joseph 1827
Moss, Joseph vs Humphries, Isaac 1823
Moreland, Joseph vs Wright, James A. 1833
Moreland, William vs Gaulden, Scriven 1831
Morgan, William vs Dicken, Richard 1852
Morris, Mrs. E. H.; Kranke & Finke for Officers of Court vs Sciple & Sons 1884
Morris, James vs Sheril, Joseph D. 1841
Morton, John vs Cobb, John A. 1840
Morton, John vs Turner, James 1824
Morton, Joseph vs Hightower, Charnel 1822
Morton, Joseph F. vs Tenney, Shubnel; Sansom, Thomas; Admin. of Lord, Benjamin B. - 1841
Morton, William M. vs Jackson, Asa M.; Harden, William P.; Admin. of Harden, Robert A. 1844
Morton, William M. vs Jackson, Asa M.; Harden, William P. 1844
Morton, William M.; Morton, Joseph F. vs Barnett, John F. 1826
Morton, William M.; Morton, Joseph F. vs Hayes, Hyram 1826
Morton, William; Morton, Joseph vs Hightower, Charnell 1823
Mosely, Peter; Mosely, Sally; Executor of Brown, Bedford vs Elder, Joshua 1819
Mosely, Peter; Mosely, Sally vs Robison, David; Mavable, Matthew 1819
Moseley, Peter; his wife Moseley, Sally; Executors of Brown, Bedford vs Smith, James; Kilgore, John L. 1822
Moses, Aaron J. vs Patman, William A. 1850
Moss & Billips vs Doggett, Thomas 1827
Moss, John D. vs Harrison, James J. 1841
Moss, Joseph vs Booth, Thomas 1821
Moss, Joseph vs Harden, Robert R. 1827
Moss, Joseph vs Harris, Virginia B. 1822
Moss, Joseph vs Humphries, Isaac ND
Moss, Joseph vs Rosseter, White 1809
Motes, Zachariah for use of Rosseter, White vs Crews, John 1821
Moultrie, Briggs H. vs Arther, Lewis; Bailey, John A. 1829
Murdock, Joseph vs Colbert, Thomas 1808
Murdock, Robert; Gray, Alexander for use of Arther, Lewis vs Wade, Thomas 1834
Murphey, Paschal vs Cabell, Robert 1812
Murphy, Paschal vs Hightower, Thomas 1812
Murray & Humphrays vs Birch, Charles C. 1828
Murray & Humphrays vs Brown, William 1828
Murray & Humphreys vs Cogburn, Moses H. 1828
Murray & Humphreys for use of Edward Quinn & Co. vs Gardner, Robert 1828
Murray & Humphreys vs Harden, Robert R. 1828
Murray & Humphreys vs Harris, Walton B. 1827
Murray & Humphreys vs Harvey, Elijah B. 1828
Murray & Humphreys for use of Edward Quinn & Co. vs Haynes, Parmeuas 1828
Murray & Humphreys for use of Edward Quinn & Co. vs McCree, William 1828
Murray & Humphreys vs Stewart, Alfred 1827
Murray & Humphreys vs Wood, Thomas 1828
Murray, Samuel vs Anderson, Mathew 1821
Murray, Samuel J. vs Wilson, Richard 1823
Murray, William vs Bayers, Henry 1829
Murray, William vs Danniell, Jeriah 1868
Murray, William vs Dicken, Richard ND
Murray, William vs Dicken, Richard 1842
Murray, William vs Dismukes, William H. 1825
Murray, William vs Dismukes, William H. 1826
Murray, William vs Harden, Edward R. 1841
Murray, William vs Harper, Nathaniel 1840
Murray, William vs Harris, Walton B. 1827
Murray, William vs Haynes, Parmenas 1844

Murray, William vs Hopkins, Eurebius A. 1840
Murray, William vs Jeffries, Thomas 1840
Murray, William vs Manley, William 1832
Murray, William vs Moffett, Gabriel; Cocke, William A. 1832
Murray, William vs Moore, Robert H. 1842
Murray, William vs McRee, Robert A.; McRee, William 1828
Murray, William vs Vickers, Elias H.; Admin of Vickers, Absalom; McRee, William B. 1869
Murray, William vs Patton, J. B. 1858
Murray, William; Humphreys, William vs Quin, Edward; Campbell, John 1828
Murray, William vs Reed, Isaac D. 1838
Murray, William vs Richardson, Richard; Vincent, Isaac L.; Admin. of Ligon, Robert 1842
Murray, William vs Ridgeway, Drury 1830
Murray, William vs Sledge, Wile; Cooper, Archer 1831
Murray, William vs Stephens, David 1841
Murray, William vs Warden, Robert R. 1842
Murray, William J. vs Burt, James F.; Elder, David 1826
Nabers, James B. vs Fryerson, James D.; Ripley, Obedience B.; Adm. of Ripley, Sylvanus 1841
Neely, Charles L. vs Whitehead, Sandford; Whitehead, Ransom A. 1852
Neisler, Hugh vs Blackburn, Nancy 1806
Nelso, John; Nelson, Samuel vs Hunt, William H. 1816
Nesbit, John vs Arthurs, Caleb 1829
Nesbit, John vs Yarbrough, William; Harper, Anselm L.; Harper, John W. 1830
Nesbit, Mary A. vs Brydie, Archibald 1846
Newell, Lott vs Johnson, Daniel H. 1821-22
Newhall, George; Remshart, William vs Shaw, George W.; Edwards, James C. 1832
Newton, Ebanezer vs Jackson, John 1841
Newton, Ebenezer vs Rogers, Right; Houghton, Robert B. 1835
Newton, Elizur L. vs Dunn, John T. 1831
Newton, Elizur L. vs Harden, Edward 1839
Newton, Elizur L. vs Jackson, William H. 1831
Newton, Elizur L. for use of Nesbit, John vs Jones, Richard; Moore, George 1831
Newton, Elizur L. vs Wolbright, Jacob 1826
Newton, Elizur L.; Newton, Ebinezar vs Sanson, Thomas; Adm. de bonis non Lord, Ebinezar; Left unadministrated by Lord, Benjamin B. 1841
Newton, Elizur L.; Newton, Ebinezar vs Sansom, Thomas 1841
Newton, Elizur L. vs Sledge, Wiley 1832
Newton, Elizur L. vs Taylor, William B. 1828
Newton, Elizur L. vs Vinson, Obediah 1832
Newton, J. H. vs Daniell, E. E.; Admin. de sontor of Daniell. Josiah 1869
Newton, John H. vs Cobb, John A.; Moore, Finney 1843
Newton, John H. vs Jackson, James 1841
Newton, John H. vs Jackson, John 1841
Newton, John H.; Lucas, Frederick W. vs Wood, John L. 1846
Newton, John H. vs McKinley, Charles G. 1841
Newton, John H. vs Walthall, Adelaide 1847
Newton, John H.; Lucas, Frederick W. vs Saye, Richard W. 1852
Newton, John S. vs Smith, Sion 1843
Newton, John V. vs Harden, Ed 1840
Newton, Josiah vs Gathright, Asuburn M. 1832
Niblett, Robert L.; Taylor, James vs Stephens, Michael 1846
Nichols, Ransom vs Gresham, Hinson Exec. Gresham, Young 1826
Nichols, Ransom vs Rogers, Right; Witter, James 1834
Nichols, Wolsey; Comstock, William S. vs Moore, Richard D. 1845
Nichol, Wosley; Comstock, William S. vs Waddel, James P. 1845
Nicholson, James S. vs DeGraffenreid, Boswell R. 1829
Nicholdson, John B. vs DeGraffenreid, Boswell B. 1830
Nisber, Thomas C.; Adm. of Nisber, John vs Dearing, William 1843
Nisbet, John vs Bradford, James T.; Rowland, Andrew; Palmer, Edmund; Cobb, John A.; Shaw, Oliver P. 1835
Nisbet, John vs Galliher, Samuel; Cobb, John A.; Barefield, Loyd K. 1835
Nisbet, John vs James, William; James, John 1831
Nisbet, John vs Wright, John C.; Oliver, Francis H.; Oliver, John Sr.; Oliver, John L. 1840
Nisbet, John vs Shaw, George W. 1835

Nisbet, John vs Shaw, George W.; Shaw, Oliver P. 1835
Nisbet, Thomas C. vs Clayton, Philip; Flint, William 1846
Nisbet, Thomas C. Adm. of Nisbet, John vs Clayton, Philip 1846
Nisbet, Thomas C. Trustee of LeConte, Harriet vs D'Autel, Jules 1844
Northington, Samuel vs Cox, Jno J. 1823
Norwood, Caleb M. vs Harris, West 1824
Nunnally, Aaron F. vs Adams, Edmund B. 1843
Nunnally, Aaron vs Winston, Joseph B. 1843
Nunnally, John vs Gordon, John 1825
Oats, Richard W. vs Cannon, William 1808
Oconee Building & Loan Assoc. vs Bell, A. A. 1879
Oglesby, George S. vs Mercer, William A. 1841
Orr, Christopher vs Jackson, Samuel; Crain, William 1811
Orr, Phillip vs Thurman, Benjamin 1812
Osburn, John vs Wooldridge, Isma W. 1840
Osgood, Daniel vs Lomice, Simson 1806
Pace, Drury vs Jones, James 1810
Pace, Drury; Jones, James; Hyde, William vs Ramey, John; Crain, William 1811
Paine, Edward vs Bonner, Jordan; Bankston, Abner 1807
Paine, Edward vs Bonner, Jordan 1808
Paine, Edward vs Bowen, William 1830
Paine, Edward vs Doolittle, Abraham 1827
Paine, Edward vs Mitchell, Henry; Boner, William H.; Simms, Arthur L. 1831
Paine, Edward vs Moore, George W.; Moore, Joshua G. 1830
Paine, Edward vs Shields, Samuel; Manley, William 1832
Paine, Edward; Jones, William vs Brown, William 1831
Paine, George D. for use of Haygood, Green B. vs Paine, Edward C. 1845
Parkson, John vs Burton, James M. 1826
Parmalee, Thomas J. vs Conner, Bowlin 1840
Parmalee, Thomas J. vs Wooldridge, Isma W.; Stephens, Harris 1840
Parmetee, Thomas vs Foster, George W.; Barnett, Nathan C.; Brightwell, William B. 1840
Pascoe, John vs Steel, George W. 1840
Patman, William vs Cobb, John A.; Cobb, Howell; Hancock, Thomas 1840
Patrick, William vs Billups, Richard 1808
Patton, James W.; Isborn, Joseph vs Christy, John H. 1847
Paulett, Lewis M. vs Hargrove, John R. 1827
Paulett, Lewis M. vs Leonard, Patrick as Bail for Hargrove, John R. 1833
Paulett, Lewis M. vs Williams, John 1827
Paullain, Felix vs Wilkinson, Robert B. 1841
Peck, David vs Harden, Robert R. 1834
Peck, David; Stevens, William B. vs Harden, Robert R. 1834
Peck, George M. vs Paine, Edward C. 1845
Pentecost, John W. vs Calehan, William 1819
Pentecost, John W.; Guice, Arnold J. vs Greathouse, Jacob 1820
Pentecost, John W. vs Hightower, William 1819
Pentecost, John W. vs Hudson, Archibald 1820
Perry, William H. vs Selman, John W.; Dickeman, Wilburn L. 1842
Phelps, Glenn vs Cogburn, Moses H. 1826
Phelps, Glenn vs Neisler, Hugh 1821
Philips, John vs Akins, James 1803
Philips, Joseph vs Stewart, Robert 1809
Phillips, B. & C. vs McDermond, P. W. 1879
Phillips, George guardian vs Brown, Joseph; Gresham, Young; Turner, James 1815
Phillips, George guardian of Strong, Temple; Strong, Pinina vs Trammel, Daniel; Lea, Temple 1812
Phillips, John vs Aikins, James 1803
Phillips, Jonathan vs Lawrence, Joseph 1808
Phillips, Joseph vs Stuart, Robert 1808
Phinizy, Fredinand vs Brown, Joseph; Ramey, John, Jr. 1812
Phinizy, Ferdinand; Phinizy, Jacob; Shields, Samuel vs Clarke, Lucy 1812
Phinizy, Ferdinand; Phinizy, Jacob; Shields, Samuel vs Evans, John 1809
Phinizy, Ferdinand vs Jackson, Asam; Hurden, William P.; Exects. of Hardin, R. R. 1844
Phinizy, Ferdinand vs Jackson, Asam; Harden, William P.; Admin of Harden, Robert R. 1844
Phinizy, Ferdinand; Malone, John; Houston, John vs Shaw, William 1820

Phinizy, Jacob vs Bradford, James Y.; Rowland, Andrew; Palmer, Edmund; Cobb, John A.; Shaw, Oliver P.; Jackson, John 1835
Phinizy, Jacob vs Butler, Lewis R. 1845
Phinizy, Jacob vs Collier, Charles W.; Tinsley, James 1835
Phinizy, Jacob vs Cobb, John A. 1834
Phinizy, Jacob vs Cobb, John A. 1834
Phinizy, Jacob vs Cobb, John A.; Martain, John 1834
Phinizy, Jacob vs Hancock, Thomas 1842
Phinizy, John F. vs Reynolds, Thomas S. 1853
Phinizy, Jacob vs Robinson, Jesse 1841
Phinizy, Son & Shields vs Turner, James 1812
Phinney, Elihu vs Legg, Thomas 1822
Pitrier, J. C. & Co. vs Stovall, B. A.; as trustee for his wife M. W. Stovall & Minor children Alex, Jennie, Lizzie, Nelly & Bolling 1878
Pittard, James D. serving partner of Pittard, Samuel vs Daniell, E. E. Admin. of Daniell, Josiah ND
Planters Company vs Hill, Isaac; Crawford, Archibald 1812
Planters Company vs Hunton, Hannah 1810
Pope, Henry vs McKinley, Charles G. 1840
Pope, Henry J. for use of Reece, William M. vs Taylor, James Jones 1842
Pope, John H. vs Verone, William 1833
Pope, Robert vs Wood, John ND
Pope, Robert; Hill, Myles vs Wright, William G.; Cocke, Jack F. 1812
Pope, Sarah K.; Hill, Blanton M.; Strong, Elisha; Hill, Abram S. Executors of Pope, Burwell vs Barnett, Nathan C. 1841
Pope & Watkins vs Easley, Benjamin 1807
Pope & Watkins vs Easley, Benjamin 1808
Pope, Zachary vs McCree, William 1815
Porter, James H. vs Harden, Robert R. 1834
Porter, John W. vs Swinney, Mark E. 1848
Porter, Oliver M. vs Admin. Hezekiah D. 1835
Porter, William; Burney, Thomas J. vs Wright, John C. 1840
Potter, Pleasant vs Bickerstaff, Johnston; Jackson, Samuel 1805
Potter, Pleasant vs Bickerstaff, Johnston; Jackson, Samuel; Ramey, William 1805
Poullian, Felix vs Wilkinson, Robert B. 1840
Poullain, Thomas N. for use of Durham, Lindsey vs Burton, James M.; Moore, Joshua G. 1832
Poullain, Thomas N. vs Robertson, James A. 1834
Powel, Starling vs Earnest, William H. 1812
Powell, John for Moon, George W. vs Erwin, Leander A.; Holmes, David 1819
Powell, John vs Starns, William 1808
Powell, William vs Kelly, Drury 1807
Pressley, Jane vs Harden, Edward 1846
Pressley, Jane vs Maynard, Robert J. 1846
Price, H. W. William vs Rogers, Right 1837
Price, John for use of Ramey, John vs Taylor, Roland; Strong, Johnson 1806
Price, John for use of Ramey, John vs Taylor, Roland; Strong, John 1807
Price, John for use of Ramey, John vs Taylor, Roland; Strong, Johnson; Strong, William Jr. 1807
Prince, Garland W. vs Kirkpatrick, John 1838
Prince, Noah vs Jackson, James 1832
Princeton, Mft. Co. vs Jenkins, Moore & Co. 1883
Puryear, John Guardian of Puryear, Mary Ann vs Bird, John A.; Rogers, Right 1834
Puryear, John for use of Lumpkin, Joseph Henry vs Cobb, John A. 1834
Puryear, Lucy A. vs Puryear, William H. 1850
Puryear, Peter vs Neisler, Hugh 1820
Puryear, William H. vs Irwin, Robert 1817
Rakestraw, Robert vs Andrew, John; Davenport, William 1827
Rakestraw, Robert G. vs Cock, Jack F. 1812
Rakestraw, Robert D. vs Cocke, Jack F. 1813
Ramey, David vs Hinton, James; Allen, Phillip 1822
Ramey, John vs Arthur, Tolbert 1808
Ramey, John vs Arthur, Tolbot 1810
Ramey, John guardian of Heard, George vs Boyd, Drury B. 1809
Ramey, John guardian of Heard, George vs Boyd, Drury B. 1817
Ramey, John vs Brown, William 1806
Ramey, John vs Sewall, Lewis 1807

Ramey, John vs Sewell, Lewis 1806
Ramey, Sanford L. for use of Sims, John H. vs Moffett, Gabriel A. 1808
Ramey, Seaborn vs Daniell, Josiah 1846
Randolph, James E. vs Lavender, William; Wages, James 1877
Randolph, James B. vs Lavender, William; Wages, James 1877
Randolph, Peter & Co. vs Merewether, Tony; Merewether, David 1820
Ranfield, Loyd K. vs Willingham, Henderson; Crawford, John 1849
Rankin, Andrew vs Wooldridge, Isma W. 1840
Rankin, Andrew; Boggs, Archibald; Evans, Thomas vs Wooldridge, Isma W.; Conner, Daniel 1840
Rankin, Andrew; Boggs, Archibald; Evans, Thomas vs Wooldridge, Isma W. 1840
Rankin, Andrew; Evans, Thomas vs Pettey, John; Pettey, Henry 1834
Rasberry, Joseph vs Echols, Robert E. 1811
Rathbone, William P.; Baker, Alfred vs Davenport, Thomas 1842
Ray, John vs Gresham, David; Butler, George 1810
Ray, Solomon vs Dicken, Richard 1806
Redd, Charles A. for trustees of Academey, Mison vs Hearing, Cyrel 1812
Redd, William for use of Cunningham, Thomas; Cunningham, John vs Trammell, John; Trammell, Francis M. 1826
Reece, Nancy vs Nall, Martin 1807
Reed, Luke; Goble, Lucher; Thomas, Frederick S. vs Manly, William 1830
Rees, John; Anderson, John S. vs Strong, James M. 1833
Rees, John; Beall, Egbert B. vs Green, Raleigh 1841
Rees, John; Beall, Egbert B. vs Wooldridge, Isma W.; Conner, Bowlin; Stephens, David 1840
Rees, Thad B. vs Brown, Alexander W. 1835
Rees, Thaddeus B. vs Strong, James M. 1833
Reese, Charles M. vs Kirkpatrick, John 1842
Reese, Charles M.; Ware, Edward R. vs Swinney, Mark E. 1848
Reese, G.; Reese, W. C. vs Vandiford, Richard 1821
Reese, John C.; Reese, Williamson C. vs Ball, John 1821
Reese, John C.; Reese, Williamson vs Hunton, James 1821
Reese, John C.; Reese, Williamson C. vs Jordan, Henry 1821
Reese, John C.; Reese, Williamson C. vs Lasiter, James 1821
Reese, John C.; Reese, Williamson C. vs Vandiford, Richard 1821
Reynolds, Coleman vs Runnels, Preston 1807
Reynolds, Gallant vs Craft, Daniel 1809
Reynolds, Gallant vs Craft, Daniel 1810
Richards, Rebecca Admx. of Richards, Royal vs Gilleland, James 1842
Richards, Thomas vs Jones, William E. 1835
Richards, Thomas; Ganatt, Francis vs Shaw, George W. 1835
Richards, Thomas vs Totty, John 1842
Richardson, James vs Jackson, John 1840
Richardson, John vs Nunnally, William B. 1822
Richardson, John H. vs Gerrald, Isaac F. 1826
Richardson, John H. vs Richardson, James G. 1830
Richardson, John W. vs Whitlow, John Admi. of Whitlow, Warren 1850
Richardson, Richard vs Moore, George W.; Cox, Richard 1829
Richardson, Richard vs Turner, James 1823
Richardson, Richard D.; Vincent, Isaac S. Admin. of Ligon, Robert vs Burton, James M.; Hendon, James ND
Richardson, Robert vs Crow, Aaron 1839
Richardson, Robert vs Crow, Aaron 1852
Ridgeway, Nelson vs Howell, James D. 1823
Ridgeway, Nelson vs Hewell, James D. 1823
Robbins, George; Robbins, Allen vs Mitchell, William L. 1831
Robbins, Samuel W. vs Cobb, John A. 1840
Roberts, & Co. vs Saulter, R. R. 1877
Roberts, & Co. vs Ware, E. H. 1877
Roberts, Edwin vs Roberts, Wilie 1805
Roberts, Jesse vs Trammel, Francis M; Trammel, Fannie 1816
Roberts, Jesse vs Trammell, Francis; Trammell, Fanny Executors of Trammell, Daniel 1817
Robinson, Jesse vs Burk, Rhesa, H. H. 1835
Robinson, Jesse vs Jackson, James 1841
Robison, Alexander L. vs Paine, George M. 1836
Robison, Alexander S. vs Paine, George M. 1838
Robison, John L. vs Wozencraft, James L. 1845
Robson, John vs Hamby, Joseph; Weaver, David 1836
Robson, John vs Harden, Edward 1833

Robson, John vs Vickers, Martin ND
Roby, Matthew for use of Morgan, Stokely vs Easly, Roderick; Holleway, George 1807
Rochfort, George vs George, William 1809
Rochfort, George vs George, William 1810
Rochfort, George vs King, Sarah 1819
Rodgers, John vs Sanders, Julius; Sanders, John L. 1809
Roe, John vs Gentry, Martin; Gentry, Neaama ND
Roe, John vs Hogue, James 1806
Rosseter, White vs Crews, John 1821
Rogers, Moses for the use of McKinne, John vs Reese, Cuthbert; Reese, Williamson; Reese, Joseph C. 1821
Roll, Luther vs Clark, Eli; Young, Benjamin 1832
Roll, Luther vs Van Houten, Daniel; Barrett, Michaels 1851
Roosevelt, Henry L.; Barker, Samuel vs Selman, James J. 1846
Ross, David vs Barber, James; Strong, Johnson 1806
Ross, David vs Barber, James; Strong, Johnson 1808
Ross, William vs Petty, John; Petty, Henry 1833
Ross, William; Brown, James, Sr.; Brown, James, Jr. vs Shaw, William 1809
Rosseter, White vs Crews, John 1821
Roundtree, George R. vs Wright, John L. 1832
Rousseau, Hiram vs Stanley, Charity M. 1830
Rowe, Chauncy Administrator of Rowe, Adna vs Holbrook, Nathan 1837
Rowe, Chauncy Adm. of Rowe, Adna vs Vervnee, William 1837
Ruckersville, Banking Co. vs Harris, Sarah H. 1843
Runnels, Hardin vs Clarke, Lucy; Brown, Joseph 1810
Runnels, Harman & Others vs Sims, John H.; Hill, Thomas 1811
Runnels, Preston vs Camp, Cicel 1805
Runnels, Preston; Runnels, Annis his wife vs Camp, Cicel 1805
Runnells, Sophia vs Bankston, Lesley 1810
Runnells, Sophia vs Bankston, Lesly 1811
Rupert, John; Rakestraw, Robert for use of Rakestraw, Robert vs Andrew, John; Davenport, William 1826
Rushin, Bryant for Millsaps, Thomas vs Lowe, John H. 1812
Russell, Alexander for use of Moss, Joseph vs Reese, Williamson C. 1821
Russell, W. O. Adm. of Brumby, R. T. vs Potts, John 1878
Rutledge, James S. vs Niblack, Samuel 1803-04
Ryle, James vs Neely, David 1812
Saffold, William; Stokes, Henry for use of Moffett, Gabriel A. vs Hinton, John 1820
Sage, William F. vs Lombard, Charles B. 1852
Sage, William P. vs Lombard, Charles B. 1852
Salmons, Lewis S. vs Selman, James J. 1845-46
Salmons, Lewis S. vs Tarpley, Augustus A. 1845
Salms, Kirby vs Sherling, Richmond 1816
Sanford, Adolphus M. vs Wright, James A. 1833
Sansom, James vs Richardson, John H. 1831
Sanson, Thomas Adm of Lord, Benjamin B. vs Wadd l, James P. 1841
Saulter, Martha Alias Brazelton, Martha for use of Officers of Court vs Saulter, Wesley Alias Cooly, John W. 1877
Saulter, Richard R. vs Flournoy, Howell C. 1847
Saunders, Julius vs Wallace, Samuel 1805
Saunders, Peter vs Pinckerton, David 1805
Saunders, Petter vs Pinkerton, David 1806
Saye, James vs Hendon, James W. 1852
Scherenell, L. & Co. vs Lumpkin, M. G. 1884
Schroder, Mathilda vs Sussdroff, Gustamus 1840
Scott, Edward vs Schoonmaker, Lodowick 1832
Scott, George vs Odgen, Joseph H. 1824
Scott, James Sr. vs Lawrence, Richard; Lawrence, Joseph 1808
Scott, William vs Alexander, John; Barber, Robert 1801
Scott, William vs McGowen, Robert 1808
Scovell, H. W. vs Thomas, William R.; Wright, Thos. A.; Brewer, Z. R. ND
Scovell, Hezekiah W. vs Booth, Benjamin H. 1821
Scovell, Hezekiah W. vs Burt, Henry 1824
Scovell, Hezakiah W. vs Freeman, Allen 1826
Scovell, Hezekiah W. vs Hendon, Isham 1821
Scovell, Hezekiah vs Love, William 1826
Scovell, Hezekiah W. vs Thomas, William R.; Wright, Thomas A.; Brown, Littleton R. 1829

Scovell, Hezekiah W.; Hall, Oliver vs Harden, Robert R.; Johnston, John C. 1832-33
Scranton, Philmon A.; Shark, William H.; Davis, Stephen E. vs Ritch & Stovall 1851
Seaman, John B.; Word, Samuel vs Jones, James M. 1838
Seale, John for use of Napier, Thomas vs Suttle, Jesse 1812
Sears, Abner vs Love, Daniel H.; Oliver, Francis H. 1834
Sears, Albert; Sears, Marcus A. vs Akridge, Ezekiel 1828
Sears, Albert vs Brown, William T.; Booth, Thomas; Merriwether, George 1830
Sears, Albert vs Brown, William T.; Ligon, Robert 1830
Sears, Albert vs Brown, William T.; Merriwether, George W. 1830
Sears, Albert vs Cherry, Vincent I.; Wright, John C. 1834
Sears, Albert vs Conner, Edward; Parker, John 1832
Sears, Albert vs Glenn, William B.; Harris, Samuel; Butler, John W.; Scott, Archibald H. 1834
Sears, Albert vs Hanson, James Sr.; Hanson, James Jr. 1834
Sears, Albert vs Harris, Samuel; Scott, A. H.; Butler, John W. 1834
Sears, Albert vs Jones, Robert A. 1832
Sears, Albert vs Kirkpatrick, John; Wooldridge, Isma W. 1834
Sears, Albert vs Knott, James 1829
Sears, Albert vs Love, David; Oliver, Francis H. 1831
Sears, Albert vs Love, Robert 1828
Sears, Marcus A. vs Gordon, Robert S. 1828
Sears, Marcus A. vs Wright, William 1828
Selman, John W. vs Harden, Robert R. 1841
Sewell, H. W. vs Lowe, William; Oates, James 1826
Sewell, Jonathan vs Collier, Charles W. 1834
Seymour, Eralbon vs Brown, William T. 1830
Seymour, Eralbon vs Brown, William alias Brown, William T.; Gaine, John M. 1830
Shannon, Thomas vs Kelough, Ebenezar 1803
Shaw, Elizabeth vs Birch, Charles C.; Birch, John N. 1828
Shaw, George W. vs Bradley, Chaney 1823
Shaw, Oliver P.; Bacon, William B. vs Adams, Edmund B. 1841
Shaw, Oliver P.; Bacon, William B. vs Barnett, Nathan C. 1841
Shaw, Oliver P.; Bacon, William B. vs Paulett, Jesse C. 1841
Shaw, Oliver; Bacon, William B. vs Thurmond, John 1841
Sheats, Benajah L.; Burton, Jeremiah vs Talbot, Elizabeth; Fullilove, Barnwell P. 1844
Sheats, Benajah S. vs Tucker, Richard O.; Moore, Robertur B. 1841
Sheats, Benajah S. vs Tucker, Richard O.; Moore, Robert W. B.; Jackson, Stephen 1841
Sheats, Benajah S. vs Witter, James; Kirkpatrick, John 1836
Sheats, Benajah S.; Sheats, Marshall M. vs Dickin, Richard 1841
Sheats, Benajah S.; Sheats, Marshall M. vs Gann, James 1841
Sheats, Benjamin J.; Sheats, Marshall M. vs Wozencraft, Thomas 1843
Sheets, Nicholas vs Hicks, Daniel 1816
Shenalt, Stephen vs Hopkins, Denney 1805
Shepherd, James vs Ridgway, Drury 1826
Shields, Josiah vs Britain, Thomas; Farra, George Y. 1810-11
Shields & Manley vs Adams, John 1826
Shields & Manly for use of Shields, Samuel vs Brown, William 1828
Shields & Manly vs Bryan, Laury 1826
Shields & Manly vs Clifton, William 1826
Shields & Manley for use of Haygood, Green B. vs Conner, David; Conner, Edward 1831
Shields & Manley for use of Haygood, Green B. vs Conner, Edward; Conner, John 1832
Shields & Manley vs Crow, Aaron 1826
Shields & Manley vs Gibbs, Thomas F. 1822
Shields & Manley vs Harden, Robert R. 1826
Shields & Manley vs Harris, Samuel B. 1826
Shields & Manley vs Haynie, James 1827
Shields & Manley vs Hendon, Isham ND
Shields & Manley vs Hendon, Isham 1821
Shields & Manley vs Langford, James 1826
Shields & Manley for use of Shields, Samuel vs Melton, Eleel 1827
Shields & Manley vs McCree, William 1826
Shields & Manley vs McCree, William 1826
Shields & Manley vs Moore, Francis 1822

Shields & Manley vs Nixon, Edward P. 1826
Shields & Manley vs Nunnally, Aaron F. 1826
Shields & Manley vs Nunnally, John A. 1826
Shields & Manley vs Pendleton, John B. 1819
Shields & Manley vs Ward, Leonard 1826
Shields & Manley vs Whatley, Willis 1826
Shields & Manley vs Whitehead, Elizabeth 1826
Shields & Manley vs Winfield, Joel 1821
Shields, Samuel vs Chandler, John B. 1810
Shields, Samuel B. vs Stringer, James 1805
Shields, William vs McCree, William 1821
Shorter, Eli S. vs Crews, John 1818
Shorter, James vs Greene, Willis 1837
Shorter, James vs Greene, Willis; Camack, James 1837
Shilman, John vs Paulett, Richard 1801
Shirley, Thomas vs Kilgore, Thomas; Whitton, John 1822
Sigon, Joseph vs Puryear, John 1834
Simms, Albert G. vs Paine, Courtney 1833
Simms, Arther T. vs Jack, Green B.; Elder, David; Turner, James 1812
Simms, Arthur L. vs Lowe, Thomas F. 1840
Simms, Arthur L. vs Turner, James; Trammell, Daniel 1812
Simms, Richard L. vs Harden, Robert R. 1842
Simms, Richard L. vs Vandiford, R.; Vandiford, A. C.; Arthur, Lewis 1839-40
Simonton, Thomas vs Kennon, John W. 1839
Sims, Arthur S. vs Lowe, Thomas F. 1840
Sims, David vs Browning, Joshua Sr. 1806
Sims, David vs Davis, Edward 1807
Sims, David vs Harper, George 1800
Sims, David for use of Hightower, John P. vs Hubert, Gabriel 1813
Sims, David vs Hunton, Hannah 1807
Sims, Loroner vs Sims, James 1828
Sims, David vs Williamson, Peter 1805
Sims, David; Sims, John H. vs Armstrong, James W.; Ramey, Sanford L. 1809
Sims, James vs Meadows, Enoch 1838
Sims, John H. for use of Crawford, Peter vs Briscoe, Nathan; Bennett, John F. 1824
Sims, John H. vs Crenshaw, James G.; Moffett, Gabriel A. 1829
Sims, John Hughes vs Bond, Edward 1810
Sims, William vs Neisler, Hugh 1828
Sims, Zachariah vs McEven, John 1809
Sims, Zachariah vs Walton, John C. 1823
Skinner, Ebenezer vs Clarke, Eli K. 1834
Sledge, Wiley vs Odum, Jordan 1830
Sledge, Wiley vs Odum, Jourdan 1830
Sloman, S. J. vs Demon, W. R. & Co. 1879
Smith, Benajah vs Hopkins, William; Benge Micajah 1803
Smith, Benajah vs Hopkins, William; Benge, Micajah 1804
Smith, Charles vs Harden, Robert R. 1841
Smith, Dan; Evans, E. W. vs Livingstone, Emiline 1879
Smith, David vs Meriweather, David 1826
Smith, George M.; Boothe, Charles A.; Alfford, Asa T. vs Griffeth, Charles T. 1834
Smith, George M. vs Harris, West 1824
Smith, Hill vs Boyer, Henry ND
Smith, Hill vs Boyers, Henry 1828
Smith, Hugh vs Reynolds, John 1833
Smith, James M. Governor of the State of Georgia vs Emrick, Joseph H. 1876
Smith, John vs Farrar, George Y.; Redd, Charles A. 1812
Smith, John vs Ritchey, James F. 1822
Smith, John vs Selman, John 1814
Smith, John vs Ward, Leonard 1826
Smith, John S. vs Carrol, David 1825
Smith, Joseph Sr. vs Weatherly, William 1838-39
Smith, Leven for use of Daniell, Jesse vs Gann, John 1843
Smith, Nathaniel vs Moore, George W. 1830
Smith, Peyton vs Jones, John P. 1810
Smith, Thomas vs Cruise, John 1822

Smith, Vines vs Hanson, James; Garner, William; Adms of Garner, Elijah 1830
Smith, William E. vs Wood, Thomas Sr. 1839
Smith, Yelverton P. vs Crocker, William 1806
Snead, Patrick H. for use of the Augusta Ins. Banking Company vs Hicks, Burton 1839
Smede, Abraham K.; Smede, George M.; Camfield, Abiel vs Rakerstraw, Gainham L. 1819
Snowden, Gilbert T.; Shear, William vs Thomas, Lovie P. 1834
Soloman, S. J. vs Demon, W. R. 1879
Sondheim, Lissan vs Schevenell, Leonard & Yancy; Goodbee H.L.; Schevenell & Co. 1877
Son (Suvivor), Andrew vs Birch, John N.; Anderson, James C. 1830
Sparks, Martin P. vs Humphries, Isaac 1823
Spear, Alva; Patten, Jonathan vs Jones, James W. 1839
Spears, Rollins B. vs Wright, John C. 1834
Spencer, William vs Beal, Courtney W. 1879
Sperry, F. L. vs Benton, Loyd 1881
Squire, Charles; Silliman, Gold S. vs Land, Jonathan; Land, Theophilis; Hunt, William H.; Espy, Robert 1822
Squire, Charles; Tillman, Gold vs Rakestraw, Gainham L. 1819
Squire, Charles; Rogers, Silas vs Billups, Joseph 1833
Stallings, John E. vs Treadway, Elijah 1819
Stamps, Timothy for use of Ector, John vs Spain, John; Stewart, Charley 1809
Stanton, James vs Cabell, Robert 1812
Stanton, James vs Cabell, Robert J. 1813
Stark, Bowling W. vs Dorsett, Theodon ND
Stark, Bowling W. vs Dorsett, Theodore 1828
Stark, John W. vs Cocke, Jack F. ND
Stark, William vs Ramey, John 1809
State of Ga. vs Bealsey, James 1845
State of Ga. vs Cash, Joel H. 1839
State of Georgia vs Elijah (a Slave) ND
State of Ga. vs Farrell, John; Dee, James 1852
State of Ga. vs Fulbright, Elizabeth 1848
State of Ga. vs Gardner, Daniel B. 1844
State of Ga. vs Gardner, Daniel B. 1844
State of Ga. vs Gilliland, Coil 1839
State of Ga. vs Jacks, John; Maxey, Edward H. 1826
State of Ga. vs Johnson, William ND
State of Georgia vs Jones, Edward H. 1841
State of Ga. vs Kennedy, David; Wood, Merrit 1822
State of Ga. vs Land, L. B. ND
State of Ga. vs Little, Thomas 1831
State of Ga. vs Miller, Rondia alias Fullbright, Rosetta 1848
State of Ga. vs Patrick, John N. 1847
State of Ga. vs Murdock, Bartlett W. 1840
State of Ga. vs Royal, William H. 1850
State of Ga. vs Smith, Ann (Polly) 1848
State of Ga. vs Stevens, Thomas; Garret, Abraham 1847
State of Ga. vs Thomas, Joseph 1824
State of Ga. vs Thompson, Robert & Co. 1837
State of Ga. vs Thurmond, Nancy 1848
State of Ga. vs Treadway, Elijah 1835
State of Ga. vs Watkins, Julia; Watkins, Rebecca 1844
State of Ga. vs Webb, M. K. ND
State of Ga. vs White, William 1847
State of Ga. vs Wilkinson, James 1837
Stedman, James or Stidman vs Stuart, Robert 1809
Steedly, Georgetta vs Waltall, E. G. 1894
Steel, James C. vs Campbell, Walter 1812
Steel, John vs Doster, James 1830
Steele, John H.; Thweatt, Peterson for use of Thweatt, Peterson vs Harden, Edward 1842
Stephens, Alexander vs Martindale, John 1808
Stephens, David vs Echols, Absalom 1810
Stephens, David vs Humphries, Elijah; Humphries, George W. 1834
Stephens, Joshua; Stephens, Harris; Executors of will of Stephens, David vs Wooldridge, Isma W.; Thomas, James L. 1840

Stern, Charles vs Hodgson, E. R. Admin. of Estate of Maupin, Fayette 1879
Stern, Charles vs Long, H. R. I. 1878
Sterns, William vs Randolph, Peter; Shaw, Margaret; Admin. of Shaw, William 1812
Stewart & Hargrave vs Jones, Robert A. 1828
Stewart, Alexander T. vs Jones, James W. & Bacon, William 1840
Stewart, Alfred vs Brown, Robert 1822
Stewart, Charles vs Holmes, David & Marable, John 1809
Stewart, Charles H. for use of Hargrave, George vs Gresham, Hinson Exec. of Gresham, Young 1824
Stewart, Charled D. vs Trustees of the University of Georgia 1817
Stewart, Charles P. & Hargraves, George vs Shepherd, Thomson 1826
Stewart, Thomas vs Wood, John L. 1847
Stewart, William for use of Connell, John M. vs Ligon, James 1817
Stewart, William for use of McConnell, John Jr. vs Earnest, Thomas & Earnest, George 1817
Stewart, William for use of McConnell vs Earnest, Thomas & Earnest, George 1817
Stewart, William vs Ramey, John 1813
Stokes, Archibald vs McDonnell, Alexander 1810
Stokes, Thomas vs Ford, James 1809
Stokes, William; Strong, Sherwood; Executors of Strong, William vs Brown, Joseph ND
Williams, Edward vs Brown, Joseph ND
Gill, William vs Brown, Joseph 1818
Stokes, William M.; Strong, Sherwood; Executors of Strong, William vs Brown, Joseph & Brown, Russell 1816
Stokes, William; Strong, Sherwood; Executor of Strong, William vs Brown, Russell & Moore, George W. 1817
Stokes, William; Strong, Sherwood; Executors of Strong, William vs Brown, Joseph & Mark, John ND
Stone, D. M. vs Bassett, J. M. 1879
Stone, D. M. vs Bassett, J. M. 1879
Stoneham, Joseph vs Brown, Joseph 1811
Stovall, Augustine vs Adams, Edmond B. & Barnett, Nathan C. 1841
Stovall, Charles vs Hampton, John; Shaw, William; Executors of Malone, John 1809
Stovall, Charles vs Mavable, John 1813
Stovall, John vs Hendon, Isham 1821
Stovall, John vs Morris, Garrett ND
Stovall, Pleasant & Davis, John vs Graham, William P. 1830
Stovall, Wilburn & Co. vs Winfield, Joel 1821
Strand, John vs Boman, Isom 1807
Straus, Joseph vs Lighfield, M. A.; Nordham 1851
Stringer, James vs Brewer, William 1808
Stringer, James vs Gentry, Elijah 1805
Strong, Charles; McCoy, Thomas M.; Executors of Thompson, John vs Cocke, Jack F. & Moss, John 1812
Strong, Charles; Executors of Strong, William Sr. for use of Bowen, Christopher vs Strong, William E. & Strong, John 1829
Strong, Charles Sr. vs Newton, Josiah 1826
Strong, Charly vs Wright, William & Wright, John 1812
Strong, Elisha Admin. of Price, William vs Wood, William; Cousons, John; Osborn, Nicholas 1838
Strong, Sherwood vs Cooper, Vining 1804
Strong, Sherwood vs Wright, John 1812
Strong, William vs Flippen, Jesse 1816
Strong, William vs Bridgewater, Samuel 1805
Strong, William vs Hartsfield, Anderson; Browning, Joshua; Seamans, William; Bankston, Henry 1806
Strong, William vs Murphy, John W. 1805
Strong, William Executors of vs Brown, Joseph & Brown, Russell 1815
Strong, William Executors of vs Heard, George; Brown, Joseph; Moore, George W. 1815
Strong, William Executors of vs Moore, George W.; Moore, John; Biggs, Aaron 1815
Strong, William Executors of vs Ward, Leonard; Brown, Joseph; Brown, Russell 1815
Strong, William Executors of vs Hinson, Tapley; Garner, Presley 1812

Strong, William; Turner, James Executors of Roberson, William vs Ramey, Sanford L. & Ramey, John 1810
Strong, William Executors of vs Wright, John L. 1812
Stroud, William; Daniel, Josiah vs Ammons, Josiah 1827
Stroud, William vs Harper, Joseph M.; Harper, Nathaniel; Harper, Anselm; Shaw, William Admins. of Harper, John W. 1838
Stuart, Robert vs Stedman, James 1809
Sturdivant, John vs Allen, Charles 1840
Sturdivant, John vs Fullilove, William W. & Davenport, Moses N. 1840
Summerford, William for use of Collier, Isaac vs Heard, George 1810
Summey, Peter A.; Summey, John S.; Wammell, Causuell G. vs Thomas, Lovick P. 1852
Sunderland, William vs Epps, Nathaniel 1849
Suttles vs Akins; Akins 1818
Suttles, Jessie vs Sims, David; Sims, John H. 1811
Suttles, William vs Akins, William; Akins, Edmund 1817
Sutton, Joel vs Love, William 1823
Sutton, Joel vs Stoneham, Henry 1822
Sutton, Williams & Co. vs Summery, Peter A.; Newton, John F. 1876
Swanson, John; Connally, Bryan vs Hendrick, John R. 1842
Swanson, S. vs Nixon, N. ND
Swanson, Samuel vs Nixon, Nahun 1823
Swift, William A. vs Robison, Pleasant 1838
Talbot, Elizabeth guardian of Fullilove, Burwell P. vs Selman, James J. Adm. of Fullilove, Seaborn J. 1841
Talmadge, Mrs. E. A. Admin. of Talmadge, W. P. vs Burch, John B. 1879
Talmadge, M. A. vs Burch, John B. 1879
Talmadge, Mrs. E. W. Admin. of Talmadge, William P. vs Parr, V. J. 1879
Talmadge, Hodgson & Co. vs Barnard, F. J. 1879
Talmadge, John vs Barefield, Lloyd R. 1835
Talmadge, John vs Frost, Samuel 1830
Talmadge, John vs Barefield, Lloyd K. 1835
Talmadge, John vs Gann, William 1840
Talmadge, W. A. vs Christy, W. D. 1879
Talmadge, W. A. vs Crawford, Horace L. 1879
Talmadge, William A. vs Burns, S. W. 1879
Talmadge, John vs Legg, Thomas 1826
Talmage, John vs Whitman, Nathan W. 1826
Talmage, John vs Shepherd, Thomas 1826
Talmage, John vs Taylor, William B. 1826
Talmage, John vs Clarke, Eli; Young, Benjamin 1831
Talmage, John vs Jackson, James & Prince, Noah F. 1831
Talmage, Lewis T. vs Paine, Edward C. 1844
Tanner, John vs Runnels, Preston 1802
Tanner, John vs Runnels, Preston 1803
Tanning, L. J. vs Robeson, William & Gay, Gilbert 1805
Taylor, Benjamin vs Ormond, James & Ormond, John 1813
Taylor, Benjamin; Fullilove, Ludwell vs Biggs, Aron; Armstrong, John 1802
Taylor, Benjamin; Fullilove, Ludwell vs Biggs, Aaron; Armstrong, John 1803
Taylor, Daniel vs Pryer, Oley 1815
Taylor, James; Niblett, Robert L. vs Stephens, Michael 1846
Taylor, Peter vs Conner, Daniel; Conner, David 1809
Taylor, Peter B. vs Galliher, Samuel; Cobb, John A. 1834
Taylor, Peter B.; Wheeler, Joseph vs Sledge, Willie 1834
Temple, Lea vs Gaddy, David 1812
Tennell, Francis vs Wheeler, Thomas; Jack, Green B. 1812
Tenney, Shubael vs Barnett, Nathan C.; Brightwell, William B. 1841
Tenney, Shubael vs Galliher, Samuel 1834
Tenney, Shubael vs Harden, Edward 1841
Tenney, Shubael vs Jackson, James 1841
Tenney, Shubael vs Poore, Benjamin P. 1841
Tenney, Shubael vs Waddel, James P. 1841
Terrell, David vs Harris, West 1825
Terrell, James D. vs Bankston, Henry 1811-13
Terrell, John D. vs Bankston, Jacob 1812
Terrell, John D. vs Hubert, Gabriel 1813
Theats, Charles vs Fluker, Robert; Teaman, William 1813
Thomas, Ben vs White, Ulary 1879
Thomas, Benjamin F. vs Mandeville, A. S. 1879
Thomas, H. P. vs Read, Isaac D. 1839-40
Thomas, Henry vs Echols, Robert 1807

Thomas, Henry vs Echols, Robert & Ramey, John 1808
Thomas, Henry; Thomas, Ralf vs Shaw, Margaret; Randolph, Peter, Adm. of Shaw, William 1812
Thomas, Jett vs Wright, William 1805
Thomas, John vs Wright, John L. 1832
Thomas, John W. vs Robertson, James S. 1813
Thomas, Lawrence; Thomas, Jett vs Gaddy, David 1808
Thomas, Merrill vs Wozencroft, Thomas 1841
Thomas, Penina W. Executorix of Thomas, Stevens vs Elliot, Benjamin; Wells, Paschal M.; Moore, Finny H.; Towns, Benjamin 1841
Thomas, Peninah W. Executrix of Thomas, Stevens vs Jackson, John 1841
Thomas, Peninah W. vs Jackson, William H.; Cobb, Howell; McKinley, Charles G. 1842
Thomas, S & J vs Cabaness, William; Conally, Charles 1809
Thomas, Stephens vs Clift, Henry 1808
Thomas, Stephen vs Deane, Nathaniel; Lea Temple 1818
Thomas, Stephens; Thomas, Jett vs Gaddy, David 1809
Thomas, Stevens vs Brown, William 1809
Thomas, Steven vs Cabness, William 1809
Thomas, Stevens vs Cobb, Howell 1840
Thomas, Stevens vs Cobb, John A. 1840
Thomas, Stevens vs Cocke, William 1832
Thomas, Stevens vs Cocke, William 1832
Thomas, Stevens vs Cogburn, Moses H. 1830
Thomas, Stevens vs Cox, John J. 1823
Thomas, Stevens vs Cox, John J. 1828
Thomas, Stevens vs Deane, Nathaniel 1808
Thomas, Stevens vs Doggett, Thomas; Sheats, Nicholas 1831
Thomas, Stevens vs Durham, Joseph; Elder, David 1831
Thomas, Stevens vs Echols, Thomas E.; Harper, Joseph M. 1833
Thomas, Stevens vs Hancock, Thomas 1836
Thomas, Stevens vs Hodges, William; Barber, William; Harper, John W. 1830
Thomas, Stevens vs Holmes, Isaac 1819
Thomas, Stevens vs Humphries, Elijah; Woolbright, Jacob; Humpries, Nancy; Humphries, Joseph 1826
Thomas, Stevens vs Kirkpatrick, John; Hicks, Burton; Cabell, William B. 1836
Thomas, Stevens vs Langford, Bedford Admr. of Langford, James 1833
Thomas, Stevens vs Manley, William; Ligon, Robert; Moore, Joshua G. 1833
Thomas, Stevens vs Newton, Josiah; Espy, Thomas 1838
Thomas, Stevens vs Oliver, Francis W.; Oliver, John L.; Oliver, John, Sr.; Sheats, Nicholad; Wright, John C. 1831
Thomas, Stevens vs Powell, Campbell 1818
Thomas, Stevens vs Rogers, Right; Hancock, Thomas 1836
Thomas, Stevens vs Sanpford, Bezabel 1833
Thomas, Stevens vs Sansom, James 1809
Thomas, Stevens vs Sledge, Charles M. 1828
Thomas, Stevens vs Strong, James M. as bail for Cocke, William 1833
Thomas, Stevens; Thomas, Jett vs Cabaness, William 1808
Thomas, Stevens; Thomas, Jett vs Mayo, Samuel as bail for Brown, William 1810
Thomas, Stevens; Thomas, Jett vs Moore, George W.; Cowen, Isaac; Cowen, Moses Admr. of Cowan, Thomas 1810
Thomas, Stevens; Thomas, Jett vs Wright, William 1810
Thomason, William vs Hopkins, Eusebius A.; Booker, John M. 1838
Thompson, Charles; Thompson, Thomas B. vs Love, David 1831
Thompson, Robert vs Dickin, Richard 1842
Thompson, Robert for use of Manning, James; Bibb, Thomas 1808
Thompson, Robert C. vs Knott, James; Choat, Jacob 1831
Thompson, William Sr. vs McDonnell, Alexander 1809
Thorton, Charles vs Patton, Arthur 1827
Thrasher, Barber vs The Madison Stevens Mill Co. 1833
Thrasher, Bartlow vs Davenport, Thomas 1840
Thrasher, Barton vs Barnett, James W. 1842
Thrasher, Barton vs Clark, Thomas C. 1842
Thrasher, Barton vs Davenport, Thomas 1840
Thrasher, Barton vs Fleming, Abel; Folly, John; Hungerford, Anson; Hungerford, Darcy 1831
Thrasher, Barton vs Garrett, John H.; Folly, John; Hungerford, Dana; Hungerford, Anson 1832
Thrasher, Barton vs Johnston, Benjamin F. 1842

Thrasher, Barton vs Oliver, John L. 1841
Thrasher, Barton vs Price, William N. W. 1841
Thrasher, Barton vs Ralls, James F. 1845
Thrasher, Barton vs Ramey, Sanford L. ND
Thrasher, Barton vs Ramey, Sanford L. 1817
Thrasher, Barton vs Scott, Archibald H.; Davenport, Henry 1834
Thrasher, Barton vs Scott, Archibald H.; Thompson, Thomas B. 1834
Thrasher, Barton vs Wright, John C.; Oliver, Francis H. 1840
Thrasher, Barton vs Smith, Anderson W.; Smith, Robert W. 1843
Thrasher, Barton vs Totty, John 1841
Thrasher, Barton vs Totty, John; Hay, John W. 1841
Thrasher, Barton vs Wozencraft, Thomas 1842
Thrasher, Barton vs Wright, John C.; Oliver, Francis H.; Oliver, John L.; Oliver, John 1840
Thrasher, Barton vs Williams, Joel 1830
Thrsaher, Barton vs Taylor, John H. 1830
Threlkeld, J. J. vs Downing, R. H. 1879
Thurman, James; Thurman, Philip vs Cocke, Jack F.; Moore, George W. 1812
Thurman, James; Thurman, Phillip vs Cocke, Jack F.; Moore, George W. 1813
Thurman, James & Phillip vs Taylor, Roland 1816-19
Thurman, James; Thurman, Philip vs Taylor, Roland; Hightower, Thomas 1812
Thurman, James; Thurman, Phillip vs Taylor, Roland; Hightwoer, Thomas 1813
Thurman, Lynch M. for use of Wooddard, Caleb vs Harden, Edward 1839
Thurman, Micajah vs Trammel, Daniel 1811
Thurmond, Harris vs Hightower, John P. 1826
Thurmond, Harris vs Turner, James 1824
Thurmond, Henry vs Hicks, Daniel; Arnold, Francis 1810-11
Thurmond, S. P. vs Harris, William 1879
Thurmond, S. P. vs Richards, J. C.; Richards, F. S. 1879
Thurmond, William Adm. of Taylor, Roland 1812
Tilman, Dickson; Trout, Sarah Executors of Trout, Nathaniel vs Espy, John 1822
Tilman, James vs Selman, James J.; Selman, John W. 1843
Tomlinson, Humphrey vs Rogers, Right 1837
Tomlinson, Humphrey vs Weatherly, William S. 1838
Tomlinson, Humphrey vs Weatherly, William S.; Weatherly, Joseph 1838
Tompkins, Nathaniel U. vs Cobb, John A. 1840
Torrence, William H. vs Callier, Charles W. 1835
Tory, Alexander Indorsee of Craig, William vs Fullwood, Robert 1803
Totherrow, Isiah and his wife Totherrow, Martha vs Jackson, Stephen 1846
Totty, John vs Fielding, William 1838
Totty, John vs Flemming, Abel 1835
Totty, John vs Maxey, Edward H. 1833
Totty, John; Hay, John W. vs Vickers, Martin 1838
Totty, John vs Vickers, Martin 1837
Towns, Benjamin vs Clarke, Ely K. 1833
Towns, Benjamin vs Harden, Edward 1842
Trammell, John vs Barnett, John F. 1821
Trammell, John vs Trammell, Francis 1817
Treadway, George; Blinn, Hosen vs Johnston, Benjamin F. 1842
Truet, Riley vs Browning, Joshua Sr. 1807
Truett, Riley vs Browning, Joshua 1806
Trummell, John vs Handon, Isham 1821
Trustees of Mason Academy (Oglethorpe Co.) vs Shaw, William 1809
Trustees of the Univ. of Ga. vs Nance, John 1811
Trustees of the Univ. of Ga. vs Ryan, Berry; Nance, John 1810
Tuck, Richard vs Clarke Co. 1828
Tuck, Thomas G. vs Stephens, Harris; Stephens, Joshua Executor of Stephens, David 1840
Tucker, H. H. vs Mayne, Charlie 1879
Tucker, H. H. vs Payne, Howard; Blanton, David 1879
Tucker, H. H. vs Thomas, Ruida; Akridge, Troup 1879
Turner, James G. vs Sims, Zachariah 1816
Turner, James G. vs Sims, Zachariah 1816
Turpin, William H.; D'Antignac, William vs Harden, Robert R.; Johnson, John C. 1834
Tye, Job vs Boyers, Henry 1828
Tyson, Eugene H.; Deane, John vs Billups, Robert R. 1820
Univ. of Ga. (Trustees) vs Ward, Leonard; Brown, Samuel 1810
Upson, Stephen vs Rakestraw, Gainham L. 1820

VanAntwerp, Edwin; Wright, William; Bull, Andrew G. vs Harden, Robert R.; Johnson, John C. 1832
Vandifer, Richard vs Adams, Godfrey 1808
Verstill, Tristram; Furman, Joseph vs King, George; King, Sarah ND
Vickers, Young vs Braswell, Joseph; Sheats, Marshall M. 1848
Vickers, Young vs White, John 1853
Vincent, Isaac H. vs Bryan, Laney 1831
Vincent, Isaac S. vs Craft, Daniel; Craft, Edward 1832
Vincent, Isaac S. vs Garwood, Johnson 1842
W. B. Wells & Co. vs Poore, Benjamin P. 1840
Waddle, John vs Clarke, Lucy; Brown, Joseph 1810-11
Wade, Robert; Wakeman, Adams vs Shaw, George W. 1833
Wages, James vs Hughes, H. S. 1879
Wakeman, Mark H. vs Shaw, George M.; Edwards, James C. 1833
Walker, Abram vs Sledge, Willie; Newton, Elizer L. 1828
Walker, James for use of Vanbibber, George vs Barnett, John F. 1827
Walker, Joseph vs Wright, William Sr. 1815
Wallace, James for use of Kellough, Allen vs Scroggin, Chatten D.; More, Abednego 1803
Wallis, John F. vs Frost, Samuel; Adams, Nathaniel A. 1834
Wallis, John F. vs Moffett, Gabriel A. 1830
Walsh, Eliza vs Coleman, Andrew 1879
Walton, George vs Brown, William 1828
Walton, James W. Y. vs Hancock, Thomas 1842
Walton, John vs Freeman, George W.; Freeman, Allen 1821
Walton, John vs Martindale, John 1810
Walton, John C. vs Hunton, John 1805
Walton, Robert vs Ligon, James 1818
Ward, Leonard vs Atkins, Ransome 1812
Ware, Bennet M. vs Love, Robert 1827
Ware, Edward R. vs Holbrook, Nathan; Moody, John W. 1843
Ware, Thomas vs Lambert, William; Lambert, Elijah; Lambert, Elisha 1803-04
Watkins, Edward vs Welch, James 1827
Watkins & Garlington vs Atkinson, Robert 1809
Watkins, Henry M. vs Moffett, Gabriel A. 1824
Watkins, John vs Love, William 1824
Watkins, John vs McDonnell, Alexander 1810
Watkins, Robert vs Welch, James 1826
Watson, Anderson vs Hambleton, Henry 1800-03
Watson & Chaffee vs Fenn, David J. 1834-37
Watts, James vs Morgan, James 1808
Watts, Jeremiah vs Davis, Edward 1808
Watts, L. B. vs Dunkins, Peter 1833
Waynman, William; Perry, Dwight vs Allen, James; Allen, Joseph 1831
Weatherly, William vs Bradford, James T. 1837
Weatherly, William vs Fleming, Abel 1837-38
Weatherly, William vs Treadway, Elijah 1837
Weaver, T. A. D. for use of Hungerford, Anson; Hungerford, Dana vs Brown, William 1829
Webster, Hosea; Parmelee, Thomas J. vs Wright, Thomas A. 1828
Webster, Hosea vs Jackson, John; Hicks, Burton 1832
Webster, Hosea; Parmelee, Thomas J.; Webster, Edwin B. vs Jackson, John; Hicks, Burton 1832
Webster, Hosea; Webster, Edwin B.; Parmalee, Thomas J. vs Ligon, Joseph; Wooldridge, Isma W. 1835
Webster, Hosea; Parmelee, Thomas J. vs Manley, William 1832
Weed, Nathaniel B.; Weed, Henry D. vs Shaw, George W.; Edwards, James C. 1832
Weir, John N. vs Hood, Wiley F. 1879
Wellborn, Abner vs Barnett, John F. 1824
Wells, William B.; Newton, Ebenezer vs Cobb, John A. 1841
Wheeler & Wilson vs Booth, A. J.; Booth, A. E. 1879
White, Thomas; Sisson, Rhodman 1827
White, William H. H.; Baynon, Watkins vs Bacon, William 1842
Whitehead, George vs Easley, Richard; Thurman, Richard 1802-03
Whitehead, John P. vs Cora, William A. 1840
Whitehead, Sanford vs Whitehead, Ransom A. 1847
Whitehead, Sanford vs Whitehead, Ransom A. Admr. of Doggett, George 1850
Whitlow, John for use of Paine, Edward vs Beardin, John 1827
Whitmore, Robert C. vs Manley, William 1830

Wier, Samuel vs Robinson, Jesse; Cobb, Howell 1841
Wilburn, Abner vs Kirkpatrick, John 1838
Wiley, L. M.; Parish & Co. vs Melton, Tabitha 1841
Wiley, Leroy M.; Banks, Hugh R.; Lane, William E.; Lane, Vandinger; Lane, Edmond H. 1852
Wiley, Leroy M.; Lane, William G.; Banks, Hugh R. vs Hester, Robert H. H. 1842
Wiley, Leroy M.; Parish, Henry; Parish, Daniel; Parish, Thomas; Banks, Hugh vs Houghton, James C. 1841
Wilhite, John vs Sledge, Charles M.; Sledge, Willie 1827
Wilhite, Meshack Admr. of Wilhite, Phillip for use of Whilhite, John R. vs Christian, John; Posey, Humphrey 1822
Wilkerson, Daniel for use of Jackson, Samuel; Jackson, John vs Booth, Thomas 1819
Wilkins, William vs Bagley, Davis 1805
Wilkins, William vs Byrd, John A.; Edwards, James C. 1832
Williams Sims & Co. vs Peavy, Peter; Wells, Thomas 1818
Williams, Albert vs Butler, Littleton R. 1846
Williams, Ebenezer; Marsh, Mordicai L.; Stilwell, Richard vs Colt, Joseph C. 1840
Williams, Edward vs Brown, Joseph 1812
Williams, Edward vs Brown, Joseph 1813
Williams, Edward vs Brown, Joseph 1816
Williams, Edward vs Caldwell, James 1819
Williams & Garrison vs Saye, Richard W.; Saye, A. H. 1879
Williams, George W. & Co. vs Collins, J. W. ND
Williams, George vs Shaw, George W. 1836
Williams, Isaac vs Braswell, Allen 1805
Williams, Isaac vs Braswell, Allen 1805
Williams, Jane for Officers of Court vs George, Maria 1881
Williams, John vs Moore, George W. 1810
Williams, John A. vs Mitchell, Green M. 1827
Williams, John A. vs Mitchell, Green M. 1835
Williams, Lewelling vs Ramey, Stanford L. alias Ramey, S. L. 1808
Williams, Nathaniel vs Beasley, John; Bealsey, James 1811
Williams, Nathaniel vs Hunton, Hannah; Hunton, John 1811
Williams, Nathaniel vs Ligon, James; Ligon, McWhorten 1812
Williams, Nathaniel vs Ligon, James; McWhorton, Hugh 1813
Williams, Paul vs Earley, Daniel 1813
Williams, Paul vs Hubert, Gabriel 1811
Williams, Robert L. vs Gordon, John D. 1838
Williams, Sutton & Co. vs Summy, Peter R.; Newton, John H. 1877
Williams, Temple C. for use of Shaw, Joseph vs Twitty, Thomas 1823
Williams, Thomas for use of Smith, James H. vs Turner, James 1821
Williams, William vs Adare, Whitmill H.; Bone, John; Adare, William; Bullock, Alexander G.; Talbot, James 1835
Williams, William vs Alexander, A. Sr. 1844
Williams, William vs Barnet, Nathan 1828
Williams, Zachariah vs Cole, Richard 1803
Williamson, Charles vs Gaines, Zenophan P. 1812
Williamson, Charles vs Gaines, Zenophon P. 1813
Willich, Ernest C. vs Deane, Burkite 1808
Williman, Gold S.; Squire, Charles vs Land, Jonathan 1822
Willingham, Henderson vs Baldwin, Banjamin; Witter, James 1836
Willis, Banjamin for use of Mahony, William vs Carnes, Thomas; Gresham, Young 1813
Willoughby, David vs Whitehead, Sanford 1870
Wills, Benjamin for use of Mahony, William vs Carner, Thomas P. 1812
Wills, Jacob V. vs Jackson, William H. 1831
Wilson, J. F. vs Johnson, Henry 1879
Wilson, James F. vs John, Austin 1879
Wilson, James F. vs Harden, Anthony 1879
Wilson, James F. vs McKinnon, West 1879
Wilson, James F. vs Reid, Thomas 1879
Wilson, R. S. vs Saye, R. W. 1879
Wilson, James F. vs Scott, Simeon 1879
Wilson, William Executors of vs Easley, Roderick 1812
Wingfield, Augustin S. Attorney for Holman, Francis; Wheeler, Joseph vs Elder, Joshua P. 1852
Wingfield, John; Wingfield, Marcellus A. vs Swinney, Mark E. 1849

Wingfield, John; Wingfield, Marcellus vs Taylor, James Jones 1848
Wingfield, John; Wingfield, Marcellus A. vs Thompson, Thomas 1848
Wingfield, Marcellus vs Swinney, Mark 1849
Winstead, Sarah vs Cobb, Howell; Fellows, George P. 1842
Winstead, Sarah vs Hicks, Burton; Jackson, John ND
Winstead, Sarah vs Owen, Alfred; Reese, Charles M. 1842
Winston, Thomas vs Stewart, Reuben 1833
Witter, James vs Edwards, James C. 1835
Wolfe, Christopher; Clark, Richard S.; Clark, Daniel L. vs Jones, James W. 1838
Wood,; Jones, vs Brown, Alfred 1828
Wood, Elias vs Moon, George W. 1828
Wood, Elizer; Jones, James S. vs Carr, William 1827
Wood, Elizer vs Colquit, Walter; Dyer, Sarah Adm. of Ayer A. ND
Wood, Elizur vs Dunn, John T. 1830
Wood, Elizur; Jones, James S. vs Ligon, Joseph 1834
Wood, Elizur vs Jackson, William H. 1830
Wood, Elizur vs Pope, Wilie 1830
Wood, John vs Arthur, Talbot 1803
Wood, John vs Barnett, Nathan C. 1834
Wood & Jones vs Brown, Alfred 1828
Wood & Jones vs Brown, Alfred 1828
Wood & Jones vs Crenshaw, James J.; Moore, Thomas 1828
Wood & Jones vs Davis, William 1828
Wood, Oreen vs Baldwin, Samuel 1843
Wood, Tabitha vs Miller, Armstead 1808
Woodliff, George vs Crawford, John M. 1823
Woodrough, William B. vs Petty, John; Petty, Henry 1833
Woods, Middleton; Lindsay, John vs Camaron, James 1802-03
Woods, Middleton; Martin, Robert vs Steavy, William; Ramey, Absalom 1806
Woods, Oreen vs Baldwin, Samuel 1842
Woolridge & Hancock vs Brown, William 1828
Wooldridge & Hancock vs McCree, William 1828
Wooldridge & Hancock vs McKee, Robert A. 1828
Wooldridge, Isma W. for use of McKinley, Charles G. vs Appling, William 1840
Wooldridge, Isma W. vs Ball, John P. 1839
Wooldridge, Isma W. vs Clifton, John 1839
Wooldridge, Isma W. vs Crow, Stephen 1839
Wooldridge, Isma W. vs Fielding, William 1839
Wooldridge, Isma W. vs Greer, William 1839
Wooldridge, Isma W.; Hancock, Thomas vs Briscoe, Phillip 1827
Wooldridge, Isma W.; Hancock, Thomas for use of Murray, William vs Boyers, Henry 1829
Wooldridge, Isma W.; Hancock, Thomas vs Crenshaw, James J. 1829
Wooldridge, Isma W. vs Harden, Edward 1834
Wooldridge, Isma W. vs Harrell, Susannah 1845
Wooldridge, Isma W. vs Hewell, Susannah 1834
Wooldridge, W. Isma vs Hunt, Wilburn 1839
Wooldridge, Isma W. vs Laughford, Bezubel 1839
Wooldridge, Isma W. vs Mastin, James G. 1839
Wooldridge, Isma W. vs McCure, George W. 1839
Wooldridge, Isma W. vs Meadows, Enoch 1838-40
Wooldridge, Isma W. vs Sheats, Linsey 1839
Wooldridge, Isma W. vs Thomas, John 1839
Wooldridge, Isma W. for use of Vincent, Isaac S. vs Spinks, Enoch 1841-42
Wooldridge, Isma W. for use of Vincent, Isaac S. vs Talmadge, John 1841
Wooldridge, Isma W. for use of Vincent, Isaac S. vs Vinson, Moses 1841
Worrill, Ransom for use of Low, Andrew; Isaac, Robert; McHenry, James vs Gibbs, Thomas F. 1822
Worthan, William vs Heard, Stephen 1807
Wortham, William vs Heard, Stephen 1808
Wray, Phillip vs Brown, Joseph; Redd, Charles A.; Rositer, White 1815
Wright, Albert vs Williams, George 1841
Wright, Albert vs Williams, George 1841
Wright, Benjamin vs Barnes, Lewis 1872
Wright, William; Bull, Andrew G.; Nichols, Barak; Sherman, Elgar vs Wooldridge, Isma W. 1840
Wright, William; Bull, Andrew G.; Nichols, Barak T. vs Weatherly, William S.; Weatherly, William Sr. 1838
Wright, William vs Crossland, William as bail for Stewart, Lazarus 1808

Wright, William vs Crossland, William; Stewart, Lazarous 1809
Wright, William; Van Antwerp, Edwin; Bull, Andrew G. vs Reynolds, John 1833
Wright, William; Van Antwerp, Edwin; Bull, Andrew G. vs Reynolds, John; Cobb, John A. 1833
Wright, William; Bull, Andrew; Nichols, Basak: Sherman, Eagan vs Connor, Bowlin 1840
Wright, William vs Stewart, Lazarus 1806
Wyatt, Edmund; McBurney, William; Wyatt, Nathaniel vs Appling, William 1840
Wyley, James R.; Cleveland, Benjamin vs Trammel, Daniel 1814
Wyllie, Hugh vs Ligon, Joseph 1810
Yarborough, William vs Glasson, Henry 1833
Young, Sanford W. vs Maxey, Jeremiah 1826
Young, Sanford W. vs McCree, William; McCree, Robert A. 1826
Zackry, Clemencha R. vs Barnett, Nathan C.; Brightwell, William B.; Paulett, Jesse C.; Hubbard, William 1840
Zuber, Abraham vs Taylor, Roland; Brown, Joseph 1810-11
Miscellaneous - 1808; 1814; 1817; 1820

PART I: LOOSE ORIGINAL RECORDS (RECORD GROUP 129)

3. Miscellaneous Records, 1800-1925 (Record Group 129-2-4)

This series consists of original miscellaneous documents, dated 1806-1912, created by the Inferior Court (later Court of Ordinary now Probate Court) of Clarke County.

There is no consistency to the types of records found in this series. Included are such items as (not an inclusive list):

(1) military records
(2) voters lists
(3) miscellaneous information on roads and bridges
(4) miscellaneous deeds, indentures, land warrants and mortgages
(5) miscellaneous oaths
(6) insolvency petitions and lists

The records have been foldered by subject. Since the types of records have no correlation to each other, there is no real arrangement to this material. The last segment of records are too miscellaneous to be broken down further into different subject headings.

Many of these records are abstracted in part ii.

<u>Misc. Records of County Poor</u>

Poor List
- -1825
- -1826
- -1827
- -1832
- -1837

Pauper Farm Inmates
- -1879
- -1880

Vouchers to Commission of the Poor
- -1878
- -1879

Poor Farm Records
- -1886
- -1889

Poor Farm Accounts
- -1882
- -1883

Pauper Farm Co-op Cotton Sales & Other Accounts
- -1879
- -1884

Estray Records
- -1837-58 1820-23
- -1848-88 1837-93
- -1843-64

Voters Lists
- -1830
- -1891
- -1891
- -1896
- -1899
- -1900
- -1902
- -1910
- -1912
- -1877

Roads & Bridges
- -Misc. Records & years (13 folders)

Retailers Bonds (liquor)
- -1819-23
- -1824-29
- -1830-38
- -1839-55
- -1859-80

Miscellaneous Bonds

Bond
- -Doster, James

Bonds for free Persons of Color
- -1836

Bail Bond
- -Rosseter, White vs Crews, John; Harris, West 1821

Constables Bond
- -1861
- -1912-16

Misc. Bonds
- -1850

Apprentice Bonds
- -Misc. Years

County Officials Bonds
- -1891

Peace Bond
- -Cotton, Orin 1856

Bastardy Bond
- -Patrich, Ezekiel; Vichery, Anna 1847

Land Grant (Wilkerson Co.)
- -Freeman, William 1806

Miscellaneous County Expenses

County Receipt Books
- -1815-25

Papers Relating to Building Clerk's Office
- -1822

County Expenses
- -1825-28

Receipts by C. C. Birch for Building Court House
- -1827

County Buildings
- -1828

County Expenses
- -1828-29

County Purchases
- -1831

Misc. County Expenses
- -1832

Appointments to County Office
- -1834

Accounting of Robert Ligon, Dec'd Clerk of Court
- -1837

Insurance on County Property
- -1877-85

Misc. Payments by County Treasurer 1840

Claims Against the County
- -1881-86

County Buildings
- -1882

Misc. County Expenses
- -1897-98

Misc. Receipts
- -Misc. Years

Misc. County Expenses
- -Misc. Years

Misc. Deeds, Indentures, Land Warrents Mortgages

Deeds
- -Floyd, Wilihmina to Murray, John F. 1859
- -Griffeth, Michael R. to Vickers, Absalom 1860
- -Paine, George M. to Harden, William P. 1845

Indentures
- -1810
- -Maynard, Robert to Griffin, Hermon; Walker, Joseph 1853
- -Newton, Josiah vs Newton, Ebenzer 1825-26
- -Taylor, William B. to Thomas, Stevens 1827
- -Love, Robert to Moore, Thomas 1828
- -Wood, Thomas to Bowen, Christopher 1828
- -Moore, Thomas to Wooldridge, Isma 1828

Indentures (continued)
- -Winn, David H. to Winn, Charles J. 1843
- -Wright, John L. to Wooldridge, Isma; Hancock, Thomas 1828
- -Brown, Samuel to Puryear, Peter Guardian of McKigney, Rebeakah 1825
- -Love, Robert to Moore, Thomas 1828

Indentures
- -Misc. Years

Land Court Records
- -1824

Headright Warrants
- -Misc. Years

Land Warrant
- -Taylor, Rolin 1809
- -1820

Mortgage
- -Maxey, Jeremiah to Maxey, Edward H. 1826
- -Love, Henry H. to Love, Robert 1822
- -1811
- -Langford, Bazabal to Richardson, Richard 1831
- -Thurmond, Philip to Bailey, William 1832
- -Byrd, John A. to Billups, Thomas C. 1830

Misc. Oaths

Oaths of Office
- -1889
- -1913
- -1914
- -1916

Oath of Allegiance
- -White, Hugh 1838

Oath of Office
- -1836

Oath of Allegiance
- -Lloyd, James Harmon

Misc. Taxes

County Tax
- -1828

Tax Information
- -1893-94
- -1825
- -1827
- -1830

Taxes
- -1827-30
- -1825

Tax Fi Fa's
- -1872-75

Tax Information Misc.
- -1820

Insolvency Petitions & Lists
- -Kellett, William 1806
- -Earnest, Geo 1807
- -Moody, Samuel 1808
- -Echols, Robert E. 1811
- -Laurence, Richard 1809
- -Jones, Thomas 1811
- -Brown, Philip 1811
- -Prior, Allen 1817
- -Sanders, Julius 1817
- -Clark, Michael N. 1825

Insolvency Petition
- -Ralls, James F. 1846

Insolvent List
- -1813

Insolvency Petition
- -Williams, Timothy 1826

Insolvency Oath
- -Booth, Benjamin H. 1827

Insolvency Petitions & Lists (continued)

Insolvent
- -Finleston, Elizabeth 1806
- -Nutt, William 1817
- -Hobbs, Joseph 1819
- -Sims, David 1819
- -Patterson, Douglas 1819

Military Records, Misc. Records & Years

Annesty Oaths
- -1865

Confederate Veterans receiving Artificial Limbs
- -1867

Confederate Records
- -1862-92
- -1863
- -1864
- -1890-91

Indian War Records
- -1893

List of Person Subject to Military Duty
- -1862

Militia Fines
- -1814-33

Militia Fines & Oaths
- -1804-31
- -1804-41
- -1812-37

Militia Records
- -1810-20
- -1810-21
- -1810-23
- -1816-21
- -1819

Misc. Conf.
- -Misc. Years

Reports to the Grand Jury
- -1889-93

Receivership (Princeton Factory)
- -1886

Jury Lists
- -1836

Misc. Record
- -Hambreck, Meshack 1804

Jury List
- -1879

Requests by Court for Prisoners
- -1818-1843

Post Office Account
- -1840

Election Notice (Stock Law)
- -1885

Accounts of Purchases
- -Harris, Mrs. Virginia B.
- -1821-26

Contract
- -Hudson, Thomas F. & McCleskey, Henderson, McCleskey, Alice & Harrison, Clarissa, 1874

Loose Papers from Receipts Y Disbursements Journal
- -1830-38

Birth Records
- -1876

Jail Guards
- -1820-21

Grand Jury Recommendations
- -1882

Lists of Destitute Persons
- -1867

Witnesses Trial of
- -Maxey, Edward; Jacks, John 1826

Military Records, Misc. Records & Years (continued)

Cancelled Checks
- -1889

Jury Summons
- -1879

Pittard Ginnery Seed Cotton Receipts
- -1925

Petition of Benjamin Pharr-Rev. Soldier
- -ca 1837

Lunacy Hearing
- -Brockman, Moses 1850

Justices of the Peace
- -1858

Stockholder Athens Factory
- -1899

Free Person of Color
- -Henderson, Robert 1819

Power of Attorney
- -Thompson, Ruth 1810

Head of Families - Athens District
- -ND

Request for Prisoners
- -Misc. Years

Treasurers Vouchers Amity Lodge
- -1851-53

Bastardy Payment
- -1821

Criminal Trials
- -1832

Launacy Hearing
- -Talmadge, John 1847

Peddlars License Application
- -Brock, John 1847

Orders of the Court
- -1833

Grand Jury Reports
- -1854-62

Trial Information
- -Wells, Thomas

Athens Manufacturing Co.
- -1896

Custody Suit
- -Matthews, Doc. M. vs Matthews, Ella 1899

Resignation of William Center, J.P.
- -1887

Inquest
- -Meriweather, James 1860

Clark County, Criminal Case File
- -State vs Henry Snowdon 1/4/1876

Arrest Warrant
- -Akeridge, William 1845

Marriage License
- -1875

Personal Letter
- -Walker, Julia M. 1867
- -Weir, John N. 1873
- -Lockhart, Judith 1866
- -Langford, U. W. 1874
- -Edwards, Jasper N. 1873
- -Rice, W. C. 1879
- -Matthews, Wm. F. 1875
- -Boggs, Richard 1874

Misc. Papers
- -Strong, William M. 1806

Seed Cotton Purchase Reports
- -Pittard, Ginnery 1920

Misc. Papers
- -1822
- -1827
- -Misc. Years (16 Folders)

PART II: ABSTRACTS FROM THE MISCELLANEOUS FILES (RG 129-2-4)

Part IV. Records in Miscellaneous Box 1.

POOR LISTS, 1825-1826-1827

Sterling Elder for Miss Susannah Crawford, 28 June 1820 (?)
M. Stokes, 19 September 1825
Mrs. Fort, 19 September 1825
No Date: Mary Hicks, Sally Robertson, Mary Ray, Ester Chesser, Ann Burger, Hardy H. Andrews
John Downs, February 1825
Nathaniel Mobbs, Elizabeth Wills, and David Beard, 1 January 1827
Mrs. Jemma Ellit, 2 January 1826
Hardy Harben Andrew, 6 March 1826
Elizabeth Wells, 6 November 1826

POOR LIST, 1832

Easter Chester, Burwell Lea, Mrs. Hodges, David Beard, Mrs. Beard, Benona Carter, Ann Burger, Mary M. Collins, Hardy H. Andrew, Saml. McCullock, Mrs. Kelgore, Umphrey Beardin. Approved by Wm. Stroud; Wm. Decken; and Joseph Hodges, Justices of the Inferior Court, 3 January 1832

Poor List, 1837

Ann Berger, Polly Chesser, Richard Perry, Lucy Thompson, Mrs. Barnes near Athens, Mrs. Margarett Willson, Mrs. Drury Gee (Gill?), Sarah Coursen, Mrs. Christina Williams, Wm. Williams, Mrs. Rodes 2 children, Mrs. Collier 1 child, C. J. Fenn, Mrs. Hannah Morris, Alexander Bell, Barsheba Silvey, Miss Parr (Insane), Lemuel Crawford, Tabitha Floyd.
Approved by E. L. Newton, J. W. Wooldridge, Wm. Dicken, Wm. Stroud, and John H. Lowe, Justices of the Inferior Court, January 1837.

ESTRAY DECLARATIONS, 1820

Oglethorpe County. Edmund Sutherland swears that the ox that was posted and sold in Capt. Garlington District, Clarke County, to Richard Jones was sold to Robert Freeman by Matthew Varner. Sworn to 19 October 1820 before Jas. Luckie, JP. Similar deposition by Robert Freeman, Oglethorpe County, 18 January 1821 before Charles B. Lee, JP. similar depositions signed by Edmd. Sutherland and Robert Freeman, Oglethorpe County, 27 July 1820, before Joseph Watters, JP.

ESTRAY RECORDS, 1820

Receipt by David Meriwether for posting notice of stray horse in Capt. Jack's District, May 1820.

Receipt by Joseph Durham for making a postscript on a horse reported by Abraham Spivey, 3 March 1822.

ESTRAY, 1823

Receipt of Winfield (?) J. M. Wright, 18 April 1823, before Sterling Elder.

ESTRAY RECORDS, 1837-1873

(Only the estrays through 1849 are listed below.)
Stephen Jackson, 9 August 1834, appraised by Jarrett Davenport and James L. Griffeth, before Wm. Fenn, JP.
Appraisement by J. N. Glenn and Abraham Rowan, 26 November 1836, before Willis J. Biggs, JP.
Aron Crow, 221st District, 3 January 1837, appraised by Waine Will and William Ball, before Richard Duken, JP.
A. Branham Silvey, 225th District, 7 May 1836, appraised by William Greer and Joshwary Miller, before John L. Wood, JP.
Wm. C. Limon, 225th District, 22 June 1836, appraised by Green Evins and James W. Baret, before Willis J. Biggs, JP.

Thomas Wood Sr., 225th District, 2 April 1836, appraised by John Kines and Thomas Wood Junr., before John L. Wood, JP.
Wilis Biggs, 221st District, 17th February 1836, appraised by John L. Wood and Uriah Boing, before Richard Duken, JP.
Enoch Meder, 225th District, 21 May 1836, appraised by Jousua W. Glenn and William Jones before Willis J. Biggs.
Appraisement by Robsen H. Seogin and Joshok H. Seogin before William Fenn, JP, 11 July 1835 (?).
Wm. Henry Kent, 10 October 1835, appraised by George M. Lanier and James Edwards before Wm. Epps, JP.
Jonathan Beard, 220th District, 3 December 1835, appraised by Humphree Pettard and John Pettard before Wm. H. Jackson, JP.
William Jones, 225th District, 21 December 1835, appraised by James Sims and Enoch Medders before Levi Akridge, JP.
Obadiah Vinson, 241st District, 23 February 1836, appraised by Richard Landers and John Thompson before Hiram Clifton, JP.
Thomas Espy of Carson's District, 9 February 1836, appraised by James Tolbert and Thomas Lester before Everett Yearly, JP.
Obadiah Vinson, 241st District, appraised by Joseph Allen and George Graham before Wm. Epps, JP, 23 February 1836.
John F. Barnett, 218th District, 22 July 1833, appraised before Wm. H. Puryear and Banjamin Lane before Robt. Cameron, JP.
Mathew Landers, 216th District, 8 January 1835, appraised by William Aikin and Jesse Nix before John J. Cheatham, JP.
James Wright, 7 November 1834, appraised by John L. Wright and William G. Wright before Benjamin Davis, JP.
Wm. Jones, 15 April 1837, before Willis J. Biggs, Esq.
Moses T. Wright, 13 May 1834, before Edwin F. Cox, JP.
John Thompson, 240th District, 4 March 1837, appraised by Richard House and Isaac D. Read before L. P. Thomas, JP.
Thomas H. Lester, 10 March 1838, before John Pittard, JP.
Thomas Espry and Darius T. House, February 1837, before Robert Siuon, clk.
William Davenport and Caleb Arthur, 9 December 1826 and 22 October 1828, before John Parker.
Willis Biggs, 19 February 1836, before Willis J. Biggs, Esq.
Obadiah Vinson, 23 February 1836 before Wm. Epps, JP.
William Jones, 21 December 1835, before Levi Akredge.
Thomas Wood Sr., 19 February 1836, before John L. Wood, JP.
Enoch Meadders, 1836, before Willis J. Biggs.
List of estrays sold in 1848-1849, animals reported by: Benj. McRae before Willis J. Biggs, Wm. R. Talmadge before John Kirkpatrick, Robert Marable before Thomas F. Lowe, George Williams before John Kirkpatrick, Wm. Dicken, John H. Newton before James J. Jennings, A. L. Harper before Hillman Jackson, and Willis J. Biggs before John L. Wood, JP. (Estrays for 1850 and later are not abstracted here.)
Isaac P. Aycock, 15 December 1837, appraised by Bennett H. McClain and William Marable before Thomas F. Lowe, JP.
Isaiah Jothenon, 1837, appraised by Albert Sears and William Leard, 5 March 1838; and John Williams Sr., 1 November 1837, before Danl. Major Jr., JP.
John Espy, 219th District, 1837, appraised by Thos. Espy and Osburn Tolbert before E. Yerbey, JP.
Stephen Crow, 22 December 1839, appraised by John P. Haynes and Isaac S. Vincent before Stephen Jackson, JP.
Abraham Silvey, 29 June 1837, appraised by Wm. Grayer and Joshua Miller before J. L. Wood.
Receipt by Abraham Spivey for money received from Jno. C. Johnson, clerk of Inferior Court, before John L. Wood.
John White, his brother Robert White, and Stroud Melton, 26 February 1839, before Jophn Calvin Johnson, clk.
Elder T. Jordan, 7 March 1838, claims horse posted by Stephen Crow before Stephen Jackson, on 22 December last. Signed 7 March 1838, before Jno. Calvin Johnson, clk.
Philip Thurmond, 222nd District; Isaiah Totheraw; and James J. Silman, 31 July 1838, before Phillip Thurmond.
Abner Graham, 217th District, 8 August 1838, appraised by Robert Moore and Wm. Epps, before Thomas Sansom, JP.
Isaac C. Vincent, 10 February 1838, appraised by John Jackson and P. Cook, before Stephen Jackson, JP.
George Tunnell, 225th District, 10 January 1838, appraised by Rowan McRee and John Wood before John L. Wood, JP.

William Jiles, 15 January 1838.

Mrs. Elizabeth Lee, 221st District, 27 February 1838, appraised by Henry L. Brittain and Moses N. Davenport before Allen Barber, JP.

Strom Melton, 221st District, 13 April 1838, appraised by William Haggood and Littleberry Burnett before Rhmd. Duken, JP.

James Stewart, 217th District on the North Oconee River near the Georgia Factory, 21 June 1839, appraised by Dennis Shay and James Carter before Samuel Brightwod, JP.

William M. Harris, 218th District, 23 February 1839, appraised by Henry L. Edwards and Benjamin Davis before Wm. P. Puryear, JP.

James Crawford, overseerer for Stevens Thomas in the 219th District, 6 June 1839, appraised by William Yearby and Selum H. Pemberton before Everett Yerbey, JP.

Fetherstand Cross, 223rd District, 14 December 1839, appraised by John A. Fambrough and Gadial Fambrough before Thomas F. Lowe, JP.

Silas Crawford, 223rd District, 7 September 1839, appraised by Moab Hale and Wm. Morable before Thomas F. Lowe, JP.

Martin G. Ledbetter, Elizabeth Lee (by Wm. Lee), and Joseph Allen, 4 March 1839, before Allen Barber, JP.

William Nabers, 220th District, 6 January 1840, appraised by Humphrey Pitard and Doctor Tuck before Wm. Hy. Jackson, JP.

Randolph Willss, 219th District, 11 January 1840, appraised by John A. Hale and Lemuel Swann before Hawkins S. Bullock, JP.

Edwin A. Walker, 222nd District, 8 January 1840, appraised by Thomas E. Williamson and Ezekiel Akridge before John B. Hawkins, JP.

Thomas Stephenson and Walter Carson, 24 January 1840, before Saml. Frost, JP.

Thomas Epps, 221st District, 17 January 1840, appraised by Stephen Daniel and James D. Hewell before Allen Barber, JP.

Thomas B. Cooper, 219th District, 9 February 1840, appraised by John Martin and Archibald McDonald before Hawkins J. Bullock, JP.

William Brewer, 218th District, 30 April 1840, appraised by Thomas H. Young and John Morton before William H. Puryear, JP.

Samuel Bail-y, 225th District, 4 April 1840, appraised by Green Evans and William Bright before John L. Wood, JP.

Samuel Bailey, 225th District, 7 March 1840, appraised by Green Evans and David Christopher before John L. Wood, JP.

Joseph Braswell, 222nd District, 4 May 1840, appraised by Samuel Braswell and Aaron Bearden before John B. Hawkins.

Hiram G. Johnston and Fleming Mobley, May 1840, before John L. Wood, JP.

Elias Busby, 16 May 1840, appraised by William Cook and John Jackson before Stephen Jackson, JP.

Nicholas Osburn, 225th District, 13 August 1840, appraised by Rowan McRee and George Tunnell before John L. Wood, JP.

Thomas A. Tuck, 241st District, 22 September 1840, appraised by Josiah Daniell and Abram Dolittle before Solomon P. Kent, JP.

Gordon Greggory, 2 October 1840, appraised by John H. Lowe, Sr. and Moab Hail before Thomas F. Lowe, JP.

Anna House, 240th District, 23 December 1840, appraised by Joel Thompson and Zachriah Sikes before F. J. Freeman, JP.

Reuben Moss, G. W. Varnum, and Thoas. A. Tuck, 10 October 1840, before Solomon P. Kent, JP.

Edmund Elder, 220nd District, 5 November 1840, appraised before Isaac Jacks and Jesse Fambrough before Thomas F. Lowe, JP.

Appraisal by Jacob Klutts and Jesse Browning before Allen Barber, JP, 18 January 1840.

Gray B. Lasseter, 222nd District, 13 November 1841, appraised by Samuel Braswell and Virgil W. Akridge before John A. Nunnally, JP.

Malinda Sheats, 239th District, 12 April 1842, appraised by Middleton Thompson and Henry Fullilove before Hartwell Jackson, JP.

William Dicken, 221st District, 26 November 1842, appraised by Richard B. Dicken and John C. Nunnally before Aaron Crow, JP.

Augustus Vanderford, 224th District, 20 July 1842, appraised by Stephen Jackson and Isaac Treadwell, before Josiett Davenport, JP.

Lindsy Durham, 223rd District, 5 April 1842, appraised by Jackson Durham and James B. Lowe before Thomas F. Lowe, JP.

Aaron Boggs, 219th District, 16 July 1842, appraised by Moses Wilson and Jeremiah G. Grey, before Archibald McDonald, JP.

James B. Fambrough, 223rd District, 8 October 1842, appraised by John A. Fambrough and Jesse Fambrough before Wm. Marable, JP.

Thomas Steworte, 217th District, 5 December 1842, appraised before Henry L. Wood and Abraham Rowan before John L. Wood, JP.
Thos. E. Williamson, 222nd District, 13 May 1843, appraised by John Sturges and James L. Wozencraft before W. F. Wozencraft, JP.
William Davis, 220th District, 14 February 1843, appraised by William Mather and James Jennings before Wm. Nabers, JP.
Federick J. Freeman, 26 May 1843, appraised by James Cook and William H. Kent before James W. Cook, JP.
John H. Lowe, Jr. and William J. Christopher, 18 February 1843, before Hartwell Jackson, JP.
William J. Christopher, 18 February 1843, before Hartwell Jackson, JP.
A. C. Middlebrook, 261st District, 4 April 1843, appraised by Joseph B. Wenston and John H. Richardson before John Knott, JP.
Wm. A. Carr, 220th District, 12 August 1843, appraised by Wiley Haeles and James Gilleland before Wm. Nabers.
William P. Harden, 221st District, 29 August 1843, appraised by Richard Dicken and Thomas Simonton before M. M. Sheats, JP.
James White and Washington Greene of Cobb County, 16 December 1843, before M. M. Sheats, JP.
William Greer, 225th District, 6 April 1844, appraised by Seborn Burger and Absalom Vickers before John L. Wood, JP.
John A. Baugh and Henry C. Seymour of Greensboro, Greene County, 22 May 1844, before John Calvin Johnson, clerk of Inf. Ct.
Wedford Barber, 220nd District, 8 May 1844, appraised by James Pace and Richry Wilson before James D. Mathews, JP.
Lewis Eidson, 241st District, 23 January 1844, appraised by William Epps and Giles Jennings before Wm. Shaw, JP.
Thomas E. Williamson, Robert McCombs of Milledgeville, and Thomas Johnson, 12 April 1844, before John Calvin Johnson, clerk.
William Wood, 219th District, 26 December 1844, appraised by Randolph Wills and Garet W. Parks before Robert C. Wilson, JP.
Moses J. Holland, 223rd District, 27 December 1844, appraised by David Willoughbey and Joel J. Morton before Thomas F. Lowe, JP.
Ezekiel Boggs, 239th District, 25 January 1845, appraised by Roderick Hill and Williamson R. Whitehead before Hartwell Jackson, JP.
Wm. Jones, 225th District, 26 March 1845, appraised by Marshall M. Sheats and James W. Barrett before Richard Dicken, JP.
Henry Jenning, 241st District, 13 May 1845, appraised by James Jennings and Lewis Eidson before Wm. Shaw, JP.
David Elder, 223rd District, 3 March 1845, appraised by John P. Elder and David Holloway before James P. Holloway, JP.
Isaac Thrasher, 261st District, 26 July 1845, appraised by John L. D. Ward and R. H. Hester before Jas. J. Selman, JP.
Andrew J. Brightwell, 223rd District, 20 December 1845, appraised by Edmund Elder and Thomas C. Clarke before Thomas F. Lowe, JP.
Henry Stephens, 241st District, 8 August 1856 (1846?), appraised by Thomas Nopps and William Shaw before Wm. Epps, JP.
James Lester, 240th District, 15 January 1846, appraised by Henry Jennings and Lucian B. Burnett before James W. Cook, JP.
Wm. Nabors, 220th District, 5 August 1846, appraised by Wm. Mathis and John Hale before James D. Mathes, JP.
Randolph Wills, 219th District, 13 February 1846, appraised by Wm. Hail and L. Swan before Jeremiah G. Gray, JP.
Aaron Boggs, 219th District, 13 February 1846, appraised by David Conger and B. J. Parr before Jeremiah G. Gray, JP.
Andrew J. Lynch, Thomas Stewart, and Philip Thurmond (of Walton County), 1 May 1846, before Thos. Simonton, JIC.
John Wood, 219th District, 20 August 1846, appraised by David Conger and B. J. Parr before Jeremiah G. Gray, JP.
George Williams, 216th District, 20 July 1847, appraised by Thomas Sansom and L. P. Thomas before John Kirkpatrick, JP.
William E. Dearing and Asbury Hull, 1 June 1847, before J. C. Johnson, clerk.
Robert Marable, 223rd District, 24 April 1847, appraised by John H. Lowe, Sr. and James Crass before Thomas F. Lowe, JP.
John Felton, 241st District, 22 June 1847, appraised by Joseph Lee and James M. Williams before William Shaw, JP.
Benjamin McRee, 6 March 1847, appraised by George Tunnell and Rowan McRee before Willism J. Biggs, JP.
Obediah Jackson, 19 February 1847, appraised by William C. Jackson and John P. Robinson before Anselum L. Harper, JP.

William P. Talmadge, 216th District, 22 April 1847, appraised by Thomas Sansom and Levie P. Thomas before John Kirkpatrick, JP.
Hardaway Smith, 28 January 1849, before John Calvin Johnson, clerk Inf. Ct.
Middleton Thompson, 221st District, 18 January 1849, appraised by William P. Harden and James J. Selman before Richard Dicken, JP.
Willis J. Biggs, 225th District, 27 February 1849, appraised by Rowan McRee and Richard McRee before John L. Wood, JP.
Thomas Mitchell, Thomas Stephenson, and John N. Wier, 216th District, 15 February 1849, before John Kirkpatrick. JP.
William G. Overby, 261st District, 14 May 1849, appraised by Thomas G. Macon and Richard M. Thompson before S. H. Thompson, JP.
William Stroud, 221st District, 7 December 1849, appraised by Thomas A. Tuck and Seaborn J. Ramsey before Thomas Simonton, JP.

ESTRAY RECORDS, 1837-1858

(Only the estrays through 1849 are listed below.)
Abraham Silvey and William Mason, 7 June 1837, before John Calvin Johnston.
John B. Kilgore, 23 June 1837, before V. W. Akredge.
Aaron Crow and Wm. Appling, 3 January 1837, before Allen Barber, JP.
John Williams Sr., May 1838, before Daniel Major, JP.
George Turnell, June 1838, before John L. Wood, JP.
Isaiah Totheron, July 1838, before Daniel Major, JP.
Isaac V. Aycock, January 1839.
Abner Graham, 5 November 1839, before Thomas J. Lowe and John Calvin Johnson.
Wm. Giles, June 1838, before Thomas Sansom.
Wm. M. Harriss, 23 February 1839, before Wm. Giles and M. J. Durham, JP.
Saml Baily, June 1840, before John L. Wood, JP.
Nicks, Osburn, December 1840, before John L. Wood, JP.
Thomas Epps, 221st District, July 1840, before Allen Barber, JP.
Saml. Bailey, October 1840, before John L. Wood, JP.
Wm. Nabors, 14 November 1846, before James Mathews (?), JP.
Henry Jennings, 13 May 1845, before Wm. Shaw, JP.
William Jones, April 1846, before Richard Dicken, JP.
Ezekiel Boggs, January 1846, before Hartwell Jackson, JP.
Wm. Wood, 26 December 1844, before Robert C. Wilson, JP.
Lewis Eidson and Joseph Lee, May 1845, before William Shaw, JP.
David Elder, August 1845, before Jas. P. Holloway, JP.
Wm. Greer, July 1844, before John L. Wood, JP.
Frederick J. Freeman, June 1844, before James W. Cook.
Linsey Durham, May 1843, before John Calvin Johnson, clerk.
Gray B. Laseter, December 1842, before John Calvin Johnson, clerk.
Aaron Boggs before Archd. McDonald, 26 January 1843.
Philip T. Elder, December 1842, before John Calvin Johnson.
Wm. Dicken, July 1841, before Aaron Crow, JP.
Aaron Crow, July 1841, before Allen Barber.
Wm. Nabors, February 1841, before Wm. H. Jackson.
Featherstone Cross, January 1841, before Thomas F. Low.
Randolph Wells, 11 January 1840, before Hawkins S. Bullock, JP.
B. R. Hillsman, February 1838, before John Knott, JP.

ESTRAYS, 1848-1888

Joseph Hale, 222nd District, 18 November 1848, appraised by Ezekiel Basset, before John Knott, JP.
(The papers filed after 1849 are not abstracted here.)

ESTRAYS, 1843-1864

Anderson C. Middlebrooks, May 1843, before John Knott, JP.
Alfred J. Stewart, 225th District, and John White, 14 July 1864, before Wm. G. Evans.
Benj. McRee, 1 April 1848, before Willis J. Briggs, JP.
Deposition of Joseph Smith Jr. for a cow sold in the Scull shoals District and another belonging to a free person of color named Foot, 11 February 1839, before Jno. H. Lowe, Sr., JIC.
A. L. Harper, January 1849, before William Jackson, JP.
George Williams and Thomas Sansom, August 1848, before John Kirkpatrick.
Wm. P. Talmadge and Asa M. Jackson, May 1848, before John Kirkpatrick.

Robt. Marable, May 1848, before Thos. F. Lowe.
Benj. McCree and John P. Snow, March 1848, before Willis J. Biggs.

BONDS FOR FREE PERSONS OF COLOR, 1836

Thomas E. Williamson is appointed guardian for Charles Chubb, free person of color, May 9, 1836. Daniel Major (?), JP, attests that he has known Chubb for four years. Francis Farrar and Thos. E. Williamson also attested to Chubb's character and to having known him for several years, 9 May 1836, before Robert Ligon, Clerk.

Wesley Nance petitions to be appointed guardian of Jacob, a free person of color, May term 1836.

Bond for Rhoda Hamilton as guardian of Edy Moore, free person of color, with Reuben Hamilton and Julius G. Darby as securities, 2 May 1836, before Stephen Jackson, JP.

APPRENTICE BONDS

(The following apprenticeships usually also spell out the obligations of what is to be provided by the person accepting the apprentice. The security is to insure that those obligations were met.)

Edmund Adams, orphan of Edmund Adams, age 16, is apprenticed to learn the trade of a blacksmith until he is age 21, 2 September 1822. James Espey holds the apprenticeship and John Espey is security.

Christopher Marable, orphan of Robert Marable, is apprenticed to James Epps to learn the tailor trade until age 20. George W. Moore is security. 2 November 1818.

Kessiah Roberts, age 3, is apprenticed to David Shay to learn husbandry until age 18. William Shaw is security. 5 August 1816.

Washington Herd, age 13, is apprenticed to Aaron Crow to learn husbandry until age 21. Security is Stephen Crow. 3 August 1818.

Francis Shearley, age 8, orphan of Robert Shearley, is apprenticed to Zacahariah Clift to learn husbandry until age 21. Security is Robert H. Moore. 15 February 1839.

Joseph Lane, orphan, age 2 years and 6 months, child of Suzanah Hambrick, is apprenticed to Joseph Lane. John Ramey is security. 15 February 1805.

Martha Beasley, age 11, orphan of Chapman Beasley, is apprenticed to Samuel H. Everett to learn house keeping until age 18. Security is Sherod G. Everett. 5 April 1841.

Ashley Camron, age 15, orphan of Ambrose Camron, is apprenticed to Daniel Ramey until age 21 to learn husbandry. Security is Gabriel A. Moffett. 1 July 1822.

David Alley, age 5, son of William Alley, is apprenticed to Ranson Nichols to learn farming until age 21. Security is William Akin. 25 January 1819.

Simeon Malone, age 5, illegitimate child of Polly Malone, is apprenticed to Lemuel Lansford to learn husbandry until age of 20. Security is Samuel Jackson. 2 August 1819.

Edmund Adams was bound to a Mr. Espy in September term 1822 but Espy has since died and therefore Adams is apprenticed to John Talmadge under the same terms. No date.

Peter Lawless, age about 1 year, orphan of Patsey Lawless, is apprenticed to Richard B. Dicken to learn the blacksmith trade for three years. Richard Dicken is security. 6 September 1847.

Frances Thompson, age 5, bastard child of Ruth Thompson, is apprenticed to Bezaleel Langford to learn husbandry until age 21. Security is Henry Paulett. 1 July 1822.

Zack Brand, age 10, orphan of Thomas Brand deceased, is apprenticed to Walter Boswell. Emanuel James is security. 15 February 1805.

Francis Shearly, orphan of Robert Shearly deceased, is apprenticed to Zachariah Clift but since Clift is illegally mistreating Shearly, the court will declare the apprenticeship revoked. 4 July 1842.

Joseph Lane is apprenticed to learn farming from Leroy Hambrick for eighteen years and six months. 15 February 1805.

William T. R. Gunter, age 7 on 7 January next, orphan of James Gunter, is apprenticed to Zechariah Gunter to learn husbandry. Zachariah Clift is security. 2 November 1841.

Richard H. Edwards, age 17 and the son of Wm. Edwards deceased, is apprenticed to John T. Dunn to become a carpenter. S. Brown is security.

2 February 1829.

Marshall S. T. Hill Lassiter, illegitimate son of Sally Lassiter, is apprenticed to William Carmichael to learn the trades of mill wright and house carpenter. Wm. Murray is security. 5 March 1827.

Osburn Woodward Gunter, age 9 years and 1 month, the orphan of James Gunter, is apprenticed to Zechariah Clift to learn husbandry. Security was Thomas Moore. 2 November 1841.

Jerusha Beasley, age 2 years and 8 days, illegitimate, is apprenticed to Hiram Beasley to learn house keeping. John L. Wood is security. 4 September 1843.

John Thompson, son of John Thompson deceased, age 8 years, 4 months, and 27 days, is apprenticed Benajah S. Sheats to learn husbandry. Middleton Thompson is security. 6 December 1852.

James Carly, age 10, the illegitimate child of Nancy Moore Carty (Carly?), is apprenticed to Richard W. Oates to learn husbandry. Security is David Stephens. 4 September 1826.

Thomas Brand is apprenticed to Benjamin Brand to learn farming. Zachariah Brand is security. 27 January 1808.

Richard Lewis, age 17, orphan now bound to Thomas Shannon, is apprenticed to William Strong Jr. Thos. Hill is security. 29 June 1803.

Ransom Thompson, age 12, son of Ruth Thompson, is apprenticed to John Ramey Jr. to learn husbandry. Security is Saml. Jackson. 5 July 1819.

Elisha Smith is apprenticed to Saml. Stedman. George Whitehead is security. 6 March 1815.

Wyturoy Stone, age 8, the son of Betsey Stone, is apprenticed to William James to learn the hatters trade. Geo. W. Moore is security. 5 March 1827.

The following indentures are from after the Civil War and usually apprentice black children. The indentures almost always give some information about each child's age and parents: Nilly Durham; William Williamson; Emma Williamson; Marshall Durham; Cato Cowart; John O. Thrasher; Ella and Albert Elder; Alethia Johnson; Amelia, Jeffrey, Charity, Eliza, Phillis, and Martha Fullilove; Mary A. J. and Wallis Glenn; James Warren Hill Thrasher; Bailey Hilliard Thrasher, Vara Thrasher, and Flora Thrasher; Bailey Smith; Sarah Ann Jones (white?); Maria Fuller; Caroline, George, and Robert S. Elder; Henry Braswell; George Lee; Jerry son of Creasy, apprenticed to Payton G. Thompson of Macon County, Ala.; Willie Shields; Robert Parks; Nod Potman; Cato Cowart; Susie Watkins; William and Annie Panion; Mary Annie Elizabeth Elder; William Clarke; William Annie Florence (female); Addington Herestern; William Kenny; Milly and Henry Owen (?); Thomas Gober; Amanda Robinson, alias Smith alias Wallis; John Thomas; Judy Crawford; Emily Mayne; Simpson, George Washington, and Marzer Thrasher; Milly and Henrietta Owens (?); Perry Hardigree; Massey and Tilman; Marshall, Luckey, Frank, Louisa, and Frances Tindall; Willie Shields; James Henry Thomas; Green Whitlow; Anderson Snowden (?); Allison Mayne; and Henry W. Fullilove.

V. Record Group 129-2-4, Miscellaneous, Box 2

HEADRIGHT WARRANTS

(For related records see the loose files in the Georgia Surveyor General Department, 330 Capitol Ave. SE, Atlanta, GA 30334.)

Edwd. L. Thomas, 11 acres, 1834.
John H. Richardson, 50 acres, 1834.
James Lankford, 200 acres, 1791.
James Caldwell, 300 acres, 1820.
William Thompson, 117 acres, 1807.
Nancy Crane, 200 acres, 1784.
Wm. Thompson, 109 acres, 1808.
Hinchey Winn, 350 acres, 1816.

TAXES 1827-1830

(This 1829 list includes the designations of the land lots won by each of the following.)

McLeroy's District; John James & as administrator of Asahel Greer.
Capt. Wells Dist.; George Muse.
Applings District; John H. Lowe, admr. of Wm. McCree.
Capt. Simms District; Thomas T. Tye.
Capt. Vincent Dist.; H. F. M. M. Lepford (Sepford?).
Capt. Lynches Dist.; Wm. Lrnold; Levi Stewart, minor; Joshua T. Dyer & as agent for orphans of John Dyer; William T. Graham.
Capt. Duponts Dist.; Noah F. Prince; G. W. Prince; Wenefred Calloway; Jonathan Beard; Geo. Shavers, man of color; Wm. W. Waddel.
Capt. Flemmings Dist.; John Whitlow; Charles Cheatham; Obadiah Vinson; Washington Holmes.

(The following list is for 1827. Also included is a letter from G. A. Moffett in 1827 listing his taxable property.)
Mrs. Sarah Tweining.
Capt. Frost's; Mathew Yates; Elisha Trammell.

TAX INFORMATION 1825, 1827, 1830

(The following lists the persons whose property is mentioned in this file.)
George W. Moore; Estate of Micajah Williamson, Gabriel A. Moffett; Mathew Yates; Elisha Trammell; Mrs. S. Twining; Robert Stuart; Martin Crow; Philip Allens.

TAX 1825

(The following lists persons whose taxable property is listed in this file.)
William Davis; Thomas T. Tye; George Muse; William McRee; William Arnold; H.F.M.M. Lipford; Levi Stewart's minor; Winefred Calloway; Williamson C. Reese; Richard W. Oates; Gabriel T. Mathis; Eleanor Hardigree; Barton Hamilton.

AMNESTY OATHS 1865

(The following list also gives each person's physical description and signature. All persons except where noted are listed as residents of Clarke County. Also see the Civil War pardons and amnesty files on microfilm reel 287/40-8 at the Georgia Department of Archives and History.)

"UNITED STATES OF AMERICA. We, the undersigned, do solemnly swear, or affirm, in presence of almighty God, that we will henceforth faithfully support, protect and defend the Constitution of the United States and the Union of the States thereunder; and that we will, in like manner, abide by and faithfully support all laws and proclamations which have been made during the existing rebellion with reference to the emancipation of slaves.--SO HELP US GOD."

55. Enon F. Anderson, age 35
56. Milledge S. Durham, age 53
57. Susan D. Mayne, age 77
58. John Watson, age 63
59. Isaac Thrasher, age 71
60. Henrietta V. Daniell, age 37

61. Marcus Jennings, age 63
62. Burr Harris, age 45
63. John W. Bearden, age 36
64. William F. White, age 30
65. Mary Strickland, age 30
66. Lucinda A. Fambrough, age 23
67. Mary E. Wise, age 28
68. Mattie J. Jacks, age 29
69. John L. Elder Jr., age 39
70. Nathan T. Elder, age 40
71. William B. Haygood, age 41
72. Camelia M. Durham, age 26
73. Ann Eliza Woodson (Newton County), age 24
74. Alexander Woodson (Newton County), age 54
75. John L. Wood, age 66
76. Thomas B. Wood, age 18
77. David E. Sims, age 23
78. George Turnell, age 57
79. Seaborn Burger, age 54
80. John O. Thrasher, age 38
81. R. C. Williams, age 25
82. Clarissa Williams, age 60
83. Susan O. Salter, age 38
84. Mary D. Dawson, age 42
85. Andrew B. Jackson, age 46
86. David Mc Davenport, age 45
87. James L. Henson, age 23
88. Benjamin P. Gregory, age 44
89. David J. Myrick, age 38
90. William T. Wray, age 33
91. Milly Klutts, age 60
92. Aaron N. Weaver, age 21
93. Ashley D. Turnell, age 32
94. William Davis, age 47
95. Saml. J. Hale, age 36
96. William H. Thrasher, age 38
97. Benjamin H. Palmer, age 30
98. Sarah A.H.N. Dicken, age 28
99. William Dicken, age 75
100. Elias McCarters, age 19
101. Celestia A. Thrasher, age 18
102. Harboard G. Hardigree, age 38
103. William T. Walker (Morgan County), age 22
104. Charles D. Cook, age 26
105. Benjamin C. Langford, age 22
106. Ann E. Hull, age 23
107. Finnie E. Adam (Richmond County), age 25
108. Isaac Treadwell (Walton County), age 31
109. Saml. D. Durham, age 23
110. Andrew J. Welter (Cherokee County, Al.), age 18
111. Sarah J. Murray, age 28
112. George W. Anderson, age 59
113. William H. Goler, age 71
114. James W. Turnell, age 22
115. William R. Daniel, age 55
116. Elizabeth Lee, age 44
117. Martha S. Wilson, age 39
118. Matilda A. Thomas, age 37
119. Lott M. Leguire, age 66
120. David M. McCleskey, age 47
121. James M. Rhodes, age 45
122. Thomas D. Threlkild, age 49
123. James R. Hardiman, age 49
124. John C. Walker, age 31
125. James F. Wilson, age 45
126. Thomas J. Poss, age 19
127. Erwin C. Cosby, age 32
128. Julia A. Grady, age 17
129. William H. Thurmond, age 43
130. James Camak. age 42
131. Henry C. Shaw, age 21
132. William Prather (Walton County), age 55
133. Jesse Bennett (Greene County), age 48
134. Joseph W. Graves (?), age 35
135. Bedford Langford, age 58
136. Wiley W. Hinesley, age 43
137. Thomas Harris, age 46
138. Benjamin B. Lanier, age 27
139. Silas W. Vickers, age 27
140. John M. Smith, age 38
141. Robert L. Harris, age 58
142. John J. Chaplin, age 22
143. Thomas Robertson, age 68
144. James T. Miller, age 45
145. Elizabeth H. Harris, age 54
146. Hlkiah Hardman, age 29
147. Elias L. Bennett (Greene County), age 21
148. Enoch A. Allgood, age 35
149. Evan P. Prather (Walton County), age 22
150. Mariam Pearman, age 68
151. James T. Adams, age 27
152. George Harper, age 38
153. Samuel H. Smith, age 47
154. David Camp (Greene County), age 54
155. Darius N. Houze, age 22
156. Thomas M. Hall, age 34
157. William Brassnell, age 71
158. John H. Lee, age 17
159. Nancy H. Ridgeway, age 61
160. Wm. A.C. Stinchcomb, age 42
161. James H. Thompson, age 34
162. George W. Durham, age 25
163. James W. Hendon, age 43
164. James J. Jennings, age 43
165. James W. Bradberry, age 20
166. James R. Malcom, age 23
167. Henry M. Fullilove, age 50
168. William H. Hinton, age 29
169. William P. Bennett, age 50
170. Eliza L. Jarrell, age 55
171. James S. Griffith, age 36
172. John C. Weatherford (Walton County), age 30
173. Andrew J. Medlin (Morgan County), age 39
174. Drury B. Jackson, age 28
175. Stephen E.F. Jackson, age 31
176. Abraham G. Jackson, age 40
177. James P. Milligan, age 30
178. Laborn P. Delay, age 48
179. James L. Griffeth, age 65
180. George E. Griffeth, age 36
181. Francis P. Griffeth, age 22
182. Robert S. Griffeth, age 20
183. David H. Moncrief, age 56
184. William McLeroy, age 58
185. James M. Crow, age 28
186. Simeon Crow, age 32
187. Mark L. McLeroy, age 23
188. Thomas Lecroy (Walton County), age 56

189. Benj. Reynolds (Morgan County), age 65
190. Edward Hill (Walton County), age 65
191. Edw. P. Blair (Walton County), age 28
192. William H. Thacker (Walton County), age 49
193. James T. Moseley (Walton County), age 31
194. James H. Salmon (Walton County), age 24
195. John H. Lowe, age 52
196. Wiley A. Thornton, age 41
197. Isaac Lowe, age 38
198. John N. Ridgeway, age 34
199. William T. Lowe, age 47
200. Johnathan Montgomery, age 42
201. Elisha Prater (Walton County), age 20
202. Edward S. Peeler (?) (Walton County), age 21
203. William K. Lecroy (Walton County), age 19
203. William J. Dobbins, age 36
204. John W. Stroud, age 38
205. Mark Stroud, age 42
206. Isaac Milligan, age 55
207. Joseph C. Milligan, age 20
208. Mattie A. Anderson, age 24
209. Mollie J. Hampton, age 29
210. Richard J. Wilson (Walton County), age 40
211. John C. Spenks (?), age 37
212. John W. Miller, age 21
213. William Pulnatt (.), age 28
214. John W. Whatley, age 25
215. Frances A. Crow, age 45
216. Ann E. Cone (Bone?), age 31
217. Azariah P. Cobb, age 52
218. Mary Ann McKern, age 51
219. John H. Eads, age 58
220. Mary Davidson, age 25
221. Eli Crow, age 26
222. Stephen F. Jackson, age 19
223. James M. McLeroy, age 19
224. Rolin J. Delay, age 22
225. James W. Jackson, age 17
226. James B. Peeler (Walton County), age 23
227. William C. Peeler (Walton County), age 24
228. Sandford Mathews, age 53
229. Ausburn L. Harper, age 69
230. Jonathan Harper, age 35
231. Asbury B.C. Delay, age 23
232. Virginia E. Mayne, age 32
233. Emeline E. Thompson, age 51
234. William Butler, age 56
235. Charles H. Allen, age 27
236. William Dinnington, age 28
237. Cecero N. Baxter (Walton County), age 23
238. Joseph H. McRee, age 37
239. John K. Dorsett, age 19
240. Henry F. Winn, age 24
241. David H. Winn, age 25
242. James W. herod, age 46
243. Joseph T. Naunius (?) (Walton County), age 30
244. Cader Peeler (Walton County), age 66
245. Joseph T. Medley (Morgan County), age 19
246. Cater H. Ginn (Morgan County), age 18
247. Thomas A. Allgood (Walton County), age 18
248. Henley H. Dickson (Walton County), age 43
249. Matthew G. Watkins (Walton County), age 49
250. John Adams, age 63
251. Willis N. Autry, age 25
252. Bedford L. Adams, age 29
253. Barton C. Thrasher, age 42
254. William H. Dicken, age 42
255. John J. Branch, age 30
256. James E. Murray, age 31
257. James S. Graves, age 33
258. Wiley J. Miller, age 35
259. John T. Turnell, age 23
260. Thomas P. McRee, age 56
261. John Whitlaw, age 60
262. Henry E. Jackson, age 27
263. William H. Hail, age 23
264. Ansel L. Harper, age 27
265. John P. Jones, age 32
266. Joseph H. Murray, age 21
267. John T. Griffin, age 28
268. William Wilson, age 52
269. Elizabeth Jackson, age 35
270. Frederick J. Freeman, age 56
271. James Jiles, age 44
272. James M. Willoughby, age 45
273. James L. Fowler (?), age 27
274. James Lester, age 45
275. John F. Murray, age 34
276. John A. Fambrough, age 79
277. David Welloughby, age 70
278. John E. McDougle, age 33
279. Middleton Thompson, age 62
280. Jesse Darnell, age 45
281. Duke A. Darnell, age 23
282. John W. Jennings, age 31
283. Seaborn Waggener, age 65
284. John D. Williamson, age 59
285. Augustus R. Maxey, age 41
284. George W. Veal, age 61
285. Charles G. Burger, age 77
286. Thomas Hinsley, age 35
287. William Montgomery, age 36
288. John S. Robison, age 48
289. Joseph B. Langford, age 26
290. Janius H. Langford, age 26
291. James W. Davenport, age 24
292. Andrew J. Pickrell, age 30
293. Benajah S. Thompson, age 23
294. Mary C. Huff, age 42
295. Alfred D. Huff, age 42
296. Silas B. Kent (Fulton County), age 21
297. John M. Allgood (Walton County), age 23
298. Isabella Gunter (Walton County), age 43
299. Nancy Allgood (Walton County), age 60
300. Mary Allgood (Walton County), age 32
301. Jerritt A. Veal, age 24

302. Isaac T. Culberson, age 15
303. Jacob L. Warren, age 22
304. Anderson C. Middlebrooke, age 80
305. Elizabeth Burger, age 38
306. Robert Frazer, age 26
307. Nancy Burger, age 49
308. Charles L. Burger, age 22
309. Samuel Braswell, age 69
310. Joseph Smith (Morgan County), age 63
311. Sarah L. Colclough, age 31
312. Amanda E. Giles, age 36
313. Elizabeth E. McRee, age 18
314. Ann Osborn, age 38
315. William Williams, age 54
316. Mary Ann Carter, age 31
317. William Huff, age 16
318. Seaborn Burger, age 18
319. Jane Rowan, age 70
320. Alfred W. Williams, age 18
321. Thomas Smith, age 20
322. William B. Hale, age 62
323. Litha F. Miller, age 20
324. Martha Burger, age 44
325. Frances J. Kines, age 42
326. Mary J. Kines, age 18
327. Clarinda B. Jones (Morgan County), age 50
328. William J. Miller, age 41
329. William H. Watkins (Walton County), age 17
330. Elizabeth Anglin, age 37
331. Marinda Laseter, age 27
332. Sallie Wheeler, age 55
333. Sallie Chaplin (Walton County), age 42
334. Joseph L. Miller, age 17
335. William D. Burger, age 25
336. Benjamin F.M. Anglin, age 18
337. Matilda Maxey, age 30
338. Harrett Maxey, age 50
339. George H. McRee, age 38
340. Christopher C. Swann, age 29
341. John F. Osborne, age 18
342. Malinda East, age 24
343. John Wood, age 58
344. William F. Fambrough, age 27
345. Silas Hail, age 74
346. James M. Giles, age 23
347. Erastus F. Harper, age 27
348. Hartwell J. Thomas, age 32
349. James M. Garner, age 38
350. Sidney R. Ward, age 49
351. David B. Elder, age 36
352. John H.C. Malcom, age 22
353. Sarah E. Adams, age 23
354. Jonathan Burgess, age 38
355. Thomas B. Wade, age 100
356. Jeremiah D. Elder, age 23
357. Martha Wade, age 59
358. Wiley J. Huff, age 32

CONFEDERATE VETERANS RECEIVING ARTIFICIAL LIMBS, 1867

(The applications for the following men ususally give for each veteran his age, physical description, and the circumstances in which he was wounded during the Civil War.)

William A. Gilleland
James R. Thompson
William B. Haygood
Thomas J. Fain
John W. Whatley
Thomas J. Fain
John W. Miller
Richard T. McMullen
John W. Whatley
John Lacy
Thomas E. Middlebrooks
David E. Sims
Daniel McKenzie
Robert Dougherty
William P. Mitchell
John W. Whatley
James R. Thomson
W. P. Bearden
J. W. Miller

VI. Record Group 129-2-4 Miscellaneous, Box 2: Civil War Era Files

CONFEDERATE RECORDS, 1862-1892

"Returns of Soldiers &c" (Apparently the following are lists of persons to receive salt from the State of Georgia during the Civil War. Also see the county by county state copy of the salt lists on microfilm reel 73/4 at the Georgia Department of Archives and History. The abbreviation "Full" apparently stands for Fuller, an officer under whom some Clarke Countians were serving.)

SOLDIERS WIDOWS:

Elizabeth Parks
Elizabeth Buchannon
Frances S.E. Ledbetter
Susan J. Peeler
Matilda C. Lawson
Emily Wetherford
Nancy A. Whitacur
Carolen Tolbert
Elizabeth W. Fishur
Mary Jane Ballew
Susan Elliott
Martha C. Loven
Redia Akin
Susan S. Hunt
Frances E. Williams
Mary E.C. Echals
Parliner Betts
E. F. Kenney
Nancy Lee
Sarah Ramson
Sarah Dean
Margret Bushin
Mary Ray
Susan Patten
Elzia Caussons
Elizabeth Tippens
Milly C. Benadicks

GUARDIAN OF PERSON HAVING CHARGE OF ORPHAN OF DECEASED SOLDIER:

F. B. Thompson
F. S. E. Ledbetter
Elizabeth Parks 4 children
Elizabeth Buchananus
Elizabeth White
Susan J. Peeler 5 children
Matilda C. Lawson & 1 child
Emily Witherford & 4 children
Nancy A. Whitacur
Caroline Talbert
Elizabeth Fishur
Mary Jane Ballew
Susan Elliott
Martha C. Lovin
Rhedia Akin
Susan S. Hunt
Frances E. Williams
J. B. Gardener
Mary E. C. Echols
Paulim (?) Betts
Eliza F. Kenney
Nancy Lee
Sarah Rawsen
Sarah Dean
Margret Busbin
Mary Ray
Susan Pattan
Eliza Coussers
Elizabeth Tippins

PERSONS DEPENDENT ON DECEASED SOLDIERS FOR SUPPORT:

Mary Nix
J. B. Gardner
Rebecca G. Lard
Lucinda Sweart

SOLDIERS CRIPPLE FOR LIFE:

G. M. Nichals

EACH AGED OR INFIRM WHITE PERSON:

M. K. Mcdarman
Susan Gully
Mary Hill
Ann Wilson
Thomas Brooks
Martha Hill
Elizabeth Nix
John Carson
Rebeca Carson
Martha Carsen
Fanny Cousins
Rhoda Cousins
Elizabeth Welch

(THE FOLLOWING NAMES APPEAR ON THE BACK OF THE LIST. THESE PEOPLE APPEAR TO BE BLACKS AND THE NUMBERS MAY BE EACH PERSON'S AGE IN YEARS & MONTHS.)

Venus Epps, 12-4
Esther Lee, 100-7
Bridget Elder, 100-12
Nancy Thrasher, 80
Pheebe Thrasher, 75
Rheda Thrasher, 60 cripple
Mary Thrasher, 70
George Murray, 70-10
Betty Harris, 55-8
Patience Elder, 75-8

Poledore Doolittle, 80
Frankey Wray, 90
Cain Murray, 81-8
Hannah Murubl, 85
Scip Williams, 85-8
Clementine Wade, 90
Amey Lowe, 85

Hannah McRenold, blind 2-10
Braswell Clarke, 82
Delila Clarke, 86
Nancy Crow, 85
Smith Griffeth, 89
Nameless, 10

"Names of Souldrens folalyrg (soldiers' families?) in Punyens district January 21st 1864"

Mrs. S.M. Jones widow and 2 children: W.O. Jones 6 years and S.R. Jones, 2 years.
Widow Susan Edwards, 2 sons in service, one dead, 2 children under 12: T. C. Edwards, age 10, F.E. Edwards, age 8½.
Widow Sonnon, age 63, 6 sons in service, 1 dead.
Heynry Hinson boys all went to the war and he is grite infirm.
Martha Mclain, wife of soldier, 2 children: M.A. Mclain, 5 years old, and Wm. T. Mclane, age 2½.
N.E. Tunnel wife of soldier, 2 children: Wm. T. Butler, 5 years old, and A.S. Butler, 2 years.
Sarah Brewer, wife of soldier, 1 child: Wm. H. Brewer, 2 years.
Martha Bradberry, wife of soldier, 3 children: W.A. Bradberry, age 7; E.R. Bradberry, age 5; S.A. Bradberry, age 2½.
Malessa Butler, wife of soldier, 5 children: N.S. Butler, age 9½; S.F. Butler, age 8; C.A. Butler, age 7; W.S. Butler, age 4; H.M. Butler, age 2.
Sarah Spinks, wife of soldier, six children under 12: L.L. Spinks, age 6; M.L. Spinks, age 4; V.B. Spinks, age 1½.
W.E. Canton, wife of soldier, 1 child: W.L. Canten, age 1 3/4.
P.F. Cooper, wife of soldier, 2 children: S.A. Cooper, age 7; H.E. Cooper, age 2
List was made by A.H. Edwards, J.P.

(List of persons to receive salt.)
Mrs. James Gunn, Benj. Peeler, Mrs. Ann Bene, Mrs. Kelly, Mr. Berry, Mr. Whatles (one arm), Wm. P. Beardin, Mrs. Margaret Parker, Mrs. Sarah Allen, Mrs. Jno. Yarborough, Mrs. Millan wife & 3C, Miss Annie Bartow (orphan), Mr. Carson.

Aged & Infirm

Chs. G. Burger & wife, 75 & 70
Mary Ann McCuen, widow
Alfred Stewart, 91 years old
Mary Cross & daughter
Wyatt Lee 100 years old & 5 C non workers
Elizabeth Lee at Saml. Ganus
William Braswell & wife
Mrs. Strickland & 1 C
Mary Jeffries & daughter

Mary Doolittle
~~Mary Whitting~~
Willy Whatley (written over Caty Whatley.)
Martha Humblett
~~Eatey Whatley-90~~ see other side
Tigner Gann 30
Peggy Ray 90
Antonia Gunn 65
Drusilla Hale 85
Mrs. Wm. Gunn
Reuben G. Dunnahoe

Persons Dependent on Soldiers for Support

Mary Spencer, 55
Jame Whitehead, 60
Amos Whitehead, 55
John Bell & wife 53

Louisa Tiller widow, 65
Sarah M. Allen, 66
~~Mrs. Allin 1 B and L~~

Soldiers Widows:

30 Mary Davison & 1 son 6 years
50 Elizabeth Cox & 1 son 9 years
33 Susan E. Adams & 4 children under 12
40 Julia Ann Whitehead & 3 children under 8
40 Martha Sunderland & 1 child under 11
~~Frances S.E. Ledbetter~~
34 Martha A. Croft & 5 children under 13
27 Judy Caroline Berry & 2 children
29 Susan Craft & 4 children

23 Louisa Thornton
32 Amanda McLeroy & 6 children
26 Amanda Sykis & 2 children
22 Agnes Kinney & 3 children
24 Margaret Thurmond & 2 children
36 Mary T. Furgersin & 6 children
34 Amanda Collier & 6 children
36 Mary E. McLeroy & 2 children
25 Nancy Jane Hill
Mary Reed

Guardian of Orphan of Deceased Soldier:

Catherine Evans for 2 orphans
Sarah A. Bradberry for 3 orphans from 5 to 10 years
Cynthia Butler for 2 orphans from 3 to 5 years
~~F.S.E. Ledbetter for 4 orphans~~
~~F.B. Thompson for 3 orphans~~
Susan E. Michael for 2 orphans
Marietta Bradberry

John W. Miller, soldier crippled for life

(List of the destitute, 15 April 1864.) Whites.

1. Mrs. McCuen
2. Mary Davison & child
3. Susan E. Adams & 2 (3?) children
4. Julia A. Whitehead & 3 children
5. Martha Sunderland and 1 child
6. Martha A. Craft & 4 children
7. Judy C. Berry & 2 children
8. Susan Craft & 4 children
9. Louisa Thornton
10. Amanda McLeroy & 5 children
11. Amanda Sykes & 2 children
12. Agnes Kinney & 2 children
13. Margaret Thrumond & 2 children
14. Mary T. Furguson & 5 children
15. Amanda Collier & 5 children
16. Mary E. McLeroy & 2 children
17. Nancy Jane Hill & 1 child
18. Mary Reed
19. Catherine Evans & 2 children
20. Sarah A. Bradberry & 2 children
21. Cynthia A. Butler & 2 children
22. Susan E. Michael & 2 children
23. Mary Spender
23. Jane Whitehead
25. Amos Whitehead
26. Louisa Tiller
27. Sarah M. Allen
28. Martha Hamblett
29. Tignor Gunn
30. Peggy Ray
31. Antonia Gann
32. Drusilla Haile
33. Mrs. Wm. Gunn
34. Rubun G. Dunnahoo
35. Charles G. Burger
36. Alfred Stewart
37. Mrs. Cross
38. Wyatt Lee
39. Elizabeth Lea
40. Wm. Braswell & wife
41. Mary Strickland & 1 child
42. Mary Jeffries
43. Sarah Jeffries
44. Mary Doolittle
45. John W. Miller
46. Mrs. Anne Bone & 3 C
47. Mrs. Pickerell
48. Mrs. Mary Brown
49. Benj. Peeler
50. Margaret W. Parker
51. Judy Lee
52. Serena Finn
53. Mrs. Miller
54. Mrs. Biggs
55. Mrs. Amanda Giles
56. Mrs. Mary Wood
57. Mrs. Jame Giles
58. Mrs. Martha Burger
59. Mrs. Elizabeth Burger
60. Mrs. McLaughlin
61. James Gann & wife
62. Mrs. Mary Chadwick
63. Mrs. Pendergrass
64. Abram Jackson
65. Cornelia Griffeth
66. Newton Hanson & wife

Blacks:

1. Mary Cook (at Brownings)
2. Betty Giles (at Thrashers)
3. Hard Hester
4. Emaline Durham
5. Sylvia Jackson (At M. Thompson)
6. Rhode Mayne
7. Celia Sheets
8. Braswell Clarke
9. Dilla Clark
10. Ellen Murray
11. Venus Epps
12. Amy Roberts
13. Esther Lee
14. Bridget Elder
15. Nancy Thrasher
16. Betty Harris
17. Patience Elder
18. Polidire Doolittle
19. Frankie Wray

20. Cain Murray
21. Hannah Marable
22. Scip Williams
23. Clementine Wade
24. Amey Lowe
25. Hannah McRee
26. Nancy Crow
27. Smith Griffeth
28. Rhoda Thrasher
29. Phobe Thrasher
30. John Brown
31. Phoebe Elder
32. Jacob Brightwell
33. Esther Brightwell
34. America Thrasher for mother
35. Thomas Osborn
36. Pleasant Evans
37. Sarrocey Elder
38. Aaron Lee
39. Mary Tindal
40. James Hutcheson
41. Mary Hampton
42. Thos Whittamore

The following lists appear to be of classes of dependents arranged by catagory. The catagories were class 1. widows of soldiers killed during the war in the Confederate service or as a result of that service; class 2. disabled and indignet soldiers whose disabilities are a result of the war; class 3. women whose means of support is from or was from having a husband or son serving, disabled, or killed as a result of Confederate service; class 4. orphans under age 12 whose fathers were killed as a result of Confederate service; class 5. names of children under age 12 of women whose means of support are men serving in the Confederate service; class 6. children under age 12 of disabled and discharged Confederate veterans without means of support; and class 7. children over age 12 of disabled and discharged Confederate veterans without means of support.

First Class.
Mrs. Francis Bailey, husband died at home from sickness contracted in the army.
Mrs. Sarah Rossen, husband killed at Fredericksburg.
Milly Catherine Benadick, husband died in the army.
Sarah L. Brown, husband died from sickness in the army.
Mariah Peeler, husband died from sickness in the army.
Mrs. M.C. Lawson, husband believed to be dead in the army.
Nancy Hill, husband in the army and believed to be dead.
Cyntha Stephens, husband died from sickness in the army.
Mary C. Loven, husband killed at South Mills.

Third Class.
Martha P. Hill, husband in service.
Lidda L. Hall, husband in service or dead.
Littilia Nolan, son absent in service and wounded.
Charlotte Davis, husband absent in the service.
Nancy Kelly, son absent in the army.
Nancy Jane Roberts, husband in army and afflicted.
Susan Meads, husband in the army.
Margaret Kettle, son in the army and prisoner.
Martha Peeler, husband absent in the army.
Caroline Giles, husband absent in the army.
Elizabeth Wood, husband in the army wounded prisoner.
Neathy C. Maroney, husband in the army and wounded.
Rozana McLendon, son absent, in the army.
Mary Giles, husband absent in the army and prisoner yankees.
Mrs. Candis Bates, husband at home on sick furlough.
Emily Wetherford, husband absent in the army.
Jane Connally, son died in the army.
Elizabeth Brooks, husband absent in the army.
Elizabeth Tippens, husband absent in the army.
Elvira Pledger, husband absent in the army.
Martha Roberts, widow son absent in the army.
Emaly Giles, husband absent in the army.
Elizabeth Pledger, husband absent in the army.
Mary A. Cooper, widow son in service.
Mrs. Obedience Couch, husband absent in service.
Elizabeth Porter, husband absent in service.
Sarah Adams, husband absent in the army.
Sarah A. Jonas, husband absent in the army.
Ann Talbert, two sons absent in the army.
Nancy Ann Allen, husband absent in the army.
Mary Wood, husband absent in the army.

Fifth Class.
Mrs. Hill, one child under 12 age.
Mrs. Charlotte Davis, two children under 12 years age.
Mrs. Candis Bates, two children under 12 years age.
Mrs. Susan Meads, five children under 12 years age.
Mrs. F. Bailey, six children under 12 years of age.
Mrs. Mary Peeler, two children under 12 years of age.
Mrs. Caroline Giles, one child under 12 years of age.
Mrs. Sarah Rosser, three children under age 12 and one over.
Milly Catherine Benadich, one child under age 12.
Mary Giles, three children under 12 years age.
Emily Weatherford, four children under 12 years.
Elizabeth Brooks, four children under 12 years age.
Elizabeth Tippens, one child under 12 years age.
Elvira Pledger, three children under 12 years age.
Emaly Giles, four children under 12 years age.
Elizabeth Pledger, two children under 12 years age.
Mrs. Obedience Couch, four children under 12 years age.
Elizabeth Porter, two children under 12 years age.
Sarah Adams, two children under 12 years age.
Mariah Peeler, seven children four under 12 years age.
Sarah A. Jones, one child under 12 years age.
Mrs. M.C. Lawson, one child under 12 years age.
Nancy A. Allen, one child under 12 years age.
Cyntha Stephens, one child under 12 years age.
Mary Wood, four children two under 12 years age.
Mary C. Loven, one child under 12 years age.

Seventh Class.
Elizabeth Royester, Susan Royester, and Oris Royster (Elamus Royester killed in the fight at Richmond; brother of the three girls).
Elizabeth Connally, indigent over 12 years age.
Martha T. Maxwell, indigent over 12 years age can't walk.
Robert S. Mullins, indigent over 12 years age can't walk.

Fifth Class. Children under age 12 of women whose husbands or sons are in the Confederate service without any other support.

Frances O. McLeroy
William McLeroy
Georgian McLeroy
Mary H. McLeroy
Martha W. McLeroy
Nancy Luke
Joseph Luke
Frances Luke
Margry E. Luke
Susan A. Jennings
Nancy A. Jennings
Aley Cook
Mary Cook
Asbury Cook
Harriett Perryman
David E. Perryman
John Hardeman
Mary Jane Craft
William M. Craft
Elijah T. Craft
Martha A. Ferguson
Charles Ferguson
Sarah Ferguson
Frances Ferguson
John Ferguson
James A. Tiller
Amanda Tiller
Margrate Tiller
John Tiller
James Delay
Emer J. Delay
Sarah C. Osbourn
John N. Osbourn
Eveline O. Osburn

Sixth Class. Children under age 12 of disabled and discharged Confederate soldiers.

Benjamin Williams
Virginia Williams
Eli D. Hereall
James F. Hereall
Mary L. Hereall
Sarah F. Crow
Catheen Crow
Anna Crow
James B. Crow
Misouri McLeroy
Georgia McLeroy
Joseph M. Leroy

Seventh Class. Children and all others dependent upon a soldier for support.
Miss Mary Dosster and Miss Elizabeth Eidson

Fourth Class. Orphans of deceased soldiers.

Martha J. Kenney
William McLeroy

David McLeroy
Harriett Perryman
David E. Perryman
John A. Berry
Mary L. Berry
Martha Cody
James Cody
John W. Cody
Sarah E. Hooppaugh
John C. Hooppaugh
Nancy O.C. Hooppaugh
Loty A. Sikes
Joseph B.C. Sikes
Mary A. Craft
Edward F. Craft
John C. Craft
Elizabeth F. Craft

Third Class. Wives of Soldiers in Service or Discharged soldiers on whose son or other person upon whom Dependent for a support Killed, Discharged or absent in Service.
Mrs. Permilla Eidson, mother of M. J. Eidson.
Mrs. Mary Fugerson, wife of J. S. Fugerson.
Mrs. Sarah Perryman, wife of R. D. Perryman.
Mrs. Martha Craft, wife of Elijah Craft.
Mrs. Eliza Thornton, wife of J. N. Thornton.
Mrs. Amanda Cook, wife of Hartwell Cook.
Mrs. Barbary H. Orsbon, wife of A. C. Orsborn.
Mrs. Cathren Huell, wife of N. H. Huell.
Mrs. Caroline Crow, wife of J. M. Crow.
Mrs. Martha Delay, wife of John M. Delay.
Mrs. Amanda McLeroy, wife of S. J. McLeroy.
Mrs. Mary Jennings, wife of John Jennings.
Mrs. Amanda Wall, wife of James E. Wall.
Mrs. Jerusha Jennings, wife of James J. Jennings.
Mrs. Elenor Lester, wife of James Lester.
Mrs. Martha Daniel, wife of Jesse Daniel.
Mrs. Martha Ann Lester, wife of Talbot N. Lester.
Mrs. Martha Patman, wife of Thomas H. Patman.
Mrs. Luticia Hardeman, wife of Thomas H. Hardeman.
Mrs. Sarah J. Sims, wife of George W. Sims.
Mrs. Louisiana McLeroy, wife of Cicero H. McLeroy.
Mrs. Martha Luke, wife of Henry B. Luke.
Mrs. Elizabeth Tiller, wife of James R. Tiller.
Mrs. Mary Williams, wife of George Williams.
Mrs. Anna Crow, mother of Simeon Crow.

Second Class. Soldiers discharged.
Nathaniel H. Hull, Confederate service.
James M. Crow, state service.
Jessee Daniel, state service.
Cicero H. McLeroy, state service.
George Williams, Confederate service.

(No Class Given.)
Mrs. Yown Miller & 2 children under 12
Mrs. W. Miller, no child
Mrs. Ben Lanier, no child
Mrs. Thos. McRee, 2 children (under age 12?): John Thomas age 9 and Matilda Johnson age 5; Susan Jane McRee age 13; Eliza Ellen McRee age 16

First Class. Widows of Soldiers.
Mrs. Amanda Sikes, widow of Richard Sikes
Mrs. Elizabeth Cody, widow of Martin Cody
Mrs. Judy C. Berry, widow of Thomas H. Berry
Mrs. Agness Kenney, widow of John F. Kenney
Mrs. Susan Craft, widow of John Craft
Mrs. Maryann McLeroy, widow of James McLeroy
Mrs. Sarah E. Evans, widow of Arden Evans
Mrs. Susan Hooppaugh, widow of Allen Hooppaugh
Mrs. Harty D. Cook

Fourth Class, 225th District.
Joseph Green Elder, age 8
Lindsey Jacks Elder, age 5
David Thomas Elder, age 2
Atven Lee Thompson, age 6
John Park Thompson, age 3
James Hanon Strickland, age 7
Geo. Washington Strickland, age 5
Monroe Strickland, age 3
George David Gloer, age 8

Martha McRee, age 58 (7th Class, 225th District)

Fifth Class. 225th District.
Mary F. Stewart, age 7
Alford W. Stewart, age 4
Mary Frances Poulnot, age 1'
Noar Burge, age 10
Mary Elizabeth Burger, age 7
Jacob Silas Burger, age 2
Susan Emerline Miller, age 8
Mary Elizabeth Miller, age 6
Julia Ann Miller, age 4
Thomas Mortimer Miller, age 2
Mary Emer Thomas, age 8
Doctor Hook Thomas, age 7
Malind Caroline Thomas, age 5
Lorenia Eveline Huff, age 9
Benjamin Franklin Huff, age 7
John Thomas Huff, age 6
Henry Marion Huff, age 4
Mary Jane Dunnahoo, age 9
Joseph Henry Dunnahoo, age 6
Susan Almer Dunnahoo, age 3
Andrew Johnson Maxey, age 4
William Dawson Maxey, age 3
Ido Udoro Maxey, age 1
Missouri L. Treadwell, age 4
Harrill E.E. Treadwell, age 3
Steven Treadwell, age 1

First Class, 225th District.
Mrs. Eliza Ann Elder, age 35
Mrs. Harriett Stan Thompson, age 28
Mrs. Mary Strickland, age 29
Nancy M. Gloer, age 51

Third Class. 225th District.
Mrs. Aletha C. Stewart, age 30
Mrs. Matilda Huff, age 54
Mrs. Susan Jane Poulnon, age 35
Mrs. Martha Ann Burger, age 42
Aletha Miller, age 30
Almira Catharine Thomas, age 28
Mrs. Lucy Jane Huff, age 28
Telithia Ann Dunnehoo, age 34
Mary Catherine Maxey, age 25
Sarah Alexander Treadwell, age 31

"Names of Widows of Soldiers unable to Support Themselves"
Amanda Giles; Sarah O'Dillon; Mary J. Eblin

Seventh Class. 239th District.
John E. Spinks, son of John C. Spinks
George Cross, son of Allen Cross

Fourth Class. 239th District.
Aldora J. Butler and James M. Michael, children of Thos. Michael .
Joseph E. Bradberry, John L. Bradberry, and Emma L. Bradberry, children of John Bradberry.
John Michael, Rean Michael, and Eliza J. Michael, children of Thos. Michael.

First Class. 239th District.
Susan E. Michael, widow of Thomas Michael
Sarah Bradberry, widow of John Bradberry

Third Class. 239th District.
Juliann Whitehaed, wife of Lewis Whitehead
Martha M. Autry, wife of Willis N. Autrey
Catherine Adams, wife of B. L. Adams
Serina Crow, wife of Aaron Crow
Penina Parker, wife of West W. Parker
Eliza E. Spenks, wife of John C. Spenks
Mary A. Cross, wife of Allen Cross
June Foster, wife of Geo. W.

Fifth Class. 239th District.
Children of Lewis Whitehead: Henry C. Whitehead, Sophronia A. Whitehead, Hiram R. Whitehead, and Emma J. Whitehead.
Children of William Davis: Mary E. Davis, William Davis, Martha A. Davis, and James H. Davis.
Children of Aaron Crow: Pulaska Crow and Charles Crow.
Children of Sheffield Parker: Harvey Parker and Frank Parker.
Children of West W. Parker: Rufus H. Parker, Frances B. Parker, James A. Parker, Wesley P. Parker, and Robert L. Parker.
Children of John C. Spenks: Henry Spenks, Allen Spenks, and Cicero Spenks.
Children of Allen Cross: Martha F. Cross, Sarah J. Cross, and Anselmn L. Cross.
Children of Geo. W. Foster (?): Saml. Foster, age 10; Frances Foster, age 7; Anna Foster, age 5; Geo. W. Foster, age 3; and infant.

No. 1 Widows of Deceased Soldiers

Mrs. H. L. Aaron
Mrs. Addy Adams
Mrs. A. M. Parks
Mrs. Nancy W. Gaff
Mrs. N. W. Clower (Full)
Mrs. Nancy Eason (Full)
Mrs. Marth Parrish
Mrs. H. L. Aaron
Mrs. Sarah Tuck
Mrs. Fich Patrick
Mrs. D. A. McDonald
Mrs. M. Aaron
Mrs. Lunian (?) Liles(?)
Mrs. Wm. Akin
Elizabeth Parks
Mary E. Echols
Nancy Hoppaugh
Mary Ledbetter
Mrs. T. F. Pitard
Sarah Gee
M. Stuart
Sarah Stuart
C. Bradshaw
Julia (?) Walker
C. Lyle
Emily King
Mrs. Wm. G. Delany
Vilia A. Walker

Wives of Deceased Soldiers.

Mrs. Mariah Peeler

No. 2 Wives of Soldiers.

Mrs. W. C. Cabbert
Mrs. H. E. Lucus
Mrs. Drews W. Jackson
Mrs. Clark Sherly
Mrs. Albert F. Tobbert
Mrs. L. A. Hudson
Mrs. T. G. Macon
Mrs. Emely Muse
Mrs. Jesse Gann
Mrs. Elizabeth Buchanan
Mrs. Susan Towns
Mrs. Mary E. Echols
Mrs. O. Vinson
Mrs. Mary C. Wallraven (Cobb)
Mrs. C. K. Wright (Fuller)
Mrs. P. H. Black (Cobb)
Mrs. M. A. Bass (Cobb)
Mrs. Elizabeth Kinley
Mrs. A. Bryant
Mrs. T. C. Tobbert
Mrs. Francis Hagwood
Mrs. R. W. Say
Mrs. Malissee Bice (Rice?)
Mrs. Harriett Williams
Mrs. Marth Poss
Mrs. Katherine O. Farrel
Mrs. Burrel Yerby
Mrs. Nancy Lee (Gee?)
Mrs. L. Jiles (?)
Mrs. Elvira Pledger
Mrs. Elizabeth Tiffens
Mrs. Jessee Gan
Mrs. Clark Bane
Mrs. Milley Bane
Mrs. J. R. Gunals
Mrs. T. Wetherly
Mrs. Calinder Martin
Mrs. A. Moorehod
Mrs. F. Clower
Mrs. Vinson
Mrs. Elizabeth Childers
Mrs. Katherine Bradshaw
Mrs. Wm. S. Grady
Mrs. D. Ballenger
Mrs. Malcom Stafford
Mrs. Sarah Richards
Mrs. Biddy Couch
Mrs. Catharin Garison
Mrs. Glover
Mrs. Mardaret Mealer
Mrs. Cathern Wheeler
Mrs. E. Kinly
Mrs. E. Gurrick
Mrs. Mary Jiles
Mrs. Sarah Edwards
James Williams
Mrs. A. Williams
Mrs. S. L. Russell
Mrs. Marga Pledger
Francis Hayood
Rebecca Vickery
James Salesbery

No. 3 Widows Having a Son or Sons in Service

Mrs. H.F. Palmer
Mrs. Milley Childers
Mrs. Susan A. Moon
Mrs. V. L. Brazelton
Mrs. Sarah P. McAlpin
Mrs. Jane Ingram
Mrs. Elizabeth Beames (Bearnes?)
Mrs. V. L. Braselton
Mrs. Elizabeth Bridges
Mrs. Elizabeth Williams
Mrs. Milly Childers
Mrs. Elizabeth Daughtery
Mrs. S. H. Yerly
Mrs. Betsey Watkns (?)
Mrs. May Chasteen
Mrs. May Cooper
Mrs. May Nix
Mrs. S. Roberts
E. C. Barrett
Nancy Whitaker
F. E. L. Royal
Mrs. Prudy White
Mrs. Elizabeth White
Mrs. M. D. Whitmon
Mrs. G. (?) Chancy
R. A. Spencer
Mrs. Bash Watters

No. 4 Families Depending on Disabled Soldiers

J. B. Burfee
Levi Hasey
Mrs. C. D. Riden
Mrs. Marth Carsen
Mrs. Charlotte Newton
Mrs. Barby Beer (Burr?)
Wm. Ledbetter orphans
Mrs. C. Goodman
Elizabeth Allen
Mrs. James W. White
Mrs. Charlotte Weil (?)
Mrs. F. J. Pridgeon
Mrs. A. M. Grogan
Mrs. D. Clowers
Mrs. W. W. Clowers (Fuller)
Mrs. May Pledger
Mrs. Francis T. Nelms
Mrs. Mary Nix
Mrs. W. H. Buckhanan
Mrs. J. A. Garabald
Mrs. Susan Towns
Mrs. V. Walker
Mrs. E. Wright
Mrs. M. Childes
Mrs. Marth Wheele (?)
Mrs. N. Allen
Ana Parish
M. A. Byron (Fuller)
Mrs. James Nickas (?)
James Johnston orphs
Milly Bone
Mrs. William Braseten
Katharine Epps
Sarah Adams
Cynthia Stevens
Elizabeth Stephens
~~Mary Pledger~~
Jane Canly
Patsy Herring
Emely Wetheford
Miss J. Mcdonald
Stephen Shields
Mary Lord
Susan Patts
A. M. Grogan
Hezekiah Kidds
Mrs. Kathaine Davis
J. W. Dunn
W. E. Dickson
Mrs. Margarett Dugless
Mrs. Millhallan
Mrs. J. Rasson
Mrs. Wm. B. Mcay (McKay? May?)
Mrs. Thomas Dean (Gearr?)
Wm. Starns (Cobb)
Mrs. Job Bird

No. 5 Discharged Soldiers

Mrs. Elizabeth Allgood
Mrs. Julies Glaze
W. R. Kent (Fuller)
Mrs. Mariah Peeler

No. 5, 216th District, Children under 12 years

Lucy A. Vinson, 11
July Vinson, 7
John T. Vinson, 4
J. W. Louza Buchhan, 12
Allis Vinson, 4
Finny Vinson, 2
James H. Towns, 11
Margaret A. Towns, 8
Wm. H. Towns, 5
Joel T. Tobbert, 3
Ana Grogan, 10
Julia Grogan, 8
Harrison Bryant, 7
Alex Bryant, 5
Thomas Bryant, 3
Charles Hardy, 4
Joseph Hardy, 1
M. L. Allgood, 2
Charley Allgood, infant
~~Marshall W. Parks, 7~~
~~John T. Parks, 11~~
Martha O. Ledbetter, 8
Sally Winfhry, 10
Wesly Winfhry, 7
Robert Winfhry, 5
Celesta Epps, 5
Joseph E. Jonas, 2
Wm Y. Lee, 12
Mary A. Lee, 11
Isaac Y. Lee, 9
Rebecca A. Lee, 7
Thomas Lee, 5
Julia Lee, 4
John Lee, 2
Rosetta Lee, 1
Elerar A. Tippans, 4
Alfonslow Giles, 9
Johnston Giles, 6
Katherine Giles, 4
Jane Y. Pledger, 12
Lerana J. Pledger, 7
James P. Pledger, 4
Willy W. Walker, 2
Alvin Stewart, 3
Lieucinda Rosson, 12
Thomas Rosson, 5
Emeline Rosson, 3
Joseph A. Pealer, 8
Robert B. Pealer, 5
Hiram S. Pealer, 2
~~Howel C. Mcdonald, 11~~
~~David A. Mcdonald, 7~~
Theadore Weal, 9
Robert Weal, 6
Joseph A. Say, 8
Mary T. Gary, 7
Elizabeth Say, 2
Henry Bone, 7
Darius Bone, 5
John W. Bone, 1
Marth A. Gann, 5
Sarah J. Gann, 2
Wm. C. Pedgeon, 8

No. 5, 216th District
Mary F. Lyle, 5 years
Winney E. Lyle, 4 years
Joseph R. Lyle, 1 year
Chas. Cheatham, 3 years
Mary C. Nichols, 9 years

Emma Nichols, 4 years
Lular Wages, 1 year
Wm. Fowler, 4 years
Thos. Fowler, 2 years
David B. Fowler, 1 year

No. 5, 216th District
Mary J. Talbot, 11 yrs.
Frances Talbot, 9 yrs.
Sarah L. Talbot, 5 yrs.
Emma C. Talbot, 2 yrs.
Wm. Talbot, 6 yrs.
Geo. J. Talbot, 3 yrs.
Henry L. Talbot, 3 mos.
Mary E. Williams, 7 years
Matilda Williams, 5 years
Geo. W. Williams, 3 years
Eliza A.E. Martin, 3 years
Emma Barnett, 4 years
Wm. Davis Barnett, 3 years
Mary J. Barnett, 3 mos.
Joseph J. Shields, 11 yrs.
Jas. B. Shields, 10 yrs.
Frank C. Shields, 8 yrs.
Susan Shields, 6 (7?) yrs.
Octavia Shields, 4 yrs.
Nancy E. Shields, 4 mos.
Mary R. Bridges, 7 years
Martha J. Bridges, 6 years
Jas. O. Bridges, 4 years
Elisabeth K. Meader, 1½ years
Jas. A. Meaders, 3 (2?) years
Sarah F. Meaders, 6 years
Amanda Meaders, 9 years
Alverado Meaders, 11 years
John Drake, 2 mos.
Arrilla Drake, 2 years
Julia L. Wamaling, 9 years
Sarah F. Wamaling, 5 years
Edward B. Wamaling, 2 years
Henry F. Williams, 3
Lady J. Williams, 6
Alexander Shurley, 3
Mary Childers, 3
Wiley Riden, 8
Rufus Riden, 11
John H. Meeler, 8
Mary J. Meeler, 11
Sarah J. Dunnaway, 2
John A. Bone, 3

Jas. Wm. Bone, 5
Jas. Willis Bone, 1
Darius Bone, 4
Jos. H. Bone, 7
Parrish, 4
Parish, 7
Jas. J. Bates, 9
Martha J. Bates, 11
Nancy E.P. Aikin, 5
Mary A.F. Aikin, 8
John C. Aikin, 11
twins: Robert A. and Agnes A. Saye, 2
John N. Saye, 4
Sarah F. Saye, 5
Mary E. Saye, 7
Nancy C. Saye, 9
~~Wm. J. Saye, 16~~
Sis Ledbetter, 10
Jas. T.R. Kinley, 3 mos.
Hester Ann Kinley, 3 yrs.
Margaret E. Kinley, 5 yrs.
Wm. F. Kinly, 8 yrs.
Sarah L. Kinley, 10
Mary F. Kinley, 11
Robert Kirkley, 6 years
Henry Bice, 3 years
Carleton M. Bice, 5 years
Columbus Bice, 7 years
Georgia Ann Bice, 8 years
Saml. Couch, 2 years
Wm. Couch, 4 years
Mary C. Couch, 6 years
Thos. Couch, 8 years
~~Mrs. Julia A. Hardy, 1 child 4, 1 child 1~~
Jas. E. Chastine, 11
Mary Ann Chastine, 9
Henry Chastine, 10
John F. Vincent, 4
Julia Vincent, 7
Lucy A. Vincent, 11

No. 4, 216th District
William S. Whitaker, 2 yrs.
Augustin C. Bailey, 3 yrs.
Telitha A.E. Bailey, 4 yrs.
Geo. W. and Andrew Bailey, twins, 6
John Wesley Bailey, 9
Sarah E. Bailey, 10
Andrew J.C. Fitzpatrick, 1
Mary J. Fitzpatrick, 3
Howell R. Fitzpatrick, 5
Silas G. Fitzpatrick, 8
~~Harvey J. Fitzpatrick, 10~~
William G. Fitzpatrick, 10
Chs. Wesley Kidd, 7
Harriett E. Kidd, 4
Wilson L. Parks, 5

Howell C. Parks, 7
Jno. Wm. H. Parks, 9
Sarah A. Parks, 11
Mary F.H. Johnson, 2
Sarah C. Johnson, 5
Mary E. Gee, 7
Lelia Barrett, 3
Ella Barrett, 5
Elizabeth Barrett, 7
Mary Aaron, 5
Saml. Aaron, 3
Willie Barrett, 11
Doct M. Barrett, 9
Nancy J. Barrett, 6
Thos. A. Barrett, 5
Z.A. Fowler Barrett, 3

No. 4, 216th District
Ida Echols, 1 year
Sarah Hunt, 11 years
Meretta Hunt, 9 years
Mary Hunt, 7 years
Obey Hunt, 5 years
Victory Kinney, 8 years
Joseph C. Kinney, 6
John Kinney, 4
Eliza Kinney, 1
Howell P. Batts, 4
Anna Parish, 4
Marshel W. Parks, 7
John J. Parks, 11
Howell Mcdonald, 11
Davd A. Mcdonald, 7

No. 3, 216th District
Candis Bates
Sarah A. Aiken
Margarett A. Saye
Emily C. Barrett
Mary Ledbetter
Elisabeth Bridges
Juda Hill
Elisabeth Kinley
Elisabeth Kirkley
Malissa Bice
Elisabeth Williams
Edney Gentry
Sarah Gardiner
Mary Ann Cooper
Obedience Couch
Catherine Garrison
Emily Smith
Sarah Short
Julia A. Hardy
Sarah L. Russel
Mary Chastain
Mrs. Elizabeth Tippins
Mrs. Alvira Pledger
Mrs. Martha Vincent

No. 3, 216th District
Mrs. R. Gleason
Mrs. Calender Martin
Mrs. Elizabeth Watkins
Mrs. M. C. Talbot
Mrs. Mary A. Talbot
Mrs. Emeline Williams
Mrs. Julia V. Martin
Mrs. Laura Jane Barnett
Mrs. Mary Nix
Mrs. Mary Martin
Mrs. Mary Chasteen
Mrs. Milly Williams
Mrs. Nancy Doolittle
Mrs. Nancy Shields
Mrs. Lucenda Bridges
Mrs. Patsey Herrin
Mrs. Susan Meader
Mrs. Saphrona Drake
Mrs. Elizabeth Beavers
Mrs. George Ann Wamaling
Harriett Kidd
Harriett Williams
Sarah Perkins
Malida Williams
Ann Williams
Emily Lampkin
Harriett Shurley
Elisabeth Wright
Malinda Childers
Ailsey Riden
Mrs. Margarett A. Meeler
Mrs. Nancy L. Dunnaway
Mrs. Nancy J. Bone
Mrs. Nancy Bone

No. 5, 216th District, Married Soldiers Wives & Widows
Martha Vinson
Sarah A. Vinson
Mrs. Elizabeth Childus
Mrs. Elizabeth Bridges
Mrs. Edna Jentry
Mrs. Caroline Tolbert
Mrs. Elizabeth Hagerewood
Mrs. Susan Towns
James H. Towns
Mrs. Emily Smith
A. M. Grogan
Mrs. Amand Bryant
Mrs. Sarah Short
Mrs. Julia A. Hardy
Mrs. E. F. Allgood
~~Mrs. A. M. Parkes~~
Catheren Epps
Mrs. Elizabeth Mullins
Sarah A. Jones
Mrs. Mary A. Pledger
Mrs. Nancy A. Lee
~~Mrs. Elizabeth Tippans~~
Mrs. Lurana Jiles
~~Mrs. Alvira Pledger~~
Mrs. Jane Conly
Mrs. Elizabeth Moan (Moon? Moore?)
Mrs. Vilant Waker
Mrs. Ann Robertson
Mrs. Nancy W. Goff
Mrs. Sarah E. Stewart
Mrs. Sarah Rossen
Mrs. Eliza E. Glover
Mrs. Susan J. Pealer
Nancy C. Hoofan
~~Hulda A. Mcdonald~~
Charlotte Weil
Mrs. Epsy Staffer
Mrs. Eliza C. Say
Mrs. Nan A. Bone
Mary A. Gann
Francis J. Prigeon

N. 3, 216th District
Margaret C. Lyle
Catherine Chatham
Mary A. Nichols
Rachel V. Magee
Martha A. Fowler
Sarah F. Fowler
Sarah Magee
Hannah Echols

No. 1, 216th District
Mary C. Echols
Susan Hunt
Eliza Kinney
Paulina Betts
Malissa McHannon

No. 1, 216th District, Names of Widows whose Husband died in the War
Mrs. A. M. Parks
Mrs. Hulda A. Mcdonald

No. 7, 216th District
Robert Martin, 14
Nancy Bridges, 16
Wm. J. Bates, 13
Bud Ledbetter, 14
Jas. D. Williams, 14
Mary E. Vincent, 13
George H. Hagwood, 13
Susan J. Towns, 13
Mauivia E. Ledbetter, 13
Walter Wimphey, 12
Virginia Wimphey, 14
Joseph Patat, 13
Elizabeth Patat, 11
Francis Patat, 7
Sarah Patat, 5
Sarah McHanna, 8
Mary Mchanna, 5

No. 1, 216th District
Nancy Whitaker
Francis Bailey
C. J. Fitzpatrick
Elisabeth Parks
Sarah Gee
Martha E. Aaron
Harritt L. Aaron

Martha Ward, three orphans: Emma, age 9; Creducy, age 6; and Susan, age 3
Sarah Braswell, one orphan: Milton, age 6
Elizabeth Bell, one orphan: William, age 4
Mrs. Pendagrass, no children
Mrs. Rutledge, no children
Mrs. Carter, three orphans
Wm. M. Elder, one orphan
David B. Elder, four orphans
Elizabeth Hail, no children
Mrs. Joseph Hetton (?), four orphans
Mrs. Wm. R. Willoughby, two orphans

Names of Mothers and Wives Dependent Upon Soldiers for Support and Wives of Disabled Soldiers
Sarah M. Allen, widow
Sarah A. Allen, wife of Charles Allen
Mary R. Little, wife of Cyrus W. Little
Fannie H. Few, wife of Lucous (?) H. Few
Mary E. Elder, wife of William M. Elder
Elizabeth Fielding, mother of Wm. J. Fielding

Names of Children of Wives of Soldiers now in Service (under 12)
Children of Cyrus W. and Mary R. Little: George Little, Robert Little, Charles Little, Cyrus Little, and Saml. Little
Children of Charles and Sarah A. Allen: Sarah F. Allen, Mary E. Allen, and Joseph T. Allen
Children of Lucious H. and Fannie H. Few: Luceous C. Few and Saml. L. Few
Wm. A. Elder, child of Wm. M. and Mary E. Elder

The Children and other Indigent persons over 12 years old dependent on the Soldiers for Support
Children of Widow Allen: Sarah Allen, Susan Allen, and Oly Allen
Children of Widow Giles: Josephene Giles, Taylor Giles, and Eveline Giles
John Wood, blind and helpless living with Mrs. Giles

Names of Orphans of deceased soldiers under 12 years old
Geoge Giles, William T. Giles, Lidia Giles, Augusta A. Eblen, and Ann L. Eblen

Buncum District.
Martha A. Craft, widow of Eliza Craft (soldier): 1 girl age 16; 1 girl age 15; 1 girl age 13; 1 boy age 12 or 8
Judy Carolin Berry, widow of Thomas Berry (soldier): 1 boy age 6; 1 boy age 4
Susan Craft, widow of John Craft (soldier); 1 girl age 13; 1 boy age 11; 1 boy 8 or 6

Luiza Thornton, widow of Newton N. Thornton (soldier)
Manda Mcleroy, widow of Stephen Mcleroy (soldier): 1 boy 15 years old; 1 girl age 13; 1 boy age 11; 1 girl age 10; 1 girl age 8; 1 girl age 6; 1 girl age 4
Mandy Sikes, widow of Richard Sikes (soldier): 1 girl age 9; 1 boy age 6
Agness Kenney, widow of John Kenney (soldier): 1 boy age 16; 1 girl age 14; 1 girl age 6
Margareta Thurmand, widow of Philip Thurmond (soldier): 1 girl age 6; 1 boy age 4
Mary T. Fergason, widow of James Fergason (soldier): 1 boy age 16; 1 girl age 12; 1 girl age 10; 2 girls (twins) age 7; 1 boy age 4; 1 girl age 2
Wyett Lee old and Blind and a Large family
Levisa Tiller widow of Elisha Tiller age 65 Lost three sons in the army
Samuel Gann for the use of Elizabeth Lee Who has bin on the County for a number of years and Idiot
Amanda Colyer, widow of Francis Colyer (soldier), 7 Children: 1 girl age 15; 1 boy age 13; 1 boy age 11; 1 boy age 9; 1 girl age 7; 1 boy age 5; 1 girl age 3
Mary E. McLeroy, widow of James R., 2 children eldest age 7

Return to Inferior Court From the Dark Croner Dist., Jan 16'64
1. Widows of Soldiers and number of children under age 12: Mrs. Ann Bone, 4; Cornelia Griffith, 3; Elizabeth McLaughlin, 1; Louisa Gurmin; Mary E, Griffith, 1.
2. Discharged Soldiers: A.B.C. Delay disabled by wound: Jas. P. Milligan, disabled by wound but not discharged.
3. Mrs. Cynthia W. Hopkins; Mrs. Elizabeth Hunt; Mrs. E. Ann L. Cooper; Mrs. Mat Crow; Mrs. Elizabeth McDougall; Mrs. Frances Vicars; Mrs. Louisa Griffith; Mrs. Martha Vicars.
4. (Numbers indicate children under age 12.) Mrs. Hopkins, 2; Mrs. Cooper, 6; Mrs. Crow, 1; Mrs. M. Dougal, 1; Mrs. J.P. Whatley, 1; Mrs. W. Hunt, 2; Mrs. E. Hunt, 2; Mrs. Griffith, 7; Mrs. Martha Vicars, 4.
5. Children of Disabled, Discharged Soldiers: None.
6. Mrs. Nancy McLaughlin; Polly McLaughlin; Miss Claudia A. Griffith; Miss Sarah Darby; Miss Nancy Hunt; Miss M. Hunt; Miss B.A. Hunt; Miss C. Hunt; Mrs. Mary Hunt; Mrs. Whatley; Miss Lucy Whatley; Miss Nancy Whatley; Miss Margaret Whatley.

(The following persons may be black and the numbers may be their ages.)

10. Venus Epps, 12
70. Amy Roberds, 12
100. Esther Lee, 7
100. Bridget Elder, 12
86. Nancy Thrasher
70. George Murray, 10
55. Betty Harris, 8
75. Patience Elder
80. Poldore Doolittle, 12
71. Frankey Wray
81. Cain Murray, 8
85. Hannah Marable
85. Scip Williams, 8
Clemintine Wade
85. Amey Lowe
80. Hannah McRee blind, 10
82. Braswell Clark, 14
86. Delila Clark, 14
85. Nancy Crow, 14
89. Smith Griffeth, 34
70. Nameless, 10

(The following list has no identification.)

Cain Murray
James Hutchison
Cupid Elder (alias Sumney)
Isham Tyrrell
John Thornton alisas Vincent
Aaron Lee
Hurd Hester blind
Polodore Doolittle
Scepio Williams
Braswell Clarke
Smith Griffeth
James Lewe
George Richardson
Ziba Howze
Simon Klutts
Robert Durham
~~Orange Thrasher~~
Abraham Durham Cripple
Big John Thrasher
Caleb Thrasher
Curry Durham
Daniel Davenport
Mariah Hampton
Abraham Walker
Jacob Brightwell alias Jackson
Esther Lee
Mary Tindal Cripple
Bowlegs Tindal Deformed
Isaac Jackson
William Foster
Peter Durham (one Eyed and Crippled)
Locklin
B. Harris 1 leg
Robert Jones
Thomas Elder
Jack Fimbrough

Edward Cooper
Jesse Durham
Titus McRee
Richard Thrasher
Simen Williams
Amos Elder
Burton Jackson
Isham Harris
Thomas Daniell
Eph: Williams

Aaron Lester
Peter Durham Sr.
Jacob Foster
Oliver Hurden cripple
Jonas Haile
Pleasent Evans
Peter Thrasher
Thomas Osborn
Primus Thrasher

List of wives of soldiers and their children under age 12 in the 219th District, January 22, 1864
Mrs. Eliza Smith, husband in state service, 5 children under age 12
Mrs. Mary L. Pittard, husband died in the Confederate service, 2 children under 12 years old
Mrs. Rodey A. Doster, husband in Confederate service, 3 children under 12 years
Mrs. Rebecca Lord, son in the Confederate service, 1 child under 12 years old
Mrs. Sarah E. Hale, husband in Confederate Service, 5 children under 12 years old
Mrs. Susan Hale, husband in the Confederate Service, 2 Children under 12 years old
Mrs. N. C. Doster, husband in the Confederate Service, 2 Children under 12 years old
Mrs. Sarah Williams, husband in the Confederate Service, no children
Mrs. Sarah Martin, husband in the Confederate Service, 3 Children under 12 years old
Mrs. Francis Ledbetter, husband died in Confederate Service, 1 child under 12 years old

Widows of Soldiers
Mrs. Susan E. Adams & 4 Children: James T., 9; Albon D., 7; Ann T., 5; Williams, 2

Women Wives & Mothers of Soldiers Now in Service
Mrs. Sarah A. Maulding & 2 children: Josephine E., 9; Cassiad, 4
Mrs. Sarah A. Dicken & 5 children: Nancy T., 11; Alma T., 9; Lucy E., 6; Matilda C., 4; Henry C., 2
Mrs. Sarah M. Hinsley & 5 children: Letha A., 10; Philo B., 8; John T., 6; Emily F., 4; babe, 1 month
Mrs. Mary White & 3 children: Thomas W., 5; Saml. H., 4; Willie F., 1
Mrs. Martha H. Vinson & 1 child: Mary V., 11
Mrs. Eveline V. Manus & 2 children: Thomas A., 7; George E., 5
Mrs. Mary V. Harris & 2 children: Cicero C., 8; Susan F., 4
Mrs. E. S. Montgomery & 4 children: Osker, 8; Emmett, 6; Sarah, 4; Thomas, 2
Mrs. Catherine H. Evans & 2 children: Tapley, 8; Sissey, 5
Mrs. Francis S. Maxey & 4 children: John, 11; James, 9; Millard, 7; Isaac J., 5
Mrs. E. Hampton
Mrs. Clarissa Williams & 1 child over 12 Rebecca M.
Mrs. Rebecca Burton

Destitute Soldiers &c June 1867
Mrs. Mary Strickland
Mrs. Julia A. Whitehead
Jain Whitehead
Levi M. Carter
Mrs. Sarah Spinks
Mrs. Susan E. Michael
Mrs. Judy Caroline Berry
Mrs. Susan Adams
Mrs. Mary Strickland
Mrs. Mary Davison
Mrs. Kitty Evans
Mrs. Elizabeth Cox
S. E. Revell
John W. Miller
Mrs. Eliza Elder

Orphans Green Huff
Mrs. Mary Strickland
Mrs. Mary C. Huff
Mrs. Susan E. Michael
Mrs. E. Burger
Mrs. Muriah Gregory
Mrs. Martha Sunderland
Mrs. Sarah Spinks
Levi M. Carter
Orphans Jacob Burger
Mrs. Eliza Coussens
Orphans Wm. Giles
Mrs. Eliza Elder
Orphans N. G. Eblin
Orphans Green Huff

Orphans Jacob Burger
Orphans Green A. Evans
Orphans Thos. Michael
Mary Strickland
Orphan Saml. Cox
Orphan Wm. P. Davidson
Orphan Thos. G. elder
Orphan Ansil Strickland
Mrs. Arun (?) E. Bone
S. E. Ruell (?)
Orphan William Davis
Julia A. Whitehead
John W. Miller
Susan E. Michael
Orphans Wm. Giles
Orphans Thos. G. Elder
Orphans Jacob Burger
Susan Adams
Mary Strickland
Orphans Green Huff
Orphans Greene Evans
Orphans Samuel Cox

Mary Davison
Elizabeth Burger
Judy Berry
Martha Sunderland
Elizabeth Cox
Mahala Hall
Susan A. Craft
Martha Craft
Mariah Gregory
Polly Chadwick
Orphns. T. G. Elder
Orphns. Jacob Burger
John W. Miller
Kitty Evans
Orphs. A. Strickland
cash M. J. Eblin
cash Mrs. Kelley
Mrs. E. Burger
Mary Davison
Mrs. E. Burger
Mary Strickland
Ketty Evans

(The following list is unidentified.)
Sarah Jane Brooks, 14
Mrs. Hancock and six children: Edmond 12, Mary 10, Benjamin 9, Cintha 6, Betty 5, Emily 1
Mrs. Stephens has 3 children under 12: Joseph 10, Lucenda 8, Matha Ann 5
Mary Butler has 1 chi Eliza 1 yr.
Mrs. Caroline H. Giles: Mary 11, Eliza J. 8, George 5, Martha 2
Nancy Doolittle

(The following list is unidentified.)
Sarah A. Williams
Francis Wilson, wife Jas. Wilson
Mary Carson
Sherwood Wise
Mrs. Jane Eidson
J.E. Patrick, widow Robert P.
Mrs. Mary Smith, widow
Shadrack Doggett
Caraoline E. White
Mary Stone, wife John
Sue Moon
Rebecca Segraves
Rosannah Gleason
Mary E. Swan, wife C.C. Swan
Rena Cape
T.W.B. Leserver
Mrs. Thomas House
Nancy Sailor
Mahala Stephens
W.M. Walker
Mrs. Kenard
Mrs. James
Matilda Couch
Jas. Lindsey
M.A. Honey
Robert Gibbs
Elezabeth Dodger
Silas Sanders
John Guire
Martha Cousins
E. Cousins
M.E. Saye
L.A. Bradberry
Susan Gulley
Newton Teat
Wm. Brimer
E.K. Clark
Jas. N. Carter

Charlie Harris child
Hiram Couch
Elizabeth Dottery
Martha Dawson
Nancy Bushell
Jas. Edward
Mary Lester
Martha Trammell
G.A. Culbertson
Mary A. Birum
Ana Tolbert
Nancy Hill
Jesse Tolbert
Mary Kendrick
Caroline Bates
~~Nancy Sailors~~
Mrs. Jerry Ritch
Nancy Stone
Nancy Gean
Sarah Dottery
Elizabeth Jones
Elizabeth Cox
Isaack Vinson
A.D. Womerlerling
D.A. Vincent
Emily Morton
Rebecca Page
Dicey Whiting
F.J. Nelms
M.M. Autery
S.J. Erwin
Caroline Tolbert
Mary Marten
Emily E. Walker
Anise Joiner
Mrs. S.H. Oglesbey
Mary Ray
Nancy Kelly

G.W. Flournoy
Jas. R. Tiller
Elizabeth Iler
Andrew J. Wages
Wm. H. Gardner
John Hancock
Joseph Daniel
Hillman Jackson
Louisa Fitzpatrick
John Tolbert
Wesley W. Wilson
Louisa Michael
G.W. Nichols
Patrick Busey
Almer Gilmore
Caroline Giles
Lucy J. Lampkin
Mrs. Nancy Bell
Louisa L. Hardin
Alpha Smith
Martha M. Durham
Mary C. Burns
Sarah Rawson
A. Miligan
J.H. Dorand
Joseph Heffley
S.A.E. Jordan
Elizabeth Reynolds
C.E. Beaver

Nancy Segraves
Susan Sailors
Mrs. John Nichols
Mrs. John Couch
Mrs. James T. Mozeley
Mrs. Thomas W. Salter
Mrs. Mary Turner, Buncombe
Mrs. Ben Lanier, Watkinsville
Mrs. Catherine Adams, High S.
~~Mrs. Jabez Jones~~
Mrs. Thos. M. Hall, S.S.
Mrs. Lindsey Durham, S.S.
~~Mrs. Chas. G. Burger~~
Mrs. Catherine Rutledge, S.M.
Letitia Richardson
Samantha Lanier
Willis Whatley
Francis Collier
Leroy Huff
Matilda Huff
Elizabeth Dicken
Lucinda Pendergrass
Mary Miller
Mrs. Elejah Carr
John Ermenger orphan
Frances Colcough
Firmongton
Geo. W. Durham
James W. Henden

"Return of Soldiers Wives, Widows &c entitled to Salt under the public notice of Col. Jared J. Whitaker Commessary General, dated Macon Ga Octr. 1st, 1864"

SOLDIERS WIDOWS

Marzee Reaves
Susan Adams
Amanda Sikes
Eliza Cody
Judy C. Berry
Agness Kinney
McLeroy
Mary T. Furguson
Sarah W. Perryman
Mrs. John Jennings
Mrs. John Craft
Mrs. Mary Davison
Mrs. Sarah Bradberry
Mrs. Kitty Evans
Mrs. Julia Whitehead
Mrs. Susan E. Michael
Mrs. Mary Bradberry
Mrs. Elizabeth Cox (Con?)
Gloer
Mrs. Eliza Elder
Mrs. Jacob Burger
Mrs. Strickland
Mrs. Sarah M. Jones
Mrs. John Miller

Mrs. Elizabeth Mclaughlin
Mrs. Cornelia Griffeth
Mrs. Mary E. Griffeth
Mrs. Ann Bone
Mrs. Elizabeth McDougald
Mrs. Louisa Gunnin
Mrs. Needham F. Hunt
Mrs. Judge Whatley
Mrs. Viola Walker
Mrs. Adam Wheeler
Mrs. Sarah Rawson
Mrs. Sarah A. Stewart
Mrs. Sarah Willoughby
Mrs. Martha Ward
Mrs. Thomas Bell
Mrs. Mary J. Eblin
Mrs. Frances A. Puerman
Mrs. Amanda E. Giles
Mrs. Sarah E. Dillon
Mrs. Cynthia Butler
Mrs. Henrietta Daniell
Mrs. Nancy Hoopaugh
Mrs. Elizabeth Burger
Mrs. Nancy Burger

SOLDIERS WIDOWES

Mrs. Amanda Sikes
Mrs. Eliza Cody
Mrs. Mary Jennings
Mrs. Susan Hooppaugh
Mrs. Hardy Cook
Mrs. Caroline Berry

Mrs. Susan Craft
Mrs. Agness Kenney
Mrs. Mary Feregeson
Mrs. Mary Ann McLeroy
Mrs. Sarah Evans
Mrs. Mary Davis

SOLDIERS WIVES
Mrs. T.H. Patman
Mrs. Martha Luke
Mrs. Martha Craft
Mrs. Eluiza Thornton
Mrs. W.R. Daniel
Mrs. Cathern Howell
Mrs. C.P. Morton (in Lumpkin's)
Mrs. Rebecah Hodge (Cook Armory)
Mrs. Amanda Hodge (Cook Armory)
Mrs. A. Jackson
Mrs. C.H. McLeroy (in Lumpkin's)
Mrs. Sarah Perryman
Mrs. T.D. Threlkeld
Mrs. J.M. Rhoads (Cook Armory)
Mrs. Amanda Wall
Mrs. G.W. Malcomb
Mrs. Uriah Poss (in Lumpkin's)
Mrs. Harret Millican (Cook Armory)
Mrs. J.B. Turnner (Cook Armory)
Mrs. Katy Bailey (Cook Armory)
Mrs. Mary Bennett
Mrs. J.H. Thompson (in Lumpkin's)
Mrs. Amanda McLeroy (detailed militia)
Mrs. Caroline Crow (in Lumpkin's)
Mrs. L. Hardeman
Mrs. S.J. Sims
Mrs. J.J. Jennings
Mrs. A.C. Osbern
Mrs. T.J. Cox (detailed militia)
Mrs. O. Nichols (in Lumpkin's)

WIDOWS HAVING SON IN SERVICE
Mrs. L. Jackson
Mrs. A. Crow
Mrs. P. Eidson
Mrs. F. Royal
Mrs. V. Tiller

DISCHARGED SOLDIERS
James Lester (in Cook Armory)
Jesse Daniell (in Cook Armory
J. R. Tiller

POLICE
R. Jennings
G. Williams
F.J. Freeman
C.T. Griffeth
John Wallace

From Athens
WIDOWS HAVING SONS IN SERVICE
Mrs. M.M. Adams
Mrs. Mary A. Allman
Mrs. Tinsley Rucker
Mrs. James M. Herrll (?)
Mrs. Wm. S. Grady
Mrs. Mary Baxter
Mrs. T.R.R. Cobb
Mrs. Helen Camak
Mrs. N.B. Richardson
Mrs. U.L. Cooper
Mrs. F.E. King
Mrs. Mary A. Bass
Jane D. Young
Jane D. Richardson

FAMILIES SONS IN SERVICE
Mr. D.M. Clower
Mr. E.K. Clark
Mr. A.C. Patman
Mr. John Kirkpatrick
Capt. Wm. H. Dorsey
~~John Calvin Johnson~~
Wesley Nance
Mrs. John Hampton
Mrs. John Patman
Mrs. Wm. Mathews
Mrs. A.G. Turner
Mrs. Patrick Barry
Mrs. Robert Turnell

WIVES OF SOLDIERS
Marth Fouler
Sarah Fouler
Sarah Crow
L. (?) J Barnett
J.V. Martin
Mary Smith
Jane Patrick
M.T. Queen (?)
Eurena Cape
Elizabeth Williams
Margaret A. Say
Mahaly Elbehert
Mary Westmoreland
Malita Williams
Susan Hunt
H. Echols
Candis Bales
Nancy Lee
Susan Mead
Milly Williams
Elizabeth Porter
Susan Peeler
Elizabeth Tissans (Tippans?)
Elvira Pledger
Sarah Lewis
Elizabeth Mullins
Martha Roberts
Elizabeth Brooks
Hariett Sherly
Lieucdy Bridges
Laura Williams
Marion Watson
Mary Wood
Emeline Williams
Elizabeth Hale
Mrs. McGuire (full)
Emely Giles
A. Plunger (full)

M.C. Walraven
M.A. Bass (full)
Margaret Burlim
Francina Williams
P.H. Black
Edwd. Hale
Robert Hale
Sarah Williams
S.A. Martin
Clisha Daster
R.A. Daster
Celisha Mchanan
Marth A. Tucker
M.A. Huff
Frances Ledbetter
Sarah Fisher
Lieusa Fisher
Sarah Pierce
Safharn Drake
Susan Bridges
Julia Hardy
Selina Bank (full)
Ginnet Isam
G.W. Fisher
Carline Lucky (full)
Amtenet Peeler
Mrs. Palley White
Mrs. W.A. Sanders
Mrs. J.M. Ginn
Mrs. T.W. Anthony
Mrs. David Vickrey
Mrs. Malcom Hany
James Darey
Mrs. Anderson Smith

Salt for Soldiers families 1864
SOLDIERS WIDOWS

Watkinsville
Murzee Reaves
Susan Adams

Buncombe
Amanda Sikes
Eliza Cody
Judy J. Berry
Agness Kinney
Mary Ann McLeroy
Mary T. Fergerson
~~Sarah T. Perryman~~
John Jennings
John Craft
Mary Davison
Susan J. Hoopaugh
Harty Cook
Sarah Evans

High Shoals
Sarah Bradberry
Kitty Evans
Julia Whitehead
Susan E. Michael
Mary Bradberry widow of C.C. Bradberry
Elizabeth Cox for (?) Thos. W. Butler

Wild Cat
Mrs. Gloer
Eliza Elder
Mrs. Jacob Burger
Mrs. Strickland
Mrs. John Miller
Mrs. Peter M. Hayes

Puryears
Sarah M. Jones
Mrs. J.D. Young

Dark Corner
Elizabeth McLaughlin
Camelia Griffeth
Mary E. Griffeth
Ann Bone
Elizabeth McDougald
Louisa Gunnion
Mrs. Needham F. Hunt a widow
Mrs. Judge Whatley

Georgia Factory
Viola Walker
Mrs. Adam Wheeler
Mrs. Sarah Rawson
Mrs. Sarah A. Stewart

Scull Shoals
Sarah Willoughby
Martha Ward
Mrs. Thomas Bell

Salem
Mary J. Eblin
Francis A. Pearman
Amanda E. Giles
Sarah E. Dillon

DEPENDENTS

Watkinsville
~~Nancy Burger~~
~~Elizabeth Burger~~

Wild Cat
C.G. Burger
Gordon Gregory
Alfred Stewart
Thomas Miller
Wm. Braswell
Sally Dicken

Puryears
Newton Houson

Watkinsville
Mrs. Susan Winn
Mrs. C.J. Winn
John Hughes
Saml. Simonton

Salem
Saml. Fielding
John Wood

High Shoals
Thos. P. McRee
D.H. Malcomb
Skit Carter

SOLDIERS WIVES
Watkinsville
Elizabeth Montgomery
Frances S. Maxey
Sarah Ann Dicken
Mary A. White
Sarah Mauldin
Mereming Hinesley
Bettie Booth
Miss Parker
Cornelia A. Hindrix
Mary Harris
Eva Manus
Amanda Durham
Emma Durham
Cary Woodis
Hester Ann Williams
Eliza Foddrill

Buncombe
Amanda McLeroy
Louisa Thornton
Barbara A. Osburn
Mrs. Richard Tiller
~~Susan P. Hoopaugh~~
~~Herty Cook~~
Mrs. Archd. Milligan
Mrs. O. Nichols
Mrs. Uriah Poss
Mrs. Rebecca Ann Cofer
Mrs. Sarah W. Perryman
Mrs. L. Hardeman
Mrs. S.J. Sims
Mrs. J.J. Jennings
Mrs. T.J. Cox
Mrs. G.W. Malcom
Amanda Wall
Mrs. Cicero McLeroy
Mrs. J.M. Crow
Mrs. Serena Thompson

High Shoals
Elizabeth Malcom
Martha Awtry
Serena Crow
Eliza Spinks
Mrs. Allen Cross
Mary H. Dickson
Mary Cobb Huff
Sally Dicken

Wild Cat
Elizabeth Marshall
Alethia Miller
Florida Osborn
Lucy Jane Huff
Lethia E. Stewart
Tulithia Dunnahoo
Mrs. Hartwell Thomas
Mrs. Hartwell Thompson
Elizabeth Haile
Mrs. Rich. D. Thurman

Puryears
Mrs. Levi M. Carter
Sarah Spinks
Martha McClain
Martha Bradberry
Sarah Brewer
Parmelia F. Cooper

Dark Corner
Louisa Griffeth
Martha Crow
Frances Vickers
Lucinda W. Hopkins
S.E.T. Jackson
Mrs. Absalom Vickers
Mrs. Joshua Vickers
Mrs. Drury W. Jackson

Georgia Factory
Emily Weatherford
Elizabeth Cooper
Martha J. Hill
Huldoh Hill
Caroline Marony
Mrs. Mac Peeler
Mrs. Martha Peeler
Mrs. Mary Giles
Mrs. Charlotte Davis
Mrs. Catherine Benedict
Mrs. Hester Ann Williams
Mrs. Wm. Davis

Schull Shoals
Susan J. Poulnot
Susan McRee
Mrs. S.J. Haile
Mrs. David B. Elder

Mrs. B.F. Castrey
Mrs. Wm. Rutledge
Mrs. Wm. T. Miller
Mrs. Frances Giles
Mrs. John W. Walker

Salem (wives)
Sarah A. Allen
Rebecca Little

Salem (Widows)
Mary J. Eblin
Amanda E. Giles
Francis A. Pearman
Sarah E. Dillon

Widows having sons in the service &c
Watkinsville
Elizabeth Collus
Mary Reed
E. Hampton
Elizabeth Lee
Rebecca Barton
Clarissa Williams
Nancy Crow
Margaret Parker
Mrs. Hugh Millicam
Mrs. Martha Patman
Mrs. Martha Luke
Mrs. Martha Craft
Mrs. Wm. R. Daniel
Mrs. Catherine Howell
Mrs. C.P. Morton
Mrs. Rebecca Hodges
Mrs. Amanda Hodges
Mrs. A. Jackson
Mrs. T.D. Trelkeld
Mrs. J.M. Rhodes
Mrs. J.B. Turner
Mrs. Amanda Wall
Mrs. Cicero McLeroy
Mrs. J.M. Crow
Mrs. Serena Thompson
Mrs. Katey Bailey
Mrs. Mary Bennett

Salem
Mrs. Miriam Peasman
Sarah M. Allen

Buncombe
L. Jackson
W. Crow
P. Eidson
F. Royal
V. Tiller

Watkinsville
Elizabeth Lee
Elizabeth Collier
Rebecca Burton
Clarissa Williams
Nancy Crow
Mary Reed
Elizabeth Hampton
Margaret Parker
Martha W. Durham
Pendergrass

Buncombe (Discharged)
Richd. Tiller
D.H. Malcom

VII. Record Group 129-2-4 Miscellaneous: Militia Records

The following are names of men found in records of militia fines and related records with the year of each document given when available. The documents are reproduced in the order in which they appear in the folders.

MILITIA FINES & OATHS 1804-1831

1831
James Fowler
Thomas Wells
J. Puryear
W.D. Bowling
J. Greenwood
John Jack
Henry Smith
David Archer, JP

(No date, Bradberry's District?)
Sgt. John C. Morgan
Corporal Ransom A. Whitehead
James Davenport
M.J.D. Moore
Garret Craft
Rezon (?) Whitehead
John Greer
Joshua Morris
Robert Craft

1831, 225th District
4th Sergeant Robert F. Smith
John N. Smith
Levi Acridge
John Hinesly
Evan Hinesly
F. McRee, clerk
Nathan C. Barnett, captain

(No date)
Wm. Humpreys
Wm. Manley
James D. Hewel
James M. Burton
John Kirkpatrick
Edward Fullwood
Simpson Carson

(No date) Capt. Edens Company
E.F. Cox
William Clark
Harris Thoumond
Corpl. James P. Elder
John A. Formby
Hartwell M. Elder
John Hardegree
Harmond Hardegree
John Riley
John G. Jacks

John Mallard, 1831, letter

1831
Lemuel Robertson
Wm. Taylor
John Gilbert
Wm. Hale
Landers (Sanders)
S. Terry
B. Whit
~~Mallard~~
John Baker
Wm. W. Wigins

(No date)
Bazelee Langford
James Hooppan

1831
James Davenport
Stephen Jackson, JP

T.W. Battey, 1832

Shubael Turney, 1831

(No date)
James C. Anderson
Cordy Durnel
Barton Thrasher
Thomas hester
W.P. graham
Joshua smith
tabby Henson
JaCob Choat
lewis bennet
James branch
Ben Jaman howard

Georgia }
Clark County } Personally appeared before me Jeremiah Barnett, who being duly sworn, deposith & saith, that he was absent from the county three or four days previous to our last general muster on some important business, and this deponent further saith that he did not absent himself from the county for the purpose of evading said muster — and he further states that it is inconvenient for him to attend Court martial to day — in consequence of his having to attend a justices court —

Sworn to before me
this 10th July 1819 — Jeremiah Barnett

Wm Manley J.P.C.

Jeremiah Barnett

Pages 104, 105 and 106 show samples of the documents abstracted on these pages.

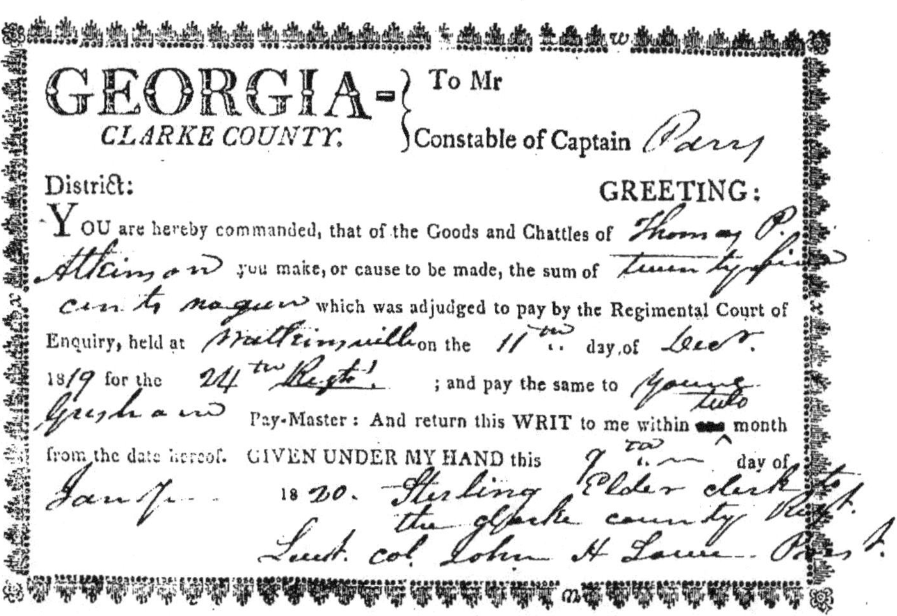

GEORGIA— } To Mr
CLARKE COUNTY. } Constable of Captain Parr

District: GREETING:

YOU are hereby commanded, that of the Goods and Chattles of Thomas P. Atkinson you make, or cause to be made, the sum of twenty five cents [illegible] which was adjudged to pay by the Regimental Court of Enquiry, held at Watkinsville on the 11th day of Dec. 1819 for the 24th Regt.; and pay the same to Young Gresham Pay-Master: And return this WRIT to me within two month from the date hereof. GIVEN UNDER MY HAND this 7th day of Jany 1820. Sterling Elder clerk of the Clarke county Regt.

Lieut. Col. John H Lowe Prest.

SAMPLE OF MARRIAGE LICENSE

Georgia
Clarke County

To ... Constable of Captain ... District. Greeting.

You are hereby commanded that of the goods & Chattles of Thomas Rutledge you Cause to be made the Sum of two dollars which was adjudged for him to pay, by the Regimental Court of Enquiry held at Watkinsville on the 27th day of October 1821 for the 24th Regiment and pay the same to Edward Paine Paymaster and return this writ to me within two months from the date hereof. Given under my hand this 26th day of November 1821

[illegible] Elder Clk to Regmt
H. W. Scovell Colonel

1831
Corporal James H. Barton
Corporal Garret M. Greer
Jarrett Deavenport
John L. Griffeth
Lewis Arthur
Elias Busbay
Allen Thompson
William Vanderford
Benjamin Norris
Purnal Cook
Edward Craft
Daniel Craft Junr.
William Fenn
Joshua Greer

1830
Wm. S. Hogue
Robert Ligon, clerk
John W. Harper, major

(No date)
Doctor W. Elder, captain, 223rd District

1829
Robert Dougherty
John Morton, colonel

1829
George L. Earnest
John Morton, colonel

1829
John H. Borders (?)
Wm. Moore
Jas. H. Barton
Isaiah Bohannon
S. W.(?) Moore
Benteen Stark (?)
Jesse H. Cogburn

1829
William Manly
John Morton, colonel

1804
Abner McCoy
Edmond B. Jenkins, paymaster

1804, Abraham Duke

1808, Ford Cotter

1804, Willobough Fann

1804, Joseph Seaglar

1804, Alexander Voss

1804, Isaac Tredwell

1804, Robert Conner

1804, William Cook

1808, Thomas Wilkins

1804, Anderson Berry

1804, William Robertson, Henry Nasworthy, Jesse Hayes, William Madaws, Richard Turner

1808, Jessey Custard, Jas. W. Armstrong, Jno. Marable

1805, Absalom Ramey, Wm. Sterns of Jackson County, Chattin D. Scroggin

1804, James Cunningham, Mohn Marable, ~~Owen Lowery~~, Daniel Allin, Wm. Marable, Robt. Marable, Wm. Starns, David Harris

1808, Davd. Simms, Francis Garner, Wm. Bugg, Jno. Spain

1804, Thomas Shannon, Moses Hartsfield, Keace (?) Barber, William Wilkins, Samuel Holloway

1804, Joseph Alexander, Ludwell Earnest, Hugh Glesson, Absalem Eachels, Miller Eachels, George Harper, Jordon Baker

1804, Robt. McCune, William Wilbourn, James Smith, Abner Herrin, Reuben Lockett

1805, David Dukes

1808, John Tweedle, John Maner, Wm. Crosley, Simon Autry, Wm. Gray, Leonard Ward

MILITIA FINES 1814-1833

1831, Jacob J. Choat, Robert Ligon, George W. King

1831, Cerdy Daniel, Wm. L. Mitchell

1832, James D. Hewell, William Janus (James?), Littleberry Land, William Humphreys, Eleel Melton, A. Barber

1832, James D. Hewell, William Manley, John Kirkpatrick, William E. Fullwood, Bolin Conner (Davenport's District)

1832, William James, James M. Davison, William Murray, Burton Hicks, Walton B. Harris, John Morton, James Pogue

1833, Joel Hardigree, John Beardin, Joseph M. Elder, John Jacks, Aaron Beardin, Gaddial Fambrough, Ellis Williby, William Holland, John Jacks, William Fambrough, Benjamin Jones, Aaron Beardin, Edward Hagins, William Hardigree, John Beardin, Jonathan Hardegree

1828, Joseph M. Elder, Robert Ligon, John Morton

1833, Joseph M. Elder

1828, William Holland

1831, John G. Jacks, George W. King, colonel

1828 & 1833, Joel Hardegree

1833, John G. Jacks, John A. Fambrough

1826, Benjamin Jones, Edward Paine, Joseph Ligon, Robert Ligon

1828, John Jacks

1827, John Jacks, William Manley

1833, John Jack

1831 & 1833, John A. Fambrough

1828 & 1833, Gaddial Fambrough

1826, Solomon Kilgore

1827, John Beardin

1827, William Hardegree

1826, Arthur Jameson

1827, William Fambrough

1827, Benjamin Jones

1827, Edward Hogans

1828, John Beardin Senr.

1833, Solomon Kilgore, Joseph Elders, Arthur Jamesons, Benjamin Jones, Jonathan Hardegree

1831, William P. Graham

1831, Barton Thrasher

1831, James C. Anderson

1828, Ellis Williby

1828, Aaron Beardin

1832, John C. Pope, Wade White, Samuel Miller, Garrett Morris, Garrett Craft, Gilbert Fry

1832, John Brewer, Edwin Edwards, Tollison Ray, Ransom A. Whitehead, Obadiah Jackson, Zachariah Rhodes, James T. Whitehead, Reuben Stewart

1827, Aaron Beardin

1832, James Davenport, John Greer, Joshua Morris, Robert Craft, Thomas House, Edward G. Harvey, Garrett Craft

1832, Stinson S. Jarrell, Garrett Craft, Robert Craft, Thomas Conner, Richard Landers, Thomas Twitty, Isaiah B. Goolsby, Wm. Fenn

1832, Jourett Davenport, Edward Craft, Lewis Arthur, Joshua Greer, John L. Griffeth, Purnal Cook, William Fenn, Daniel Craft Junr., Joseph J. Griffin, Garland Sims

1832, William P. Graham, Jacob T. Choat, ~~Barton Thrasher~~, ~~James C. Anderson~~, Cordy Daniel, Isaac Thrasher

1832, William Price, ~~Reubin Stewart~~ (Martin's District), ~~Zachariah Rhodes~~ (Martin's District), William M. Morton, William H. Puryear, John L. Wright, Thomas Jeffreys, William Price, Saml. Garner

1832, Wm. Price, John Smith, Charles Strong, Saml. Gray, William Whitton, Jos. F. Morton, Lewis Murphey, Wm. Morton

1832, Thomas Wood, John M. Edwards, James Hanson, Henry Boyers, Joseph F. Morton, William M. Harris, James Childers, Silas Hamon, Christopher Kimbell, Henry Mitchell, Henry Carter, Kennon Cooper

1832, Henry Haralson, John C. Greer, William Edwards, John H. Richardson, John Gardner

1832, John C. Greer, John Deane, Eugene S. Tyson, Henry Kneeland, Lemuel Robertson, Hugh L. Henderson, Edward Ware, James J. Crenshaw, James Tinsley, Benjamin Towns, Richard Harrison, Robert E. Belcher, John W. Whitman, Jordan Odum, Edward Ware, John Jack, George Fellows, Adrian N. Mayer, John Greenwood, William D. Bowling, James Pinckard, Jones Gresham, William Harris, Adam Foster, Colden Ketchum, Joseph Hutchinson, John Dearing, James Cosby, Joseph Hutchinson, Edward Carter, David Blount, James C. Edwards, Lemuel B. Robertson, Burton Hicks, George W. Shaw, William B. White, William Hale, William Taylor, John Gilbert, Aaron Lewis, John Baker, Wiggins, Sanders, R. Nichols

1832, George W. Jones, James S. Jones, James Smith, Adnan N. Mayres, Wm. B. Taylor, George B. Judd, Rodman Sesson, Richard Ross, John Heard, James Welch, George B. Judd, William Wilkins, lieutenant; William Neighbors, Elijah Croxton, John Kirkpatrick, John Smithwick, Richard Harrison, Thomas Blakemon, Smith Alexander, Benjamin C. Graves, Richard Nowlan, John Akin, John Jack, Thomas Fowler, Thomas Nowlan, Joseph Bergen, James Martin, Serenus A. Mayer, Joseph Ledbetter, A.N. Mayer, James Tinsley, Ebenezer B. McKinley, John W. Womack, A.L. Sims, John Rutherford, Charles H. Dupont, Abram Hill, Henry Hull, Richard Nowland, William Smith, John L. Lewis, James Smith, John Wiggins, William Jack, Robert Fowler, John Moulton, Richard Harrison, David Smith, A.N. Mayer, George B. Judd, James S. Jones, James Tinsley, G.A. Moffett, James Rasbury

1832, Owen Wood, Richd. Glass, Archibald Millegan, Joseph Durham, Robt. A. McCree, lieutenant colonel; Silas Durham, captain; Presley Garner, Jr., Banester J. Pringle, C.G. Burger

1832, Joseph Durham, William M. Morton

1832, James Haynie, David Weaver, Newton Hanson, Benjamin Grimes, John Owens, Joseph Durham, Edward Beardin, Richard Glass, Robert Whitton, John W. Smith Isaac Jacks, Wesley Williams, Charles B. Hunton.

1820, Amos Crow, John H. Lowe

1815, Jeremiah Burnett, Sterling Elder, Farr H. Trammell

1817, James Mathews, John Silman

1814, Jeremiah Burnett

1816, Elisha Earnest

MILITIA FINES & OATHS, 1804-1831

John Moore, 1823, 217th District, captain

Marcus A. Sears, 1823, 222d District, second lieutenant

John Scott, 1823, ensign

John G. Rutherford, 1823, captain

1840:
Doctor W. Elder, major
Daniel Clower, major
Sol. P. Kent, major
Thos. T. Holder, lieutenant
Smith Alexander, lieutenant
Reuben Hamilton, lieutenant
James A. Whaley, lieutenant
William Adams, lieutenant
Jacob E. Wise, lieutenant
Eli Bradberry, lieutenant
James A. Reeves, captain
Robert Daniell, captain
Philip J. Starks, captain
Wm. H. W. Price, captain
Edwards, captain
Wm. Johnson, lieutenant
Joab Jones, provost marshal
John Calvin Johnson, clerk
Wm. H. Crawford, captain
Robert C. Wilson, captain
John S. Linton, lieutenant
Wm. Bacon, lieutenant
Benjamin F. Johnston
Abel Fleming
Edward W. Roberts
John Beasley Jr.
James Beasley
Capt. Wm. H. W. W. Price, captain
Joseph A. Hughey
T. R. Hendrix
Tarleton Eades
Joseph Johnson
Robert Daniell, captain
Wm. Alexander
James P. Elder
George W. Foster
Jackson M. Thrasher, sergeant
Zeno D. E. Swinney, corporal
Mark E. Swinney
Cordy Darnill (Daniell?)
Ezekiel Boggs
Wm. A. Swift
George W. Davenport
Augustus Tarpley
Robert E. Burton
John Norton
Lewis G. Anderson
Richard Thompson
Samuel Thompson
Archibald H. Wadsworth
Julius A. Askew
Thomas G. Hester
John W. Hay
Thos. G. Wright, captain
Jonathan Montgomery
Alsa Moore
Curtis Dupree
James Berryhill
Wm. Murray
Nathan C. Barnett
John F. Lee
David Conner
David Strateham
Jacob E. Wise, captain
Eunebius A. Hopkins
Tollison Ray
William B. Daniell (Darnell?)
James A. Reeves
James Allen

1835:
Nathan C. Barnett, colonel
Joseph Billups, major
Lovick P. Thomas, major
Benj. C. Yancey, captain
Andrew J. Cook, lieutenant
Walter Carson, captain
~~James Jones~~
~~Walter Carson, sergeant~~
Moses Venson, captain
Wayne Wise, captain
James J. Taylor, sergeant
Wm. Cook, lieutenant

1834:
Waller Carson, captain
John A. Martin
Osborne Wiley
Thompson McGivins (?), captain
Benjamin Baldwin
Cicero Buffington
John Rolin
Gideon Dowse
Elias Busby
James Thomas
Pernal Cook
Garrett Parks, sergeant
John Tolbert, sergeant
Benjamin Davis
Wm. D. Maddox, major
Willis J. Biggs
Thomas Bowen
Jesse Hanson
John L. Doyle
Joseph Durham
Bob Henderson

1841:
Given (Green?) B. Haygood
Frances A. Crow
Jas. W. Cook

1820:
Harrison Huff

1841:
Jesse Daniell, captain
Stephen Jackson, second lieutenant
William Jackson, second lieutenant
Robert Jennings, first lieutenant
Thomas Booth, second lieutenant

1842:
Solomon P. Kent, major
William Williams, captain
Elias B. Pritchard, captain
Stephen Jackson, lieutenant
Francis Crow, lieutenant
James W. Cook, lieutenant
Jennings, lieutenant
William A. Fambrough
John R. Banks
Joel C. Barnett
J. B. E. Overby
R. S. Neal
Francis Fuller
John Sturges
William Sturges
Joseph Allen
James Shaw
Wm. M. Cawley
John G. Maxey
William M. Cook

1841:
Hiram Beasley
Doctor W. Elder, major
Thomas G. Elliott, captain
William A. Adams, captain
Owen Wood, first lieutenant
Joel W. Haile, first lieutenant
David G. Blakely, first lieutenant
Edmunds G. Elder, first lieutenant
Robert H. H. Hester
Jackson M. Thrasher
Cordy Daniel
John Norton
Elisha Holland
John W. Huy (?)
George W. Foster
William H. W. Price
Littleberry Stovall
John J. Whitlow
James J. Selman
Wiley Edmondson
James Boggs
Joseph A. Hughey
Linsey Jacks
Jacob Autrey
William I. Webster
James Calahan
John L. Ward

Militia Fines, 1809-1819 (specific dates are not given)
John H. Lowe
James Price
Thomas Cousins
Aaron Biggs
Archabald Crawley
Abraham Johnston
Charles Burgore
James Sims
John Tye
Greenberry Reynolds
John Wood
William Hickman
Joseph Durham
Burril Yearby
William Brumberton
John L. Ponder
William Bone
Hugh Bailey
William Wallace
Arter Walls
George Mckinzey
Samuel McKee
Joseph Brown, major
Murdock Martin
Jack F. Cock (Cook?)
Willis Kilgore
William Sansom
David Watson
William Wortharm
Peter Milner
Francis Marshall
Randolph Hester
John Marrable
Boling Cox

Thomas Moore
William L. Wallace
Burrel Yearby
Jacob Martin
John L. Wright
Gresham Vickers
Boling Cox
Robert Conner
Arthur Cooper
Thomas Jones
James Bruce
Abraham Pennington
John Ray
John Watson
Radford Lassiter
Charles Wilsey
Edward Bond
John Ball
Abner Ball
Warrington Spillers
William Rains
Weldon Easley
Hugh Hall
Henry Bugg
Thomas Jones
Samuel Garner
Gresham Vickers
Ballard McDormont
Elisha White
Benjamin Kirkland
Lemuel Brown
Samuel (?) Brown
Burwell Mathews
Benjamin Wheeler
David Holmes
Cyrel Herring
Whitehead Ryan
William Clements
Gilbert Copeland
William Broach
Hugh McWhorter
William Weatherly
Archebald Crawford
William Mitchell
Lazarus Summerlin
Green B. Jacks
John Simpson
Joseph Ector
John Giles
Thomas Simmons
James Sims
Walter Connel
William Davis
Thomas Spiur
William Wilkins
William G. Wright
William Crow
Alexander Crow
Jerimiah Burnett
John A. Cogburn
Thomas Booth
Jeremiah Burnett
White Rosseter
Isaac Adams
Mark J. Allen
John Richardson
James Ormond
Elijah Garner
Archablad Crawford
M. B. Patten
Leander Erwin

Eli Baxter
William Johnston
Allen Brown
Jre E. Paschall
Isaac Kindrick
Thomas Earnest
Elisha Earnest
Robert Powell
John Parmer
James Smith
William Proctor
Whiton Oliver
Richard Easley, Jr.
Jessee Freeman
John Dunaway
Joseph Ligon
Robert Hutson
William Simpson
Robertson Fambrough
James Haney
John McCree
Robert McCree
Enoch Henson
Seabourn Brown
William P. Easley, captain
David Kinney, lieutenant
William Thompson
Whitehead Ryan
George R. Hunter
Johnson Freeman
Johnson Frost
Aaron Biggs
Abraham Johnson
Richard Dicken
Louis Lampkins
Howell Elder
James Epps
James Mathews
George M. Lanier
Joseph Bridges
Thomas Lowe
John Kemp
John Warren
Allen Pryer
William Garner
Lemuel Brown
Samuel Marss
Aaron Biggs
John L. Wright
William G. Wright
Charnel Hightower
Stevens Thomas
William Manly
Zachariah Sims
Sandy Marbury
William H. Hunt
James Steret (?)
William Banks
Samuel Weir
Thomas Garrison
Robert Morris
Alexander McCane
Edmund Jones
Burwell Traweek
Needham Sorrell
Walter Johnston
William Reynolds
William G. Wright
John L. Wright

William Wood
Phillip Easton
Thomas Wortha, lieutenant
Mathew Marrable
Washington Young
Richard Richardson
William Moss
Graham Vickers
John Wood
John Wooton
Tapley Short
George Y. Farrar
Robert Conner, sergeant
Saml. Collins
Sterling Helton
William Johnston, sergeant
John C. Parr
Joseph Ector
Joshua Famborough
Jesse Martindale
John J. Pass
Humphrey Poss
Joel Lassiter
John M. Clark
Hardy Johnston
Thomas Cammell
William Thompson
Arthur Ayers
Gallant Reynolds
Martin Lea
John Y. Maynor
Henry Mitchell
Lewis Moore
Martin Kinney (Kines?)
Henry Mitchell, sergeant
John Flint
~~John Borman~~ (?)
Stephen Malone
Joseph Jolly
Alexander Farr
John H. Paschal
Joseph C. Morton
Wm. H. Puryear
Wm. W. Brown
Lemuel Swanson
Lemuel Lasseter
Tapley Short
Willis Kilgore
Thomas Kilgore
Solomon Kilgore
Elijah Garner
Wm. G. Wright
Cain Cavender
Edward L. Thomas
Nathaniel Whitman
Wm. Williamson
William Hickman
George Huse

1819:
Jas. J. Moore, captain
Jas. Treadwell, captain
Saml. Garner, ensign
Jesse Jones
Anderson Statum
Wm. Clark
R. J. Cabell
Obed Haile
Lemuel Lansford
Jno. Greer
Nathaniel Epps
Jno. Pace
Washington Holms
Philip Woodley
Huderson Bailey
Wm. Mattox
Henry Stoneham
Philip Pryor
Jno. Nance
Wm. J. Wright
Lemuel Lasseter
Jno. L. Wright
Thomas Kilgore
Newton Henson
Willis Kilgore
Elijah Garner
Jas. F. Morton
Thos. Pinson
Charnell Hightower
Jno. R. Morton
Thomas Tye
Seaborn Summers
Bnj Langford
Sylvanus C. Dolittle
Jos. Rasbury
Thomas Bradley
Jas. Daniel
Wm. P. Jackson
Cyrus Henderson
V. Watkins
Jas. Hinson
Francis Marshall
Barton Thrasher
John Broom
Zedekiah Scates
Thomas Campbell
John Crell
Charles Stewart
Edward Maxey
Wm. L. Fambrough
Joshua Fambrough
Harris Thurmond
Edward Bearden
John Penner
Jas Haynie
Jesse Garner
Aron Bearden
Wm. Whitton
Silas Northan
Jas. Buckley
Lewis Moore
Willis Moore
Elijah Bearden
Jno. Connell
Henry Mitchell, captain
Thos P. Atkinson
Jno. Hutchinson
Thos. Jeffries
Jas. Briden
Wm. Nutt
Wm. P. Jackson
Cyrus Henderson
Cornelious Jackson
Saml. Henderson
Allen Freeman
Jas. Heard
Malcolm Johnston
Middleton Hartsfield
Jas. L. Thomas
Wm. Kimbro
Joseph Summerlin
Stephen Williams
Joseph Moss
Amus Crow
Abell Crow
Thos. Fench
Jos. F. Morton
Wm. G. Wright
Levi H. Carter
John H. Paschal
Lemuel Lasseter
Jno. F. Barnette
Nathaniel Epps
John Pace
Hampton W. Hill
Allen Fambrough
Humphrey Posey

1820:
Frances Thornton
Wm. G. Wright
Jno. B. Marable
Lemuel Lasseter
John Wood
Tapley Short
Thos. Finch
Thomas Morton
Malcom Johnston
Harrison Huff
Williamson C. Reese
Wm. Caldwell
Jas. Beasley
Middleton Hartsfield
Stokeley Evans
Samuel Henderson
Cyrus Henderson
Garling Simms
Tapley Short
Jno. L. Wright
Wm. G. Wright
Elijah Garner
Tarpley Short
Wm. Williamson
Jno. H. Paschall
Wm. H. Puryear
N. C. Whitman
Allen Freeman
Jas. Whitehead
Young Vickers
Jno. Green
Jno. C. Pearson
Edward Cox
Edward Paine
Russell Crawford
Christopher Garlington
Eugene H. Tyson
Levi Brewer

1821:

Jno. Wood
Ucebrous Hopkins
Jas. Grimes
Jno. W. Graves
Saml. Collins
William Whitton
Merret Wood
William Garnes
Wm. Jones
Edward H. Maxey
Gresham Vickers
Tarpley Short
Levy H. Carter
Wm. G. Wright
Wm. H. Puryear
Lemuel Lasseter
Wm. Flippin
Saml. Garner
Inman Whitton
ebenezer Pedegrew
Jno. L. Wright
Newton Hinson
Bennett Pedigrew
Lemuel Swanson
Samuel Garner
Henry Jennings
Nathan W. Whitman
Marshall Peck
Jas. Wheeler
Thos. Littlepage
Torrance Conner
Wm. Hodge
Frances Wcelhannon
Josiah Mcekelhannon
Hy Mcekelhannon
Moses McCalahan
Robert Walker
Ebenezer Newton
William Woodley
Jas. Parrish
Littlebury Woodley
Wm. Maddox
Thomas Jeffries
Philip Ryan
James A. Bailey
Henry White
Jno. McAlpin
Solomon Bearden
John Hunton
Charles Hunton
Elijah Bearden
Wm. Garner
Robert A. McRea
James Hinson Junr.
James Hinson Senr.
Elisha Holland

1821

Barton Thrasher
Middleton Hill
Eleazer Talley
Ed L. Thomas
Hope H. Tegner
Wm. P. Graham
Jacob L. Abrahams
Jas. F. Ritchie (?)
Vincent Watkins, lieutenant
Telman McDaniel
Jno. A. Hopkins
Littlebury Barnett
Jos. F. Ritchie
Amos Crow
Jesse Howell
Jas. O. Ragland
Garrett Craft
Daniel Summers
John Hunton
Jno. W. Graves
John Jacks
Jacob Abrahams
William Hutchinson
Loyd Marrs
Madison B. Mitchell, lieutenant
John Greer, lieutenant
Natahan W. Whitman
Alexander Webster
James Tinsley
Jas. F. Waddle
Jas. Martin
Lott Lagwin
Pinckney Thrasher
Coleson Copeland
Jacob Abrahams
Ambrose Hill
Henry Carlton
John Wood
Wm. Garner
John Hunton
Jos. Rutledge
John Massey
Wm. Graham
Levi Stroud
Abraham Perkins
Jeremiah Burnette
Edwin S. Smith
Robert Brown

1822

George L. Earnest
Thos. R. Mitchell
Saml. Gann
Charles Broach
Julius Davis
Thos. Hancock
Laban Moncrief
Harris Andrews
Thos. Rough
Marta Smith
Jas. W. Harris, lieutenant
Drury Ridgeway
Nathan Fowler
Sherrard Harper
Jno. F. Stephens
Thos. F. Gibbs
Pinckney Thrasher
John Jacks
Freeman Biggs
John Gaton
Jas. F. Ritchie
Richard Glass
Newton Huson
Marrit Wood
Wm. Garner
Reuben Johnson

Cashwell Brand
Jesse Jones
Jonas Brand
William Bailey (Barley?)
Jos. Parrish
Thos. Jeffries
R. Espy
Gabriel T. Mathis
John Jack
Isaac Baldwin
Charles Barnett
Moses Bryant
Archebald Bryant
Wm. B. Cobb
John F. Dunn
Joseph Talley
Ezekiel Lamar
Cutliff Lembaugh
Jonathan M. Peck
James Wheeler
Tucker Whitfield
Moses P. Calahan
Laban Moncrief

Lemuel Swanson
Tapley Short
Wm. Flippin
Lemuel Lasseter
Tyrie Harris
John W. Smith
Jonas Brand
Joshua Morgan
Cashwell Brand
Jesse Jones
Wm. Atkinson
Jno. D. Swift
Wm. P. Graham
Jno. R. Hargroves
Bryant Williams
Luke Garner
Garland Sims
Reuben Stewart
Thomas Campbell
Edwin F. Smith
Robert Brown
Allen G. Fambrough
John Flint
John Greer

1823
John F. Stephens
Jesse Howell
R. R. Billups
John H. Richardson

John Kilgore
Jno. C. Pearson
George Ball

Henry Deane, 1823
Hugh Glosson, 1804
Henry Nasworthy, 1804
David Conner, 1804
John Marable, 1805
George Harper, 1804
Miller Echols, 1804
James Witton (?), 1804
James McCulloch, 1804
John Whitten, 1804
Aaron Butler, 1804
William Arnold, 1804
Lazarus Summerland, 1804
James Smith, 1804
William Welbourn, 1804
Robert Marable, 1804
James Cuningham, 1804
John Marable, 1804
Reace Barber, 1804
Moses Hartifield, 1804

Thomas Shannon, 1804
Abner Herrin, 1804
Stephen Tredwell, 1804
Jesse Hayes, 1804
William Meadows, 1804
Edmund Dukes, 1804
Nathan Smith, 1804
Richd. Marable, 1805
Absolon Echols, 1804
Joseph Alexander, 1804
William Pearson, 1804
Robert Marable, 1804
Stephen Nobles, 1805
Edwin Cox, 1820

(No date)
David Meredith
Saml. Harris
R. Nichols
Wm. Garner (?)

Jno. C. Pearson
Saml. Garner
Leonard Ward

(No date)
Thos. Bradley
Jas. C. Ragland

A. Crow
Levi Stroud

Geo. L. Earnest
J. Davis
J. F. Ritchie
Jno. A. Hopkins
J. F. Ritchie
R. Crawford
Lewis Lampkin
John Palmer
Robert Powel
Wm. Crow
Jas. Epps
Isaac Kendrick
A. Crawford
Amos Crow
Jrie Paschal
Jesse Howel
Abram Perkins
Jeremiah Barnet
A. Crawley
John Fye
Wm. Hickman
Wm. Broach
Hugh McWhorter
Robert Hutson
Wm. Simpson
Robert A. McRea
Charles Welsey
Henry Bugg
Radford Lasseter
A. Pennington
Jas. Bruce
William Thompson
Jas. Serrit
Wm. Banks
Lemuel Brown
Gilbert Copeland
Sandy Marbury
Eli H. Baxter
Thomas Garratson
George R. Hunter
Burwell Traywick
Wm. Welkins
Wm. Clements
Wm. Moss
John Pace
Wm. Wood
Jos. Ligon

Josiah Newton, 1819

Bob & Ned Henderson, 1819

John A. Cogburn, 1815

James Smith, 1816

Samuel Collins, 1818, sergeant

Stephen Williams, 1820

(No date)
Abell Crow
Allen Brown
W. Rosseter
Joseph Moss
Thos. Booth
Edward Paine
Goe W. Merewether
Duel Suwences
Joseph Rasbun
A. C. Doolittle

(No date)
M. Marable
W. Holmes
N. Epps
Willis Kilgore
R. Richardson
Wm. H. Hunt
Wm. Manley
Edward Jones
Jno. L. Wright
Thos. Kilgore
David Kenney
Johnson Freeman
Jonson Frest
A. McCane
Robt. Morris
Stevens Thomas
Zach Sims

(No date)
Jos. T. Morton
Jno. R. Morton
Beng Langford
Jas. Daniel
Frances Marshal
Jos. Brown
J. Burnett
Amos Crow
J. Burnete
Elisha Earnest
Jos. Mathers

Edmund Ramey, 1810

1805
Thos. Mitchell, captain
James Smith, lieutenant
Robt. Kinney, ensign

Samuel Brown, 1809, captain

David Kinney, no date, captain, 216th District

1831
Jo. Hutchenson, lieutenant
John Milledge, lieutenant
Francis Boon
Thos. Batty
David Blunt
Edward Carter
James Cosby
John Dearing

Adam Foster
Jones Gresham
Wm. Harris
Hershel Johnson
Colden Ketchum
Pinkard
John Whitehead

1808
James Hitchcock, captain
Thomas Mitchell, captain
Robert Martin, captain
Charles Read, captain
Leonard Ward, captain
William Starn, lieutenant
James Daniel, lieutenant
Hardy Sparks, lieutenant
William Wright, lieutenant
Robert Kenney, lieutenant
John Dean, ensign
Edward Nixon, ensign
Jesse Serwner, ensign
John A. Carter, ensign
William Talbott, ensign
James Thomason
James D. Cole
John Marable
James W. Armstrong
Jesse Castarl
James Dabney
John Patton
Hugh Neisler
Elijah Davis
John Pettis
Francis Garner
Thos. Washhaun
Spencer Reynolds
John Mock
William Crosby
Simon Awtry

1808
Obadiah Echols
Gresham Vicars
Norris Hendon
William Bugg
John Gordon
Wm. Matthews
Saml. McKee
Benjamin Wilson
William Gray
John Tweedwell
John Nance
John Dean
Wm. G. Wright
Thomas Mitchell, captain

1804
Edmund B. Jenkins
David Sims
Joseph Lane

1831
Geo. W. King, colonel
A. L. Simms, major
Joseph Billups, major
Richd. Dicken, major
Wm. McLeroy, captain
Wm. Bradberry, captain
Doctor W. Elder, captain
Thomas Echols, captain
David J. Fenn, captain
Nathan C. Barnett, captain
Young Jacks, captain
Jiles Jennings, captain
Levin W. Thomas, captain
Seaborn Ramsey, lieutenant
Walden Wise, lieutenant
Wayne Wise, lieutenant
Bolling Conner, lieutenant
James Whaley, lieutenant
Wm. Appling, lieutenant
Owen Wood, lieutenant
Levin W. Thomas, captain
John C. Morgan, sergeant
Ransom A. Whitehead, corporal
James P. Elder, corporal
James A. Barton, corporal
Garret M. Greer, corporal
Robert E. Belcher, second lieutenant
Wiggins, sergeant
Joseph Huchinson, lieutenant
Frances Boon, corporal
John Milledge, lieutenant
Joseph Hutchinson, lieutenant
Thomas Batty
David Blount
Edward Carter
James Cosby
Jno. Dearing
Adam Foster
Jones Gresham
Wm. Harris
Hershal Thomas
Colden Ketchem
James Pinckard
Jno. Whitehead
Bazaleel Langford
James Hooppan
John C. Morgan, sergeant
James Davenport
Memory J. D. Moore
Garrett Craft
Reason Whitehead
John Greer
Joshua Morris
Robert Craft
James D. Hewell
John Kirkpatrick
Wm. Edwd. Fullwood
Sampson Carson
Wm. Manley
Jowett Davenport
John L. Griffeth
Lewis Arther
Elias Busboy
Allen Thompson
Wm. Vandeford
Benjamin Norris
Purnal Cook

Edwd. Craft
Danl. Craft Jr.
Wm. Fenn
Joshua Greer
Robert Smith
Jno. W. Smith
Levi Akredge
John Hinsley
Wm. M. Morton
Joseph Durham
Samuel Klutts
Joseph H. Hambey
Benjn. Bowles
Edwin F. Cox
Wm. Clarke Junr.
Harris Thurmond
James P. Elder
Hartwell E. Elder
John Hardigree
Harmond Hardegree
John Riley
John G. Jacks
John A. Famborough
James C. Anderson
Corday Daniel
Barton Thrasher
Thos. Hester
Wm. P. Graham
Joshua Smith
Tarpley Henson
Jacob T. Choat
Lewis Bennett
James Branch

1830
John W. Harper, major
Arthur L. Sims, major
John Deane, captain
Isaw S. Vincent, captain
Giles Jennings, captain
Saml. D. Mitchell, captain
Benj. Davis, captain
Richard Dicken, captain
Robert Belcher, lieutenant
Daniel Dodson, lieutenant
Obadiah Vincent, lieutenant
A. M. Gathright, ensign
Jos. J. Griffin, captain
Thomas House, captain
James C. Edwards
Edward Ware
Lemuel Robertson
A. M. Gathright, ensign
Hugh L. Henderson
Hugh M. Neisler
Henry Kneeland
Chas. Dougherty
Wm. Murray
John C. Johnson
Wm. Humphreys
Bruton Hicks
Wm. T. Brown
Green B. Haygood
Marcus A. Sears
George L. Earnest
Burwell Perry
Jos. Ligon
Richard Hughes
Walton B. Harris
George D. Paine
Allen Barber
Joshua G. Moore
Isma W. Wooldridge
John Morton
George L. Earnest
Robert Dougherty
William Manley
Robert Ligon
Geo. W. Merewether

1830
John W. Harper, major
J. S. Vincent, captain
Richd. Deckins, captain
Jiles Jennings, captain
Elisha Herndon, captain
Wm. Bradberry, lieutenant
John Gann, lieutenant
William J. Bradberry, first lieutenant
Garrett Crafton
E. G. Harvey, corporal
William Hogue, captain

(no date)
A List of men of 217th Dist., John Deane Capt.

1. John J. Cox
2. Walter B. Harris
3. Wm. Whitten
4. Winfield Hand
5. John C. Greer
6. Henry Jennings
7. Green Holmes
8. Wm. B. Herring
9. Daniel B. Deboard
10. Daniel Ramey
11. James M. Strong
12. Adamson T. Cox
13. John B. wofford, captain
14. Turner Cobb
15. Robt. Moore
16. Blake Cooper
17. John Reynolds
18. Wm. E. Strong
19. John Power
20. Thos. Morton
21. Wm. Edwards
22. Boyd Tuck
23. John Garner
24. Saml. Garner
25. Joseph Tuck
26. Robt. Hayes
27. Woodson Raney
28. William Lane
29. Nathan Bigers
30. Isaac Garner
31. Levi Stewart
32. Arthur Smith
33. Duke Richardson
34. John Richardson
35. Richd. Richardson
36. Philip Lane
37. Harper Conally
38. John Moore

39. John A. Strickland
40. Elijah Hendon
41. Wm. H. Kent (?)
42. Thos. Simonton
43. Saml. Simonton
44. Thos. Simonton
45. Robinson Scoggins
46. Eugene H. Tyson
47. Thos. Sansom
48. James Sansom
49. David Biggers
50. Josiah M. Kent
51. John Smith
52. John Bowen
53. Benning Moore
54. Richard Hooker
55. Robert Whitton
54. Cobb
55. Eli B. Tuck
56. William E. Strong
57. Levi Crawford
58. Thomas Bowen

1830
Richard Dicken
William Murray
Jno. Calvin Johnson
Wm. Humphreys
Burton Hicks
Wm. T. Brown
Greene B. Haygood
Marcus A. Sears
George L. Earnest
Burwell Perry
Joseph Ligon
Walton B. Harris (removed from the county)
Richard Hughie
George D. Paine
Charles Dougherty
Allen Barber
Joshua G. Moore
Isma W. Wooldridge
Lewis McGwier
John Morton
Joseph T. Stokes, sergeant

1831
Levin Thomas
Thomas Wills
John Puryear
Wm. Bowling
John Greenwood
John Jack
George Fellows (?)
Edward Ware
Jno. W. Whitman
A. N. Mayer
James Tinsley
Jordan Odum
Richard Harrison
James J. Crenshaw
Benj. Towns
Aaron Lewis
Burton Hicks
Geo. W. Shaw
Leml. B. Robertson
Wm. Taylor
Jno. Gilbert
Wm. Hale
Sanders
S. Tenny
Wm. B. White
John Baker
John Mallard
Wearing
Robert Ligon
J. S. Vincent

MILITIA FINES & OATHS, 1812-1837

James Henson Sr., 1821

James Hinson Jnr., 1821

Elisha Holland, 1821

John W. Graves, 1821

James Grimes, 1821

Usebius Hopkins, 1821

Samuel Gardner, 1821

Graham & Harper vs. William Fielding, 1837

Malcom Johnston, 1820

Malcom Johnston, 1819

Whitehead Ryan, 1816

(petition, no date)
Col. F. P. Taylor
Eli Bradberry
Smith Alexander, lieutenant
Moses Vinson, lieutenant
Robert Jennings, lieutenant
John Osborn, lieutenant
Edmunds G. Elder, lieutenant
Wm. Fielding, lieutenant
D. W. Elder
Solomon P. Kent, major
Thomas G. Elliott, captain
Jesse Daniel, captain
Jones Stark, captain
Greene B. Haygood, captain
Jacob E. Wise, captain
William Pratt, captain
Jas. W. Cook, lieutenant
Hillman Jackson (Packson?)
Joel Whale (?), lieutenant
Stephen Jackson, lieutenant
F. A. Crow, lieutenant
Thomas Booth

William Davis, 1813

William Mitchell, 1812

Walter Connel, 1813

Thomas Speers, 1813

Robert J. Cabell (?), 1819

Phillip Woodley, 1819

Whitehead Ryan, 1812
William Mattox, 1819
Henry Stoneham, 1819
Obed Haile, 1819
Anderson Bailey, 1819
John Nance 1819
Philip Ryan, 1821

1816
Gabriel A. Muffett, captain
Gabl. J. Mathews
Wm. Thompson
Whitehead Rean
Fil A. Gleason
Wm. Paris
Nicholas Freeman
John Freeman
Lieutenant David Kinny
Peter Dodd
George R. Hunt
Johnston Freeman
Johnston Frost
Nicholas Lawrence
James Ligon, captain
William Simpson
William Hightower, captain
Aron Biggs, sergeant
Abram Johnston
Richard Dicen
Umphrey Edwards
Isaac Adams
James Stewart, captain
John Parker, captain
John Oliver, captain

Henry White, 1821
John A. Bailey, 1821
Thomas Jeffries, 1821
William Maddox, 1821

1827
John Morton, colonel
R. A. McRea, lieutenant colonel
Wm. S. Mitchell, major
Jno. W. Harper, major
Jas. G. Masten, captain
H. C. Lea, captain
Thomas Echols, captain
David A. Love, captain
Wm. Appling, captain
Sol Frost, captain
Robert Espy, captain
Jas. McLeroy, captain
A. L. Simms, captain
C.C. Birch, captain
Virgil Akredge, lieutenant
David Majors, lieutenant
Thomas Elard (?), lieutenant
Jonas Haile, lieutenant
Clarke T. Williams, ensign
A. M. Gathright, ensign
Lemuel Robertson, ensign
William Humphreys
L. B. Land
William James
Levan W. Thomas
William Clifton
John Bradley
Israel P. Harvey
William Norris
Lord Kilgore
John Bearden
William Hardegree
Edward Hagins
Joseph Braswell
Aron Bearden
Benjamin Jones
William Fambrough
John Jacks
John Gardner
John M. Richardson
William Edwards
John C. Greer
Henry Harralson
James Tinsley
Adrian Myers
Joseph Ledbetter
Serenus A. Myers
James Martin
Joseph Bergen
William H. Puryear, sergeant
William Price, sergeant
Richard Fleming, lieutenant
William D. Bowling
Hugh B. Leeper
Randolph Wills
Mastin Wills
John B. Adair
George Mews
Uriah Bryant

Deposition by Robt. Fullwood that the Bible of his father Major Wm. Fullwood dec'd, in the possession of his mother in South Carolina, shows Robert Fullwood to have been born 3 January 1766. Made 12 June 1812.

1822
J. Newton, colonel
Benjn. David (?), captain
Thomas Wells, captain
W. J. Wright, captain
William Appling, captain
Richard Thompson, lieutenant
Charles Parr (?), lieutenant
Charles M. Heard
Laban Moncrief
Harris Andrews
Thomas Keough
Martin Smith
Robert Billups

Hinchey Winn, 1819
George Walton, 1821

Jeremiah Burnet, 1819

John H. Paschall, 1819

1820
Josiah Newton, major
John Dean, captain
Thos. L. Lowe, captain
Jackson Smith, second lieutenant
Richd. Thompson, first lieutenant
Zachariah Wortham, ensign
Wm. Bailey, second lieutenant
Jonas Brand, second lieutenant
Edwin G. Rogers, first lieutenant
John Dean, captain

Charnal Hightwoer
Tapley Short
Inman Whitton
John L. Wright
William G. Wright
Elijah Garner
William Williamson
John H. Paschal
Wm. H. Puryear
Tapley Short
Nathaniel W. Whiteman

1819
Alexander Farr
John H. Paschal
Joseph C. Morton
William H. Puryear
William W. Brown
Lemuel Swanson
Lemuel Laseter
Taply Scott
Willis Kilgore

Thomas Kilgore
Solomon Kilgore
Elijah Garner (?)
William G. Wright
Cain Cavender
Edward L. Thomas
Nathaniel Whitman
William Williamson

Thomas P. Atkinson, 1819
Stephen Malone, 1818
Thomas Hancock, 1822
William Graham, 1821
Thomas Rutledge, 1821
Henry Carleton, 1821
John Massey, 1821
Levey (Leroy?) Brewer, 1820

James Beasley, 1820
Garret Craft, 1821
Williamson C. Reese, 1820, sergeant
John Greer, 1821
Malcom Johnston, 1820
Thomas Morton, 1820
James Daniel, 1819
John B. Marable, 1820

Deposition of Pleasant Bryant that he is over forty-five years of age. January 12, 1815.

Bazaleel Langford, 1819
Anderson Statum, 1819
Wm. Starns, 1815
Elijah Garner, 1816
John Richardson, 1816
Samuel Collins, 1821
Zedekiah Skates, 1819
Thomas Lowe, 1817
John Creek, 1819
John Broom, 1819

Thomas Campbell, 1819
Barton Thrasher, 1819
Frances Marshall, 1819
John Henson, 1819
Lemuel Lansford, 1819
Philip Pryor, 1819
Henry Jennings, 1821
James Hayney, 1819
Josiah Nunelly, 1824
W. C. Dobbins, 1824

(No date given)
John Ramey
Benj. Booth
William Stroud
Henry Bowling
Henry Paulett
John Haygood
Isham Hendon
David Shay
Asbury Hull
John Smith
Wm. L. Parr
Ransom Nichols

James Bransford
Arthur C. Akinsons
John Shepherd
Gabl. Mathews
G. Y. Farrar
James Caldwell
Thomas Edmundson
Jno. H. Lowe
John M. Dobbins
Wm. McColm
Roland Taylor

MILITIA RECORDS, 1810-1820

Edmund Jones, 1816
Nathaniel Epps, 1818 & 1819
Richard Richardson, 1818
Phillip Easton, 1817
Washington Holmes, 1819
Thomas Kilgore, 1819
John L. Wright, 1819
Willis Kilgore, 1819
Stevens Thomas, 1817
William H. Hunt, 1816
Johnson Freeman, 1817
Johnston Frost, 1817
Alexander McCane, 1817
Robert Morris, 1817
Zachariah Sims, 1816
David Kinney, 1817
Mathew Marrable, 1818

Enoch Henson, 1816
Robertson Famborough, 1816
Samuel Brown, 1812
Whiton Oliver, 1816
John Watson, 1810
John Ray, 1810
John L. Wright, 1810
Randolph Hester, 1809
William Sansom, 1809
Francis Martial, 1809
Jack F. Cocke, 1809
Joseph Durham, 1809
John Wood, 1809
John H. Lowe, 1809
Charles Burgon, 1809
Abram Jonston, 1809
James Price, 1809

(No date)

1. John E. Ward
2. Lucian B. Burnett
3. Berry Gann
4. James Mc Sumter
5. Joseph L. Gardner
6. John W. Cook
7. Nathaniel Richardson
8. Hiram Richardson
9. Wm. T. Tyson
10. Spenser Barber
11. Joseph Beall
12. David Conner
13. Chas. G. Gregory
14. A. B. Jackson
15. Wm. Durham
16. John W. Kennon
17. Robert Moore
18. Richard Carmichael
19. John Carmichael
20. Purnal Cook
21. John P. Haynes
22. Thomas Lowe
23. Pretchet
24. Famborough
25. Hardegne
26. Giles
27. Holland
28. Middleton
29. Rouland
30. Blakeley
31. David Elder
32. A. M. Jackson
33. Wm. Lampkin
34. Hardeway Smith
35. Isaac S. Vincent
36. Wm. B. McRee
37. Jesse Darnel
38. Sandford Sims
39. James Cook
40. Lewis J. Lampkin
41. James Lester
42. Elijah Clifton
43. Nathan Cook
44. Alexander Melton
45. Samuel S. Sledge
46. John A. Mathews
47. Martin Thompson
48. Willis Thompson
49. Daniel Reed
50. Mathew Caygle
51. Pulaski Crow
52. A. G. Garner (?)
53. G. M. Parin (Pain?)
54. Francis M. Haygood
55. Overton Stephens
56. Robert Swan
57. Mathew Rhodes
58. Thomas Garison
59. Benjamin F. Drake
60. Wm. Fleming
61. James Williams
62. Wm. Buchannon
63. J. F. Nason
64. Washington Ivins
65. Alx Brown
66. George Rutledge
67. James Garrison
68. Jackson Richardson
69. Wm. Thomas
70. James Garner
71. Samuel Parish
72. Edward Jeffreess
73. Wm. A. Greer
74. William Simms
75. E. A. Hopkins
76. Berford Brooks
77. James Reeves
78. John Edwards
79. James Henson
80. James Conner
81. Stephen Leonard
82. Wiley Hayles
83. Masters Daniel

A. M. Jack

J. S. Vincent
R. H. Moore

MILITIA RECORDS, 1810-1821

Jre. E. Paschal, 1816
Jesse Howell, 1821
Jeremiah Burnitt, 1821
Abram Perkins, 1821
Thomas Earnest, 1816
Amos Crow, 1821
Archabald Crawford, 1812
James F. Ritchey, 1821
Isaac Kendrick, 1816
John A. Hopkins, 1821
Russell Crawford, 1820
James Eppes, 1816
Lewis Lampkins, 1816

William Crow, 1814
John Parmer, 1816
Robert Powel, 1816
William Weatherly, 1812
Charles Willey, 1810
Robert McCree, 1816
Hugh McWhorter, 1812
William Broach, 1812
William Hickman, 1809
John Tye, 1809
Archabel Crowley, 1809
Gadeal Fambrough, lieutenant, 1809
Saml. Boyd, ensign , 1809
Amos Ponder, 1809

John L. Wright, captain 218th District, and John G. Mayne, lieutenant 217th District, 1814

Ferr K. Trammell, no date, captain, 239th District

Travis Straughn, captain, 241st District, and Parks Middleton, lieutenant, 239th District, 1814

Robert Hutson, 1816

MILITIA RECORDS, 1810-1823

Burwell Trawick, 1816
James McKleroy, 1822, captain
Bob and Ned Henderson, free persons of color, 1819 (several documents)
Benjn. Nutting, 1822
John Richardson, 1810
William Wood, 1817
John Pace (Parr?), 1819
Julius Davis, 1822
George L. Earnes, 1821

William Clements, 1812
Thomas Garretson, 1817
George R. Hunter, 1817
William Proctor, 1816
Sandy Mabury, 1816
Levy Stroud, 1821
Eli Baxter, 1816
James O. Ragland, 1821
Alexander Crow, 1814
Thomas Bradley, 1819
Joseph Ligon, 1816

Aster Walls, William Baumbutons, George McKenzy, Hugh Baty, Berell Yearby, William Bone, John L. Ponder, Samuel McRee, william Wallard, 1820 (?)

Lemuel Brown, 1812
Gilbert Copeland, 1812
William Banks, 1817
James Bruice, 1810
William Thompson, 1817

James Steret, 1816
Radford Lassater, 1810
Abraham Pennington, 1810
William Wilkins, 1813
Henry Bugg, 1811

1820 (1810?)
Joseph Durham
William Hickman
John Wood
Greenbury Reynolds
John Tye

Charles Burgon
Abraham Johnston
Archebel Crowley
Aron Biggs

MILITIA RECORDS, 1816-1821

1818
John Selman, lieutenant colonel
John H. Lowe, major
Josiah Newton, major
James Meriwether, major
Edward Conner, captain
William L. Parr, captain
John Deane, captain
James McCleroy, captain
Richd. Maxfield, ensign
James Akins, lieutenant
John Morgan, ensign
John Conner, lieutenant
Charles Stewart, ensign
Josiah Daniel, lieutenant
John Harper, ensign
Hezekiah D. Adams, lieutenant
William Carnes, sergeant
John Tekle, sergeant
Robert Conner, sergeant
Green B. Jacks, lieutenant
William Starnes, captain
William Flippen, lieutenant
Samuel Collins, sergeant
Sterling Helton, sergeant

1816
Thomas Stamps
John H. Lowe, major
James Wright, captain
James Meriwether, captain
Hezekiah D. Adams, lieutenant
Francis M. Trammel, lieutenant
Drewry Cooper, ensign
James Smith, ensign
James Sims, ensign
David Willoughby, ensign
Jesse Martindale
Joseph Ligon
Robert Hutson
William Simpson
John Simpson
Robertson Fambrough
Francis W. Trammel, lieutenant
James Hayney, sergeant
John McCree
Robert McCree
Enoch Henson
Seabourn Borwn
Charles Burgore
James Wright, captain

1817 (1819?)
Duel Summers
Sebron Summers
Bazeleel Langford
S. C. Doolittle
Jas. Rasberry
Thos. Bradley
James Cook
James Daniel
Arch Hudson
William P. Jackson
Cyrus Henderson
James Wilkins
Vinsan Watkins
John Wilkins
Edward Paine
George W. Moore
Wm. Murray
David Johnson
Thos. Smith
Wm. Appling
Wm. Stover
Jerh. Burnitt
Amos Crow
Job Wilkins

1816
F. H. Trammel, major
Parks Middleton, captain
William P. Easley, captain
James Stuart, captain
John Oliver, captain
John Parker, captain
Wade White, lieutenant
Nathan Gann, lieutenant
Jacob Treadwell, lieutenant
James McCleroy, lieutenant
Isaac Hill Jr., lieutenant
Martin Crow, ensign
Sherwood Harper, ensign
Zachariah Dickinson, ensign
William Clifton, ensign
Wade White, lieutenant
Allen Brown, sergeant
Starling Helton, sergeant
Capt. William P. Easley
Richd. Easley Jr.
Jesse Freeman
John Dunaway
Absalom Camron
Richd. Cole
John Parker, captain
John Alexander
William Bugg
Whiton Oliver
Parks Middleton, captain
James Smith
William McMurray
William Proctor
John A. Cogburn
James Stewart, captain
Jre E. Paschal
Isaac Kindrick
Edmund Baughn
Thomas Earnest
Elisha Earnest
Robert Powell
Lewis Lampkin
John Parmor
John Deane
Sherwood Porch
Joseph Seaglar

(No date)
Robert Orr
Jesse Jones

Otho H. Appling

1819
James J. Moore, captain
Alexander Moore, first lieutenant
Henry Pope, ensign

James Tredwell, captain
John Poss, first lieutenant
wm. Hennard, second lieutenant
John Hendon

(No date)
Rebun Winfrey, sergeant
Anderson Statund, sergeant

Robert McCree, corporal
William Clark, sergeant

Request in 1819 for running the line between James Tredwell's and James Moore's districts.

John Lea, no date, certificate that he cannot do militia duty

(No date)
John Dean, captain
John Garner
Lemuel Lansford
Nathaniel Epps

John Pace
Washington Holmes
Gabriel A. Moffett

James Treadwell and Sharrard Harper, no date

1819
John Selman (?), colonel
Jno. A. Lowe, lieutenant colonel
Josiah Newton, major
James Oates, captain
Wm. L. Parr, captain
Henry Mitchell, captain
Henry Harris, captain
Jno. M. Dobbins, captain
Wm. B. Holt, captain
Otho H. Applin, captain
Christopher Garlington, captain
Sherwood Harper, captain
Jos. Ligon, first lieutenant
Wm. J. Wilburn, second lieutenant
Hiram Beasley, lieutenant
Reuben Stewart, lieutenant
Hezekiah D. Adams, lieutenant
Green B. Jacks, lieutenant
James E. Brown, lieutenant
Robert Espy, lieutenant
Joshua Morgan, lieutenant

John White, lieutenant
Richard Thompson, lieutenant
William Clifton, lieutenant
Josiah Daniel, lieutenant
Elijah Traedway, lieutenant
Loyd Mares, ensign
James Galwson, ensign
Zachariah Wortham, ensign
Francis Thornton, ensign
Robert Kendrick, ensign
James J. Moore
Alexander Moore, lieutenant
Wm. Hinnard, ensign
Henry Pope
James Tredwell, captain
John Pass, 1st lieutenant
William Hinnard, ensign
Saml. Garner, ensign
Reuben Winfrey, sergeant
Anderson Statum, sergeant
Robert Orr, sergeant
Jesse Jones, corporal

1819
Elijah Treadway, William Hester, Thos. Thompson

1819
James Wilkins, John Wilkins, James Cook, Aaron Clifton

1819
John J. Moore, S. Harper

1817
Abner Bradley, captain
John Hodge, lieutenant
John M. Harper, ensign
Patterson Wise, 1st sergeant
Robert M. Echols, 2nd sergeant
James Yates, 3rd sergeant
Otho A. Apling, 4th sergeant
William L. Parr, captain
Jeremiah Mathews Jr. lieutenant
Joshua Morgan, ensign

John Fletcher, 1st sergeant
Robert M. Grower, 2nd sergeant
Thomas Shepherd, 3rd sergeant
Reuben Johnson, 4th sergeant
William Starnes, captain
William Flippen, lieutenant
Charnold Hightower, ensign
Jonathan Oakes, 1st sergeant
William G. Wright, 2nd sergeant
Richard Farrar, 3rd sergeant

Willis Moss, 4th sergeant
John Bearden, captain
James F. Richey, lieutenant
Charles G. Moore, ensign
Martin Kines, 1st sergeant
John Warren, 2nd sergeant
Robert McCree, 3rd sergeant
Edmund Bearding, 4th sergeant
David Kinney, captain
James Akins, lieutenant
William Jolley, 2nd sergeant
George Kinney, 3rd sergeant
John Puryear, 4th sergeant
John Deane, captain
John G. Maine, lieutenant
Asa Powell, ensign
Jesse Hayes, 1st sergeant
Malcom Johnston, 2nd sergeant
Isaac Powell, 3rd sergeant
Thomas Simonton, 4th sergeant
James Sims, captain
Francis Miller, lieutenant
James Henson, ensign
Charles Stamps, 1st sergeant
Jesse Jones, 2nd sergeant
James Nicholson, 3rd sergeant
Jesse Arnold, 4th sergeant
Thomas Wortham, lieutenant
Elijah Crule, ensign
Arthur Heirs, 1st sergeant
William Davis
Thomas Campbell
Thomas Caldwell
William P. Easley, captain
James Muckle, lieutenant
William Clifton, ensign
Aaron Filghman, 1st sergeant
Aaron Greathouse, 2nd sergeant
Isaac Cohoon, 3rd sergeant
John Allen, 4th sergeant
Needham Muckle, 4th sergeant
Edward Conner, captain
Jacob Tredwell, lieutenant
Ambrose Hill, ensign
George W. Merewether
Jesse Cannada
Thomas Vanderford
John Hammilton
James Stewart, captain
Joel Wingfield, lieutenant
James Straughn, ensign
John Hogwood
Alford Moss
Micajah Gann
Elisha Earnest
James Merewether, captain
Hezekiah D. Adams, lieutenant
Joshua Elder
Joseph Giles
Edward A. Maxey

Edward Paine and Robert Ligon, 1821

(No date), 219th District
Phillip Woodly, sergeant
William Roberds, sergeant
Henry Harris

1819
Robert Espey, 2nd lieutenant
Francis Thornton, ensign
Thos. Farrar, ensign
John Dane, captain
Wm. J. Wilburn, 2nd lieutenant
Henry Mitchell, captain
John Pennell, ensign

1816
John Selman, lieutenant colonel
Alex McDonnall, major
Gabriel A. Moffett, captain
John G. Maine, lieutenant
David Robertson, ensign
John Hatchett, 1st sergeant
Gabriel T. Mathews, 1st corporal
Jesse Hays, 1st corporal
John L. Wright, captain
John F. Barnett, lieutenant
David Harris, ensign
Richd. Thompson, 1st sergeant
William Thompson, 2nd sergeant
Jonathan Oakes, 3rd sergeant
Saml. Tye, 4th sergeant
Josiah Newton, captain
David Kinney, lieutenant
William Callaham, ensign
George G. Holt, 1st sergeant
Robert Morris, 2nd sergeant
Edwd. Calaham, 3rd sergeant
James Croxton, 4th sergeant
Ange Dillerpreer, captain
Thomas Wortham, lieutenant
Whitehead Ryan, sergeant
William Thompson, sergeant
Robert J. Caleell, captain
John Fletcher, lieutenant
James Kinney, lieutenant
Christopher Garlington, ensign
Farr H. Trammell, major
William P. Easley, captain
James McCleroy, lieutenant
William Clifton, ensign
Barnett Downs, 1st sergeant
Stokley Evans, 2nd sergeant
Eldridge Nall, 3rd sergeant
John Allen, 4th sergeant
John Donaway, 1st corporal
Aaron Hightower, 2nd corporal
Isaac Cohoon, 3rd corporal
Thomas Owens, 4th corporal
Parks Middleton, captain
Wade White, lieutenant
Zachariah Dickerson, ensign
Sterling Helton, 1st sergeant
Alexander Terry, 2nd sergeant
Jesse Kinney, 3rd sergeant
John Parker, captain
Nathan Gann, lieutenant
Sherwood Harper, ensign
James Glossen, 1st sergeant

Alson L. Harper, 1st sergeant
William Hodge
Humphrey Edwards
John Oliver, captain
Jacob Tredwell, lieutenant
Elisha Hood, ensign
Henry Mitchell. 1st sergeant
Ludwell Malone, 2nd sergeant
Isaac Adams, 3rd sergeant
Ely Fann, 4th sergeant
James Stewart, captain
Isaac Hill, lieutenant
Martin Crow, ensign
Allen Brown, 1st sergeant
William Haggood, 2nd sergeant
Richd. Dicken, 3rd sergeant
Lea Melton, 4th sergeant
John H. Lowe, major
James Merewether, captain
Hissekiah Adams, lieutenant
David Willibey, ensign
Edward Maxey, 1st sergeant

Joshu Elder, 2nd sergeant
Joshua Famborough, 3rd sergeant
David Elder, 4th sergeant
Francis M. Trammel, lieutenant
James Smith, ensign
James Haney, 1st sergeant
James Williams, 2nd sergeant
William Garner, 3rd sergeant
Thomas McCree, 4th sergeant
James Wright, captain
Drury Cooper, ensign
John Kemp, 1st sergeant
Alexander Caldwell, 2nd sergeant
George Street, 3rd sergeant
Jonas Hale, 4th sergeant
Isaac Thrasher, lieutenant
James Sims, ensign
Martin Lee, 1st sergeant
Alesalom Arnold, 2nd sergeant
Micajah Williamson, 3rd sergeant
John Nott, 4th sergeant

1819
Jno. Selman, colonel
Jno. H. Lowe, lieutenant colonel
James Meriwether, major
Josiah Newton, major
John M. Dobbins, captain
~~James Sims~~
Hezekiah D. Adams, 1st lieutenant
Elijah Tredway, 2nd lieutenant
Alred Ruthledge, ensign
Stephen Hester, 1st sergeant
Charles Rutledge, 2nd sergeant
Thos. Williamson, 3rd sergeant
Rulew Winfrey, 4th sergeant
Jesse Jones, 1st corporal
Douglas Patterson, 2nd corporal
Theophilus Fowler, 3rd corporal
Wm. R. Moore, 4th corporal
Jas. Oates, captain
Hiram Beasley, 1st lieutenant
Greene Eudin (?), 2nd lieutenant
Ruben Stewart, ensign
Jas. Harris, 1st sergeant
John Haile, 2nd sergeant
Young Vickers, 3rd sergeant
Anderson Staturn, 4th sergeant
Henry Mitchell, captain
James Irwin, 1st sergeant
Wm. Jones, 2nd sergeant
Abraham Silvey, 3rd sergeant
Thomas Wade, 3rd sergeant
Robert McCree, 1st corporal
James Williams, 2nd corporal
Charles G. Burgon, 3rd corporal
Thos. Allen, 4th corporal
Wm. B. Holt, captain
Green B. Jacks, 1st lieutenant
Robert Kendrick, ensign
Thos. Robertson, 1st sergeant
Wm. Clark, 2nd sergeant
Wm. Hardigree, 3rd sergeant
Wm. Fambrough, 4th sergeant
Wm. L. Parr, captain
Joshua Morgan, 1st lieutenant
Thomas Farrar, ensign
John G. King, 1st sergeant
Robert J. Coleell, 2nd sergeant
Joseph H. Atkinson, 3rd sergeant

Otho H. Applin, captain
James E. Brown, 1st lieutenant
Robert Espey, 2nd lieutenant
Frances Thornton, ensign
Wm. W. Callaham, 1st sergeant
Moses Barler, 2nd sergeant
Robert Orr, 3rd sergeant
Mathew Allen, 4th sergeant
Wm. Runnells, 1st corporal
Wm. Yates, 2nd corporal
Jesse Jones, 4th corporal
John Deane, captain
Eugine H. Tyson, 1st lieutenant
Zachariah Wortham, ensign
~~John Gardner, 1st sergeant~~
~~James Sansom, 2nd sergeant~~
~~Gilbert Kent, 3rd sergeant~~
~~William Price, 4th sergeant~~
Jackson Smith, 1st sergeant
Mathew Mayne, 2nd sergeant
James Sansom, 3rd sergeant
Wm. Price, 4th sergeant
John Gardner, 1st corporal
James Fields, 2nd corporal
Gilbert Kent, 3rd corporal
Phillip Easton, 4th corporal
Christ. Garlington, captain
Richd. Thompson, 1st lieutenant
Saml. Gardner, ensign
Bannaster Pringle, 1st sergeant
Thomas Tye, 2nd sergeant
Henry L. Britton, 3rd sergeant
Richard Farrar, 4th sergeant
Henry Harris, captain
John White, 1st lieutenant
John Stephens, ensign
Phillip Woodley, 1st sergeant
Thos. Wills, 2nd sergeant
John Jack, 3rd sergeant
William Roberts, 4th sergeant
H.W. Scowell, Captain, 221st Dist.
Joseph Ligon, 1st lieutenant, 221st District
Wm. J. Wilbern, 2nd lieutenant, 221st District
Lloyd Marr, ensign, 221st District

Allen W. Brown, 1st sergeant 221st District
Robt. Ligon, 2nd sergeant 221st District
Eleel Melton, 3rd sergeant, 221st District
James Brewer, 4th sergeant, 221st District
Thos. Booth, 1st corporal, 221st District
Thos. Eppes, 2nd corporal 221st District
Thos. Dicken, 3rd corporal, 221st District
Joseph Moss, 4th corporal, 221st District
John W. Penticost, captain
Wm. Clifton, 1st lieutenant
Thomas Fand (?), 1st sergeant
Peter Whitehead, 2nd sergeant
George Whitehead, 3rd sergeant
Aaron Clifton, 4th sergeant
James J. Moore, captain
Alexander Moore, 1st lieutenant
Henry Pope, ensign
Sherwood Harper, captain
Josiah Daniel, 1st lieutenant
James Glowson, ensign
Henry Glowson, 2nd sergeant
Humphrey Edwards, 3rd sergeant
Belton Daniel, 4th sergeant
James Tredwell, captain
John Poss, 1st lieutenant
Wm. Hinnard, 2nd lieutenant

1819
Wm. Appling, Wm. Stroud, Jeremiah Burnett, Amos Crow, Job Wilkins

1819
James Haynie
Jesse Garner
Aron Bearden
Wm. Whitton
Silas Norton
Jno. Hinesly
Jas. Backley
Louis Moore
Willis Moore
Elijah Beardin
Jno. Connel
Samuel Fielding
James Henson
Francis Marshal
Barton Thrasher
John Thrasher
John Brown
John Brewer
Zed Skates
John D. Ward
Thos. Campbell
Wm. Beasley
Jas. Beasley Jr.
John Creel
David Anderson
Wm. B. Holts
Thos. Lowe
G. Hue Crumpton
Chas. Stewart
Edwd. Maxey
Loveless Fambrough
Joshua Fambrough
Harris Thurman
Wiley Harris
Edwd. Beardin
Jno. Pinner
Wiley Smith
Elijah B. Brown
Inman Whitton

John Nance, 1819

George D. Paine, 1814

1812
Wm. Buachs
Wm. Finch
Hugh Mcgarter
John Bruce
John Martindale, captain
Richard Maxwell

Robert F. Smith 1815

Corporal Joseph Moss, Amos Crow, Ed Paine, John Trammill, Abel Crow, Captain H. W. Scovell, 1819

(No date)
Thomas Firch, Joseph F. Morton, William G. Wright, Levi H. Carter, John H. Paschel, Lemuel Lassetter, John F. Barnett

(No date)
Martin Smith, Nath. Epps, John Pace, Hampton W. Hill

1819
Samuel Heald and Thomas D. Atkinson

John C. Parr, 1819; Reuben Gower, 4th sergeant

(No date)
William W. Carnes, John Hutchinson, Loyd Thomas, Thos. Jeffries

1819
Samuel Heald, John C. Parr, Thomas P. Atkinson

(No date)
Jas. Briden, Barnet Downes, Jas. Hunter, Wm. Nutt, Wm. Jackson, Cyrus Henderson, Cornelius Jackson, Saml. Henderson

(No date)
George L. Earnest and Robert Canterbury

Peter Miller, 1810
Sterling Elder
James Hitchcoke

1816
A. McDonald, major
Robt. J. Cabell, captain
John L. Wright, captain
Josiah Newton, captain
A. Delapierre, captain
Gabl. Moffett, captain
John F. Barnett, lieutenant
David Robinson, ensign
David Harris, ensign
John L. Wright, captain
Mark Allen
John Richison
James Ormand
Elijah Garner
Archibald Crawford
William G. Wright
M. B. Patten
Walter Biscane
Wm. W. Carnes
Miles C. Nesbett
Richd. H. Randolph
Wm. C. Dawson
Etheldred Langston
James Stewell
Leander Erwin
Zachariah Sims
Archd. Mathis
Eli Baxter
William Johnston

(No date)
Saml. Jackson, colonel
Joseph Brown, major
Thomas Mitchell, major
John Selman, major
Isaac Funderburgh, captain
Richard S. Cosby (Easley?), captain
Ruben Hill, captain
White Rosseter, captain
Samuel B. Hutchinson, captain
Augustin S. Clayton, captain
Alford Stewart, captain
James Boyle, captain
John Martindale, captain
Robt. Martin, captain
Wm. Arnold, captain
Robt. F. Smith, captain
John H. Lowe, adjutant
Joseph Moss, quartermaster
John Ector, quartermaster sergeant
Young Gresham, pay master
John Gerdine, surgeon
Sterling Elder, clerk
George Fann, provost marshall
Zadock Bonner, lieutenant
John Cohoon, lieutenant
Moses Lloyd, lieutenant
John Dickinson, ensign
Richd. Loving, sergeant
John Pounds, sergeant
Alexr. Terry, sergeant
Boykin Bridges, lieutenant
Thomas Kinney, fifer
Isaac Daniel, lieutenant
William Stroud, sergeant
Mathew Mitchell, sergeant
Christopher A. Carter, sergeant
Thomas Epps, sergeant
Paton Cary, ensign
Cary Wood, ensign
Jesse Lane, sergeant
John Kinny, sergeant
George Kinny
Edmund Akins
John L. Wright, lieutenant
Wm. Flippen, ensign
Moses Bledsoe, sergeant
Robert Strong, sergeant
James Cunningham
James Robinson, lieutenant
Saml. Robinson, ensign
Robert Simonton, sergeant
Gabreel Murphet, sergeant
John Ewing, sergeant
Arthur Herring, sergeant
John Richardson, fifer
Pinson Drew, drummer
Joshua Morgan, sergeant
Arthur Wall, sergeant
Wm. Yarborough, sergeant
Richd. Laurens, lieutenant
James Talbert, ensign
H. Powell, sergeant
Thos. McCune
Reuben Stewart, lieutenant
Joel Laseter, sergeant
David Akredge, sergeant
John Hale, sergeant
Francis Trammel, lieutenant
Joseph Durham, ensign
Aaron Biggs, sergeant
John B. Kilgro, sergeant
Abraham Johnson, sergeant
Joseph Darnal, sergeant
Green B. Jacks, lieutenant
Isaac Thrasher, sergeant
James Ligion, sergeant
Joshua Welch, lieutenant
Saml. Welch, ensign

Alexander Quesenbery, sergeant
Alexander Bacheller, sergeant
James Sims, sergeant
Patrick Eaves, sergeant
John Dorman, sergeant
Permenes Hanes, sergeant
Isham Robinson, sergeant
James Barnet, sergeant
Elisha Hood, fifer
John Nutt, sergeant
Wm. Hightower, sergeant
George Clifton, sergeant
Jeremiah Pace, sergeant

John Pace, 1819

William Moss, 1818

MILITIA RECORDS, 1819

John Selman, colonel
John N. Lowe, lieutenant colonel
Josiah Newton, major
James Oats, captain
Henry Mitchell, captain
John M. Dobbins, captain
William B. Holt, captain
Otho Appling, captain
Christ. Garlington, captain
H. W. Scovell, captain
John W. Penetcost, captain
Jos. Ligon, lieutenant
Wm. J. Welburn, lieutenant
Hiram Beasley, lieutenant
Hezekiah D. Adams, lieutenant
James E. Brown, lieutenant
Robert Espy, lieutenant
Richd. Thompson, lieutenant
William Clifton, lieutenant
James Glawson, ensign
Zachariah Wortham, ensign
Frances Thornton, ensign
Robert Kendrick, lieutenant
Ejune H. Tyson, lieutenant
Elijah Treadway, lieutenant
Robert J. Cabbell, sergeant
Obed Haile
John Greer
Nathaniel Epps
John Pace
Washington Holmes
Lemuel Lansford
Phelep Woodley
Anderson Bailey
William Mattox
Henry Stoneurn
Philip Pryor
John Nance
William G. Wright
Lemuel Lasseter
John L. Wright
Thomas Kilgore
Newton Henson
Willis Kilgore
Elijah Garner
Joseph F. Morton
Thomas Penson
Charnel Hightower
Thomas Tye
John R. Morton
Seaborn Summers
Bazabel Langford
S. C. Doolittle
Jas. Rasbury
Thomas Bradley
John W. Pentecosts, captain
James Daniel
Wm. P. Jackson
Syras Henderson
Venson Watkins
James Henson
Francis Marshall
Barton Thrasher
John Brown
Zedekiah Skates
Thomas Campbell
John Creel
Captain Wm. B. Holts
Charles Stewart
Edward Maxey
Wm. L. Fambrough
Joshua Fambrough
Harris Thurmond
Edward Beardin
John Penner
James Hayney
Jesse Garner
Aaron Beardin
William Whitten
Silas Norton
John Henesley
James Buckley
Lewis Moore
Wells Moore
Elijah Bearden
John Connel
James J. Moore, captain
James Treadwell, captain
Samuel Garner, ensign
Jesse Jones, corporal

VIII. Record Group 129-2-4, Miscellaneous, Box 3

Stirling Helton, 1838, at the request of Wm. B. Daniel
John Nutt, 1818
Henry Duke, 1828
Garrett Craft, 1837, at report of Stephen Crow
Charles Burger, 1827
Benton Starks, 1842
John Talmadge (lunatic), 1841, by his guardian Stephen C. Talmadge

BIRTH RECORDS

(Birth records for the following persons in this file gives usually incomplete information on each person's date of birth, name of parent, sex/number of child of mother, color, and names and place of birth of parents. These records are for 1876.)

Richard Walton, black
Edward Pittard, white
Musette Kate Thompson, white
Bessa Leana Moseman, white
Isham thomas Cosby Barnett, white
dead child of Calvin James Bridges, white
William Walton Barnett, white
Susan Amanda Thompson, white
Andrew Jackson Newton, black
Paul Bell Mathews, white

IX. Record Group 129-8-3, Poor School Records, Box 1

Later records in this collection begin with 1852. Given below are names of children with their respective ages and parents, from the lists for 1823 and 1837. Later lists can also be found in this box starting with 1852.

POOR SCHOOL, 1823

(The following lists were compiled in accordance with the Act of the Georgia Legislature of December 23, 1822. The act provided scholarships to children between the ages of 8 and 18 who had not been given public education for more than three years and whose parents had not paid more than fifty cents above the state poll tax.)

Capt. Wright's District
Ann Anderson, widow: George Washington, Wm. M., Edmund, Noah & Elizabeth.
James Brown: Alexr. W. & Nancy.
Henry Turner: Reuben, Belsey, Polly & Nancy.
Belsey Lard: Mary.
John Kilgore: William L., Brown, Smith, & Mary.
Thomas Campbell: Howell, William, Walter, Mariah, & Malinda.
John Knott: Elizabeth.
Hosa Haile: Benjamin.
Timothy Williams: William, Salley, & Rebecca.
Lucetea Thacker, widow: Garrett, James, & Ostin H.
Susannah Busby, widow: Richard.
Gray Lassiter minor in care of Joel Haile.
Joel Lasseter: John, Richard, Lucinda, Syntha, senone, & Julian.
Henry Bass: Noah & Thursey.
Brecy M. Owins: Coleman P. and Sarah J.
Jesse Martendale: three, names not known.
Signed John Selman.

Captain Hearndon's, formerly Captain Blankinship's District.
Levi Foster's children: Reuben, Paley (female), Elizabeth.
Elizabeth Whitehead's children: Rebecca and Sanford.
Sarah Whitehead's child: Richard.
Reason Whitehead's child: Caleb.
Elizabeth Whitehead, widow, her children: Rawsom, Williamson, Leutisha (female), Berry, and John.
William Ball's children: John and Mary.
Mrs. Wilkins, widow, her children: Susanna and Fredric.
George W. Allen: Louisa and Jones.
John Ball's children: Dison and William.
Silas Vikus' children: Hollensworth, Silas, and Pollyann.
Mary Hannor's child: James T. Hannor.
Lewis Bradberry's children: Eli and Nathan.
Margerett Ray's child: Toleson.
George Cagle: Mary and Nancy.

Captain Ward's District.
William Hightower: Jesse, Sally, John, and James.
Simeon Salter: John.
James McKleroy: Christianna, William, and Anna.
Barnett Downs: Peggy, Floyd, Elizabeth, and Nemiah.
Jesse Walker: Elizabeth, Josiah, and Jessee.
Massa Duke: Allen, Edington, and William.
William Thompson: Lenora, Teresea, and Hugh.
Wiat Leigh: Sally, Elizabeth, Joseph, Hartwell, and Mary.
Lany Hagin an orphan.
Tilmon McDonald: Kesiah.

Captain Sorrell's District.
John Dolton's children: Martha, Susannah, Nancy, and Vincent.
David Hollaway's children: Wm. B., Elizabeth, and Melinda.
Wm. Hardigree's child: John Hardigree.
Wm. Loginn's step child: Elizabeth Hudson.
Jehu Crumpton's children: Thomas, Richard, and Sally.
James Pike's children: Sion and Lucinda.

David Godfrey's child: John Godfrey.
John O'Conner's children: Juriah and Henry.
David Lynch's children: Eliza, Jane, Munroe, and Ulysses.
Orphans of John Robertson deceased: Sally, Katherine, Wm., and James.
Richard Barnet's child: Smith Barnett.
Wm. Meadow's children: Reuben, Theophilus, and Anna.
Thomas Crane's child: Thomas Crane.
Orphan of Wm. Coleman: Mary Coleman.
Captain Wm. Holt, guardian: Joseph Biggs.
Joshua Miller's child: Matilda Miller.

Captain McRee's District.
Robert Childers' children: James, William, and Samuel.
Aaron Biggs' children: William and Willis.
Josiah Maxey's children: Lucenda, Harriott, and John H.
Wm. Garner's children: Nancy, Elijah, Delila, and Lucinda.
Lemuel Lasseter's children: Henry and Elizabeth.
Mrs. McRee's children: Thomas, Peggy, and William.
Alexr. Smith's child: William Smith.
John Pinner's children: Cintha and Lucinda.
William Greer's children: Elvirah, Mary An, Eliza, Nancy, and Welmoth.
William Hutchinson's children: Susannah, Wm. C., Joshua, and Daniel.
Richd. Lewis: Martha, Polly, and Massey.
James Moore's children: Sarah, Nancy A., and Janet E.
Charles Burger's children: William, Seaborn, and Susannah.
Wm. Elliott's children: Richard, William, and Sarah.
Mrs. William's children: Peggy and William.
Elizabeth Hagan's children: Elizabeth, Polly, and Permelia.
John B. Hutchinson's child: Jane.
Washington Lanton, orphan.

Captain Richard Dicken's District.
William Adams' children: Richard, Charlotte, and Elizabeth.
Samuel Harris' children: William and Sophia.
James Barbur's children: Jane and Susannah.
Polly Haygood, widow, her children: 1 male and Anna and Sarah.
Racheal Burnett, widow, her children: Bedford, Lusham, Jula, Linda and Omma.
Nancy M. Carter's child: James.
Willia Whatley's children: Willis, Judge, and Penina.
Misses Moseby's child: Thomas Jefferson.
Robert Velvin's children: Jethro, Nancy, Tempy, Susannah, Ceiley, and Mary.
John Delloach's children: Jesse Gaston, Fanny, and Elizabeth.

Poor Children in Captain Appling's District.
Martha Aikin, Joseph Alexander, Smith Alexander, Nathan Alexander, Mary P. Blankenship, Catherine P. Blankenship, Elsey R. Blankenship, William W. Johnston, George W. Johnston, Eliza R. Johnston, Hulda H. Johnston, Marth Z. Johnston, Gilbert Martin Ledbetter, Joseph Henry Ledbetter, Sophia Ledbetter, Mary Ann Ledbetter, Femmy Ledbetter, Mary Ann Minor, Elizabeth Minor, Helena Minor, William Henry Minor, Wilson Mooneyham, William Mooneyham, Rebecca Mooneyham, Thomas J. Rogers, Charlotte P. Rogers, Eliza Ann Rogers, Augustin C. Rogers, James H. Rogers, Nice Whitfield, Louisa Whitfield.

Captain Hewell's District.
Pritchett's child: William G. Pritchett.
James Wilson's children: Richard, Milton, Albert, and James.
Nancy Wilson's child: Sally.
Malcolm McLeod's children: Sally B., Neal, and John.
John Hamilton's children: James, Eli, Nancy, and John W.
James Greer's children: Joshua and Martha.
Briant Williams' child: John Williams.
Betty Edgars' child: John.
John Varner's children: Mary H. and Eli.
Jonathan Hogue (parent? child?).
Frances Mitchell's children: Andrew B. and Nancy Mitchell.
John H. Paschal's children: Harriott, Emily, Eliza, and Caroline.

Note that Miss Fort was received 19 September 1825, deceased on 26 November 1825, and buried 27 November 1825 by David Stephens. (Apparently some records of the poor fund are misfiled in these poor school records.)

Order that John Turner, Mercer Bradshaw, Nathaniel Mobbs, Mary Wilkes, and ----- Weaver (?) be struck from the poor list and Miss Kilgore, Burwell Lee, and Humphrey Bearden be added.

Captain Davis' District.
(Apparently the names below are parents and the numbers are the number of children in each family who are poor school children.)
Thomas Angle, 3; Thos. Jeffreys, 2; Ben Parr, 3; Sarah Twedewell, 1; Mary Kennon, 1; and Samuel Heald, 1.

POOR SCHOOL, 1837

Amanda Lee, age 8, daughter of James Lee deceased.
Wm. Gunn's daughters Nancy and Mahala, 10 to 12.
Mary Fuller, age 15.
Gray Stevens, age 13.
Minerva Stevens, age 9.
Sarah Brewer, age 12.
James Grewer, age 10.
Panina Brewer, age 8.

Children between 8 and 15 years of age. 241st District.
Katherine Lanier of Geo. W. Lanier.
Angeline Lanier of Geo. W. Lanier.
Langford Lanier of Geo. W. Lanier.
Martha Lanier of Geo. W. Lanier.
Joseph Lea of John Lea.
Elizabeth F. Lea of John Lea.
John Davis of John Davis.
Elizabeth Davis of John Davis.
Sarah Ann Langford of Bazelell Langford.
Henry Langford of Bazelell Langford.
George Langford of Bazelell Langford.
James Langford of Bazelell Langford.
Stephen C. Gann of Samuel Gann.
Martha Gann of Saml. Gann.
William Summers of Daniel Summers.
Francis Summers of Daniel Summers.
Harden Summers of Daniel Summers.

Children between 8 and 16.
Wm. Floyd, son of Tabitha Floyd.
John Floyd, son of Tabitha Floyd.
Camella Floyd, daughter of Tabitha Floyd.
Panina Floyd, daughter of Tabitha Floyd.
~~George Thomas, son of Levi Thomas~~.
Richard H. Carmical, son of William Carmical.

Thomas Bowles, age 8, son of widow Bowles.

217th Georgia Militia District.
Thomas Cockron, age 8.
Frances Holland (female).
Thomas Lee, age 9.

Elizabeth Bradberry, age 12, daughter of William Bradberry.
Martha Bradberry, age 10, daughter of William Bradberry.

Elizabeth Sisson, widow, her children: William, about 11; Merinda, about 10, and Ann Eliza, 8.

James Vaughn, age 9
Children between 8 and 14: Katherine Thacker and Lucinda Thacker.

Richard Akin, age 13
James Akin, age 12
Sarah Akin, age 9

Henry Akin, age 9
James Kelly, age 10
John Kelly, age 8

Jesse Fenn, age 14

Richard Nason, between age 9 and 10, son of James Nason.
Hugh M. Nason, between ages 11 and 12, son of James Nason.
Joseph Moreland, between ages 12 and 13, son of William B. Moreland.
Jesse Hadley, between ages 15 and 16, son of Mrs. Bates.
Charles A. Wadkins, between ages 10 and 11, son of Moses Wadkins.
Joseph H. Ogden, age 13, son of Ogden deceased.
Thomas Barnes, between ages 11 and 12, son of Daniel Barnes deceased.

Elizabeth Stewart, age 10, daughter of Thos. Stewart.
Parmelia Wood, age 10, daughter of Lucy Wood.
Wm. Stewart, age 8 or 9, son of Thos. Stewart.
Anderson Fambrough, age 14, son of Joshua Fambrough.
James Rutledge, age 12, son of widow Rutledge.
John Rutledge, age 10, son of widow Rutledge.
Joseph McRee, age 13, son of widow Frankie McRee.

PART iii: ORIGINAL MARRIAGE RECORDS (RECORD GROUP 129-2-1)

X. Losse Orignial Marriage Licenses, Box 1, 1803-1850s

The Georgia Department of Archives and History also has boxes of later loose Clarke County marriages starting circa 1853 and microfilm copies of the books of recorded marriages.

Fround on the marriage records listed below although usually not included on the abstracts below, is the date that the marriage license was taken out, the date and book where the marriage is recorded, and the name of the official who conducted the wedding.

Also see the following books by Mary Bondurant Warren: Georgia Marriages 1811 Through 1820 (Danielsville, GA, 1988); Marriage Book A (1805-1821) Clarke County, GA Including Previously Unrecorded Marriage Licences in the Office of Ordinary (Danielsville, GA, 1966); her abstracts of Georgia marriage records to 1810 in Georgia Genealogist in part ii, State Records --Marriage Records; and Marriages and Deaths Abstracted from Extant Georgia Newspapers (2 vols., Danielsville, GA, 1966 and 1972). (Covers 1763 to 1829).

GEORGIA. Clarke County.

To any Judge, Justice of the Inferior Court, Justice of the Peace, or Minister of the Gospel:

EITHER of you are hereby authorized to join in HOLY MATRIMONY Henry Bishop & Rebecca Hamilton if they be of Lawful age, and authorized by the LEVITICAL DEGREES. You will certify when the Matrimony was solemnized, and return this License to me, that the same may become of Record of said County.

GIVEN under my hand this 30th day of Augt 1825

Jno H. Lowe[illegible]

GEORGIA, Clark County,

TO any Judge, Justice of the Inferior Court, Justice of the Peace, or Minister of the Gospel:

YOU are hereby authorized to join together in the holy State of Matrimony, ~~Miss Mahaley Hadley and~~ Mr Allen Bates & Mahaley Hadley and to make your return on this licence to this office, of their actual intermarriage, and of the day on which the same was solemnized.

Given from under my hand and Seal, this 23rd Day of May 1836

Joseph Ligon C. C. O.

I do certify that ~~Mahaley Hadley~~ and Allen Bates & Mahaley Hadley were this day joined together in the bonds of Matrimony before me, this twenty third Day of May 1836

Sam L. Frost J.P.

GEORGIA,
Clarke County.

To any Minister of the Gospel, Judge, Justice of the Inferior Court, or Justice of the Peace.

YOU *are hereby authorized to join* Mr Mercer Bradshaw *and* Miss Sarah Gordon *in the Holy state of Matrimony, according to the Constitution and Laws of this State; and for so doing, this shall be your sufficient License.*

GIVEN *under my hand and seal, this* 15th *day of* December 1852

Asa M Jackson Or.
Ordinary

L.S.

Georgia,
Clarke County.

I DO CERTIFY, That Mercer Bradshaw *and* Sarah Gordon *were duly joined in Matrimony by me, this* 16th *day of* December 1852

WM Epps J.P.

Joseph Albright to Elizabeth Maddox, 9 October 1809. Executed 12 October 1811.

Starting Acree to Susannah Meddows, 16 February 1811. Executed same day.

William Aplin to Elizabeth Loyal, 8 October 1808. Executed 13 October 1808, /s/ Isaiah Hales.

Jonathan Adams to Rachel McClendon, 17 October 1807. Executed 22 October 1807.

John Allen to Elizabeth Davis, 15 December 1810. Executed the same day.

Edward Akin to Patsy Parr, 1 December 1812. Executed 22 December 1812 by Reverend Isaiah Hales.

Thomas Anderderson to Poley Barnett, 11 August 1812. Executed 13 August 1812.

Frapein Arnold to Epsybeth Arandale, executed on or after 19 March 1806.

Thomas Allen to Polly Cole, 23 November 1813, executed 24 November 1813.

Otho H. Appling to Jane W. Brown, 11 October 1815, executed the same day.

Volentine Atkinson to Elizabeth Brand, 7 April 1815, executed 9 April 1815 by Isaiah Hales, minister.

Isaac Adams to Nancy Bankston, 17 July 1816, executed 1 August 1816.

Mark J. Allen (Millen?) to Mahaly Farrar, 8 February 1816, executed 15 February 1816.

David Anderson to Ellender Hill, 9 January 1816, executed 12 January 1816.

Lewis Arthur to Nancy Hartsfield, 16 January 1816, executed 18 January 1816 by Isaiah Hales, minister.

Uriah E. Amonds to Prudence Kemp, 20 October 1818, executed the same day.

William Akins to Mary Quarterus, 2 March 1819, executed 17 March 1819.

Phillip Allen to Sarah Robinson, 20 October 1819, executed the same day.

John Anderson to Nancy Smith, 12 December 1821, executed 13 December 1821.

Richard Adams to Rebecca Whitehead, 20 September 1823, executed 21 September 1821.

William L. Anderson to Eudocia M. Hill, 2 February 1825, executed the same day by William H. Gray, minister.

Thomas Angle to Mary Watkins, 14 September 1824, executed 15 September 1824.

Joshua Ammons to Martha Echols, 1 March 1824, executed 4 March 1824.

Charles Allen to Elizabeth Lea, 25 December 1826, executed 26 December 1826.

James Allen to Nancy Wood, 27 December 1826, executed 27 December 1826 by Wm. Alexander.

Smith Alexander to Nancy Stephens, 23 September 1827, executed same day.

Wm. M. H. Adrian to Clementine Mattox, 28 March 1831, executed 13 April 1831.

Joseph Alexander to Lucinda Weir, 1 April 1832, executed 3 May 1832.

William Amis to Jane E. Pinson, 9 December 1833, executed 10 December 1833 by Miller Bledsoe, minister.

Nathan Alexander to Delila Barber, 3 January 1833, executed 3 January 1833.

Joseph Amis to Elizabeth Price, 10 October 1836, executed 13 October 1836 by John Lary, minister.

George W. Anderson to Ann Hamlett, 5 January 1835, executed 7 January 1835.

Virgil W. Akridge to Mariah M. Walker, 1 April 1834, executed 3 April 1834 by John Hendricks, minister.

Wm. Alexander to Penina Gann, 2 October 1834, executed 2 October 1834.

Reuben H. Adams to Martha Ann Matthews, 8 November 1854, executed 9 November 1854.

Walter A. Appling to Victoria A. Greer, 7 February 1853, executed 8 February 1853 by A. Church, D.D.

Emory F. Anderson to Susan M.F. Foster, 4 November 1853, executed 8 November 1853 by W. J. Cotter, minister.

William T. Adams to Susan E. Spps, 30 March 1853, executed 31 March 1853 by Bedford Langford, M.G.

William G. Allen to Jane Camelia Wigley, 1 May 1852, executed 2 May 1852.

Andrew J. Allen to Sarah Ann Lee, 20 March 1852, executed 25 March 1852 by Henry Crawford, minister.

John Q. Allison to Arminda E. Parker, 25 May 1852.

George A. Archer to Martha Luke, 22 December 1848, executed 24 December 1848.

Jessee W. Aaron to Catherine Taylor, 18 April 1848, executed 20 April 1848 by Sylvanus Landrum, minister.

William Akridge to Artealeer Overby, 26 November 1848.

Jas. H. Anderson to Pamelia J. Elder, 7 January 1847, executed 10 January 1847 by Jno. L. Oliver, minister.

William W. Anderson to Francis Thrasher, 14 September 1847, executed 15 September 1847 by M. H. Hubbard, minister.

William H. Allen to Anna C. Sledge, 30 June 1846, executed 1 July 1846 by A. Church, D.D.

William J. Archer to Charlotte Ann Weir, 4 May 1846, executed 7 May 1846 by Nathan Hoyt, D.D., minister.

James G. Adams to Martha A.E. Whitehead, 27 June 1846, executed before Jno. L. Oliver, minister, 28 June 1846.

John L. Amis to Lucy Smith, 24 November 1845, executed by Willis C. Norris, minister, Walton County, 24 November 1845.

David H. Alexander to Miss Margarett J. Fulton, 5 August 1845, executed 5 August 1845 by N. Hoyt, minister.

Snowden T. Anchon to Eleanor S. Patterson, 8 February 1845, executed by P. F. Burgess, minister, 9 February 1845.

Ransom Allen to Susan Moss, 27 June 1844, executed 30 June 1844.

Daniel Allen to Susan E. Hester, 21 November 1844, executed before J.N. Glenn, minister, 21 December 1844.

Pinckney Ayers to Elizabeth Gordon, 25 April 1844, executed 25 April 1844.

William H. Ashford to Louisa Booth, 19 December 1844, executed 19 December 1844 before J. N. Glenn, minister.

William W. Anderson to Anna Jane Whitaker, 10 January 1843, executed 10 January 1843.

William D. Appling to Miss Martha C. H. Boothe, 10 January 1842, executed 11 January 1842 before J. N. Glenn, minister.

Lewis G. Anderson to Susan Thrasher, 28 July 1842, executed 28 July 1842 by J. N. Glenn, minister.

William L. B. Akin to Sarah Ann O. Perry, 27 January 1841, executed 28 January 1841.

John Alexander to Emily Weire (Ware?), 25 October 1841, executed 25 October 1841.

Augustus Adams to Solita Ann Silvy, 13 February 1841, executed 18 February 1841.

William A. Appling to Elizabeth W. Billups, 17 August 1840, executed 17 August 1840 by Henry Safford, minister.

Jesse Ansley to Sidney Ann Wood, 19 October 1840, executed 20 October 1840.

William Barber to Rachel Daniel, 5 January 1810, executed the same day.

Ezekiel Bassett to Sarah Thomas, 3 October 1810, executed 4 October 1810.

Samuel Brown to Martha Mckigny, 23 June 1810, executed 24 June 1810 before John Hodge, V.S.M.

James N. Brown to Patsey McCoy, 23 December 1809, executed 26 December 1809.

Joseph Bridges to Salley Lovin, 31 March 1809, executed 2 April 1809 before M. J. Bankston.

John Black to Nancy Haing (?), 22 September 1809, executed 12 October 1809 by Elnathan Davis, minister.

John Bankston to Elizabeth Maho, 17 October 1809, executed October 26, 1809.

Thomas Banus (Baccus?) to Lucy Gilbert, 11 January 1809, executed 12 January 1809.

John Butler and Jenny Hurd, 24 October 1804, executed 28 October.

Charles Burger to Malinda Garner, 25 October 1808, executed 27 October 1808.

William Brodnex to Mary N. Gleeson, 29 April 1808, executed 29 April 1808.

Charles Broach to Poley Smith, 20 December 1810, executed the same day.

Christopher Bowen to Elizabeth McCay, 21 March 1808, executed 31 March 1808.

Lesley Bankston to Elizabeth Brewer, 13 August 1808, executed August 18, 1808.

Jacob Bankston to Nancy Brewer, 3 October 1808, executed 5 October 1808 before Jeremiah Burnitt, D.D.

James Black to Sally Dean, 11 September 1807, executed 24 September 1807.

Lewis Balden to Jency Taide, 26 April 1806, executed 27 April 1806.

James Briant to Rancy Hammock, 29 May 1806, executed 1 June 1806.

Jordan Bonner to Polly Adams, 2 October 1811, executed 3 October 1811.

Thomas Bolding (?) to Miley Dean, 18 October 1806, executed 18 October 1806.

James Blakley to Susanah Strong, on or after 18 December 1804.

William Beavers to Sucky Talbot, 5 October 1812, executed 15 October 1812.

Samuel Briant to Poley Barber, 30 October 1812, executed 1 November 1812.

Nathan B. Barnett to Salley Lumsden, 13 November 1810, executed the same day.

William Beasley to Charity Cook, 23 December 1813, executed 24 December 1813.

Lemuel Brown to Betsy Mitchell, 11 June 1813, executed 13 June 1813.

Alexander Baker to Sarah Wilson, 26 April 1814.

Simeon Bankston to Salley Brewer, 13 February 1815, executed 16 February 1815.

John Binnion to Polly Cook, 7 November 1815, executed the same day.

James Brewer to Sinthey Kilgore, 31 October 1805, executed 1 November 1815.

John Browning to Jinney Houze, 19 June 1815, executed 20 June 1815 by H. Hull.

Abner Baker to Cintha McKey, 17 September 1816, executed 19 September 1816.

Obed Baker to Isabella Wilson, 24 September 1816, executed 26 September 1816 before Isam Goss.

Greay Barber to Charlotte Stidman, 15 August 1816, executed 15 August 1816.

Josiah Bradley to Patsey Brooks, 12 December 1816, executed 12 December 1816 before Jacob Bankston.

Samuel Braswell to Frankey Thomas, 16 January 1816, executed 17 January 1816.

John W. Brewer to Jane Fann, 12 November 1816, executed 14 November 1816.

Thomas Booth to Patsey Hall, 15 December 1817, executed 17 December before West Harris, minister.

William Brand to Elizabeth Gill, 13 August 1817, executed 21 August 1817.

John Burks to Lewcy Hutson, 11 April 1817, executed 17 April 1817.

Robert R. Billups to Elizabeth W. Fullwood, executed 11 September 1818.

Benjamin H. Boothe to Lecy E. Harris, 24 September 1818, executed 24 September 1818 before West Harris, minister.

Bailey Bostick to Tabitha Wood, 8 December 1818, executed same day by Jno. Haygood, D.D.

Nathan Bransford to Sarah Powell, 2 November 1818, executed 3 November 1818.

George Braswell to Nancy Freeman, 10 February 1818, executed the same day.

Jacob Burgor to Rosse Garner, 29 January 1818, executed same day.

Allen Barber to Frances Crawford, 8 November 1819, executed 11 November 1819.

Christopher Bass to Lucy Marrable, 30 August 1819, executed 30 August 1819 by M. Waddel, D.D.

John F. Beavers to Nancy Hill, 1 June 1819, executed 2 June 1819.

William Bryant to Elizabeth Busbey, 10 September 1819, executed 12 September 1819.

John Burks to Martha Whitehead, 23 January 1819, executed 28 January 1819.

Frances Belcher to Jincey P. Connel, 5 December 1820, executed same day.

Nicholas H. Bacon to Sarah Mathews, 20 December 1820, executed same day.

Thomas Bell to Babby Bohannon, 22 August 1821, executed August 26, 1821.

Thomas J. Biggs to Martha Osburn, 3 October 1821, executed 4 October 1821 by West Harris, P.G.

James Brewer to Frances Moss, 16 May 1821, executed 17 May 1821.

William Burks to Sally Green, 23 July 1821, executed 2 August 1821.

Charles Beal to Harrett Holmes, 16 February 1822, executed 17 February 1822 by Isam Goss, minister.

Chapman Beasley to Elizabeth Thacker, 13 August 1822, executed same day.

John Brewer to Cintha Barber, 27 April 1822. executed 7 May 1822.

Asbury Burks to Rutha M. Whitehead, 18 June 1822, executed 20 June 1822.

James Busby to Rebecca Thacker, 5 August 1823, executed 7 August 1823.

George Bell (Ball?) to Elizabeth Ball, 4 February 1823, executed 4 February 1823.

Jonathan Burges to Martha Haile, 27 October 1823, executed 30 October 1823.

Noah Burroughs to Lucenda Gann, 5 March 1823, executed 6 March 1823.

Henry Burt to Sarah Hearndon, 11 March 1823, executed 13 March 1823.

James M. Burton to Martha Gilbert, 22 July 1824, executed 24 July 1824 before Wm. B. Barnett, minister.

Henry Bishop to Rebecca Hamilton, 30 August 1825, executed evening of 30 August 1825.

Zadock Bonner to Lucy Jackson, 22 December 1825, executed 28 December 1825.

Henry Boyers to Sally Collier, 26 October 1825, executed the same day.

William Britton to Mary Harris, 20 July 1825, executed 20 July 1825 by Miller Bledsoe, minister.

Richard E. Burke to Mary R. Elliott, 27 January 1825, executed same day.

David H. Barnes to Miley Bateman, 21 February 1826, executed 23 February 1826.

William Bradberry to Catherine Ball, 25 April 1826, executed 25 April 1826.

Peter Bradshwa to Mary Lee, 27 July 1826, executed the same day.

Wm. Braswell to Nancy Joiles, 4 December 1826, executed 5 December 1826 before John A. Hurst, minister.

Josiah Barrat to Mary Raines, 2 March 1827, executed 4 March 1827.

Benjamin Bowles to Mary Moore, 8 January 1827, executed 9 January 1827.

Nathan Beggers to Mary Cooper, 3 November 1828, executed 3 November 1828.

William J. Biggs to Lodusky Jones, 17 April 1828, executed the same day.

Eli Bradberry to Louisa Wise, 1 January 1828. executed 3 January 1828.

Lewis Bryan to Fortine Hinton, 4 December 1828, executed 9 December 1828 before Tho. J. McGaughey, minister.

John P. Ball to Nancy C. Martin, 30 December 1829, executed December 31, 1829.

Littleberry Burnett to Elizabeth Daniell, 23 May 1829, executed 28 May 1829.

Richard Barber to Martha Hopkins, 22 December 1830, executed 23 December 1830.

Seaborn Booles (Boales?) to Susan M. McRee, 23 January 1831, executed 23 January 1831.

Alexander W. Brown to Ann Silvey, 16 December 1831, executed 18 December 1831.

James M. Beasley to Margarett Gibson, 4 December 1832, executed 6 December 1832.

Thomas Bell to Sarah Ann Lloyd, 9 August 1832, executed same day.

John Brooks to Sarah T. Baldwin, 12 April 1832, executed 15 April 1832.

Archibald Brydie to Jane Johnson Hancock, 29 February 1832, executed 1 March 1832 by Nathan Hoyt, minister.

George W. Borum to Mary Gardner, 26 January 1833, executed 31 January 1833.

John McD. Borders to Emaline L. Jones, 16 December 1833, executed 17 December 1833 before James Shannon, pastor of the Baptist Church, Athens, GA.

Jeptha Browning to Sarah G. Houze, 4 December 1833, executed 8 December 1833.

Edmund Bryant to Sarah Wilkerson, 7 December 1833, executed same day.

Elijah Bradshaw to Q. Anne Kines, 26 November 1833, executed 27 November 1833.

Jonathan Burgess to Elizabeth Haile, 29 November 1834, executed 4 December 1834.

Daniel Brown to Tabitha Cothram, 15 October 1837, executed 15 October 1837.

Ruben K. Brown to Miss Jane E. Milton, 21 October 1837, executed 23 October, before Jeremiah Norman, M.M.E.C.

Hardy Bryant to Miss Levina Higgdon, 18 June 1837, executed 18 June 1837.

David Beasley to Susan Burger, 27 May 1837, executed 30 May 1837.

Willis J. Biggs to Eliza Osborn, 23 January 1837, executed 26 January 1837.

James M. Bevers to Elizabeth Gill, 26 April 1836, executed 26 April 1836.

John T. Baker to Francis E. Dobbins, 17 March 1836, executed the same day by Nathan Hoyt, minister.

Allen Bates to Maholey Hadley, 23 May 1836, executed same day.

Robert Beasley to Elizabeth Weaver, 24 December 1835, executed 27 December 1835.

Exekiel Boggs to Eliza A. Nichols, 1 April 1835, executed 2 April 1835.

Richard Boggs to Caroline L. Nichols, 10 January 1835, executed 13 January 1835.

James Boggs to Leanah Tolbert, 17 August 1835, executed 18 August 1835.

Alexander Rowling (Bowling?) to Nancy Bryant, 24 April 1834, executed 27 May 1834.

John C. Bailey to Matilda F. Spurlock, 18 November 1834, executed 20 November 1834 before J. N. Glenn, minister.

F. R. Bowen to Alsey L. Glaze, 30 April 1834, executed 30 April 1834.

Seaborn Burger to Lucenda Maxey, 28 October 1834, executed 21 January 1834.

Wm. P. Brewer to Sarah Coussons, 11 January 1834, executed 12 Janaury 1834.

Jesse Butler to Nancy Maxey, 16 January 1834, executed 19 January 1834.

Frances A. Bell to Olly Jackson, 25 August 1834, executed 28 August 1834 before James Cook, L.D.

Joseph Braswell to Sarah Hardigree, 20 December 1855, executed 20 December 1855 before James P. Holloway, minister.

George H. Blair to Elizabeth Kirkley, 9 February 1855, executed 18 February 1855.

William Blackman to Sarah Starnes, 30 January 1855, executed 1 February 1855.

Edward P. Bishop to Miss Martha M. Bingham, 10 December 1855, executed 13 December 1855 by Nathan Hoyt, minister.

Henry Beusse to Miss Menecies Evans, 5 November 1856, executed 6 November 1856 before A. M. Wynn, minister.

William G. Bentley to Mary F. A. Brightwell, 20 October 1855, executed 25 October 1855.

Joseph S. Bell to Nancy E. Kenney, 26 November 1855, executed 27 November 1855.

James L. Bailey to Mary Ann S. Reynolds, 9 February 1855, executed 18 February 1855.

John W. Bearden to Miss Eliza A. Turnell, 4 February 1854, executed 7 February 1854.

John M. Bradberry to Sarah A. Daniell, 21 October 1854, executed 22 October 1854 by George W. Malcomb, minister.

John James Branch to Virginia Croswell, 5 October 1854, executed the same day before J. J. Wallace, minister.

William Bradberry to Martha J. Butler, 27 December 1854, executed 28 December 1854.

James A. Bentley to Louisa Patman, 1 May 1854, executed 2 May 1854 before James M. Gunter, minister.

Jasper Newton Bone to Miss Ann Wadley, 20 December 1852, executed 6 January 1853.

Benjamin H. Blackburn to Miss Martha J. Talbert, 9 September 1853, executed 10 September 1853.

John W. Baker to Miss Nancy T. Beardin, 7 December 1853, executed before Henry Crawford, minister of M.E. Church, 8 December 1853.

James Ellis Beasley Jr. to Elender Hill, 9 October 1853, executed 23 October 1853.

Jonathan B. Burgess to Eliza H. Elder, 5 December 1853, executed 8 December 1853 before James P. Holloway, minister.

Henry Brown to Polley Minerva Kelley, 5 August 1853, executed 7 August 1853.

Charles L. Bolton to Miss Mary Stroud, 17 November 1853, executed 17 November 1853 by Charles M. Irwin, minister.

N. D. (L.?) Barnard to Miss Francis Dougherty, 30 September 1853, executed

5 October 1853 before A. Church (?), D.D.

William Blackman to Miss Emily Mobley, 9 December 1852, executed 9 December 1852 by Alfred T. Mann, minister.

Dillard H. Brown to Miss Penelope Rhodes, 21 July 1852, executed 22 July 1852 before Benjamin Thornton, minister.

Christopher C. Bradberry to Marietta Crow, 14 December 1852, executed 14 December 1852 before Bedford Langford, minister.

Thomas Y. Booth to Miss Delila Wood, 15 December 1852, executed 19 December 1852.

Mercer Bradshaw to Mrs. (?) Sarah Gordon, 15 December 1852, executed 16 December 1852.

John H. M. Barton to Miss Eliza A. Klutts, 14 December 1852, executed 15 December 1852.

John C. Bone to Miss Nancy Hamilton, 25 December 1852, executed 26 December 1852.

Samuel Baldwin to Frances D. Burk, 13 September 1852, executed 14 September 1852 before A. Church, D.D.

James B. Burpee to Mary Rumney, 7 January 1851, executed 10 January 1851 by Thompson L. Smith, minister.

R. J. Butler to H. H. Parsons, 17 September 1850, executed same day by Nathan Hoyt, minister.

Francis M. Beardin to Lucy W. Harris, 27 January 1850.

James B. Burger to Delilah Phillips, 12 February 1850.

Robert Booth to Susan Caroline Gray, 30 May 1850.

Peter Bradshaw to Mrs. Ann House, 14 November 1850.

David Buchannon to Susannah Loving, 22 September 1850.

James Brewer to Frances East, 3 November 1850.

Walton H. Booth to Nancy A. Crow, 13 December 1849.

Charles J. Buchanon to Elizabeth White, 25 March 1849.

Thomas Boyd to Martha J. Corsly, 2 August 1849.

Samuel Linsy to Miss Susan Ann Tuck, 22 February 1849.

Sandors Bone to Miss Martha Benton, 20 February 1849.

Lloyd Benton to Mary Lester, 16 November 1848.

Francis J. Brown to Elizabeth Antonett Pressley, 6 December 1848.

John W. Burke to Caroline A. White, 14 September 1848.

David E. Blakely to Sarah White, 5 December 1847.

Joel Abbott Billips to Susan Harris, 4 November 1847.

Jacob Burger to Miss Martha Wood, 30 December 1847.

John M. Bonnell to Mary Ann Morton, 31 January 1847.

Edward S. Billups to Martha C. Richardson, 6 October 1846.

John M. Billips to Miss Sarah M. Phinizy, 5 February 1846.

George Brown to Sarah Williams, 13 August 1846.

James S. Benton to Miss Narcisa Williams, 22 February 1846.

William Mc. Burt to Sarah Ann Ward, 17 May 1846.

Joseph Burger to Nancy Read, 17 December 1846.

James M. Bearden to Nancy M. Towns, 3 November 1846.

John Barber to Miss Martha E. Weir, 15 October 1846.

Marien Blackburn to Miss Eliza Benton, 5 July 1846.

William Bell to Callander Brightwell, 8 January 1846.

Michael Barnett to Elen P. Williams, 11 February 1846.

Andrew Baxter to Martha Williams, 28 January 1846.
William T. Bailey to Miss Elizabeth P. Winstead, 13 April 1846.
William B. Benit to Eliza J. Brown, 25 December 1845.
Daniel Brown to Gillis Stephens, 8 May 1845.
John M. Brown to Dorcas Farrar, 14 September 1845.
William Britt to Elizabeth Davis, 22 October 1845.
Isham J. Brown to Sophenia A. Mobley, 10 August 1845.
Asa Browning to Mirna Brown, 5 March 1844.
James A. Bell (Beall) to Lucy J. Treadwell, 27 June 1844.
William Buchanan to Frances Crawford, 6 June 1844.
S. D. Bridgeman to Miss Priscilla Ware (Wier), 3 January 1844.
John Beasley to Margaret Brown, 31 December 1843.
Newman Burger to Henrietta Buchannan, 21 December 1843.
Charles Jasper Burger to Sarah Yearnest, 17 May 1843.
Milton A. Battle to Eliza V. Stroud, 2 May 1843.
Silas M. Bradshaw to Scidney Davis, 23 October 1842.
Bedford Burnett to Mary Jeffries, 14 July 1842.
Stephen Bradshaw to Rachael Summers, 22 December 1842.
William T. Baldwin to Susan M. Harris, 3 March 1841.
Andrew J. Brightwell to Almira Preston, 20 January 1841.
Nathan C. Barnett to M. A. Cooper, 15 April 1841.
William Bennett to Mary Hamilton, 11 March 1841.
William B. Bolton to Sarah Ann Jennings, 2 December 1841.
Adison B. Brown to Anne Elder, 9 December 1840.
Samuel Bailey to Alethia A. Lyman, 2 February 1840.
John F. Biggers to Laticia Yearby, 3 December 1840.
William B. Brightwell to Elizabeth Clotelda Bell, 15 October 1839.
Josiah A. Browning to Nancy Cook, 28 November 1839.
Patrick Barry to Charlotte McDerment, 26 September 1839.
Moses Brown to Esther Smith, 28 July 1839.
Samuel Bowman to Eliza Costler, 4 July 1839.
William Burger to Eliza Garner, 23 May 1839.
James Barber to Mahala Stephens, 16 January 1838.
Greensby W. Barber to Frances Barber, 7 January 1838.
Watkins Raymon to Jane E. Bryan, 7 November 1838.
Newman Burgher to Margaret Beasley, 18 December 1838.
James Franklin Bowden to Miss Emily A. Shankle, 4 October 1855.
James Cuningham to Lucy Holmes, 4 July 1809.
Thomas Conners (Couzens?) to Patsy Tye, 19 December 1809.
Robert J. Cabell to Ann R. Billups, 20 July 1809.
Martin Crow to Rachel Parker, 24 November 1808.
Boling Cox to Rebekah Carvness, 19 April 1808.
William Collins to Betsy Caldwell, 25 December 1808.
Henry Cannon to Polley Martin, 24 February 1808 (?).
Jhhn Clement to Patience Hendon, 11 June 1806.
Amos Crow to Elizabeth Stephens, 6 September 1807.
William Curtis to Nancy Jones, 31 January 1807.

George Cagle to Izable Ray, 30 December 1810.
Jack F. Cock to Salley Strong, 27 August 1807.
Edward Cary to Lucinda Clayton, 15 September 1811.
George Clifton to Milley Brown, 23 February 1807.
Isham Cagle to Milindy Rea, 12 January 1812.
Aaron Crow to Nancy Walden, 29 October 1812.
John Cagle to Barbary Cagle, 24 December 1813.
Wiley Carter to Polly Powell, 16 December 1813.
Edward Conner to Miss Rebecca Cook, 12 April 1813.
Joseph Cotton to Mary Greenwood, 30 March 1813.
Edward Craft to Whinney Tankersley, 17 March 1813.
Robert Conner to Nancy Selerets (Stewart?), 2 October 1806.
Wm. Clement to Patsy Stidman, 23 January 1805.
John J. Cox to Betsy Herring, 12 July 1814.
Jeremiah Culberson to Patsey Mcalphin, 26 December 1804.
John Cockrill to Salley Norton, 26 October 1816.
Richard Cole to Sarah Freeman, 29 November 1815.
Absaton Clark to Rebecca Wetton (Wilton?), 18 December 1816.
William Cole Junr. to Mary Freeman, 26 December 1816.
David Christopher to Lucy Jones, 7 January 1818.
James Clandining to Rebecca Turner, 29 May 1818.
Aaron Clifton to Jane Nutt, 25 July 1819.
James Croxton to Sarah Buship, 31 August 1819.
Purnal Cook to Nancy McCoy, 21 September 1820.
Daniel Craft Jr. to Sarah Tankersley, 27 January 1820.
Russell Crawford to Maria Holder, 9 November 1820.
Zachariah Cagle to Polly Jackson, 23 December 1821.
George H. Connally to Jane Marable, 24 January 1822.
Silas Crawford to Frances Stewart, 30 May 1822.
Edwin Cox to Sally Hardegree, 9 September 1824.
Abel Crow to Henrietta Mash, 8 January 1824.
Jacob Crow to Mary Burnett, 6 January 1824.
Michael N. Clark to Millissi Hinton, 17 March 1825.
James Calahan to Frances Jiles, 19 December 1826.
Isaac Clark to Tabitha C. Thrasher, 12 October 1826.
Cuthbert S. Collier to Mary H. Collier, 27 July 1826.
Bryan Connally to Serena Hunt, 5 October 1826.
Blake Cooper to Elizabeth Scogin, 2 November 1826.
Robert Camron to Penina Hinton, 15 March 1827.
Clement Clifton to Nancy Jackson, 7 June 1827.
Robert Camron to Pheriba Hinton, 18 May 1828.
Thomas Conner to Martha Ann Cogburn, 22 January 1828.
Willis Cooper to Biddy Hales, 17 February 1828.
John Cobb to Sally Strong, 23 August 1829.
John Clifton to Elizabeth McClure, 26 January 1830.
Peyton H. Colbert to Caroline Mathews, 25 August 1830.
James Conner to Illender Pitts, 7 January 1830.

Robert Craft to Elizabeth Fostin, 27 November 1830.
John Crawford to Sarah E. Bass, 27 July 1830.
Thomas Campbell to Arquilla Ware, 25 December 1831.
Wm. M. Cawley to Elizabeth Simms, 20 January 1831.
Ellington Credille to Catherine Davenport, 4 January 1831.
Eli Crow to Anna McLeroy, 7 December 1831.
Thomas M. H. Cummin to Charlotte Partain, 11 September 1831.
Hiram Clifton to Sarah McCune, 18 November 1832.
Neal F. Cochran to Martha A. Nunnally, 28 September 1832.
Joel T. Crawford to Sarah Ann Watson, 27 December 1832.
John Clark to Eliza J. Tenney (Turner?), 17 December 1833.
David C. Crawford to Catherine Watson, 20 August 1833.
Jesse Chadwick to Mary Ann Whitehead, 30 December 1833.
Joseph B. Cobb to Almira D. Clayton, 5 October 1837.
Patrick McCann to Celia Chester, 7 November 1837.
David H. Culberson to Martha Jane Young, 28 December 1837.
Appleton Chisolm to Mary Ann Glasson, 31 August 1837.
James Carmichael to Elizabeth Smith, 4 June 1837.
Marlin T. Crow to Sarah M. Browning, 22 August 1837.
Leonard E. Case to Martha Greer, 15 April 1836.
Deane W. Chase to Alcy Johnson, 30 July 1836.
Levi H. Carter Jr. to Gabrielle Ward, 22 December 1836.
Josiah A. Clark to Miss Mary D. Cheatham, 8 December 1836.
Thomas Cooper to Mary Taylor, 16 September 1836.
David Carr to Nancy Sims, 6 January 1835.
Thomas Conner to Lucenda Thomas, 8 December 1835.
Samuel Chancey to Miss Priscilla Whitfield, 20 December 1835.
Howell Cobb to Mary Ann Lamar, 26 May 1835.
Hugh H. Cox to Mary M. Moreland, 8 October 1835.
Asa Simmons to Martha H. Scoggin, 27 December 1835.
Bowlin Conner to Lucinda Hodges, 30 September 1834.
Walter Carson to Rebecca N. Martin, 21 August 1834.
Calvin J. Crow to Miss Sarah Ann Reynolds, 4 March 1855.
John T. Crosby to Miss Elizabeth Dennis, 12 August 1855.
Winston O. Cooper to Pamelia F. Jones, 28 December 1855.
Charles P. Cooper to Miss Hessie M. Jackson, 2 April 1855.
Nathan Cook to Sarah Snellings, 29 March 1855.
David Conner to Miss Peninnah J.L. Carter, 14 December 1855.
Edward L. Close to Margarett H. Carter (Center?), 27 December 1855.
Benjamin F. Carter to Miss Mary Ann Hail, 9 December 1855.
N. P. Carreker to Miss M. E. Newton, 30 October 1855.
Hendley V. Callaway to Sarah H. Pope, 7 March 1854.
John L. Collier to Frances R. Simonton, 26 January 1854.
George Washington Couch to Obedience Cooper, 9 February 1854.
Aaron Crow to Miss Sarena F. Parker, 26 January 1854.
William Creighton to Miss Sarah Bone, 30 April 1854.
Thomas L. Clown to Mary A. Shackelford, 27 May 1854.

Gideon P. Close to Miss Georgia A. Morgan, 29 December 1853.

Benjamin Wofford Couch to Elizabeth Cooper, 25 January 1852.

James B. Couch to Nancy Garrison, 9 May 1852.

Ephraim B. Clayton to Damarius E. Putman, 8 January 1852.

William Crow to Louiza E. Griffin, 5 September 1852.

Abijah Congo (Conger? Couger?) to Miss Elizabeth D. Rounsevall, 23 December 1852.

Jackson Chapplin to Mary Leason, 7 March 1852.

John Z. Cooper to Eliza Ann Laticia Jackson, 18 December 1851.

Thomas Cooper to Matilda Griffith, 6 November 1851.

John E. Craft to Susannah Johnson, 28 September 1851.

Stephen C. Cartledge to Mary F. Garthright, 30 September 1851.

Anderson F. Crawford to Elizabeth Aiken, 14 November 1850.

Francis M. Carson to Sarah Ann Wood, 4 April 1850.

Jacob N. Cox to Nancy Jackson, 25 October 1849. (Jacob is also called Joel N. Cox elsewhere on the document.)

Jeremiah A. Cross to Mary Harper, 9 December 1849.

Thomas Collier to Elizabeth Burnett, 19 August 1849.

Orren J. Cotton to Martha Ann Stewart, 22 January 1849.

Henry A. Curry to Mary Eppse, 6 April 1848.

Paul M. Center to Lantha L. Pridgeon, 25 July 1848.

Hughey A. Carthers to Mary A. Griffith, 16 November 1848.

John Colley to Miss Martha E. Willson, 4 March 1847.

Joseph Costler to Miss Arnminta Haggard, 4 November 1847.

James Crow to Frances Mary Ann Allen, 1 February 1846.

Daniel Conner to Nancy Buchannon, 6 April 1845.

Francis A. Clark to Sultana Smith, 23 September 1845.

Michael J. Claney to Mary Ann Jones, 18 November 1845.

Bannister Cockram to Caroline E. Cogburn, 21 October 1845.

David Conner to Frances E. Adams, 6 January 1845.

William Center to Mary Lee, 2 May 1844.

John Cousens to Sarah A. A. Trammell, 21 November 1844.

Benjamin G. Connell to Nancy Beasley, 11 February 1844.

Felix L. Clotfetter to Nancy Jackson, 16 January 1844.

Stephen Crow to Elizabeth Allen, 4 December 1844.

George A. Croom to Julia M. Church, 21 February 1843.

Calvin H. Chauncey to Elizabeth Gee, 23 March 1843.

Lewis S. Craig to Miss Elizabeth Church, 8 June 1843.

Hugh H. Cox to Cynthia Glower, 1 December 1842.

Richard Chauncey to Sarah Fenn, 10 December 1842.

Richard Charmichael to Elizabeth Spinks, 6 April 1842.

John R. Caruthers to Elizabeth Griffith, 6 September 1842.

Benjamin Conley to Sarah H. Semmes, 7 June 1842.

Timothy Conner to Mary Elizabeth Stephens, 6 September 1840.

John W. Cook to Emily Greer, 7 February 1839.

William Copher to Anna Cavin, 25 August 1839.

William M. Cook to Frances A. Jennings, 31 October 1839.

Joseph Dunaway to Cathren McAllough, 16 February 1809.

George A. Dilworth to Cathrin A. Jones, 8 December 1808.
William Dobben to Nancy Stanly, 7 February 1809.
James Daniel to Sariah Mixson, 21 January 1808.
David Day to Mary Johnston, 22 October 1807.
Danby (?) Brown to Asa Garratt, 3 September 1807.
John M. Dobbins to Sena Sawyers, 10 November 1807.
David Darnel to Jean Lard, 5 November 1807.
Thomas Daniel to Patsey Smith, 12 November 1807.
John Durham to Metildah Reynolds, 20 October 1810 (1810?).
Stephen Dukes to Suckey Keener, 3 October 1810.
Edmond Duke to Clocy Fannen, 24 July 1806.
Josiah Daniel to Sally Burrow, 19 July 1811.
Thomas Duken to Elizabeth Ramsey, July 24, 1806.
Thos. Deeakes (Dukes?) to Temperance Bridges, June 1, 1804.
Seprenus Dolittle to Mary Glossen, 23 September 1812.
Moses W. Dobbins to Edith Smith. 22 December 1812.
Nimrod Dickens to Nancy Roberts, 26 July 1813.
William Dickens to Nancy P. Earnest, 15 March 1814.
William H. Dismukes to Mary Cook, 19 January 1815.
William Doggett to Nancy Addams, 7 December 1815.
Jeremiah M. Daniel (McDaniel?) to Nancy Burnett, 22 January 1817.
James Dickerson to Aryann (?) Adams, 27 August 1818.
John Dickinson to Frances Thompson, 26 July 1818.
John Dean to Mary Scott, 15 July 1819.
Boswell B. Degrafenried to Sarah King, 17 August 1819.
Beaton Daniel to Martha Hodges, 12 April 1821.
Abraham Doolittle to Mary Glasson, 22 December 1822.
John P. Dickinson to Eliza Legg, September 1, 1822.
Charles Dougherty to Elizabeth T. Moore, 7 December 1823.
William W. Downs to Henaretta Sparks, 10 August 1823.
Thomas Doggett to Elizabeth Creal, 22 April 1824.
William J. Davis to Mary Wells, 8 December 1825.
James Delay to Peggy Duncan, 23 December 1825.
Obed Dyer to Elizabeth Brown, 31 August 1825.
Andrew Danielly to Elizabeth Cook. 7 September 1826.
William A. Davis to Tabitha Kelley, 26 January 1826.
Daniel Deupree to Francina B. Cox, 28 February 1826.
Thomas Doggett to Rutha McCallum, 4 January 1827.
Joseph Durham to Loancy Huff, 8 December 1827.
Moses N. Davenport to Mary E. Fullilove, 17 December 1828.
Nathaniel Daniel to Mary Parker, 29 December 1829.
Chatten Doggett to Matilda W. Campbell, 8 July 1830.
Edington Duke to Johannah House, 15 August 1830.
William Daniel to Julia Burnett, 26 July 1831.
Milledge S. Durham to Elizabeth T. Sorrell, 28 December 1831.
William R. Daniell to Clementiney Hamilton, 11 October 1832.
Thomas B. Davenport to Susan M. Clark, 29 November 1832.

Robert Dougherty to Susan Watkins, 3 January 1833.
Robert Davenport to Miss Martha Hester, 13 June 1833.
Lorenzo D. Duncan to Virginia C. Paschal, 10 October 1836.
George Dent to Miss Frances E. Thomas, 2 June 1836.
Minos D. (S.?) Doolittle to Elizabeth Statehaur, 19 September 1836.
Robert Daniel to Naomi Burnett, 11 August 1836.
James Davis to Holly Moore, 29 October 1835.
Shadrack Doggett to Jane Vickers, 10 September 1834.
John Dean to Tabitha Morton, 7 January 1834.
Leonard T. Doyal to Matilda Thompson, 16 January 1834.
Henry Dukes to Mary Mathews, 17 December 1834.
Callvill Dial to Miss Catherine Canady, 15 March 1855.
James M. Dennis to Frances Blackman, 14 October 1855.
Thomas M. Dean to Miss Susan Y. Swift, 28 November 1853.
Green Doughtry to Elizabeth Moone, 9 March 1854.
Shadrack Doggett to Mary Curry, 29 November 1854.
Geo. W. Dosster to Miss Sarah Waggoner, 7 December 1854.
Charles W. Deming to Anna R. Hale, 14 June 1854.
Robert E. Davenport to Miss Mary A. Royal, 15 May 1854.
LaFayette Dautrey to Sarah Evans, 17 March 1853.
James H. Dunnahan to Talitha A. Elder, 10 October 1852.
William H. Dicken to Sarah Ann Osburn, 23 October 1851.
James Defoor to Malinda Willingham, 2 October 1851.
Jeremiah M. Daniell to Sarah Ann Wise, 16 May 1850.
Argyle Troublesome Dunaway to Elizabeth Mullin, 3 February 1850.
Irvin Dickson to Eliza Kinney, 3 March 1850.
William Davis to Rachel Whitehead, 7 July 1850.
Henry T. Dickinson to Theodosia M. Floyd, 22 October 1850.
Henderson Davis to Julia E. Salter, 20 December 1849.
Edward W. Dillashaw to Sarah L.S. Aken, 19 July 1849.
John M. Devenport to Martha J. Freeman, 27 December 1849.
Jason M. Delay to Francis Gober, 14 November 1849.
Lewis J. Dupree to Martha J. Adams, 9 December 1849.
Alonzo Lawrence Doolittle to Nancy Annis Langford, 26 April 1849.
Lindsey Durham Jr. to Littleton J. Richardson, 11 January 1848.
James Dautry to Susan B. Stone, 9 September 1847.
Hiram R. Delany to Mary Duncan, 13 January 1847.
George Davis to Eliza Whitton, 17 June 1847.
William B. Daniell to Henrietta V. Jennings, 10 July 1845.
William W. Durham to Sarah Lowe, 14 January 1845.
Josiah Daniells Jr. to Elizabeth S. Lester, 16 January 1845.
Richard B. Dicken to Mahalz Klutts, 11 November 1845.
William T. Dennis to Anne R. Neisler, 7 March 1844.
Albin P. Dearing to Miss Eugenia E. Hamilton, 21 November 1844.
Nathaniel Daniel to Eliza Ann Harper, 17 November 1844.
Wilson L. Davenport to Mary Brightwell, 9 May 1844.
Jesse Davenport to Sarah Hail, 29 June 1843.

Fielding Dillard to Frances A. Chaffin, 18 March 1841.
F. J. Drummon to Mary G. Epps, 30 November 1841.
James Dillon to Tereza Burges, 6 January 1841.
Laban Patrick Delay to Eliza Gray Martin, 5 August 1840.
Mathew G. Dicken to Elisabeth C. Klutts, 31 August 1840.
Elijah M. Dearing to Martha Ann Lawrence, 10 December 1840.
James W. Darbey to Lucinda Hamilton, 15 March 1840.
Josiah Daniell to Elizabeth Jeffriess, 4 April 1839.
Thomas Davenport to Elizabeth Smith, 3 January 1839.
Wilburn T. Dickerson to Eliza B. Sheats, 17 October 1839.
Mark Dogett to Phetney Nalls, 14 October 1810.
William Edwards to Caty Cole, 6 October 1808.
Samuel Echols to Elizabeth Wood, 5 June 1808.
Buckner Easley to Polley Merideth, 22 April 1808.
William East to Rachel Castleberry, 25 September 1806.
Edmonds Elder to Nancy Tigner, 23 September 1810.
Jeremiah Early to Ann Billups, 22 August 1811.
David Elder to Elizabeth Allen, 23 April 1813.
Joshua Elder to Anne Gray, 11 October 1812.
Sterling Elder to Polley Hening (Herring?), 7 May 1812.
Joseph Ewing to Elizabeth Newton, 15 September 1812.
John M. Edwards to Sucky Harris, 25 December 1811.
Robert M. Echols to Polly Melton, 8 February 1816.
Leander A. Erwin to Elizabeth B. Marrable, 5 September 1816.
Hartwell Elder to Permelia Tignor, 21 December 1817.
Howell Elder to Rebecca P. Herring, 16 October 1817.
Elisha Evans to Pressey Williams, 22 January 1818.
James S. Elkin (?) to Francis M. Edwards, 28 December 1819.
Thomas Epps to Pricilla Hodges, 3 February 1819.
Green Evans to Polley Edmundson, 30 December 1819.
Stokely Evans to Lucinda Hightower, 25 March 1819.
Isaac H. Elliss (?) to Jincy Croxton, 15 February 1820.
Martin East to Sarah Parker, 19 April 1821.
Thomas Echols to Polly Harper, 6 February 1821.
Peter Edmunds to Mahala Hudson, 25 September 1821.
Francis Eberhart to Kiddy Norris, 22 August 1822.
Jeremiah Elder to Elvirah Herring, 25 November 1822.
Robert Earnest to Salley Busby, 10 December 1823.
Joseph Elder to Sarah Ausbern, 13 February 1823.
Joseph Elder to Sally Jacks, 16 April 1823.
Wetch Elder to Mary Burt, 12 October 1823.
David Elder to Elizabeth Orsburn, 21 December 1824.
Silas East to Harrett Houze, 3 July 1825.
William S. Echols to Katherine Holder, 18 October 1825.
Edwin Edwards to Sarah Ball, 29 December 1825.
Joseph Elder to Nancy Blakeley, 24 August 1825.
Daniel Elder to Lucy Wood, 31 December 1828.

William Eppes to Sarah Alexander, 23 January 1826.

Obediah Echols to Hannah Holder, 30 January 1827.

William Epps to Elizabeth Connally, 7 February 1827.

William Evans to Ann Reid, 13 January 1829.

James Espy to Margarett Spence, 28 May 1833.

Leander N. Ewing to Jenette Welch, 18 October 1836.

Nathaniel Epps to Mrs. Elizabeth Carter, 9 December 1835.

Lewis H. Edwards to Mildred Ann Lane, 8 February 1835.

Phillip T. Elder to Telitha Bassett, 12 March 1835.

James W. Espey to Ann F. Prince, 13 February 1834.

John Eidson to Pamelia Jennings, 7 August 1834.

John D. Edwards to Louisa M. Houghton, 2 December 1834.

William E. Eppes to Miss Emily Bancraft, 28 July 1834.

James V. Evans to Mary S. Wagoner, 21 December 1854.

Greene A. Evans to Catherine Crawford, 17 December 1854.

Franklin Glen Eblen to Mary June Thompson, 22 June 1853.

David B. Elder to Martha E. McRee, 21 April 1853.

Thomas N. Epps to Cecilia P. Jennings, 31 March 1853.

Joseph Epps to Miss Nancy Adams, 23 June 1853.

James H. Edler to Elizabeth C. Durham, 8 January 1852.

Joshua P. Elder to Manerva Bassett, 4 March 1852.

John O. Edwards to Cornelia E. E. Jones (given as Elizabeth Jones elsewhere on the document), 29 July 1852.

Daniel A. England to Miss Nancy C. Riden, 10 January 1851.

William N. Evans to Selina Ann Williams, 26 January 1851.

Thomas N. Epps to Penelope S. Crittenden, 30 December 1850.

James H. Eidson to Sirena Daniell, 25 October 1849.

Franklin Epps to Winney Smith, 10 November 1848.

John L. Elder to Lucy A. Davis, 19 October 1848.

John Elder to Elizabeth Hester, 5 October 1848.

Pleasant Ellington to Rachel Timms, 18 January 1847.

Thomas G. Elder to Eliza A. Hail (Hale), 12 December 1847.

Nathan T. Elder to Lucy G. Brown, 15 December 1847.

Giles B. Eidson to Elizabeth Ann Daniell, 4 June 1847.

John E. England to Miss Sophia A. Wells, 24 February 1846.

Edmonds G. Elder to Susan Huey, 4 February 1846.

Wiley G. Evans to D. A. Jones, 23 September 1846.

Wych M. Elder to Nancy Hardegree, 25 November 1845.

Alvan B. Ewing to Miss Louisa Newton, 7 May 1845.

John Epps to Catherine Buckhannon, 7 October 1845.

Richard J. Evans to Elizabeth Summers, 8 February 1844.

William Epps to Dolly Lee, 27 December 1844.

William Evans to Mariah Stewart, 5 October 1843.

Jasper N. Edwards to Permilia A. Watkins, 3 February 1842.

William Y. Elder to Emily C. Thurmond, 19 October 1841.

David R. Elder to Minerva C. Clark, 23 September 1840.

Joshua Epps to Mary Bent, 27 September 1840.

Henry Easterling to Martha Greene, 10 December 1838.
William Fench (Finch? French?) to Lidda Davis, 24 November 1809.
John Finch to Elizabeth Easley, 8 February 1809.
William Fears to Nancy Thrasher, August 8, 1809.
Gadiel Fambrough to Nancy Elder, 2 February 1809.
Jesse Fann to Nancy Bagget, 18 December 1806.
Anderson Fambro to Elizabeth Hester, 12 December 1810.
Jesse Freeman to Catherine Jackson, 21 August 1812.
Henry Funderburg to Patsey Conner (Comer?), 26 January 1813.
Henry Funderburgh to Debby Wilson, 28 December 1814.
John Faulkner to Charlott Jones, 6 February 1806.
Joseph Few to Polly Fielder, 25 July 1804.
John Freeman to Susannah Baker, 13 April 1815.
William Freeman to Martha Cole, 30 November 1815.
Wm. H. Flournoy to Eliza Kello Brown, 20 September 1816.
Thomas M. Fagg to Elizabeth M. Echols, 23 October 1817.
William L. Famborough to Innicence Tigner, 21 July 1817.
John Flint to Hennaritta Hatchett, 27 October 1817.
William Flippen to Elizabeth Morton, 28 December 1817.
William Finch to Tellethy Bearden, 16 December 1819.
Johnson Freeman to Easther Traywick, 4 June 1819.
Labun T. Freeman to Elenor T. Brown, 28 December 1819.
Joshua Fambrough to Polly Jacks, 31 January 1820.
Minter Fouler to Mary Nixon, 20 January 1820.
Freeman Fuller to Susannah Daniel, 16 July 1820.
Gilbert Fry to Anne Cagle, 14 January 1821.
Bluford Fuller to Rebecca Farrarl, 3 January 1822.
Allen Freeman to Rutha Stephens, 25 May 1825.
Stephen Felker to Missippina Melton, 4 October 1827.
John Fullilove to Malinda Deane, 25 January 1827.
Samuel Fielding to Elizabeth Noth (North?), 22 May 1827.
John F. Foster to Frances Thrasher, 28 April 1829.
Anderson Fambrough to Elizabeth Holloway, 29 June 1830.
James Faris to Rebekah Gann, 5 December 1830.
Frederick J. Freeman to Catherine Hamilton, 3 November 1831.
Harrison H. Freeman to Cassey Snow, 10 July 1831.
Samuel Fitzgerald to Rachel Wilkerson, 24 August 1833.
John Floyd to Wilhilmina Rosseter, 28 January 1833.
Frederick Foster to Philania Shadwick, 6 December 1837.
Henry M. Fullelove to Asenith Jackson, 18 February 1836.
Lewis M. Fowler to Elizabeth A. Conger, 20 December 1836.
James D. Frierson to Margaret R. H. Bostwick, 24 February 1835.
Robert K. Foster to Elizabeth A. Allen, 21 May 1835.
James O. Farrell to Frances Wiggins, 15 September 1835.
Pleasant L. Foster to Ann T. Thompson, 23 February 1834.
Stephen Foster to Elizabeth Thompson, 23 February 1834.
Henry F. Fullilove to Matilda A. Deane, 25 August 1852.

William Fulcher to Mary E. Rogers, 17 October 1852.
M. C. Fulton to Miss V. F. Hamilton, 4 November 1851.
Hartwell Cook to Amanda Falkner, 11 December 1851.
Absalom Farrar to Amanda Daniell, 17 December 1851.
James W. Figgens to Elizabeth Willoughby, 19 November 1850.
William W. Furgerson to Adaline Brown, 14 August 1849.
Stephen McLeroy to Admanda Freeman, 18 February 1849.
Howell C. Flournoy to Eliza Parrish, 4 June 1847.
Anderson Fambrough to Mary Holloway, 13 November 1844.
Charles L. Fielding to Eliza Blakeley, 17 January 1844.
George W. Foster to Jane D. Fielding, 2 February 1843.
William H. Felton to Miss Mary Ann Carlton, 21 November 1843.
Jesse W. Fann to Nancy McCune, 10 November 1842.
John Ferrell to Catherine McDonald, 21 April 1842.
Louis Friedman (Lewis Freedman) to Catherine Jordan, 31 October 1841.
William Fulcher to Catherine Hamilton, 1 July 1841.
John Felker to Martha Harper, 20 May 1841.
Avry J. Fielder to Elizabeth Edwards, 29 January 1841.
Burwell P. Fullilove to Ariann Adams, 22 October 1840.
John E. Fambrough to Elizabeth Haile, 21 October 1840.
Jeremiah A. Fairfield to Jane Close, 9 July 1839.
Calven J. Fall to Sarah B. Stroud, 21 November 1839.
James F. W. Freeman to Amanda L. E. Gordon, 1 March 1838.
Nathan Gan to Nancy Sumers, 5 January 1809.
Edmond Greer to Francis Hodnett, 31 January 1810.
William Gamble to Jiney Laurance, on or after 17 January 1810.
Aasa Goodwin to Peggy Sayers, 20 October 1808.
Baley George (George Baley?) to Delila Greer, 18 June 1807.
Charles Garrett to Nancy Yarborough, 16 July 1807.
William Gann and Elizabeth Summers, 5 February 1812.
Joseph Giles to Sesley Mitchell, 13 October 1814.
Micajah Gann to Polly Stone, 10 September 1815.
James Glasson to Jincy Shaw, 31 July 1815.
Jesse Gilbert to Jane Hanner, 29 June 1816.
Richard Glass to Nancy Cole (Collings?), 24 July 1817.
Harbert Grimes to Mary Moore, 12 January 1817.
Henry Glawson to Nancy Lea, 3 December 1818.
John W. Glenn to Mary Jones, 17 December 1818.
Thomas Greer to Sintha Mayne, 8 December 1818.
William Gann Junr. to Polly Stephens, 15 July 1819.
William Giles to Salley Willeby, 23 December 1819.
Robert M. Gower to Mary M. Smith, 22 March 1820.
Rolley Green to Elizabeth Floyd, 28 December 1820.
Nathan Gann to Sally Westly, 11 March 1821.
Samuel Gann to Sally Lee, 3 December 1821.
Jesse H. Garner to Elizabeth Whitten, 7 November 1821.
Thomas F. Gibbs to Caroline K. Harris, 27 September 1821.

William L. Griffeth to Mary Norris, 2 January 1821.
John Gage to Eliza Ector, 17 April 1822.
James Garner to Sophia Whitten, 9 January 1822.
Seaborn Garrett to Sarah Elder, 9 May 1822.
James D. Gray to Feby H. Marshall, 30 November 1822.
Thomas Gallaway to Margaret Deane, 19 November 1823.
John Greer to Malinda Pace, 23 February 1823.
John Gardner to Nancy Bolling, 22 December 1824.
Whitson H. George to Mary W. George, 22 January 1824.
Ezekeil Gilham to Nancy A. Andrews, 25 October 1824.
Jeremiah G. Gray to Naomi White, 29 September 1824.
John M. Gresham to Mariah Strong, 18 November 1824.
Josiah C. Garrett to Susannah Atkinson, 20 December 1825.
William P. Graham to Frances Graves, 3 November 1825.
Albert Y. Gresham to Lucy A. Grimes, 21 April 1825.
Thomas Glass to Elizabeth Bearden, 26 February 1826.
Robert S. Gordon to Sophronia A. Gerald, 14 September 1826.
William S. Goss to Sarah Atkinson, 10 October 1826.
John C. Greer to Francina E. Cox, 17 January 1826.
John Gann to Sally Stephens, 18 September 1828.
Isaac F. Gerrald to Elethia Kent, 7 February 1828.
William Gilham to Isabella McCree, 3 November 1829.
Joshua Greer to Susan Doggett, 12 March 1829.
Allen Griffith to Susan Barber, 15 December 1829.
James B. Griffith to Elizabeth M. White, 11 June 1829.
David Gibson to Mary Hinesley, 26 June 1831.
Allen Gilbert to Mary Lea, 9 December 1831.
John Gann to Elizabeth Kent, 5 August 1832.
Robert Gann to Julia Ann Gann, 3 June 1832.
Samuel Gann to Sarah Epps, 4 October 1832.
William Gardner to Sally Garrison, 25 May 1832.
John Gann to Mary Ann Allen, 27 September 1833.
Charles T. Griffith to Louiza Ried, 27 January 1833.
Nathan Gann to Mary Wilkins, 10 November 1833.
Garrett M. Greer to Lancy Hagins, 25 December 1833.
William C. Gathright to Eliza Ann Parker, 26 October 1837.
Coil Gilleland to Caroline Vesey, 29 June 1837.
Jackson Grady to Miss Elizabeth E. Philips, 27 August 1837.
John Gann to Mary Clifton, 30 May 1837.
Owen Wood to Caroline Godfrey, 23 February 1837.
William D. Grimes to Frances Booth, 3 January 1837.
Patterson Garrison to Frances R. Carr, 31 March 1836.
William Gamble to Sarah Ann Thomas, 7 April 1836.
James R. Glenn to Ann Williams, 9 June 1836.
William Garner to Mary Ann Wise, 22 December 1836.
George Graham to Mary O. Hattaway, 6 January 1835.
John D. Gordon to Sarah Robison, 1 October 1835.

James W. Barrett (Garrett?) to Mary Ann Puryear, 4 June 1835.

James Gann to Frances Gann, 5 February 1835.

Philip Gerard Gottenberger to Emily Antenette Muse, 8 May 1834.

Isaac Gardner to Harriett A. Floyd, 27 February 1834.

John Glaze to Martha Durham, 28 October 1834.

John T. Grant to Martha C. Jackson, 23 December 1834.

R. P. Griffith to Miss Mary Mitchell, 23 October 1856.

Robert J. Gardner to Miss Mary Parish, 20 December 1855.

John Pendleton Grimes to Lucy Jane Wood, 5 January 1854.

Thomas Giles to Elizabeth Maxwell, 19 February 1854.

Johnson Garwood to Miss Harriet T. Rust, 5 March 1854.

George Washington Giles to Calinder C. Merrett, 14 May 1854.

George E. Griffith to Nancy A. Elder, 2 March 1854.

James C. Gray to Susan Bell, 4 October 1854.

James Giles to Caroline Jones, 22 December 1854.

Thomas W. Geans to Miss Nancy B. Bone, 29 November 1854.

John Jiles (Giles?) to Lorina Pledger, 25 December 1853.

James Glasson to Sarah Allen, 20 September 1853.

James S. Griffeth to Martha A. Jackson, 4 December 1853.

Henry Gee to Sarah Gully, 5 September 1852.

Richard A. Godfrey to Francis L. Hail, 21 December 1851.

Edward P. Gordon to Matilda V. Osburn, 6 February 1851.

Henry Gann to Sarah T. Alexander, 17 January 1850.

Ruel Kinkade Giles (Jiles?) to Emily Martha Ann Sanders, 20 October 1850.

James Gallaway to Annie N. Doble (Dobbs?), 15 November 1849.

Benjamin Gregory to Francina Mobley, 5 March 1849.

David Gann to Malinda Lee, 10 June 1849 (Written at the bottom: "Please be to their Ashes").

Clarke Glasson to Martha Bradberry, 3 August 1848.

James B. Gunter to Parentha Cothran, 14 February 1847.

Edward Gee to Winney F. Williams, 23 December 1847.

Silas M. Garrison to Miss Mary M. Williams, 12 January 1847.

John Griffith to Zarephath Jackson, 21 January 1846.

Stephen C. Gann to Susan Evans, 21 January 1846.

Charles B. Garwood to Elvira G. Close, 13 July 1845.

George Gates to Harriett E. Cavin, 2 June 1844.

Martin Garrison to Mary Boram, 6 November 1844.

Caleb Garrison to Sarah Iler, 11 January 1843.

Richard A. Green to Miss Rebecca A. Iverson, 16 November 1843.

Anthony C. Gamel to Caroline Gilleland, 9 June 1842.

Luther J. Glenn to Mildred L. R. Cobb, 27 April 1849.

Daniel B. Gardner to Mary Wheeler, 1 August 1841.

Lucius J. Gartrell to Miss Louisiana O. Gideon, 16 November 1841.

Littleberry Gann to Eleaner Gann, 7 October 1840.

Allen Gilbert to Sarah Mead, 17 May 1840.

Henry Gann to Elizabeth Crow, 26 April 1838.

James M. Grubbs to Elizabeth Carmichael, evening 5 July 1838.

Joseph F. Garrison to Polly Eiler, 18 March 1838.

William H. Hunt to Nancy Stuart, 23 February 1809.
Fredrick Hays to Elizabeth Lambert, 23 February 1809.
John Hodnett to Elizabeth Tigner, 30 May 1809.
Harwood Harper to Elizabeth Smith, 9 July 1809.
Absalom Harper to Elizabeth Hughey, on or after 12 July 1806.
John Holafield to Elizabeth "Betsey" Kilgore, 6 February 1806.
James Hogwood to Salley Stroud, March 22, 1807.
John Huston to Betsy Maddox, 22 September 1808.
Thomas Hester to Sarah Boyd, 28 December 1808.
John Harris to Frankey Loyd, 14 July 1808.
William Hagwood to Polly Stroud, 24 March 1808.
Richard Helton to Milley Davis, 22 October 1807.
Samuel Hamby to Barsheba Hayden, 8 February 1807.
Norris Hendon to Aley Clements, 2 November 1807.
James Hambrick to Polley Bankston, 29 September 1806.
John Hagler to Nancy Dodson, 10 August 1806.
James Hughey to Anny Harper, 31 December 1805.
John Haywood (Haygood?) to Polley Moss, on or after 28 January 1804.
Joseph Haywood to Fanny Silmon, 2 September 1803.
Charles Eaton Haynes to Martha H. Harrison, 1 July 1810.
James Haynie to Alla Smith, 26 January 1810.
John Henning to Judith Merewether, 27 November 1810.
John Himsly to Mary Huff, 21 November 1810.
Martin Hines to Elizabeth Woods, 18 March 1810.
Charles Houghton to Sarah Thompson, 24 October 1810.
William Hester to Elizebeth Stone, 13 January 1811.
Jeremiah Hill to Virginia Phillips, April 21, 1811.
William Hinyard to Mary Spinks, 30 January 1812.
Aaron Hopkins to Salley Strong, 18 April 1812.
Nicholas Howard to Judith Campbell, 6 July 1812.
Samuel S. Hunter to Betsey Horton, 7 October 1812.
Edward Hagans to Hearty Poarch, 29 October 1812.
Enoch Henson to Cindy Ruly Barber, 25 February 1813.
Daniel Hagins to Elizabeth Newson, 1 June 1813.
William Hardegree to Leah Moore, 24 June 1813.
William Herrin to Elizabeth Wilson, 7 April 1813.
Elisha Hood to Polly Wilson, 25 April 1813.
William Hall (Hale?) to Delilah Wheeler, 9 October 1814.
Jesse Hammock to Polly Jones, 2 November 1819.
Jonathan Hardigree to Polley Giles, 28 August 1814.
Joseph Hodge to Salley Epps, 2 February 1815.
William Hodge to Salley Adams, 30 November 1815.
Pleasant Hardegree to Betsey Grimes, night of May 2, 1816.
Charles W. Harris to Polly Strong, 25 April 1816.
West Harris to Martha G. Harvie, 17 December 1816.
Aaron Hendon to Elizabeth Stidman, 10 July 1816.
Joseph Harper to Mariah Stephens, 14 August 1817.

Newton Henson to Haney Garner, 27 January 1817.
Tapley Henson to Mariah Kilgore, 14 December 1817.
Martin Holloday to Mariah D. Henson, 19 January 1817.
Samuel Hopkins to Elizabeth Parker, 2 January 1817.
James Hunton to Catherine Marrable, 9 October 1817.
William Hutson to Ann D. Johnson, 12 November 1818.
Jesse Howell to Levency Harris, 15 October 1818.
William B. Hath to Nancy Meriwether, 5 May 1818.
Mathew Hobson to Elizabeth M. Mounger, 13 February 1818.
Hendey Harris to Susannah Oakes, 15 November 1818.
John Hales to Jane Williams, 15 January 1818.
Joel Haile to Nancy Lassiter, 9 January 1818.
Hosa Haile to Drusilla Haile, 21 February 1819.
Peter Hamilton to Mary Malone, 19 December 1819.
Robert R. Harden to Mary Antoinette Gauvain, 1 August 1819.
William Hardiman to Silvey Powell, 9 December 1819.
William Hayes to Nancy Hatchett, 9 December 1819.
Aaron Hightower to Dianah Brits, 17 January 1819.
Henry Hightower to Lucy Green, 8 April 1819.
Rolly Hightower to Betsey House, 29 April 1819.
Asbury Hull to Lucy C. Harvey, 20 April 1819.
Reuben Hambleton to Mary G. Heard, 28 September 1820.
Nathan Hamilton to Rebecca Findley, 17 March 1820.
Samuel Hancock to Mary B. Atkinson, 30 November 1820.
Henry Hightower to Temperance Ray, 13 January 1820.
John Hunton to Nancy McColm, 10 March 1820.
William M. Harris to Lucenda Scogin, 5 December 1821.
Merrimon Herndon to Ann Watson, 6 May 1821.
Samuel Hicks to Pamela Holmes, 4 December 1821.
Ansleum L. Harper to Lucinda Melton, 18 July 1822.
James Henderson to Lucinda Kellum, 19 December 1822.
Samuel Higgenbotham to Mary Ball, 9 September 1822.
Isaac Hightower to Elizabeth Luke, 3 October 1822.
Archibald M. Hill to Mary F. Rutledge, 15 August 1822.
John Hodges to Carut Daniell, 21 November 1822.
William S. Hogue to Elizabeth Cook, 4 May 1822.
Joseph A. Hughey to Susan Thrasher, 12 December 1822.
John Hutchinson to Milly Robinson, 12 March 1822.
Appleton Haygood to Charlotte Adams, 15 April 1823.
Nathaniel H. Harper to Susannah Stephens, 3 April 1823.
Jesse Hightower to Mary Kagle, 28 August 1823.
Archibald Holland to Elizabeth Hagin, 30 December 1823.
Cicero Holt to Emily G. Moore, 9 June 1823.
Henry Hall to Mary Agness Bacon, 31 July 1823.
Elijah Humphries to Betsey Alexander, 12 March 1823.
James Haile to Anna McCarly, 11 January 1824.
John Hale to Rebecca Hailes, 12 February 1824.

James B. Herrell to Martha Stephens, 4 June 1824.
Stephen C. Hester to Virginia B. Nunnally, 22 December 1824.
Jonathan Hightower to Mariah Wiggins, 5 October 1824.
Harris House to Anna Luke, 31 March 1824.
James Hamilton to Nancy Parker, 23 August 1825.
Walton B. Harris to Jane F. Herring, 22 March 1825.
Joseph Hester to Ann C. Hester, 2 August 1825.
William Haile to Elizabeth Cooper, 5 October 1826.
William Haile to Cassinda Whitton, 15 January 1826.
Edward G. Harvey to Olivia W. Hill, 15 June 1826.
Silas Henson to Mary Ann Whitton, 21 December 1826.
William Hopkins (?) to Mary Perkins, 15 August 1826.
John W. Harper to Drucella Hodges, 10 July 1827.
Elijah B. Harvey to Elizabeth S. Williams, 12 July 1827.
John Hinson to Betsey Ann Sims, 17 June 1827.
Mathew Haile to Matilda Hailes, 20 November 1828.
Samuel B. Harris to Cintha Silvey, 5 November 1828.
Tyre Harris to Lucy Pinson, 23 December 1828.
Robert Raymond Hardin to Matilda Harison Morton (?), 1 December 1829.
Stephen Hester to Susan Gordan, 1 October 1829.
John F. Hillyer to Mary Briscoe, 24 March 1829.
Samuel Harrison to Minervia Bell, 3 December 1830.
John Hiner to Nancy Beasley, 23 June 1830.
Robert W. Hunter to Margarett Watson, 28 December 1830.
William B. Holloway to Elizabeth M. Elder, evening of 30 December 1831.
Wylie Huff to Mitilda Miller, 18 December 1831.
Joseph H. Hamby to Malissa Wright, 5 July 1832.
Jesse Hanson to Mitilda Wade, 20 December 1832.
Joel Hardigree to Jane Blakeley, 5 December 1832.
Thomas Harris to Caroline Brown, 23 December 1832.
James J. Harrison Jr. to Mentoria B. Cox, 26 August 1832.
Sterling Helton to Pheoba Foster, 1 February 1832.
Stephen C. Hester to Margaret F. Foster, 27 December 1832.
Benjamin B. Hopkins to Elizabeth Edwards, 13 December 1832.
S. (L.?) B. Huff to Polly Collier, 3 January 1832.
Lasley Garner to Catherine Connally, 3 January 1833.
James Hanson to Wealthy Freeman, 8 February 1833.
David Hamby to Olley Daniell, 17 September 1833.
John Hinesley to Susan Garner, 29 July 1833.
William Henry Hunt to Mary Jane Taylor, 7 November 1833.
Richard Hughs to Mary E. Nunnally, 11 July 1833.
John Hambleton to Susan Smith, 29 December 1834.
William Hoopaugh to Mariah Garner, 19 February 1837.
Peterson Hawkins to Miss Mary A. C. Dyer, 12 July 1836.
Joel W. Hale to Nancy Elder, 8 September 1836.
Thomas H. Harden to Margaret Ann Dearing, 29 March 1836.
William Hodges to Martha Conner, 22 December 1836.

John J. Huggins to Emily G. Holt, 27 January 1835.
Hardin Haygood to Elizabeth Ann Locklin, 18 February 1835.
William F. Hailes to Martha Griffeth, 30 September 1835.
Charles Wallace Howard to Miss Susan Jett Thomas, 30 April 1835.
Joel Hutsell to Elizabeth Hart, 15 May 1834.
Wm. George Haun to Catherine Edmondston, 27 March 1834.
John Hinton to Math Kelly, 29 May 1834.
James C. Houghton to Lucinda M. Jones, 30 January 1834.
Darius T. Howze to Nancy W. Hendon, 23 January 1834.
Harmon H. Hardigree to Polly Williby, 9 December 1834.
William W. Hopper to Martha A. H. Allison, 12 August 1855.
Thomas Hinesly to Julia Ann Elder, 3 June 1855.
John J. Hawkins to Miss Oreno Susan Pittard, 30 December 1855.
Thomas Harris to Miss Mary V. Turnell, 18 February 1855.
Stephen A. Hamilton to Miss Emma Moore, 30 December 1855.
James S. Hale to Elizabeth C. Rutledge, 2 September 1855.
William T. Hale to Susan A. Hale, 23 December 1855.
John H. Harris to Eudosia Lowe, 10 January 1854.
Samuel F. Hester to Sarah F. Elder, 31 October 1854.
John C. Haggard to Miss Rebeca Mabery, 9 March 1854.
John W. Hamilton to Martha W. Lanier, 15 March 1854.
Francis M. Haynes to Miss Elizabeth Bailey, 10 April 1853.
Benjamin W. Humphreys to Mary Jane Meriwether, 19 November 1853.
John Hampton to Miss Eliza A. Hayes, 14 December 1853.
Thomas Hendricks to Miss Mary J. Smith, 12 August 1853.
William A. Harp to Lucy J. Biggers, 25 March 1852.
Wiley James Huff to Martha Ann Owen, 14 March 1852.
Steven A. Harris to Lavinah R. White, 24 August 1852.
Edward T. Hale to Susan Lumpkin, 6 October 1852.
John Hill to Lucinda Pitman, 12 May 1851.
James W. Hinton to Susan C. Dyer, 15 October 1851.
John M. Hunt to Susan Echols, 5 October 1851.
Wiley Madison Hinesley to Sarah M. Owens, 29 January 1851.
N. W. Handrup to Miss Sarah E. Bridges, 30 Dec. 1851.
Elisha L. Holland to Margaret Ann Cross, 19 December 1850.
Nathaniel H. Herrell to Catherine Crow, 7 July 1850.
Almerin Hall to Elizabeth Thurmond, 25 April 1850.
William P. Harrison to Elizabeth J. Parker, 28 August 1850.
Col. Hopkins Holsey to Miss Mary J. Nisler, 26 September 1850.
William B. Haygood to Malinda A. Thompson, 17 October 1850.
Juan Honfleur to Annie E. Whitaker, 2 October 1850.
William P. Harden to Sarah J. Murray, 2 October 1849.
John B. Hattaway to Miss Ann W. Moore, 12 July 1849.
Thomas Hodges to Amanda Cogburn, 10 May 1849.
William T. Hamby to Susan Ann Daniell, 1 March 1849.
David Hodges to Rebecca Vaughn, 5 May 1848.
Peter W. Haynes (Hayes?) to Lucy Ann Veal, 2 November 1848.

Francis D. Harrel to Sarah Bangers, 4 January 1848.
Josiah W. Hale to Susan Blakeley, 13 January 1848.
Robert R. Harden to Martha W. Durham, 23 May 1848.
Harbert G. Hardigree to Mary Williby (or Willoughby), 5 Dec. 1847.
Daniel Van Houten to Lucinda H. Whitten, 23 May 1847.
Jeptha C. Harris to Martha R. Upshaw, 7 September 1847.
Daniel G. Hughes to Mary H. Moore, 20 October 1847.
Burwell House to Julian Amanda Crow, 27 September 1846.
Willis B. Harris to Mary A. J. Mortin, 17 December 1846.
Charles B. Hunt to Martha Lord, 26 November 1846.
Hezekiah Hobgood to Keziah Britt, 24 July 1845.
John Howse to Miss Claudia Caroline Clayton, 1 October 1845.
Benjamin H. Hill to Caroline E. Holt, 27 November 1845.
Napoleon B. Hardin to Mary Louisa Appling, 2 December 1845.
Obed Haile to Sarah Edwards, 6 December 1845.
Joel A. Higgins to Caroline V. Moore, 18 June 1844.
Henry Hull Jr. to Miss Ann M. Thomas, 9 October 1844.
George W. Hanye (Hanze?) to Elizabeth J. Wilson, 10 October 1844.
William T. Harris to Nancy N. Dunnway, 9 February 1844.
Frances C. House to Permelia Lee, 17 August 1843.
George R. Hendree to Cornelia J. Paine, 5 October 1843.
Josiah M. Hunt to Sarah C. Spinks, 28 September 1843.
Green Huff to Mary Cobb Stewart, 19 October 1843.
John W. Hamilton to Catherine Lanier, 12 January 1843.
Duke Hamilton to Nancy D. Luke, 26 August 1843.
A. J. Harndon to Miss Mariah Laverin, 18 April 1843.
David Harper to Mary Ann Dupree, 6 November 1842.
Joseph Hodges to Hannah Kennedy, 10 October 1842.
Benjamin F. Hardiman to Arabella R. Harris, 31 May 1842.
Joseph F. House to Eliza Ann Ridgeway, 2 January 1842.
Edward R. Hodgson to Anna Bishop, 18 January 1842.
James P. Holloway to Miss Sarah Elder, 5 January 1842.
John Haney to Francis S. Brightwell, 22 April 1841.
Joseph Haile to Elizabeth Ann Blakeley, 27 December 1841.
William Harris to Harriett Davenport, 11 November 1841.
John J. Hardigree to Mary R. Fambrough, 17 November 1841.
John Hibbert to Laura Ann Garwood, 7 May 1840.
Seaborn Howse to Elizabeth Smith, 2 August 1840.
James M. Hendon to Lorena Jackson, 24 December 1840.
Hilliard J. Hill to Amanda M. Moss, 15 September 1840.
Robert H. Hammilton to Louisa James (Jane?) Hodges, 16 June 1839.
William Herring to Eliza Edwards, 6 January 1839.
John Harris to Elizabeth Spurlock, 27 April 1839.
Earven Hinsley to Lucinda Robinson, 18 April 1838.
Mosses J. Holland to Fanny Hardigree, 7 October 1838.
Elisha Hardegree to Sarah Willoughby, 18 February 1838.
Greene B. Haygood to Martha Ann Askew, 11 March 1838.

Frederick S. S. Hunt to Martha H. Puryear, 10 September 1838.
William S. Hemphill to Sarah Fowler, 20 December 1838.
John Haygood to Mary A. W. Fuller, 20 December 1838.
Willis Head to Frances Bassitt, 26 December 1838.
A. W. Iler to Miss Elizabeth J. Richards, 2 April 1846.
Robert Iverson to Miss Frances E. Neisler, 7 June 1836.
Abraham Johnston to Margret Ray, 4 January 1810.
Drury W. Jackson to Lucy B. Ridgeway, evening of 2 August 1821.
Henry Johnson to Elizabeth Hednet, 28 November 1810.
Philip Jones to Peggy Johnston, 29 September 1809.
John Jackson to Susannah Hicks, 12 December 1808.
James Johnston to Betsy Ray, 3 March 1807.
Zachariah Jourdan to Tabitha Stokes, 27 September 1807.
Jesse Jennings to Mary Adams, 17 January 1811.
George Jonston to Susannah Clifton, 29 October 1806.
John Johnson to Prudence Farley, 6 September 1804.
Richard Jeils to Lilley Dean, 26 June 1806.
Charles C. Jackson to Lucy W. Connelly, 22 December 1813.
William Johnson to Mary Shye, 26 January 1813.
Joseph Jolly to Polly Freeman, 7 October 1813.
Edward Johnston to Syna McCartney, 7 September 1814.
Walter Johnston to Ruthey Shepherd, 23 June 1814.
Cornelious Jackson to Elizabeth Green, 7 September 1815.
John Johnson to Morning Britton, 16 February 1815.
Reuben Johnson to Cady Mathews, 7 November 1816.
James Jinnings to Francis A. Greer, 24 November 1817.
Jesse Jones to Rebecca Miller, 1 October 1820.
Henry Jackson to Mary Smith, 24 January 1822.
Stephen Jackson to Charlotte Collins, 21 March 1824.
John G. Johnson to Mary Johnson, 22 July 1824.
Young Jacks to Judith Adams, 25 December 1827.
Hartwell Jackson to Salley Jackson, 31 January 1828.
William P. Jackson to Jane L. Suttle, 25 December 1828.
Benjamin Jones to Lidia Huff, 16 October 1828.
Robert Jennings to Louisa Stark, 21 July 1831.
John Calvin Johnson to Elizabeth P. Waddel, 3 November 1831.
William L. Justess to Vianna Barton, 23 February 1832.
Wiley A. Jones to Sarah M. Edwards, 21 May 1833.
Stinson J. Jarrall to Susan T. Davenport, 19 January 1837.
Willis Jordan to Nancy Wheeler, 28 February 1837.
Andrew B. Jackson to Elizabeth Ann Thomas, 3 January 1836.
Kindred Jacks to Lucinda Fambrough, 15 December 1836.
George A. Jarrall to Eliza Ann Yearby, 22 October 1835.
Ahashabia Johnston to Francis W. Ward, 29 October 1835.
John Jones to Frances Ann Crawford, 31 December 1835.
Frances Jackson to Luticia Jackson, 23 October 1834.
John Jackson to Abi Haygood, 31 July 1834.

William Jeffriess to Martha N. Ramsey, 17 April 1851.
Nathan Johnson to Rebecca A. McRee, 21 November 1855.
W. B. Jackson to Mary W. Adams, 13 October 1853.
Milton C. Jackson to Sophian E. Pridgeon, 14 September 1852.
Oliver Porter Johnson to Eliza Hardigree, 27 March 1850.
James J. Jennings to Jarusha A. Conner, 21 October 1849.
John Calvin Johnson to Matilda Harrison Harden, 13 May 1848.
James D. Jones to Almedia Klutts, 13 April 1848.
Charles H. Johns to Lilly A. Williams, 3 February 1847.
Drewry W. Jackson to Martha Ann Hayes, 1 October 1846.
Hilman Jackson to Mary Ann Haygood, 20 January 1846.
David Jiles to Mary Stricklin, 11 October 1846.
Abraham G. Jackson to Catherine Barrett, 5 October 1845.
William Jiles to Frances Robertson, 4 May 1845.
William Johnston to Nancy W. Pearman, 22 September 1844.
Linsey Jacks to Lucinda Haile, 26 December 1843.
William Johnston to Mary Daniels, 7 February 1843.
Kabez Jones to Elizabeth Crawford, 19 October 1843.
Asa M. Jackson to Eveline R. J. Harden, 1 September 1842.
Benjamin F. Johnston to Lucy Ann McCoy, 20 July 1841.
William Jackson to Martha Greear, 14 October 1841.
Cary Johnson to Frankey Stephens, 22 December 1840.
John S. Jackson to Martha Kenny, 13 February 1840.
Harris Jiles to Martha Hardigree, 10 January 1839.
Solomon Kilgore to Anney Heard, 14 March 1809.
John Kent to Lausey Hambrick, 8 June 1809.
James Kilgo to Frances Pearman, 30 October 1808.
John Kelley to Hannah Kagenet, 15 December 1808.
Durum Kelly to Meriam Oraer, 7 August 1806.
James Keenum to Polly Keenum, 1 December 1811.
Mathew Kilgore to Rebekah Beasley, 23 June 1811.
Alexander Kenedy to Darcus Walker, 28 April 1812.
William Kimbrow to Martha Gann, 24 January 1812.
Gideon Kimbrel to Ann Maxey, 18 March 1813.
Jesse Kinney to Fanney Doggett, 10 August 1813.
Solomon Kilgore to Tegey Maxey, 18 January 1818.
Samuel Key to Mary Cockrill, 27 February 1819.
Thomas Kilgore to Peggy Maxey, 30 December 1819.
William Kimble to Mary Hinton, 16 October 1823.
Gilbert Kent to Susan Wortham, 5 February 1824.
Robert Kimbell to Sarah Hinton, 8 February 1824.
John J. King to Emila Nichals, 14 December 1827.
Solomon P. Kent to Elizabeth Summers, 6 April 1831.
Joseph Kennedy to Hannah Gardner, 19 April 1832.
Josiah Kent to Lovina Gann, 9 September 1832.
William H. Kent to Martha Hopkins, 22 May 1832.
Frances Kilgore to Mary Connally, 10 January 1832.

Charles Kinney to Lousa Wier, 12 April 1832.
Isaiah Kent to Anny Landers, 19 November 1835.
Hesekiah M. Kidd to Sarah J. Hinton, 23 December 1855.
Isaac Mc Kenny to Candis A. Ross, 28 April 1855.
Calvin P. Kirkley to Elizabeth Judy Blackman, 27 July 1854.
Michael Kettle to Susan Kelley, 17 September 1854.
James D. Kisselberg to Miss Armind Smith, 4 August 1853.
Porter King to Miss Callie M. Lumpkin, 19 February 1852.
George W. Knox to Aliathia W. Tindall, 4 March 1851.
Thomas Kinney to Mary Jane Dixon, 20 July 1851.
William King Junr. to Augusta C. Clayton, 8 October 1851.
Thomas O. Kimble to Miss Elizabeth Evins, 7 December 1848.
John F. Kinney to Miss Mary A. Jackson, 15 June 1848.
William Kimber to Emily Gann, 28 November 1847.
John Kittle to Martha Connal, 9 November 1845.
James D. Kelley to Sarah Ann Spurlock, 4 September 1842.
Isaac M. Kenney to Sarah Ann Richardson, 20 March 1842.
William Kelly to Mary Ann Mastin, 9 August 1840.
Thomas Kines to Frances Wood, 12 May 1839.
John W. Kennon to Sarah C. Moore, 3 October 1839.
Henry Lane to Martha Herring, 1 January 1809.
Henry Langford to Nancy Patterson, 20 April 1809.
John Loyd to Sarah Harris, 20 October 1808.
John Loyd to Betsey Holt, 22 October 1808.
Samauel Leard to Linda Lincecum, 12 September 1808.
Thomas Legg to Olivia McFalls, 1 April 1807.
Edward Lloyd to Sarah Anderson Hatchett, 6 December 1810.
Samuel Lawrence to Florow Camron, 13 November 1806.
Green Lea to Peggy Muffitt, 16 July 1807.
Joel Lamberth to Mary Morgan, 15 December 1807.
Joseph Lane to Elizabeth Hill, 24 March 1807.
Richard Lewis to Betsey Jiles, 31 December 1805.
Zebede Luis to Mckey Gill, 13 October 1805.
John H. Lowe to Kiddy Hill, 29 June 1809.
Richard Luven to Sally Kinny, 28 February 1811.
Jessey Levans to Whiney Levins, 10 June 1813.
Ryan (Myas?) Lord to Renchy Whitehead, 18 July 1813.
Samuel Lawrence to Ruthy Butler Finley, 13 January 1814.
Elijah Loving to Elizabeth Robertson, 7 April 1814.
Robert Lord (Lard?) Jr. to Sinthy Martin, 13 July 1815.
Geo. M. Lanear to Polly Langford, 1 February 1816.
Samuel (Lemuel?) Lasseter to Mary Sims, 30 September 1817.
Thomas Loving to Nancy McCartney, 19 December 1818.
William Love to Rebecca Crews, 24 September 1818.
Henry Lipham to Nancy Bearding, 25 October 1818.
Burrell Lea to Elizabeth Eatherton, 18 June 1818.
Sterling Lanier to Sarah V. Fullwood, 28 September 1818.

Bazellton Langford to Elizabeth Adams, 17 December 1818.
James Lasseter to Nancy Hailes, 27 August 1820.
Edmund Lea to Rachael Garrett, 5 July 1821.
George W. Lumpkins to Alleathy Jones, 5 July 1821.
Lott M. Lagwin to Mary McRee, 14 March 1822.
Robert Legon to Wilhelmina Fullwood, 1 October 1822.
William Little to Burchry Powell, 6 March 1822.
William Loguin to Polly Hudson, 29 December 1822.
John Lee to Dorcas McGowan, 1 April 1824.
Bedford Langford to Mary Thompson, 15 December 1825.
Britain Lasseter to Martha McCallum, 1 September 1825.
Philip Lane to Salley Stewart, 16 August 1826.
Joseph Lea to Peggy Gann, 23 December 1827.
John Lea to Patsey Kent, 18 July 1827.
Henry C. Lea to Serena R. Rootes, 26 August 1828.
Joseph Leadbetter to Delila Davis, 21 May 1829.
James Lea to Fanny Crow, 23 September 1828.
Abraham Letlow to Susannah Luke, 28 June 1829.
James E. Locklin to Nancy Haygood, 18 December 1828.
Gray B. Lesseter to Frances N. Cooper, 16 December 1830.
John F. Lasseter to Elizabeth Dorrell, 27 June 1830.
Thomas O. Lloyd to Seytha Marable, 3 January 1830.
Eli Landers to Margaret McRee, 8 August 1833.
William LeConte to Sarah A. Nisbet, 10 October 1833.
Henry Lester to Emily Mathews, 21 May 1833.
John Landers to Alethia Wortham, 14 July 1833.
Burwell Lea to Lucinda Ramsay, 31 December 1833.
John H. Lowe to Sarah Hill, 31 May 1833.
William S. Lowry to Miss M. A. E. Stephens, 2 August 1837.
Lewallen W. Lloyd to Ann Wood, 15 July 1837.
Charles B. Lyle to Julia E. Carlton, 14 December 1837.
John H. Lowe Jr. to Elizabeth A. Maxey, 18 August 1836.
John R. Stanford to Cordelia J. Charlton, 17 May 1836.
James Harman Lloyd to Julia Tanner, 12 January 1835.
James B. Lowe to Matilda C. Fambrough, 27 December 1835.
Mereda Landers to Mary Ann Martha Akin, 8 September 1835.
Philip Lampkin to Ann Eliza Hanson, 15 December 1835.
Gilbert Ledbetter to Dicey Tribble, 27 March 1834.
Wyatt Lee to Mary Wellbourn, 9 December 1834.
Grandirson F. Loveing to Elizabeth Hemrick, 15 July 1855.
John Lloyd to Miss Mary E. Johnson, 18 October 1855.
Thomas Lee to Nancy Bridges, 14 March 1855.
Phillip F. Lamar to Catherine E. Lowe, 1 October 1854.
John W. F. Lowery to Elanor Overby, 6 December 1854.
Isaac Lowe to Julia Ann M. Hester, 8 November 1853.
James B. Landrum to Salina Gregory, 3 August 1852.
Nathan Lee to Sarah House, 9 January 1851.

Charles B. Limbard (Lambard) to Julia E. Kellogg, 6 April 1851.
Wyatt Lee Jr. to Nancy Ann Fletcher, 10 January 1850.
Thomas R. Loving to Susan Fambrough, 29 December 1850.
Winfrield L. Lampkin to Miss Harriett H. Wagnon, 20 February 1850.
Charles W. Lane to Louisa Matthews, 3 December 1850.
Bezleel Langford Lanier to Almanza Jane Conner, 28 June 1849.
Henry B. Luke to Martha Gann, 1 February 1849.
Augustin S. Langford to Martha A. S. Tuck, 5 July 1849.
John S. Linton to Miss Lucy Ann Hull, 18 December 1849.
Thomas J. Lester to Amanda J. Sansom, 19 December 1848.
William Lanier to Elizabeth Daniell, 5 August 1847.
William C. Loving to Louisa Scenter, 26 October 1847.
Patman Lester to Susannah Daniell, 5 August 1847.
John Leonard to Eliza Beggars, 10 January 1847.
Dr. H. R. I. Long to Miss Susan J. Stroud, 26 May 1847.
Terrell M. Lampkin to America F. Adams, 15 April 1847.
William A. Langford to Sarah C. Hale, 31 January 1847.
Robert F. Ligon to Emely E. Paine, 30 December 1846.
John W. Langford to Susan Turnell, 7 August 1845.
Harrison G. Lane to Miss Judith Maddux, 15 September 1844.
Lewis J. Lampkin to Miss Lucy P. Haines, 27 May 1844.
William Lanier to Lucy Jane Billups, 8 October 1844.
Lewis LeConte to Miss Harriett Nisbet, 25 July 1843.
Andrew J. Lamar to Mary A. Jackson, 18 December 1842.
Edmund Lilley to Sarah Smith, 15 June 1841.
Lewis Lester to Martha Hendon, 14 October 1841.
Walter Lanier to Eliza M. Mead, 17 September 1840.
Francis C. Langford to Harriett Hamilton, 31 December 1840.
Peter E. Love to Martha E. Stroud, 21 November 1839.
Arthur Irwin Leet to Judith Scott Branch, 12 May 1839.
James Lester to Eleanor Daniell, 1 August 1839.
Nevill M. Lumpkin to Susan E. Mayne, 11 October 1838.
James N. Leanier to Maryann Kent, 25 July 1838.
Benjamin Laine to Elizabeth Gardner, 21 August 1834.
James McCarty to Elizabeth McCarty, 12 October 1809.
James McColough to Elizabeth McColough, 26 July 1807.
Leroy McCoy to Nancy Hicks, 4 January 1810.
Felix McGee to Elizabeth Walls, 15 January 1807.
John McGee to Esther Hutson, 20 September 1807.
William McMichael to Lucy S. Packlett (?), on or at 24 July 1809.
Hugh McWhirter to Heleney Ligon, 25 January 1810.
Jno. McAlpin to Susanna Smith, 26 March 1812.
John McAlphin to Jincy Hicks, 24 October 1811.
Lewis McKee to Ann Atkinson, 3 January 1813.
James McCullough to Anna Cain (Cusern?), 25 December 1816.
John McDanniel to Peggy Anderson, 3 January 1819.
James G. Martin to Ann Ramsey, 14 December 1809.

Lloyd Marrs to Matilda Cooper, 2 May 1819.
Semeon D. Maning to Nancy Summerlin, 3 August 1820.
Green M. Mitchell to Leana Williams, 18 May 1820.
William St. L. Musgrove to Rebecca Pendergrass, 8 June 1820.
Jesse Martindale to Polly Coleman, 8 February 1821.
Sterling Mayes to Mary Thompson, 18 June 1820.
Mathew Moseley to Betsey Roberson, 2 January 1821.
Robert Moore to Eleanor Craig, 15 July 1824.
William McKleroy to Margarett Parkerson, 17 August 1828.
Francis M. McCree to Martha Biggs, 19 January 1832.
Nathaniel McLaughlin to Nancy Collier, 14 November 1833.
James F. McKnight to Frances D. Maddox, 13 February 1837.
Andrew J. McGaughey to Sarah W. Cook, 7 March 1837.
William McKinzie to Miss Lucretia Gardner, 27 December 1836.
James W. McCleskey to Lucretia Wier, 11 March 1835.
John E. McCain to Martha Smith, 13 October 1835.
Charles G. McKinley to Elizabeth Julia Flournoy, 9 September 1834.
Jacob R. McRee to Susan McRee, 2 October 1855.
William L. McLeroy to Miss Margaret Wallace, 16 December 1855.
Cicero McLeroy to Louisiana Lesuere, 11 March 1855.
E. J. McCall to Miss Charlotte R. Blair, 22 April 1855.
Jefferson G. McNorton to Miss Matilda F. Hayes, 5 January 1853.
John Thomas McCoy to Lucy Jane Elder, 19 May 1853.
Joseph H. McCree to Susan Frances Elder, 10 April 1851.
George H. McRee to Mary P. Elder, 3 January 1849.
Francis M. McLeroy to Lucinda Eidson, 9 September 1849.
Wiliam J. McLeroy to Nancy E. Jackson, 13 January 1848.
Richard B. McRee to Mary E. Elder, 14 March 1847.
John McDaniell to Eliza Couch, 25 May 1847.
James H. McGaughey to Martha Fambrough, 3 June 1847.
Danil McDonald to Miss Mary M. Taylor, 31 October 1843.
Wm. B. McRee to Frances A. Jones, 12 March 1843.
Charles G. McKinly to Miss Frances C. Jackson, 16 November 1842.
Thomas P. McRee to Moriley Ann Briant, 2 April 1840.
Charles F. McCay to Miss Narcissa Williams, 11 August 1840.
Alexander McCalpen to Sarah P. Dyer, 23 April 1838.
Ballard McDurment to Margaret Kerr, 2 December 1838.
Robert S. Mckleroy to Nancy H. Ridgeway, 16 December 1838.
Thomas Macburnet to Sarah Smith, 5 July 1806.
Alexander Mash to Sary Strawn, 15 September 1811.
John Moore to Nancy Hindon, 6 January 1811.
Robert Morris to Denah Akins, 18 November 1808.
Isaac Midlebrooks to Betsey Thompson, 11 January 1809.
Robert R. Minter to Sarah S. Puryear, 8 December 1808.
Burwell Mathews to Sally Smith, 15 October 1807.
Isaac Martin to Polley Caldwell, 30 November 1806.
Robert Middleton to Prulah Finley, 25 September 1806.

Robert Marable to Cathern Vickors, 20 September 1806.
Gabreal F. Mathis to Leatia C. Billups, 25 December 1810.
Robert Mitchel to Jamimi Ponder, 20 December 1810.
Elbert Mathews to Sually Hails, 13 February 1812.
John Mathews to Mary Adams, 17 (January?) 1812.
William Mitchell to Judith Brown, 25 November 1813.
Joseph Moss to Sophia Easley, 8 July 1813.
Matthew Marrable to Maria Fullwood, 15 October 1815.
Edward Maxey to Polley Elder, 28 May 1815.
James Mathews to Sally Evans, 1 August 1816.
Jeremiah Mathews to Lucy Hales, 28 November 1816.
Benjamin Middleton to Mary Satterwhite, 3 October 1816.
Gabriel A. Moffett to Salley Cocke, 11 July 1816.
William Manley to Mary R. Brown, 13 November 1811.
James Mathews to Mariah Booth, 11 December 1817.
Henry Mitchell to Nancy Biggs, 16 December 1817.
John F. Mapp to Elizabeth Steele, 1 October 1818.
Jeremiah Maxey to Tabitha McBee, 26 March 1818.
William Miles to Agnes Nutt, 11 March 1818.
Fuller Milsaps to Elizabeth Stephens, 18 June 1818.
Jissey Mobly to Margarett Beasley, 2 October 1818.
Peter Moseley to Sarah S. Brown, 27 December 1818.
James G. Martin to Elizabeth Chisholm, 11 April 1822.
Willis Moss to Milley Britton, 4 June 1822.
Lanty Mattocks to Nancy Malone, May 17, 1823.
David Meriwether to Henrietta Callier, 24 February 1825.
Samuel Miller to Elizabeth Ann Tipper, 28 September 1825.
Stroud Melton to Sally Lea, 17 October 1826.
Daniel Major to Mary Akridge, 4 January 1827.
John G. Maxey to Millison Whitton, 28 June 1827.
Memory J. D. Moore to Elizabeth Bryan (?), 5 August 1827.
Thomas Mason to Milley Stone, 30 October 1828.
Robert Martin to Sarah Mayfield, 24 May 1829.
Randal W. Mastin to Mary Crow, 15 September 1829.
Thomas V. Mecune (?) to Martha Mecune, 24 October 1830.
Reuben R. Medder to Nancy Martindale, 23 December 1830.
John Monroe to Emilia H. Paschal, 21 December 1830.
George Marable to Prudence S. Jennings, 26 September 1831.
William Mason to Elizabeth Conner, 12 May 1831.
Gabriel A. Moffett to Elizabeth Dickinson, 28 August 1831.
Jonathan Morgan to Christanah Gardner, 23 September 1832.
William C. Martin to Elivira Jacks, 17 December 1833.
A. C. Middlebrooks to Mary Thrasher, 22 July 1833.
Thomas J. Mozely to Rebecca Roberson, 12 November 1833.
William Mason to Emily Pyron, 28 December 1837.
John Moore to Jane A. Moore, 4 February 1836.
Nathaniel J. Mitchum to Eudocia Hubbard, 14 April 1836.

Josiah Jackson Moncrief to Mary Hopkins, 13 November 1836.
John Mathews to Margaret Crow, 3 December 1835.
John H. Maxey to Mary Ann McCree, 15 November 1835.
Enoch Medders to Martha B. Sims, 3 January 1834.
Joshua Morris to Martha Foster, 16 September 1834.
Elijah Moore to Barbary J. Barber, 16 December 1834.
A. D. Moore to Adeline Moore, 29 December 1834.
John William Mayne to Virginia Elizabeth Graham, 10 September 1848.
Joshua M. Miller to Miss Phoebe Gray, 5 December 1855.
Frederick Miller to Mary E. Gurvin, 4 September 1853.
William H. Murray to Miss Sarah J. Vincent, 19 September 1854.
Elijah F. Major to Sarah A. Blakeley, 13 October 1853.
Pendleton Mortimer Miller to Lethia A. Owens, 23 June 1853.
Hiram B. Meridith to Frances M. Hale, 28 August 1853.
William J. Masters to Rebecca Rhoads, 27 January 1852.
George B. Morgan to Mary Ann Giles, 1 April 1852.
L. C. Matthews to Miss Agnes Matthews, 20 February 1851.
John G. Maxey to Susan Silvey, 28 July 1850.
William Miller to Mary Fenn, 31 October 1850.
Alexander Martin to Roseda Miller, 24 April 1849.
Lafayette Marshall to Martha E. Elder, 3 January 1849.
George T. Mastin to Amanda F. Dicken, 27 December 1849.
William H. Marshall to Arianna Elder, 19 October 1848.
Thomas Montgomery to Elizabeth S. Dickin, 19 September 1848.
Rufus L. Moss to Mary A. Anthony, 8 August 1848.
Jonathan Montgomery to Sarah E. Hendon, 26 January 1848.
James A. Mealer to Margarett Stone, 23 December 1847.
Robert Moore to Miss Catherine N. Kirkpatrick, 16 November 1847.
Pleasant J. Moon to Miram A. Hoopugh, 11 August 1847.
William W. Moore to Miss Mary A. Semms, 2 October 1845.
Greene M. Maxwell to Martha A. Royal, 5 June 1845.
Pinckney Masters to Jane Williams, 2 September 1845.
John R. Mathews to Catherine Matthews, 2 March 1845.
Daniel W. Miller to Miss Susan H. Neisler, 1 January 1845.
Jesse Mercer to Alsey Brown, 2 October 1845.
Joel J. Morton to Nancy C. Lowe, 22 February 1844.
John R. Mounce to Miss Jane M. Finley, 27 August 1844.
Milford Masters to Martha Walker, 17 December 1843.
Thomas Miller to Emily Owen, 7 July 1843.
John A. Matthews to Permelia A. Bearden, 3 August 1843.
Nathaniel Mott to Elizabeth Ann Hinsley, 28 December 1841.
Francis A. Mead to Mary Ann Jennings Smith, 31 May 1840.
Thomas Moore to Miss Martha Jackson, 2 April 1840.
Alsa Moore to Sarah A. Park, 7 February 1839.
Joseph F. Morton (Martin?) to Mildred Elizabeth Matthews, 18 Feb. 18
Isaac Newton to Clarecy Stewart, on or after 5 August 1809.
John Nutt to Polley East, 23 November 1808.

Thomas Norton to Elizabeth Gill, 12 May 1811.
James Nicholson to Polly Stone, 7 October 1813.
Joseph Nail to Elisa Easley, 19 October 1815.
Nathan Nalls to Lucrecy Burks, 8 October 1818.
Silas M. Norton to Sarah Bransford, 19 July 1820.
William Norton to Matilda Durham, 20 April 1820.
James Nixon to Joicey Malone, 16 October 1821.
Thomas Noland to Martha B. Thrasher, 4 December 1821.
Henry Niles to Ann Maddocks, 9 October 1823.
Henry Nixon to Theodotia Fowler, 23 November 1823.
Edward P. Nixon to Mary S. Elder, 13 April 1828.
William B. Nutt to Mariah Gathright, 6 October 1830.
William Nabers to Sarah H. Cheatham, 24 March 1835.
William M. Nance to Statery E. Weatherly, 19 June 1835.
John W. Nicholson to Martha M. Gartrell, 18 November 1852.
Robert Nichelson to Susan A. Elder, 12 September 1852.
William Hailes to Delana Thomas, 14 August 1838.
John Nunnally to Zarephath Griffith, 5 September 1848.
Josiah Newton to Mrs. Charlotte Sisson, 2 November 1848.
James Negle to Catherine Reeves, 25 October 1848.
John C. Nunnally to Elizabeth A. Dickin, 22 October 1840.
Whiting Oliver to Rebecca W. Puryear, 14 December 1815.
John Osbourn to Patsey Pace, in the house of Isaac Pace, 5 November 1815.
Jonathan Oakes to Susannah Ramey, 30 December 1818.
John Owens to Sharlott Osbern, 16 February 1820.
Joseph Ogden to Cintha Barber, 12 June 1822.
Thomas Overby to Elenor Thompson, 25 January 1823.
Francis H. Oliver to Mary Love, 1 May 1828.
N. J. Omberg to Sarah C. Fulton, 8 June 1837.
Jacob Awtry to Sarah Ann Manlay, 25 September 1837.
Basil H. Overby to Asenath C. Thrasher, 18 May 1837.
Augustus A. C. Osborn to Barbary A. Maxey, 19 October 1854.
John Osborn to Ann Willoughby, 20 October 1853.
David Owen to Ann D. Hudson, 30 May 1852.
Francis W. Osborn to Martha Willoughby, 16 December 1845.
John Osburn to Martha Elder, 10 January 1843.
William Oliver to Margaret E. Tuck, 11 July 1841.
Edward Owen to Susan McCane, 10 January 1843.
Andrew J. Pickrell to Louisa Francis Allgood, 4 October 1857.
James Pruet to Polly Leard, 2 June 1808.
John Puryear to Lucy Smith, 26 September 1809.
Andrew Pettefils to Fanny Thompson, 24 July 1809.
William Powel to Clearey Eastridge, 24 September 1806.
John Parker to Fanney East, 23 November 1808.
Jeremiah Pace to Betsy Hails, 16 July 1807.
Edward Paine to Matilda Brenton, December 1807.
Aqullah Phelps to Giney Henson, 1 December 1807.

John Pace to Salley Anderson, 3 December 1807.
John Powel to Sally Watters, 20 November 1806.
Henry Phillips to Nicy Ward, 23 November 1810.
Joseph Pickering to Marian Cook, 7 February 1810.
Robert Polley to Polley Darnold, 12 July 1810.
Aaron Parker to Margret Browning, 26 June 1806.
Levi Powell to Frances Bradbury, 10 January 1811.
James Prophet to Lereisa Runnels, 24 March 1811.
John Phillips to Salley Kirkwood, on or after 12 February 1806.
Henry N. Pope to Elizabeth Henton, 21 May 1812.
Joseph Pickering to Rebecca Belcher, 26 February 1813.
John Parker to Milley East, 18 January 1814.
Peter Puryear to Lucy B. Holmes, 30 November 1815.
Sherrod Porch to Seleah Bued (Boid?), on or after 9 December 1816.
Allen Prior to Sally Thornton, 14 January 1816.
William Parker to Elizabeth Hopkins, 22 July 1817.
William Puryear to Unisey Wooton, 9 February 1817.
James Parish to Nancy Byford, 22 January 1818.
William Patterson to Rodey Runnels, 29 January 1818.
William Price to Fanney Strong, 18 June 1818.
Daniel Ramey to Polly Morton, 24 May 1818.
Whitmill Pearman to Mirian Ward, 28 January 1819.
Elisha Powell to Elizabeth Malone, 9 May 1820.
John C. Pearson to Anna Ball, 6 April 1820.
William M. Peters to Gracy Powell, 18 May 1820.
Nathaniel Pendergrass to Elizabeth Burks, 23 April 1822.
Coleman Prindle to Catherine Fambrough, 3 January 1822.
Peyton Parker to Sarah Hopkins, 26 February 1823.
Abraham Perkins to Mary Ann C. Smith, 22 February 1821.
William H. Parker to Margaret W. Whatley, 13 March 1823.
Nathaniel Priggeon to Polly Williby, 12 December 1824.
James B. Patmon to Sarah Price, 24 April 1825.
John N. Patrick to Edith Hailes, 1 December 1825.
Samuel Peppers to Jane Smith, 21 January 1825.
Oliver M. Porter to Alpha T. Adams, 13 July 1826.
John Park to Sarah T. Robertson, 25 October 1827.
James Parker to Catharine Bradbury, 29 November 1827.
James Patterson to Nancy Howard, 28 October 1827.
Robert A. Pryor to Louisa Houghton, 22 December 1829.
John J. Pass to Sarah Bradberry, 16 October 1831.
John Piercall to Elizabeth Stewart, 6 January 1821.
William Pinson to Martha W. Morton, 14 August 1832.
John H. Ponder to Margaret A. Williams, 19 December 1832.
Wylie H. Pope to Arianna N. Twineng, 25 September 1832.
Thomas Preston to Elmira Clark, 9 February 1832.
Azariah M. Pinson to Lucinda Wilson, 28 November 1833.
Josiah Pyrant (Bryant?) to Elizabeth Williby, 31 December 1833.

Samuel Parr to Louiza Humphries, 21 February 1833.

William Pratt to Roselinda Everitt, 30 March 1837.

John T. Palmer to Elizabeth A. Barber, 24 December 1837.

Napoleon Potts to Susan Hodges, 18 February 1835.

Littleberry Parker to Elizabeth C. Thomas, 7 January 1835.

William Pittard to Elizabeth Palmer, 7 April 1835.

Leonard Parr to Mary Jane McDaniel, 27 August 1834.

Littleton Patterson to Elizabeth Dupree, 13 Febraury 1834.

Robert Page to Rebeckah Watkins, 16 January 1851.

John C. Pitner to Miss Sarah C. Weir, 21 October 1852.

Ruel K. Prigen to Miss Frances Wallice, 18 December 1853.

Jacob Peeler to Martha P. Merritt, 16 October 1853.

Albert G. Pitner to Mrs. (?) Martha E. Barber, 16 June 1853.

Elisha A. Plidger to Mary Ann E. Saunders, 23 June 1853.

Francis P. Prater to Miss Ann C. Kinney, 21 April 1853.

David Phillips to Malinda Johnson, 26 September 1854.

Dr. William H. Phillips to Martha Almira Marable, 4 October 1854.

John F. Pittard to Mary L. Ware, 6 April 1854.

Jacob N. Parsons to Elizabeth Tuck, 12 September 1854.

Wiley Peeler to Susannah Addams, 18 January 1855 (Performed by John Kirkpatrick, justice of the peace, who added: "and do further certify that I never want to be at such another Fandango, yours &c.")

John Patillo to Armanda L. Winfield, 6 December 1855.

Thomas H. Patman to Martha Epps, 13 May 1855.

Thomas J. Price to Martha B. Cavin, 1 April 1850.

Henry Peeler to Elizabeth Susan Culbreath, 30 May 1850.

Moses Parks to Martha E. Dickson, 16 January 1849.

Benjamin J. Parr to Sarah C. Sison, 12 February 1849.

Thomas Jefferson Pain to Mary Ann Nance, 15 March 1849.

West W. Parker to Perminah C. Brewer, 3 December 1848.

Lewis J. Parr to Lucy P. Dicken, 19 December 1848.

John A. Pledger to Elvira Crew, 10 December 1848.

James M. Patterson to Elizabeth W. Barber, 13 April 1847.

Elisha M. Pealor to Maria Loving, 15 July 1847.

Thomas J. Pinner to Mary Calahan, 1 October 1846.

Edward C. Paine to Lourania Broughton, 20 May 1845.

Allen Pearce to Sabra Francis Britt, 14 October 1845.

James W. Parker to Gazelle P. Morgan, 17 July 1845.

Sidney B. Paine to Agnes M. Hendron, 7 January 1845.

William R. Potter to Mary S. Garner, 17 March 1844.

West W. Parker to Sarah Brewer, 16 December 1844.

George M. Paine to Clementine Sansom (Lansum?), 21 March 1844.

A. B. Perry to Carolin Thrasher, 15 January 1843.

Augustus Patman to Margaret Barber, 26 January 1843.

John N. Pate to Lucy H. Moore, 21 April 1842.

W.H.W. Price to Perlina Knott, 10 February 1841.

George Powers to Tabitha J. Williams, 1 November 1841.

Robert C. Park to Sarah A. Crawford, 22 October 1840.

Joseph G. Paxton to Martha S. Deane, 6 February 1840.
Elias B. Pritchard to Susan A. Crawford, 19 January 1840.
Jonathan Parrish to Mary A. Brown, 15 March 1840.
William L. Parr to Sarah Williams, 5 September 1839.
Samuel J. Parish to Margaret A. Brown, 29 January 1839.
Jeptha V. Perry to Sarah F. Nunnally, 5 April 1838.
Dennis R. Puryear to Elizabeth J. Puryear, 24 December 1838.
Benjamin B. Parker to Lettitia Glenn, 15 March 1838.
Noel F. Roberds to Highley Carter, 10 March 1808.
Briant Rushing to Charity Obarr, 12 April 1806.
Sandford L. Ramey to Nancy Heard, 3 February 1807.
Preston Runnels to Dyce Cannon, 9 July 1806.
Jesse Rippy to Marcy Mecune, 16 September 1806.
Thomas Roberts to Amey Eastridge, 28 July 1810.
James Robeson to Sally Haynes, 9 January 1810.
Joseph Rasberry to Polly Sharard (?), 19 December 1812.
James Robeson to Margaret Simonton, 20 November 1812.
Osburn Rodgers to Mary Thorne, 20 April 1813.
Edmund Ramey to Jane L. Haynes, 25 August 1814.
Charles A. Redd to Elizabeth Gresham, 22 February 1814.
Willis Richards to Harriett Lee, 27 April 1814.
William Roberts to Sarah Byford, 23 February 1817.
Reuben Ransom to Nancy Holmes, 17 November 1818.
Henry Reese to Mary Bonner, 7 September 1819.
Green Runnels to Erwin Allen, 18 February 1819.
Fryer Robertson to Peggy Spillers, 26 August 1817.
Nelson Ridgeway to Nancy H. Jackson, 4 May 1820.
Thomas Roberson to Silvana Hayes, 14 March 1821.
Sylvanus Ripley to Obedience B. Cheatham, 1 December 1822.
William Roberts to Mary Finn, 25 June 1822.
Right Rogers to Elizabeth C. Houghton, 14 May 1822.
Edward Runnells to Delana Laseter, 10 May 1822.
Josa Ragan to Matilada Deane, 9 February 1823.
Richard Richardson to Letitia Johnston, 14 January 1823.
John G. Roberts to Sarah Clark, 27 February 1823.
Henry Reese to Mary Morris, 20 November 1825.
Grant Roberds to Frances Pass, 14 August 1825.
James Rasberry to Sarah Moon, 9 September 1826.
Thomas Reynolds to Matilda Thomas, 9 November 1826.
William O. Rutledge to Melena Foster, 7 December 1826.
James Robinson to Nancy Hinson, 31 December 1828.
Absalom B. Ross to Nancy Echols, 22 April 1828.
Purmedus Reynolds to Nancy Foster, 13 April 1831.
Jeremiah Robertson to Terisa Moore, 10 March 1831.
James Richardson to Nancy Jordan, 21 December 1837.
John J. Robertson to Hinson G. Holder, 8 September 1836.
Isaac D. Read to Mary F. Brightwell, 23 April 1835.

John Richardson to Amelia Sims, 11 March 1835.
David Richardson to Selina F. Gerald, 3 December 1835.
Duke Richardson to Emily H. Nunnally, 3 September 1835.
David Royster to Mertis Ann Wood, 13 July 1834.
William T. Roberson to Manerva E. Thompson, 16 January 1851.
James Rhoades to Miss Polley Rowlan, 11 November 1852.
Seaborn J. Ramey to Wildey Wiggins, 22 August 1852.
James M. Ridgeway to Martha F. Thompson, 16 September 1852.
John N. Rigway to Miss Sarah A. Harper, 27 January 1853.
Andrew Ray to Mary Kettle, 9 November 1854.
William T. Robertson to Martha Ann Elizabeth Elder, 18 December 1855.
S. C. Rose to Sarah F. Weatherly, 26 September 1850.
Francis Rawson to Miss Ann B. Evans, 27 December 1850.
Robert Randolph to Mary Brown, 8 May 1849.
Eugenius Rawson (Ransom?) to Permelia Angeline Stewart, 28 January 1849.
Reuben R. Ransom to Mary J. Dobbins, 26 September 1848.
John A. Reynolds to Caroline Pamelia Wooldridge, 8 August 1848.
James S. Ralls to Martha Hewell, 5 October 1848.
Lafayette Runyan to Charity M. Blackman, 12 November 1848.
Anderson Ray to Nancy Cook, 17 December 1848.
Jesse Robison to Martha Couch, 6 May 1847.
Sydney C. Reese to Caroline M. Hardin, 9 September 1847.
James F. Ralls to Sarah Ann Branch, 5 December 1846.
Tolerson Ray to Nancy Ann Rutledge, 22 January 1846.
Joseph Ratchford to Miss Mary A. Willson, 17 December 1845.
John P. Robinson to Sarah E. Danielly, 31 December 1843.
Robert (?) Martin Reynolds to Alla Thomas, 2 May 1843.
John S. Robison to Rebecca A. Montgomery, 11 March 1841.
James M. Royal to Frances E. Rumney, 9 August 1840.
Charles M. Reese to Elizabeth W. Gerardine, 6 May 1839.
Charles Roberts to Martha Buckhannon, 24 November 1839.
Henry H. Richardson to Malinda Skeats (Sheats?), 21 February 1839.
John W. Richardson to Martha Whitlow, 14 March 1839.
James Miner Sturgus to Sarah E. Brooks, 27 December 1849.
Richard Stewart to Polley Culbertson, 21 December 1809.
William Saunders to Ann Gilmore, 1 January 1809.
Nimrod Smith to Patsy Baker, 26 January 1806.
Levi Stroud to Fanny Hagwood, 24 November 1807.
Robert Stuart to Pricilla Greer, 7 July 1807.
William Simon to Polley Wood, 11 August 1807.
Elijah Strong to Polly Mathews, 30 October 1806.
Charles Sawers to Meary Hopkins, 30 July 1806.
James Smith to Edny Arnold, on or about 29 December 1806.
John Skeen to Eady Hancock, 15 November 1808.
Eli Stroud to Betsy Durby, 12 October 1808.
John Simons to Betsy Whatley, 2 January 1808.
John Sansom to Elizabeth Dunn, 13 November 1815.

John Selmon to Biddy Wright, 12 March 1805.
Joseph Self to Rachel Bearden, 25 February 1810.
Samuel H. Swinney to Nancy Laseter, 25 September 1810.
Laban Shephard to Agnes Smith, 7 December 1811.
Tapley Straughan to Nancy Straughan, 1 August 1811.
James Simmons to Pacience Smith, 18 September 1812.
Thomas Seates to Prudence Peaney, 12 September 1813.
John Shaw to Patsey Grimes, 11 April 1813.
Ezekiel Stanley to Elizabeth Rutledge, on or after 9 June 1813.
Francis Stranger (Straun?) to Nancy Parker, 23 December 1813.
Dewel Summers to Patsey Harper, 24 November 1813.
Paul Satterwhite to Catherine Powell, 30 March 1814.
Ralph Smith to Susannah Turner, 25 October 1814.
Nicholas Smith to Courtney Deane, 9 February 1815.
John Stevens to Polly White, 4 May 1815.
Reuben Stewart to Charity Hale, 19 December 1815.
Wm. M. Stokes to Jane Bridgewater, 16 November 1815.
Daniel Summers to Charlotte Morris, 9 July 1815.
Joseph Sanders to Gilley Buckney, 22 February 1816.
Benjamin Selman to Matilda Wright, 9 January 1816.
William Stroud to Serrena Battles, 8 November 1814.
Martain Smith to Rutha Gamble, 16 October 1816.
William Spinks to Bedy Bohonnon, 8 February 1816.
George S. Streat to Mary C. Colling, 5 December 1816.
Edwin Studiven to Lucinda Hicks, 25 February 1816.
Richard Shackleford to Polley McSparren, 20 January 1817.
James Stevens to Gilley Barber, 24 December 1817.
Orin Stroud to Milcah Trammell, 18 September 1817.
James Shepherd to Nancy Moton, 8 February 1818.
Thomas Smith to Nancy Edmondson, 2 April 1818.
William Stephens to Nancy Gray, 10 December 1818.
James Smith to Polly Harris, 2 August 1818.
Joseph Shaw to Polly Callahan, 11 March 1819.
George Shipley to Salley Spenks, 26 December 1819.
John Smith to Keziah Bridion, 2 September 1819.
Anderson Statom to Charlotty Moore, 20 April 1820.
Sanders J. Scroggin to Martha Pendergrass, 15 May 1821.
William Shaw Jr. to Sarah Harper, 4 October 1821.
John Sherling to Rebecca Hancock, 25 November 1821.
Alford Stewart to Polly Crawford, 13 August 1820.
Thomas Stewart to Peggy Holder, 22 October 1821.
John F. Stevens to Martha Harper, 4 February 1819.
Millington Scogin to Mary H. Carter, 26 February 1822.
Job Smith to Charlotte Endens (Evans?), 7 February 1822.
William Smith to Sally Moss, 16 May 1822.
Montford Stokes to Cealia A. McMurphy, 22 December 1823.
Washington Strickland to Miss Elizabeth Gray, 18 January 1843.

James R. Smith to Elizabeth Mathews, 17 November 1822.
William J. Strong to Sally Bowling, 26 August 1822.
Seabourn Summers to Nancy Shaw, 14 November 1822.
Stephen Tredwill to Sarah Bonner, 7 March 1822.
Lindsey Sheats to Martha Wade, 8 February 1824.
Daniel S. Smith to Elizabeth M. Winn, 11 March 1824.
Joshua Stephens Jr. to Mary Gann, 22 July 1824.
Timothy Swinney to Elizabeth Alldred, 16 November 1823.
James J. Scoggin to Cintha Harris, 24 June 1825.
Daniel Shores to Susan Bearding, 4 January 1825.
Loree Sims to Vicy McCallum, 10 February 1825.
Tolbert G. Smith to Elizabeth B. Harris, 12 December 1825.
Wm. J. Smith to Thena Duncan, 13 February 1825.
John A. Strickland to Elizabeth Simonton, 19 December 1826.
Noah Strickland to Charlotte Vandeford, 10 March 1826.
John H. Sims to Ann R. Wade, 20 December 1827.
George Stettman to Ellen Lowe, 6 February 1827.
George W. Shaw to Mary P. Jackson, 28 February 1828.
David Smith to Epsey T. Sanford, 10 July 1828.
Harris Stephens to Mary Daniel, 21 February 1828.
Joseph T. Stokes to Hannah (?) Carty, 16 December 1828.
James M. Strong to Mary A. S. Lumpkin, 13 December 1828.
John Stroud to Tensey Stroud, 28 December 1828.
Almis M. Singleton to Lucinda Burrough, 25 March 1829.
James Shaw to Polley Gann, 30 September 1829.
Robert Smith to Gilly Smith, 20 October 1829.
Joseph Smith to Nancy Whitlow, 24 December 1829.
David Statum to Sarah Conner, 10 November 1829.
Levy Stewart to Elizabeth Holder, 2 February 1829.
Thomas Stewart to Lucinda Wood, 23 August 1829.
James Shaw to Polly Gann, 11 February 1830.
John A. Strickland to Mary Scoggin, 14 October 1830.
Samuel Simonton to Ann C. Brightwell, 12 May 1831.
Thomas Simonton to Sophronia Ann Gordon, 24 November 1831.
Charles Spiller to Elizabeth Wiggins, 17 November 1831.
Hardy Strickland to Sarah Daniel, 4 October 1831.
John W. Selman to Minerva L. Sheats, 15 March 1832.
Benjamin L. Sims to Jane Sherley, 30 September 1832.
Charles A. Smith to Mary F. Davenport, 22 June 1832.
Fielding M. Smith to Susan A. Nunnally, 12 January 1832.
Joshua Smith to Emily Allen, 20 December 1832.
John Strong to Harriett Hinton, 13 December 1832.
John Sturdivant to Mary James, 10 May 1832.
John D. Swift to Maryann Harris, 21 February 1832.
Ansel B. Strickland to Miss Polly Braswell, 26 August 1855.
Marten Luther Strong to Miss Georgia A. Hill, 14 October 1852.
Robert M. Smith to Miss Rosa J. Pringle, 9 August 1853.

James Summergill to Rosanna Parker, 2 December 1853.
Osborne D. Shaw to Mary Ward, 13 November 1853.
Henry P. Staples to Elizabeth Ward, 16 January 1853.
Malcom Strafford to Epsey Herron, 31 January 1853.
Milton Sayre to Miss Minerva J. Winstead, 11 August 1853.
Marcellus Stanley to Miss Julia A. T. Pope, 8 November 1854.
Abram Smith to Frances Klutts, 19 January 1854.
William B. Stewart to Mary L. Nabers, 8 December 1854.
William Sanders to Sarah Jane Smith, 24 January 1855.
Silas C. Stewart to Alethia E. Huff, 31 December 1855.
Alfred Stewart to Miss Mary Tennessee Haggard, 4 November 1855.
Presley B. Starnes to Jemima Blackman, 8 July 1855.
Benjamin M. Spurlock to Miss B. Lucretia Starnes (Stone?), 2 September 1855.
John Seay (Sears?) Jr. to Sarah J. Lowery, 20 December 1855.
Richard A. Saye to Martha I. Gathright, 19 March 1850.
Washington F. Stark to Lucretia E. Daniel, 1 April 1856.
Robert M. Stephenson to Aseneth S. Dobbins, 14 November 1850.
Thomas W. Stephenson to Miss Martha J. Crenshaw, 31 July 1850.
John Cicero Spinks to Eliza Brewer, 28 July 1850.
William Sims to Martha Ann Cox, 21 August 1849.
John Sikes to Prudence E. Jennings, 5 April 1849.
Wm. Sanders to Mary Ann Epps, 3 December 1848.
William A. C. Stinchcomb to Elizabeth T. Ridgeway, 1 October 1848.
John William Shaw to Nancy Catherine Echols, 2 January 1848.
John M. Stone to Mrs. (?) F. A. Smith, 30 April 1848.
William J. Small to Mary Ann E. Willson, 13 June 1848.
Jackson Shirley to Nancy Mullens, 31 January 1847.
Harman Schevenell to Nancy Mary Towns, 16 December 1847.
Joher Smith to Nancy Perry, 3 October 1847.
J. D. Sherrill to Miss Sarah E. Costler, 1 September 1847.
Walker Sims to Frances Mary Ann Elder, 26 January 1846.
Anthony S. Smith to Isabella Robison, 22 December 1846.
James J. Selman to Susan Walker, 8 December 1846.
Wiley O. Saunders to Rachel Emeline Smith, 8 October 1846.
Burey Smith to Nicy Griffeth, 24 December 1846.
Marion T. Sexten to Elaland McDummond, 21 August 1846.
Richard R. Salter to Miss Sophiah E. Welch, 19 November 1846.
John H. Smith to Eliza Connel, 9 January 1845.
Vardy H. Shelton to Sarah A. R. Brown, 4 December 1845.
William Sunderland to Martha Epps, 10 August 1845.
William P. Smith to Juda Jackson, 19 September 1844.
Sherman J. Simms to Amanda Jane Donoho, 10 October 1844.
Samuel H. Smith to Icey Blakeley, 26 October 1843.
E. Sanford Sims to Nancy McRee, 24 March 1843.
Daniel Statham to Orrey Connor, 1 January 1843.
Bradford H. Spinks to Sarah G. McDonough, 10 December 1843.

Augustus D. Short to Miss Jane G. Smith, 25 December 1842.

Henry O. Silvey to Martha Ann Ward, 4 November 1841.

James Shaw to Joannah Davis, 18 February 1841.

Lewis S. Salmons to Permelia Ann Garpley, 15 January 1840.

Daniel Summers to Elizabeth Whitman, 19 February 1840.

Henry Thomas Stephens to Elizabeth Epps, 26 March 1840.

Overton Stephens to Sarah Ann Humphreys, 14 January 1840.

Thomas Stephens to Mary Conner, 24 January 1840.

James J. Selman to Margaret F. Hester, 15 December 1840.

David Stephens to Anzalina Howse, 18 April 1839.

Young J. W. H. Stephens to Rebecca Connor, 28 April 1839.

William Sunderlin to Lovicy Beasley, 24 February 1839, Sunday morning about 9 AM.

William Simms to Eavmin Elder, 1 January 1839.

Dennis Shay to Rachael Carr, 11 April 1839.

John B. Smith to Julia Ann M. Ryan, 14 March 1839.

George Sherwood to Nancy Parish, 11 July 1839.

Seaborn J. Smith to Levicia Davenport, 22 December 1839.

Robert Swan to Mary Roades, 3 May 1838.

William A. Steedley to Zeliann Britt, 25 September 1838.

Daniel R. Stephens to Mary E. Starks, 29 November 1838.

John Shannon to Frances C. Moore, 28 June 1837.

James M. Shepherd to Mary Varner, 25 January 1837.

William Silvey to Mary Brown, 26 January 1836.

George W. Sims to Adaline Glasson, 10 February 1836.

Paul J. Semmes to Emily J. Hemphill, 14 June 1836.

James Shepherd to Mary Vickers, 2 April 1835.

Anderson W. Smith to Sarah H. Pendergrass, 16 July 1835.

Theodoric L. Smith to Frances A. Broadnax, 21 September 1835.

William Snead Sr. to Nancy M. McDuffie, 4 May 1834.

Nicholas Sheats to Martha Fullilove, 9 April 1834.

Elem W. Smith to Susan W. Floyd, 17 April 1834.

Bennet Sims to Mary Ann Mathews, 27 February 1834.

Russell Shepard to Mary Treadwell, 3 April 1834.

Jones Stark to Avarilla Kent, 18 December 1834.

Robenson H. Scogin to Catherine Smith, 18 December 1834.

Robert W. Tuck to Elizabeth G. Embrey, 14 November 1833.

Thomas Thompson to Sarah Reese, 16 January 1833.

David Trammel to Fanny Boid, 24 November 1809. (Note on back that Coleman Runnels married Betsy Durham on the same day.)

Robert Tremble to Ruth Thrasher, 7 September 1808.

Thomas Townsend to Nicy Taylor, 3 February 1808.

William Thompson to Patsy Keenum, 13 November 1808.

William Tegner to Jincy McAlphin, 21 February 1808.

Benjamin Thurmond to Polly Brownfield, 10 November 1807.

James Taylor to Salley Oats, 28 April 1808.

Joshua Tileyry to Salley Fussell, 29 October 1807.

Allen Trawick to Sally Kinney, 13 January 1807.

John Trammel to Polly Dickenson (?), 13 July 1807.

Permission from Saml. Hester for Philamon Thompson to marry Hester's daughter Sarah Leigh Hester, 28 December 1807.

Philamon Thompson to Sarah (Marah?) Hester, 31 December 1807.

Josiah Taylor to Epsebeth Looker, 1 October 1807.

Stephen Thomas to Eliza P. Carey, 11 February 1807.

Edmond W. Taylor to Salley Stuart, on or after 11 April 1806.

James Tommason to Elizabeth Hendon, 4 August 1806.

Allen Thornton to Ann Heard, 11 September 1805.

Andrew Townsend to Delilah Peirce, 5 May 1803 (1805?).

Richard Thompson to Fanne Middlebrooks, 12 September 1810.

Robert Trawick to Elizabeth Powel, 25 January 1810.

Harris Trammell to Sally Hagwood, 13 August 1812.

Nathaniel Twining to Salley Hunton, 26 July 1814.

Micajah Thomas (?) to Eliza Turner, 25 June 1811.

Alexander S. Tait to Darcus R. Billups, 23 November 1815.

Thomas Tanner to Jane R. Dougherty, 9 November 1815.

Jacob Tredwell to Polly Bonner, 3 August 1815.

John Tyner to Nancy Bryant, 30 April 1811.

Isaac Treadwell to Patsey Wilson, 5 September 1816.

Thomas Tye (?) to Fanny Maxey, 9 February 1816.

Reuben Turner to Mary Nall, 27 December 1821.

Martin Taneer to Patsey Miller, 19 February 1818.

Theophilus Thomas to Elizabeth M. Colley, 23 August 1819.

Benj. F. Tucker to Jane Hunter, 8 October 1822.

Francis Trammell to Sarah Copeland, 25 February 1819.

John Turner to Henry Nall, 7 December 1820.

Drury Thomas to Lucinda Hinton, 1 February 1824.

James A. Thornton to Sarah Craig, 16 September 1824.

William Tindall to Elizabeth J. Harwill, 15 January 1824.

John Trammell to Jane Harris, 13 November 1823.

James Turner to Elizabeth Fambrough, 16 April 1823.

Tapley B. Tolbert to Sarah Tolbert, 9 December 1824.

Richardson Tuck to Martha M. Embry, 28 September 1825.

Miles Tolbert to Ann Tolbert, 2 March 1826.

John Taylor to Frances Whitton, 25 October 1829.

Samuel Thomas to Peggy Craft, 21 February 1828.

James Thompson to Lucy Greer, 2 April 1828.

Middleton Thompson to Martha R. Sheats, 10 December 1829.

Thomas Thompson to Rebecca B. Smith, 13 August 1829.

William Talbot to Elizabeth Fullalove, 12 June 1830.

Robert Thompson to Mary S. Hendon, 14 January 1830.

Allen E. Thompson to Ellender Fenn, 4 July 1831.

Thomas A. Tuck to Nancy Ann Summers, 8 November 1831.

Shubael Tenney to Mary Ann Fulwood, 10 January 1832.

Frederick Thompson to Eliza House, 29 February 1832.

John Thomas to Milison D. Thomas, 13 March 1836.

William Thompson to Emily House, 7 February 1836.
Stevens Thomas Jr. to Miss Isabella L. Hays, 20 June 1836.
George Turnell to Martha F. Sansom, 2 October 1835.
Henry Waring Todd to Emily E. Watkins, 20 October 1835.
Lovick Pierce Thomas to Martha Ann Bedell, 6 May 1834.
John Talbot to Emily Kinney, 14 August 1834.
Harris Thurmond to Easlena S. Tarpley, 16 June 1834.
Asbury Thompson to Ann M. Cheatham, 28 January 1834.
Robert G. T. Taylor to Tallulah L. Harris, 23 October 1851.
Robert Turnell to Elizabeth A. Hunt, 50 (?) December 1851.
Robert Trammell to Martha E. Veal, 16 October 1851.
James H. Thompson to Sarenia Haygood, 16 (15?) September 1852.
John F. Thurman to Mary W. Thompson, 22 February 1852.
Hartwell J. Thomas to Almira C. Elder, 22 December 1853.
Richard D. Taylor to Miss Sarah J. Billips, 6 October 1853.
Thomas C. Threatt to Salina Floid, 17 July 1853.
Tavner Threatt to Martha Lee, 8 May 1853.
Coalman Tucker to Harriet Kidd, 14 November 1854.
Isaac Treadwell to Sarah A. McRee, 1 February 1855.
William T. Thornton to Miss Jinnie A. Barrett, 15 November 1855.
G. G. Thompson to Miss Mary Stovall, 1 January 1855.
William Thomas to Matilda Ann Elder, 25 October 1853.
John G. Thomas to Miss Susan A. Carr, 12 November 1856.
Henry Tuggle to Hannah R. Stewart, 8 November 1850.
John M. Tilly to Miss Sarah A. Pringle, 3 January 1850.
James Thompson to Mrs. Martha Roberts, 20 January 1850.
George N. Thompson to Elizabeth A. Jackson, 25 April 1850.
James Talbert to Mary C. Haden, 1 February 1849.
Richard O. Thurman to Caroline E. Tindall, 23 December 1849.
Beverly A. Thornton to Georgia A. Lamar, 22 November 1849.
John C. Thurman to Sarah Ann T. Welch, 8 March 1849.
Wiley A. Thornton to Sarah Haygood, 5 October 1848.
Moland H. Thornton to Miss Aley Crow, 5 October 1848.
James H. Towns to Nancy C. Cavin, 12 October 1848.
Robert Timms to Sarah Morris, 13 June 1847.
Caswell G. Transwell to Nancy E. Sansom, 22 December 1847.
James R. Thurmond to Julia A. Hamilton, 25 June 1846.
William H. Thurmond to Miss Mariah L. Herden, 6 October 1845.
Wiley Thompson to Martha N. McLeroy, 25 September 1845.
Richard M. Thompson to Mary Bassett, 24 December 1845.
John M. Towns to Amelia Frances Towns, 15 October 1844.
Willism Thompson to Dolly Lee, 15 February 1843.
Aaron Thompson to Mary Moss, 10 February 1842.
William P. Talmadge to Elizabeth A. Royal, 17 March 1842.
William Thomas Jr. to Mary Ann Whitlaw, 16 March 1842.
William Thomas III to Jane Burney, 2 January 1842.
Barton C. Thrasher to Mary S. B. Elder, 23 December 1841.

Isaiah Totherrow to Martha Craft, 24 December 1839.

Washington Thomas to Martha M. Hale, 3 January 1839.

Henry B. Tenney to Elizabeth W. Punchard, 12 April 1839.

Jet Thomas to Sarah P. Haile, 7 February 1839.

Anthony Toney to Awrena Gann, 27 May 1839.

James D. Thomas to Sarah E. Billips, 7 August 1838.

John Urnhart to Lucinda Pinnar, 12 May 1834.

Isaac S. Vincent to Delia Ann Haynes, 30 June 1833.

Ferdinand Vickers to Anna Vickers, 7 March 1820.

James Vickers to Elizabeth Lassiter, 23 September 1817.

John Vaughan to Pricilla D. Edwards, 9 September 1823.

Absalom Vickers to Elizabeth Moore, 11 May 1825.

William Vandiford to Delila Miligan, 3 April 1827.

David A. Vason to Miss Cordelia Ann Pope, 6 November 1837.

Young Vickers to Mary Laird, 5 September 1837.

Isaac V. Vinson to Rebeccah E. F. Aikin, 28 February 1837.

Martin Vickers to Maryann Stevens, 20 December 1836.

William F. M. Veal to Sarah Jacks, 30 September 1852.

B. F. Venable to Mildred Wallice, 8 October 1854.

Obadiah Vinson to Martha Gunter, 8 March 1849.

Moses Vincent to Martha Shaw, 4 June 1840.

Alexander Veal to Sarah Jane Godfrey, 5 December 1839.

Allen C. Vanderford to Delia Ann Greer, 18 June 1839.

Jack Welborn to Elizabeth "Betsey" Jackson, 19 October 1809.

William Wood to Betsy Sims, 30 May 1809.

James Wheeler to Betsy McCune, 1 February 1809.

Petter Williamson to Betsey Spurlock, 16 March 1808. (Note on back: "Mr. Williamson Please Excuse the situation I was Log Roling Jno. Smith, Register of Probates".)

Thomas Washam (Worsham?) to Salley Herren (?), 26 July 1807.

William Henry Walden to Betsy Mercer, 11 September 1806.

Samuel Wallace to Lyda Beazley, 3 August 1806.

Daniel West to Polley Middleton, 21 August 1806.

Robert Williams to Ann Crawford, 17 March 1810.

William Wright to Nancy McCoy, 1 July 1810.

Elijah Wilkeson to Polley Holt, 9 September 1806.

William Weatherby to Elizabeth Smith, 6 May 1811.

Tucker Whitfield to Elizabeth Cookson, 26 September 1811.

Samuel Wier to Ann Wheler, 10 December 1811.

Thomas A. Williams to Gilly Mannig, 18 April 1811.

John Webb to Faithey Alford, 30 August 1812.

Walton Whatley to Indy Childers, 3 June 1805.

Thomas Willoughbe to Agness Hays, 7 January 1813.

Obediah Ward to Susan Fambraugh, 8 September 1814.

Moses Watkins to Elizabeth Angle, 7 December 1814.

Reason Whitehead to Celia Bell, 29 April 1814.

Vincent Watson to Prudence Hill, 13 July 1815.

John H. Watts to Prudence Hill, 27 April 1815.

Thomas Wortham to Nancy Bickerstaff, 30 November 1815.

Collins Waters to Matilda Britton, 28 July 1816.

Andrew White to Elizabeth Childers, 19 August 1817.

Wade White to Salley Traylor, 24 October 1816.

William Whitton to Catherine Henson, 24 November 1817.

Richard L. Wilkerson to Nancy Powell, 22 September 1817.

Benjamin Williams to Patsey Pounds, 1 October 1816.

James Whitehead to Edy Ball, 8 December 1818.

Inman Whitton to Susannah Warren 28 June 1818.

Job Wilkins to Rutha Thompson, 21 June 1818.

Merrit Wood to Catherine Garner, 19 July 1818.

John Wood to Nancy Wooton, 28 May 1817.

Benjamin Ware (Ward?) to Rebecca Hagin, 11 May 1819.

Leonard Ward to Susannah McCallam, 22 July 1819.

Littleberry Watts to Margaret Harvey, 20 April 1819.

Wm. J. Wilbun to Louisa H. Darby, 27 January 1819.

Benjamin Williams to Kessey L. Hancock, 3 February 1819.

Nathan Ward to Elizabeth Cannada, 26 December 1820.

James Wilkins to Lucy Adams, 11 June 1820.

Robert Wilkins to Charity Cagle, 7 January 1820.

James R. Walker to Nancy Smith, 19 November 1821.

Robert Williby to Elizabeth Medows, 14 December 1820.

Jonathan Ward to Mariah Sims, 22 November 1821.

Puckett Wood of Jackson County to Miss Patsey Barbour of Clarke County, 4 January 1821.

A. W. Wright to Sarah Hailes, 22 February 1821.

James P. Waddel to Frances Hull, 28 October 1822.

William Waller to Eliza Gann, 19 September 1822.

John Ward to Catherine Carmichael, 26 November 1822.

Nathan C. Williams to Sarah East McMurphay, 4 September 1822.

Robert Whitten to Elizabeth Kelley, 29 December 1823.

William Shitton to Nancy Garner, 30 December 1823.

Isham Wheeler to Mahala Hayes, 13 May 1824.

John White to Luzina H. Gray, 30 September 1824.

Job Wilkey to Mary Summers, 12 August 1824.

Wayne Wise to Susan Thompson, 9 December 1824.

William Watson to Margaret Barber, July 21, 1825.

Joel Williams to Mary Smith, 13 October 1825.

William Wright to Mary Madox, 6 July 1825.

Isma W. Wooldridge to Mariah W. Thomas, 30 December 1824.

William W. Ward to Sally S. Carmichael, 18 October 1826.

John Wilkins to Lur Nall, 9 October 1823.

Thomas Wood Jr. to Nancy Garner, 30 October 1823.

Joseph Wells to Elizabeth A. Gerrald, 14 December 1826.

Charles Wilson to Jane Barber, 23 July 1823.

Abijah Wise to Rutha Wise, 11 October 1826.

Merritt Wood to Nancy Jeffs, 17 November 1826.

William Wright to Sidney Hailes, 21 December 1826.
Robert Whitfield to Charity Daniell, 18 October 1827.
Jesse Whitlow to Frances C. Allen, 4 January 1827.
Nathan W. Whitman to Elizabeth Stone, 13 September 1827.
William Whitlow to Permelia H. Allen, 2 October 1828.
George Whitton to Peggy Garner, 7 February 1828.
James Williams to Sarah McCarty, 21 December 1828.
Paschal J. Whatley to America J. Marable, 19 November 1829.
Ransom A. Whitehead to Marilda Doggett, 16 July 1829.
Ellis Williby to Elizabeth Durham, 31 December 1829.
Josiah Wallis to Julia Ann Ramey, 27 June 1830.
Edward Rowell Ware to Margaret Elizabeth Bacon, 13 April 1830.
Williamson Whitehead to Nancy Cagle, 6 December 1830.
Thomas Whitfield to Rene Gann, 10 October 1830.
John Wright to Lucy Andrew, 12 May 1830.
Sanford Whitehead to Elmira Wise, 22 December 1831.
Jesse M. Wilson to Nancy A. Moore, 17 February 1831.
John Wood to Martha Brightwell, 2 June 1831.
Lucian R. Wheeler to Mary Williams, 5 January 1832.
Joseph Cleggins to Pamelia Brown, 6 November 1832.
Samuel Wilkes to Elizabeth Garner, 28 December 1832.
John A. C. Williams to Mary Ann L. Smith, 18 December 1832.
A. D. Wooldridge to Susan J. H. Wooldridge, 26 April 1832.
Clark P. William to Harriett Jossey, 12 March 1833.
William G. Wright to Milly Moss, 22 December 1833.
William Williams to Pressie Thompson, 22 February 1833.
Joseph C. Wilkins to Mary E. Grant, 27 June 1837.
Richard M. Whitehead to Ann Glasson, 13 November 1837.
William Williams to Martha Haile, 26 December 1837.
Greene Wiggins to Ann Smith, 21 May 1837.
Caleb Whitehead to Martha Craft, 9 January 1837.
William White to Elisa Greer, 12 March 1837.
John Wade to Martha H. Maxey, 3 January 1836.
Wilson O. B. Whatley to Elizabeth W. Lumpkin, 15 December 1836.
Charles J. Winn to Rebeckah Young, 23 April 1835.
Edward Williams to Elizabeth Wilkerson, 5 March 1835.
William Wood to Matilda Kines, 9 February 1835.
Joe E. Whitfield to Miss Emenline Summers, 25 December 1835.
R. S. Williams to Lucy Jane Puryear, 8 December 1835.
David Weaver to Sarah Hinesly, 4 September 1835.
George Williams to Elizabeth H. Allen, 19 June 1834.
John T. Williams to Elizabeth Williby, 15 April 1834.
Samuel Walker to Sarah McCollum, 6 May 1834.
William B. Wood to Mary Durham, 18 December 1834.
James M. Willoughby to Martha F. Hester, 1 May 1851.
William James Weatherford to Emily Hemrick, 25 May 1851.
Joseph Sinclear to Sarah Louise Morton, 6 May 1851.

Freeman Westmoreland to Mary Vinson, 11 February 1851.
James C. Williamson to Frances A. Fellows, 6 May 1852.
James R. Woods to Matilda B. Hillsman, 2 June 1852.
John Wimberly to Martha Ann Barnes, 5 December 1852.
James C. Wilson to Nancy P. Park, 29 January 1852.
Clark W. Welch to Marth J. Parker, 26 August 1852.
J. R. Wilson to Miss R. A. Rust, 4 November 1852.
Notle Wortham to Nancy Peeler, 27 March 1853.
John C. Whitner to Miss Martha S. Cobb. 28 September 1853.
David Waggoner to Susan E. Jennings, 20 January 1853.
John B. Ward to Miss Martha A. Griffith, 24 March 1853.
Abraham C. Warren to Margaret Peeler, 15 May 1853.
Wm. W. Wilson to Miss Caroline A. Elder, 8 November 1853.
Wm. A. Woodis to Miss Sarach C. Jackson, 16 April 1853.
James W. Wilson to Elizabeth A. White, 31 August 1854.
William J. Wadkins to Elizabeth Nix, 25 June 1854.
Midleton M. Williams to Miss Lida J. Williams, 3 August 1854.
Adolphus D. Wamaling to Miss Georgia Ann Fellows, 6 April 1854.
Thomas W. Walker to Julia M. Adams, 22 November 1854.
Nicholas Ware to Frances A. Yerby, 3 December 1854.
Henry Wise to Sarah A. Stewart, 25 October 1855.
Westly W. Willson to Mary E. Bailey, 6 May 1855.
Robert T. Williams to Emaline Haile, 29 November 1855.
Charles W. Wallace to Miss Sarah A. Culp, 23 December 1855.
James A. Ward to Martrha Jacks, 3 January 1850.
John White to Cary Harelson, 24 July 1850.
Henry D. Wiggins to Jane White, 29 December 1850.
Jacob M. Weaver to Virginia B. Boothe, 19 December 1850.
Joseph Wise to Mary Ann Jarrell, 10 December 1850.
Robert W. Wier to Sarah J. Kirkpatrick, 12 July 1849.
Lewis Whitehead to Julia Ann Norris, 14 August 1849.
Dawson Williams to Elizabeth Haggard, 1 October 1848.
James C. Williamson to Miss Evelina Sisson, 3 October 1848.
Samuel White to Mary Timms, 6 July 1847.
Joseph T. Williams to Artemicia R. A. S. Vandivere, 28 October 1847.
Wiley Wood to Harriett N. Wozencraft, 5 July 1847.
William Wood to Mary Loving, 25 February 1847.
Jesse Whitehead to Mary Earnist, 15 July 1847.
John W. Wood to Ketty Elizabeth Stewart, 10 February 1847.
Thomas S. Williamson to Miss Cornelia C. Newton, 22 July 1847.
Moses M. Wilson to Miss Sarah Jane Stone, 25 February 1847.
Burdy O. Williams to Miss Martha Ann S. Maddux, 29 January 1846.
Charles J. Winn to Eliza J. Langford, 17 December 1846.
William T. Ward to Eliza Ann Burt, 19 April 1846.
Andrew J. Williamson to Nancy E. Kinney, 2 November 1845.
Sherwood Wise to Mary Eidson, 2 October 1845.
Stephen Wilbanks to Angelina Lanier, 18 December 1845.

William A. Whitlow to Almedea Jackson, 21 August 1845.
William Williams to Ruth Bell, 26 August 1845.
James C. Wilson to Elizabeth Fielding, 23 December 1845.
Archibald B. Whitlow to Susan Thrasher, 2 January 1845.
William Willborn to Ann Bolls, 29 June 1843.
Silas A. Wilson to Sarah A. Fambaugh, 9 November 1843.
John G. Woddail to Matilda Adeline Nunnally, 22 December 1842.
Robert T. Wright to Martha H. Cook, 15 December 1842.
Reuben Wallis to Frances Arthur, 14 October 1841.
Thomas H. S. Wiley to Mary Thurmond, 19 October 1841.
William T. Wozencraft to Amelia G. Oliver, 8 September 1840.
James P. Wilson to Jemima Barber, 17 April 1840.
Jett T. Wright to Mary S. Davenport, 18 April 1839.
John Wood to Fanny Kelly, 29 December 1839.
Nicholas Welter to Sofrona Ann Weaver, 2 May 1839.
Abner Wood to Louisiana Silvey, 7 June 1838.
George K. Williams to Elvira Hamilton, 26 August 1838.
William H. H. White to Jemima Simpson, 12 November 1838.

PART iv: MICROFILMED RECORDS

XI. Inventory of County Records on Microfilm at the Georgia Department of Archives and History

For references to printed abstracts of some of the records listed below see James E. Dorsey, Georgia Genealogy and Local History: A Bibliography (Spartanburg: The Reprint Co., 1983).

ORDINARY OR PROBATE COURT

Microfilm reel	
102/29	Register of Agents, 1881-1896
102/32	Apprentice Book, 1837-1911
37/80	Apprenticeship Records and Bonds, Book A, 1802-1822
102/32	Miscellaneous Bonds, 1869-1882

Register of Births:

102/31	Scattered, incomplete, and not indexed, 1808-1852
19/77	Not indexed, 1875-1876

Bonds to Support Families of Confederate Soldiers:

37/97	1861-1869
97/3	1861-1869

County Copies of Federal Censuses (Note: The Georgia Department of Archives and History also has microfilm of Federal copies of Federal census records for Clarke County, 1820-1880 and 1900-1910, with state-side indexes to the same):

38/76	County Copy of 1850 Census
38/77	County Copy of 1860 Census
49/75	County Copy of 1860 Census
38/78	County Copy of 1880 Census
97/4	County Copy of 1880 Census

102/30	Chain Gang Records, 1883-1886
102/36	Lists of State Pensioners for Confederate Service, 1888-1934 (Note: Clarke County tax digests for 1906-1916, 1918-1934, and 1936-1938 have lists of Confederate veterans and widows, see below for tax digest microfilm.)
102/31	Peddlers Licenses for Disabled Confederate Veterans, 1909-1914
37/79	Pension Records, 1884-1912
97/3	same

(Mote: The Georgia Department of Archives and History has state penison files and lists of pensioners, arranged by county, for veterans and widows of veterans of the Southern Cause.)

37/79	Confederate Discharge Certificates, 1864
97/3	same

102/30	Coroner's Book, 1877-1892

County Commissioner Minutes (also see Inferior Court Minutes for County Purposes):

96/51	1898-1908, Indexed
98/40	1909-1927, Books B-D, Indexed
98/41	1927-1948, Books E-G, Indexed

County Officers Bonds:

96/48	1847-1957, Books A, B, F
97/24	1864

19/77 Register of Deaths, not indexed, 1875-1876

102/79 Register of Dentists, 1882-1945

Letters of Administration:
96/49 Temporary Letters, 1871-1893
96/50 And Guardianship, Volume C, 1890-1924

Administrators, Executors, and Guardians Books:
96/46 1811-1831, Book 1, not indexed
19/80 1829-1847, Book A, pt. i, indexed
97/24 1839, indexed
264/36 1845-1866, indexed
96/48 1847-1876, Book B, indexed
96/46 1849-1852. 1852-1876, not indexed
19/80 1856-1874, Book A, pt. ii, indexed
97/23 1867-1914, indexed
96/47 1876-1898, indexed; 1891-1949, not indexed
96/46 1889-1909, Guardians Bonds, not indexed
List of Administrators and Executors, 1811-1821

Annual Returns:
98/33 1905-1915, Books NN-OO
98/34 1915-1927, Books PP-SS
98/35 1927-1938, Books TT-VV
98/36 1938-1952, Books WW-YY
98/37 1855-1959, Books ZZ, I

96/8 Index to Estate Records, Books J-GG

19/80 Inventories and Appraisements, 1811-1828

102/32 Inventories and Sales of Estates, 1850-1860, 1859-1871

Miscellaneous Estate Records:
96/19 1799-1817, Books A-H
96/18 1815-1830
96/20 1818-1851, Books C-D
96/21 1827-1845, Books F-G
96/22 1838-1867, Books H-J
96/23 1847-1872, Books K-L
96/24 1847-1872, Book M
96/25 1853-1855, Book N
96/26 1853-1859, Book O
96/27 1856-1866, Book P
96/28 1858-1863, Book Q
96/29 1857-1866, Book R
96/30 1859-1871, Book S
96/31 1860-1863, Book T
96/32 1861-1866, Book U
96/33 1862-1868, Book V
96/34 1863-1866, Book W
96/35 1862-1873, Book X
96/36 1866-1883, Books Y-Z
96/37 1868-1885, Books AA-BB
96/38 1873-1883, Books CC-DD
96/39 1878-1914, Books EE-FF
96/40 1881-1956, Books GG-HH
96/41 1885-1894, Book JJ
96/42 1889-1898, Book KK
96/43 1893-1897, Book LL
96/44 1897-1905, Book MM
96/45 1881-1913, Book A

Letters Testamentary:
96/49 1871-1893
96/50 1892-1926, Book C

Wills (also see Ted O. Brooks, <u>In the Name of God Amen</u>: <u>Georgia Wills 1733-1860</u> (Atlanta, 1976):
<u>96/7</u> 1802-1859, Books A-C

96/8 1859-1911, Books D-E: undated general index
100/14 1912-1955, Books F-H

Years Support Estate Records:
96/54 1881-1925, Books A, 2
100/15 1924-1952, Books 3-4

97/23 Deeds and Mortgages, 1807-1814 (also see the more extensive deeds and mortgages under Superior Court below)

Homestead Records:
242/45 Docket and Applications, 1846-1869
96/54 Book A, 1869-1943
102/34 Pony Homesteads, 1884-1926

96/50 Ordinary's Expense Book, 1871-1882

97/24 Register of Free Persons of Color, 1847-1862

97/5 Headright Grants, 1803-1832
(Note: The Georgia Department of Archives and History has more extensive records of headright grants for the whole state on microfilm. See _Index to Headright and Bounty Grants of Georgia, 1756-1909_ (Easley, SC: Southern Historical Press, 1970.)

264/36 Inferior Court Dockets, 1841-1851

102/34 Inferior Court Funds, 1840-1871

Inferior Court Minutes (also see Ordinary Minutes):
97/16 County and Court Purposes, 1802-1840, not indexed
96/9 Ordinary Purposes, 1803-1829, not indexed
96/9 County Purposes, 1815-1836, not indexed
96/10 Ordinary Purposes, 1822-1830, 1830-1845, 1831-1846, no index
96/10 County Purposes, 1838-1855, no index
97/17 Court Purposes, 1839-1846, 1846-1852, 1852-1856, 1856-1865, no index
96/11 Ordinary Purposes, 1845-1851, indexed; 1846-1852, no index
96/11 County Purposes, 1854-1863, 1864-1872
102/34 County Purposes, 1866

Inferior Court Receipts:
264/35 1829-1835
97/22 1830-1831, 1841-1852

Inferior Court Writs:
97/18 1801-1810
97/19 1810-1820
97/20 1820-1829
97/21 1827-1840
97/22 1841-1852

96/53 Lunacy Records, Book 1, 1895-1909

Marriages:
80/59 1805-1821, Book A, indexed
96/3 1805-1867, Books A-C, indexed
96/4 1848-1872, Books D-E, indexed
96/5 1871-1890, Books F-H, indexed
96/6 1890-1901, Books I-J, indexed
100/5 1901-1917, Books K-M, indexed
100/7 1909-1916, Book 1 (Black), indexed
100/8 1916-1943, Books 2-4 (Black), indexed
100/6 1917-1945, Books N-P, indexed
100/9 1943-1956, Book 5 (Black), indexed
100/7 1945-1956, Books Q-R, indexed

Ordinary Minutes (see also Inferior Court Minutes for Ordinary Purposes):
96/12 1851-1863
96/13 1863-1873
96/14 1873-1885

96/15	1879-1890
96/16	1890-1901, Books A-B
96/17	1872-1879, also includes oaths
100/16	1902-1917, Books C-E
100/17	1917-1928, Books F-H
100/18	1928-1943, Books I-L
100/19	1943-1952, Books M-O
100/20	1852-1960, Books P-S
96/17	Index for 1889-1946

96/51 Miscellaneous Ordinary's Records, 1873-1882

97/24 Partnership Records, 1842-1872

102/30 Paupers Records, 1883-1886

102/29 Physicians Register, Books 1-2, 1895-1910

102/28 Poor School Funds, 1876-1879

97/23 Powers of Attorney, 1807-1814, 1835-1868

96/52 Road Register, 1908

School Board Records:

102/32	1839-1896
102/31	1864-1870
97/1	1858-1912, Free School Reports
	1846-1849, Scholars Reports
	1852-1872, Poor Children Records

102/19 Sheriff's Sales, 1842-1889

Treasurer's Book:

97/2	1857-1868, not indexed
264/35	1857-1868, not indexed
102/34	1889-1896, not indexed

102/32 U. S. Marshall's Book, 1878-1882

Voters Lists:

102/36	1890-1894, indexed
97/2	1896-1898, not indexed
97/15	1908, not indexed

SUPERIOR COURT

Microfilm reel

50/77 Bonds for fractional lots in leased in Baldwin and Wilkinson counties, early 1800s

102/25 Bonds and Writs, 1818-1834, 1811-1873

Registration of Charters:

102/24	Record of Charters, 1891-1909
98/38	Books 2-3, 1909-1944
98/39	Books 3-4, 1944-1958

100/2 Register of Decrees, Book 1, 1920

General Index to Deeds and Mortgages:

97/26	1801-1907, Grantees, A-K
97/28	1801-1907, Grantees, L-Z
97/25	1801-1907, Grantors, A-K
97/27	1801-1907, Grantors, L-Z
97/29	1890-1907, Filing Docket
97/30	1891-1899, Grantor and Grantee
97/31	1899-1908, Grantor and Grantee
99/46	1908-1913, Grantor and Grantee
99/48	1913-1941, Grantee, A-Q
99/49	1913-1941, Grantee, R-Z

99/46 1913-1941, Grantor, A-Dewberry
99/47 1913-1941, Grantor, Dewberry-Z
99/51 1941-1960, Grantee, A-Howe
99/52 1941-1960, Grantee, Huggins-Z
99/49 1941-1960, Grantor, A-G
99/50 1941-1960, Grantor, H-T
99/51 1941-1960, Grantor, U-Z

Deeds and Mortgages (also see Mortgages below.):
97/32 1802-1804, Book A
97/33 1803-1811, Book B
97/34 1805-1807, Book C
97/35 1807-1809, Book D
97/36 1809-1814, Books E-F
97/37 1811-1815, Book G
97/38 1814-1820, Book I

Deeds:
97/39 1815-1818, Book K
97/40 1818-1821, Book L
97/41 1821-1828, Books M-N
97/42 1828-1836, Books O-P
97/43 1836-1843, Books Q-R
97/44 1844-1850, Books S-T
97/45 1851-1859, Books U-V
97/46 1860-1866, Books W-X
97/47 1867-1873, Books Y-Z
97/48 1873-1876, Book AA
97/49 1876-1881, Books BB-CC
97/50 1881-1883, Book DD
97/51 1884-1887, Book EE
97/53 1887-1889, Book FF
97/52 1889-1890, Book GG
97/54 1890-1891, Book HH
98/1 1890-1892, Book JJ
98/2 1891-1897, Book KK
98/3 1892-1893, Book LL
98/4 1893-1894, Book MM
98/5 1894-1899, Book NN
98/6 1896-1899, Book OO
98/7 1896-1897, Book PP
98/8 1897-1899, Books QQ-RR
98/9 1899-1908, Book SS
98/42 1900-1903, Books TT-WW
98/43 1903-1906, Books XX-ZZ
98/44 1905-1907, Books 1-3
98/45 1907-1912, Books 4-6
98/46 1908-1912, Books 7-10
98/47 1911-1913, Books 11-13
98/48 1913-1918, Books 14-16
98/49 1914-1920, Books 17-19
98/50 1916-1917, Books 20-22
98/51 1917-1919, Books 23-26
98/52 1919-1920, Books 27-29
98/53 1920-1921, Books 30-33
98/54 1921-1923, Books 34-36
99/1 1923-1924, Books 37-40
99/2 1924-1925, Books 41-43
99/3 1925-1927, Books 44-47
99/4 1927-1928, Books 48-50
99/5 1928-1930, Books 51-54
99/6 1930-1931, Books 55-57
99/7 1931-1933, Books 58-60
99/8 1933-1934, Books 61-64
99/9 1935-1937, Books 65-67
99/10 1936-1938, Books 68-71
99/11 1937-1939, Books 72-74
99/12 1938-1940, Books 75-78
99/13 1939-1941, Books 79-81
99/14 1941-1942, Books 82-85
99/15 1942-1944, Books 86-88

99/16 1944-1945, Books 89-92
99/17 1945-1946, Books 93-95
99/18 1946, Books 96-98
99/19 1946-1947, Books 99-102
99/20 1947, Books 103-105
99/21 1947-1948, Books 106-109
99/22 1948-1949, Books 110-112
99/23 1948-1949, Books 113-116
99/24 1949-1950, Books 117-118
99/25 1949-1951, Books 119-122
99/26 1950-1951, Books 123-125
99/27 1951, Books 126-128
99/28 1951-1953, Books 129-132
99/29 1952-1953, Books 133-135
99/30 1953, Books 136-138
99/31 1953-1954, Books 139-142
99/32 1954-1955, Books 143-145
99/33 1954-1955, Books 146-148
99/34 1955-1956, Books 149-152
99/35 1955-1956, Books 153-155
99/36 1956, Books 156-159
99/37 1956-1957, Books 160-162
99/38 1957, Books 163-165
99/39 1957-1958, Books 166-169
99/40 1958, Books 170-172
99/41 1958, Books 173-175
99/42 1959-1959, Books 176-179
99/43 1959, Books 180-182
99/44 1959-1960, Books 183-185
99/45 1959-1960, Books 186-187

97/23 1807-1814, Copies in Ordinary's Office

General Index to Mortgages (also see General Index to Deeds above):
99/52 1908-1941, Realty Mortgages and Liens
99/53 1943-1955, Direct, A-Z; Reverse, A-C
99/54 1943-1955, Reverse, D-Z: 1956-1960, Direct, A-K
100/1 1956-1960, Direct, L-Z; Reverse, A-S
100/2 1956-1960, Reverse, T-Z

Mortgages (also see Deeds and Mortgages above):
98/10 1820-1838, Books K-M
98/11 1838-1854, Books N-P
98/12 1855-1879, Books Q-S
98/13 1879-1889, Books T-U
98/14 1887-1893, Books V-W
98/15 1893-1897, Books X-Y
98/16 1897-1907, Book Z
98/17 1889-1901, Book 1

Execution (on property) Docket:
100/10 1851-1925, Books 1-3
100/11 1926-1941, Books 4-5
100/12 1942-1953, Books 6-7
100/13 1953-1960, Book 8 (only to page 274)

Issue Docket:
100/3 1869-1932 Cases 1-6312, Books 1-4
100/4 1932-1958 Cases 6313-13, Books 5-9

102/28 Estray Records, 1817-1897

102/26 Grand Jury Minutes, 1814-1868, Book Q

223/27 Justice of the Peace Docket, 1837-1847 (241 District), 1850, 1858-1870, no index

102/27 Jury Lists, Civil Cases, 1879-1911

97/5 Land Court Minutes, 1834-1875

102/28 Marks and Brands, 1802-1869

Superior Court Minutes:

98/18	1801-1820, Books 1-5, no index
98/19	1820-1834, Books 6-11, no index
98/20	1834-1850, Books 12-16, no index
98/21	1850-1856, Books 17-19, no index
98/22	1857-1864, Books 20-21, no index
98/23	1864-1871, Books 22-24, no index
98/24	1872-1875, Books 25-26, no index
98/25	1875-1880, Book 27, no index
98/26	1880-1886, Books 28-29, indexed
101/42	1883-1891, Books 29-30, indexed
101/43	1889-1891, Book 31, indexed
98/27	1891-1895, Books 32-33, indexed
98/28	1896-1898, Book 34, indexed
98/29	1898-1900, Book 35, indexed
98/30	1900-1903, Book 36, indexed
100/25	1903-1911, Books 37-40
100/26	1911-1914, Books 41-42
100/27	1914-1919, Books 43-45
100/28	1919-1925, Books 46-49
100/29	1925-1929, Books 50-52
100/30	1929-1933, Books 53-55
100/31	1933-1936, Books 56-58
100/32	1936-1940, Books 59-61
100/33	1940-1943, Books 62-64
100/34	1943-1947, Books 65-67
100/35	1947-1950, Books 68-71
100/36	1950-1953, Books 72-74
100/37	1953-1956, Books 75-77
100/38	1958-1959, Books 81-82
100/39	1956-1958, Books 78-80

Plats (Surveys of Land):

100/2	Index; Book A
100/21	Books 1 & 3 (Book 2 was not filmed)
100/22	Book 4
100/23	Book 5
100/24	Book 6

100/2	Title Register, 1920-1938, Book 1

Veterans Discharge Records:

102/19	1918-1945, Book 1
102/20	1945-1946, Books 2-3
102/21	1946, Book 4
102/22	1946-1960, Books 5-6
102/23	1916-1919, World War I

Writs:

101/50	1802-1805, Books A-B, indexed
101/51	1805-1807, Books C-E, indexed
101/52	1806-1811, Books F-G, indexed
101/53	1805-1811, Books H-I, indexed
101/54	1804-1813, Books K-L, indexed
102/1	1815-1817, Books O-P, indexed
102/2	1816-1820, Books R-S, indexed
102/25	1818-1834, indexed
102/3	1819-1825, Books T-U, indexed
102/4	1822-1842, Book V, indexed
102/5	1822-1829, Book W, indexed
102/6	1837-1841
102/7	1841-1843
102/8	1843-1859
102/9	1844-1859, Book 28
102/10	1851-1861, Book 26
102/11	1852-1862, Book 29
102/12	1838-1876, Books 30-32
102/13	1877-1885, Books 33-34
102/14	1874-1891, Book 35
102/15	1891-1894, Books 36-37
102/16	1894-1897, Books 38-39

102/17	1897-1900, Books 40-41
102/18	1900-1904, Book 42

TAX DIGESTS

An index to names of tax payers in the 1799 and 1801 tax digests of Jackson County and the 1802, 1805, 1809, and 1815 tax digests of Clarke County can be found in R. J. Taylor, Jr. Foundation, An Index to Georgia Tax Digests (5 vols., Spartanburg: The Reprint Company, 1986).

Microfilm reel	
97/6	1802-1814
61/8	1815-1818
97/7	1819-1832
97/8	1833-1840
97/9	1841-1845
97/10	1846-1855
61/8	1848
97/11	1856-1866
97/12	1867-1870
97/13	1867-1869, Wild Lands
97/14	1871-1875, list of insolvant tax payers
102/36	1893-1894, insolvant tax payers
250/34	1960

The Georgia Department of Archives and History also has on microfilm the tax digests for 1900-1952 and 1960. Original tax digests for Clarke County (and all Georgia counties) at the Georgia Archives survived from c1872 to almost the present. The National Archives Atlanta Branch in East Point, GA has Federal direct tax records for Clarke County and the rest of Georgia for 1865 to 1873 (1865-1866 are on microfilm).

PRIVATE RECORDS ON MICROFILM

Microfilm reel	
23/76	American Legion Womens Auxilliary, Unit No. 20, Athens, GA, Minutes 1921-1949, Books 1-5
252/24	Athens Fire Company, Number 1. Minutes 1857-1879. Miscellandous Records, 1870, 1873, 1889, 1904.
9/80 & 10/81	Emmett Jopling Bondurant Letters, 1889-1899
97/5	Clarke County Agricultural Ass. Minutes, 1859-1873
18/71	Andrew Jackson Cobb Papers, 1880-1827. Includes certificate of appreciation for WW I service to Lowell Cobb.
218/21	Martha (Atalanta) Lumpkin Receipt Book, 1871-1878
18/71	Davison Family School Certificates from Yaarab Temple and Athens High School, 1920-1937.
18/71	Deed between William Dearing and John Nesbit, 1875
212/14,15, 52,53	Georgia Railroad and Banking Company 1835-1957, Minutes
188/20	Joseph Finch Morton Store Account Books, 1822-1826.
18/71	Moss Genealogy; Rufus L. Moss Biography; Julia P. Moss Letters.
18/71	Annie Noble Sims Collection of Military Service Records and Other Records. Includes Exum, McKine, Hill, Walton, and Pope. Some records from Isle of Wight County, VA.
18/59	Milton B. Smith Collection 1829-1865. Includes personal and Civil War letters, miscellaneous loose records, 1785-1828.
102/28	Clarke County States Rights Association, 1834-1840.

18/80 S. B. Wingfield Private Papers and Genealogy, 1838-1944

18/80 _Athens Banner_, pamphlet, 1906

18/80 _Handbook of Athens and Souvenir of the Carnival, October 1-6, 1900_ (1900)

18/80 Sylvanus Morris, _Strolls About During the Early Seventies_ (nd)

18/73 Charles Morton Strahan, _Clarke County, Georgia and the City of Athens_ (Atlanta, 1893)

Athens First Baptist Church:
22/78 Minutes of the Female Mite Society of Athens, 1819
22/79 Church Minutes, 1830-1913, Books 1-4

18/59 Bethany Methodist Church Minutes, 1878-1909

252/5 Buena Vista Baptist Church Minutes & History, 1858-1885

19/79 Crooked Creek Baptist Church Minutes, 1850-1873

Emanual Episcopal Church:
18/80 Minutes, 1843-1907
18/59 Minutes, 1907-1908

18/80 First Christian Church of Athens, History, 1875-1958

196/53 First Methodist Church, History & Minutes, 1801-1953

18/59 First Methodist Episcopal Church South, Athens. History, Members, and Infant Baptisms

First Presbyterian Church of Athens:
18/59 Minutes and Members, 1820-1860
76/50 Miscellaneous Deeds and Papers, 1820-1921
18/59 Minutes and Members, 1861-1890
76/50 Minutes and Church Register, 1897-1907

Prospect United Methodist Church, Athens:
240/24 Church Register, 1845-1900s

Winterville First Methodist Church, Winterville:
18/71 Quarterly Conference Records, Womens Foreign Missionary Society, 1899-1902; Annual Meetings, 1891-1893, 1895, 1898
18/72 Minutes, 1881-1918; Treasurers Book, 1890-1914; Sunday School records, 1889-1897, 1919

18/59 Georgia Domestic Missionary Society Minutes 1844-1893

PRIVATE RECORDS NOT ON MICROFILM BUT AT THE GEORGIA DEPARTMENT OF ARCHIVES AND HISTORY

Athens, GA. Petition, 1871.

Atkisson Family Papers, 1839, 1861-1890, 1914-1923, 1945.

Atlanta Alpha Chi Omega Mothers Club, 1938-1978.

Mell Marshall Barrett Memoir, 1950.

Bass Family Papers, 1807, 1820, 1848-1862.

Patrick S. Burney, Jr. Papers, 1919, 1939, 1955-1959.

Church Microfilming Project, 1967-1968.

Martha Lumpkin Compton Family Papers, 1832-1903.

Eagle Tavern Journal, 1818-1820.

Gathright/Mathews Legal Papers, 1823-1848, 1870, 1871 (concerns mining and Lumpkin County)

Lemuel Pratt Grant Papers, 1838-1844 (concerns railroads)

Georgia Association of Young Children Records, 1974-1979

Gunison/Griswold Papers, 1854-1969

Harden/Pruitt Family Papers, 1814-1899

Edward Harden Family Papers, 1840, 1918, 1925

Thomas Walton Harris Family Papers, 1775, 1819-1857

Ivey/Saulter Business Papers, 1848-1930

Drury W. Jackson Family Collection, 1673-1978

Lucian Lamar Knight Collection, 1862-1951

Archibald Thompson MacIntyre Papers, 1802, 1828-1925

Jack Martin Papers, 1963-1972

Moina B. Michael Collection, 1916-1964

Mitchell/Fondren Papers, 1847, 1851, 1861-1865

Morcock/Baldy/Smith/Williams Family Papers, 1772-1921, 1978

John Newton Real Estate Account Book, 1842-1887

Ogletree Family Papers, 1810-1890, 1985

Robert Ousley Smith Papers, 1877-1924, 1986

Travellor's Rest/Jarrett Manor Collection, 1747-1977

Mary Carter Winter Collection, 1797, 1843, 1867-1868, 1902-1966

John Hartwell Woodward Collection, 1861, 1871-1872, 1918

Goodloe Harper Yancey Papers, 1877-1894

NEWSPAPERS

The following is a list of the Athens newspapers on microfilm at the Georgia Department of Archives and History. Consult the card catalog for the microfilm reel numbers and the exact dates. A larger collection of Athens newspapers can be found at the University of Georgia Libraries in their Georgia Newspaper Project microfilm.

Athens Banner, 21 December 1906, 1967-1976

Athens Blade, 31 October 1879; a few issues 1880

Athens Evening Chronicle, 18 September 1889

The Banner Watchmen, 9 May-29 August, 1882

Foreign Correspondent & Georgia Express, 5 January 1811

Athens Gadfly, c1927

Iconoclast, 14 March 1927

Liberalist, 1927

Red and Black, 1968-1971 (on several reels)

Richards Weekly Gazette, 5 May 1849-27 Apr. 1850

Southern Banner, 1832-1882

Southern Recorder, 24 May 1842

Southern Watchman, 1855-1882

ATHENS CITY RECORDS

Microfilm reel	
Minutes:	
98/31	1879-1885, Book 1
98/32	1885-1895, Books 2-3
101/44	1895-1898, Book 4
101/45	1898-1902, Book 5
City Court Writs:	
101/46	1879-1894, Book 1

101/47	1893-1900, Book 2
101/48	1895-1897, Book 3
101/49	1897-1900, Book 4

STATE GOVERNMENT RECORDS NOT ON MICROFILM BUT AT THE GEORGIA DEPARTMENT OF ARCHIVES AND HISTORY

Record Group 1-1-108
Returns of Qualified Voters for Clarke County, 1867-1868. This volume is a registration book of voters qualifying to participate in a special state election for bringing Georgia back into the Union. Black and white adult males registered. Oaths of allegiance to the Union are in oath books in Record Group 1-1-108. These volumes survive for every Georgia county and major city except for Haralson County.

Record Group 4-2-46
File II Counties, Clarke County. Includes various miscellaneous published and manuscript materials including tax insolvant lists for 1806, 1807, 1809, 1813, 1814, 1818, and 1824.

XII. Militia Records From Duke University, 1804-1820s

Militia records of Clarke County from the Clarke County records that were formally at the William R. Perkins Library but which are not at the Georgia Department of Archives and History. These records are compiled from the microfilm copy on reel 281-71 at the Georgia Archives.

Given below are the names and years that appear on each record. Almost all of these documents are excuses for failing to appear for militia duty or, ususally in the 1820s, lists of persons who failed to show up for drill and loose, individual, signed commissions.

Nottey, Wortham, 1812

James Bell (Belk?), 1812

James Ligon, 1812

Major T. Mitchell, Captain Alfred Stewart, Captain Robert J. Cabell, Captain James Boyle, Lieutenant Richd. Lawrence, Ensign Wm. Flippins, Ensign James Talbott, Ensign C. Wood, and Ensign Saml. Ribeson. Defaulters in Captain Stewart's District: Charles Smith, Cyeel Harring, Arthur Harring. Defaulters in Capt. Boyles Company: Phillip Ryan, Whitehead Ryan, Walter Connel, Jacob Martin, and John Parish. Defaulters in Captain Clayton's District: Wm. H. Hunt, Wm. Clements, , Gilbert Copeland, and Geo. Hyche. Also cited were Captain Wm. Starnes, lieutenants John P. Cary, John L. Wright, and James Robison. 7 August 1812.

William Clements, 1812

Hugh McWhorter, 1812

James Sims, 1813

Major Thomas Mitchell, captains Wm. Starnes, Robert J. Cabell, Jos. Boyle, John P. Cary, Lieutenant Jas. Kensey, and ensigns Saml. Robison, Wm. Flipping, and John Fletcher. Defaulters in Captain Cabells' District: John Shepherd, Wm. Davis, and Thos. Spirir. Defaulters in Captain Casey's District: Wm. Watkins and Robert Thurmond. Also cited were sergeants Joseph Jolly and Thornton Stone of Captain Casey's company; Captain J.F. Cooke, lieutenants Jacob Burns, John L. Wright, Richd. Laurence, and Davd. Kenney; and Ensign Milse Smith. 15 July 1813.

Captains Rob. J. Cabell, John Johnson, John L. Wright, J. F. Cock; lieutenants James Kenney, David Kenney, John G. Mayne; and ensigns Miles Smith, and John Fletcher. Defaulters in Capt. Cabell's District; Robert Rakeshaw. Defaulters in Captain Wright's District: Moses Bledsoe, John Cunningham, Burwell Brewer, Charnol Hightower, Moses Davis, William G. Wright, James Ormond, and Phillip Gleeson. 20 May 1814.

Captains Isaac Funderburg, Thomas Boothe, ~~Harrison-Trammell~~ (?), Travis Straughn, Parks Middleton; ensigns Garrett Craft, James Stewart, and Elijah Lovin. Defaulters in Captain Boothes Company: William Crow, Alexander Crow, and Jeremiah Burnett. 21 May 1814.

Jonathan Hardigree, 1815

James Barber, over age 45, January 13, 1815

John Crouch, 1815

Stephen Hester, 1815

George Fann, over age 45 as of 22 July last. 12 January 1815.

Josiah Daniel, Wm. Dyson, 1815

Robt. Martin, Charles Smith, John Sanders, and Joseph Ewing, 1812

Charles A. Redd, 1812

Thomas Hall and son Hugh Hall who is under 18. 27 May 1811

Col. Saml. Jackson, Major Thomas Mitchell, Major John Selmon, captains Isaac Funderbaugh, Robert Martin, Thomas Butts, Wm. P. Easley, John P. Casy (Cary?), James Merewether, John Johnston, John L. Wright, Farr H. Trammell, ~~William-Johnston~~; lieutenants Jack Fambrough, Thomas Owen, John

Williams, Nathan Gann, John Fletcher, Parker Middleton, John F. Barnett, Isaac Tharasher, ~~John Williams, Parker Middleton~~; ensigns James Stewart, David Williby, James Sims, David Harris, Sherwood Harper, John Conner, William Wright, and Isaac Thrasher. Deliquents: William Davis, Obed Hail, Thomas Stamps, William H. Hunt, Benjamin Wills, John Crouch, John Pinner, Jeptha Stewart, Jesse Suttles, Russell Brown, Norris Hendon, Henry Taylor, Andrew F. Ewing, Joshua Calaham, Henry Boling, Stephen Hester, Henry Funderburgh, Barnett Downs, Stephen Merewether, Philo Smith, Josiah Daniel, Charles Meriwether, William Clements, John Camron, Robert Hudson, Henry Clift. January 15, 1815.

Major Farr H. Trammell; captains Parks Middleton, Isaac Funderburgh, John Parker, William P. Easley, Paul Satterwhite; lieutenants Wade White, Nathan Gann; ensigns James Dickerson, Martin Crow, Robert Conner, and Sherwood Harper. Deliquents in Captain William P. Easley's Company: Richard Cole and John Cockral. Deliquents in Captain John Parker's Company: John Henning and James Oliver. Deliquents in Captain Parks Middleton's Company: John A. Cogburn, Bayley George, Garrett Craft, Bullard McDurmond. Deliquents in Captain Paul Satterwhites District: Thomas Booth, William Crow, Jeremiah Burnett, and White Rossiter. Deliquents in Captain Isaac Funderburgh's District: Isaac Adams. 16 September 1815.

Wm. Proctor, 1816

John Simpson, 1816

Drury Cooper and David Willeby, 1816

Colonel John Silman, Major H. F. Tramell, Major Jno. H. Lowe, captains Ange Diliprier, Benjamin Williams, James Stewart, John Parker, Gabl. A. Moffett, William Starn, James Wright, Jams. Ligon, William Hightower, John Oliver, William P. Easley, William L. Parr; lieutenants Isaac Helt, Nathan Gann, Thomas Worsham, Isaac Thrasher, H. D. Adams, Francis Trammel, Jacob Tredwek, John Flitcher; ensigns John Shepard, Sherwood Harper, James Sims, Joseph Ligon, and Elisha Wood. Deliquents were Captain William P. Easley, Lieutenant David Kinney, 1st Sergeant William Thompson, and Whitehead Ryan. Deliquents in Captain Newton's Company: George R. Stewart, Johnson Freeman, and Johnson Frost. Deliquents in Major Lowe's Battalion: Aaron Biggs and Abraham Johnson. Deliquents in Major Trammell's Battalion: Richd. Duckin. 17 October 1816.

James Ormond, 1816

Mark J. Allen, 1816

Officers of the Clarke County Regiment, 27 September 1816: Col. John Silman, Major John L. Lowe, Major Farr H. Trammell, Captain Benjamin Williams, Lieutenant Elijah Loving, Ensign Zachariah Dickenson, sergeants: Sterling Helton, Alexander Torry, Jesse Kinney, and Richard Whitehead; Captain James Stewart; Lieutenant Isaac Hill, Ensign John Shepherd, sergeants Allen Brown, Charles E. Stewart, William Haygood, and Richard Dicken Jr.; Captain John Parker, Lieutenant Nathan Gann Jr., Ensign Sherwood Harper, sergeants James Glasson, Ansala Harper, William Hodge, and Humphrey Edwards; Captain Gabriel A. Moffett, Lt. John G. Mayne, Ensign David Robertson, sergeants John Hatchett, Jesse Hays, and Gabriel F. Mathews; Captain Ange Dillipree, Lieutenant Thomas Wortham, sergeants Westly Talbott, John Pace, Jack White, and Thos. Taylor; Captain William Starnes, sergeants Lemuel Swanson, Archabald Crawford, Phillip A. Glasson, and Isaac Middlebrooks; Captain Francis Arnold, Lieutenant Isaac Thrasher, Ensign James Sims, sergeants John Nott, Martin Lea, Absalom Arnold, and Micajah Williamson; Captain James Wright, Lieutenant John Kemp, Ensign James Stephens, sergeants David Akridge, Joseph Ray, Thomas Kemp, and Joel Lassiter; Captain James Ligon, Lieutenant Hezekiah D. Adams, Ensign Joseph Ligon, sergeants Pleasant Hardegree, Robertson Fambrough, John Fambrough, and William Simpson; Captain William Hightower, Lieutenant Francis Trammell, Ensign James Smith, sergeants Aaron Biggs, Granesson Moore, Abraham Johnson, and Enoch Hanson; Captain John P. Ulmer, Lieutent Jacob Treadwell, Ensign Elisha Hood, and sergeants Ludwell Malone, Isaac Adams, and Eli Farr (?); Captain William P. Easley, Lieutenant James McCleroy, Ensign William Clifton, sergeants Eldred Nalls, John Allen, and Barna Downy; Captain William L. Parr, Lieutenant John Fletcher, sergeants Nicholas Freeman, John Freeman, Reuben Traylor, and Peter Dodd; Captain

Josiah Newton, Lieutenant David Kenney, Ensign Wm. Callahan, and sergeants George R. Hunter, Johnson Freeman, Johnson Frost, and Nicholas Laurence. 27 September 1816.

Needham Sorrell and Obed Hail, 1816

James Oates, 1818

Walter Johnson and Elijah Strong, 1816

Nicholas Laurence, Robert Morris, Alexander McKane, Edmond Jones, Burwell Trawick, and Josiah Newton, 1816

William Manly, Stephen Thomas, Robert Espey, William Manly, Zachariah Sims, Sandy Mayberry, William H. Hunt, James Steret, and William Banks, 1816

Johnson Freeman and Samuel Winn, 1816

Edward Callihan, Isaac Winn, Hiram Pendergrass, Nathaniel Pendergrass, Edward L. Thomas, and Thomas Garrison, 1816

Col. John Silman, Major Farr H. Trammell, captains William Starn, William Hightower, James Ligon, William L. Parr, John Parker, Josiah Newton, James Stewart, James Wright, Benjamin Williams, Gabriel A. Moffett, William P. Easley; lieutenants Nathan Gann, Hezekiah Adams, James McCleroy, Sherwood Harper, Elijah Loving; and ensigns John Shepherd and Zachariah Dickerson. Deliquent in Captain James Stewart's Company: Lewis Lampkins, Howell Elder, James Epps, James Mathews, Isaac Daniel; Capt. John Parker's Company: George M. Lanier; Captain William P. Easley's Company: Joseph Bridges, Absalom Camron, James Pittman, James Meriwether, and John Pounds; Capt. James Ligon's Company: Thomas Lowe; Captain James Wright's Company: John Kemp, John Warren, and Burwell Johnston; Captain William Hightower's Company: Allen Pryer, William Garner, Lemuel Brown, Samuel Murf, and Aaron Biggs; Captain William Starns' Company: John L. Wright, William G. Wright, and Charnal Hightower; Captain Josiah Newton's Company: Stevens Thomas, Robert Aspey, William Manley, Zachariah Sims, Sandy Mabury, William Hunt, James Steret, William Banks, Samuel Weir, Isaac Wier, Hiram Pendigrass, Nathaniel Pendergrass, Edward L. Thomas, Thomas Garrison, Robert Morris, Elxander McCane, Edward Jones, and Burwell Trawick; Captain William L. Parr's District: Needham Sorrel, Walter Johnston, William Proctor, Seaborn Brown, James Hayney. 27 December 1816.

Josiah Newton, 1817, commission as major

List of officers in the Clarke County regiment, 6 October 1818: Col. John Silman, Major John H. Lowe, Major Josiah Newton, Major James Merewether, Captain James Oates, Lt. Hiram Beasley, sergeants James Stevens, Timothy Williams, Allen Edmondson, John Earnest; Captain James Sims; Lieutenant Hezekiah D. Adams, Ensign James Hanson, sergeants Benjamin Ellread, William McCullough, William Foster, and Samuel S. Minor; Captain James Meriwether, Lieutenant Green B. Jacks, Ensign Richard Maxwell, sergeants Jesse Martindale, David Holloway, Thomas Willeby, and Robert Willeby; Captain William L. Parr, Lieutenant Jeremiah Mathews, Ensign Joshua Morgan, sergeants Benjamin Davis, Joseph Jolly, John Hunt, and William Johnson; Captain Edward Conner/James Treadwell, Lieutenant John Conner, Ensign William Hinnard, and sergeants William Fenn, John Tukle, James Wilson, and Robert Conner; Captain James McCleroy/J. W. Pentecoust, Lieutenant William Clifton, sergeants Campbell Powell, Elisha Powell, Aron Hightower, and William Doggett; Captain James Stewart, Lieutenant Joel Winfield, Ensign Charles E. Stewart/L. Mane (?), sergeants John Haywood, Lloyd Mares, Armstead Henson, and Christ. a Carter; Captain James J. Moore, Lieutenant Alexander Moore, Ensign Jesse Kinney, sergeants Samuel Collins, Henry Pope, and Sterling Helton; sergeants Joseph Durham, Henry Mitchell, Francis M. Trammell, and Wiley Harris; Captain David Kinney, Lieutenant James Akin, sergeants William Callahan, John Yates, William Carnes, and William Norris; Captain John Dean, Lieutenant Uje Tyson, Ensign Zachariah Wortham, sergeants Thomas Simonton, Jonathan Oakes, Mathew Maine, and Isaac Holmes; Captain Henry Harris, Lieutenant John White, Ensign John Stevens, sergeants William Mattocks, George Muse, William Beavers, and Samuel Jack; Captain William Starns, Lieutenant William Flippen, and Ensign Charnal Hightower; Captain Sherwood Harper,

Lieutenant Josiah Daniel, Ensign John W. Harper, sergeants James Glawson, Humphrey Edwards, Beaton Daniel, and Henry Glawson. 6 October 1818.

Henry Duke, John J. Pass, Humphrey Posey, and William Hawkins, 1818

Henry Mitchell, Lewis Moore, Martin Kines, James Haynie, and Frances M. Trammell, 1818

John Darman, Asia Hulig, and Campbell Powell, 1818

Allen Edmonson, Wm. Wright, Jas. Wright, Joel Lassetter, Jno. M. Clark, Henry Carlton, Jno. Carner, Hardy Johnson, Thomas Kemp, Thos. Campbell, Jno. Kemp, Wm. Thompson, Charles Linder, Timothy Williams, Wm. Caldwell, Arter Heirs, Garland Reynolds, Elizabeth Basset, James Stephens, David Akridge, Martin Lea, Robert Lassetter, Jno. Y. Manor, Jno. Brewer, 1818

Richard Maxwell, commission of ensign, 1818

John W. Harper, commission of ensign, 1818

Edward Conner, commission of captain, 1818

Joint commission for Lieutenant Colonel John Silman, Major John H. Lowe, Major Josiah Newton, Captain William L. Parr, Lieutenant John Conner, Lieutenant Hezekiah D. Adams, Ensign Joshua Morgan, 1818

Asa Hulsey, 1818

James Henson, 1818

James McKleroy, 1818

Hiram Busby (Beasley?), 1818

John Flink, 1818

Col. John Silman, majors John H. Lowe, Josiah Newton, James Meriwether; captains William L. Parr, James McCleroy, James Oates, John Deane, William Starns, James Meriwether, James Stewart, Edward Conner, James Sims; lieutenats Josiah Daniel, Hiram Beasley, James Akins, John Conner; ensigns John W. Harper, Richard Maxfield, Joshua Morgan, and James Henson. Deliquents: William Johnson, Joel Stone, John C. Parr, Jesse Crumpton, Joseph Ector, Joshua Famborough, Jesse Martindale, Henry Duke, John J.Pass, Humphrey Posey, William Hawkins, Joel Lasseter, James Wright, William Wright, John M. Clark, Henry Carlton, Hardy Johnston, Thomas Camp, Thomas Canncil, John Kemp, William Thompson, Charles Lender, William Caldwell, Arthur Ayers, Galland Reynolds, Ezekiel Bassett, David Akridge, Martin Lea, Robert Lassiter, John Y. Maynor, John Brewer, John Connel, Henry Mitchell, Lewis Moore, Martin Moore, Martin Kiny (?), James Haney, Henry Mitchell, John Deanes, John Flint, John Dorman, and Asa Hulsa, Jesse Mitchell, Hesekiah Scovell, Middleton Hartsvield, George W. Moore, James Epps, John Jackson, William Manley, Stephen Malone, John Haygood, George Huse, and Joseph Jolly. 7 October 1818.

Ensign Reuben Stewart, Lieutenant Hezekiah D. Adams, Lieutenant Green B. Jacks, Captain David Kenney, Lieutenant Uje Tyson, Ensign Zachariah Wortham, Captain Henry Harris, Lieutenant John White, Ensign John Stevens, Lieutenant William Flippen, Ensign Charnel Hightower, Ensign Wm. Hinnard, Lieutenant William Clifton, Lieutenant Joel Winfield, Captain James J. Moore, Lieutenant Alexander Moore, Ensign Jesse Kinney, and Captain Sherwood Harper. 4 November 1818.

James J. Moore, commission, 1818

Alexander Moore, commission, 1818. Mentions Joel Winfield

James E. Brown, 1819

J. W. Pentecost, 1819

Christopher Garlinton, 1819

Francis Thornton, 1819

Eugene H. Tyson, 1819

Robt. Espy, 1819

Otho H. Appling, 1819
Zachariah T. Wortham, 1819
Thomas Farrar, 1819
William B. Holt, 1819
Jos. Ligon, Jr., 1819
Hezekiah D. Adams, 1819
Reuben Stewart, 1819
John M. Dobbins, 1819
Hezekiah W. Scovell, 1819
Robert Kendrick, 1819
Henry Mitchell, 1819
James Glasson, 1819
Daniel Jackson, 1819
Young Gresham, 1819
Elijah Treadway, Jr., 1819

Thomas Lowe, Jehue Crumpton, Charles Stewart, Edward Maxey, Wm. L. Fambrough, Joshua Fambrough, Harris Thurman, Wiley Harris, Edward Bearden, John Pinner, Wiley Smith, Elijah Brown, Inman Whitman, James Hayney, Jesse Garner, Aaron Beardin, William Whitton, Silas Norton, John Hinesley, James Buckley, Lewis Moore, Willis Moore, Elijah Bearden, John Connell, Anderson Statum, Robert McCree, Wm. Clark, John McDonnell, Robert J. Cabell, Obed Haile, John Greer, Lemuel Lansford, Nathaniel Epps, John Parr, Washington Homes (?), Gabriel A. Moffett, William Roberts, Phillip Woodly, Philip Ryan, Anderson Bailey, William Mattock, Henry Stoneman, Phillip Pryor, John Nance, William Flippen, William G. Wright, Tapley Short, Wm. H. Puryear, William W. Brown, Lemuel Lasseter, John H. Passchal, John L. Wright, Thomas Kilgore, Newton Henson, Wilis Kilgore, Elijah Garner, Joseph F. Morton, Thomas Pinson, Charnal Hightower, Thomas Tye, John R. Morton, Francis Thornton, Lemuel Lansford, Thomas Tye, John R. Morton, James Croxton, Dewel Summers, Seaborn Summers, Bazaliel Langford, S.C. Doolittle, Jas. Rasberry, Thomas Bradley, James Cook, James Daniel, Archibald Headdon, Wm. P. Jackson, Syres Henderson, James Wilkins, Vinson Watkins, John Wilkins, Edward Paine, George W. Moore, William Murray, David Johnson, Thomas Smith, William Appling, William Stroud, Jeremiah Burnett, Amos Crow, Jole Wilkins, Samuel Fielding, James Henson, Francis Marshal, Barton Thrasher, John Thrasher, John Broom, John Brewer, Zedekiah Skates, John D. Ward, Thomas Campbell, William Beasley, James Beasley, John Creel, David Anderson, Thomas Lowe, Jehu Crumpton, Charles Stewart, Edward Maxey, Wm. J. Fambrough, Joshua Fambhrough, Harris Thurman, Wiley Harris, Edward Bearden, John Pinner, Wiley Smith, Elijah Brown, Inman Whitman, James Hayney, Jesse Garner, Aaron Beardin, William Whitton, Silas Norton, John Hinesley, James Buckley, Lewis Moore, Willis Moore, Elijah Bearden, and John Connell. 10 July 1819.

Thomas A. Fenn, 1819

List of officers, 29 October 1819. Col. John Selman, Lt. Col. Jno. H. Lowe, Major Josiah Newton, Major James Meriwether, Major James Oates, Adjutant Isham Harden, Capt. Otho H. Appling, 1st Lt. James E. Brown, 2nd Lt. Robert Espey, Ensign Francis Thornton, sergeants Wm. M. Callahan, Moses Barber, Robert Orr, Mathew Allen, corporals Wm. Runnells, Wm. Yates, Capt. Wm. L. Parr, 1st Lt. Joshua Morgan, 2nd Lt. Jonas Brand, Ensign Thos. Farrar, sergeants John G. King, Robert J. Cabell, Jos. H. Atkinson, Reuben Gower, corporals Mark McCleroy, Daniel Brand, Merril Embry, Wm. Mathews, Capt. John Dean, 1st Lt. E. Tyson, 2nd Lt. Jackson Smith, Ensign Zachariah Wortham, Capt. Christ Garlington, 1st Lt. Thompson (?), sergeants Banister Perndle, Henry Briton, Richd. Farrar, Capt. Henry Harris, 1st Lt. Jno. White, 2nd Lt. Wm. Bailey, Ensign Anderson Bailey, sergeants John Jack, Wm. Roberts, Phil Woodliff, Capt. Sherwood Harper, Lieut. Josiah Daniel, Ensign James Glawson, sergeants James Edwards, David Stephens, Patterson Wise, Wm. Epps, Capt. Hezekiah W. Scovall, lieutenants Jos. Ligon, Wm. J. Wilborn, Ensign Loyd Mare, sergeants Allen W. Brown, Robert Ligon, Seal Melton, James Brown (Brewer?), corporals Jos. Moss, Thos. Booth, Thos. Dicken, Thos. Epps, Capt. Jno. W. Penticost, lieutenants Wm. Clifton, Eldridge Nall, Ensign Thos. A. Fann, sergeants Campbell Powell, George Whitehead, Peter Whitehead, Aaron Clifton, Capt. James Treadwell, sergeants John Wilson, Glen Phelps, Harney Treadwell, John Vanidford, corporals Edwd. Conner, John Oliver, Edmund Dukes, Wm. Vandiford, Capt. James Hinton, lieutenants Danl. Jackson, Wm. Parker, Ensign Mremon Hendon, Capt. John M. Dobbins, lieutenants Hezekiah D. Adams, Elijah Treadway, Ensign Alna Rutledge, sergeants Steven Hester, Charles Rutledge, Thomas Williamson, Reuben Winfrey, Capt. Owen Spurlock, lieutenants Hiram Beasley, Green Evans (?), Ensign Reuben Stewart, sergeants

James Harris, John Haile, Robert Hunter, Anderson Statum, corporals Thomas Caldwell, Wiley Ward, William Lard, Henry Carleton, Capt. Wm. B. Holt, Lieutenant Allen Fambrough, sergeants Thos. Robertson, Wm. Hardigree, Wm. Clarke, Wm. Fambrough Jnr., Capt. Henry Mitchell, Ensign John Pinner, sergeants Robert McCrea, Thos. Wade, Wm. Jones, and Abraham Silvey.

Ensign Francis Thornton, Ensign Thos. Farrar, Capt. John Dean, Lieut. William Wilborne, Capt. Henry Mitchell, and Ensign John Pinner, 1819.

Allen Freeman, James Herd, Malcom Johnson, Hinchy Wier (Ewin?), John Rainy (Ramy?), Middleton Hartsfield, James (?) Thomas, William Cimbre, Joseph Summerlin, Steven Williams, Willis Whatley, Jessey Ball, 1819.

Eldridge Nall, 1819

John White, 1819

John Riddle, 1812

William Bailey, 1819

Joseph Moss, Amos Crow, Abel Crow, Edward Paine, John Trammell, and Robert Ligon, 1819

William H. Parker, 1819

Jackson Smith, 1819

John Pimer (Pinner?), 1819

John Baily, 1819

Saml. Heals, John C. Parr, Thos. P. Atkinson, Phillip Woodley, Wm. Roberts, William Carnes, Jno. Hutcheson, Lloyd Thomas, Thos. Jefries, James Briden, Barnett Downs, William Nutt, Wm. P. Jackson, Cyrus Henderson, Cornelius Jackson, Samuel Henderson, James Hunter, John Deane, Wm. J. Wilburn, Saml. Heald, John Deane, Allen Freeman, James Heard, Malcomb Johnston, John Ramey, Midleton Hartsfield, James L. Thomas, Hinchey Winn, Wm. Kimbrew, Joseph Summerlin, Stephen Williams, Willis Watley, Jesse Ball, Phillip Woodliff, William Carnes, Joseph Moss, Amos Crow, Abel Crow, Edward Paine, Thos. Finch, Joseph F. Morton, William G. Wright, Lucy Carter, John H. Paschall, Lemuel Lasseter, John F. Barnett, Martin Smith, Nathaniel Epps, John Pace, Hampton W. Hill, Allen Fambrough, Robert Sewart, Enoch Spinks, Garlland Sims, and Humphrey Posey. 10 December 1819.

Hampton W. Hill, 1819

Jonas Brand, 1820

List of Officers, April 16, 1823. Capt. Sherwood Harper, lieutenants Josiah Daniels, Bazabel Langford, Ensign James Galwson, sergeants James Edwards, William Epps, Patterson Wide, Capt. James Hinton, lieutenants Daniel Jackson, Wm. Parker, sergeants Thos. Robertson, James Mathews, Jesse Ball, corporals Lowry Bryant, Robert Wilkins, Middleton Hartsfield, West. Parker, Capt. Richard Dickens, lieutenants Joseph Ligon, Wm. Manly, Ensign Richard E. Bush, sergeants Robert Ligon, Joshua G. Moore, Eleel Melton, James Brewer, Capt. Wm. L. Parr, lieutenants Joshua Morgan, Jonas Brand, Ensign Eugene H. Tyson, sergeants Wiley Hailes, James Hale, Martin Smith, Samuel Pittard, corporals Joseph Billups, Phillip Watkins, John Varner, Elijah Embrey, Capt. John Deane, Lieut. Jackson Smith, Ensign Zachariah T. Wortham, sergeants Wm. Humphrey, Allen Barber, John G. Mayne, Daniel Ramey, corporals John H. Richardson, Elijah hendon, Wm. Edwards, Dyson Bowling, Capt. Theophilus S. Lane, lieutenants Edwin Rogers, Maddison Mitchell, Ensign Francis Thornton, Capt. Christ. Garlington, lieutenants Richard Thompson, Tyree Harris, Ensign Nelson Anderson, sergeants Willis Moss, Christ. Kilnbest, Wm. Wright, James Fields, Capt. Reuben Stewart, lieutenants Thomas A. Wright, James Harris, Ensign Samuel Collins, sergeants Thomas Kermichael (Carmichael?), John Taylor, John Hunter, Wmson. C. Reese, corporals William Nunally, Solomon Kilgore, Edmund Camp, Calvin Wilkerson, Capt. Green B. Jacks, Lieutenant Edward H. Maxey, sergeants Anderson Burt, Allen Fambrough, Francis Belcher, Benj. Sims, Capt. John M. Dobbins, lieutenants William Foster, John Thrasher, Ensign Alna Rutledge, sergeants Airs Conant, Richard Downs, Thomas Wells, Daniel McDonald, Capt. Henry Mitchell, Capt. Henry Harris, Lieutenant William Baley, sergeants Leander Boggs, Christopher White, Phillip Rian, and Robert Billups.

Reuben Stewart, 1820

Thomas A. Wright, 1820

James Harris, 1820

Green B. Jacks, 1820

William Foster, 1820

John B. Marable, Charles Royster, William G. Wright, Martin Kines, Lemuel

Lasseter, John Wood, John F. Barnett, Levy H. Carter, Tapley Short, Thomas Finch, Wm. H. Puryear, James Fields, Winfield J. Wright, Leroy Puteller (Patillo?), Thomas Wells, Ambrose Smith, Thomas Morton, Malcomb Johnston, Williamson C. Reese, David Anderson, Wm. Callahan, Harrison Hoeffer, Wmson. C. Reese (Ruse?), Samuel Braswell, Robert Lassiter, Henry Jordan, John Earnest, Richard Beasley, Owen Spullock, Wm. Caldwell, James Beasley, Middleton Hartsfield, Stokey Evans, George Evans, Saml. Henderson, Cyrus Henderson, James Henderson, Barnett Downs, John McDaniel, Garling Sims, John Vandeford, Henry Pope, William H. Puryear, and Henry Jordan. 20 May 1820.

H. W. Scovell, 1820

Tyre Harris, 1820

Nelson Anderson, 1820

John Conner, 1820

William Manley, 1820

Johnson Frost, 1820

Thos. A. Fann, 1820

Richard E. Burke, 1820

Edward Ward, 1820

William Clifton, 1820

Richard Dickens, 1820

Reuben Y. Hamilton, 1820

John Thrasher, 1820

John J. Pass, 1820

John G. Rutherford and Alfred W. Hamilton, students at Franklin College, 1821

Wiley W. Mason and Wm. R. Crabb, students at Franklin College, 1821

William Caldwell, 1820

List of officers, 25 September 1820. Col. John Silman, Lt. Col. John H. Lowe, majors Josiah Newton, James Oates, Hezekiah W. Scouvall, Capt. John M. Dobbins, lieutenants William Foster, Dicken Walker, Ensign William Weatherly, sergeants Adans Counett, Richard Downs, Thomas Wells, Daniel McDonnell, corporals Augusin Smith, John Dalton, James Heard, Capt. William L. Parr, lieutenants Eugene H. Tyson, Jonas Brand, sergeants Wiley Hailes, James Haile, Martin Smith, Martin Smith, Samuel Pittard, corporals Joseph Billups, Phillips Watkins, John Varner, Elijah Eanbrey, Capt. John Deane, Lieutenant Jackson Smith, Ensign Zachariah T. Wortham, sergeants William Humphrey, John G. Maine (?), Phillip Baileer, Daniel Ramey, corporals John H. Richardson, William Edwards, Dison Bowling, Capt. William Clifton, lieutenants Thomas A. Fenn, Jason Marriton (?), Ensign Henry Hightower, sergeants Purnel Cook, Keelin Cook, William Nixson, Capt. Green B. Jackson, Lieutenant Edward H. Maxey, sergeants Anderson Burt, Allen Fambrough, Francis Belcher, Benjamin Sims, Capt. Reuben Stewart, lieutenants Thomas A. Wright, James Harris, sergeants Thomas Camichael, John Taylor, Isaac Martin, Wmson. C. Reese, corporals James Robinson, Solomon Kilgore, Calvin Wilkinson, Elisha Dotson, Capt. Sherwood Harper, lieutenants Josiah Daniel, Bazaleel Langford, Ensign John Adams, sergeants Alfred Moss, Haywood Harper, Nathan Shaw, Silas East, Capt. Henry Harris, lieutenants Peter Ashley, William Bailey, Ensign Abner Wells, sergeants Leander Boggs, Christopher White, Phillip Ryan, Robert Billups, Capt. Thos. J. Lane, lieutenants Edwin G. Rodgers, Madison Mitchell, sergeants James Vinson, John Kinney, Asbury Hull, Jonathan Kinney, Captain Johnston Frost, lieutenants John J. Pass, Reuben Hamilton, Ensign John Conner, sergeants Wm. Shepherd, Wm. Tankersley, corporals John Wilson, Thomas Twitty, Edward Craft, Capt. Richd. Dicken, lieutenants Joseph Ligon and Wm. Manly

William Caldwell, 1820

Jason Minton, 1820

William Hennard, Moses A. Cogburn, 1820

Peter Ashley, 1820

Ned and Bob Anderson, free persons of color, 1820

Eugene H. Tyson, Christopher Garlington, William Roberts, Wmson. C. Reese, Leroy Brewer, John Wood, James Erwin, Pernal Cook, Barnett Downs, Edward Paine, Obadiah Jackson, John Flint, James Erwin, 28 October 1820

Reuben Stewart, 1820

Henry Hightower, 1820

Pernal Cook, Barnell Downs, and Edward Paine, 1820

John Wood and James Erwin, 1820

Levy Brewer and Wm. Foster (?), 1820

John Penur, Henry Freman, Robert Kimbell, Gresham Vickery, John F. Barnett, Tapley Short, Levy H. Carter, Wm. G. Wright, Wm. H. Puryear, Lemuel Lasseter, Lewis M. Paulett, William Wells, Jonathan Ward, James Gray, William Flippin, Samuel Garner, Inman Whitten, Ebenezer Pedigrew, Jehu L. Wright, Newton Hinson, Winfield J. Wright, Newton Hinson, Winfield J. Wright, Bennett Bidegrew, Lemuel Swanson, Nathaniel Epps, Samuel Gardner, Isaac Smith, Henry Jennings, Charnell Hightower, Isaac Davis, William Wright, Samuel Heald, Charley Heard, Nathan W. Whitman, Marshall Peck, James Wheeler, Thomas Littlepage, William Carr, Tarrance Conner, Wm. Hodge, Francis Mucklehannen, Isaiah Mucklehannon, Hezekiah Mucklehannon, Moses W. Callahan, Allen Johnston, Alexander Wester, Charles Daugherty, Alfred Hamilton, John G. Rutherford, James Thornton, Wm. Roberts, Wm. Mason, Wm. R. Crabb, M. Scott, James Gage, Wm. Cobb, Thos. Meriwether, Robert McLiet (?), Alfred Scott, Ezekiel Lamar, Cuttey Lumbaugh, Samuel Plummer, Thomas Sullivan, Pucket Wood, Robert Walker, Ebenezer Newton, John Fowler, James Martin, Gabriel T. Mathis, Richard Wilson, William Woodley, James Parish, Littleberry Woodley, William Maddox, Thomas Jeffries, Phillip Ryan, John A. Bailey, Henry White, John McAlphin, William Whitten, John Hunton, Charles Hunton, Elijah Bearden, William Garner, Robert A. McRee, James Henson, Jr., James Henson Sr., Elisha Holland, Barton Thrasher, Middleton Hill, Eleanor Talley, Edward L. Thomas, Hope H. Tigner, William Graham, William L. Fambrough, Jacob Abrams, Loyd Murr, Abram Perkins, James F. Ritchee, Amos Crow, Vincent Watkins, Enoch Spinks, Charnall Hightower. 9 June 1821.

Gresham Vickers, Tapley Short, Levy H. Carter, Wm. G. Wright, Wm. H. Puryear, Lemuel Lasseter, William Flippin, Samuel Garner, Inman Whitten, Ebenezer Pedegrew, John B. Wright, John McAlpin, Solomon Beardin, John Hunton, Charles Hunton, Elijah Beardin, William Garner, Robert A. McRee, James Hinson Jr., James Hinson Sr., Elisha Holland, Barton Thrasher, Middleton Hill, Eleaner Talley, Edward T. Thomas, Hope H. Tigner, William Graham, Jacob Abrahams, James F. Ritchee, Vincent Watkins, Felghman McDaniel, Newton Hinson, Bennett Pedigrew, Lemuel Swanson, Samuel Gardner, Henry Jennings, Nathan W. Whitman, Marshall Peck, James Wheeler, Thomas Littlepage, Torance Conner, Wm. Hodge, Francis Mucklehannon, Isaiah Mucklehannon, Hezekiah Mucklehannon, Moses W. Callihan, Robert Walker, Ebenezer Newton, William Moodley, James Parish, Littleberry Woodley, William Maddox, Thomas Jeffries, Philip Ryan, John A. Bailey, Henry White. 11 June 1821

Usbious Hopkins, Jas. Grimes, Samuel Collins, John W. Graves, Thomas Strickland, Samuel Whitehead, Robt. Childers, John McAlpin, William Whitten, Welborn Newton (?), Martin Thimes, Merit Wood, Williams Garner, John Bearden, William Jones, John Connell, Abraham Silvey, Edward H. Maxey. 26 May 1821

A. H. Webster, 1821

Charles M. Heard, 1821

Samuel Gray, 1821

Jonathan M. Peck, 1821

Edward Paine, 1821

John A. Hopkins, George Walton, Littleberry Burnett, James F. Ritchey, Amos Crow, Jesse Howell, Abraham Prokins, James O. Ragland, Henry Duke (over age 45), Garrett Craft, Edwin Craft, George Meriwether, Alfred Moss, Dewell Summers. 7 July 1821

Henry Carlton, Joel Lassetter, John Wood, William Garner, John Hunton, Richard Glass, Thomas Rutledge, John Massy, Drury Gardner, William Graham. 18 September 1821

R. W. Burdell, Wm. Hightower, E. Talley, James Nixon, Madison R. Mitchell, John Greer, Timothy Williams, John Pinner, Drakeford L. Trammell, Stevens Thomas, Nathan Whitman, Alexander Webster, Wm. Johnston, John Suley, James Croxton, James Tinsley, James F. Waddel, James Martin, George J. Dodd, Robert Watkins, Lott Lagevin, Wm. L. Fambrough, Pinkney Thrasher,

Colson Copeland, Jacob Abraham, Abrose Hill, Henry Carlton, Joel Lasseter, John Wood, William Garner, John Hunton, Richard Glass, Thomas Rutledge, John Massey, William Greham, Leroy Stroud, Abraham Perkins, Jeremiah Burnett, Robert R. Billups, James Stewart Jr., Edwin S. Smith, Robert Brown, George L. Earnest, James F. Ritchee, Umphrey Hurst, Sharrard Harper, George W. Meriwether, Payton Parker. October 1821

Eleanah Talley, William Hightower, Jas. Nixon, Robert W. Burdell, Madison Mitchell, John Greer, Timothy Williams, and Jno. Pinner. September 27, 1821

John W. Graves, Henry Carlton, William Jones, William Whitton, John Hunton, Robt. Childers, Sterling Collier, David Wiloby, Jesse Robertson, John Jacks, Richd. Barnet, Jacob Pike, Jacob Abrahams, Ambros Hill, Anderson Birt, William Hutchenson, Lloyd Mars, Leroy Patillo, James Hinson. 13 October 1821

Humphrey Pittard, George J. Dodd, Robert Wadkins, and Benjamin Davis, 1821

Wm. Fambrough, 1821

Lott Legwyn, Wm. L. Fambrough, Pincknye Thrasher, Coleson Copeland, Jacob Abraham, and Ambrose Hill, 1821

Levy Stroud, James Stroud Jr., Abram Perkins, Robert Brown, Jeremiah Burnett, James F. Ritchey, Robert R. Billups, George L. Earnest, Edward L. Smith. October 27, 1821

John Anderton, 1821
Charles D. Parr, 1821
Robert Brown, 1822
Jett Wright, 1821
John Wilson, 1822
Laban Moncrief, 1822
Jesse W. Hewell, 1822
Thomas Keough, 1822
Edwin L. Cox, 1822
Hezekiah Blankenship, 1822
James Wilson, 1822
Harris Andrews, 1822
Lemuel Swanson, 1822
Laban Moncrief, 1822
Ezekiel Lamar, 1822
William Appling, 1822
Robert A. McRee, 1822
John Mathews, 1822
George Whitehead, 1822

John R. Hargrove, James Hinson Jr., John D. Swift, and William D. Graham, 1822

Robert Orr, Jonas Brand, and William Atkinson, 1822

David Patterson, Joshua Morgan, Cashwell Brand, and Jesse Jones, 1822

James W. Harris, 1822
Thomas F. Gibbs, 1822
Archd. Bryant, 1822
Cutliff Limbaugh (Fambough?), 1822
James Wheeler, 1822
Tucker Whitfield, 1822
John Jack, 1822
Isaac Baldwin, 1822
Charles Barnett, 1822
Laban Moncreef, 1822
Robert Espey, 1822
Gabriel T. Mathis, 1822
Moses P. Calahan, 1822
Jonathan M. Peck, 1822
Pinckney Thrasher, 1822
John Gaton, 1822
William Bailey, 1822
James Parish, 1822
Jonas Brand, 1822
Cashwell Brand, 1822
Cashwell Brand, 1822
Jesse Jones, 1822
Reuben Johnson, 1822
William Garner, 1822
Merrit Wood, 1822
Newton Hinson, 1822

Richard Glass, 1822

John Brewer, 1822

John F. Stevens, 1822

John Jacks, 1822

Tyre Harris, 1822

Lemuel Lassiter, 1822

Martin Smith, 1822

Tyre Harris, 1822

Nathan Fowler, 1822

Sherwood Harper, 1822

William Flippin, 1822

Wm. B. Cobb, 1822

Tapley Short, 1822

John F. Dunn, 1822

Joseph Talley, 1822

James F. Richee, 1822

Freeman Biggs, 1822

Drury Ridgeway, 1822

Thomas A. Wright, 1822

James Wright, 1822

List of Officers, 1822 (?). Capt. Etheldred Sorrell, lieutenants William Aldred, William D. Godfrey, sergeants Benja. Leroy, John Fambrough, Robertson Fambrough, Pleasant Hardigree, Capt. Thomas A. Wright, lieutenants James W. Harris, Allen Freeman, Ensign Timothy Williams, sergeants Reuben Stewart, Thomas Campbell, Edmund Jackson, Thomas Daggett, corporals Willis Kilgore, Edward Runnells, Wiley Edmundson, Samuel Baswell, Capt. Robert A. McCree, Lieutenant John W. Smith, Ensign Martin Rieves, sergeants James Hainey, Greene M. Mitchell, John Varnum, Henry H. Grimes, corporals Thomas Kilgore, James Williams, Harris Firbish, Lewis Moore, Captain Elkaner Tally, lieutenants Stephen Hester and Thomas Rutledge, sergeants Hezekiah D. Adams, John C. Wright, William Carmichael, Thomas Miller, corporals John Thrasher, John Williams, John M. Dobbins, Robert F. Smith, Captain Thomas Wills, sergeants William Maddox, Richard Wilson, George Murr, Captain Benja. Davis (?), lieutenants Charles D. Parr, Nicholas Baker, sergeants David (Daniel?) Patterson, John B. Suler (?), James Ferguson, Robert Orr, Captain William Applin, lieutenants Micajah W. Thweatt, James A. Thornton, William W. Callahan, Wiley Pope, Puckett Wood, Johnston Freeman, corporals Jacob Woolbright, John L. Wheten (?), Moses P. Callahan, James Landers, Captain Winfried J. Wright, Lieutenant Richard Thompson, sergeants Laban Moncrief, Thos. Cousons, William M. Morton, Willis Moss, corporals Lemuel Swanson, James R. Buckley, Tyre Harris, Nathan Braseal, Colonel Hezekiah W. Scovall, Lieutenant Colonel Josiah Newton, Major James Oates, Major Joseph Ligon, Quartermaster John H. Lowe, Quartermster Sergeant John W. Graves (?), Paymaster Edward Paine, Surgeons Mate Henry Hull, Adjutant Robert Ligon, Sergeant Major William Nunnally, Captain Hezekiah Blankinship, lieutenants John Brewer, Lewis Bryant, sergeants John Greer, Daniel Jackson, James Dickerson, James House, Captain James McCleroy, Lieutenants John Mathews, George Whitehead, sergeants William Hogue, Stokley Evans (?), Archibald Hutson, Jacob Jones, Captain Jesse M. Hewett, lieutenants John Wilson, James Wilson, sergeants David Simmons, Bryant Williams, John Varner, William Tankersley, Captain Richard Dickens, lieutenants William Manley, James W. Harris, sergeants Benja. H. Booth, William Humphries, John L. Kilgore, and Tarpley Holder

John W. Smith, 1822

Reuben Stewart, 1822

William Manley, 1822

Richard Hughes, 1822

John H. Paschal, 1822

James W. Harris (Hanes?), James Wilson, John Wilson, Joseph Moss, Drury Ridgeway, Archabald Hutson, William Milsaps, William Fowler, Thomas Smith, Sherwood Harper, Allan Barber (?), John F. Simms (?), James M. Burton, James Nixon, Thos. F. Gibbs, Richard Barnett, Richard Aycock, Pinckney Thrasher, John Jacks, Sowel Braswell, Joel Lassiter, Freeman Biggs, John Gatlin, James F. Richey, Charles G. Burgood, Edward Bearden, Richard Glass, Newton Henson, Merrit Wood, William Garner, John Varnum (?), Reuben Johnson, Cashwell Brand, Jesse Jones, John Shepherd, Isaac Davis, Thos. P. Atkinson, Jonas Brand, Thos. Wells, William Bailey, James Parish, Thos. Jeffries, Robert Espey, Gabriel T. Mathis, Martin Smith, George Muse (?), John Jack, Wm. W. Callahan, Isaac Baldwin, Charles Barnett, Moses Bryant, Archabald Bryant, John Blankinship, Wm. B. Cobb, John T. Dunn (?), Joseph Humphries, Joseph Talley, Ezekeil Lamar, Cutliff Linnebourg (?), William Glece (?), Jonathan H. Peck, Henry Fitzsimmons, Nathan W. Whitman, James Wheeler, Tucker Whitfield, Stephen Fulker, Moses P. Calahan, James Landers, Laban Moncrief, Lemuel Swanson, Willis Moss, Tapely Short, William Flippin,

Lemuel Lasseter, Tyre Harris, Christ. Kimbel, and Nathan Brisco (?). 13 July 1822

John B. Sulvey, Jonas Brand, Joshua Morgan, Cashwell Brand, Jesse Jones, John H. Paschall, Phillip Easton, Wm. Atkinson, Gabriel T. Mathews, James Mclleroy, Robert Billups, Peter Ashby, John M. Crawford, Thos. Jeffries, John D. Swift, Wm. P. Graham, John R. Hargrove (?), James Hinson, Larkin L. Baldwin, Thos. A. Wright, Wm. Stroud, Eliel Milton, Martin Crow, H. Blankinship, Joseph Moss, Garrett Morris, Wm. Pritchard, James Jackson, John C. Pearson, Ruben Foster, Elder Mitchell, Bryant Williams, Luke Garner, Henry Deane, Garland Sims, James Wright, Reuben Stewart, Thomas Campbell, Edwin S. Smith, Robert Brown, Allen G. Fambrough, John Flint, John Greer, Hampton W. Hill, and John F. Stevens. 16 November 1822

John Deane, 1822

Jonas Brand, 1823

Thomas Campbell, 1823

Reuben Stewart, 1823

John R. Hargroves, 1823

John W. Smith, 1823

Cashwell Brand, 1823

Bryant Williams, 1823

Jesse Jones, 1823

Luke Garner, 1823

Wm. P. Graham, 1823

John D. Swift, 1823

Garland Sims, 1823

William Hodges, 1823

Job Wilkins, 1823

Elisha Herndon, 1823

William Barber, 1823

James Oates, Zachariah Rhodes, Reuben Stewart, Wm. M. Morton, Wm. H. Puryear, John L. Wright, Thomas Jeffries, Wm. Price, John Wagnon, David Smith, Adrian N. Mayse (?), James Tinsley, John Moulton, George B. Jodd, James F. Jones, Richard Harrison, Robert Fowler, Gabriel Moffett, James Smith, James Rasbery, Henry Hull, Irvin Dixon, Richard Nowland, Charles H. Dupont, Abraham Hill, John Rutherford, A. L. Lewis, Ebenezer B. McKinley, John W. Womack, John Wiggins, John L. Lewis, Wm. Smith, Wm. Jack. 10 March 1827. Also mentions Bob and Ned Henderson, musicians.

APPENDIX A: A Missing Page From the 1840 Census of Clarke County

Page 216 of the microfilm of the 1840 Federal Census of Clarke County cannot be read because it is blured. Consequently, it is omitted in the indexes to the 1840 Census of Georgia. Reproduced below are the names that appear on that page.

Alex Moore	July Clayton
Warren Grant	Rieclio Gowan
Patrick Benj	Bob Parr
William Wamer (Warner?)	James M. Royal
Elizabeth Mathison	Wilson Lumpkin
Nathan Hoyt	Nancy Hunt
Nathan Holbrooks	H. B. Jackson
Ebencar Newton	W. E. Dickson
Hopkins Newbury	W. Fitzpatrick (Kitzpatrick?)
Henry Cade	Sarah Coal
Penina Rolason	John Butterworth (?)
Adolso Wolhol	W. H. M. Waiter (McCallar?)
B. C. Thompson	B. Lords
Sarah Thomas	Charles H. Gay
Sarah Winsted	W. S. Constance

****

APPENDIX B: Land Court Minutes, 1803-1832

The following document was found in Clarke County, File II Counties, Georgia Department of Archives and History.

	Jan. 3rd. 1803	
Thomas Findley	Proved his rights; warrant issued for	50 acres
	Mch. 7th. 1803	
Eley Nuron	Proved his rights for self, wife & ch. warrant issued	26 a
Stephen Nobles	Proved his rights for	50 a
Eley Nuron	Proved on his head rights 6 a to David Shay	6 a
Alexander Voss	Proved his rights for self, wife & one Child	150 a
Archibald Bryant	Proved his rights for 2	200 a
	Nov. 7th. 1803	
Samuel Halaway	Proved his rights for	150 a
	Feb. 6th. 1804	
Isaac Crow	Proved his rights for	200 a
Samuel McKee	Proved his rights for	200 a
William Polk	Proved his rights for	600 a
Thomas Lin	Proved his rights for	450 a
Jeremiah Milton	Proved his rights for	400 a
	June 4, 1804	
Joshua Browning	Proved his rights for	550 a
Zedoc Cook	Proved his rights for	650 a
James Perry	Proved his rights for	350 a
Moses H. Cogbourn	Proved his rights for	200 a
William Dyseen	Proved his rights for	400 a
Daniel Craft	Proved his rights for	550 a
John Strother	Proved his rights for	600 a
Samuel Johnston	Proved his rights for	150 a
Gabriel Hubert	Proved his rights for	600 a
Jonathan Melton	Proved his rights for	750 a
Aaron Parker	Proved his rights for	550 a
James Downs	Proved his rights for	500 a
Samuel Henderson	Proved his rights for	300 a
Puellah Bankston	Proved his rights for	
Johnanon Ricks	Proved his rights for	300 a
Davis Bagley	Proved his rights for	400 a
John Cook	Proved his rights for	400 a
James Cook	Proved his rights for	500 a
David Shay	Proved his rights for	50 a

James Johnston	Proved his rights for	600 a
Williby Fann	Proved his rights for	500 a
Jesse Fann	Proved his rights for	300 a
Elijah Runnels	Proved his rights for	200 a
William Loyd	Proved his rights for	450 a
Joseph Calen	Proved his rights for	350 a
Jacob Bankston	Proved his rights for	100 a
Thomas Davis	Proved his rights for	550 a
Elijah Bankston	Proved his rights for	
John Armstrong Jr.	Proved his rights for	400 a
John Armstrong Sr.	Proved his rights for	300 a
William Nobles	Proved his rights for	600 a
William Johnston	Proved his rights for	350 a
Swan Thompson	Proved his rights for	650 a
Henry Huff	Proved his rights for	650 a
Johnson Runnels	Proved his rights for	350 a
Mitchel Burford	Proved his rights for	550 a
John Blair	Proved his rights for	550 a
Job Springer	Proved his rights for	450 a
William Williams	Proved his rights for	250 a
Anderson Fambro	Proved his rights for	500 a
John Kilgore	Proved his rights for	500 a
Thomas Blair	Proved his rights for	450 a
Spencer Reynolds	Proved his rights for	450 a
John Henderson	Proved his rights for	550 a
Bartley Wootten	Proved his rights for	750 a
Philip Tigner	Proved his rights for	550 a
James Stewart	Proved his rights for	400 a
Jeptha Stewart	Proved his rights for	400 a
John Folsom	Proved his rights for	450 a
William Smith	Proved his rights for	550 a
William Bankston	Proved his rights	
William Pitman	Proved his rights for	300 a
Martha Stewart	Proved her rights	
Abner Bankston	Proved his rights	
James Langford	Proved his rights	
John Edwards	Proved his rights for	350 a
William Brown	Proved his rights for	300 a
Tabitha Wood	Proved her rights for	100 a
Benjamin Hagood	Proved his rights for	400 a
William Kelly Jr.	Proved his rights	
William Shaw	Proved his rights for	550 a
George Shall	Proved his rights	
John Stephens	Proved his rights for	200 a
Elijah Milton	Proved his rights for	200 a
James Stringer	Proved his rights for	200 a
George Clifton	Proved his rights for	200 a
William Grimes	Proved his rights for	350 a
James McGee	Proved his rights for	400 a
Roland Taylor	Proved his rights for	850 a
Wilie Roberts	Proved his rights	
Nimrod Taylor	Proved his rights	
Burkitt Dean	Proved his rights for	750 a
Johnson Strong	Proved his rights for	550 a
Joseph Ray	Proved his rights	
William Filney	Proved his rights	
William Jones	Proved his rights	
Hannah Croxin	Proved her rights for	400 a
Isaac Hill	Proved his rights for	650 a
William Hannah	Proved his rights for	200 a
John Ramey	Proved his rights for	1000 a

Gabriel Hubert renewed an old warrant, granted for Jackson Co. 500 a

Solomon Bearfield renewed an old warrant for 230 acres in the Reserven, A Bounty, dated Dec. 1790, issued from Jackson Co. in lieu of an old warrant in the above name.

Jacob Bankston, renewed an old warrant granted in Wilkes Co. in part of his own headrights.

Uriah Humphreys renewed an old warrant, Jackson Co. for 850 acres on his family head rights.

Asa Morgan renewed an old warrant, Jackson Co. for 200 acres

Name	Entry	Acres
Philip Tigner and) John Henderson)	On their head rights previously proved	1000 a
Anderson Fambro &) John Kilgore)	On their head rights previously proven	1000 a
William Nobles &) Henry Huff)	On their head rights previously proven	1000 a
William Johnson &) Swan Thompson)	On their head rights previously proven	1000 a
John Blair &) Spencer Reynolds)	On their head rights previously proven	1000 a
John Armstrong &) Job Springer)	On their head rights previously proven	1000 a
Bartley Wootten &) Johnson Runnels)	On their head rights previously proven	1000 a
William Nobles &) Henry Huff)	On their head rights previously proven	1000 a
William Brand	Proved his rights for	100 a
Thomas Crain	Proved his rights for	450 a
Joseph Hunden	Proved his rights for	200 a
Isaac Milton	Proved his rights for	650 a
Abner Bankston	Received a warrant on head rights prev. proven	50 a
Nod. Nelson	Proved his rights for	600 a
	1st. Monday Sept. 1804	
William Polk	On head rights previously proven	475 a
Bozman Adear	Proved his rights for	200 a
Nathan Merony	Proved his rights for	150 a
Preston Runnels	Proved his rights for	200 a
Jesse Green	Proved his rights for	204¼ a
John Bone	Proved his rights for	212⅕ a
Edward Moore	Proved his rights for	750 a
George Hampton	Proved his rights for	100 a
Levin Rumbley	Proved his rights for	450 a
Aaron Causey	Proved his rights for	163 a
Henry Williams	Proved his rights for	450 a
Jonathan Nobles	Proved his rights for	400 a
David King	Proved his rights for	400 a
Preston Runnels	Proved his rights for	100 a
Johnathan Lee	Proved his rights for	300 a
	October 1, 1804	
Henry Williams	On head rights previously proven	100 a
Thomas Crain	Proved his rights for	100 a
Joseph Cox	Proved his rights for	200 a
Stephen Cardner	Proved his rights for	250 a
John Neilson	Proved his rights for	200 a
	1st. Monday Dec. 1804	
William Crocker	Proved his rights for	400 a
	1st. Monday Feb. 1805	
Joseph Lane	Proved his rights for	600 a
	Mch. 4, 1805	
Obediah Baker	Proved his rights for wife and one child	100 a
	1st. Monday April 1805	
Joseph Lane	On rights previously proved for 600 a	800 a
	May 5th. 1805	
Richard Dickens	Proved his rights for	350 a
Robert Leak	Proved his rights for	300 a
	July 1st. 1805	
Hope Hull	Proved his rights for	950 a
Moses Henson	Proved his rights for	650 a
	Aug. 5th. 1805	
William Ramey	Proved his rights for	450 a
Roland Taylor	Proved his rights for	50 a
William Johnston	Proved his rights for	200 a
	1st. Monday Oct. 1805	
Richard Laurence	Proved his rights for	350 a
Nicholas Baker	Proved his rights for	275 a
Solomon Dawson	Proves his rights for	400 a

	May 5th. 1806	
Thomas Scrivner	Proved his rights for	200 a
	Oct. 6, 1806	
William Ramey	On head rights proved Aug. 15, 1805	650 a
	Nov. 3rd. 1806	
William Ring	Proved his rights for	350 a
	Feb. 2nd. 1807	
William Porch	Proved his rights for	200 a
	Sept. 7th. 1807	
William Herring	Proved his rights for	200 a
	1st Monday Oct. 1807	
William Thompson	Proved his rights for	500 a
Young Gill	Proved his rights for	350 a
	Dec. 7, 1807	
William Thompson	Prayed warrant for balance of above warrant	117 a
William Cole	Proved his rights for	800 a
	1st. Monday Jan. 1808	
William Mitchel	Proved his rights for	750 a
	Mch. 7, 1808	
Daniel Easley	Proved his rights for	199 a
	Apl. 4, 1808	
William Mitchel Sr.	Prayed on hear rights previously proven	100 a
William Mitchel Jr.	Proved his rights for	450 a
	Sept. 5, 1808	
Richard Deekin	Renewed an old warrant for	350 a
Robert Leak	Renewed an old warrant for	300 a
	1st. Monday Nov. 1808	
Lemuel Wootem	Proved his rights for	350 a
Daniel Ramey	Proved his rights for	200 a
Thomas Lag	Proved his rights for	200 a
	1st Monday Jan. 1809	
Roland Taylor	Proved his rights for	100 a
John Taylor	Proved his rights for	300 a
	May 1, 1809	
Roland Taylor	Prays warrant for 35 acres short on first warrant	35 a
	Aug. 7, 1809	
Judith Morton	Proved her rights for	200 a
	Nov. 6, 1809	
Jeptha Stewart	On head rights previously proven	250 a
	Mch. 5, 1810	
David Sims	Proved his rights for	200 a
	Nov. 5, 1810	
Joseph Laramore	Proved his rights for	550 a
	Mch. 4, 1811	
Obediah Baker	Proved his rights for	200 a
	1st. Monday May 1811	
Joseph Brown	Proved his rights for	1000 a
William McCue	Renewed an old warrant for	1000 a
	Nov. 4, 1811	
Robert Caruth	Proved his rights for self, wife and three children, Jan. 6, 1812	
Daniel Ramey	Renewed an old warrant, in lieu of same amount granted in Greene Co.	200 a
	1st. Monday Apl. 1812	
Thomas Hill	Proved his rights for	200 a
Jonathan Milton	Proved his rights for	100 a
	July 6, 1812	
Hugh Neisler	Proved his rights for self and 7 in family, 1st. Monday Sept. 1812	

Hugh Neisler	Prayed on above	65 a
	Mch. 5, 1813	
Hugh Neisler	Prayed on above	100 a
	May 3, 1813	
Thomas P. Carnes	Proved on his rights for	100 a
	Jan. 4, 1814	
Joseph Brown	Renewed an old warrant for	1000 a
	Jan. 2, 1815	
Henry Boling	Proved his rights for	650 a
	Apl. 3, 1815	
George Rockfort	Proved his rights for	300 a
	May 1, 1815	
Josiah Freeman	Proved his rights for	950 a
Stephen Crow	Proved his rights for	950 a
	Sept. 4, 1815	
Alexander Torry	Proved his rights for	950 a
Russell Brown	Proved his rights for	550 a
William Thompson	Renewed an old warrant for	109 a
	Jan. 1, 1816	
Drury Pace	Proved his rights for	400 a
Ludwell Armstrong	Proved his rights for 4 of his ch. for	200 a
	Feb. 5, 1816	
David Stephens	Proved his rights for	1150 a
	May 6, 1816	
Hope Hull	Renewed his head rights previously proven	350 a
	June 3, 1816	
Hinchley Winn	Proved his rights for	550 a
Henry Harris	Proved his rights for	350 a
	Aug. 5, 1816	
Solomon Betton	Proved his rights for	1500 a
Thomas Wheeler	Proved his rights for	450 a
	Sept. 2, 1816	
David Holmes	Proved his rights for	950 a
Robert J. Cabell	Proved his rights for	750 a
	Feb. 3, 1817	
Thomas McCoy	Proved his rights for	1000 a
	Mch. 3, 1817	
David Elder	Proved his rights for	1000 a
Sterling Elder	Proved his rights for	800 a
Joseph Ligon	Proved his rights for	200 a
	Apl. 7, 1817	
James Hayes	Proved his rights for	450 a
George Hayes	Proved his rights for	1950 a
	May 5, 1817	
William Clark	Proved his rights for	2350 a
	Oct. 6, 1817	
John Pounds	Proved his rights for	450 a
George Rochfort	Renewed an old warrant for	350 a
Andrew Burt	Proved his rights for	450 a
John Bearden	Proved his rights for	200 a
	Jan. 5, 1818	
William Dickens	Proved his rights for	400 a
Willis A. Johnston	Proved his rights for	200 a
	Feb. 1, 1819	
James M. Burton	Proved his rights for	750 a
	Sept. 6, 1819	
James Stewart	Renewed his head rights for	400 a
Edward S. Callahan	Proved his rights for	350 a
	Apl. 30, 1820	
Jonathan Lane	Proved his rights for	750 a

	June 5, 1820	
John Jackson	Proved his rights for	400 a
	July 3, 1820	
James Caldwell	Proved his rights for	350 a
	Aug. 7, 1820	
Hundley Brunson	Proved his rights for	1000 a
Hiram Hays	Proved his rights for	1000 a
Thomas Booth	Proved his rights for	600 a
	Sept. 4, 1820	
John F. Barnett	Proved his rights for	700 a
	Mch. 5, 1821	
Richard Dickens Jr.	Proved his rights for	200 a
Gabriel A. Moffett	Proved his rights for	1000 a
	Sept. 2, 1822	
Joseph Jiles	Proved his rights for	400 a
	Mch. 3, 1823	
Hundley Brewer	Proved his rights for (Renewed)	678 a
	May 5, 1823	
Gabriel A. Moffett	Renewed his head rights for	1000 a
	Mch. 1, 1824	
Martin Crow	Proved his rights for	700 a
John H. Lowe	Renewed his head rights for	130 a
	Sept. 6, 1824	
David Homes	Renewed his head rights for	950 a
	Oct. 4, 1824	
John M. Richardson	Proved his rights for	200 a
	Jan. 3, 1825	
William D. Harris	Proved his rights for	400 a
James Hendon	Proved his rights for	450 a
	Mch. 7, 1825	
William Clark	Proved his rights for	2222 a
	June 6, 1825	
Gabriel A. Moffett	Renewed his head rights for	900 a
	Sept. 5, 1825	
David Richardson	Proved his rights for	800 a
Malcom McLeod	Proved his rights for	650 a
William Jackson	Proved his rights for	350 a
	Feb. 6, 1826	
James Tinsley	Proved his rights for	900 a
	Mch. 6, 1826	
William Jones	Proved his rights for	550 a
	Apl. 3, 1826	
Wyatt Lea	Proved his rights for	850 a
	May 1, 1826	
William McCollum	Renewed his head rights for	250 a
	Jan. 1, 1827	
Green M. Mitchell	Proved his rights for	350 a
	Mch. 5, 1827	
Thomas Moore	Proved his rights for	1000 a
	Mch. 5, 1828	
Ransom Nichols	Proved his rights for	700 a
	June 6, 1828	
Thomas Mitchell	Applied for duplicate warrant for The original lost 7 or 8 years ago by Jackson Co. Surveyor. Granted.	1000 a
	July 7, 1829	
Edward G. Harvey	Proved his rights for	400 a
William H. Brewer	Proved his rights for	450 a

	Oct. 6, 1829	
Eucebius A. Hopkins	Proved his rights for	400 a
Thomas House	Proved his rights for	350 a
	Jan. 3, 1832	
Jonathan Hardigree	Proved his rights for	500 a
	May 1, 1832	
Francis M. McCree	Proved his rights for	500 a
	Aug. 7, 1832	
Lewis Arthur	Proved his rights for	650 a
	Oct. 1, 1832	
Frederick I. Freeman	Proved his rights for	250 a

(Last page gone)

****

APPENDIX C: Some Clarke County Deaths, 1834-1877

The following document was found in Clarke County, File II Counties, Georgia Department of Archives and History.

John Browning	3/25/1854	
Sarah Crow	3/21/1838	
Mother	7/24/1838	(Sarah Anne Daniell)
Grandfather	9/5/1840	(William, Rev. Soldier)
Susan Burnett	5/21/1841	
Frances Daniell	3/31/1852	
Jonathan Lee	5/27/1842	
Margaret Browning	8/13/1842	
Rachel Johnson	11/27/1842	
Abner Bradley	2/5/1843	
Grand Mother	10/3/1843	(Mary Melton)
Masters Daniell	7/5/1844	
Solomon Kent	8/13/1884	
James Hendon	2/14/1845	
Berry Burnett	2/23/1845	
Father	6/22/1845	(Josiah, Sr.)
William Parker	8/4/1845	
Harriet East	3/7/1846	
Enoch Spinks	3/22/1846	
Eli Bradberry	3/23/1846	
Mary Ball	3/27/1846	
Sarah Parker	4/8/1846	
Aaron Crow	5/25/1846	
Melinda Wise	12/27/1846	
Nancy Daniell	3/15/1847	
Nancy Tuck	5/12/1847	
Sarah McLeroy	7/18/1847	
James Barber	7/31/1847	
William Ball	9/12/1847	
Marian Crawford	9/18/1847	
Francis Jackson	4/21/1848	
Thomas Jeffries	9/30/1848	
William Thomas, Sr.	4/3/1849	
Mary Bradshaw	4/27/1849	
William Haygood	7/30/1849	
Young W. Harper	9/6/1869	(1949?)
Sarah E. Daniell	10/4/1849	
John Furnell	4/8/1850	
Old Mrs. Edwards	10/15/1850	
Elizabeth Dannily	5/24/1850	
Elizabeth Leneer	4/17/1851	
Joel Colley	10/11/1851	
Levin Smith	10/26/1851	
Catherine Hamilton	7/14/1852	
Gracy Ramsey	7/12/1852	
Mrs. William Eppe	8/4/1852	

Mr. Dawson (or Mc)	10/28/1852
E. A. Hopping	4/23/1853
William Cook (Sheriff)	9/23/1853
Mrs. Nathan Cook	10/27/1853
Charles Dougherty	11/26/1853
George Loanoar	7/25/1854
John Jackson, Sr.	6/25/1854
Thomas Epps (shot)	7/25/1854
O. Richardson	3/2/1855
Joseph Hodges	/ /1855
James Cook	5/18/1855
Julius Darby	6/10/1855
John Cook Esqu.	8/4/1855
Susan Lester	10/12/1855
David Hamby	1/16/1856
Mrs. E. A. Hopkins	2/19/1856
Mrs. Mary Daniell	4/15/1856
Richard Dickon	2/15/1857
Catherine Hodges	3/1/1857
Calab Barber	3/13/1857
James McLeroy	4/21/1857
Martha Jennings	4/28/1857
Keolin Cook	9/4/1857
Catherine A. Lester	10/17/1857
Frances Johnson	5/5/1860
Bedford Burnett	--------
Henry Stephens	9/25/1860
Azeriah Cobb	10/10/1860
W. J. Norris	10/23/1860
Wm. H. Murray (shot)	1/8/1861
J. S. Vincent (Isaac S. Vincent?)	9/27/1861
Josiah Weatherly (shot)	10/17/1861
Caroline Autry	10/25/1861
C. W. Murray	1/8/1861
Reason Whitehead	3/20/1862
William Burnett	6/13/1862
James Wise	7/10/1862
Judy Lee	7/10/1862
John M. Bradberry	10/20/1862
Mrs. Wm. Davis	9/16/1862
Julia T. Bradberry	10/25/1862
Jacob Bradberry	10/5/1862
P. W. Bradberry	1/21/1862
Catherine McEntire	11/7/1862
Licien Burnett	11/9/1862
Naomi Daniell	11/12/1862
Martha Ann Durham	11/16/1862
Green B. Haygood	12/30/1862
William Yearboro	2/1/1863
Aaron Whitehead	3/16/1863
Col. John Low	3/9/1863
John B. Daniell	5/2/1863
Rachel Burnett	6/4/1863
Zadoo Cook	8/3/1863
C. C. Bradberry	10/28/1863
Richard Huges	11/9/1863
Dr. Blant Elder	11/13/1863
Elder Geo. W. Malcomb	1/27/1864
John J. Jackson	2/12/1864
Mary Wise	2/14/1864
Barnett Malcomb	5/27/1864
Mrs. John Cooper	5/30/1864
Miss Mary Whitehead	6/15/1864
John Haygood	7/17/1864
Mrs. Duke Hamilton	9/12/1864
Miss Mandy Cook	9/14/1864
Harvey Parker	9/22/1864
Francis Parker	10/4/1864
Cicero Cook	1/10/1865
Hinson Jones	1/25/1865
William Epps Esq.	1/31/1865

Mrs. Jane Parker	2/15/1865
John Acock	3/12/1865
Mrs. Fannie Brewer	3/23/1865
Mrs. Richard Whitehead	3/29/1865
Simion Acock	4/14/1865
Giles Jennings	4/16/1865
N. J. Daniell	4/17/1865
Miss Sarah Whitehead	6/30/1865
Bradford Spinks	7/7/1865
William Shaw Jr.	7/10/1865
Old Lady Whatley	12/9/1865
Stephen Jackson Sr.	10/16/1865
Moses Melton	12/5/1865
Mrs. J. P. Whatley	3/14/1866
Hartness Cook	5/15/1866
Nancy Crow/Aaron Crow's baby	6/7/1866; 6/22/1866
Mrs. Martha Morton	7/22/1866
Francina Lester	12/22/1866
Wm. H. Dorsey	3/27/1867
Joseph J. Lumpkin	6/4/1867
Mrs. Thomas Malcome	5/8/1867
Miss Lelia Lester	7/24/1867
Old Mrs. Doolittle	10/11/1867
Jamês Edwards	10/15/1867
Gilbert Kent	10/3/1867
James D. Malcome	10/28/1867
Mrs. Peggy Ray	11/2/1867
Mrs. George Harrill	2/2/1868
Silas East	2/28/1868
Emma Harper	7/3/1868
A. A. Harper	7/3/1868
James R. Malcom's baby	7/1/1868
Brother Josiah Daniell	3/13/1869
Nancy Ann Hawk	6/10/1869
Lewis Lester	9/25/1869
Mrs. George Foster	9/17/1869
Mrs. Clemontina Daniell	1/10/1870
Archey Knott	1/23/1870
William Strouc	2/10/1870
Mrs. Ponder	3/15/1870
Mark Stroud	3/26/1870
John Harris	4/7/1870
William Puyear (shot)	5/28/1870
Thomas Threlkeed	6/6/1870
Miss Selina Acock	6/12/1870
Lewis Eidson	7/5/1870
Wyatt Lee	7/10/1870
O. B. Autry's baby	7/31/1870
Mary Lou Thornton	8/26/1870
Mrs. Mariette Jarren	8/26/1870
Jacob Autrey's baby	1/ / 1871
Old Man Pidore	1/2/1871
James Daniell's little boy	1/7/1871
Willis Watley	1/17/1871
Richard Cheatam	1/21/1871
James Almond	2/21/1871
Miss Martha Jackson	4/5/1871
Mrs. Beaton Daniell	2/10/1871
Mrs. Nelly Bradberry	5/13/1871
Mrs. Whitehead's little boy	6/13/1871
Elder J. W. Walker	5/15/1871
Richard Richardson	7/2/1871
Mrs. Benjamine Peeler	7/14/1871
Nathaniel P. Kent	8/14/1871
William H. Ashford	9/27/1871
Mrs. Margaret Bradberry	9/13/1871
John Griffiths Sr.	9/17/1871
Japer Maxey	12/5/1871
Augustus J. Malcome	1/17/1872
William Jones (Wm. H. Jones)	2/22/1872

Boze Maxey	3/22/1872
B. S. Sheets	5/1/1872
Mrs. Sally Smith	5/25/1872
Mrs. Betty Lester	9/4/1872
Beaton Daniell	6/13/1872
Mrs. Mary Lester	9/4/1872
G. W. Malcome's Jimmy	9/23/1872
G. W. Malcome's Albert	9/24/1872
Brother Nathaniel	---------
C. Daniell	10/10/1872
John C. Malcome's Lillian	10/15/1872
James R. Malcom's Molly	10/30/1872
Serena Crow	2/3/1873
Polly Haygood	2/25/1873
Hann Echolds	3/12/1873
William Lewis	7/4/1873
John B. Ward	6/27/1873
John C. Adams	7/8/1873
Samuel Simonton	7/2/1873
Mrs. Robert (?)	7/19/1873
Helman Jackson	12/5/1873
William R. Daniell	3/29/1874
Grandma Johnson	3/29/1874
James Johnson	4/5/1874
Mrs. Abe Jackson	3/28/1877
W. B. Hale	4/13/1877

Daniell

Josiah
b. 2/26/1792
d. 6/22/1845
m. 7/19/1811

Sarah Ann Owens (Burrough) widow
b. 6/10/1782
d. 7/25/1838

William B.
b. 5/12/1812
d. ---------
m. 7/26/1831

Kept all of these records of the deaths in Clark County, in an old Ledger, which finally came into the possession of his grandson, Josiah Bradberry, and not belongs to Ellie Bradbury, his daughter.

Josiah
b. 9/24/1824
d. 3/13/1869
m. 1/16/1845

Kept the Almanac Diary (1849-1862). This Almanac was printed on the left side of the page, thus leaving the right side for the written records. Quotations, dates of events, weather reports were all written, nothing printed.

The Almanac belonged to O. H. Bradbury of Bogart, Ga., but was lost when the Post Office burned several years ago.

(?): Josiah, Sr.,219;
(?): Robert, Mrs., 222
AARON: H. L., Mrs., 090; Harritt L., 094; Jessee W., 142; Lodie B., 005; M., Mrs., 090; Martha E., 094; Mary, 092; Saml., 092; Samuel T., 005; W. M., (chldn. of), 005
ABBOTT: D. Q., 005
ABNEY: Martin J. (chldn. of), 005
ABRAHAM: Jacob, 209
ABRAHAMS: Jacob L., 114; Jacob, 114, 208, 209
ABRAMS: Jacob, 208
ACHOLS: Essie, 039
ACOCK: Isaac P., 023; John, 221; Selina, 221; Simion, 221
ACREE: Starting, 141
ACRIDGE: Levi, 103
ADAIR: John B., 120; Joseph M., 005
ADAM: Finnie E., 080
ADAMS: Addy, 090; Albon D., 096; Alpha T., 174; America F., 169; Ann T., 096; Ariann, 157; Aryann (?), 152; Augustus, 142; B. L., 089; Bedford L., 081; Catherine, 089, 098; Charlotte, 134, 161; Edmond B., 023, 056; Edmund B., 042, 043, 049, 053, 076; Edward, 023; Elizabeth, 134, 168; Florida V., 005; Frances E., 151; Godfrey, 060; H. D., Lt., 202; Hezekiah D., 1st Lt., 127; Hezekiah D., 205; Hezekiah D., Lt., 124-126, 130, 202-205; Hezekiah D., Sgt. 210; Hezekiah Lt., 203; Hissekiah, Lt., 127; Isaac, 112, 120, 141, 202; Isaac, 3rd Sgt. 127; Isaac, Sgt., 202; James G., 142; James T., 080, 096; James, 023; John C., 222; John M., 023; John Maxie, 005; John, 005, 023, 053, 081; John, Ens., 207; Jonathan, 141; Judith, 165; Julia M., 187;
ADAMS: Lucy, 185; M.M., Mrs., 099; Martha J., 153; Mary M., 005; Mary W., 166; Mary, 165, 171; N. A., 044; Nancy, 155; Nathaniel A., 029, 033, 042, 044, 046, 060; Nolie G. H., 005; Polly, 143; Reuben H., 141; Richard, 023, 032, 134, 141; Samuel J., 005; Sarah E., 082; Sarah, & 2 chldn., 087; Sarah, 086, 091; Susan E. & (4 chldn.), 084; Susan E. & 2(3?) chldn., 085; Susan E., 096; Susan, 005, 096-098, 100; W. B. P., 005; William A., 005; William A., Capt., 111; William C., 005; William T., 142; William, 023, 134; William, Lt., 110; Williams, 096
ADARE: Whitmill H., 061; William, 061
ADDAMS: Nancy, 152; Susannah, 175
ADEAR: Bozman, 215
ADKINS: Francis, 038
ADRIAN: Wm. M. H., Rev.141
AIKEN: Betsey, 005; Elizabeth, 151; Frances, 005; Henry M. (chldn. of), 005; Martha, 134; Polly, 005; Rhoda, 005; Sarah A., 093; Tabitha, 005
AIKIN: John C., 092; Mary A. F., 092; Nancy E. P., 092; Rebeccah E. F., 184; William, 072
AIKINS: James, 049
AKEN: Sarah L. S., 153
AKERIDGE: David, 023; Ezekiel, 023; William, 069
AKIN: Edward, 141; Henry, 135; James S., 027; James, 005, 023, 135; James, Lt., 203; John, 109; Mary Ann Martha, 168; Rhodia, 083; Richard, 135; Rodia, 083; Sarah, 135; William L. B., 142; William, 076; Wm., Mrs., 090
AKINDIGE: William, 025
AKINS: --, 057; Denah, 170; Edmund, 057, 129; James S., 023; James, 023, 049; James, Lt., 124, 126, 204; William, 057, 141
AKREDGE: David, Sgt., 129; Levi, 072, 118; V. W., 075; Virgil, Lt., 120
AKRIDGE: Calvin Walker, 005; David, 035, 204; David, Sgt., 202; Ezekiel, 005, 023, 037, 053, 073; Levi, 045, 072; Mary, 171; Troup, 005, 059; Virgil K., 073; Virgil W., 005, 141; William, 040, 142
ALBITZ: Nancy J., 005
ALBRIGHT: Joseph, 141
ALBRITTON: J. M., 024
ALDRED: William, Lt., 210
ALEIN: James J., 023; William, 023
ALEXANDER: A., Sr., 061; Aaron, 023, 034, 039; Betsey, 161; David H., 142; John, 005, 052, 124, 142; Joseph, 005, 107, 115, 134, 141; Mary E. (chldn. of), 005; Nathan, 134, 141; Samuel P., 005; Sarah T., 159; Sarah, 155; Smith, 109, 134, 141; Smith, Lt., 110, 119; W. S. (chldn. of), 005; Wm., 110, 141
ALFFORD: Asa T., 054
ALFORD: Faithey, 184
ALLAN: David, 044
ALLDRED: Elizabeth, 179
ALLEN (MILLEM?):: Mark J., 141
ALLEN: Andrew J., 142; Ben, 023; Benjamin, 023; Charles H., 081; Charles, 057, 094, 141; Daniel, 142; Elizabeth A., 156; Elizabeth H., 186; Elizabeth, 091, 151, 154; Emily, 179; Erwin, 176; Frances C., 186; Frances Mary Ann, 151; George W., 132; George, 039; Hannibal, 038; Henry J., 023; James (chldn. of), 005; James, 023, 039, 045, 060, 110, 141; John, 043, 141; John, 4th, Sgt., 126; John, Sgt., 202; Jones, 132; Joseph T., 094; Joseph, 060, 072, 073, 111; Louisa, 132; Margaret, 005; Mark J., 112, 202; Mark, 129; Mary Ann, 158; Mary E., 094; Mathew, 4th Sgt., 127; Mathew, Sgt., 205; Mose, 005; N., Mrs., 091; Nancy A., & 1 ch., 087; Nancy Ann, 086; Oly, 094; Permelia H., 186; Phillip, 050, 141; Ransom, 142; Samuel L., 037, 038; Sarah A., 094, 102; Sarah F., 094; Sarah M., 084, 085, 094, 102; Sarah, 084, 094, 159; Susan, 094; Thomas P., 045; Thomas, 141; Thos., 4th Cpl., 127; William G., 142; William H., 142; William M., 005; Woodson, 023
ALLENS: Philip, 079
ALLEY: David, 076; William, 076
ALLGOOD: Charley, 091; E.F., Mrs., 093; Elizabeth, 091; Enoch A., 080; James (chldn. of), 005; James F., 005; John M., 081; Louisa Francis, 173; M.L., 091; Mary, 081; Nancy, 081; Thomas A., 081
ALLIN: B., 084; Daniel, 107; L., 084
ALLISON: John Q., 142; Martha A. H., 163; Robert, 023
ALLISTON: Charles, 005
ALLMAN: Mary A., Mrs., 099
ALMOND: James, 221
ALRED: Jonathan, 005
AMIS: J. W. (Chldn. of), 005; J. W., 005; John L., 142; Joseph, 141; William, 141
AMMONS: Joshua, 141; Josiah, 057
AMONDS: Uriah E., 141
ANCHON: Snowden, 142
ANDERDERSON: Thomas, 141
ANDERSON: Albert Elmers, 005; Amanda, 005; Ann, 132; Bob, 207; Charles E. H., 005; David, 128, 141, 205, 207; Edmund, 132; Elizabeth, 132; Emery F., 005; Emory F., 142; Enon F., 079; Frances E., 005; George W., 080, 141; George Washington, 132; J. H., 005, 023; James B., 023; James C., 005, 023, 036, 037, 055, 103, 108, 109, 118; James, 005, 023; Jas. H., 142; John S., 051; John T., 023; John, 141; Lewis G., 110, 142; Mathew, 047; Mattie A., 081; Ned, 207; Nelson, 207; Nelson, Ens., 206; Noah, 132; Peggy, 169; Robert, 023; Salley, 174; Thomas, 033; William L., 141; William W., 005, 142; Wm. M., 132
ANDERTON: John, 209
ANDREW: Hardy H., 071; John, 050, 052; Lucy, 186
ANDREWS: Garrell, 028; Hardy H., 071; Hardy Harben, 071; Harris, 114, 120, 209; John, 027, 036; Nancy A., 158
ANESLEY: Madison, 005
ANGLE: Elizabeth, 184; Thomas (3), 135; Thomas, 141
ANGLIN: Benjamin F. M., 082; Elizabeth, 082
ANSLEY: Jesse, 142
ANTHONY: Cicero H. (chldn. of), 005; Mary A., 172; Robert, 005; T. W., Mrs., 100
APLIN: William, 141
APLING: Otho A., 4th, Sgt., 125
APPERSON: Thomas, 023
APPLIN: Otho H., Capt., 127; William, Capt., 210
APPLING: Capt., 134; Mary Louisa, 164; Otho H., 005, 125, 141, 205; Otho H., Capt., 125, 205; Otho, Capt., 130; Thomas, 023, 024, 030; Walter A. (chldn. of), 005; Walter A., 023, 032, 142; William A., 142; William D., 142; William, 005, 023, 035, 037, 046, 062, 063, 205, 209; William, Capt., 120; Wm., 075, 124, 128; Wm., Capt., 120; Wm., Lt., 117
APPLINGS: --, 079
ARANDALE: Epsybeth, 141
ARCHER: Cicero S., 005; David, 103; George A., 005, 142; Nina N., 005; William J., 142
ARMSTED: Miller, 033
ARMSTRONG: James W., 043, 044, 054, 117; Jas. W., 044, 107; John, 057 215; John, Jr., 214; John, Sr., 214; Jonathan, 045; Ludwell & 4 ch., 217
ARNOLD: Absalom, Sgt., 202; Alesalom, 2nd Sgt., 127; Charles W., 005; Clarence B., 005; Daniel, 005; Edny, 177; Elijah B., 023; Fielding W., 023; Fields W., 023; Francis, 059; Francis, Capt., 202; Frapein, 141; Jesse H., 023; Jesse, 4th, Sgt., 126; Mary V., 005; Park E., 024; William, 079, 115; Wm.,Capt., 129
ARNOLD?: Wm., 079
ARTHER: Lewis, 045, 047, 117
ARTHUR: Barney, 024; Caleb, 005, 028, 072; Frances, 188; Lewis, 033, 054, 107, 109, 141, 219; Mary, 006; Talbot, 024, 035, 036, 045, 050, 062; Tolbert, 050
ARTHURS: Caleb, 048
ARTREE: Alexander, Jr., 006
ARZE: Barnardo J., 006
ASH: John E., 006; Millie M., 006; W.C. (chldn. of), 006
ASHBY: Peter, 211
ASHFORD: William H. (chldn. of), 006; William H., 006, 142, 221
ASHLEY: Peter G., 032; Peter, 207; Peter, Lt., 207
ASKEW: Josiah F., 006; Julius A.,

110; Martha Ann, 164
ASPEY: Robert, 203
ASPY: Joseph, 006
ATKINS: Ransome, 060
ATKINSON(?): Thomas P., 105
ATKINSON: A. C., 024; Ann, 169; Arthur C., 006; Fannie, 024; Jos. H., Sgt., 205; Joseph H., 3rd Sgt. 127; Mary B., 161; Robert, 060; Sarah, 158; Susannah, 158; Thomas D., 128; Thomas P., 024, 121, 129; Thos. P., 113, 206, 210; Volentine, 141; Wash. G., 024; Washington G., 024; William, 209; Wm., 115, 211
ATKINSONS: Arthur C., 121
ATKISSON: Family, 197; Fannie A. H., 006
AUSBERN: Sarah, 154
AUTERY: M. M., 097; Baby, 221; Jacob, 111, 221; William, 024
AUTRY: Baby, 221; Caroline, 220; Martha M., 089; Mary Cleo, 006; O. B., 221; Simon, 108, 117; Willis N., 081, 089; Jacob, 173
AWTRY: Martha, 101
AYCOCK: Isaac P., 006, 072; Isaac V., 075; James (orpns. of), 006; James, 006; Richard, 210
AYER: A., 062
AYERS: Arther, 204; Arthur, 112; Pinckney, 142
BACHELLER: Alexander, Sgt., 130
BACKLEY: Jas., 128
BACON: Margaret Elizabeth, 186; Mary Agness, 161; Nicholas H., 144; Robert, 006; William B., 053; William, 029, 034, 056, 060; Wm., Lt., 110
BAGGET: Nancy, 156
BAGGETT: Stephen, 024
BAGLEY: Davis, 061, 213
BAIL-Y: Samuel, 073
BAILEER: Phillip, Sgt., 207
BAILEY (BARLEY?): William, 115
BAILEY: Anderson, 120, 130, 205; Anderson, Ensgn, 205; Andrew, 092; Augustin C., 092; Eliza, 024; Elizabeth, 163; F., Mrs., & 6 chldn., 087; Francis, 094; Francis, Mrs., 086; Geo. W., 092; George Albon, 006; Huderson, 113; Hugh, 111; James A., 114; James L., 146; John A., 033, 045, 047, 120, 208; John C., 146; John Wesley, 092; Katey, 102; Katy, 099; Lula K., 006; Mary E., 187; Richard, 024; Saml., 075; Samuel, 073, 148; Sarah E., 092; Telitha A. E., 092; Wesley E. (chldn. of), 006; William (chldn. of), 006; William T., 148; William W. (chldn. of), 006; William W., 006; William, 024, 032, 045, 067, 206, 209, 210; William, Lt., 207; Wm., 2nd Lt., 121, 205
BAILY: Green, 024; John 206; Saml., 075
BAIN: W. A., 030
BAKER: Abner, 143; Alexander, 143; Alfred, 024, 051; Chas. (chldn. of), 006; James L., 045; John H., 045; John T., 006, 145; John W., 146; John, 024, 046, 103, 109, 119; Jordan, 024; Jordon, 107; Joshua, Sr., 024; Nicholas, 215; Nicholas, Lt., 210; Obed, 024, 143; Obediah, 216; Obediah, wife & ch., 215; Patsy, 177; Susannah, 156
BALDEN: Lewis, 143
BALDWIN: Benj. C., 036, 045; Benjamin C., 031; Benjamin, 061, 111; Catherine W., 024; Cyrus G., 024; Damacis C., 024; Damaris, 024, 030; Damarius, 024; Damavis C., 024; Elijah, 024; Francis G., 030; Isaac, 115, 209, 210; James G., 024, 043; James J., 006; Joseph, B., 024; Larkin L., 032, 211; Loami, 024; Samuel, 062, 147; Sarah T., 145; William T., 148
BALDY: Family, 198
BALES: Candis, 099; Stephen, 025
BALEY: William, Lt., 206
BALL: Abner, 112; Catherine, 145; Dison, 132; Edy, 185; Elizabeth, 144; George, 115; Jesse, 206; Jesse, Sgt., 206; Jessey, 206; John P., 032, 062, 145; John, 051, 112, 132; Mary, 132, 161, 219; Sarah, 154; William, 006, 071, 132, 219
BALLENGER: D., Mrs., 090
BALLEW: Mary Jane, 083
BANCRAFT: Emily, 155
BANCROFT: Edward (chldn. of), 006; George L., 006
BANE: Clark, Mrs., 090; Milley, Mrs., 090
BANEFIELD: Loyd K., 024
BANGERS: Sarah, 164
BANK: Selina, 100
BANKS: Hugh R., 061; Hugh, 061; John R., 111; Linton, 024; William, 112, 123, 203; Wm., 116
BANKSTON: Abner, 024, 039, 049, 214, 215; Elijah, 214; Henry (chldn. of), 006; Henry, 006, 031, 036, 056, 057; Jacob, 057, 143, 214; John, 031, 143; Lesley, 052, 143; Lesly, 052; Levi, 031; M. J., 143; Nancy, 141; Peter, 006; Polley, 160; Puellah, 213; Sarah, 024; Simeon, 143; William, 006, 024, 214
BANNER: Polly, 024
BANUS(BACCUS?): Thomas, 143
BARBER(?): Allan, 210
BARBER: A., 108; Allen, 024, 036, 041, 073, 075, 118, 119, 144; Allen, Sgt., 206; Arnie L., 006; Barbery J., 172; Calab, 220; Cindy Ruly, 160; Cintha, 144, 173; Delila, 141; Elizabeth A., 175; Elizabeth W., 175; Frances, 148; George, 024; Gilley, 178; Greay, 143; Greensby W., 006, 148; James, 006, 028, 036, 037, 041, 052, 148, 201, 219; Jane, 185; Jemima, 188; John, 147; Keace (?), 107; Margaret, 175, 185; Martha E., 175; Moses, Sgt., 205; Poley, 143; R. C., 006; Reace, 115; Richard, 145; Robert, 006 051; Sarah, 006; Spenser, 122; Susan, 158; Wedford, 074; William, 023, 025, 046, 058, 142, 211
BARBOUR: Patsey, 185
BARBUR: James, 134; Jane, 134; Susannah, 134
BARCLEY: John, 023
BAREFIELD: Jemimah, 006; Lloyd K., 057; Lloyd R., 057; Loyd K., 048
BARET: James W., 071
BARFIELD: Brown, 006
BARKER: Samuel, 052; William, 025, 027
BARLER: Moses, 2nd Sgt., 127
BARNARD: Annis L., 006; F.J., 057; Mollie, 006; N. D. (L.?), 146; Nathaniel L., 032
BARNES: Daniel, 136; David H., 144; Henry Marshall, 006; Lewis, 062; Martha Ann, 187; Mrs., 071; Thomas, 136
BARNET: James, Sgt., 130; Jeremiah, 116; Nathan, 061; Nathaniel B., 025; Richard, 134; Richd., 209
BARNETT (GARRETT?): James W., 159
BARNETT: Caroline, 006; Charles, 115, 209, 210; Claborn, 006; Elisha, 126; Emma, 092; Isham Thomas Cosby, 131; James W., 058; Joel C., 111; John F., 025, 026, 034, 038, 042, 046, 047, 059, 060, 072, 128, 206-208, 218; John F., Lt., 126, 129, 202; John H., 025, 027; John, 006; L.(?) J., 099; Laura Jane, 093; Lewis, 006; Littlebury, 114; Margaret Ann, 006; Mary J., 092; Michael, 147; Nathan B., 143; Nathan C., 023, 025, 027, 029, 030, 032, 036, 042, 049, 050, 053, 056, 057, 062, 063, 110, 148; Nathan C., Capt., 103, 117; Nathan C., Col., 110; Nathan E., 025; Nathan, 006, 042; Nathaniel B., 025; Nathaniel C., 042; Poley, 141; Richard, 210; Smith, 134; Uriah, 025; William B., 025; William Walton, 131; Wm. B., Rev., 144; Wm. Davis, 092; Zilla A., 006
BARNETTE: Jno. F., 113; John, 023
BARNEY: John, 024
BARNHARD: Frances Elizabeth, 006
BARR: Michael J., 025
BARRAT: Josiah, 145
BARRET: James M., 025
BARRETT: --, 025; Benjamin H., 006; Catherine, 166; Doct. M., 092; E.C., Mrs., 090; Elizabeth, 092; Ella, 092; Emily C., 093; James W., 074; James, 025; Jinnie A., 183; John F., 041; Joseph S., 006; Lelia, 092; Mary Ann, 025; Mell Marshall, 197; Michaels S., 030; Michaels, 052; Nancy J., 092; Thomas, 025; Thos. A., 092; William B. (chldn. of), 006; William G., 006; Willie, 092; Z. A. Fowler, 092
BARRFIELD: Lloyd K., 030
BARROW: Clara E., 006; David C., Sr., 006
BARRY: Frank, 006; J. M., 025; Joseph M., 006; Patrick, 025, 148; Patrick, Mrs., 099
BARTON: Benjamin, 037; Caleb J., 006; Gincy, 006; James A., Cpl., 117; James H., Cpl., 107; James M., 041; Jas. H., 107; John H. M., 147; Rebecca, 006, 102; Vianna,165
BARTOW: Annie, Miss, 084
BARWICK: Stancil, 006
BASS(COBB): M. A., Mrs., 090
BASS: Christopher, 144; Family, 197; Henry, 132; M.A., 100; Mary A., 099; Noah, 132; Sarah E., 150; Thursey, 132; William F. (chldn. of), 006; William F., 006; William, 039
BASSET: Elizabeth, 204; Ezekiel, 075
BASSETT: Ezekiel, 142, 204; J.M., 056; Manerva, 155; Mary, 183; Telitha, 155
BASSITT: Frances, 165
BASWELL: Samuel, Cpl., 210; W. P., 025
BATEMAN: Miley, 144
BATES: Allen, 145; Candis, 086, 093; Candis, Mrs., & 2 chldn., 087; Caroline, 097; Jas. J., 092; John R., 025; Martha J., 092; Mary, 025; Mrs., 136; Wm. J., 094
BATTEY: T. W., 103
BATTLE: Milton A., 006, 148
BATTLES: Serrena, 178
BATTS: Howell P., 093
BATTY: Thomas, 117; Thos., 116
BATY: Hugh, 123
BAUGH: John A., 074
BAUGHN: Edmund, 124
BAUMBUTONS: William, 123
BAXTER: Andrew, 025, 148; Cecero N., 081; Eli H., 116; Eli L., 006; Eli, 112, 123, 129; Mary, 006, 099; R. B., Jr., 006; Thomas W., 006, 025, 029
BAYERS: Henry, 047
BAYLEY(?): George?, 157

BAYMON: Watkins, 025
BAYNARD: Ephraim M., 006
BAYNON: Watkins, 060
BAZELL: Isham, 034; James, 025
BAZZELL: James, 025
BEAL: C. W., 025; Charles, 144; Courtney W., 055; Nathan H., 025; Nathan, 035; Zephariah, 006
BEALL: C. W., 039; E. B., 025; Egbert B., 025, 051; Elias, 025; Joseph, 122; Theophelus, 025
BEALSEY: James, 055, 061
BEAMES(BEARNES?): Elizabeth, 090
BEANE: Nathaniel, 038
BEARD: David, 071; Jonathan, 072, 079; Moses, 006; Mrs., 071
BEARDEN: Aaron, 006, 025, 073, 108; Aron, 113, 120, 128; Edward, 113, 205, 210; Elijah, 113, 114, 130, 205, 208; Elizabeth, 158; Humphrey, 135; James M., 147; John W., 080, 146; John, 025, 120, 208, 217; John, Capt., 126; Permelia A., 172; Rachel, 178; Richard, 006, 025, 036; Solomon, 114; Tellethy, 156; W. P., 082
BEARDIN: Aaron, 109, 130, 205; Edward, 110, 130; Edwd., 128; Elijah, 128, 208; John, 060, 108; John, Sr., 108; Nancy T., 146; Sarah (Adams), 036; Solomon, 208; Umphrey, 071; Wm. P., 084
BEARDING: Edmund, 4th, Sgt., 126; Nancy, 167; Susan, 179
BEARFIELD: Solomon, 214
BEASLEY: Chapman, 076, 144; David, 145; Hiram, 077, 111; Hiram, 1st Lt., 127; Hiram, Lt., 125, 130, 203-205; James Ellis, Jr., 146; James Jr., 128; James M., 145; James, 110, 121, 205, 207; Jas., 113; Jerusha, 077; John A., 006; John, 034, 042, 061, 148; John, Jr., 110; Lovicy, 181; Margaret, 148; Margarett, 006, 171; Martha, 076; Nancy, 151, 162; Rebekah, 166; Richard, 207; Robert, 145; William, 143, 205; Wm., 128
BEAVER: C. E., 098
BEAVERS: Elizabeth, 093; John F., 025, 144; W. R., 045; William, 143; William, Sgt., 203
BEAZLEY: Lyda, 184
BECK: Thomas J., 025
BEDELL: Benjamin, 025; Martha Ann, 183; Pendleton, 006; Robert, 006
BEECHER: Samuel T., 025
BEEGLES: William, 033
BEER(BURR?): Barby, 091
BEERS: William P., 025
BEGGARS: Eliza, 169
BEGGERS: Nathan, 145
BELCHER: Francis, 144; Francis, Sgt. 206, 207; Rebecca, 174; Robert E., 109; Robert E., 2nd Lt., 117; Robert, Lt., 118
BELL (BEALL): James A., 148
BELL (BELK?): James, 201
BELL(BALL?): George, 144
BELL: Alexander, 071; Anna, 174; Celia, 184; Daniel C., 006; Elizabeth Clotelda, 148; Elizabeth, 094; Frances A., 146; George, 035, 037; James, 025; John, 039, 084; John, Mrs., 084; Joseph S., 146; Joseph, 032; Minervia, 162; Nancy, 098; Ruth, 188; Susan, 159; Thomas, 144, 145; Thomas, Mrs., 098, 100; William, 094, 147
BELLAH: Moses, 006
BELTON: Soloman, 025
BENADICH: Milly Catherine, & 1 ch., 087
BENADICK: Milly Catherine, 086
BENADICKS: Milly C., 083
BENARD: (chldn. of), 006
BENE: Ann, Mrs., 084
BENEDICT: Catherine, 101; Jno. A. (chldn. of), 006; John A., 006; Mary Louise, 006; S.R., 006
BENGE: Micajah, 024, 054; William, 023
BENIT: William B., 148
BENNET: Edward, 025; Lewis, 103
BENNETT: Elias L., 080; Jesse, 080; John F., 054; Lewis, 118; Mary, 099, 102; Nancy, 006; William P., 080; William, 148
BENT: Mary, 155
BENTLEY: James A., 146; M. A., 006; William G., 146
BENTON: Eliza, 147; Emma Dora, 006; James S., 147; Lloyd S., 006; Lloyd, 147; Loyd, 055; Martha, 147; Mary C., 006; William L., 006; William M., 006
BERADIN: Francis M., 147
BERGEN: Joseph, 109, 120
BERGER: Ann, 071
BERRIAN: Martha P., 006
BERRY: Anderson, 107; Caroline, 098; John (chldn. of), 006; John A., 088; Judy C. & 2 chldn., 085; Judy C., 088, 098; Judy Carolin (2 boys), 094; Judy Caroline & 2 chldn., 084; Judy Caroline, 096; Judy J., 100; Judy, 097; Mary L., 088; Mr., 084; Thomas H., 088; Thomas, 094
BERRYHILL: James, 110
BERTLING: Jane E., 006; Marie Louise, 006; Robert, 006
BESSMAN: John W., 025
BETHUNE: William M., 025
BETTON: Solomon, 217
BETTS: Parliner, 083; Paulim (?), 083; Paulina, 094; Z.H. (chldn. of), 006
BEUSSE: Henry, 146; J. H. D.,025
BEVERS: James M., 145
BIBB: --, 044; Thomas, 039, 058
BICE(RICE?): Malissee, 090
BICE: Carleton M., 092; Columbus, 092; Georgia Ann, 092; Henry, 092; Malissa, 093
BICKERSTAFF: Johnston, 031, 050; Nancy, 185
BIDDLE: Pendleton T. (chldn. of), 006
BIDEGREW: Bennett, 208
BIGERS: Nathan, 118
BIGGARS: Nathan, 025
BIGGERS: David, 119; James, 041; John F., 025, 148; Lucy E., 006; Lucy J., 163; Mary, 006; Nathan, 006
BIGGS: Aaron, 006, 025, 026, 041, 056, 057, 111, 112, 134, 202, 203; Aaron, Sgt., 129, 202; Aron, 123; Aron, Sgt., 120; Freeman, 027, 114, 210; James P., 006; Joel, 006; Joseph, 134; Martha, 170; Mrs., 085; Nancy, 171; Thomas J., 144; Wilis, 072; William J., 074, 145; William, 134; Willis J. (chldn. of), 006; Willis J., 006, 071, 072, 075, 076, 111, 145; Willis, 072, 134
BILLIPS: --, 047; Edward S., 147; Joel Abbott, 147; John M., 147; John, 031; Joseph, 025; Richard, 034; Sarah E., 184; Sarah J., 183
BILLUPS: Ann R., 148; Ann, 154; Darcus R., 182; Edward S., 006; Elizabeth W., 142; James, 023; John, 006, 026, 027, 031; Joseph, 026, 028, 029, 042, 055; Joseph, Cpl., 206, 207; Joseph, Maj., 110, 117; Leatia C., 171; Lucy Jane, 006, 169; R. R., 115; Richard, 049; Richard, Jr., 026, 030; Robert R., 006, 026, 059, 144, 209; Robert T., 026; Robert, 026, 047, 120, 211; Robert, Sgt. 206, 207; Thomas C., 067; William, 006
BINGHAM: Martha M., 146
BINNION: John, 143
BINYON: Burton, 006; George, 032
BIRCH: C.C., 066; C.C., Capt., 120; Charles C., 047, 053; Charles, 038; John N., 053, 055; John, 038
BIRD: Henry, 032; Job, Mrs., 091; John A., 050; Joseph, 046
BIRT: Anderson, 209
BIRUM: Mary A., 097
BISCANE: Walter, 129
BISCOE: Phillip, 026
BISHOP: Anna, 164; Brice H., 026; Edward P., 006, 146; Henry, 144; Joseph, 007; Mary C., 007; Thomas, 007, 026
BLACK (COBB): P. H., Mrs., 090
BLACK: J. W., 032; James, 143; John, 143; P. H., 100
BLACKBOURN: Nancy, 026
BLACKBURN: Benjamin H., 146; Marien, 147; Nancy, 048
BLACKMAN: Charity M., 177; Elizabeth Judy, 167; Frances, 153; Jemima, 180; William, 146, 147
BLACKMON: E. M, Mrs., 007
BLAIR: Charlotte R., 170; Dickson, 026; Edw. P., 081; George H., 146; Green, 006; J. C. (chldn. of), 007; John, 026, 214, 215; Nathan P., 007; Thomas, 007, 214; William M., 026
BLAKE: William, 026
BLAKELEY: --, 122; Eliza, 157; Elizabeth Ann, 164; Icey, 180; Jane, 162; Nancy, 154; Sarah A., 172; Susan, 164
BLAKELY: David E., 147; David G., 1st Lt., 111
BLAKEMON: Thomas, 109
BLAKINSHIP: William, 007
BLAKLEY: James, 143; Samuel, 007
BLALOCK: William, 036
BLANKENSHIP: Catherine P., 134; Elsey R., 134; H., 211; Hezekiah, 209; Mary P., 134; Capt., 132; Hezekiah, Capt., 210; John, 210
BLANTON: Benjamin, 026; David, 059; James A., 026
BLASINGHAM: John, 034
BLEDSOE: Miller, Rev., 141, 144; Moses, 201; Moses, Sgt., 129; Robert, 026
BLINN: Hosen, 059
BLOOMFIELD: R. K. (chldn. of), 007; Robert K., 007
BLOUNT: David, 109, 117
BLUNT: David, 116
BOADERS: John H., 024
BOARDMAN: Elijah, 045; Hannah C., 045; Hannah, 045
BOGGS: --, 046; Aaron, 007, 026, 073, 074, 075; Archibald, 026, 051; Exekiel, 145; Ezekiel, 074, 075, 110; Harriet, 007; James, 111, 146; John M., 007; Joseph A., 026; Leander, Sgt. 206, 207; Richard, 069, 146; Sarah Caroline, 007
BOHANNAN: Duncan, 007; Isaiah W. D., 007; Wiley (chldn. of), 007; William, 007
BOHANNON: Babby, 144; Isaiah, 107; Bedy, 178
BOID: Fanny, 181
BOING: Uriah, 072
BOLDING(?): Thomas, 143
BOLING: Henry, 202, 217; Samuel, 007
BOLLING: Nancy, 158
BOLLS: Ann, 188
BOLTON: Charles L., 146; William B., 148
BOMAN: Isom, 056
BOND: Edward, 029, 042, 054, 112
BONDURANT: Emmett Jopling, 196; Mary J., 007
BONE: Ann (4 ch), 095; Ann, 098, 100; Anne, Mrs., & 3 Chldn., 085; Arun (?) E., Mrs., 097;

Darius, 091, 092; Henry, 091; Jas. Willis, 092; Jas. Wm., 092; Jasper Newton, 146; John A., 092; John C., 147; John W., 091; John, 061, 215; Jos. H., 092; Mildred, 007; Milly, 091; Nan A., 093; Nancy B., 159; Nancy J., 093; Nancy, 093; Sandors, 147; Sarah, 150; William, 032, 111, 123
BONER: William H., 049
BONES: John, 026; Samuel, 026
BONNELL: John M., 147
BONNER: Allen, 007; Frances E., 007; Jordan, 043, 143; Jorden, 026; Jordon, 026, 049; Junsha, 007; Mary, 176; Melvin, 007; Polly, 182; Sarah, 179; Thomas, 007; William H., 007; Zadock, 042, 144; Zadock, Lt.129
BOOKER: John M., 058
BOOLES(BOALES?): Seaborn, 145
BOON: Frances, Cpl., 117; Francis, 116
BOORAM: Thomas L., 029
BOOTH: A. E., 060; A. J., 060; Benj., 121; Benja. H., Sgt. 210; Benjamin H., 046, 052, 067; Bettie, 101; Frances, 158; G.M., 026, 031; George J., 026, 035; J. M., 031; J. N., 031; John, 035; Louisa, 142; Mariah, 171; Mary F., 007; Robert, 035, 147; Thomas Y., 147; Thomas, 026, 036, 041, 042, 047, 053, 061, 112, 119, 144, 202, 218; Thomas, 2nd Lt., 111; Thos., 116; Thos., 1st Cpl., 128; Thos., Cpl., 205; Walton H., 007, 147
BOOTHE: Benjamin H., 144; Charles A., 054; Martha C. H., 142; Thomas, Capt., 201; Virginia B., 187
BORAM: George W., 007
BORAM: Mary, 159
BORDERS (?): John H., 107
BORDERS: John H., 029, 031; John McD., 145; John, 038; Michael A., 026
BORMAN(?): John, 112
BORMAN: Henry D., 043
BORNE: Daniell, 007
BORUM: George W., 145
BORWN: Seabourn, 124
BOSTICK: Bailey, 144; Floyd, 035; Margarette, 035; Rebecca, 035; Rebekah, 007; William, 035
BOSTWICK: Margaret R. H., 156; Rebecca, 025; William, 026
BOSWELL: Walter, 076
BOUCHELLE: Jesse C., 024, 028
BOUCHELLS: Jesse C., 034
BOWDEN: James Franklin, 148
BOWDRE: Albert, 026; Hays, 026
BOWEN: Christopher, 026, 027, 056, 066, 143; F.R., 146; John, 119; Mary Jane, 007; Thomas, 111, 119; Uriah N., 007; William, 049
BOWES: John, 027
BOWIE: James, 027; Langders, 027
BOWLES: Benjamin, 145; Benjn., 118; Thomas, 135; Widow, 135
BOWLING: Dison, Cpl., 207; Dyson, Cpl., 206; Henry, 121; Sally, 179; Thomas, 007; W. D., 103; William D., 109, 120; Wm., 119
BOWLS: Thomas, 007
BOWMAN: Samuel, 148
BOYD: Drury B., 050; George, 027; Robert, Jr., 007; Saml., 123; Sarah, 160; Thomas, 147
BOYER: Elias, 027; Henry, 054
BOYERS: Henry, 045, 059, 062, 109, 144
BOYLE: James, Capt., 129, 201
BOYLES: Jos., Capt., 201
BOYLSTON: Dubose, 007
BRACKENRIDGE: William A., 027
BRADBERRY: --, 103; C. C., 100, 220; Christopher C., 007, 147; E. R., 084; Eli, 119, 133, 145, 219; Eli, Lt., 110; Elizabeth, 135; Emma L., 089; Jacob, 220; James W., 080; John L., 089; John M., 146, 220; John, 089; Joseph E., 089; Josiah, 222; Julia T., 220; L.A., 097; Lewis, 133; Margaret, 221; Martha, 084, 101, 135, 159; Mary, 098, 100; Nathan, 133; Nelly, 221; P.W., 220; Rutha, 007; S. A., 084; Sarah A. & 2 chldn., 085; Sarah, 089, 098, 100, 174; W. A., 084; William J., 1st Lt., 118; William, 135, 145, 146; Wm., Capt., 117; Wm., Lt., 118
BRADBURY: Catharine, 174; Ellie, 222; Frances, 174; O. H., 222
BRADEM: Lewis R., 007
BRADFORD: Anna L., 007; James T., 048, 060; James Y., 050
BRADLEY: Abner, 219; Abner, Capt., 125; Chaney, 053; Elijah, 027; John, 040, 120; Josiah, 143; Lodie, 005; Minnie (chldn. of), 007; Thomas, 113, 123, 130, 205; Thos., 115, 124
BRADSHAW: C., 090; Elijah, 145; Katherine, 090; Mary, 219; Mercer, 135, 147; Peter, 145, 147; Silas M., 148; Stephen, 148
BRADSHWA(?): Peter, 145
BRANCH: Armstead, 034; Armsted, 034; Charity, 007; Dicey, 007; James C., 007, 029; James, 103, 118; John J., 081; John James, 146; Judith Scott, 169; Sarah Ann, 177; William S., 007
BRAND: Benjamin, 077; Cashwell, 115, 209, 210, 211; Daniel, Cpl., 205; Elizabeth, 141; Jonas, 115, 206, 209-211; Jonas, 2nd Lt., 121, 205; Jonas, Lt., 206, 207; Malaciah, 007; Thomas, 076, 077; William, 144, 215; Zack, 076; Zachariah, 077
BRANSFORD: James, 029, 121; Nathan, 144; Sarah, 173
BRASEAL: Nathan, Cpl., 210
BRASELTON: V. L., Mrs., 090
BRASETEN: William, Mrs., 091
BRASSNELL: William, 080
BRASWELL: Allen, 027, 031, 036, 061; George, 144; Henry, 077; Joseph, 060, 073, 120, 146; Milton, 094; Polly, 179; Samuel, 027, 028, 041, 073, 082, 143, 207; Sarah, 094; Sowel, 210; William, 084; William, Mrs., 084; Wm., 085, 100, 145; Wm., Mrs., 085
BRAY: B. A., 040; Benjamin A. (chldn. of), 007
BRAZELTON: Martha, 052; V. L., Mrs., 090
BREEDLOVE: John A., 027
BRENT: Kendal C., 046
BRENTON: Matilda, 173
BREWER: Burwell, 201; Eliza, 180; Elizabeth, 143; Fannie, 221; Hundley, 007, 027, 218; Hunley, 027; James, 135, 143, 144, 147; James, 4th Sgt., 128; James, Sgt., 206; Jno., 204; John W., 144; John, 109, 128, 144, 205, 210; John, Lt., 210; L.R., 027; Leroy, 207; Levey (Leroy?), 121; Levi, 113; Levy, 208; Littleton R., 027; Nancy, 143; Panina, 135; Perminah C., 175; Salley, 143; Sarah, 084, 101, 135, 175; William (chldn. of), 007; William H., 218; William, 027, 033, 041, 056, 073; Wm. H., 084; Wm. P., 146; Z. R., 052
BRIANT: James, 143; Moriley Ann, 170; Samuel, 143
BRIDEN: James, 206; Jas., 113, 129
BRIDGEMAN: S. D., 148
BRIDGES: --, 027; Arminda, 007; Boykin, Lt.129; Calvin James (Ch. of), 131; Elisabeth, 093; Elizabeth, 007, 090, 093; Jas. O., 092; John W., 027; Joseph, 112, 143, 203; Killis C., 027; Lieucdy, 099; Lucenda, 093; Martha J., 092; Mary R., 092; Nancy, 094, 168; Sarah E., 163; Susan, 100; Temperance, 152
BRIDGEWATER: Jane, 178; Samuel, 056
BRIDION: Keziah, 178
BRIGGS: Willis J., 075
BRIGHT: William, 073
BRIGHTWELL: Andrew J., 007, 074, 148; Andrew, 041; Ann C., 179; Callander, 147; Esther, 086; Frances A., 007; Francis S., 164; Jacob, 086, 095; John M., 007; John, 007, 027, 044; Martha, 186; Mary F. A., 146; Mary F., 176; Mary, 153; Samuel, 027; William B., 025-027, 032, 049, 057, 063, 148
BRIGHTWOD: Samuel, 073
BRIMER: Wm., 097
BRISCO (?): Nathan, 211
BRISCO: John (chldn. of), 007; Sallie, 007
BRISCOE: Mary, 162; Nathan, 027, 054; Phillip, 062
BRITAIN: Thomas, 053
BRITON: Henry, Sgt., 205
BRITS: Dianah, 161
BRITT: Agnes (chldn. of), 007; Keziah, 164; Sabra Francis, 175; William, 148; Zeliann, 181
BRITTAIN: Henry L., 073; John, 007; Thomas, 007
BRITTEN: James, 043; James, Jr., 043
BRITTON: Henry L., 3rd Sgt. 127; Matilda, 185; Milley, 171; Morning, 165; William, 144
BRMORD: John, 026
BROACH: Charles, 114, 143; James, 007; William, 112, 123; Wm., 116
BROADNAX: Frances A., 181; William (chldn. of), 007
BROCKMAN: Moses, 069; W. H., 041
BRODNEX: William, 143
BROOKS: Berford, 122; Elizabeth, & 4 chldn., 087; Elizabeth, 086, 099; George G., 027; Georgia, 007; John, 145; Lucile, 007; Oliver C., 027; Patsey, 143; Robert P., 003; Sarah E., 177; Sarah Jane, 097; Ted O., 190; Thomas, 083
BROOM: John, 113, 121, 205
BROUGHTON: Lourania, 175
BROWN (BREWER?): James, Sgt., 205
BROWN: --, 027, 028, 038; Adaline, 157; Adison B., 148; Alexander W., 051, 145; Alexr. W., 132; Alfred, 062; Allen W., 1st Sgt., 128; Allen W., Sgt., 205; Allen, 112, 116; Allen, 1st Sgt., 127; Allen, Sgt., 124, 202; Alsey, 172; Alx, 122; B., 027; Bedford, 007, 027, 040, 047; Betsy Ann, 007; Caroline, 162; Carrie M., 043; Carter, 007; Danby (?), 152; Daniel, 145, 148; David, 027, 038; Dillard H., 147; Dolly, 007; Earnest Stewart, 007; Elenor T., 156; Elijah B., 128; Elijah, 007, 205; Eliza J., 148; Eliza Kello, 156; Elizabeth, 152;
BROWN: Frances, 007; Francis J., 147; Gary (chldn. of), 007; George, 007, 147; Hattie Lou, 007; Henry, 007, 146; Isham J., 148; Jacob, 039; James E., 1st Lt., 127, 205; James E., 204; James E., Lt., 125, 130; James N., 143; James, 027, 132; James, Jr., 052; James, Sr., 052; Jane W., 141; Jeremiah (chldn. of), 007; Jeremiah, 007; John B. J.,

007; John H., 025, 028; John M., 148; John, 086, 128, 130; Jos., 116; Joseph, 025, 027, 029, 033-035, 037, 040, 045, 049, 052, 056, 060-063, 216, 217; Joseph, Maj., 111, 129; Judith, 171; Lemuel, 033, 040, 112, 116, 123, 143, 203; Littleton R., 027, 052; Lucy G., 155; Margaret A., 176; Margaret, 007 148; Mary A., 176; Mary R., 171; Mary, 085, 177, 181; Milley, 149; Minor W., 007; Minta, 007; Mirna, 148;
BROWN: Moses, 148; Murphy, 027; Nancy, 132; Nellie, 007; Pamelia, 186; Philip, 067; Robert, 056, 114, 115, 209, 211; Ruben K., 145; Russell, 056, 202, 217; S., 076; Samuel (?), 112; Samuel T., 028; Samuel, 025, 027, 030, 033, 034, 059, 067, 122, 143; Samuel, Capt., 116; Sarah A. R., 180; Sarah L., 086; Sarah S., 171; Seaborn, 203; Seabourn, 112; Thomas, 007; Viny, 007; W., 027; Wes, 027; William F.,043; William T., 028, 037, 053; William W., 043, 046, 121, 205; William, 024, 027, 032, 043, 044, 047, 049, 050, 053, 058, 060, 062, 214; Wm. T., 118, 119; Wm. W., 112
BROWNDIELF: John, 007
BROWNE: William M., 007
BROWNFIELD: Jincey, 007; Polly, 181
BROWNING: --, 085; Asa, 148; Frances H., 007; James H., 007; Jeptha, 145; Jesse, 073; John (chldn. of), 007; John, 007, 143, 219; Joshua, 007, 056, 059, 213; Joshua, Sr., 054, 059; Josiah A., 148; Josiah, 007; Lucy Ann Susan, 007; Margaret, 007, 027, 219; Margret, 174; Sarah M., 150; William, 027
BRUCE: James, 112; Jas., 116; John, 028, 128
BRUICE: James, 123
BRUMBERTON: William, 111
BRUMBY: Ephraim R. (chldn. of), 007; John W. (chldn. of), 007; Lucy Lee, 007; R. T., 052; Richard T., 007
BRUNELY: Trapier, 007
BRUNSON: Hundley, 218; Isaac W., 028
BRUX: --, 028
BRYAN(?): Elizabeth, 171
BRYAN: Eli, 028; Felix, 028; Isaac, 028; Jane E., 148; Laney, 060; Laury, 046, 053; Lewis, 145
BRYANT: A., Mrs., 090; Alex, 091; Amand, 093; Archabald, 210; Archd., 209; Archebald, 115; Archer, 028; Archibald, 213; Edmund, 145; Hardy, 145; Harrison, 091; Lewis, Lt., 210; Lowry, Cpl., 206; Moses, 115, 210; Nancy, 146, 182l Pleasant, 121; Samuel, 046; Thomas, 091; Uriah, 120; William, 144
BRYANT?: Josiah, 174
BRYDIE: A., 028; Archibald, 028, 029, 039, 043, 048, 145; Camilla (chldn. of), 007; Eugene W. (chldn. of), 007
BRYON: M. A., Mrs., 091
BRYSON: Harper C., 032; Harper, 028; William, 028
BUACHS: Wm., 128
BUCHANAN: Elizabeth, 090; William, 148
BUCHANANUS: Elizabeth, 083
BUCHANNAN: Charles J., 007; Frances E., 007; Henrietta, 148
BUCHANNON: David, 147; Elizabeth, 083; Nancy, 151; Wm., 122
BUCHANON: Charles J., 147
BUCHER: --, 028
BUCHHAN: J. W. Louza, 091
BUCKHANAN: W. H., Mrs., 091
BUCKHANNAN: Catherine, 007
BUCKHANNON: Catherine, 155; Martha, 177
BUCKLEY: James K., 028, 044; James R., Cpl., 210; James, 130, 205; Jas., 113
BUCKLY: James K., 028
BUCKNEY: Gilley, 178
BUED (BOID?): Seleah, 174
BUESSE: H., 028
BUFFINGTON: Cicero, 111
BUGG: Henry, 112, 116, 123; Sarah A., 007; William, 117, 124; Wm., 107
BULL: Andrew G., 060, 062, 063 Andrew, 063
BULLOCK: Alexander G., 061; Eliza S., 007; Hawkins J., 073; Hawkins S., 073; Mark S., 075; W.S., 007
BURBANK: E. L., 007, 028
BURCH: Charles C., 028; J.B., 039; John B., 057; William R., 028
BURDELL: R.W., 208; Robert W., 209
BURFEE: J. B., 091
BURFORD: Mitchel, 214
BURGE: Noar, 089
BURGER: Ann, 071; C. G., 100, 109; Charles G., 081, 085; Charles Jasper, 148; Charles L., 082; Charles, 131, 134, 143; Chas. G., Mrs., 098; Chs. G., 084; Chs. G., Mrs., 084; Daniel N. (chldn. of), 007; E., Mrs., 096, 097; Elizabeth, 082, 085, 097, 098, 100; Jacob Silas, 089; Jacob, (Orphs.), 096, 097; Jacob, 147; Jacob, Mrs., 098, 100; James B., 147; John A., 007; Joseph, 147; Martha Ann, 089; Martha, 082, 085; Mary Elizabeth, 089; Nancy, 082, 098, 100; Newman, 148; Seaborn, 080, 082, 134, 146; Seborn, 074; Susan, 145; Susannah, 134; William D., 082; William, 134, 148
BURGES: Jonathan, 144; Tereza, 154
BURGESS: Jonathan (chldn. of), 008; Jonathan B., 146; Jonathan, 082, 145; Linton S., 008; P. F., Rev., 142
BURGHER: Newman, 148
BURGON: Charles G., 3rd Cpl., 127; Charles, 122, 123
BURGOOD: Charles G., 210
BURGOR: Jacob, 144
BURGORE: Charles, 111, 124
BURK: Frances D., 147; Rhesa H. H., 051
BURKE: Betsey Ann, 034; John W., 147; Richard E., 028, 037, 144, 207; Theophilus, 008; Thomas (chldn. of), 008; Thomas A., 008; William B., 028
BURKS: Asbury, 144; Elizabeth, 174; John, 144; Lucrecy, 173; Rheea H. H., 034; William, 144
BURLESON: Bowie, 042
BURLIN: Margaret, 100
BURNET: Jeremiah, 121
BURNETE: J., 116
BURNETT: Bedford, 008, 134, 148, 220; Berry, 219; Elizabeth, 151; J., 116; Jeremiah, 008, 028, 042, 110, 112, 128, 201, 202, 205, 209; Jula, 134; Julia, 152; Licien, 220; Linda, 134; Littleberry, 073, 145, 208; Lucian B., 074, 122; Lusham, 134; Margaret Ann, 008; Mary, 149; Nancy, 152; Naomi, 153, 220; Nathan C., 028, 041; Omma, 134; Racheal, 134; Rachel, 220; Susan, 219; William, 046, 220
BURNETTE: Jeremiah, 114
BURNEY: Jane, 183; Patrick S., Jr., 197; Thomas J., 050; William V., 028
BURNITT: Jeremiah, 123; Jeremiah, D. D., 143; Jerh., 124
BURNS: Jacob, Lt., 201; Mary C., 098; S. W., 057
BURPEE: A.L., 028; James B., 147
BURROUGH: Lucinda, 179; Sarah Ann, 222
BURROUGHS: B. W. N., 008; Noah, 144
BURROW: Sally, 152
BURT: Anderson, Sgt. 206, 207; Andrew, 217; Eliza Ann, 187; Henry, 052, 144; James F., 048; Mary, 154; William Mc., 147
BURTON: James M., 008, 033, 034, 036, 045, 046, 049-051, 053, 103, 144, 210, 217; James, 028; Larry M., 026; Rebecca, 096, 102; Robert E., 008, 034, 110
BUSBAY: Elias, 107
BUSBEY: Elizabeth, 144
BUSBIN: Margaret, 083
BUSBOY: Elias, 117
BUSBY (BEASLEY?): Hiram, 204
BUSBY: Elias, 029, 073, 111; James, 144; Richard, 132; Salley, 154; Susannah, 132
BUSEY: Patrick, 098
BUSH: Richard E., Ensgn, 206
BUSHELL: Nancy, 097
BUSHIN: Margaret, 083
BUSHIP: Sarah, 149
BUSTIN: Edward, 028; Musgrove, 028
BUTLER: A. S., 084; Aaron, 115; Aldora J., 089; C. A., 084; Cynthia A. & 2 chldn., 085; Cynthia D., 008; Cynthia, 098; E. L., 008; Eliza, 097; George, 051; H. M., 084; Henry S., 036; Jesse, 146; John W. (chldn. of), 008; John W., 053; John, 143; Lewis R., 050; Littleton R., 036, 061; Lucy, 008; Malessa, 084; Martha J., 146; Moses, 028; Mrs., 097; N. S., 084; R. J., 147; Richard, 028; S. F., 084; Thos. W., 100; W. S., 084; William, 081; Wm. T., 084
BUTTERWORTH(?): John, 213
BUTTS: Thomas, Capt., 201
BUZZELL: James, 028
BYFORD: Nancy, 174; Sarah, 176
BYNTON: Hollis, 028
BYNUM: Alfred, 008
BYRD: John A., 028, 032, 044, 045, 061, 067
BYRDIE: John A., 032
BYRNES: Thomas, 032
BYRUM: John W., 028
CABANESS: William, 058
CABBELL: Rob I., 047; Robert J., 008; Robert J., Sgt., 130; Robert W., 008
CABBERT: W. C., Mrs., 090
CABELL(?): Robert J., 119
CABELL: R. J., 113l Rob. J., Capt., 201; Robert J., 026, 027, 055, 148, 205, 217; Robert J., Capt., 201; Robert J., Sgt., 205; Robert S., 026; Robert, 047, 055; Robt. J., Capt., 129; William B., 058
CABNESS: William, 058
CADDY: David, 035
CADE: Henry, 213; Thomas L., 030
CAFFIN: Patience, 008
CAGLE: Anne, 156; Barbary, 149; Charity, 185; George, 133, 149; Isham, 149; John, 149; Mary, 133; Nancy, 133, 186; Zachariah, 149
CAHOON: Isaac, 3rd, Sgt., 126
CAIN (CUSERN?): Anna, 169
CAIN: William, 045
CALAHAM: Edwd., 3rd, Sgt., 126; Joshua, 202
CALAHAN: James, 111, 149; Mary, 175; Moses P., 039, 115, 209, 210
CALDWELL: Alexander, 2nd Sgt., 127; Betsy, 148; James, 061, 079, 121, 218; Polley, 170l Thomas, 126; Thomas, Cpl., 206; William, 033, 204, 207; Wm., 113, 204, 207
CALEELL: Robert J., Capt., 126
CALEHAN: William, 049

CALEN: Joseph, 214
CALLAHAM: William, Ens., 126; Wm. W., 1st Sgt., 127
CALLAHAN: Edward S., 217; Moses P., 046; Moses P., Cpl., 210; Moses W., 208; Polly, 178; William W., Lt., 210; William, Sgt., 203; Wm. M., Sgt., 205; Wm. W., 210; Wm., 207; Wm., Ensgn, 203
CALLAN: Thomas, 028
CALLAWAY: Hendley V., 150
CALLENDER: Benjamin, 034
CALLIER: Charles W., 038, 059; Henrietta, 171
CALLIHAN: Edward, 203; Moses W., 208
CALLOWAY: Wenefred, 079
CAMACK: James, 054
CAMAK: Annie T., 008; James W., 008; James, 008, 028, 080; Lewis, 008; Margaret Ann, 008; Thomas, 008
CAMARON: James, 062
CAMERON: Ambros, 026; Robt., 072
CAMFIELD: Abiel, 055
CAMMELL: Thomas, 112
CAMP: Abner, 028; Cicel, 052; David, 080; Edmond, 028; Edmund, Cpl., 206; Thomas, 204
CAMPBELL: C. D., 008; Charles D., 008; Duncan G., 008; Howell, 132; Isaac, 034; Jesse I., 008; John, 048; Judith, 160; Malinda, 132; Mariah, 132; Matilda W., 152; Thomas, 030, 033, 113, 115, 121, 126, 130, 132, 150, 205, 211; Thomas, Sgt. 210; Thos., 128, 204; Walter, 055, 132; William, 132
CAMRON: Absalom, 124, 203; Ambrose, 076; Ashley, 076; Florow, 167; John, 202; John, Jr., 008; Robert, 149
CANADY: Catherine, 153
CANLY: Jane, 091
CANNADA: Elizabeth, 185; Jesse, 126
CANNCIL: Thomas, 204
CANNON: Dyce, 176; Henry, 148; William, 008, 049
CANNY: Thomas P., 028
CANTEN: W. L. 084
CANTERBURY: Robert, 129
CANTON: W. E. 084
CAPE: Eurena, 099; Rena, 097
CARAWAY: John, 024, 028
CAREY: Eliza P., 182
CARHART: --, 028
CARITHERS: Edy H., 008; Johnnie L., 008; Martha F., 008
CARLETON: Gabriel, 038; Henry, 121; Henry, Cpl., 206
CARLTON: Henry, 114, 204, 208, 209; J. B., Dr., 008; Julia E., 168; Mary Ann, 157
CARLY: James, 077
CARMICAL: Richard H., 135; William, 135
CARMICHAEL (?): Thomas, Sgt., 206
CARMICHAEL: Andrew W., 028; Catherine, 185; Elizabeth, 159; James, 150; John C., 028; John, 122; Richard, 122, 151; Robert D., 027; Sally S., 185; Thomas, Sgt., 207; William P., 028; William, 077; William, Sgt. 210
CARNES: Thomas P., 008, 025, 028, 217; Thomas Petters, 028; Thomas Pl, 040; Thomas, 061; William W., 028, 128; William, 206; William, Sgt., 124, 203; Wm. W., 129
CARR: David, 150; Elejah, Mrs., 098; Elijah W., 008; Frances R., 158; Rachael, 181; Susan A., 183; Thomas, 028; William A., 028, 037; William, 062, 208; Wm. A., 074
CARREKER: N. P., 150
CARREWAY: John, 024
CARREY: Thomas P., 025
CARRITHERS: E. H., Mrs., 032; Lucy, 032
CARROL: David, 054
CARROLL: David, 028
CARSEN: Marth, 091; Marthy, 083
CARSON: --, 072; Francis M., 151; John, 083; Mary, 097; Mr., 084; Rebeca, 083; Sampson, 033, 117; Simpson, 103; Waller, Capt., 111; Walter, 073, 150; Walter, Capt., 110
CARTER: Benjamin F., 150; Benona, 071; Christ. A., Sgt., 203; Christopher A., 028; Christopher A., Sgt., 129; Edward, 109, 116, 117; Elizabeth, 155; Hawkins, 028; Henry, 109; Highley, 176; James, 073, 134; Jas. N., 097; John A., Ensgn, 117; Joseph R., 039; Levi H., 039, 046, 113, 128; Levi H., Jr., 150; Levi M., 096; Levi M., Mrs., 101; Levy H., 114, 207, 208; Lucy, 206; Margarett H., 150; Mary Ann, 082; Mary H., 178; Mrs., (3 orphs.), 094; Nancy M., 134; Peninnah J.L., 150; Skit, 101; Wiley, 149
CARTHERS: Hughey A., 151
CARTLEDGE: Stephen C., 151
CARTY(CARLY?): Nancy Moore, 077
CARTY: Hannah (?), 179
CARUTH: Robert, wife & 3 ch., 216
CARUTHERS: Edy H., 008; John R., 151
CARVNESS: Rebekah, 148
CARY: Dudley, 028; Dudly, 038; Edward, 149; John P., Capt., 201; John P., Lt., 201; John, 040; Lucy, 028, 038; Margaret, 008; Orlando, 008; Paton, Ensgn, 129
CASE: Leonard E., 028, 150
CASEY: Capt., 201; John A., 028
CASH: Benjamin W., 028; Floyd, 008; Joel H., 055
CASTARL: Jesse, 117
CASTLEBERRY: Henry, 008; Rachel, 154
CASTREY: B. F., Mrs., 102
CASY (CARY?): John P., Capt., 201
CATBELL: Robert L., 047
CATER: Charles, 028
CAUSEY: Aaron, 215
CAUSSONS: Elzia, 083
CAUTERBURY: Phillip, 008
CAVENDER: Cain, 112, 121; Eleanir, 027
CAVIN: Anna, 151; Harriett E., 159; Martha B., 175; Nancy C., 183
CAWLEY: Wm. M., 111, 150
CAWSON: John, 040
CAYGLE: Mathew, 122
CEBRA: John Y., 028
CENTER: George W., 008; Paul M., 151; William M., 008; William, 069, 151
CHADWICK: Jesse, 150; Mary, Mrs., 085; Polly, 097
CHAFFE: --, 060
CHAFFIN: Frances A., 154; Lemuel (chldn. of), 008; Patience, 008
CHAMBERLAIN: Charles V., 046
CHANCEY: John, 008; Samuel, 150; Saul J., 008
CHANCY: G (?), Mrs., 090
CHANDLER: C. H., 008; John B., 043, 054
CHAPLIN: John J., 080; Sallie, 082
CHAPPELL: Robert, 008
CHAPPLIN: Jackson, 151
CHARLTON: Cordelia J., 168
CHASE: Alban, 008; Deane W., 150
CHASTAIN: Mary, 093
CHASTEEN: Mary, 093; May, 090
CHASTINE: Henry, 092; Jas. E., 092; Mary Ann, 092
CHATHAM: Catherine, 093; Mary W., 029
CHAUNCEY: Calvin H., 151; John, 035; Richard, 151
CHEATAM: Charles, 079; John J., 072
CHEATHAM: Ann M., 183; Anthony R. (chldn. of), 008; Anthony R., 008; C. L., 008; Chas., 092; Clifford W., 008; E. S., 008; John S., 008; Laura, 008; Mary D., 150; Obedience B., 176; Thomas H., 028; Thomas, 029
CHEATUM: Richard, 221; Sarah H., 173
CHENEY: F. W. (chldn. of), 008; Frances (chldn. of), 008; Franklin W., 008; Lucas, 008; Mary Louisa, 008; Paul, 008
CHERRY: Aquilla, 026; Valentine J., 035; Vincent I., 053; William L., 029; William, 008, 025
CHESSER: Ester, 071; Polly, 071
CHESTER: Celia, 150; Easter, 071; Elisha W., 029
CHILDERS: Elizabeth, 090, 185; Henry, 032; Indy, 184; James, 109, 134; Malinda, 093; Mary, 092; Milly, 090; Robert, 134; Robt., 208, 209; Samuel, 134; William, 134
CHILDES: M., Mrs., 091
CHILDUS: Elizabeth, 093
CHISHOLM: Elizabeth, 171
CHISLOM: John, 029
CHISOLM: Appleton, 150; John, 027
CHISSOM: Appleton, 008
CHOAT: Jacob J., 108; Jacob T., 109, 118; Jacob, 058, 103
CHOICE: Cyrus, 029; John, 029; Tully, 029
CHRISTIAN: John, 061
CHRISTOPHER: David, 073, 149; William J., 031, 074; Wm. G., 033
CHRISTY: Ida Laura, 008; John H., 008, 049; W. D., 057
CHUBB(COL, FREE): Charles, 076
CHURCH: A., D.D., 142, 147; Alenzo, 029; Alonzo, 008; Elizabeth, 151; Julia M., 151
CIMBRE: William, 206
CLACK: John C. F., 040
CLANDINING: James, 149
CLANEY: Michael J., 151
CLARK: Absaton, 149; Braswell, 095; Daniel L., 062; Delila, 095; Dilla, 085; E.K., 097, 099; Eli K., 029, 039, 045; Eli, 052; Elijah, 029; Elmira, 174; Ely K., 028, 044; F., 029; Francis A., 151; Francis, 029; H., 029; Horace, 029; Isaac, 149; Jeremiah H., 029; Jno. M., 204; John M., 008, 112, 204; John, 029, 150; Josiah A., 150; Larkin, 038; Lucy (chldn. of), 008; Lucy, 027, 033; Michael N., 034, 067, 149; Minerva C., 155; Richard S., 062; Samuel, 029; Sarah, 176; Susan M., 152; Thomas C., 058; William (chldn. of), 008; William, 103, 217, 218; William, Sgt., 125; William, Sr., 029; Wm., 113, 205; Wm., 2nd Sgt., 127
CLARKE: Absalom, 029; Braswell, 084, 085, 095; Delila, 084; Eli K., 054; Eli, 028, 057; Elijah, Gen., 003; Ely K., 029, 059; Frederick A., 029; Julia, 029; Lucy, 029, 040, 049, 052, 060; Thomas C., 074; William Sr, 029; William, 029, 077; Wm., Jr., 118; Wm., Sgt. 206
CLARKSON: Joseph, 032, 033
CLAY: William H., 046
CLAYTEN: William W., 045
CLAYTON: A. J., 029; Almira D., 150; Augusta C., 167; Augustin S., 008, 029; Augustin S., Capt., 129; Augustine S., 029; Augustus S., 029; Capt., 201;

Claudia Caroline, 164; Edward P., 029; Edward, 036; Ephraim B., 151; H.B., 042; July, 213; Lucinda, 149; Philip, 036, 046, 049; Phillip, 040; William W., 024, 029; William, 036
CLEGGINS: Joseph, 186
CLEMENT: James, 029; John, 008, 029, 148; William, 029; Wm., 149
CLEMENTS: Aley, 160; Charles, 029; William, 112, 123, 201, 202; Wm., 116, 201
CLEVELAND: Benjamin, 063
CLIFF: William, 029
CLIFT: Henry, 058, 202; Zacahariah, 076; Zachariah, 076, 077
CLIFTON: Aaron, 125, 149; Aaron, 4th Sgt., 128; Aaron, Sgt., 205; Clement, 033, 149; Elijah, 122; George, 008, 029, 149, 214; George, Jr., 029; George, Sgt., 130; Hiram, 072, 150; John, 038, 062, 149; Mary, 158; Susannah, 165; William, 040, 053, 120, 207; William, Capt., 207; William, Ensgn, 124, 126, 202; William, Lt., 125, 130, 203, 204; Wm., 1st Lt., 128; Wm., Lt., 205; Young B., 008
CLINARD: A. D., 029
CLINCH: Robert T., 008
CLINE: William, 029
CLOCK: Darius, 029, 030; Jack F., 030
CLOSE: Edward L., 150; Elijah, 035; Elvira G., 159; Gideon P., 151; Jane, 157
CLOTFETTER: Felix L., 151
CLOWER: (chldn. of), 008; D.M., 099; Daniel M., 032; Daniel, Maj., 110; F., Mrs., 090; N. W., Mrs., 090
CLOWERS: D., Mrs., 091; W. W., Mrs., 091
CLOWN: Thomas L., 150
CLUTE: John D., 030
COAL: Sarah, 213
COATS: John G., 008
COBB: --, 119; A.P., 008; Andrew Jackson, 196; Azariah P., 081; Azeriah, 220; Edwin Newton, 008; Howell (chldn. of), 008; Howell, 008, 024, 029, 031, 032, 034, 035, 037, 049, 058, 061, 062, 150; John A., 024, 029-031, 034, 035, 037-039, 045, 047-051, 057-060, 063; John B., 030, 032; John, 149; Joseph B., 150; Lamar, 008, 030; Lowell, 196; Lucy B., 008; Lucy, 030, 044; Marion Thomas, 008; Martha S., 187; Mary Ann, 008; Mildred L. R., 159; T. R. R., Mrs., 099; Thomas R. R., 008; Thomas W., 030; Turner, 118; Wm. B., 115, 210; Wm., 208
COBELL: Robert J., 030, 046
COCHRAN: Neal F., 150
COCHRILL: John, 149
COCK (COOK?): Jack F., 111
COCK: J.F., Capt., 201; Jack F., 008, 050, 149
COCKE: Jack F., 025, 026, 030, 038, 040, 044, 050, 055, 056, 059, 122; Jack, 025; Salley, 171; William A., 048; William, 058
COCKRAL: John, 202
COCKRAM: Bannister, 151
COCKRILL: Mary, 166
COCKRON: Thomas, 135
CODY: Eliza, 098, 100; Elizabeth, 088; James, 088; John W., 088; Martha, 088; Martin, 088
COE: Ann A., 030
COFER: Rebecca Ann, Mrs., 101
COFFIN: Lee, 030
COGBURN: Amanda, 163; Caroline E., 151; Jesse H., 107; John A., 112, 116, 124, 202; Martha Ann, 149; Moses A., 207; Moses H., 023, 047, 049, 058, 213
COHEN: J., 030
COHN: Herman, 008
COHOON: Isaac, 3rd Cpl., 126; John, Lt.129
COIL: W. M., 030
COILE: James N. (chldn. of), 008; James N., 008
COLBERT: Peyton H., 149; Thomas, 046, 047; W. C., 008; William C. (chldn. of), 008
COLCLOUGH: John (chldn. of), 008; John, 008; Sarah L., 082
COLE(COLLINGS?): Nancy, 157
COLE: Caty, 154; James D., 117; Josiah, 008; Martha, 156; Polly, 141; Richard, 061, 149, 202; Richd., 124; Samuel, 030; Sarah, 008, 024, 030, 032, 035; Sarissa B., 008; William, 216; William, Jr., 149
COLEELL: Robert J., 2nd Sgt., 127
COLEMAN: Andrew, 030, 060; Clementine, 008; John, 030; Mary A. (chldn. of), 008; Mary, 134; Polly, 170; Wm., 134
COLLEY: Elizabeth M., 182; Joel, 219; John, 151
COLLIER: Amanda & 5 Chldn., 085; Amanda & 6 chldn., 085; Charles W., 050, 053; Cuthbert S., 149; Cuthbert, 030; Elizabeth, 102; Francis, 098; Isaac, 057; John L., 150; Mary H., 149; Mrs. (1 ch.), 071; Nancy, 170; Polly, 162; Sally, 144; Sterling, 209; Thomas, 008, 151; William, 008
COLLING: Mary C., 178
COLLINS: Bryon W., 030; Charlotte, 165; Ellen, 008; I.W., 044; J. W., 030, 031, 034, 061; James L., 040; Mary M., 071; Robert, 030; Saml., 112, 114; Samuel, 030, 121, 208; Samuel, Ensgn, 206; Samuel, Sgt., 116, 124, 203; Tom, 044; William, 148
COLLUS: Elizabeth, 102
COLLY: George W., 008; John, 008
COLORED, FREE: Foot, 075; Jacob, 076
COLORED: Mary Ann, 016
COLQUIT: John T., 030; Walter, 062
COLT: John H., 008; Joseph C., 033, 045, 061
COLYER: Amanda (7 chldn.), 095; Francis, 095
COMBS: --, 030; George D., 030; Sterling, 030
COMPTON: Lora A., 008; Martha Lumpkin, 197; Thomas M., 008
COMSTOCK: William S., 048
CONALLY: Charles, 058; George A., 030; Harper, 118
CONANT: Airs, Sgt. 206
CONDICT: Steven H., 030
CONE (BONE): Ann E., 081
CONGER: Abijab, 030; Abijah, 008, 031, 039; David, 074; Elizabeth A., 156; Hedges T., 009; Thomas, 030, 035
CONGO(CONGER? COUGER?): Abijah, 151
CONLEY: Benjamin, 151
CONLY: Jane, 093
CONNAL: Martha, 167
CONNALLY: Bryan, 057, 149; Catherine, 162; Elizabeth, 087, 155; George A., 030; George H., 149; Jane, 086; Mary, 166
CONNEL: Benjamin, 041; Eliza, 180; Jincey P., 144; Jno., 128; John, 130, 204; Walter, 112, 119, 201
CONNELL: Benjamin G., 151; Elizabeth, 009; Jno., 113; John M., 056; John, 205, 208
CONNELLY: Lucy W., 165
CONNER Daniel, 057; David, 057
CONNER (COMER?): Patsey, 156
CONNER: Almanza Jane, 169; Bolin (chldn. of), 009; Bolin, 108; Bolling, Lt., 117; Bowlin, 035, 037, 045, 049, 051, 063, 150; Daniel, 030, 051, 151; David, 053, 110, 115, 122, 150, 151; Edward, 030, 039, 053, 149; Edward, Capt., 124, 126, 203, 204; Edwd., Cpl., 205; Elizabeth, 171; James, 122, 149; Jarusha A., 166; John, 053, 207; John, Ensgn, 202, 207; John, Lt., 124, 203, 204; Martha, 162; Mary, 181; Orrey, 180; Robert, 107, 112, 149; Robert, Ensgn, 202; Robert, Sgt., 112, 124, 203; Sarah, 179; Tarrance, 208; Thomas, 109, 149, 150; Timothy, 151; Torance, 208; Torrance, 114
CONNERS (COUZENS?): Thomas, 148
CONNOR: Rebecca, 181
CONSTANCE: W. S., 213
CONWAY: P. C., 030
COOK: Aley, 087; Amanda, 088; Andrew J., Lt., 110; Arthur, 009; Asbury, 087; Charity, 143; Charles D., 080; Cicero, 220; Drury H., 038; Elizabeth, 152, 161; F.W.C., 009; Hardy, Mrs., 098; Hartness, 221; Hartwell, 009, 088, 157; Harty D., Mrs., 088; Harty, 100; Henry H., 030; Herty, 101; J. S., 030; James C., 026, 030; James W. (chldn. of), 009; James W., 009, 074, 075; James W., Lt., 111; James, 030, 074, 122, 124, 125, 205, 213, 220; James, L. D., 146;
COOK: Jas. W., 111; Jas. W., Lt., 119; John W., 009, 122, 151; John, 213; John, Esq., 220; Keelin, Sgt., 207; Kelin, 009; Keolin, 220; Mandy, 220; Marian, 174; Martha H., 188; Mary, 085, 087, 152; Nancy, 148, 177; Nathan, 122, 150; Nathan, Mrs., 220; P., 072; Pernal, 111, 207, 208; Polly, 143; Purnal, 107, 109, 117, 122, 149; Purnel, Sgt., 207; Rebecca, 149; Sarah W., 170; Susan, 009; William B., 030; William M.(chldn. of), 009; William M., 030, 111, 151; William, 073, 107, 220; Wm., Lt., 110; Zadock, 030; Zadoo, 220; Zedoc, 213
COOKE: Eugene D., 030; J. F., Capt., 201
COOKSON: Elizabeth, 184
COOLY: John W., 052
COOPER: Amelia (chldn. of), 009; Archer, 048; Arthur, 112; Blake, 118, 149; Charles P., 150; Drewry, Ensgn, 124; Drury, 202; Drury, Ensgn, 127; E. Ann L., 095; Edward, 096; Elizabeth, 101, 151, 162; Frances N., 168; H. E., 084; James A., 033; John Z., 151; John, Mrs., 220; Kennon, 109; M.A., 148; Mary A., 086; Mary Ann, 093; Mary, 145; Matilda, 170; May, 090; Mrs. (2 ch), 095; Obedience, 150; P. F., 084; Parmelia F., 101; S. A., 084; Thomas B., 073; Thomas, 150, 151; U. L., Mrs., 099; Vining, 056; Willis, 030, 037, 149; Winston O., 150
COPELAND: Coleson, 114, 209; Colson, 209; Gilbert, 112, 116, 123, 201; Sarah, 182
COPHER: William, 151
CORA: William A., 060
CORBETT: James, 030
CORD: John M., 030
CORSLY: Martha J., 147
COSBY (EASLEY?): Richard S., Capt., 129
COSBY: Erwin C., 080; James 109, 116, 117; James C., 046; James R. (chldn. of), 009
COSTLER: Eliza, 148; Joseph, 151;

Sarah E., 180
COTHRAM: Tabitha, 145
COTHRAN: Parentha, 159
COTTER: Ford, 107; W.J., Rev., 142; Joseph, 149; Orren J., 151
COUCH: Benjamin Wofford, 151; Biddy, 090; Eliza, 170; George Washington, 150; Hiram, 097; James B., 151; John, Mrs., 098; Martha, 177; Mary C., 092; Matilda, 097; Obedience, 086, 093; Obedience, Mrs., & 4 chldn., 087; Saml., 092; Thos., 092; Wm., 092
COUEY: Lizzie A. (chldn. of), 009
COULEY: Benjamin, 035
COULTER: E. Merton, 003
COUNETT: Adans, Sgt., 207
COURSEN: Sarah, 071
COUSENS: John, 151
COUSINS: E., 097; Fanny, 031, 083; Martha, 097; Rhoda, 083; Thomas, 111
COUSONS: John, 009, 056; Thos., Sgt. 210
COUSSERS: Eliza, 083
COUSSONS: Eliza, 096; Sarah, 146; Thomas, 009
COVINGTON: Henry, 009
COWAN: Thomas, 058
COWART: Cato, 077
COWEN: Isaac, 058; James, 031; Moses, 058
COX (CON?): Elizabeth, 098
COX: --, 030; Adamson T., 118; Boling, 111, 112, 148; Bolling, 045; E. F., 103; Edward, 113; Edwin F., 031, 072, 118; Edwin L., 209; Edwin, 115, 149; Elizabeth & son, 084; Elizabeth M., 009; Elizabeth, 096, 097, 100; Francina B., 152; Francina E., 158; Hugh H., 150, 151; Jacob N., 151; Jno J., 049; Joel N., 151; John J., 031, 040, 041, 058, 118, 149; Joseph, 215; Martha Ann, 180; Mentoria B., 162; Richard, 009, 031, 044, 051; Saml., (Orph.) 097; Samuel, (Orphs.)097; T.J., Mrs., 099, 101
COY: Thomas W., 031
CRABB: Wm. R., 207, 208
CRAFT: Daniel, 051, 060, 213; Daniel, Jr., 107, 109, 149; Daniel, Sr., 009; Danl., Jr., 118; Edward F., 088; Edward, 036, 060, 107, 109, 149; Edward, Cpl., 207; Edwd. 118; Edwin, 208; Elijah T., 087; Elijah, 009, 088; Eliza, 094; Elizabeth F., 088; Garret, 103; Garrett, 109, 114, 117, 121, 131, 202, 208; Garrett, Ensgn, 201; Hannah, 031; John C., 088; John E., 151; John, 088, 094, 100; John, Mrs., 098; Martha A. & 4 Chldn., 085, 094; Martha, 088, 097, 099, 102, 184, 186; Mary A., 088; Mary Jane, 087; Peggy, 182; Rebecca, 031; Robert, 103, 109, 117, 150; Susan & 4 chldn., 084, 085; Susan A., 097; Susan, (3 chldn), 094; Susan, 088, 098; William M., 087
CRAFTON: Garrett, 118
CRAFTS: David, 025
CRAIG: Eleanor, 170; Lewis S., 009, 151; Rebecca, 009; Sally C., 009; Sarah, 182; William, 009, 059
CRAIN: Thomas, 031, 215; William, 040, 049
CRANE: Benjamin F., 031; Charles A., 009; Fanny T. (chldn. of), 009; J. R., 031, 038, 045; James R., 009; John R., 009; John W., 031; Nancy, 079; Ross, 009, 031; Thomas, 134
CRASS: James, 074
CRAVIN: William M., 031
CRAWFORD: A., 116; Anderson F., 151; Ann, 184; Archabald, 123; Archabald, Sgt., 202; Archablad, 112; Archebald, 112; Archibald, 031, 050, 129; Catherine, 155; David C., 150; Elizabeth, 166; Frances Ann Dunkling, 009; Frances Ann, 165; Frances, 144, 148; H. H., 009; Henry, 031; Henry, Rev., 142, 146; Horace L., 057; James, 073; Joel T., 150; John A., 009; John M., 062, 211; John R., 009; John, 009, 051, 150; Joseph, 031;
CRAWFORD: Judy, 077; Julia F., 009; Lemuel, 071; Levi M., 040; Levi, 119; Marian, 219; Peter, 054; Polly, 178; R., 116; Russell, 113, 123, 149; Sarah A., 175; Silas, 073, 149; Susan A., 176; Susan, 009; Susannah, Miss, 071; Thomas (chldn. of), 009; Thomas, 009, 030; W. S., 025; William H., 031; Wm. H., Capt., 110
CRAWLEY: A., 116; Archabald, 111
CREAL: Elizabeth, 152
CREDILLE: Ellington, 150
CREEK: John, 121
CREEL: John, 128, 130, 205
CREIGHTON: William, 150
CRELL: John, 113
CRENSHAW: Daniel, 009; David, 045; James G., 054; James J., 027, 036, 046, 062, 109, 119; James T., 038; Martha J., 180; Zadock F., 009
CREW: Elvira, 175
CREWS: John, 009, 031, 033, 034, 041, 047, 052, 054, 066; Rebecca, 167
CRITTENDEN: Penelope S., 155
CROCKER: William, 055, 215
CROFT: Martha & 5 chldn., 084
CROMPTON: John, 045
CROOKER: William, 031
CROOM: George A., 151
CROSBY: John T., 150; William, 117
CROSLEY: Wm., 108
CROSS: Allen, 089; Allen, Mrs., 101; Anselmn L., 089; Featherstone, 075; Fetherstand, 073; George, 089; Jeremiah A., 151; Margaret Ann, 163; Martha F., 089; Mary & dau., 084; Mary A., 089; Mrs., 085; Sarah J., 089
CROSSLAND: William, 062, 063
CROSWELL: Virginia, 146
CROUCH: John, 201, 202
CROW: A., 115; A., Mrs., 099; Aaron, 051, 053, 073, 075, 076, 089, 149, 150, 219, 221; Aarow, 009; Abel, 128, 149, 206; Abell, 113, 116; Abner, 031; Alexander, 112, 123, 201; Aley, 183; Amos, 110, 114, 116, 123, 124, 128, 148, 205, 206, 208; Amus, 113; Anna, 087, 088; Aron, 071; Calvin J., 150; Caroline, 088, 099; Catherine, 163; Cathleen, 087; Charles, 089; Eli, 081, 150; Elizabeth, 159; F.A., Lt., 119; Fanny, 168; Frances A., 111;
CROW; Francis, Lt., 111; Franes A., 081; Isaac, 213; J. M., 088; J. M., Mrs., 101, 102; Jacob, 149; James B., 087; James M., 080, 088; James, 151; Jocob, 031; Julian Amanda, 164; Margaret, 009, 172; Marietta, 147; Marlin T., 150; Martha, 101; Martin, 079, 148, 211, 218; Martin, Ens., 124, 127, 202; Mary, 171; Mat, Mrs., 095; Mrs. (1 ch), 095; Nancy A., 147; Nancy, 084, 086, 095, 102, 221; Pulaska, 089; Pulaski, 122; Sarah F., 087; Sarah, 099, 219; Serena, 101, 222; Serina, 089; Simeon, 080, 088; Stephen, 009, 062, 072, 076, 131, 151, 217; Steven, 031; W., 102; William, 112, 123, 151, 201, 202; Wm., 116
CROWLEY: Archebel, 123; Charly, 031
CROXIN: Hannah, 214
CROXTON: Elijah, 109; James, 009, 149, 205, 208; James, 4th, Sgt., 126; Jincy, 154
CRUISE: John, 054
CRULE: Elijah, Ens., 126
CRUMPTON: G. Hue, 128; Jehu, 133, 205; Jehue, 205; Jesse, 204; Richard, 133; Sally, 133; Thomas, 133
CULBERSON: David H., 150; Isaac T., 082; Jeremiah, 149
CULBERTSON: G. A., 097; Jeremiah, 009; Polley, 177
CULBREATH: Elizabeth Susan, 175; Nancy, 009
CULLEN: --, 031
CULLUM: Francis, 031
CULP: B. F., 024; Henry T., 009; Peter, 009; Sarah A., 187
CUMING: Thomas B., 028
CUMMIN: Thomas M. H., 150
CUMMING: Elizabeth, 009
CUMMINGS: Thomas, 040
CUNINGHAM: Andrew, 031; James, 115, 148; John, 031; Thomas, 031
CUNNINGHAM: (chldn. of), 009; James, 107, 129; Jno., 026; John, 026, 030, 051, 201; Tho., 026; Thomas, 026, 030, 051; William R., 031
CUNNNINGHAM: John, 029; Thomas, 029
CURRY: Henry A., 151; James W., 031; John, 031; Mary, 153
CURTIS: William, 148
CUSTARD: Jessey, 107
CUTHEN: Lemuel R., 031
CUTHENS: Lemuel, 031
D'ANTIGNAC: William, 059
D'AUTEL: Jules, 049
DABNEY: James, 117
DAGGATT: Thomas, Sgt. 210
DALE: John M., 009
DALTON: John, Cpl., 207; Lewis O., 009
DAMRON: Peter, 009
DANE: John, Capt., 126
DANEILL: Joseph, 031
DANFORTH: Jacob, 031
DANIEL (MCDANIEL?): Jeremiah M., 152
DANIEL: (?), 031; Allen, 031; Amos, 031; Beaton, 152; Beaton, Sgt., 204; Belton, 4th Sgt., 128; Cerdy, 108; Corday, 118; Cordy, 109, 111; Duke A. (chldn. of), 009; Ezekiel, 031; Isaac, 203; Isaac, Lt.129; James, 121, 124, 130, 152, 205; James, Lt., 117; Jas., 113, 116; Jesse, 009, 088; Jesse, Capt., 119; Jessee, 088; Joseph, 098; Josiah(chldn. of), 009; Josiah, 031, 036, 057, 152; Josiah, 1st Lt., 128; Josiah, 201, 202, 204, 205, 206, 207; Josiah, Lt., 124, 125;
DANIEL: Lucretia E., 180; Martha, 088; Mary, 179; Masters, 122; Nathaniel, 152, 153; Rachel, 142; Robert, 037, 153; Sarah, 179; Stephen, 073; Susannah, 156; Thomas, 152; W. R., Mrs., 099; William R., 080; William, 152; Wm. B., 131; Wm. R., Mrs., 102
DANIELL (DARNELL?): William B., 110
DANIELL(?): Nathaniel, Bro., 222; William, 219
DANIELL: Amanda, 157; Asa B., 009; Beaton, 222; Beaton, Mrs., 221; Boy, 221; C., 222; Carut, 161; Charity, 186; Clemontina, 221; E. E., 048, 050; Eleanor, 169; Elizabeth Ann, 155; Elizabeth, 145, 169; Frances, 219; Francis M., 009; Henrietta

V., 079; Henrietta, 009, 098; James, 221; Jeremiah M., 153; Jeremiah, 009; Jesse, 031, 054, 099; Jesse, Capt., 111; John B., 220; Josiah, 009, 048, 050, 051, 073, 154, 221, 222; Mary, 220; Masters, 219; N. J., 221; Nancy, 219; Olley, 162; Robert, 031; Robert, Capt., 110; Sarah A., 146; Sarah Ann, 219; Sarah E., 219; Sarah, 009; Sirena, 155; Susan Ann, 163; Susannah, 169; Thomas M., 009; Thomas, 096; William B., 009, 153, 222; William R., 152, 222; William, 009, 043
DANIELLS: Josiah, Jr., 153
DANIELLY: Andrew, 152; Elizabeth, 009; Sarah E., 177
DANIELS: Mary, 166
DANNELL: Nathaniel, 031
DANNIEL: Russell C., 031
DANNIELL: Jeriah, 047
DANNILY: Elizabeth, 219
DARBEY: James W., 154
DARBY: James W. (chldn. of), 009; James W., 009; Julius G., 009, 076; Julius, 220; Louisa H., 185; Sarah, 095
DAREY: James, 100
DARMAN: John, 204
DARNAL: Joseph, Sgt., 129
DARNALD: Nicholas H., 031
DARNEL: David, 152; Jesse, 122; Nicholas H., 031
DARNELL: Duke A., 081; Jesse, 081
DARNILL (DANIELL?): Cordy, 110
DARNOLD: Polley, 174
DASTER: Clisha, 100; R. A., 100
DAUENBAUM: --, 025
DAUGHERTY: Charles, 208
DAUGHTERY: Elizabeth, 090
DAUTREY: Lafayette, 153
DAUTRY: James, 153
DAVENPORT: --, 108; Catherine, 150; Daniel, 095; David Mc, 080; George W., 110; Harriet, 164; Heney, 029; Henry, 029, 059; Henry, Jr., 029; James B., 041; James W., 081; James, 047, 103, 109, 117; Jarrett, 071; Jesse, 153; John A., 031; Jonett, 027; Josiett, 073; Jourett, 109; Jovett, 047; Jowett, 117; Levicia, 181; M.N., 036; Martin S., 034; Mary D., 009; Mary F., 179; Mary S., 188; Moses N., 034, 036, 046, 057, 073, 152; Nancy, 009; Robert E., 153; Robert, 029, 045, 153; Susan T., 165; Thomas B., 152; Thomas, 026, 029, 031, 034, 051, 058, 154; William, 027, 047, 050, 052, 072; Wilson L., 153
DAVID (?): Benjn., Capt., 120
DAVID: Martha C., 031; Robert, 031
DAVIDSON: James M., 026; John J., 031; Mary & ch., 085; Mary, 081; Wm. P., (Orph.)097
DAVIES: Edward, 042; John, 028
DAVIS (?): Benja, Capt., 210
DAVIS: --, 031; Angeline, 009; Benj., Capt., 118; Benjamin, 072, 073, 111, 209; Benjamin, Sgt., 203; Capt., 135; Charlotte 086, 101; Charlotte, Mrs. & 2 chldn., 087; Delila, 168; Edward, 031, 035, 036, 040, 044, 054, 060; Elijah, 117; Elizabeth, 135, 141, 148; Elnathan, Rev., 143; Emery, 009; Emma M., 009; Emmie, 009; Fuller, 009; George, 153; Henderson, 153; Isaac, 208, 210; J. 116; James H., 089; James, 153; Joannah, 181;
DAVIS: John, 031, 056, 135; Joseph, 046; Julius, 114, 123; Kathaine, 091; Lidda, 156; Lucy A., 155; Madison, 009; Marion T., 009; Martha A., 089; Mary E., 089; Mary, 098; Milley Ann, 009; Milley, 160; Moses, 201; Nancy A., 009; Prior L., 009; Rebecca, 032; Scidney, 148; Stephen E., 053; Thomas, 031, 214; William A., 152; William J., 152; William, (Orph.) 097; William, 009, 026, 038, 062, 074, 079, 080, 089, 112, 119, 126, 153, 202; Wm.,201; Wm., Mrs.,101, 220
DAVISON: Family, 196; Harris, 031; James M., 108; John, 032; Mary & son, 084; Mary, 096-098, 100
DAWSON: Elijah, 032; George M., 009; Henry T., 032; Lucien W., 009; Martha, 097; Mary D., 080; Mr. or Mc., 220; Sarah D. J., 009; Solomon, 215; Wm. C., 129
DAY: David, 152
DEAN(GEARR?): Thomas, Mrs., 091
DEAN: Burket, 035; Burkett, 044; Burkitt, 214; Henry G., 032; John, 009, 117, 152, 153; John, Capt., 121, 125, 203, 205, 206; John, Ensgn, 117; Lilley, 165; Miley, 143; Nathaniel, 023; Sally, 143; Sarah, 083; Thomas M., 153; Westly, 009
DEANE: Burkite, 061; Charles, 043; Courtney, 178; Henry, 115, 211; John, 059, 109, 124, 206, 211; John, Capt., 118, 124, 126, 127, 204, 205, 207; Malinda, 156; Margaret, 158; Martha S., 176; Matilda A., 156; Matilda, 176; Nathaniel, 043, 058
DEANES: John, 204
DEANS: Charles, 031
DEAR: --, 032
DEARING: Albin D., 009; Albin P., 153; Elijah M., 154; Eugenia, 009; Jno, 117; John, 109, 116; Marcella, 009; Margaret Ann, 162; Margaret, 009; Thomas H., 009; William E., 074; William, 009, 032, 037, 038, 045, 048, 196
DEARINGS: William, 032
DEAS: John, (chldn. of), 009
DEAUFIGNAC: William D., 032
DEAVENPORT: James B., 041; Jarrett, 107
DEBOARD: Daniel B., 118
DEBUTTS: Joshua, 032
DECKEN: Richard, 036; Wm., 071
DECKINS: Richd., Capt., 118
DEE: James, 055
DEEAKES (DUKES?): Thos., 152
DEEKIN: Richard, 216
DEFOOR: James, 153
DEGAFFENREID: Boswell B., 034, 152
DEGRAFFENREID: Boswell B., 048; Boswell R., 048
DELACY: Henry M., 009
DELANY: Hiram R., 153; Wm. G., 090
DELAPIERRE: A., Capt., 129
DELAY: A.B.C., 095; Asbury B. C., 081; Emer J., 087; Hiram R., 030; James, 087, 152; Jason M., 153; John M., 088; Josi-Ann, 009; Laban Patrick, 154; Laborn P., 080; Martha, 088; Rolin J., 081
DELLOACH: Elizabeth, 134; Fanny, 134; Jesse Gaston, 134; John, 134
DELONEY: Rosa E., 009; William G., 009
DELPH: Natalie, 009
DEMING: Charles W., 153
DEMON: W. R., 054, 055
DEMOND: W. A., 032; W. R., 032; William R., 032; Wm. R., 032
DEMORE: Nancy, 009; William R., 009
DENNIS: Elizabeth, 150; James M., 153; William T., 153
DENT: George, 032, 153
DENTON: John B., 032; John, 032
DERICOT: Anthony, 025
DERRICOATE: Mike, 009
DETROBRAIND: Rosalie Gauvain, 030
DEUPREE: Daniel, 152; Francina, 009; Lucy D., 009; Lucy Y., 009
DEVENPORT: John M., 153
DEWBERRY: --, 193
DIAL: Callvill, 153
DICEN: Richard, 120
DICKEMAN: Wilburn L., 049
DICKEN: Alma T., 096; Amanda F., 172; Catherine, 009; Elizabeth, 098; Henry C., 096; Lucy E., 096; Lucy P., 175; Mathew G., 154; Matilda C., 096; Nancy T., 096; Richard B. (chldn. of), 009; Richard B., 009, 073, 076, 153; Richard, 023, 032, 036-038, 040, 042, 047, 051, 074-076, 112, 119; Richard, Capt., 118, 134; Richard, Jr., Sgt., 202; Richd., 3rd Sgt. 127; Richd., Capt. 206; Richd., Maj., 117; Sally, 100, 101; Sarah A.H.N., 080; Sarah A., 096; Sarah Ann, 101; Thos., 3rd Cpl., 128; Thos., Cpl., 205; William H., 081, 153; William, 009, 025, 032, 037, 073, 080; Wm., 072, 075
DICKENS: Nimrod, 152; Richard, 207, 215; Richard, Capt., 206, 210; Richard, Jr., 218; William, 152, 217
DICKENSON(?): Polly, 182
DICKENSON: Zachariah, Ensgn, 202
DICKERS: Richard, 032
DICKERSON: James, 152; James, Ensgn, 202; James, Sgt. 210; John N., 009; Wilburn T., 154; Zachariah, Ens., 126, 203
DICKIN: Elizabeth A., 160; Elizabeth S., 172; Joseph, 032; Richard, 023, 053, 058; Thomas, 032; William, 032
DICKINS: Richard, 033
DICKINSON: Elizabeth, 171; Henry T., 153; Joel, 028; John P., 152; John, 152; John, Ens., 129; Zachariah, Ens., 124
DICKON: Richard, 220
DICKSON: Henley H., 081; Irvin, 153; Martha E., 175; Mary H., 101; Richard, 033; W.E., 091, 213
DILIPRIER: Ange, Capt., 202
DILL: Robert L., 039
DILLARD: Fielding, 154
DILLASHAW: Edward W., 153
DILLERPREER: Ange, Capt., 126
DILLIPREE: Ange, Capt., 202
DILLON: James, 154; Sarah E., 098, 100, 102
DILWORTH: George A., 152
DIMAURT: David, 028
DINKINS: Samuel H., 033
DINNINGTON: William, 081
DISMUKES: William H., 047, 152
DIXON/DICKSON: Isaac, 009
DIXON: Floyd, 009; Henry, 044; Irvin, 211; Joseph, 037; Mary Jane, 167; Thomas, 009
DOBBEN: William, 152
DOBBINS: Aseneth S., 180; Francis E., 145; Jno. M., Capt., 125; John M., 121, 152, 205; John M., Capt., 127, 130, 205-207; John M., Cpl., 210; Mary J., 177; Moses W., 152; W. C., 121; William J., 010, 081
DOBBS: S. C., 033
DOBLE (DOBBS?): Annie N., 159
DODD: George J., 208, 209; Peter, 120; Peter, Sgt., 202
DODGER: Elezabeth, 097
DODSON: Daniel, 010, 029; Daniel, Lt., 118; Nancy, 160
DOGETT: Mark, 154
DOGGETT: Chatten, 152; Chattin, 010, 033; Chattin, Jr., 010; Fanney, 166; George, 010, 041, 060; Marilda, 186; Mark (?), 046; Richard, 010, 041; Shadrack, 097, 153; Susan, 158; Thomas,

033, 047, 058, 152; William, 152; William, Sgt., 203
DOLITTLE: Abram, 073; Seprenus, 152; Sylvanus C., 113
DOLTON: John, 133; Martha, 133; Nancy, 133; Susannah, 133; Vincent, 133
DONAGHEY: Samuel, 037
DONAWAY: John, 1st Cpl., 126
DONNALD: Robert, 029
DONOHO: Amanda Jane, 180
DOOLITTLE: A. C., 116; Abraham, 049, 152; Alonzo Lawrence, 153; Mary, 084, 085; Minos D. (S.?), 153; Nancy, 093, 097; Old Mrs., 221; Poldore, 095; Poledore, 084; Polidire, 085; S. C., 124, 130, 205
DOOLY: John M., 025, 033
DORAN: Anderson, 010
DORAND: J. H., 098
DORMAN: John, 033, 204; John, Sgt., 130
DORRELL: Elizabeth, 168
DORSETT: Charles L., 033; John K., 081; Theodon, 055; Theodore, 055
DORSEY: F.S., 010; James E., 003, 189; James P., 010; William H., 010; Wm. H., 221; Wm. H., Capt., 099
DORTIC: German I., 033
DOSSTER: Geo. W., 153; Mary, 087
DOSTER: Francis M., 010; James, 055, 066; N. C. (2 ch), 096; Rodey A., Mrs. (3 ch), 096
DOTSON: Elisha, Cpl., 207
DOTTERY: Elizabeth, 097; Sarah, 097
DOUBLEHEAD: Bird, 010
DOUGAL: M., Mrs. (1 ch), 095
DOUGHERTY: Charles, 033, 044, 119, 152, 220; Chas., 118; Francis, 146; Jane R., 182; Rebecca, 033; Robert, 082, 107, 118, 153; William, 033
DOUGHTERY: Charles (chldn. of), 010; Charles, 010; Elizabeth, 010; Rebekah, 010
DOUGHTRY: Green, 153
DOUGLAS: Thomas, 010
DOWELL: Thomas, 033
DOWNES: Barnet, 129
DOWNING: R. H., 029, 059
DOWNS: Barnell, 208; Barnett, 133, 202, 206, 207; Barnett, 1st, Sgt., 126; Elizabeth, 133; Floyd, 133; James, 213; John, 071; Nemiah, 133; Peggy, 133; Richard, Sgt. 206, 207; William W., 152
DOWNY: Barna, Sgt., 202
DOWSE: Gideon, 111
DOYAL: Leonard T., 153
DOYLE: John L.,111; Patrick H., 010
DRAKE: Arrilla, 092; Benjamin F., 122; John, 092; Safharn, 100; Saphrona, 093; William A., 033
DREW: Pinson, drummer, 129
DRUMMON: F. J., 154
DUCKIN: Richd., 202
DUDLEY: Benjamin, 010
DUERDEN: P. H., 010
DUGLESS: Margaret, 091
DUKE: --, 031; Abraham, 038, 107; Allen, 133; Beverly A., 010; Edington, 133, 152; Edmond, 152; Henry, 131, 204, 208; Macy, 033; Massa, 133; Stephen, 038; Thomas, 038; William, 133
DUKEN: Rhmd., 073; Richard, 033, 071, 072; Thomas, 152
DUKES: Abram, 038; David, 107; Edmund, 115; Edmund, Cpl., 205; Henry, 153; Stephen, 038, 152
DULA: Thomas, 033
DUNAMS: David, 028; Jacob, 028
DUNAWAY: Argyle Troublesome, 153; John, 112, 124; Joseph, 151
DUNCAN: Lorenzo D., 153; Mary, 153; Peggy, 152; Robert B., 033; Terry E., 033; Thena, 179
DUNKINS: Peter, 060
DUNLAP: John C., 033
DUNN (?): John T., 210
DUNN: Elizabeth, 177; J.W., 091; John F., 115, 210; John T., 024, 025, 032, 033, 041, 048, 062, 076; John, 033; Leah, 010
DUNNAGHY: Samuel, 033, 037
DUNNAHAN: James H., 153
DUNNAHOE: Reuben G., 084
DUNNAHOO: James, 010; Joseph Henry, 089; Mary Jane, 089; Rubun G., 085; Susan Almer, 089; Tulithia, 101
DUNNAWAY: Nancy L., 093; Sarah J., 092
DUNNEHOO: Telithia Ann, 089
DUNNEL: John T., 028
DUNNWAY: Nancy N., 164
DUNSON: Obadiah, 027
DUPONT: Capt., 079; Charles A., 109; Charles H., 211
DUPREE: Curtis, 110; Elizabeth, 175; Lewis J., 153; Mary Ann, 164; William, 033
DURBY: Betsy, 177
DURHAM: Abraham, 010, 095; Amanda, 101; Betsy, 181; Brightwell, 026; Camelia M., 080; Cornelia, 010; Curry, 095; Elizabeth C., 155; Elizabeth, 186; Emaline, 085; Emma, 101; Geo W., 098; George W., 080; Henry (chldn. of), 010; Jackson, 073; Jesse, 096; John, 010, 152; Joseph, 040, 058, 071, 109-111, 118, 122, 123, 152; Joseph, Ensgn, 129; Joseph, Sgt., 203; Lindsey, 050; Lindsey, Jr., 010, 153; Lindsey, Mrs., 098; Lindsy, 073, 075; Lona, 040; M. J., 075; Marshall, 077; Martha Ann, 220; Martha M., 098, 164; Martha, 159; Mary, 186; Matilda, 173; Milledge S., 079, 152; Napoleon B., 010; Nilly, 077; Peter, 095; Peter, Sr., 096; Robert, 095; Saml. D., 080; Samuel D., 010; Silas, Capt., 109; Wiley, 032; William W., 153; Wm., 122
DURHAN: Joseph, 033
DURLEY: (chldn. of), 010
DURNEL: Cordy, 103
DYER: John, 079; Joshua T., 079; Mary A. C., 162; Obed, 152; Sarah P., 170; Sarah, 062; Susan C., 163
DYSEEN: William, 213
DYSON: William, 031; Wm., 201
EACHELS: Absalem, 107; Miller, 107
EADES: Tarleton, 110
EADS: John H., 081
EALY: Gad, 010
EANBREY: Elijah, Cpl., 206
EARLEY: Augustus W., 043; Daniel, 061; Richard, 023, 042
EARLY: Augustus W., 043; Jacob, 010; Jeremiah, 154; Sarah G., 010
EARNES: George L., 122
EARNEST: Elisha, 110, 112, 116, 124; Geo. L., 116; Geo., 067; George L., 107, 114, 118, 119, 129, 209; George, 056; John B., 044; John, 207; John, Sgt., 203; Ludwell, 107; Nancy P., 152; Robert, 154; Thomas, 056, 112, 123, 124; William H., 050
EARNIST: Mary, 187
EASLEY: Benjamin, 050; Buckner, 154; Daniel, 216; Elisa, 173; Elizabeth, 156; Richard, 023, 042, 060; Richard, Jr., 112; Richd., Jr., 124; Roderick, 010, 024, 033, 039, 045, 061; Sophia, 171; Weldon, 112; William P., Capt., 112, 124, 126, 202, 203; Wm. P., Capt., 201; Wosham, 034
EASLY: Roderick, 052
EASON: Nancy, 090
EAST: --, 030; Fanney, 173; Frances, 147; Harriet, 219; Malinda, 082; Martin, 154; Milley, 174; Polley, 172; Silas, 010, 154, 221; Silas, Sgt., 207; William, 154
EASTERLING: Henry, 040, 156
EASTON: George L., 035; Phillip, 112, 122, 211; Phillip, 4th Cpl., 127
EASTRIDGE: Amey, 176; Clearey, 173
EATHERTON: Elizabeth, 167
EAVES: Patrick, Sgt., 130
EBERHART: Ann E., 010; Edward P., 010; Francis, 154; John, 010; S. P., 039; Thomas, 032
EBLEIN: Mary J., 098
EBLEN: Ann L., 094; Augusta A., 094; Franklin Glen, 155
EBLIN: M. J., 097; Mary J., 089, 100, 102; N. G., (Orphs.), 096
ECHALS: Mary E. C., 083
ECHOLDS: Hann, 222
ECHOLS: Absalom, 033, 037, 055; Absolon, 115; Elizabeth M., 156; Emeline, 010; Ester, 025, 028; George, 010; H., 099; Hannah, 010, 093; Ida, 010, 093; James, 010, 033; Martha, 141; Mary C., 094; Mary E. C., 083; Mary E., 090; Miller, 115; Milner, 024, 029, 033; Nancy Catherine, 180; Nancy, 176; Obadiah T. (chldn. of), 010; Obadiah T., 010; Obadiah, 117; Obediah, 024, 029, 033, 155; Reuben, 033; Robert E., 032, 033, 051, 067; Robert M., 154; Robert M., 2nd Sgt., 125; Robert, 027, 033, 057, 058; Samuel, 154; Silas, 010; Susan, 163; Thomas E., 058; Thomas, 154; Thomas, Capt., 117, 120; William S., 154
ECTOR: Eliza, 158; John, 033, 055; John, Otmr, Sgt., 129; Joseph, 033, 112, 204
EDENS: Capt., 103
EDGAR: Mathais, 033; William, Jr., 033
EDGARS: Betty, 134; John, 134
EDGE: Ezekiel S., 033; Ezekiel, 033; Frank G., 010; Sarah, 010; Warren, 010
EDLER: James H., 155
EDMONDSON: Allen, Sgt., 203; Nancy, 178; Thomas, 041; Wiley, 111
EDMONDSTON: Catherine, 163
EDMONSON: Allen, 204
EDMUNDS: Peter, 154
EDMUNDSON: Polley, 154; Wiley, Cpl., 210
EDWARD: Jas., 097
EDWARDS: A. H., 084; Albert H., 033; Capt., 110; Edwin, 109, 154; Eliza, 164; Elizabeth, 157, 162; F. E., 084; Francis M., 154; Gage D., 033; Henry L., 010, 073; Humphrey, 127; Humphrey, 3rd Sgt., 128; Humphrey, Sgt., 202, 204; James C., 038, 048, 060-062, 109, 118; James, 072, 221; James, Sgt., 205, 206; Jasper N., 069, 155; Jim, 031; John D., 155; John M., 109, 154; John O., 155; John, 122, 214; Joseph, 033; Lewis H., 155; Old Mrs., 219; Pricilla D., 184; Richard H., 076; Richard J., 010; Robert H., 010; Sage D., 027; Sarah M., 165; Sarah, 090, 164; Soloman, 010; Susan E., 010; Susan, 084; T. C., 084; Umphrey, 120; William, 109, 120, 154; William, Cpl., 207; Wm., 076, 118; Wm., Cpl., 206
EIDSEN: John T., 010; Lewis, 010; Margaret (chldn. of), 010; Elizabeth, 087; Giles B., 155; James H., 155; Jane, 097; John, 155; Lewis, 074, 075,

221; Lucinda, 170; M.J., 088; Mary, 187; P., 102; P., Mrs., 099; Permilla, 088
EILER: Polly, 159
ELARD (?): Thomas, Lt., 120
ELBEHERT: Mahaly, 099
ELDER: Albert, 077; Almira C., 183; Amos, 096; Anne, 148; Arianna, 172; Asbury B., 010; Blant, Dr., 220; Bridget, 083, 085, 095; Caroline A., 187; Caroline, 077; Cupid, 095; D. W., 119; Daniel, 154; David B., 082, 155; David B., Mrs., 101; David B.,(4 Orph.), 094; David G., 010, 155; David M., 010; David Thomas, 088; David, 029, 033, 048, 054, 058, 074, 075; David, 4th Sgt., 127; David, Sr., 010; Doctor W., Capt., 107, 117; Doctor W., Maj., 110, 111; Eavmin, 181; Edmonds G., 155; Edmonds, 010, 154; Edmund, 073, 074; Edmunds G., 1st Lt., 111; Edmunds G., Lt., 119;
ELDER: Eliza Ann, 089; Eliza H., 146; Eliza, 096, 098, 100; Elizabeth M., 162; Ella, 077; Frances Mary Ann, 180; George, 077; Harrison W., 029; Harrison, 029, 033; Hartwell E., 118; Hartwell M., 103; Hartwell, 010, 154; Henderson, 010; Howard, 033; Howell, 010, 033, 112, 154, 203; James P., 110, 118; James P., Cpl., 103, 117; Jeremiah D., 082; Jeremiah, 154; John (chldn. of), 010; John L., 155; John L., Jr., 080; John P., 074; John, 010, 155;
ELDER: Jordan, 033; Joseph Green, 088; Joseph M. (chldn. of), 010; Joseph M., 010, 108; Joseph, 033, 154; Joshua P., 034, 061, 155; Joshua, 039, 047, 126, 154; Joshua, 2nd Sgt., 127; Joshua, Sr., 010; Julia Ann, 163; Lindsey Jacks, 088; Lucy Jane, 170; Martha Ann Elizabeth, 177; Martha E., 172; Martha, 010, 173; Mary Annie Elizabeth, 077; Mary E., 094, 170; Mary P., 170; Mary S. B., 183; Mary S., 173; Matilda Ann, 183; Nancy A., 159;
ELDER: Nancy, 156, 162; Nathan T., 080, 155; Pamelia J., 142; Patience, 083, 085, 095; Philip T., 010, 075; Phillip T., 155; Phoebe, 086; Polley, 171; Robert S., 077; Sarah F., 163; Sarah, 158, 164; Sarrocey, 086; Sterling, 010, 027, 033, 034, 071, 105, 110, 129, 154, 217; Sterling, Clk., 129; Susan A., 173; Susan Frances, 170; T.G., (Orphs.) 097; Talitha A., 153; Thomas G., 155; Thomas P. (chldn. of), 010; Thomas P., 010; Thomas, 095; Thos. G., (Orphs.) 097; Wetch, 154; William M., 094; William Y., 010, 033, 037, 155; Wm. A., 094; Wm. M.,(1 Orph,), 094; Wych M., 155; David, 122, 154, 217
ELDERS: Joseph, 108
ELKIN (?): James S., 154
ELLINGTON: Pleasant, 155
ELLIOT: Benjamin, 058
ELLIOTT: Benjamin, 024, 034; Mary R., 144; Richard, 134; Sarah, 010, 134; Susan, 083; Thomas G., Capt., 111, 119; William, 134; Wm., 134
ELLIS: --, 034; Thomas, 034
ELLISON: Hannah, 025; Henry G.,025
ELLISS: Isaac H., 154
ELLIT: Jemma, Mrs., 071
ELLREAD: Benjamin, Sgt., 203
EMBREY: Elijah, Cpl., 206; Elizabeth G., 181
EMBRY: Joel, 034; Martha M., 182; Merril, Cpl., 205; William, 034
EMERSON: Walter, 034
EMRICK: Joseph H., 054
ENDENS (EVANS?): Charlotte, 178
ENGLAND: Daniel A., 155; John E., 155
EPPE: William, Mrs., 219
EPPES: James, 123; Thos., 2nd Cpl., 128; William E., 155; William, 155
EPPS(?): Susan E., 142
EPPS: Catheren, 093; Celesta, 091; Elizabeth, 181; Franklin, 155; J. Milten, 010; James, 076, 112, 203, 204; Jas., 116; John, 155; Joseph, 155; Josephine, 010; Joshua, 155; Katherine, 091; Martha, 175, 180; Mary Ann, 180; Mary G., 154; N.,116; Nath., 128; Nathaniel, 057, 113, 122, 125, 130, 155, 205, 206, 208; Salley, 160; Sarah, 158; Thomas M., 036; Thomas N., 010, 155; Thomas, 073, 075, 154, 220; Thomas, Sgt., 129; Thos., Cpl., 205; Venus, 083, 085, 095; William, 010, 029, 034, 046, 074, 155; William, Esq., 220; William, Sgt., 206; Wm., 072, 074; Wm., Sgt., 205
EPPSE: Mary, 151
EPSY: John, 026; Robert, Capt., 120; Thomas, 058
ERMENGER: John (Orph), 098
ERWIN: Francis, 034; James, 207, 208; L.A., 034; Leander A., 026, 027, 029, 034, 043, 050, 154; Leander, 112, 129; Leandr A., 044; S. J., 097
ESKRIDGE: John, 034
ESPEY: James W., 155; James, 076; John, 076; Robert, 203, 209, 210; Robert, 2nd Lt., 126, 127, 205
ESPRY: Thomas, 072
ESPY: James W., 026; James, 155; John, 010, 059, 072; Mr., 076; R., 115; Robert, 034, 055; Robert, Lt., 125, 130; Robt., 204; Thomas, 026, 034, 072; Thos., 072
EUDIN(?): Greene, 2nd Lt., 127
EUSTIS: William F., 034
EVANS(?): Stokley, Sgt. 210
EVANS: Ann B., 177; Arden, 088; Arthur, 030; Benjamin J., 010; Catherine & 2 chldn., 085; Catherine H., 096; Charles, 034, 037; E.W., 054; Elisha, 154; George, 207; Green A.,(Orphs.) 097; Green, 073, 154; Green, Lt., 205; Greene A., 155; Greene, (Orphs.) 097; Henry W., 034; Henry, 044; Jacks, 034; James V., 155; Jehue, 034; John, 010, 038, 049; Ketty, 097; Kitty, 096, 097, 098, 100; Lucius P., 010; Menecies, 146; Parke, 034;
EVANS: Pleasant, 086, 096; Richard J., 155; Sallie E., 010; Sally, 171; Sarah E., 088; Sarah, 098, 100, 153; Sissey, 096; Stokeley, 113; Stokely, 154; Stokey, 207; Stokley, 2nd Sgt., 126; Susan, 159; Tapley, 096; Thomas, 051; Wiley G., 155; William N., 155; William, 155; Wm. G., 075
EVERETT: Sanuel H., 076; Sherod G., 076; Sherod, 010
EVERITT: Roselinda, 175
EVINS: Elizabeth, 167; Green, 071
EWING: Alvan B., 155; Andrew F., 202; James D., 010; John, Sgt., 129; Joseph, 154, 201; Leander N., 155; Samuel, 010
EWINGS: Arthur, 034
EXUM: --, 196
FAGG: Thomas M., 156
FAIN: Thomas J., 082
FAIRFIELD: Jeremiah A., 157
FALKNER: Amanda, 157
FALL: Calven J., 157
FALLWOOD: Robert, 039
FAMBAUGH: Sarah A., 188
FAMBOROUGH: --, 122; John A., 118; Joshua, 112, 204; Robertson, 122; William L., 156
FAMBOUGH(?): Cutliff, 209
FAMBRO: Anderson, 156, 214, 215; John N., 034
FAMBROUGH: Allen G., 115, 211; Allen, 113, 206; Allen, Lt., 206; Allen, Sgt. 206, 207; Anderson (chldn. of), 010; Anderson, 010, 136, 156, 157; Catherine, 174; Elizabeth, 182; Gaddial, 108; Gadeal, Lt., 123; Gadial, 073; Gadiel, 156; Jack, Lt., 201; James (chldn. of), 010; James M., 010; James P., 073; Jesse, 073; John A., 073, 081, 108; John E., 157; John R., 010; John, Sgt., 202, 210; Joshua, 043, 113, 128, 130, 136, 156, 205; Joshua, 3rd Sgt., 127; Loveless, 128;
FAMBROUGH; Lucinda A., 080; Lucinda, 165; Martha, 170; Mary R., 164; Matilda C., 168; Robertson, 112, 124; Robertson, Sgt., 202, 210; Susan, 169, 184; William A., 010, 111; William F., 082; William L., 208; William, 026, 033, 044, 108, 120; Wm. J., 205; Wm. L., 113, 130, 205, 208, 209; Wm., 209; Wm., 4th Sgt., 127; Wm., Jr., Sgt. 206
FAMROUGH: John A.,034; John E.,034
FAND (?): Thomas, 1st Sgt., 128
FANN: Ely, 4th Sgt., 127; George, 201; George, Prov. Mars., 129; Jane, 144; Jesse W., 157; Jesse, 156, 214; Joseph A., 040; Thos. A., 207; Thos. A., Ensgn, 205; William, 034; Williby, 214; Willobough, 107; Wiloughby, 042
FANNEN: Clocy, 152
FARIS: James, 156
FARLEY: Prudence, 165
FARR (?): Eli, Sgt., 202
FARR: Alexander, 112, 121
FARRA: George Y., 053
FARRAR: Absalom, 157; Dorcas, 148; Francis, 034, 076; G.Y., 121; George Y., 030, 035, 037, 054, 112; Mahaly, 141; Richard, 3rd Sgt., 125; Richard, 4th Sgt., 127; Richd., Sgt., 205; Thomas, 205; Thomas, Ensgn, 127; Thos., Ensgn, 126, 205, 206
FARRARL: Rebecca, 156
FARREL: Katherine O., 090
FARRELL: James O., 156; John, 036, 055
FARRER: John, 028; Thomas J., 028
FARROW: George W., 034
FAULKNER: John, 156
FEARS: William, 156
FELKER: John, 157; Stephen, 034, 156
FELLOWS(?): George, 119
FELLOWS: Almira C., 010; Ella M., 034; Frances A., 187; George P., 010, 034, 062; George, 109; Georgia Ann, 187; James, 034; Mary Ann, 010
FELTON: John, 074; R. J., 010; William H., 157
FENCH(FINCH? FRENCH?): William, 156
FENCH: Thos., 113
FENN: C. J., 071; David J., 060; David J., Capt., 117; Ellender, 182; Jesse, 135; Mary, 172; Sarah, 151; Thomas A., 205; Thomas A., Lt., 207; Willerby, 043, 044; William, 072, 107, 109; William, Sgt., 203;

Wm., 071, 109, 118
FEREGESON: Mary, 098
FERGASON: James, 095; Mary T., (7 chldn), 095
FERGERSON: Mary T., 100
FERGUSON: Charles, 087; Frances, 087; James, Sgt. 210; John, 087; Martha A., 087; Sarah, 087
FERRELL: John, 157
FERRY: Ebenezer L., 034; Ebenezer, 034; George W., 034
FEW: Fannie H., 094; Hill, 010; Joseph, 156; Luceous C., 094; Lucious H., 094; Martha (chldn. of), 010; Martha A., 010; Saml. L., 094; Seaborn, 034
FIELD: William G., 034
FIELDER: Avry J., 157; Polly, 156
FIELDING: Charles L., 157; Elizabeth, 094, 188; Jane D., 157; Saml., 101; Samuel, 128, 156, 205; William, 023, 059, 062, 119; Wm. J., 094; Wm., Lt., 119
FIELDS: Henry H., 034; James, 207; James, 2nd Cpl., 127; James, Sgt., 206
FIGGENS: James W., 157
FILGHMAN: Aaron, 1st, Sgt., 126
FILNEY: William, 214
FIMBROUGH: Jack, 095
FINCH: John, 156; T. Charles, 034; Thomas, 207; Thos., 113, 206; William, 010, 156; Wm., 128
FINDERBURGH: Isaac, Capt., 129
FINDLEY: John B., 034; Mathew, 034; Rebecca, 161; Thomas, 034, 213; William, 043, 045
FINKE: --, 047
FINLESTON: Elizabeth, 068
FINLEY: Jane M..172; Prulah, 170; Ruthy Butler, 167
FINN: Mary, 176; Serena, 085
FIRBISH: Harris, Cpl., 210
FIRCH: Thomas, 128
FIRMONGTON: --, 098
FISHER: G. W., 100; Lieusa, 100; Sarah, 100
FISHUR: Elizabeth W., 083; Elizabeth, 083
FITZGERALD: Samuel, 156
FITZPATRICK(KITZPATRICK?): W., 213
FITZPATRICK: Andrew J. C., 092; C. J., 094; Harvey J., 092; Howell R., 092; Louisa, 098; Mary J., 092; Patrick, 034; Silas G., 092; William G., 092
FITZSIMMONS: Henry, 028, 034, 210
FLANIGAN: Eliza, Mrs., 032
FLEMING: Abel, 025, 033, 037, 058, 060, 110; Able, 031, 044; Daniel F., 034; John, 035; Mary, 035; Miller, 035, 041; Richard, Lt., 120; Robert, 035; Wm., 122
FLEMMING: Abel, 023, 059; Capt., 079
FLETCHER: John, 1st Sgt., 125; John, Ens., 201; John, Lt., 126, 202; Nancy Ann, 169
FLETEHER: James, 023
FLINK: John, 204
FLINT: John, 112, 115, 156, 204, 207, 211; William, 049
FLIPPEN: Jesse, 035, 056; William, 156, 205; William, Lt., 124, 125, 203, 204; Wm., Ensgn, 129
FLIPPIN: Mary, 010; William, 035, 208, 210; Wm., 114, 115
FLIPPING: Wm., Ens., 201
FLIPPINS: Wm., Ens., 201
FLITCHER: John, Lt., 202
FLOID: Salina, 183
FLORSHEIN: --, 025
FLOURNEY: Howell C., 025
FLOURNOY: (chldn. of), 010; Elizabeth Julia, 170; G. W., 098; Howell C., 035, 043, 052, 157; Howell, 029; John G., 035; Mary M., 010; Robert (chldn. of), 010; Robert, 010; Wm.H.,156
FLOYD: Benjamin (chldn. of), 010; Cameila, 135; Elizabeth, 157; Harriett A., 159; John, 035, 135, 156; Panina, 135; Stewart, 035; Susan W., 181; Tabitha, 071, 135; Theodosia M., 153; Wilhilmind H., 010; Wilihmina, 066; Wm., 135
FLUKER: Robert, 035, 057
FODDRILL: Eliza, 101
FOLLY: John, 058
FOLSOM: John, 214
FORCE: Benjamin W., 035; John P., 035; Lewis M., 035
FORD: A. J., 034; James, 056; John, 035
FORMBY: John A., 103
FORT: Miss, 135; Mrs., 071
FOSTER (?): Wm., 208
FOSTER: Adam G., 035; Adam, 109, 117; Ann, 089; Elizabeth, 132; Emily, 010; Frances, 089; Frederick, 156; Geo. W., 089; George W., 049, 110, 111, 157; George, Mrs., 221; Infant, 089; Jacob, 096; John (chldn. of), 010; John F., 023, 156; John, 010; June, 089; Levi, 132; Margaret F., 162; Martha, 172; Melena, 176; Nancy, 176; Paley, 132; Pheoba, 162; Pleasant L., 156; Reuben, 132; Robert K., 156; Ruben, 211; Saml., 089; Samuel H., 035; Stephen, 156; Susan M. F., 142; William, 095, 206; William, Lt., 206, 207; William, Sgt., 203
FOSTIN: Elizabeth, 150
FOULER: Marth, 099; Minter, 156; Sarah, 099
FOURNOY: Martha Ann, 041
FOWLER: Cody, 010; David B., 092; Drury, 035; Ida, 010; James L., 081; James, 103; John, 208; Lewis M., 156; Martha A., 093; Marvin, 010; Nathan, 114, 210; Robert, 109, 211; Sarah F., 093; Sarah, 165; Theodotia, 173; Theophilus, 3rd Cpl., 127; Thomas, 109; Thos., 092; William, 210; Wm., 092
FRASER: Hugh A., 035
FRAZER: Robert, 082
FRAZIER: Julian, 035
FREDERICK: Felis(chldn. of), 010; Felix, 010
FREEDMAN(?): Lewis, 157
FREEMAN: Allen, 025, 027, 052, 060, 113, 156, 206; Allen, Lt., 210; Amanda, 157; Benjamin, 044; Calthriss, 011; Catherine, 035; F. J., 073, 099; Federick J., 074; Frederick I., 219; Frederick J., 075, 081, 156; George W., 060; Harrison H., 156; Heartwell, 039; Hugh, 035; James F. W.,157; James, 035; Jesse, 124, 156; Jessee, 112; John, 011, 035, 039, 120, 156; John, Sgt., 202; Johnson, 112, 116, 122, 156, 202, 203;
FREEMAN: Johnson, Sgt., 203; Johnston, 120; Johnston, Lt., 210; Josiah, 217; Labun T., 156; Martha J., 153; Mary, 149; Nancy, 144; Nicholas, 030, 120; Nicholas, Sgt., 202; Polly, 165; Robert, 035, 071; Samuel (chldn of), 011; Samuel, 011; Sarah, 149; Timothy, 042; Wealthy, 162; William, 044-046, 066, 156
FREMAN: Henry, 208
FREST: Johson, 116
FRIEDMAN: Louis, 157
FRIERSON: James D., 035, 156; Margarette, 035
FROST: Capt., 079; Johnson, 112, 202, 207; Johnson, Sgt., 203; Johnston, 120, 122; Johnston, Capt., 207; Saml., 073; Samuel, 029, 030, 057, 060; Sol., Capt., 120
FRY: Gilbert, 109, 156
FRYERSON: James D., 048
FUGERSON: J. S., 088; Mary, 088
FULBRIGHT: Elizabeth, 055
FULCHER: James, 011; Jesse, 042; Samuel, 011; William, 157
FULKER: Stephen, 210
FULLALOVE: Elizabeth, 182
FULLBRIGHT: Rosetta, 055
FULLELOVE: Henry M., 156
FULLER: --, 083; Bluford, 156; Francis, 111; Freeman, 156; Maria, 077; Mary A. W., 165; Mary, 135; William, 026
FULLILOVE: Amelia, 077; Barnwell P., 053; Burwell P., 057, 157; Charity, 077; Eliza, 077; Henry F., 156; Henry M., 080; Henry W., 077; Henry, 073; Jeffery, 077; John, 156; Ludwell, 057; Martha, 077, 181; Mary E., 152; Phillis, 077; Seaborn J., 057; William W., 057
FULLWOOD: Edward, 103; Elizabeth W., 144; Jane W., 035; Maria, 171; Robert, 011, 035, 039, 045, 059, 120; Robt., 120; Sarah V., 167; Wilhelmina, 168; William E., 108; Wm. Edwd., 117; Wm., Maj., 120
FULTON: M.C., 157; Margarett J., 011, 142; Sarah C., 173
FULWOOD: Mary Ann, 182; Robert, 043
FUNDERBAUGH: Isaac, Capt., 201
FUNDERBURG: Henry, 156; Isaac, Capt., 201
FUNDERBURGH: Henry, 156, 202; Isaac, Capt., 202
FURGERSIN: Mary T. & 6 chldn., 085
FURGERSON: William W., 157
FURGUSON: Mary T., & 5 Chldn., 085; Mary T., 098
FURMAN: Joseph, 060
FURNELL: John, 219
FUSSELL: Salley, 181
FYE: John, 116
GADDY: David, 038, 043, 057, 058
GAFF: Nancy W., 090
GAGE: James, 208; John, 158; Mathew, 035
GAHAGAN: Laurence, 035
GAILY: Joseph, 035
GAINE: John M., 053
GAINES: Zenophan P., 061; Zenophon J., 046; Zenophon P., 061
GAITHRIGHT: William M., 035
GAITHUR: Greenberry, 035
GALLAWAY: James, 159; Thomas, 158
GALLIHER: Samuel, 032, 048, 057
GALLOWAY: Arura, Mrs., 032; James, 011, 032; James, Mrs.,032
GALPHIN: Thomas, 035
GALWSON: James, Ensgn, 125, 206
GAMBLE: Rutha, 178; William, 011, 157, 158
GAMEL: Anthony C., 159; Anthony, 035
GAN: Jessee, Mrs., 090; Nathan, 157
GANATT: Francis, 051
GANN: Alex, 011; Ann, 011; Antonia, 085; Awrena, 184; Berry, 122' David, 011, 159; Eleaner, 159; Eliza, 185; Emily, 167; Frances, 159; Henry, 159; James, 053, 085, 159; James, Mrs., 085; Jesse, Mrs., 090; John, 031, 037, 041, 054, 158; John, Lt., 118; John, Sr., 011; Julia Ann, 158; Littleberry, 159; Lovina, 166; Lucenda, 144; Malenda, 011; Marth A., 091; Martha, 135, 166, 169; Mary A., 093; Mary, 179; Micajah, 126, 157; Nathan, 042, 157, 158; Nathan, Jr., Lt., 202; Nathan, Lt., 124, 126, 202, 203; Peggy, 168; Penina, 141; Polley, 179; Polly, 179; Rebekah, 156; Rene, 186;

Robert, 158; Saml., 114; Samuel, 035, 095, 135, 157, 158; Sarah J., 091; Stephen C., 135, 159; Tigner, 084; W. H., 039; William, 057, 157; William, Jr., 157; William, Sr., 011
GANNET: Jeff, 011
GANTLEY: Daniel W., 035
GANTT: Frances L., 011
GANUS: Saml., 084
GARABALD: J. A., Mrs., 091
GARDENER: J. B., 083
GARDINER: Sarah, 093
GARDNER: --, 042; Christanah, 171; Daniel B., 055, 159; Drury, 208; Elizabeth, 169; Hannah, 166; Isaac, 159; J. B., 083; John, 109, 120, 158; John, 1st Sgt., 127; Joseph L., 122; Lucretia, 170; Mary, 145; Robert J., 159; Robert, 036, 047; Saml., Ensgn, 127; Samuel, 119, 208; Stephen, 215; William, 158; Wm. H., 098
GARFIELD: Thomas B., 011
GARISON: Catharin, 090; Thomas, 122
GARLINGTON: --, 060; Capt., 071; Christ., Capt., 127, 130, 205, 206; Christopher, 026, 035, 113, 207; Christopher, Capt., 125; Christopher, Ensgn, 126
GARLINTON: Christopher, 204
GARNER(?): A. G., 122
GARNER: Catherine, 185; Charles, 035; Delila, 134; Elijah, 011, 028, 055, 112, 113, 121, 129, 130, 134, 205; Eliza, 011, 148; Elizabeth, 186; Francis, 107, 117; Haney, 161; Isaac, 118; Jael, 011; James M., 082; James, 122, 158; Jesse H., 157; Jesse, 113, 128, 130, 205; Jno., 204; John, 118, 125; Lasley, 162; Lucinda, 134; Luke, 115, 211;
GARNER: Malinda, 143; Mariah, 162; Mary S., 175; Nancy, 134, 185; Peggy, 186; Presley, 011, 056; Presley, Jr., 109; Pressley, 011; Rosse, 144; Saml., 109, 114, 115, 118; Saml., Ens., 113, 125; Samuel, 112, 114, 208; Samuel, Ens., 130; Susan, 162; Thomas P., 061; William, 055, 112, 158, 203, 208-210; William, 3rd Sgt., 127; Wm., 114, 115, 134
GARNES: William, 114
GARPLEY: Permelia Ann, 181
GARRAR: George Y., 026
GARRATSON: Thomas, 116
GARRATT: Asa, 152
GARRET: Abraham, 055; Charles, 157; John, 011
GARRETSON: Solomon, 035; Thomas, 123
GARRETT: Garrett, Sgt., 111; John H., 023, 058; Josiah C., 158; Racheal, 168; Riley, 011; Seaborn, 158
GARRISON: --, 061; Caleb, 159; Catherine, 093; J. D., 011; James, 122; Joseph F., 159; Martin, 159; Nancy, 151; Patterson, 158; Sally, 158; Silas M., 159; Thomas, 112, 203
GARTHRIGHT: Mary F., 151
GARTRELL: Lucius J., 159; Martha M., 173
GARWOOD: Charles B., 159; Johnson, 060, 159; Johnston, 039; Laura Ann, 164
GARY: Mary T., 091
GASTON: Thomas, 026
GATES: George, 159; James, 035; Lucy, 011
GATHRIGHT/MATHEWS: --, 197
GATHRIGHT: A.M., Ensgn, 118, 120; Asuburn M., 048; Ausban M., 046; Ausborne M., 035; Ausburn M., 035; Mariah, 173; Martha I., 180; William C., 158; William M., 035
GATLIN: John, 210
GATON: John, 114, 209
GAULDEN: Scriven, 047
GAURAINE: Mary Antoinette, 011
GAUVAIN: Michael A., 028, 035; Michael C., 044; Michael, 028, 040; Rosalia, 028; Mary Antoinette, 161
GAY: Charles H., 041, 213; Gilbert, 057
GAYDON: John, 036
GAYTON: John, 036
GEAN: Anna, 011; Nancy B., 011; Nancy, 097
GEANS: Thomas W., 159
GEE(GILL?): Drury, 071
GEE: Edward, 159; Elizabeth, 151; Henry, 159; Mary E., 092; Sarah, 090, 094
GENTRY: Edney, 093; Elijah, 056; Elisha, 011; Elyah, 035; Martin, 052; Neaama, 052
GEORGE: Bailey (chldn. of), 011; Bailey, 011, 035; Baley, 157; Bayley, 202; Maria, 011, 061; Mary W., 158; Travis, 011; Whitson H., 158; William B., 045; William, 035, 052
GERALD: Selina F., 177; Sophronia A., 158
GERARDEN: Adelaide V., 011
GERARDIN: John, 011
GERARDINE: Elizabeth W., 177
GERDINE: John, 011; John, Sgn., 129; Linton, 011; Marion C., 011; Mary E., 011; Sarah H., 011; Susan G., 011
GERRALD: Elizabeth A., 185; Isaac F., 036, 051, 158; Isaac, 036
GIBBS: Robert, 097; Thomas F., 053, 062, 157, 209; Thos. F., 114, 210
GIBSON: --, 027; Andrew, 036; David, 158; Francis, 036; Lewis, 027, 034, 036; Margarett, 145
GIDEON: Louisiana O., 159
GILBERT: Allen, 158, 159; Felix H., 036; Felix, 036; Jesse, 157; Jno., 119; John, 103, 109; Lucy, 143; Martha, 144; William H., 036; William, 036
GILBERTS: --, 036
GILES (JILES?): Ruel Kinkade, 159
GILES: --, 122; Alfonslow, 091; Amanda E., 082, 098, 100, 102; Amanda, 085, 089; Betty, 085; Caroline H., 097; Caroline, 086, 098; Caroline, Mrs., & 1 ch., 087; Eliza, 097; Emaly, & 4 chldn., 087; Emaly, 086; Emely, 099; Eveline, 094; Frances, Mrs., 102; George Washington, 159; George, 094, 097; Jame, Mrs., 085; James M., 082; James, 159; John, 112;
GILES: Johnston, 091; Joseph, 126, 157; Josephene, 094; Katherine, 091; Lidia, 094; Maj., 011; Martha, 097; Mary Ann, 172; Mary, & 3 chldn., 087; Mary, 086, 097, 101; Polley, 160; Taylor, 094; Thomas, 159; Widow, 094; William T., 094; William, 157; Wm., (Orphs.), 096, 097; Wm., 075
GILHAM: Ezekiel, 158; William, 158
GILL: Elizabeth, 144, 145, 173; Mckey, 167; William, 056; Young, 216
GILLELAND: Caroline, 159; Coil, 028, 158; Henderson, 011; James, 051, 074; Mary F., 011; William A., 011, 082; William, 011
GILLESPIE: James, 046
GILLILAND: Coil, 055; William D., 036; William H., 036
GILMAN: Sanders, 036
GILMORE: Almer, 098; Ann, 177
GINN: Cater H., 081; J. M., Mrs., 100
GLASCOM: Daniel, 011
GLASS: James, 030; Richard, 110, 114, 157, 208-210; Richd., 109; Thomas, 036, 158
GLASSIN: Henry, 011
GLASSON: Adaline, 181; Ann, 186; Clarke, 159; Henry, 063; James, 157, 159, 205; James, Sgt., 202; Mary Ann, 150; Mary, 152; Phillip A., Sgt., 202
GLAWSON: Henry, 157; Henry, Sgt., 204; James, Ens., 130, 205; James, Sgt., 204
GLAZE: Alsey L., 146; John, 159; Julies, Mrs., 091
GLEASON: Fil A., 120; R., Mrs., 093; Rosannah, 097
GLECE (?): William, 210
GLEESON: Mary N.,143; Phillip, 201
GLENN: J. N., 071; J. N., Rev., 142, 146; James R., 158; John W., 157; Joshua N., 036; Jousua W., 072; Lettitia, 176; Luther J., 159; Mary A. J., 077; Nicholas, Jr., 011; Robt. L., 011; Wallis, 077; William B., 053
GLESSON: Hugh, 107
GLOER: --, 098; George David, 088; Mrs., 100; Nancy C., 089
GLOSON: Henry, 042
GLOSSEN: James, 1st, Sgt., 126; Mary, 152
GLOSSON: Hugh, 115
GLOVER: Eliza E., 093; John H., 036; Mrs., 090
GLOWER: Cynthia, 151
GLOWSON: Henry, 2nd Sgt., 128; James, Ensgn, 128
GOBER: Francis, 153; Thomas, 077; Wesley B., 011; William H., 011
GOBLE: Lucher, 051
GODFREY: Caroline, 158; David, 134; John, 134; Richard A., 159; Sarah Jane, 184; William D., Lt., 210
GOFF: Nancy J., 011; Nancy W., 093
GOIN: Drury, 036
GOLDBERG: Robert, 036
GOLDING: Hunter, 011; John R., 011, 036; Sarah, 036; Sophanisba, 036; Susan, 011; Thomas (chldn. of), 011
GOLER: William H., 080
GOODBEE(?): H. L., 055
GOODMAN: C., Mrs., 091; Robert H., 036
GOODRICK: William H., 025
GOODWIN: Aasa, 157; Elizabeth, 011, 038; Heard, 038
GOODWYNN: Elizabeth, 038; Herod, 038
GOOLSBY: Isaiah B., 109; Isaiah, 036; John, 011; Lucy, 011
GORDAN: Susan, 162
GORDMAN: Robert H., 044
GORDON: Amanda L.E., 157; Edward P., 039, 159; Elizabeth, 142; James F., 036; John D., 061, 158; John, 049, 117; Robert J. (chldn. of), 011; Robert S., 011, 027, 041, 053, 158; Robert, 040; Samuel, 042; Sarah, (?), 147; Sophronia Ann, 179
GORHAM: --, 036
GORLEY: Jonathan, 011; Mary, 011
GOSS: Isam, 143; Isam, Rev., 144; William S., 158
GOTTENBERGER: Philip Gerard, 159
GOULD: Mary E., 011; Russell, 011
GOWAN: Riecllo, 213
GOWER: Reuben, 4th Sgt., 128; Reuben, Sgt., 205; Robert M., 157
GRADY: Jackson, 158; Julia A., 080; William S. (chldn. of), 011; William S., 011, 036, 040; Wm. S., Mrs., 090, 099
GRAHAM: --, 119; Abner, 011, 034, 041, 072, 075; Andrew, 011,

034, 041, 042; Doctor R., 011; George (chldn of), 011; George, 072, 158; Virginia Elizabeth, 172; W.P., 103; William D, 209; William P., 036, 056, 108, 109, 158; William T., 079; William, 121, 208; Wm. P., 114, 115, 118, 211; Wm., 114
GRANADE: Benjamin M., 038
GRANNIS: George, 036
GRANT: Aura, 036, 039; James R., 011; John T., 159; Mary E., 186; Orra, 036; Warren, 213
GRAVES(?): John W.,Qtrmr. Sgt.,210
GRAVES: Benjamin C., 109; Frances, 158; James S., 081; Jno. W., 114; John W., 036, 043, 119, 208, 209; Joseph W., 080
GRAY: Alexander, 047; Anna, 011; Anne, 154; Elizabeth, 177; George, 011; Hezekiah, 029; James C., 159; James D., 158; James, 208; Jeremiah G., 074, 158; Jeremiah G., Sr., 011; Luzina H., 185; Martha M., 011; Martha, 011; Nancy, 178; Phebe, 011; Phoebe, 172; Saml., 109; Samuel, 208; Susan Caroline, 147; William H., 141; William, 117; Wm., 108
GRAYER: Wm., 072
GREATHOUSE: Aaron, 2nd Sgt., 126; Jacob, 049
GREEAR: Martha, 166
GREEN: Elizabeth, 165; Jesse, 215; Jno., 113; John R. (chldn. of), 011; John R., 011; Lucy, 161; Raleigh, 051; Richard A., 159; Rolley, 157; Sally, 144; Thomas F., Jr., 011
GREENE: Ethel, 011; Martha, 156; Washington, 074; William P., 030; Willis, 054
GREENWOOD: J., 103; John, 109, 119; Mary, 149; Polly, 036; Thomas, 036; William, 036
GREER: Asahel, 079; Asel, 011; Cynthia W., 011; Delia Ann, 184; Delila, 157; Edmond, 157; Elisha, 186; Eliza, 134; Elvirah, 134; Emily, 151; Francis A., 165; Garret M., Cpl., 107, 117; Garrett M., 158; James, 011, 134; Jno., 113; John C., 011, 036, 109, 118, 120, 158; John, 103, 109, 115, 117, 121, 130, 158, 205, 208, 209, 211; John, Lt., 114; John, Sgt. 210;
GREER: Joshua, 107, 109, 118, 134, 158; Lucy, 182; Martha, 134, 150; Mary An, 134; Mary Ann, 036; Nancy, 134; Pricilla, 177; Richard C., 011; Thomas, 011, 157; Victoria A., 142; Welmoth, 134; William, 062, 071, 074, 134; Wm. A., 122; Wm., 075
GREGG: --, 034
GREGGORY: Gordon, 073
GREGORY: Benjamin P., 080; Benjamin, 159; Chas. G., 122; Gordon, 100; James L., 011; Mariah, 097; Muriah, 096; Salina, 168
GREHAM: William, 209
GRESHAM: Albert Y., 028, 044, 158; David, 051; Davis C., 036; Davis, 011; Elizabeth, 176; Hinson, 048, 056; John M., 158; Jones, 109, 117; Robert, 011; Young, 011, 025, 042, 048, 049, 056, 061, 105, 205; Young, PayMr., 129
GREY: Jeremiah G., 073
GRIFFETH: Allen, 158; C.T., 099; Camelia, 100; Charles T., 054, 158; Cornelia, 085; Francis P., 080; George E., 080; James B., 158; James L., 071, 080; James S., 159; John L., 107, 109, 117; Joseph J., 109; Louisa, 101; Martha, 163; Mary E., 100; Michael R., 066; Nicy, 180; Robert S., 080; Smith, 084, 086; William L.,158
GRIFFIN: Hermon, 066; John T., 081; Jos. J., Capt., 118; Louiza E., 151
GRIFFITH: Charles R. A., 011; Claudia A., 095; Cornelia (3 ch), 095; Cornelia, 098; E. (1 ch), 095; Elizabeth, 151; George E., 159; James S., 080; John L., 011; John, 159; Louisa, 095; Martha A., 187; Mary A., 151; Mary E., 098; Matilda, 151; Michael R., 011; Morgan, 036; Mrs. (7 ch), 095; R. P., 159; Smith, 095; Zarephath, 173
GRIFFITHS: John, Sr., 221
GRIMAGE: Joshua, 041
GRIMES: Benjamin, 110; Betsey, 160; George (chldn. of), 011; Harbert, 157; Henry H., Sgt. 210; James, 119; Jas., 114, 208; John Pendleton, 159; Lucy A., 158; Patsey, 178; Thomas W., 036; William D., 158; William, 214
GRIMMIT: William, 036
GRODON: Robert, 040
GROGAN: A. M., 091, 093; A. M., Mrs., 091; Ana, 091; Julia, 091
GROWER: Robert M., 2nd Sgt., 125
GRUBBS: James M., 159
GUEEN(?): M. T., 099
GUICE: Arnold J., 049
GUIRE: John, 097
GULLEY: Susan, 097
GULLY: Sarah, 159; Susan, 083
GUNALS: J. R., Mrs., 090
GUNISON/GRISWOLD: --, 197
GUNN: Antonia, 084; James, Mrs., 084; Mahala, 135; Nancy, 135; Nathan, 046; Tignor, 085; Wm., 135; Wm., Mrs., 084, 085
GUNNIN: Louisa, 098; Needham F., Mrs., 098
GUNNION: Louisa, 100
GUNNISON: John, Jr., 011
GUNTER: Ila Hall, Mrs., 011; Isabella, 081; James B., 159; James M., Rev., 146; James, 076, 077; Martha, 184; Osburn Woodward, 077; William T. R., 076; Zechariah, 076
GURMIN: Louisa (1 ch), 095
GURRICK: E., Mrs., 090
GURVIN: Mary E., 172
HABERSHAM: Robert, 036
HADEN: Mary C., 183
HADLEY: Jesse, 136; Joshua, 046; Maholey, 145
HAELES: Wiley, 074
HAGAN: Elizabeth, 134; Permelia, 134; Polly, 134
HAGANS: Edward, 160
HAGEREWOOD: Elizabeth, 093
HAGGARD: Armminta, 151; Elizabeth, 187; French, 032; John C., 163; Mary Tennessee, 180
HAGGOOD: William, 073; William, 2nd Sgt., 127
HAGIN: Elizabeth, 161; Lany, 133; Rebecca, 185
HAGINS: Daniel, 160; Edward, 011, 108, 120; James, 011; Lancy, 158
HAGLER: John, 160
HAGOOD: Benjamin, 214; John, 036
HAGWOOD: Charles E., 094; Fanny, 177; Francis, Mrs., 090; Sally, 182; William, 160
HAIL: Eliza A., 155; Elizabeth, 094; Francis L., 159; Mary Ann, 150; Moab, 073; Obed, 202, 203; Sarah, 153; Silas, 082; William H., 081; Wm., 074
HAILE: Benjamin, 132; Drucilla, 161; Drusilla, 085; Elizabeth, 101, 145, 157; Emaline, 187; Hosa, 132, 161; James, 161; James, Sgt., 207; Joel W., 1st Lt., 111; Joel, 041, 132, 161; John, 2nd Sgt., 127; John, Sgt. 206; Jonas, 096; Jonas, Lt., 120; Joseph, 164; Lucinda, 166; Martha, 144, 186; Mathew, 162; Moab, 044; Obed, 113, 120, 130, 164, 205; S. J., Mrs., 101; Sarah P.,184; William, 028, 162
HAILES: Edith, 174; Henry J., 040; Joel, Jr., 011; John, 011; Matilda, 162; Nancy, 168; Rebecca, 161; Sarah, 185; Sidney, 186; Wiley, Jr., 036; Wiley, Sgt., 206, 207; Wiley, Sr., 036; William F., 163; William, 173
HAILS: Betsy, 173; Sually, 171
HAINES: Lucy P., 169; William, 036
HAINEY: James, Sgt. 210
HAING(?): Nancy, 143
HALAWAY: Samuel, 213
HALE: Anna R., 153; Charity, 178; Drusilla, 084; Edward T., 163; Edwd., 100; Elizabeth, 099; Frances M., 172; Frances, 011; Gussie, 011; James S., 163; James, Sgt., 206; Joel W., 162; John A., 011, 073; John, 036, 074, 161; John, Sgt., 129; Jonas, 4th Sgt., 127; Joseph, 075; Josiah W., 011, 164; M. E., Miss, 011; Martha M., 184; Mary A., 011; Mary G., 011; Moab, 011, 036, 073; Noah, 011; Obed, 036; Robert W., 011; Robert, 100; S.C., 011; Saml. J., 080; Sarah C., 169; Sarah E. (5 ch), 096; Susan (2 ch), 096; Susan A., 163; W.B., 222; Wiley, 011, 040; William B., 011, 082; William J., 011; William T., 163; William, 011, 109; Wm., 119
HALES: Biddy, 149; Isaiah, Rev., 141; John, 161; Lucy, 171
HALL (HALE?): William, 160
HALL: Almerin, 163; George W., 011; Henry, 036, 161; Hugh, 112, 201; James P., 012; Lidda L., 086; Mahala, 097; Martin, 028; Oliver, 053; Patsey, 144; Thomas M., 080; Thomas, 036, 201; Thos. M, S.S., Mrs., 098; W.A.S., 012
HALSTEAD: Job S., 042; John, 042
HAMBEY: Joseph H., 118; Joseph, 033
HAMBLETON: Henry, 060; John, 036, 162; Reuben, 161
HAMBLETT: Martha, 085
HAMBRECK: Meshack, 068
HAMBRICK: James, 160; Lausey, 166; Leroy, 076; Suzanah, 076
HAMBY: David, 162, 220; Joseph H., 162; Joseph, 051; Samuel, 160; William T., 163
HAMILTON: Alfred W., 207; Alfred, 208; Barton, 012, 079; Catherine, 156, 157, 219; Clementiney, 152; Drury I., 012; Duke, 012, 164; Duke, Mrs., 220; Eleazer, 036; Eli, 134; Elvira, 188; Eugenia E., 153; Harriett, 169; Henry, 012; James S. H., 012; James, 134, 162; John W., 134, 163, 164; John, 134; Julia A., 183; Lucinda, 154; Mary E., 012; Mary, 148; Nancy, 134, 147; Nathan, 161; Peter, 161; Reuben Y., 207; Reuben, 076; Reuben, Lt., 110, 207; Rhoda, 076; Sarah S., 012; Stephen A., 163; Thomas N., 036; V. F., 157
HAMLETT: Ann, 141
HAMMILTON: John, 126; Robert H., 164
HAMMOCK: Benjamin, 025, 036; Jesse, 160; Rancy, 143
HAMMONDTREE: Sarah S., 012
HAMON: Silas, 109
HAMPTON: E., 102; E., Mrs., 096;

Eliza, 012; Elizabeth, 102; George, 215; James, 047; John, 036, 056, 099, 163; Jonathan, 012; Mariah, 095; Mary, 086; Mollie J., 081
HANCOCK: --, 062; A. C., 012; Benjamin, 097; Betty, 097; Cintha, 097; Eady, 177; Edmond, 097; Emily, 097; James, 012; Jane Johnson, 145; John, 098; Kessey L., 185; Mary, 097; Mrs., 097; Rebecca, 178; Richardson, 037; Samuel, 161; Thomas, 012, 024, 025, 029, 037, 038, 049, 050, 058, 060, 062, 067, 121; Thor, 026; Thos., 114; W.J., 012
HAND: Daniel, 037; David, 037; Winfield, 118
HANDON: Isham, 059
HANDRUP: N. W., 163
HANES: Permenes, Sgt., 130
HANEY: James, 112, 204; James, 1st Sgt., 127; John, 164
HANLAND: Risley, 037
HANNAH: Thomas, 012; William, 214
HANNER: Jane, 157
HANNIN: Abraham, 037
HANNOR: James T., 133; Mary, 133
HANSEN: Thomas, 037
HANSFORD: Mary Ella, 012
HANSON: Ann Eliza, 168; Enoch, Sgt., 202; James, 055, 109, 162; James, Ensgn, 203; James, Jr., 053; James, Sr., 053; Jesse, 025, 111, 162; Nancy, 012; Newton, 085, 110; Newton, Mrs., 085
HANY: Malcom, Mrs., 100
HANYE (HANZE?): George W., 164
HARALSON: Henry, 109
HARDEGNE: --, 122
HARDEGREE: Elisha, 164; Harmond, 103, 118; Joel, 108; John, 103; Jonathan, 108; Nancy, 155; Pleasant, 160; Pleasant, Sgt., 202; Sally, 149; William, 108, 120, 160
HARDEMAN: John, 087; L., Mrs., 099, 101; Luticia, 088; Mary E. (chldn. of), 012; Mary E., 012; Nancy S., 012; Thomas H., 088; William J., 012
HARDEN/PRUITT: Family, 198
HARDEN: (chldn. of), 012; Anthony, 061; Ed, 048; Edward R., 024, 030, 046, 047; Edward, 031, 034, 036-038, 048, 050, 055, 057, 059, 062; Edward, Family, 198; Eveline R.J., 166; Isham, Adj., 204; John, 037; Joseph, 047; Martha W., 012; Mary E.G., 012; Matilda Harrison, 166; Robert A., 047; Robert R.(chldn. of), 012; Robert R., 012, 025, 027-029, 032, 037, 040, 042, 044, 046, 047, 049, 050, 053, 054, 059-061, 164; Robert, 026; Thomas H., 037, 162; William P., 012, 047, 049, 066, 074, 075, 163; William R., 012
HARDIGREE: Eleanor, 079; Eliza, 166; Fanny, 164; Harbert G., 164; Harboard G., 080; Harmon H., 163; Joel, 108, 162; John J., 164; John, 118, 133; Jonathan, 160, 201, 219; Martha, 166; Perry, 077; Pleasant, Sgt., 210; Sarah, 146; Wm., 133; Wm., 3rd Sgt., 127; Wm., Sgt. 206
HARDIMAN: Benjamin F., 164; Benjamin, 012; James R., 080; Susan, 041, 042; William, 161
HARDIN: Aleck, 037; Caroline M., 177; Louisa L., 098; Napoleon B., 164; R. R., 049; Robert Raymond, 162; Sally, 044
HARDMAN: Hlkiah, 080
HARDY: Charles, 091; Joseph, 091; Julia A. & 2 chldn., 092; Julia A., 093; Julia, 100
HARELSON: Cary, 187
HARGRAVE: --, 056; George, 056
HARGRAVES: George, 037, 056; George, Sr., 037
HARGROVE (?): John R., 211
HARGROVE: John R., 027, 049, 209
HARGROVES: Jno. R., 115; John R., 211
HARME: John H., 037
HARMONY: John Frederick, 037
HARNAGE: Ambrose, 037
HARNDON: A. J., 164
HARP: William A., 163
HARPER: --, 119; A. A., 221; A. L., 072, 075; Absalom, 160; Alson L., 1st Sgt., 127; Amselmn L., 037; Anelmn L., 037; Anny, 160; Ansala, Sgt., 202; Ansel L., 081; Anseleum L., 161; Anselm, 057; Anselmn L., 037; Anselmn, 037; Anselum L., 031, 074; Ausburn L., 081; Daisy, 012; David, 164; Eliza Ann, 153; Emma, 221; Erastus F., 082; George, 025, 031, 033, 037, 054, 080, 107, 115; Harwood, 160; Haywood, 041; Haywood, Sgt., 207; Henry, 012; James, 037;
HARPER: Jno. W., Maj., 120; John M., Ensgn, 125; John W., 012, 032, 037, 046, 048, 057, 058, 107, 162; John W., Ensgn, 204; John W., Maj., 118; John, Ensgn., 124; Jonathan, 081; Joseph M., 057, 058; Joseph, 160; Martha, 157, 178; Mary, 151; Nathaniel H., 161; Nathaniel, 036, 047, 057; Patsey, 178; Polly, 154; S., 125; Sarah A., 177; Sarah, 178; Sharrard, 125, 209; Sherrard, 114; Sherwood, 210; Sherwood, Capt., 125, 128, 203-207; Sherwood, Ensgn, 124, 126, 202; Sherwood, Lt., 203; Young W., 012, 219
HARRAL: James, 037
HARRALSON: Henry, 120
HARRAW: Joseph, 037
HARREL: Francis D., 164
HARRELL: James, 037; Nathaniel H., 163; Susannah, 041, 062
HARRILL: George, Mrs., 221
HARRING: Arthur, 201; Cyeel, 201
HARRIS (HANES?): James W., 210
HARRIS: (chldn. of), 012; --, 037; Abner, 115; Arabella R., 164; B., 095; Baker, 012; Betty, 083, 085, 095; Buckner, 037; Burr, 080; Care Y., 012; Caroline K., 157; Charles W., 160; Charlie, 097; Charlotte, 012; Cicero C., 096; Cintha, 179; Cordella, 012; David, 025, 107; David, Ensgn, 126, 129, 202; Elizabeth B., 179; Elizabeth H., 080; Gabriel, 037; Hendey, 161; Henry, 126, 217; Henry, Capt., 125, 127, 203-207; Hugh N., 012; Isham, 025, 096; J. Otis, 012; James M., 012; James W., 043, 209;
HARRIS: James W., Lt., 210; James, 206; James, Lt., 206, 207; James, Sgt. 206; Jane, 182; Jas. W., Lt., 114; Jas., 1st Sgt., 127; Jeptha C., 164; Jeremiah, 012; Jesse, 037; John H., 163; John W., 037; John, 012, 160, 164, 221; Josh, 012; Judith, 012; Lavinia R., 012; Lecy E., 144; Levency, 161; Lucy W., 147; M. L., 042; Martha, 012; Mary S., 012; Mary V., 096; Mary, 101, 144; Maryann, 179; Myrtis (chldn. of), 012; Myrtis, 012; Myrtus, 032; Paulina T., 012; Polly, 178; Rebecca, 012;
HARRIS: Robert L., 033, 080; Robert, 039; S., 026; Saml., 115; Sampson W., 037; Samuel B. (chldn. of), 012; Samuel B., 053, 162; Samuel Baker, 012; Samuel, 053, 134; Sarah H., 012, 052; Sarah, 167; Sophia, 134; Steven A., 163; Sucky, 154; Susan F., 096; Susan M., 148; Susan, 147; Tallulah L., 183; Thomas W., 037; Thomas Walton, 198; Thomas, 012, 080, 162, 163; Turner, 012; Tye, 038; Tyre, 025, 162, 207, 210, 211; Tyre, Cpl., 210; Tyree, Lt., 206; Tyrie, 115; Virginia B., 047; Walter B., 118; Walton B., 037, 047, 108, 119, 162; Walton, 012; Webb, 043; West, 044, 049, 054, 057, 066, 160; West, Rev., 144; Wiley, 128, 205; Wiley, Sgt., 203; William D., 218; William L., 038; William M., 073, 109, 161; William T., 164; William, 012, 059, 109, 134, 164; Willis B., 164; Wm., 117; Young L. G., 012, 038
HARRISON: Alonzo T., 012; Averton, 038; Clarissa, 068; James J., 012, 047; James J., Jr., 162; James, 039; Martha H., 160; Mentoria B., 012; Richard, 038, 109, 119, 211; Samuel, 162; William P., 163
HARRISS: Hendley, 038; Wm. M., 075
HART: Angeligue, 012; Elizabeth, 163; James B., 038
HARTIFIELD: Moses, 115
HARTLEY: John B., 029
HARTSFIELD: Anderson, 056; Middleton, 043, 113, 206, 207; Middleton, Cpl., 206; Midleton, 206; Moses, 107; Nancy, 141
HARTSVIELD: Middleton, 204
HARVEY: E. G., Cpl., 118; Edward D., 162; Edward G., 025, 109, 218; Elijah B., 045, 047, 162; Israel P., 120; John, 012; Lucy C., 161; Margaret, 185
HARVIE: Martha G., 160; William, 012
HARWILL: Elizabeth J., 182
HASELTINE: William H., 038
HASEY: Levi, 091
HASTIE: William S., 035
HATCHETT: Hennaritta, 156; John, 1st, Sgt., 126; John, Sgt., 202; Nancy, 161; Sarah Anderson, 167
HATH: Willaim B., 161
HATHORN: Benjamin, 038; Hugh, 012
HATTAWAY: John B., 163; Mary O., 158
HAUN: Wm. George, 163
HAVILAND: James C., 037, 038; R. B. Z., 038; Robert B., 037; Robert, 038
HAWK: Nancy Ann, 221
HAWKINS: John B., 029, 032, 073; John J., 163; Nicholas, 038; Peterson, 162; Stephen, 038; William, 038, 204
HAWKS: Sherman B., 012
HAWTHORN: Hugh, 012
HAWTHORNE: Benjamin, 038
HAY: --, 036; John W., 027, 029, 037, 059, 110
HAYDEN: Barsheba, 160
HAYES: Edmond, 012; Eliza A., 163; George, 038, 217; Hiram, 012, 042; Hyram, 047; James, 217; Jesse, 107, 115; Jesse, 1st, Sgt., 126; John E.(chldn of), 012; John R., 012; M.T., 012; Mahala, 185; Martha Ann, 166; Matilda F., 170; Missouri, 025; Peter M., Mrs., 100; Peter W., 012; Richard, 012; Robt., 118; Silvana, 176; William, 161
HAYGOOD: Abi, 165; Anna, 134; Appleton, 161; Francis M., 122; Francis, 090; Given (Green?), 111; Green B., 038, 049, 053, 118, 220; Greene B., 119, 164;

Greene B., Capt., 119; Hardin, 163; Jno., D. D., 144; John, 011, 038, 121, 165, 204, 220; Mary Ann, 166; Nancy, 168; Polly, 038, 134, 222; Sarah, 134, 183; Serenia, 183; Son, 134; Varena, 011; William B., 080, 082, 163; William, 011, 038, 219; William, Sgt., 202
HAYLES: Wiley, 122
HAYNES (HAYES?): Peter W., 163
HAYNES: Charles Eaton, 160; Delia Ann, 184; Francis M., 163; Franklin B., 012; Jane L., 176; John P., 072, 122; Pamenas, 039; Parmenas, 038, 047; Parmenas, Jr., 040; Parmeuas, 047; Parminas, 045; Sally, 176
HAYNEY: James, 121, 130, 203, 205; James, Sgt., 124
HAYNIE: James, 053, 110, 128, 160, 204; Jas., 113; Samuel, 026; Wilkins, 038
HAYS: Agness, 184; Fredrick, 160; Hiram, 218; Isabella L., 183; Jesse, 1st Cpl., 126; Jesse, Sgt., 202; Robert, 012; William, 028, 038
HAYWOOD (HAYGOOD?): John, 160
HAYWOOD: John, Sgt., 203; Joseph, 160
HEAD: Carrie, 012; Jesse J., 012; Samuel B., 038; Willis, 165
HEADDON: Archibald, 205
HEADLY: Harvey S., 038
HEALD: Saml., 206; Samuel (1), 135; Samuel, 128, 129, 208
HEALS: Saml., 206
HEALY: Thomas, 038
HEARD: Abraham, 038; Ann, 182; Anney, 166; Charles M., 120, 208; Charley, 208; Franklin C., 038; George E., 012; George, 035, 050, 056, 057; James, 206; James, Cpl., 207; Jas., 113; Jesse, 038; John, 109; Joseph, 038; M. E., Mrs., 012; Mary G., 161; Nancy, 176; Samuel, 038; Stephen, 062
HEARING: Cyrel, 051
HEARNDEN: Sarah, 144
HEARNDON: Capt., 132
HEARNS: Jeptha, 024
HEDGE: Charles M., 024
HEDGES: Joseph, Sr., 012
HEDNET: Elizabeth, 165
HEFFLEY: Joseph, 098
HEIRS: Arter, 204; Arthur, 1st. Sgt., 126
HELT: Isaac, Lt., 202
HELTON: Richard, 160; Starling, Sgt., 124; Sterling, 112, 162; Sterling, 1st, Sgt., 126; Sterling, Sgt., 124, 202, 203; Stirling, 131
HEMPHILL: Emily J., 181; Sarah A., 012; W. S., 012; William S., 025, 033, 165
HEMRICK: Elizabeth, 168; Emily, 186; Julia, 012
HENDEN: James W., 031, 098
HENDERSON: Bob, 111, 116, 123, 211; Cyrus, 113, 124, 129, 206, 207; Elias, 038; Elijah, 024; Hugh L., 109, 118; Isabella, 038; James, 031, 038, 161, 207; John H., 038; John, 038, 214, 215; Josiah, 038; Julia, 012; Mathew H., 012; Ned, 116, 123, 211; Robert, 012, 069; Saml., 113, 129, 207; Samuel, 038, 113, 206, 213; Syras, 130; Syres, 205
HENDON: Aaron, 160; Elijah, 012, 119; Elijah, Cpl., 206; Elizabeth, 182; Isham, 028, 034, 041, 043, 046, 052, 053, 056, 121; James M., 164; James W., 052, 080; James, 012, 030, 038, 042, 051; 218, 219; Lorena, 012; Martha, 169; Mary S., 182; Mremon, Ensgn, 205; Nancy W., 163; Norris, 031, 038, 117, 160, 202; Patience, 148; Sarah E., 012, 172
HENDREE: George R., 164
HENDRICK: John R., 057; John, 038; Manvel T., 025
HENDRICKS --, 029; John, 029, 038; John, Rev.141; Thomas, 163
HENDRIX: T. R., 110
HENDRON: Agnes M., 175
HENESLEY: John, 130
HENING (HERRING?): Polley, 154
HENLEY: Albert P., 012
HENNARD: William, 207; Wm., 2nd Lt., 125
HENNING: John, 160, 202; Margaret, 012
HENRY: Jeff, 038; Samuel, 045; Thomas, 025
HENSIN: John, 162
HENSON: Armstead, Sgt., 203; Catherine, 185; Enoch, 112, 122, 124, 160; Giney, 173; James L., 080; James, 122, 128, 130, 204, 205; James, Ensgn, 126, 204; James, Jr., 208; James, Sr., 119, 208; John, 121; Mariah D., 161; Moses, 215; Newton, 113, 130, 161, 205, 210; Silas, 162; Tabby, 103; Tapley, 161; Tarpley, 118
HENTON: Elizabeth, 174
HENZE: D. N., 012
HERBERT: Gabriel, 027; Isaac, 038
HERD: James, 206; Washington, 076
HERDEN: Mariah L., 183
HEREALL: Eli D., 087; James F., 087; Mary L., 087
HERESTERN: Addington, 077
HERNDON: Elisha, 027, 211; Elisha, Capt., 118; George, 012; Isham, 037; Joseph, 045; Merrimon, 161
HEROD: James W., 081
HERRELL: James B., 162
HERREN(?): Salley, 184
HERRIN: Abner, 107; Moses, 038; Patsey, 093; William, 160
HERRING: Arthur, Sgt., 129; Benajmin, 034; Betsy, 149; Cyril, 026; Eleanor C. M., 012; Elvirah, 154; Jane F., 162; Macy, 032; Martha, 167; Patsy, 091; Rebecca P., 154; Richard, 034; Stephen W., 012; William (chldn. of), 012; William, 012, 164, 216; Wm. B., 118
HERRINGS: Cyrel, 112
HERRINS: Ann R., 012
HERRLL(?): James M., Mrs., 099
HERRON: Epsey, 180
HESTER: Ann C., 162; Charles, 012; Elizabeth, 012, 155, 156; Francis, 037, 038; Hard, 085; Hurd, 095; Joseph, 029, 162; Julia Ann M., 168; Margaret F., 181; Martha F., 186; Martha, 153; R. H., 074; Randolph, 111, 122; Robert H. H., 061, 111; Robert, 012; Saml., 182; Samuel F., 163; Samuel, 012; Sarah (Marah?), 182; Sarah Leigh, 182; Stephen C. (chldn. of), 012; Stephen C., 012, 162; Stephen, 012, 039, 162, 201, 202; Stephen, 1st Sgt., 127; Stephen, Lt., 210; Steven, Sgt. 205; Susan E., 142; Thomas G., 110; Thomas, 103, 160; Thos., 118; William (chldn. of), 012; William, 125, 160
HETTON: Joseph, Mrs., (4 orphs.), 094
HEWEL: James D., 103
HEWELL: Capt., 134; Catherine, 012; James D., 051, 073, 108, 117; Jesse W., 209; John T., 012; Martha, 177; Nathaniel N. (chldn. of), 012; Susannah, 044, 062
HEWETT: Jesse M., Capt., 210
HIBBERT: John, 164
HICKMAN: John, 031; William, 111, 112, 123; Wm., 116
HICKS: Barton, 041; Bruton, 118; Burton, 033, 038, 039, 055, 058, 060, 062, 108, 109, 119; Daniel, 012, 039, 053, 059; Jincy, 169; Lucinda, 178; Mary, 012, 071; Nancy, 169; Samuel, 161; Susannah, 165
HIGGAMBOTHAM: Oliver, 033
HIGGDON: Levina, 145
HIGGENBOTHAM: Samuel, 161
HIGGINS: Joel A., 164
HIGHTOWER: --, 012; Aaron, 161; Aaron, 2nd Cpl., 126; Aron, Sgt., 203; Charnal, 203, 205; Charnal, Ens., 203, 204; Charnall, 208; Charnel, 047, 112, 130; Charnell, 047, 113, 208; Charnol, 201; Charnold, Ens., 125; Henry, 161, 207; Henry, Ens., 207; Isaac, 161; James, 133; Jesse, 133, 161; John P., 039, 054, 059; John, 133; Jonathan, 162; Lucinda, 154; Rolly, 161; Sally, 133; Thomas, 025, 047, 059; William, 039, 049, 133, 209; William, Capt., 120, 202, 203; Wm., 208; Wm., Sgt., 130
HIGHTWOER: Charnal, 121; Thomas, 059
HILL: --, 196; Abraham, 211; Abram S., 039, 050; Abram, 109; Abrose, 209; Althea, 012; Ambros, 209; Ambrose, 114, 209; Ambrose, Ens., 126; Ann, 012; Archibald M., 161; Baker(chldn. of), 012; Baker, 012; Benjamin H., 164; Blanton A., 012; Blanton M., 050; Charles, 039; Edward, 081; Elender, 146; Elizabeth Ann, 012; Elizabeth, 167; Ellender, 141; Eudocia M., 141; Georgia A., 179; Hampton W.,113, 128, 206, 211; Hilliard J., 164;
HILL: Huldoh, 101; Isaac, 012, 050, 214; Isaac, Jr., Lt., 124; Isaac, Lt., 127, 202; Isaac, Sr., 042; J.B., 012; Jeremiah, 160; John, 163; Josiah, 039; Juda, 093; Kiddy, 167; Martha J., 101; Martha P., 086; Martha, 083; Mary, 083; Middleton, 042, 114, 208; Miles, 026; Mrs. & 1 ch., 087; Myles, 050; Nancy Jane, & ch., 085; Nancy Jane, 085; Nancy, 013, 086, 097, 144; Olivia W., 162; Prudence, 184; Roderick, 039, 074; Ruben, Capt., 129; Sarah, 168; Thomas, 013, 052, 216; Thos., 077; Walter B., 003
HILLIARD: C.M. (chldn. of), 013
HILLSMAN: B. R., 075; Matilda B., 187
HILLYER: James, 039; John F., 162; Junius, 039; Shaler, 039
HIMSLY: John, 160
HINDON: Nancy, 170
HINDRIX: Cornelia A., 101
HINER: John, 039, 162; Lewis, 039; Mary, 039
HINES: Martin, 160
HINESLEY: John, 162, 205; Mary, 158; Mereming, 101; Wiley Madison, 163; Wiley W., 080
HINESLY: Evan, 103; Irvin, 013; Jno., 128; John, 103; Sarah, 186; Thomas, 163
HINNARD: William, Ens., 125, 203; Wm., 2nd Lt., 128; Wm., Ens., 125, 204
HINSLEY: Babe, 096; Earven, 164; Elizabeth Ann, 172; Emily F., 096; John T., 096; John, 118;

Letha A., 096; Philo B., 096; Sarah M., 096; Thomas, 081
HINSLY: Martha, 013
HINSON: Armistead, 013; Heynry, 084; James, 209, 211; James, Jr., 114, 119, 208, 209; James, Sr., 114, 208; Jas., 113; Nancy, 176; Newton, 114, 208, 209; Tapley, 056
HINTON: Fortine, 145; Harriett, 179; Jacob, 039; James W., 163; James, 050; James, Capt. 205, 206; Jason, 039; John, 013, 052, 163; Lucinda, 182; Mary, 166; Millissi, 149; Penina, 149; Pheriba, 149; Rachel, 034; Sarah J., 167; Sarah, 166; Susan Tallulah, 013; Thomas, 013; William H., 013, 080
HINYARD: William, 160
HITCHCOCK: James, Capt., 117; Murry S. (chldn. of), 013; William, 039; Williams, 039
HITCHCOKE: James, 129
HITT: Charles B., 039
HOBBS: Joseph, 068
HOBGOOD: Hezekiah, 164
HOBSON: Mathew, 161
HODGE: Amanda, 099; G. J., 013; John, 013: John, Lt., 125; John, V. S. M., 143; Joseph, 160; Louisa J., 013; Rebecah, 099; William, 127, 160; William, Sgt., 202; Wm., 114, 208
HODGES: Amanda, 102; Catherine, 220; David, 163; Drucella, 162; John, 161; Joseph, 030, 032, 033, 038, 039, 071, 164, 220; Louisa James (Jane?), 164; Lucinda, 150; Martha, 152; Mrs., 071; Pricilla, 154; Rebecca, 102; Susan, 175; Thomas, 163; William, 027, 032, 058, 162, 211
HODGESON: Edward R., 025
HODGSON: --, 057; Annie, 013; Asbury H., Sr., 013; E. R., 056; E. R., Sr., 013; Edward R., 164; Edward R., Sr., 013; Julia (chldn. of), 013; Robert B., 013; Robert P., 013; Willaim V. P., 013
HODNETT: Francis, 157; John, 160
HOEFFER: Harrison, 207
HOFF: Rachael, 013
HOGANS: Edward, 108
HOGG: Sarah, 013
HOGUE: Jacob, 013; James, 052; Jonathan, 134; William S., 161; William, Capt., 118; William, Sgt. 210; Wm. S., 107
HOGWOOD: James, 160; John, 126
HOLAFIELD: John, 160
HOLBROOK: Henry M., 039; John F., 039; L. W., 039; Nathan, 013, 034, 045, 046, 052, 060
HOLBROOKS: L.W., 039; Lorenzo W., 039; Nathan, 213
HOLDER: Elizabeth, 179; Hannah, 155; Hinson G., 176; John H., 013; John, 013; Katherine, 154; Maria, 149; Peggy, 178; Tapley, 013, 039; Tarpley, Sgt. 210; Thos. T., Lt., 110
HOLLAND: --, 122; Archibald, 161; Elisha L., 163; Elisha, 111, 114, 119, 208; Frances, 135; Moses J., 074; Mosses J., 164; Neal, 029; William, 108
HOLLAWAY: David, 133; Elizabeth, 133; James, 034; Melinda, 133; Wm. B., 133
HOLLBROOK: Martha, 013
HOLLEWAY: George, 052; Ruth, 013
HOLLIMAN: B. L., 013
HOLLODAY: Martin, 161
HOLLOWAY: Anny, 039; David, 074; David, Sgt., 203; Elizabeth, 156; James P., 074, 164; James P., Rev., 146; Jas. P., 075; Mary, 157; Samuel, 107; William B., 162
HOLLOWELL: Asa, 013
HOLMAN: Francis, 039, 061
HOLMES: David, 039, 050, 056, 112, 217; Green, 118; Harriett, 144; Isaac, 058; Isaac, Sgt., 203; James, 0131 John (chldn of), 013; John, 013; Lucy B., 174; Lucy, 148; Nancy, 176; Pamela, 161; W.,116; Washington, 079, 125, 130; Washinton, 122
HOLMS: Washington, 113
HOLSEY: Albon, 013; Hopkins, Col., 163
HOLT: Betsey, 167; Caroline E., 164; Cicero, 013, 033, 038, 039, 161; Edgar, 013; Emily G., 163; George G., 1st, Sgt., 126; Polley, 184; William B., 205; William B., Capt., 130; Wm. B., Capt., 125, 127, 206; Wm., Capt., 134
HOLTS: Wm. B., 128; Wm. B., Capt., 130
HOMES (?): Washington, 205
HOMES: David, 218
HONEY: M. A., 097
HONFLEUR: Juan, 163
HOOD: Beulah (chldn. of), 013; Beulah V., 013; C. W., 039; Elisha, 160; Elisha, Ens., 127, 202; Elisha, Fifer, 130; W.F., 039; Wiley F., 028, 039, 040, 060; Wiley R., 039
HOOFAN: Nancy C., 093
HOOKER: Richard, 046, 119
HOOPAAUGH: Susan J., 100
HOOPAUGH: Nancy, 098; Susan P., 101; William, 162
HOOPPAN: James, 103, 117
HOOPPAUGH: Allen, 088; John C., 088; Nancy O. C., 088; Sarah E., 088; Susan, 088, 098
HOOPUGH: Miram A., 172
HOOVER: Lawson P., 013
HOPE: John, 042
HOPKINS (?): William, 162
HOPKINS: --, 040; Aaron, 160; Anselum L., 033; Benjamin B., 044, 162; Cynthia W., 095; Denney, 053; Dennis, 027; E. A., 122; E. A., Mrs., 220; Eleanor H., 013; Elizabeth, 174; Emily, 013; Eucebius A., 219; Eunebius A., 110; Eurebius A., 048; Eusebens (chldn. of), 013; Eusebeus A., 024; Eusebias A., 041; Eusebius A., 040, 058; Eusibas A., 029; Eusibusa, 033; Hannah, 013; Jno. A.,114, 116; John A.,123, 208;
HOPKINS; Joseph, 013; Lambeth, 013, 040; Laurabeth, 040; Lemuel, 040; Lucinda W., 101; Martha, 145, 166; Mary, 172; Meary, 177; Moses, 013; Mrs. (2 ch), 095; Rachel, 040; Samuel, 033, 161; Sarah, 174; Solomon A., 040; Ucebrous, 114; Usbious, 208; Usebius, 119; William, 013, 040, 054
HOPPAUGH: Nancy, 090
HOPPER: William W., 163
HOPPING: E. A., 220; Ephraim S., 013; Ephraim L., 040
HORTON: Alfonzo, 013; Betsey, 160; Daniel T., 013; T.A., 013
HOUGHTON: Charles, 160; Elizabeth C., 176; James C., 061, 163; Louisa M., 155; Louisa, 174; Robert B., 048
HOUSE: Ann, Mrs., 147; Anna, 073; Betsey, 161; Burwell, 164; Darius T., 072; Eliza, 182; Emily, 183; Frances C., 164; Harris, 162; James, Sgt. 210; Johannah, 152; Joseph F., 164; Rebecca Ann, 013; Richard, 072; Sarah, 168; Thomas, 109, 219; Thomas, Capt., 118; Thomas, Mrs., 097
HOUSON: Newton, 101
HOUSTON: Cobb, 039; John, 049
HOUZE: Angeline, 013; Darius N., 080; Darius, 013; Harrett, 154; Jinney, 143; Joseph (chldn of), 013; Sarah G., 145
HOWARD: Ben Jaman, 103; Charles Wallace, 163; Hiram, 013; John, 040; Nancy, 174; Nicholas, 160; Patrick, 013; Rhesa, 040; William, 040
HOWE: --, 193
HOWEL: Jesse, 116
HOWELL: Catherine, 102; Cathern, 099; Cobb, 031; James, 040; Jesse, 114, 115, 123, 161, 208; Sidney S., 036
HOWLAND: Clavin L., 040
HOWSE: Anzalina, 181; John, 164; Seaborn, 164
HOWZE: Darius T., 163; Ziba, 095
HOYT: N., Rev., 142; Nathan, 013, 213; Nathan, D. D., 142, 145, 146, 147
HUBBARD: Charles Lews, 013; Eudocia, 171; M. H., Rev., 142; Thomas, 040; William, 040, 063
HUBERT: Gabriel, 013, 026, 037, 039, 041, 046, 054, 057, 061, 213, 214; James, 013
HUCHINSON: Joseph, Lt., 117
HUCK: Thomas A., 037
HUDSON: Ann D., 173; Arch, 124; Archibald, 049; Charles L., 013; Elizabeth, 133; George W., 013; Katie (chldn. of), 013; Katie, 013; L.A., Mrs., 090; Mahala, 154; May Belle, 013; Polly, 168; Robert, 202; Shaderick, 031; Thomas F., 068
HUELL: Cathren, 088; N. H., 088
HUEY: Susan, 155
HUFF: Alethia E., 180; Alfred D., 081; Benjamin Franklin, 089; Elizabeth, 013, 040; George, 013; Green (Orphs.), 096, 097; Green, 164; Greene (chldn. of), 013; Greene B., 040; Greene, 013; Harrison, 111, 113; Henry Marion, 089; Henry, 013, 214, 215; John Thomas, 089; John, 040; Leeroy, 044; Leroy, 040, 098; Lidia, 165; Littleberry, 040; Loancy, 152; Lorenia Eveline, 089; Lucy Jane, 089, 101; M. A., 100; Mary C., 081, 096; Mary Cobb, 101; Mary, 160; Matilda, 089, 098; Rachael, 013; S.(L.?)B., 162; Valentine, 040; Wiley J., 082; Wiley James, 163; William, 082; Wylie, 162
HUGES: Richard, 220
HUGGAN: Alexander, 040
HUGGINS: --, 193; J. H., Sr., Mrs., 013; James H., 040; James, 039; John J., 040, 045, 163; John, 040
HUGHES: Daniel G., 164; George H., 040; H. S., 060; Hamden Sidney, 039; Harrisden S., 013; John, 101; Richard, 033, 037, 039, 118, 210; William, 041
HUGHEY: Elizabeth, 160; James, 160; Joseph A., 110, 111, 161
HUGHIE: Richard, 119
HUGHS: Richard, 040, 162
HULIG: Asia, 204
HULINGS: James, 040
HULL: Ann E., 080; Asbury, 013, 028, 040, 074, 121, 161; Asbury, Sgt., 207; Augustus L., 003; Elmira, 013; Frances, 185; H., 143; Henry, 024, 109, 211; Henry, Jr., 164; Henry, Sgns. Mate, 210; Hope, 040, 215, 217; Lucy Ann, 169; Lula M., 013; Nathaniel H., 088
HULSA: Asa, 204
HULSEY: Asa, 204

HUMBLETT: Martha, 084
HUMPHARIES: Elijah, 038; Uriah, 040
HUMPHRAYS: --, 047
HUMPHREY: Benjamin, 031; William, Sgt., 20; Wm., Sgt., 206
HUMPHREYS: --, 047; Benjamin W., 163; Sarah Ann, 181; Uriah, 214; William, 024, 040, 108, 120; Wm., 118, 119
HUMPHRIES: Elijah, 040, 055, 058; George W., 055; George, 040; Isaac, 047, 055; Joseph, 058; Louiza, 175; Uriah(chldn. of), 013; Uriah, 013, 040; William, Sgt. 210
HUMPREYS: Wm., 103
HUMPRIES: Nancy, 058
HUNDEN: Joseph, 215
HUNDON: Elisha, 045
HUNGERFORD: Anson, 044, 058, 060; Dana, 044, 058, 060; Darcy, 058; J., 032; John, 040; W.S., 032; William S., 040
HUNGTINTON: G. J., 040
HUNNICUTT: James Bernard, 013; Rosa May, 013; W. L. C., 013
HUNPHREYS: William, 048
HUNPHRIES: Elijah, 161; Joseph, 210
HUNT: B. A., Miss, 095; C., Miss, 095; Charles B., 164; D. J., 033; E., Mrs. (2 ch), 095; Elizabeth A., 183; Frederick S. S., 165; George R., 120; James M., 035; John M., 163; John, Sgt., 203; Josiah M., 034, 035, 164; M., Miss, 095; Mary, 093, 095; Meretta, 093; Elizabeth, 095; Nancy, 095, 213; Needham F., Mrs., 100; Obey, 093; Sarah, 093; Serena, 149; Susan S., 083; Susan, 094, 099; Thomas, 040; W., Mrs. (2 ch), 095; Wilburn, 062; William H., 028, 038, 048, 055, 112, 122, 160, 202, 203; William Henry, 162; William, 203; Wm. H., 116, 201
HUNTER: Alexander, 040; Alfred, 013; Benj. F., 029; David Van, 030; George R., 112, 116, 122; George R., Sgt., 203; Henry, 013; James, 206; Jane, 182; Jas., 129; John, 013; John, Sgt., 206; Robert W., 162; Robert, Sgt. 206; S. M. (chldn. of), 013; Sam, 039; Samuel S., 160; Sarah Ann, 013; Starkie, 013
HUNTON: Charles B., 110; Charles, 114, 208; Hannah, 050, 054, 061; James, 033, 051, 161; John, 040, 060, 061, 114, 161, 208, 209; Salley, 182
HURD: Jenny, 143
HURDEN: Oliver, 096; William P., 049
HURLEY: Langston, 013
HURST: John A., Rev., 145; Umphrey, 209
HUSE: George, 112, 204
HUSON: Newton, 114
HUSSON: Alexander, 040
HUSTON: John, 160
HUTCHENSON: Jo., Lt., 116; William, 209
HUTCHESON: James, 086; Jno., 206; Peter W. (chldn. of), 013; Peter W., 013
HUTCHINSON: Daniel, 134; Jane, 134; Jno., 113; John B., 134; John, 128, 161; Joseph, 109; Joseph, Lt., 117; Joshua, 134; Samuel B., Capt., 129; Susannah, 134; William, 114, 134; Wm. C., 134
HUTCHISON: James, 095
HUTSELL: Joel, 163
HUTSON: Archabald, 210; Archibald, Sgt. 210; Coly, 013; Esther, 169; Lewcy, 144; Robert, 045, 112, 116, 123, 124; Shadrack (chldn. of), 013; Shadrick, 031; Thomas, 040; William, 161
HUY (?): John W., 111
HYATT: Edmund, 045; Nathaniel, 045
HYCHE: Geo., 201
HYDE: William, 049
HYNDS: Ernest C., 003
IAMS: John, 038
ILER: A. W., 165; Elizabeth, 098; Sarah, 159
IMS: John, 038
INGRAM: Jane, 090
IRBY: Sarah, 013
IRVIN: Josephus, 041
IRWIN: Charles M., Rev., 146; David, 040; Francis, 040, 041; James, 1st Sgt.,127; Robert, 050
ISAAC: Robert, 062
ISAM: Ginnet, 100
ISBORN: Joseph, 049
IVERSON: Frances E., 013; Rebecca A., 159; Robert, 013, 165
IVEY/SAULTER: --, 198
IVINS: Washinton, 122
JACK: A. M., 122; Capt., 071; Green B., 040, 054, 057; James K. P., 013; John, 103, 108, 109, 115, 119, 209, 210; John, 3rd Sgt. 127; John, Sgt., 205; Margaret, 044; Samuel, 013, 044; Samuel, Col. (chldn. of), 013; Samuel, Col., 013; Samuel, Sgt., 203; William, 109; Wm., 211
JACKS: Elivira, 171; Green B., 034, 112, 206; Green B., 1st Lt., 127; Green B., Capt. 206; Green B., Lt., 124, 125, 129, 203, 204, 206; Greene B., 013; Isaac, 041, 073, 110; John G., 103, 108, 118; John, 055, 068, 108, 114, 120, 209, 210; Kindred, 165; Linsey, 111, 166; Martha, 187; Mattie J., 080; Polly, 156; Sally, 154; Sarah, 184; Young, 165; Young, Capt., 117
JACKSON (PACKSON?): Hillman, 119
JACKSON: (chldn. of), 013; A.B., 122; A. M., 122; A., Mrs., 099, 102; Abe, Mrs., 222; Abraham G., 080, 166; Abram, 085; Almedea, 188; Amanda, 041; Andrew B., 080, 165; Asa M., 041, 042, 047, 075, 166; Asam, 042, 049; Asenith, 156; Burton, 096; Camilla, 013; Catherine, 156; Charles C., 165; Cornelious, 113; Cornelius, 129, 165, 206; Daniel, 013, 205;
JACKSON: Daniel, Lt., 206; Daniel, Sgt. 210; Danl., Lt., 205; David W., 013; Drewry W., 166; Drews W., Mrs., 090; Drury B., 080; Drury W., 165; Drury W., Family, 198; Drury W., Mrs., 101; Drury, 013; Edmund, Sgt. 210; Eliza Ann Laticia, 151; Elizabeth "Betsey", 184; Elizabeth A., 183; Elizabeth, 081; Frances C., 170; Frances, 165; Francis (chldn. of), 013; Francis, 013, 219; George J., 041; Green B., Capt. 207; H. B., 213; Harriet, 013; Hartwell, 073, 074, 075, 165; Hartwell, Jr., 041; Hartwell, Sr., 013, 041; Helman, 222; Henry E., 081;
JACKSON: Henry, 013, 165; Hessie M., 150; Hillman, 013, 072, 098; Hilman, 166; Isaac R., 041; Isaac, 095; Ivery, 041; J., 041; Jacob, 095; James W., 081; James, 034, 037, 045, 047, 048, 050, 051, 057, 211; Jane, 013; John J., 220; John S., 166; John W., 014; John, 023, 027, 033, 036, 041, 042, 046, 048, 050, 051, 058, 060-062, 072, 073, 165, 204, 218; John, Sr., 014, 220; Juda, 180; L., 102;
JACKSON: L., Mrs., 099; Land, 041; Lorena, 164; Lottie B., 014; Lucy, 144; Luticia, 014, 165; Maggie, 014; Margaret, 014; Martha A., 159; Martha C., 159; Martha, 172, 221; Mary A., 167, 169; Mary P., 179; Milton C., 166; Nancy E., 170; Nancy H., 176; Nancy, 149, 151; Obadiah, 042, 109, 207; Obediah, 041, 074; Olly, 146; Polly, 149;
JACKSON: R.M., 041; Ruth M., 014; S.E.T., 101; S.J., 041; S., 041; Salley, 165; Saml., 077; Saml., Col., 129, 201; Samuel, 027, 033, 041, 049, 050, 061, 076; Sarach C., 187; Stephen E. F., 080; Stephen F., 081; Stephen, 014, 029, 031, 041, 053, 059, 071-073, 076, 103, 165; Stephen, 2nd Lt., 111; Stephen, Jr., 221; Stephen, Lt., 111, 119; Steven, 041;
JACKSON: Sylvia, 085; T., 041; Trump, 039; W.A., 014; W.B., 166; William (chldn. of), 014; William C., 042, 074; William E., 041; William H., 025, 029, 033-036, 038, 041, 045-048, 058, 061, 062; William Henry, 041; William P., 124, 165; William, 028, 029, 033, 075, 166, 218; William, 2nd Lt., 111; Wm. H., 072, 075; Wm. Hy., 073; Wm. P., 113, 130, 205, 206; Wm., 129; Zarephath, 159
JACOBSON: Rosa C., 014
JAMES: Emanuel, 076; Enoch, 036, 038; Henry, 014, 040, 041; John, 036, 038, 048, 079; Mary, 179; Mrs., 097; Samuel, 036 038; William, 040, 048, 077, 108, 120
JAMESON: Arthur, 108
JAMESONS: Arthur, 108
JANUS(JAMES?): William, 108
JARRALL: George A., 165; Stinson J., 165
JARREL: Tilman, 041
JARRELL: Eliza L., 080; George A., 014; Isaac F., 041; James S., 014; Martin, 014; Mary Ann, 187; Mike, 014; Stinson S., 041, 109
JARREN: Mariette, 221
JEFFERIES: Thos., 113
JEFFERSON: Robert (chldn. of), 014; Z. P., 039
JEFFERYS: Thomas, 109
JEFFREESS: Edward, 122
JEFFREYS: Thos. (2), 135
JEFFRIES: --, 014; Elizabeth, 154; Jeffries & dau., 084; Joseph A. (chldn. of), 014; Mary, 085, 148; Sarah, 085; Thomas, 048, 114, 120, 208, 211, 219; Thos., 115, 128, 210, 211
JEFFRIESS: William, 166
JEFFS: Nancy, 185
JEFRIES: Thos., 206
JEILS: Richard, 165
JEININGS: Henry, 024
JEMISISON: Ella, 014
JENKINS: --, 050; E. B., 041; Edmond B., PayMr., 107; Edmund B., 117; Edmund Booker, 041; John, 014; Peter, 014
JENNINGS: Calab, 025; Cecilia P., 155; David, 030; Frances A., 151; Giles, 014, 074, 221; Giles, Capt., 118; Henrietta V., 153; Henry (chldn. of), 014; Henry, 014, 074, 075, 114, 118, 121, 208; J. J., Mrs., 099, 101; James (chldn. of), 014; James J., 072, 080, 088, 166; James, 014, 041, 074; Jefferson, 024, 041; Jerusha, 088; Jesse, 165;
JENNINGS; Jiles, Capt., 117, 118; John W., 081; John, 088, 100; John, Mrs., 098; Joseph B., 014;

Lt., 111; Marcus, 080; Martha, 220; Mary T., 014; Mary, 088, 098; Nancy A., 087; Pamelia, 155; Prudence E., 180; Prudence S., 171; R., 099; Robert H., 014; Robert, 014, 165; Robert, 1st Lt., 111; Robert, Lt.,119; Sarah Ann, 148; Susan A., 087; Susan E., 187
JENTRY: Edna, 093
JEWELL: William, 041
JILES(?): L., Mrs., 090
JILES(GILES?): John, 159
JILES: Betsey, 167; David, 166; Frances, 149; Harris, 166; James, 081; Joseph, 218; Lurana, 093; Mary, 090; William, 073, 166
JIMISON: John M., 041
JINKINS: Moore?, 026
JINNINGS: James, 165
JODD: George B., 211
JOHN: Austin, 061
JOHNS: Charles H., 166; Lillie Angelina, 014; W.B., 041, 042
JOHNSON: --, 029; Abraham, 112, 202; Abraham, Sgt., 129, 202; Alcy, 150; Alethia, 077; Allen R.,014; Ann D.,161; Benjamin F., 042; Cary, 166; Daniel H., 048; David H., 014; David, 124, 205; Edwin, 039; Elsa A., 003; Fanny, 024; Frances, 220; Frankey, 014; George T., 014; Grandma, 222; Hardy, 204; Henry, 061; Hershel, 117; Isaac W., 042; Isaac, 034; J. C., 074; J. T., 014; James, 042, 222; Jno. C.,072; Jno. Calvin, 072, 119; Joe, 014; John C., 037, 059, 060, 118; John Calvin, 037, 042, 074, 075, 099, 166;
JOHNSON: John Calvin, Clk., 110; John, Capt., 201; Jophn Calvin, 072; Joseph, 110; L. G., 014; Letitia, 014; Lousia, 014; Malcom, 206; Malinda, 175; Mary E., 168; Mary F.H., 092; Nathan, 166; Nehemiah, 042; Oliver Porter, 166; Rachel, 219; Reuben, 114, 209, 210; Reuben, 4th. Sgt., 125; Sarah C.,092; Susannah, 151; Thomas, 037, 042, 074; Tunes, 014; Walter, 203; William D.(chldn of), 014; William D., 014; William, 042, 055, 204, 215; William, Sgt.,203; Wm.,Lt., 110
JOHNSTON: Abraham, 111, 123, 165; Abram, 120; Ahasabia, 165; Allen, 208; Benjamin F., 029, 035, 042, 058, 059, 110, 165; Burwell, 203; Edward, 165; Eliza R., 134; George W.,134; Hardy, 112, 204; Hiram G., 073; Hulda H., 134; James, (Orphans of), 091; James, 165, 214; John C., 053; John Calvin, 075; John, Capt., 201; Letitia, 176; Malcolm, 113; Malcom, 113, 119, 121; Malcom, 2nd Sgt., 126; Malcomb, 206, 207; Marth Z., 134; Mary, 152; Peggy, 165; Samuel, 213; Walter, 112, 165, 203; William, Sgt., 112; William W., 134; William, 112, 129, 166, 214, 215; William, Capt., 201; Willis A., 217; Wm., 208
JOILES: Nancy, 145
JOINER: Anise, 097; J. J., 042; J. W., 039; William R., 042
JOLLEY: William, 2nd Sgt., 126
JOLLY: Joseph, 112, 165, 204; Joseph, Sgt., 201, 203
JONAS: Joseph E., 091; --, 042, 062; Adaline, 014; Alleathy, 168; Andrews S. (chldn. of), 014; Benjamin F., 040; Benjamin, 108, 120, 165; Caroline, 159; Catrin A., 152; Charlott, 156; Clarinda B., 082; Cornelia E. E., 155; D. A., Miss, 155; E. E. (chldn. of), 014; Edmond, 203; Edmund, 112, 122; Edward H., 055; Edward, 042, 116, 203; Elijah, 014; Elizabeth, 097, 155; Emaline L., 145; Ephraim, 042; Frances A., 170; Frank, 014; George W., 109; Hinson, 220; Jabez, Mrs., 098; Jacob, 042; Jacob, Sgt. 210; James D., 014, 166; James F., 211;
JONAS: James M., 035, 053; James S., 062, 109; James W., 028-030, 033, 034, 042, 055; James W., 056, 062; James, 049, 110; Jesse, 113, 115, 125, 165, 209-211; Jesse, 1st, Cpl., 127; Jesse, 2nd Sgt., 126; Jesse, 4th Cpl., 127; Jesse, Cpl., 125, 130; Joab, Pvst. Mrsl., 110; Job, 028; John H., 042; John P., 054, 081; John T., 014; John, 014, 026, 165; Joseph S., 014; Joseph, 037; Kabez, 166; Lena, 014;
JONAS: Letty, 014; Lodusky, 145; Lucinda M., 163; Lucy, 149; Lydia, 014, 040; Mary Ann, 151; Mary, 014, 157; Nancy, 148; Nannie Lou, 014; P. Calvin, 014; Pamelia F., 150; Philip, 165; Polly, 160; Richard, 042, 045, 046, 048, 071; Robert A. (chldn. of), 014; Robert A., 028, 053, 056; Robert, 095; Rupel, 023; Russell, 023, 042; S. M., Mrs., 084; S. R., 084; Sarah A., & 1 ch., 087; Sarah A., 086, 093; Sarah Ann, 077; Sarah M., 098, 100; Seaborn, 042;
JONAS: Thomas, 036, 067, 112; Thomas, Jr., 023, 035, 044; W. O., 084; Walter R., 042; Wiley A. (chldn. of), 014; Wiley A., 165; William (Wm. H.), 221; William E., 038, 051; William, 014, 042, 044, 049, 072, 075, 208, 209, 214, 218; Wm., 072, 074, 114; Wm., 2nd Sgt., 127; Wm., Sgt. 206
JONSON: Henry, 165; John Calvin, 165; John G., 165; John, 165; Mary, 165; Reuben, 165; William, 165
JONSTON: Abram, 122; George, 165
JORDAN: Catherine, 157; Elder T., 072; Henry, 207; Nancy, 176; S. A. E., 098; Willis, 165
JOSEPH: Helen, 014
JOSSEY: Harriett, 186
JOTHENON: Isaiah, 072
JOURDAN: Zachariah, 165
JUDD: George B., 030, 109
JUSTESS: William L., 165
KAGENET: Hannah, 166
KAGLE: Mary, 161
KEENER: Suckey, 152
KEENUM: James, 166; Polly, 166
KEER: John, 042
KEESE: John S., 014; Theodon, 038
KEIFFER: Bros., 042
KELBOURN: Daniel, 035
KELGORE: Mrs., 071
KELLETT: William, 067
KELLEY: Elizabeth, 185; James D., 167; John, 166; Mrs., 097; Polley Minerva, 146; Susan, 167; Tabitha, 152
KELLOGG: Freeman, 037; Julia E., 169
KELLOUGH: Allen, 060
KELLUM: Lavonia, 014; Lucinda, 161; W. E., 014
KELLY: Allen, 042; Drury, 050; Durum, 166; Fanny, 188; Francis, 042; Jacob, 031; James, 135; John, 042, 135; Math, 163; Mrs., 084; Nancy, 086, 097; William, 042, 167; William, Jr., 214
KELOUGH: Ebenezer, 053
KELSEY: Charles, 042, 045; George H., 042, 045; George, 042
KEMP: Jno., 204; John, 112, 203, 204; John, 1st Sgt., 127; John, Lt., 202; Joseph, 042; Prudence, 141; Stephen, 042; Thomas, 204; Thomas, Sgt., 202; W. C., 025; William C., 014
KENARD: Mrs., 097
KENDRICK: Isaac, 116, 123; Mary, 097; Robert, 205; Robert, Ensgn, 125, 127; Robert, Lt., 130
KENEDY: Alexander, 166
KENNARD: Annabel, 014; Joel S.,014
KENNEDY: Charles, 042; David, 055; Hannah, 164; Joseph, 166; Thomas (chldn. of), 014
KENNEY: Agness (3 chldn), 095; Agness, 088, 098; Clifford A., 014; D. M., 014; David, Lt., 201, 203; E.F., 083; Eliza F., 083; George, 014; Isaac (chldn. of), 014; Isaac M., 014, 167; James S.H., 014; James S., 014; James, Lt., 201; John F., 088; John, 044, 095; Joseph A., 014; Louisa A., 014; Louisa, 014; Martha J., 087; Nancy E., 146; Robert, Lt., 117; Samuel, 014; Sarah Sophia, 014
KENNON: John W., 054, 122, 167; Mary (1), 135
KENNUM: Patsy, 181
KENNY: Isaac Mc, 167; Martha, 166; William, 077
KENSEY: Jas., Lt., 201
KENT(?): Wm. H., 119
KENT: Avarilla, 181; Elethia, 158; Elizabeth, 158; Gilbert, 042, 166, 221; Gilbert, 3rd Cpl., 127; Isaiah, 167; John, 166; Josiah M., 119; Josiah, 166; Maryann, 169; Nathaniel P., 221; Peter, 042; Patsey, 168; Silas B., 081; Sol. P., Maj., 110; Soloman P., 014, 073, 166; Solomon P., Maj., 111, 119; Solomon, 219; W. R., 091; William H., 042, 074, 166; William, 046; Wm. Henry, 072
KEOUGH: Thomas, 120, 209
KERMICHAEL: Thomas, Sgt., 206
KERR: Andrew, 042; Jesse, 042; Margaret, 170; William, 042
KESSE: Theodon, 037; Theodore, 037
KETCHUM: Colden, 109, 117
KETTLE: Margaret, 086; Mary, 177; Michael, 167; William, 014
KEY: Samuel, 166
KIDD: Chs. Wesley, 092; Gabriel, 014; Harriet, 183; Harriett E., 092; Harriett, 093; Hesekiah M., 167; James, 042
KIDDS: Hezekiah, 091
KIGNY: W. Beatty, 014
KILBOURN: Daniel, 035
KILBURN: John R., 042
KILGO: James, 166
KILGORE: Benjamin, 042; Brown, 132; Elizabeth "Betsey", 160; Frances, 166; John B., 075; John L., 047; John L., Sgt. 210; John, 042, 115, 132, 214, 215; Lord, 120; Mariah, 161; Mary, 132; Mathew, 166; Miss, 135; Peter, 014; Sinthey, 143; Smith, 132; Solomon, 108, 112, 121, 166; Solomon, Cpl., 206, 207; Thomas, 054, 112, 113, 121, 122, 130, 166, 205; Thomas, Cpl., 210; Thos., 116; Wilis, 205; William L., 132; Willis, 042, 111-113, 116, 121, 122, 130; Willis, Cpl., 210
KILGRO: John B., Sgt., 129
KILNBEST: Christ., Sgt., 206
KIMBEL: Christ., 211
KIMBELL: Christopher, 109; Robert, 166, 208

KIMBER: William, 167
KIMBLE: Thomas O., 167; William, 166
KIMBREL: Gideon, 166
KIMBREW: Wm., 206
KIMBRO: Wm., 113
KIMBROW: William, 166
KINDRICK: Isaac, 112, 124
KINES: Frances J., 082; John, 072; Martin, 1st, Sgt., 126; Martin, 204, 206; Mary J., 082; Matilda, 186; Q. Anne, 145; Thomas, 167
KING: Agnes B., 014, 035; Agness B., 030; Caroline, 014; David, 215; Ed, 039; Emily, 014, 090; F. E., 099; Francina E., 014; Geo. W., Col., 117; George W., 034, 108; George W., Col., 108; George, 060; James, 042; Jesse, 042; John G., 014; John G., 1st Sgt., 127; John G., Sgt., 205; John J., 166; Porter, 167; Sarah, 023, 030, 031, 034, 035, 052, 060, 152; William, 042; William, Jr., 167
KINLEY: Elisabeth, 093; Elizabeth, 090; Hester Ann, 092; James, 014; Jas. T. R., 092; Margaret E., 092; Mary F., 092; Sarah L., 092
KINLY: E., Mrs., 090; Wm. F., 092
KINNEBREW: B. T., 014
KINNEY (KINES?): Martin, 112
KINNEY: Agnes & 2 chldn., 085; Agnes & 3 chldn., 085; Agness, 100; Alford, 014; Ann C., 175; Charles, 167; David, 116, 122; David, Capt., 116, 126, 203, 204; David, Lt., 112, 126, 202; Eliza, 093, 094, 153; Emily, 183; George, 3rd, Sgt., 126; James, 041, 042; James, Lt., 126; Jane, 014; Jesse, 166; Jesse, 3rd, Sgt., 126; Jesse, Ens., 203, 204; Jesse, Sgt., 202; John F., 167; John, 030, 093; John, Fifer, 129; John, Sgt., 207; Jonathan, Sgt., 207; Joseph C., 093; Nancy E., 187; Robt., Ens., 116; Sally, 181; Thomas, 167; Victory, 093
KINNY: David, Lt., 120; George, 129; John, Sgt., 129; Sally, 167
KINY (?): Martin, 204
KIRK: Hampton, 014
KIRKLAND: Benjamin, 112
KIRKLEY: Calvin P., 167; Elisabeth, 093; Elizabeth, 146; Robert, 092
KIRKPATRICK: Catherine N., 172; John, 014, 025, 027, 037, 042, 045, 050, 051, 053, 058, 061, 072, 074, 075, 099, 103, 108, 109, 117, 175; Sarah J., 187
KIRKWOOD: James, 014; Salley, 174
KISSELBERG: James D., 167
KISSELLBURG: Henry J., 034
KITTLE: Clarissa, 042; Elizabeth, 014; James, 014; John H., 014; John, 014, 167; John, Jr., 042; Margaret, 014; Rufus C., 014; William, 014; Willis, 014
KLUTTS: Almedia, 166; Elisabeth C., 154; Eliza A., 147; Frances, 180; Jacob, 014, 073; Mahalz, 153; Milly, 080; Samuel, 014, 118; Simon, 095
KNAPPEN: Thomas, 027
KNEELAND: Henry, 109, 118
KNIGHT: Lucian Lamar, 198
KNOTT: Archey, 221; Elizabeth, 132; James, 025, 028, 037, 053, 058; John, 029, 074 075, 132; Perlina, 175
KNOWLAND: Solomon, 042
KNOX: George W., 167
KOLB: Charley, 040
KRANKE: --, 047
KRONER: Frank H., 014
LACKEY: James, 042
LACY: John, 082
LAFETTE: Augustus, 033
LAG: Thomas, 216
LAGEVIN: Lott, 208
LAGRE: Nathan C., 042
LAGWIN: Lott M., 168; Lott, 114
LAINE: Benjamin, 169
LAIRD: Mary, 184
LAMAR: Andrew C., 043; Andrew J. (chldn. of), 014; Andrew J., 014, 169; Ezekiel, 115, 208, 209, 210; Georgia A., 183; Mary Ann, 150; Phillip F., 168; Zachariah, 014
LAMBERT: Elijah, 060; Elisha, 060; Elizabeth, 160; John H., 014; Thomas, 014; William, 060
LAMBERTH: Joel, 167
LAMKIN: R. W., 014
LAMPKIN: Cobb (chldn. of), 014; Edward, 040, 043, 044; Emily, 093; Lewis J., 014, 122, 169; Lewis, 046, 116, 124; Lucy J., 098; Mattie, 015; Philip, 168; Robert H. (chldn. of), 015; Terrell M., 169; Washington, 015; William H., 015; Winfrield L., 169; Winnie, 015; Wm., 122
LAMPKINS: Lewis, 123, 203; Louis, 112
LAND: Archibald, 043; Elizabeth, 015; John H., 039; Jonathan, 055, 061; L. B., 055, 120; Littleberry, 108; Theophilis, 055; Wiley, 043
LANDERS (SANDERS?): Wm. Hale, 103
LANDERS: Anny, 167; Benjamin, 043; Eli, 168; James, 210; James, Cpl., 210; John, 168; Mathew, 072; Mereda, 168; Richard, 072, 109
LANDRUM: Ardella, 015; James B., 168; Sylvanus, Rev., 142
LANE: Benjamin, 072; Charles W., 169; Edmond H., 061; Harrison G., 169; Henry, 167; Isaac, 043; Jesse, 015, 043; Jesse, Sgt., 129; Joel, 040; Jonathan, 025, 027, 043, 217; Joseph, 046, 076, 117, 167, 215; Mildred Ann, 155; Philip, 033, 118, 168; Richard (chldn. of), 015; Theo S., 043; Theophilus S., Capt. 206; Theophilus, 027; Thomas J., Capt. 207; Vandinger, 061; William E., 061; William G, 061; William, 118
LANEAR: Geo. M., 167
LANEY: Charles, 043
LANG: John, 035
LANGFORD: Augustin S., 169; Bazabal, 067; Bazabel, 130; Bazabel, Lt., 206; Bazaleel, 038, 041, 117, 121; Bazaleel, Lt., 207; Bazaliel, 205; Bazelee, 103; Bazeleel, 124; Bazelell, 135; Bazellton, 168; Bedford, 058, 080, 168; Bedford, M. G., 142, 147; Beng, 116; Benjamin C., 080; Bezaleel, 076; Bnj., 113; Eliza J., 187; Francis C., 169; George, 135; Henry, 135, 167; James, 015, 0127, 038, 039, 043, 053, 058, 135, 214; Janius H., 081; John W., 043, 169;
LANGFORD: Joseph B., 015, 081; Nancy Annis, 153; Polly, 167; Sarah Ann, 135; U. W., 069; William A., 169
LANGSTON: Etheldred, 129
LANIER: Angeline, 135, 187; Ben, Mrs., 088, 098; Benjamin B., 080; Bezleel Langford, 169; Catherine, 164; Geo. W., 135; George M., 015, 072, 112, 203; George, 043; Katherine, 135; Langford, 135; Martha W., 163; Martha, 135; Sterling, 167; Walter, 169; William, 169
LANIGAN: Mary L., 043
LANKFORD: James, 079
LANOS: Charles, 043
LANSFORD: Lemuel, 076, 113, 121, 125, 130, 205
LANTON: Washington, 134
LARAMORE: Joseph, 216
LARD: Belsey, 132; Jean, 152; Mary, 132; Rebecca G., 083; William, Cpl., 206
LARKIN: Clark, 038
LARY: John, Rev.141
LASATER: Joel, 043
LASETER: Delana, 176; Gray B., 075; Joel, 043; Joel, Sgt., 129; Lemuel, 121; Marinda, 082; Nancy, 178
LASITER: James, 036, 051
LASSATER: Radford, 123
LASSETER: Britain, 168; Elizabeth, 134; Gray B., 073; Henry, 134; James, 168; Joel, 132, 209; John F., 168; John, 132; Julian, 132; Lemuel, 112-115, 130, 134, 205-208, 211; Lucinda, 132; Mary, 015; Radford, 116; Richard, 132; Samuel(Lemuel?), 167; Senone, 132; Syntha, 132
LASSETTER: Joel, 204, 208; Lemuel, 128; Robert, 204
LASSITER: Elizabeth, 184; Gray, 132; Joel, 112, 210; Joel, Sgt., 202; Lemuel, 210; Marshall S. T., 077; Nancy, 161; Radford, 112; Robert, 204, 207; Sally, 077
LAUGHFORD: Bezubel, 062
LAUNINS: S. A., Mrs., 015
LAURANCE: Jiney, 157; Joseph, 027, 034, 038, 042; Nicholas, 203; Nicholas, Sgt., 203; Richard, 043, 067, 215; Thomas, 036
LAURENS: Richd., Lt.129
LAVENDER: Nancy E., 015; William, 051
LAVERIN: Mariah, 164
LAWLES: Peter, 015
LAWLESS: Patsey, 076; Permelia, 015; Peter, 076
LAWRENCE: Camilla, 015; Joseph, 038, 049, 052; Martha Ann, 154; Nicholas, 120; Richard, 015, 052; Richd., Lt., 201; Samuel, 167
LAWSON: Lizzie (chldn. of), 015; M. C., Mrs., & 1 ch., 087; M. C., Mrs., 086; Matilda C. & (1 ch.), 083
LAZARUS: Morris, 043
LEA: Burrell, 167; Burwell, 071, 168; Edmund, 168; Elizabeth F., 135; Elizabeth, 085, 141; Green, 027, 043, 044, 167; H. C., Capt., 120; Henry C., 168; James, 168; John, 125, 135, 168; Jonathan, 037; Joseph, 135, 168; Martin, 112, 204; Martin, Sgt., 202; Mary, 158; Nancy, 157; Noal, 043; Sally, 171; Temple, 027, 043, 044, 049, 058; Wyatt, 218
LEADBETTER: Joseph, 168
LEAK: James, 015; Robert, 033, 215, 216
LEANIER: James N., 169
LEARD: Polly, 173; Samuel, 167; William, 072
LEASON: Mary, 151
LEAVENWORTH: Mark, 043
LEBEN: Joseph B., 043
LECONTE: Harriet, 049; Lewis, 169; William, 168
LECROY: William K., 081
LEDBETTER: Bud, 094; F.S.E., 083; Femmy, 134; Frances S.E., 083, 084; Frances, 100; Francis, Mrs. (1 ch), 096; Gilbert Martin, 134; Gilbert, 168; Joseph Henry, 134; Joseph, 109, 120; Martha O., 091; Martin G., 073; Mary Ann, 134; Mary, 090, 093;

Mauivia E., 094; Sis, 092; Sophia, 134; William, 043; Williamson, 043; Wm. (orphans of), 091
LEE(GEE?): Nancy, 090
LEE: Aaron, 086, 095; Amanda, 135; Burwell, 135; Charles B., 071; Dolly, 155, 183; Elizabeth, 073, 080, 084, 095, 102; Elizabeth, Mrs., 073; Esther, 083, 085, 095; George, 077; Harriett, 176; Isaac Y., 091; James, 135; Johathan, 025; John F., 110; John H., 080; John W., 015; John, 015, 043, 091, 168; Johnathan, 015, 215; Jonathan, 219; Joseph, 074, 075;
LEE: Judith, 015; Judy, 085, 220; Julia, 091; Malinda, 159; Martha, 183; Martin, 1st Sgt., 127; Mary A., 091; Mary, 145, 151; Nancy A., 093; Nancy, 083, 099; Nathan, 168; Permelia, 164; Rebecca A., 091; Rosetta, 091; Sally, 157; Sandford, 015; Sarah Ann, 142; Temple, 037; Theophilus, 043; Thomas, 091, 135, 168; Wiat, 033; William, 043; Wm. Y., 091; Wm., 073; Wyatt & 5 chldn., 084; Wyatt, 085, 168, 221; Wyatt, Jr., 169; Wyett, & fam., 095
LEEB: Arthur J., 043
LEEPER: Allen, 043; Hugh B., 120
LEET: Arthur Irwin, 169
LEFTWEEK: John T., 026
LEGG: Eliza, 152; Thomas, 050, 057, 167
LEGGETT: William, 042
LEGON: Robert, 168
LEGUIRE: Lott M., 080
LEGWYN: Lott, 209
LEIGH: Elizabeth, 133; Hartwell, 133; Joseph, 133; Mary, 133; Sally, 133; Wiat, 133
LEMAND: Robert F., 043
LEMBAUGH: Cutliff, 115
LENAES: Charles, 043
LENDER: Charles, 204
LENEER: Elizabeth, 219
LEONARD: John, 169; Patrick, 043, 049; Stephen, 122
LEPFORD(SEPFORD?): H.F.M.M., 079
LEROY: Benja., Sgt. 210; Joseph M., 087
LESERVER: T. W. B., 097
LESSETER: Gray B., 168
LESTER: A.L., 043; A.N. (chldn. of), 015; Aaron, 096; Betty, 222; Catherine A., 220; Elenor, 088; Elijah R. (chldn. of), 015; Elizabeth S., 153; Emily, 015; Francina, 221; Henry, 168; James, 043, 074, 081, 088, 099, 122, 221; Lelia, 221; Lewis, 015, 169, 221; Martha Ann, 088; Mary, 097, 147, 222; Ned, 015; Patman, 015, 169; Susan, 220; Talbot N., 088; Thomas H., 072; Thomas J., 169; Thomas, 072; William P. (chldn. of), 015
LESUERE: Louisiana, 170
LETLOW: Abraham, 168
LEVANS: Jessey, 167
LEVINS: James, 032; Whiney, 167
LEWE: James, 095
LEWIS: A. L., 211; Aaron, 109, 119; Gilley, 035; John L., 109, 211; Judith A., 015; Martha, 134; Massey, 134; Nicholas, 043; Polly, 134; Richard, 077, 167; Richd., 134; Sarah, 099; William, 222
LIGHFIELD: M. A., 056; Manried, 036
LIGON: Cesar, 015; Heleney, 169; James, 015, 028, 043, 056, 060, 061, 201; James, Capt., 120, 202, 203; James, Sgt., 129; Jos. Jr., 205; Jos., 116, 118; Jos., 1st Lt., 125; Jos., Lt., 130, 205; Joseph (Liggon), 043; Joseph, 028, 037, 043, 060, 062, 063, 108, 112, 119, 123, 124, 217; Joseph, 1st Lt., 127; Joseph, Ens., 202; Joseph, Lt., 206, 207; Joseph, Maj, 210; Joseph, Sr., 015; McWhorten, 061; Robert (chldn. of), 015; Robert F., 169; Robert, 015, 035, 048, 051, 053, 058, 066, 076, 107, 108, 118, 119, 126, 206; Robert, 2nd Sgt., 128; Robert, Adj., 210; Robert, Sgt., 205, 206; Thomas, 043
LIKENS: Thomas M., 024; Thomason, 024
LIKINS: Thoams M., 024
LILES(?): Lunian (?), Mrs., 090
LILLEY: Edmund, 169
LILLY: Edward, 015; Sarah A., 015
LIMBARD(LAMBARD): Charles B., 169
LIMBAUGH(?): Cutliff, 209
LIMON: Wm. C., 071
LIN: Thomas, 213
LINCECUM: Linda, 167
LINDER: Charles, 204
LINDSAY: John, 062
LINDSEY: Jas., 097
LINNEBOURG (?): Cutliff, 210
LINSY: Samuel, 147
LINTEN: Alexander B., 043; John S., 043
LINTON: A. B., 015; B., 045; John S., 169; John S., Lt., 110; John, Sr. (chldn. of), 015; Lucy Ann, 015
LIPFORD: H. F. M. M., 079
LIPHAM: Aaron, 043; Henry, 167
LITTLE: Charles, 094; Cyrus W., 094; Cyrus, 094; George, 094; Mary R., 094; Rebecca, 102; Robert, 094; Saml., 094; Thomas, 055; William, 168
LITTLEPAGE: Thomas W., 043; Thomas, 208; Thos., 114
LIVINGSTON: Emiline, 054
LLOYD: Edward, 167; James Harman, 168; James Harmon, 067; James W., 036; John, 168; Lewallen W., 168; Moses, Lt.129; Rebecca Francis, 015; Sarah A., 015; Sarah Ann, 145; Thomas O., 168; Thomas, 038
LOANOAR: George, 220
LOCKETT: Reuben, 107
LOCKHART: Judith, 069
LOCKLIN: --, 095; Elizabeth Ann, 163; James E., 168
LOCKWOOD: Eleazer, 043
LOFTEN: Samuel, 043
LOGAN: Charles, 044
LOGINN: Wm., 133
LOGUIN: William, 168
LOMBARD: Charles B., 015, 052
LOMICE: Simon, 049
LONG: Berry, 037; Crawford W., 015; Elizabeth, 015; Frances T., 003; H.R.I., 056; H.R.I., Dr., 169; Susan J., 015; Willie Julian, 015; Willie, 039
LOOKER: Epsebeth, 182
LORD (LARD?): Robert, Jr., 167
LORD: Archibald, 015; Benjamin B., 015, 029, 038, 044, 047, 048, 052; Ebanazer, 044; Ebenezer, 015, 029; Ebinezar, 048; Elizabeth, 015; Margaret, 015; Martha, 164; Mary, 091; Rebecca (1 ch), 096; Robinson, 044; Ryan (Myas?):167; William, 015
LORDS: B., 213
LOVE: Daniel H., 053; David A., Capt., 120; David H., 023, 032; David, 053, 058; Henry H., 067; Hugh, 044; Mary, 173; Peter E., 169; Robert, 028, 030, 032, 044, 053, 060, 066, 067; William, 044, 052, 057, 060, 167
LOVEING: Grandirson F., 168
LOVEN: Martha C., 083; Mary C., & 1 ch., 087; Mary C., 086
LOVIN: Elijah, Ensgn, 201; Martha C., 083; Salley, 143
LOVING: Elijah, 167; Elijah, Lt., 202, 203; Maria, 175; Mary, 187; Richd., Sgt., 129; Sanford (chldn. of), 015; Susannah, 147; Thomas R., 169; Thomas, 167; William C., 169
LOW: Andrew, 062; George, 043, 044; John H., 037; John, Col., 220; Thomas F., 075
LOWE: --, 037; Abram, 028; Amey, 084, 086, 095; Catherine E., 168; Ellen, 179; Eudosia, 163; Isaac, 081, 168; James B., 073, 168; Jno H., 121; Jno. A., Lt. Col., 125; Jno. H., Lt. Col., 127, 204, 207; Jno. H., Maj., 202; Jno. H., Sr., 075; Joe B., 015; John A., Sr., 044; John H., 015, 044, 052, 071, 079, 081, 110, 111, 122, 167, 168, 218; John H., Adj., 129; John H., Jr., 074, 168; John H., Lt. Col., 105; John H., Maj., 124, 127, 203, 204; John H., Q.M., 210; John H., Sr., 044, 073, 074; John L., Maj., 202; John N., Lt. Col., 130; Nancy C., 172; Robert, 044; Sarah, 015, 153; Thomas F., 054, 072, 073, 074; Thomas J., 075; Thomas, 028, 044, 112, 121, 122, 203, 205; Thos. F., 076; Thos. L., Capt., 121; Thos., 128; Walter H., 015; William T.,081; William, 040, 053
LOWERY: John W. F., 168; Levi, 044; Owen, 107; Sarah J., 180
LOWRY: William S., 168
LOYAL: Elizabeth, 141; Francis, 015
LOYD: Frankey, 160; James H., 034; John, 167; Thomas, 038; William, 214
LRNOLD?: Wm., 079
LUALLEN: William, 044
LUCAS: Frederick W., 048; Martha S., 015; Silas E., 003
LUCKIE: James, 024; Jas., 071
LUCKY: Carline, 100
LUCUS: H. E., Mrs., 090
LUCY: Cobb, 044
LUIS: Zebede, 167
LUITTE: Susan M., 044
LUKE: Anna, 162; Elizabeth, 161; Frances, 087; Henry B., 088, 169; Joseph, 087; Margry E., 087; Martha, 088, 099, 102, 142; Nancy D., 164; Nancy, 087; Susannah, 168
LUMBAUGH: Cuttey, 208
LUMPKIN: Callie M., 167; Charles M., 015; Edward P., 015; Edwin King, 015; Elizabeth W., 186; Frank, 015; George (chldn of), 015; George R., 015; George W., 015; George, 044; Joseph Henry, 015, 050; Joseph J., 221; M. G., 052; Martha (Atalanta), 196; Mary A. S., 179; Mary Bryant, 015; Miller G., 045; Minnie, 015; Nevill M., 169; Robert C., 015; Samuel P., 015; Samuel, 044; Susan, 163; William, 044; Wilson, 015, 213
LUMPKINS: George W., 168
LUMSDEN: Salley, 143
LUVEN: Richard, 167
LYLE: C., 090; Charles B., 168; David J., 028, 038; David L., 038; Fannie C., 015; James, Sr., 015; Joseph R., 092; Lee M., 042; Margaret C., 093; Mary F., 092; Winney E., 092
LYLES: Dilmus, 044; William Henry, 044
LYMAN: Alethia A., 148
LYNCH: Andrew J., 074; David,

044, 134; Eliza, 134; Jane, 134; Lettice, 044; Munroe, 134; Ulysses, 134
LYNCHES: Capt., 079
LYNDON: A. O. (chldn. of), 015; Oscar, 015
LYONS: C. H. (chldn. of), 015; C. H., 015
MABERY: Rebeca, 163
MABURY: Sandy, 123, 203
MACBURNET: Thomas, 170
MACCRERRY: William, 044
MACINTYRE: Archibald Thompson, 198
MACK: Daniel, 015
MACKY: Peter, 044
MACON: (chldn. of), 015; Alethia, 015; T. G., Mrs., 090; Thomas G., 030, 043, 044, 075
MACUIN: Anthony, 043
MACUION: Anthony, 044
MADAW: William, 107
MADDOCKS: Ann, 173
MADDOX: Betsy, 160; Elizabeth, 141; Frances D., 170; J. A., 015; James, 044; John C., 015; Joseph, 015, 044; William, 120, 208; William, Sgt. 210; Wm. D., Maj., 111; Wm., 114
MADDUX: Judith, 169; Martha Ann S., 187
MADOX: Mary, 185
MAGBEE: Hiram, 015
MAGEE: Rachel V., , 093; Sarah, 093
MAGOWEN: Robert, 036
MAHO: Elizabeth, 143
MAHONEY: Dennis, 044; William, 044
MAHONY: Dennis, 044; William, 061
MAINE(?): John G., Sgt., 207
MAINE: Alexander, 044; John G., Lt., 126; Mathew, Sgt., 203
MAJOR: Daniel, 075, 076, 171; Danl., Jr., 072; Elijah F., 172; Paul, 044
MAJORS: David, Lt., 120
MALCOM: Baby, 221; D. H., 102; Elizabeth, 101; G. W., Mrs., 101; James R., 080, 221, 222; John H. C., 082; Molly, 222
MALCOMB: Barnett, 220; D. H., 101; Edna, 015; Elder Geo. W., 220; G. W., Mrs., 099; George W., Rev., 146
MALCOME: Albert, 222; Augustus J., 221; G. W., 222; James D., 221; Jimmy, 222; John C., 222; Lillian, 222; Thomas, Mrs., 221
MALLARD: B., 103; John, 103, 119
MALLORY: Henry, 015
MALON: Martin H., 015
MALONE: Elizabeth, 174; Isaac, 015; John, 015, 036, 049, 056; Joicey, 173; Ludwell, 2nd Sgt., 127; Ludwell, Sgt., 202; Madison, 044; Mary, 161; Nancy, 171; Phoebe, 015; Polly, 076; Robert (chldn of), 015; Robert, 044; Simeon, 076; Stephen, 112, 121, 204; Steven, 044; William, 015
MAN: Milly, 015
MANDEVILLE: A.S., 057; Eliza, 015
MANE (?): L., Ens., 203
MANER: John, 108
MANGUM: T. B., 015
MANING: Semeon D., 170
MANLAY: Sarah Ann, 173
MANLEY: --, 053, 054; William, 042, 044, 045, 048, 049, 058, 060, 108, 118, 171, 203, 204, 207, 210; William, Lt., 210; Wm., 103, 116, 117
MANLY: --, 053; William, 044, 051, 107, 112, 203; Wm.,Lt., 206, 207
MANN: Alfred T., Rev., 147; Baker, 044; Jonathan (chldn. of), 015
MANNIG: Gilly, 184
MANNING: --, 044; James, 058
MANOR: Jno. Y., 204
MANTEY: William, 043
MANUEL: Millie, 015
MANUS: Eva, 101; Eveline V., 096; George E., 096; Thomas A., 096
MAPP: John F., 171; Littleton, 015, 044
MARABEL: John, 034; Mathew, 044; Robert, 043; William, 034
MARABLE: America J., 186; Augustine W. (chldn. of), 015; Augustine W., 015, 039; Christopher, 076; George, 171; Hannah, 086, 095; Jane, 149; Jno. B., 113; Jno., 107; John (chldn. of), 015; John B., 121, 206; John, 015, 026, 031, 044, 056, 115, 117; M., 116; Martha Almira, 175; Minnie S. (chldn. of), 015; Mohn, 107; Richd., 115; Robert (chldn. of), 015; Robert, 015, 072, 074, 076, 115, 171; Robt., 076, 107; Seytha, 168; William A., 015; William, 072; Wm., 107
MARBURY: Leonard, 015; Sandy, 112, 116
MARE: Loyd, Ensgn, 205
MARES: Lloyd, Sgt., 203; Loyd, Ens., 125
MARK: John, 056
MARKS: Myer, 015; S., 024; Simon, 015
MARONEY: Neathy C., 086
MARONY: Caroline, 101
MARR: Lloyd, Ens., 127
MARRABLE: Catherine, 161; Elizabeth B., 154; John, 111; Lucy, 144; Mathew, 112, 122; Matthew, 171
MARRITON(?): Jason, Lt., 207
MARRS: LLoyd, 170; Loyd, 114
MARS: Lloyd, 209
MARSH: Alex R., 015; Mordical L., 061
MARSHAL: Frances, 116; Francis, 128, 205
MARSHALL: Charlotte T., 004; Clarence, 015; Elizabeth, 101; Feby H., 158; Frances, 121; Francis, 015, 025, 111, 113, 130; Lafayette, 172; M. R., 044; W. L., 044; William H., 172; William, 044
MARSS: Samuel, 112
MARTAIN: John, 050
MARTEN: Mary, 097
MARTENDALE: 3 children, 132; Jesse, 132
MARTIAL: Francis, 122
MARTIN: --, 031, 109; Alexander, 172; Calender, Mrs., 093; Calinder, Mrs., 090; Dicy E., 016; Eliza A. E., 092; Eliza Gray, 154; George W., 016; George, 016; Isaac, 170; Isaac, Sgt., 207; J.V., 099; Jack, 198; Jacob, 016, 112, 201; James G., 169, 171; James, 044, 109, 120, 208; Jas., 114; John A. (chldn. of), 016; John A., 016, 111;
MARTIN: John, 044, 073; Julia V., 093; Mary, 016, 093; Murdock, 111; Nancy C., 145; Polley, 148; Rebecca N., 150; Robert, 016, 026, 031, 044, 062, 094, 171; Robert, Capt., 117, 201; Robt., 201; Robt., Capt., 129; S.A., 100; S. C., Miss, 016; Sarah (3 ch), 096; Sinthy, 167; William (chldn. of), 016; William C., 171
MARTINDALE: Jesse, 112, 124, 170, 204; Jesse, Sgt., 203; John, 037, 055, 060; John, Capt., 128, 129; Nancy, 171
MASEY: John, 121
MASH: Alexander, 170; Henrietta, 016, 149; Moricai, 033
MASON: --, 030; Emily, 044; Henry Lamar, 016; John C., 044; Thomas, 171; Wiley W., 207; William, 016, 075, 171; Wm., 208
MASSEY: John, 114, 209
MASSY: John, 208
MASTEN: Jas. G., Capt., 120
MASTERS Milford, 172; Pinckney, 172; William J., 172
MASTIN: George T., 172; James C., 046, 062; Mary Ann, 167; Thomas V., 171
MATHER: William, 074
MATHERS: Jos., 116
MATHES: James D., 074
MATHEWS: B. J., 016; Burwell, 112, 170; Cady, 165; Caroline, 149; Charles L., 044; Elbert, 171; Elizabeth, 179; Emily, 168; Gabl. J., 120; Gabl., 121; Gabriel F., Sgt., 202; Gabriel T., 029, 211; Gabriel T., 1st Cpl., 126; James D., 074; James, 075, 110, 112, 171, 203; James, Sgt., 206; Jeremiah, 171; Jeremiah, Jr., Lt., 125; Jeremiah, Lt., 203; John A., 122; John R., 044, 172; John, 171, 172, 209; John, Lt., 210; Leroy C., 044; Mary Ann, 181; Mary, 153; Paul Bell, 131; Polly, 177; Sandford, 081; Sarah, 144; Willie L., 016; Wm., 099; Wm., Cpl., 205
MATHIS: Archd., 129; Gabreal F., 171; Gabriel T., 079, 115, 208-210; Wm., 074
MATHISON: Elizabeth, 213
MATTHEWS: Agnes, 172; Anderson, 039; Catherine, 172; Charles L., 045; Ella, 069; James D.(chldn. of), 016; James D., 016; Jennie B., 016; Jesse, 016; John A., 172; John R. (chldn. of), 016; John R., 016; L.C., 172; Louisa, 169; Lucy O., 016; M., Doc., 069; Martha Ann, 141; Martha E., 016; Mary E., 016; Mary, 016; Mildred Elizabeth, 172; R. D. (chldn. of), 016; Robert D., 016; W. F., 045; W. H., Mrs., 016; William F. (chldn. of), 016; William F., 016; William, 016; Wm. F., 069; Wm., 117
MATTOCK: William, 205
MATTOCKS: Lanty, 171; William, Sgt., 203
MATTOX: Clementine, 141; James G., 045; William, 120, 130; Wm., 113
MAULDIN: Sarah, 101
MAULDING: Cassisd, 096; Josephine E., 096; Sarah A., 096
MAUPIN: Fayette, 056; LaFayette, 016
MAVABLE: John, 056; Matthew, 047
MAXEY: Albert J., 016; Andrew Johnson, 089; Ann, 166; Augustus R., 045, 081; Barbary A., 173; Booz, 016; Boze, 045, 222; E. E. Mc P. B., 016; Edward A., 126; Edward H., 016, 023, 033, 055, 059, 067, 114, 208; Edward H., Lt., 206, 207; Edward, 068, 113, 130, 171, 205; Edward, 1st Sgt., 127; Edwd., 128; Elizabeth A., 168; Elizabeth, 016; Fanny, 182; Frances S., 101; Francis S., Mrs, 096;
MAXEY: George W., 045; Harriett, 031, 082; Harriott, 134; Henry, 016; Ido Udoro, 089; Isaac J., 096; James, 096; Japer, 221; Jeremiah, 063, 067, 171; John (chldn. of), 016; John G., 111, 171, 172; John H., 134, 172; John, 016, 096; Joseph (chldn of), 016; Joseph, 016; Josiah, 016, 031, 134; Lucenda, 134, 146; Martha H., 186; Mary Catherine, 089; Matilda, 082; Millard, 096; Nancy, 146; Peggy, 166; Tegey, 166; William Dawson, 089
MAXFIELD: Richard, Ensgn, 204;

Richd., Ens., 124
MAXWELL: Elizabeth, 159; Greene M., 172; Martha T., 087; Richard, 128, 204; Richard, Ens., 203; Sarah H., 016
MAY: Elizabeth, 045; Lewis, 045
MAYBERRY: Sandy, 203
MAYER: A. N., 109, 119; Adrian N., 109; Serenus A., 109
MAYES: Sterling, 170
MAYFIELD: Charles, 024; Malinda, 024; Sarah, 171; Thomas, 016
MAYNARD: Robert J., 050; Robert, 066
MAYNE: Allison, 077; Charlie, 059; Emily, 077; Geo. S. (chldn. of), 016; James P. (chldn. of), 016; John A., 016; John G., Lt., 123, 201, 202; John G., Sgt., 206; John W., 016; John William, 172; Mathew, 2nd Sgt., 127; Rhoda, 085; Sintha, 157; Susan D., 079; Susan E., 169; Virginia E., 081
MAYNOR: John Y., 112, 204
MAYO: Samuel, 058
MAYRES: Adnan N., 109
MAYS: Levi, 016; Lucy Ann, 016; S. J., 045; Seaborn J., 045; Seaborn T., 045
MAYSE(?): Adrian N., 211
MCALLISTER: Joseph L., 017
MCALLOUGH: Cathren, 151
MCALPHIN: Jincy, 181; John, 169, 208; Patsey, 149
MCALPIN: Jno., 114, 169; John, 208; R. T., Dr., 017; Robert, 017; Sarah P., 090
MCAY (MCKAY? MAY?): Wm. B., Mrs., 091
MCBEE: James, 017; Tabitha, 171
MCBOYDE: James, 045; John, 045
MCBURNEY: William, 045, 063
MCCAIN: John E., 170
MCCALAHAN: Moses, 114
MCCALL: E. J., 170
MCCALLAM: Susannah, 185
MCCALLUM: Martha, 168; Rutha, 152; Vicy, 179; William, 033
MCCALPEN: Alexander, 170
MCCANE: A., 116; Alexander, 112, 122; Elxander, 203; Susan, 173
MCCANN: Patrick, 150
MCCARLY: Anna, 161
MCCARTAN: Thomas, 045
MCCARTER: James J., 045
MCCARTERS: Elias, 080
MCCARTNEY: Nancy, 167; Syna, 165
MCCARTY: Elizabeth, 169; Hannah, 017; James, 169' Sarah, 186
MCCAY: Charles F., 170; Elizabeth, 143; Thomas, 045
MCCLAIN: Bennett H., 072; Martha, 101
MCCLENDON: Rachel, 141
MCCLEROY: James, Capt., 124, 203, 204, 210; James, Lt., 124, 126, 202, 203; Mark, Cpl., 205
MCCLESKEY: Alice, 068; David M., 017, 080; Georgia Bell, 017; Greene L. (chldn. of), 017; Henderson, 068; James W., 170; William W., 017
MCCLESKY: John, 045
MCCLURE: Elizabeth, 149
MCCOLLOUGH: John J., 045
MCCOLLUM: Sarah, 186; William, 218
MCCOLM: Nancy, 161
MCCOLOUGH: Elizabeth, 169; James, 169
MCCOMBS: Nelson, 017; Robert, 074
MCCOMMON: James, 017
MCCONNELL: --, 056; John, Jr., 056
MCCORD: James L., 045; James, 017
MCCOWEN: George Francis, 017
MCCOY: Abner, 107; Henry, 017; John Thomas, 170; Leroy, 169; Lucy Ann, 166; Nancy, 149, 184; Patsey, 143; Thomas M., 056; Thomas, 217
MCCREA: Robert, Sgt. 206
MCCREE: Alexander, 045; Benj., 076; Francis M., 170, 219; Isabella, 158; John, 112, 124; Joseph H., 170; Jourdan, 017; Mary Ann, 172; Robert A., 063, 209; Robert A., Capt., 210; Robert, 112, 123, 124, 205; Robert, 1st, Cpl., 127; Robert, 3rd, Sgt., 126; Robert, Cpl., 125; Robt. A., Lt. Col., 109; Thomas, 4th Sgt., 127; William, 045, 047, 050, 053, 054, 062, 063; Wm., 079
MCCRISTON: Jesse, 024
MCCRUE: William, 024
MCCUE: William, 216
MCCUEN: Mary Ann, 084; Mrs., 085
MCCULLEN: Richard T., 082
MCCULLOCH: James, 115
MCCULLOCK: Saml., 071
MCCULLOUGH: James, 169; William, 017; William, Sgt., 203
MCCUNE: Betsy, 184; Nancy, 157; Robt., 107; Sarah, 150; Thos., 129
MCCURDY: James (chldn. of), 017; James G., 017
MCCURE: George W., 062
MCCURVIN: Anthony, 034
MCDANIEL: Felghman, 208; Henry D., 045; John, 207; Mary Jane, 175; Telman, 114
MCDANIELL: John, 170
MCDANNIEL: John, 169
MCDARMAN: M. K., 083
MCDERMED: P. W., 039
MCDERMENT: Charlotte, 148
MCDERMOND: P. W., 039, 049
MCDILL: Newton, 045
MCDONALD: A., Maj., 129; Alexander, 028, 046; Archd., 075; Archibald, 073; Catherine, 157; D. A., Mrs., 090; Daniel, Sgt. 206; Danil, 170; David A., 091, 093; Howel C., 091; Howell, 093; Hulda A., 093, 094; J., Miss, 091; Keslah, 133; Thomas, 133
MCDONNALL: Alex, Maj., 126
MCDONNELL: Alexander, 024, 056, 058, 060; Daniel, Sgt. 207; John, 205
MCDONOUGH: Sarah G., 180
MCDORMONT: Ballard, 112
MCDOUGALD: Elizabeth, 098, 100
MCDOUGALL: Elizabeth, Mrs., 095
MCDOUGLE: John E., 081
MCDOWELL: William A., 017; Willie, 017
MCDUFFIE: Nancy M., 181
MCDUMMOND: Elaland, 180
MCDURMENT: Ballard, 170
MCDURMOND: Bullard, 202
MCEKELHANNON: Hy, 114; Josiah, 114
MCELHANNON: Christopher, 025
MCENTIRE: Catherine, 220
MCEVEN: John, 054
MCFALLS: Olivia, 167
MCGARTER: Hugh, 128
MCGAUGHEY: Andrew J., 170; James H., 170; Tho. J., Rev., 145
MCGEE: Adam, 045; Felix, 169; James (chldn. of), 017; James, 017, 214; John, 169
MCGINTY: Henry C., 017
MCGIVINS(?): Thompson, Capt., 111
MCGOVERN: John, 045
MCGOWAN: Dorcas, 168
MCGOWEN: Robert, 045, 051
MCGUIRE: Lewis L., 045; Mrs., 099
MCGUIVE: Thompson, 026
MCGWIER: Lewis, 119
MCHANAN: Celisha, 100
MCHANNA: Mary, 094; Sarah, 094
MCHANNON: Malissa, 094
MCHENRY: James, 062
MCINTIRE: Charles, 045
MCKANE: Alexander, 203
MCKEE: Lewis, 169; Robert A., 062; Saml., 117; Samuel, 017, 111, 213
MCKENZIE: Daniel, 082
MCKENZY: George, 123
MCKERN: Mary Ann, 081
MCKEY: Cintha, 143
MCKIE: John S. (chldn. of), 017; Mary E., 017
MCKIGNEY: B., 045; Beattie, 045; Beaty, 017; Rebeakah, 067; William, 045
MCKIGNY: Martha, 143
MCKINE: --, 196
MCKINLEY: Archibald C., 045; Charles G., 024, 035, 037, 048, 050, 058, 062, 170; Ebenezer B., 109, 211; William, 035
MCKINLY: Archibald C., 045; Charles G., 170
MCKINNE: John, 052
MCKINNEY: Mollie, 017; R. W., 017; Samuel, 045; Zora, 017
MCKINNON: West, 061
MCKINZEY: George, 111
MCKINZIE: Alexander, 029; William, 170
MCKLEROY: Anna, 133; Christianna, 133; James, 123, 133, 204; Robert S., 170; William, 133, 170
MCKNIGHT: James F., 170
MCLAIN: M. A., 084; Martha, 084
MCLANE: Wm. T., 084
MCLAUGHIN: Gerard, 036; Mrs., 085
MCLAUGHLIN: Elizabeth (1 ch), 095; Elizabeth, 098, 100; Nancy, 095; Nathaniel, 170; Polly, 095
MCLECROY: Mark L., 080; Thomas, 080; William, 080
MCLENDON: Rozana, 086
MCLEOD: John, 134; Malcolm, 134; Malcom, 218; Neal, 134; Sally B., 134
MCLEROY: --, 079, 098; Amanda & 5 Chldn., 085; Amanda & 6 chldn., 085; Amanda, 088, 099, 101; Anna, 150; C.H., Mrs., 099; Cicero H., 088; Cicero, 170; Cicero, Mrs., 101, 102; Cornelia (chldn. of), 017; David, 088; Frances O., 087; Francis M., 170; Georgia, 087; Georgian, 087; James M., 081; James R., 095; James, 088, 220; Jas., Capt., 120; Louisiana, 088;
MCLEROY: Manda (7 chldn), 095; Martha N., 183; Martha W., 087; Mary Ann, 098, 100; Mary E. & 2 chldn., 085, 095; Mary H., 087; Maryann, 088; Misouri, 087; Needham, 017, 045; S. J., 088; Sarah, 219; Stephen J., 017; Stephen, 095, 157; William J., 170; William L., 170; William, 087; Wm., Capt., 117
MCLESTER: James G., 017; James, 045
MCLIET (?): Robert, 208
MCLLEROY: James, 211
MCMICHAEL: William, 030, 036, 169
MCMILLIAN: John B., 017
MCMURPHAY: Sarah East, 185
MCMURPHY: Cealia A., 178
MCMURRAY: William, 124
MCNAUGHT: --, 045
MCNEED: William, 027, 045
MCNEES: B. Samuel, 045; William, 045
MCNEILL: Clay King, 017
MCNEY: William, 045
MCNORTON: Jefferson G., 170
MCRAE: Benj., 072
MCREA: R. A., Lt. Col., 120; Robert A., 114, 116
MCREE: Benj., 075; Benjamin, 017, 074; Capt., 134; Eliza Ellen, 088; Elizabeth E., 082; F., 103; Frankie, Mrs.136; George H., 082, 170; Hannah, 086, 095; Isabella, 017; Jacob R., 170; James M., 017; John(chldn. of), 017; John Thomas, 088; John,

017; Joseph H., 081; Joseph, 136; Margaret, 168; Martha E., 155; Mary, 168; Matilda Johnson, 088; Mrs., 134; Nancy, 180;
MCREE: Peggy, 134; Rebecca A., 166; Richard B., 170; Richard, 075; Robert A., 048, 208; Rowan (chldn. of), 017; Rowan, 017, 072-075; Samuel, 123; Sarah A., 183; Susan Jane, 088; Susan M., 145; Susan, 101, 170; Thomas P., 081, 170; Thomas, 134; Thos. P., 101; Thos., Mrs., 088; Titus, 096; William B., 048; William, 017, 048, 079, 134; Wm. B., 122, 170
MCREYNOLD: Hannah, 084
MCSPARN: John (chldn. of), 017; John, 017
MCSPARREN: Polley, 178
MCWHIRTER: Hugh, 169
MCWHORTEN: Hugh, 061
MCWHORTER: Cassandra, 017; Hugh, 112, 116, 123, 201; James H. M., 045; Lizzie (chldn. of), 017; Lizzie, 017; Moses E., 017; William, 017
MEAD: Eliza M., 169; Francis A., 172; Joseph H., 046; Sarah, 159; Susan, 099
MEADDERS: Enoch, 072
MEADE: Henry M., 030
MEADER: Elisabeth K., 092; Susan, 093
MEADERS: Alverado, 092; Amanda, 092; Jas. A., 092; Sarah F., 092
MEADOW: Anna, 134; Reuben, 134; Theophilus, 134; Wm., 134
MEADOWS: Enoch, 045, 054, 062; William, 115
MEADS: Allen (chldn. of), 016; Susan, 086; Susan, Mrs., & 5 chldn., 087
MEALER: James A., 172; Mardaret, Mrs., 090
MECUNE(?): Randal W., 171
MECUNE: Marcy, 176; Martha, 171
MEDDER: Reuben R., 171
MEDDERS: Enoch, 072, 172
MEDDOWS: Susannah, 141
MEDER: Enoch, 072
MEDLEY: Joseph T., 081
MEDLIN: Andrew J., 080
MEDOWS: Elizabeth, 185
MEEKER: Christopher C., 016
MEELER: John H., 092; Margarett A., 093; Mary J., 092
MEGS: Josiah, 038, 044
MEIGS: Josiah, 029, 038, 044
MELL: Edward B., 004; Patrick H., 016
MELTON: Alexander, 122; Eleel, 053, 108; Eleel, 3rd Sgt., 128; Eleel, Sgt., 206; Ethen, 045; Isaac, 043, 045; Jonathan (chldn of), , 016; Jonathan, 016, 024, 042, 213; Lea, 4th Sgt., 127; Lucinda, 161; Mary, 219; Missippina, 156; Moses, 045, 221; Polly, 154; Seal, Sgt., 205; Strom, 073; Stroud, 031, 037, 072, 171; Tabitha, 031, 037, 061; William, 046
MEMNO: Elvira Lee, 016
MENNARD: William, 046
MERCER: Betsy, 184; Jesse, 172; William A., 046, 049
MEREDITH: David, 115
MEREWETHER: David, 033, 051; Geo. W., 118; George W., 126; Goe W., 116; James, Capt., 126, 127, 201; James, Maj., 203, 204; Judith, 160; Stephen, 202; Tony, 051
MERIDITH: Hiram B., 172; Polley, 154
MERIWETHER: Charles, 202; David, 016, 025, 028, 033, 043, 046, 054, 071, 171; Francis H., 029; George Ann, 016; George W., 045, 046, 209; George, 044, 208; James (chldn. of), 016; James, 016, 025, 069, 203; James, Capt., 124, 203, 204; James, Maj., 124, 127, 204; Martha M., 016; Mary Jane, 163; Nancy, 161; Richard, 016; Sarah T., 046; Thos., 208; William (chldn of), 016; William, 016, 030, 044
MERONY: Nathan, 215
MERRETT: Calender C., 159
MERRITT: Berryman G., 016; Celia, 016; Martha P., 175; W.D., 016
MERRIWETHER: George W., 053; George, 053; W. S., 032
MESSER: William, 046
MEWS: George, 120
MICHAEL: Eliza J., 089; James M., 089; John, 089; Louisa, 098; Moina B., 198; Rean, 089; Susan E. & 2 chldn., 085; Susan E., 089, 096, 097, 098, 100; Thomas (chldn. of), 016; Thomas, 089; Thos., (Orphs.) 097; Thos., 089
MIDDLEBROOK: A. C., 074
MIDDLEBROOKS: A. C., 046, 171; Anderson C., 016, 075, 082; Fanne, 182; Isaac, 026, 046; Isaac, Sgt., 202; Mattie Bell, 016; Thomas E., 082; Thos. E. (chldn. of), 016; Zack B., 016
MIDDLETON: --, 122; Benjamin, 171; John, 046; Parker, Lt., 202; Parks, Capt., 124, 126, 201, 202; Parks, Lt., 123; Polley, 184; Robert, 170
MIDLEBROOKS: Isaac, 170
MIERS: Nathan, 026
MILES: Martha, 016; William, 171
MILIGAN: A., 098; Delila, 184
MILLAN: Mrs., (Wife & 3 C), 084
MILLANDON: Laurent, 046
MILLEDGE: John, Lt., 116, 117
MILLEGAN: Archibald, 109
MILLER: Aletha, 089; Alethia, 101; Armstead, 062; Caleb, 023; Daniel W., 172; Ephrain, 046; Francis, Lt., 126; Frederick, 172; George N., 046; Horatis, 046; J. W., 082; James T., 080; James, 046; Jesse, 016; John W., 081, 082, 085, 096, 097; John, Mrs., 098, 100; Joseph L., 082; Joshua M., 172; Joshua, 072, 134; Joshwary, 071; Julia Ann, 089; Litha F., 082; Mary
MILLER: Elizabeth, 089; Mary, 098; Matilda, 134, 162; Mrs., 085; Patsey, 182; Pendleton Mortimer, 172; Peter, 129; Rebecca, 165; Rondia, 055; Roseda, 172; Samuel, 109, 171; Susan Emerline, 089; Thomas Mortimer, 089; Thomas, 100, 172; Thomas, Sgt. 210; W., Mrs., 088; Wiley J., 081; William J., 082; William, 172; Wm. T., Mrs., 102; Yown, Mrs., & 2 chldn., 088
MILLHALLAN: Mrs., 091
MILLICAM: Hugh, Mrs., 102
MILLICAN: Harret, 099; Archd., Mrs., 101; Isaac, 081; James P., 080; Jas. P., 095; Joseph C., 081
MILLIKEN: William, 025
MILLS: Alford, 016; Edward, 025
MILLSAPS: Thomas, 052
MILNER: --, 046; Peter, 111
MILSAPS: Fuller, 171; Thomas, 046; William, 210
MILTON: Eliel, 211; Elijah, 214; Ethan, 046; Hannah E., 046; Isaac, 215; Jane E., 145; Jeremiah, 213; John, 046; Jonathan, 216
MINOR: Elizabeth, 134; Helena, 134; Mary Ann, 134; Samuel S., Sgt., 203; William Henry, 134
MINTER: Robert R., 170
MINTON: Jason, 046, 207
MITCHEL: Robert, 171; Thomas, 024; William, 216; William, Jr., 216; William, Sr., 216
MITCHELL/FONDREN: --, 198
MITCHELL: --, 027; Albert L., 016; Andrew B., 134; Betsy, 143; Elder, 211; Florence, 027; Frances, 134; Giles, 016; Green M., 061, 170, 218; Greene M., Sgt. 210; Henderson, 016; Henry, 049, 109, 112, 171, 204, 205; Henry, 1st Sgt., 127; Henry, Capt., 113, 125-127, 130, 206; Henry, Sgt., 112, 203; Jesse, 204; John, 016, 046; Madison B., Lt., 114; Madison R., 208;
MITCHELL: Madison, 209; Madison, Lt., 206, 207; Mary, 159; Mathew, Sgt., 129; Nancy, 134; S. D. (chldn. of), 016; Saml. D., Capt., 118; Sesley, 157; T., Maj., 201; Thomas R., 046; Thomas, 016, 025, 046, 075, 218; Thomas, Capt., 117; Thomas, Maj., 129, 201; Thos. R., 114; Thos., Capt., 116; William L., 016, 046, 051; William L., Maj., 016; William P., 082; William, 041, 046, 112, 119, 171; William, Jr., 016; Wm. L., 108; Wm. S., Maj., 120
MITCHUM: Nathaniel J., 171
MITT: David, 046
MIXSON: Sariah, 152
MOAN(MOON? MOORE?): Elizabeth, 093
MOBBS: Nathaniel, 071, 135
MOBLEY: Emily, 147; Fleming, 073; Francina, 159; Sophenia A., 148
MOBLY: Jissey, 171
MOCK: John, 117
MOFFET: Gabriel, 046
MOFFETT: G. A., 079, 109; Gabl. A., Capt., 202; Gabl., Capt., 129; Gabriel A., 033-035, 038, 040, 041, 046, 051, 052, 054, 060, 076, 079, 125, 171, 205, 218; Gabriel A., Capt., 126, 202, 203; Gabriel, 048, 211; Gabriela, 027; Henry, 046
MONCREEF: Laban, 209
MONCRIEF: David H., 080; Josiah, 172; Laban, 114, 115, 120, 209, 210; Laban, Sgt. 210
MONROE: John, 171
MONSFIELD: Eli, 046
MONTGOMERY: Absalom (chldn. of), 016; Absalom, 016; Calista A., 016; E.S., Mrs., 096; Elizabeth, 101; Emmett, 096; Johnathan, 081; Jonathan, 110, 172; Nancy, 046; Osker, 096; Rebecca A., 177; Sarah, 096; Thomas, 096, 172; William, 081
MOODLEY: William, 208
MOODY: John W., 060; Samuel, 067
MOON: Collin, 016; Eva, 016; George W., 040, 046, 050, 062; Isaac S., 016; John W., 016; Pleasant J., 172; Sarah, 176; Sue, 097; Susan A., 090; Susan, 016; Thomas, 046; William, 016
MOONE: Elizabeth, 153
MOONEYHAM: Rebecca, 134; William, 134; Wilson, 134
MOORE (COL, FREE): Edy, 076
MOORE: --, 050; A. D., 172; Adeline, 172; Alex, 213; Alexander, 1st Lt., 125, 128; Alexander, 204; Alexander, Lt., 125, 203, 204; Alsa, 016, 024, 110, 172; Ann W., 163; Benjamin P., 028; Benning B., 046; Benning, 119; Caroline V., 164; Charles G., Ens., 126; Charlotty, 178; Duff, 046; Edward, 215; Eleanor, 016; Elijah, 172; Elizabeth T., 152; Elizabeth, 184; Emily G., 161; Emma, 016,

163; Finney H., 044, 046;
MOORE: Finney, 048; Finny H., 046, 058; Frances C., 181; Francis, 016, 053; George W., 027, 030, 037, 038, 041, 046, 049, 051, 054, 056, 058, 059, 061, 076, 079, 124, 204, 205; George, 048; Granesson, Sgt., 202; Henrietta, 016; Henry, 046; Holly, 153; J.W., 016; James J., 125, 204; James J., Capt., 125, 128, 130, 203, 204; James, 134; Jane A., 171; Janet E., 134; Jas. J., Capt., 113; John J., 125; John O., 026; John R., 046; John, 016, 025, 046, 056, 118, 170, 171; John, Capt., 110; Joshua G., 046, 049, 050, 058, 118, 119; Joshua G., Sgt., 206;
MOORE: Leah, 160; Lewis, 112, 113, 130, 204, 205; Lewis, Cpl., 210; Lizzie A., 016; Louis, 128; Lucy H., 175; M. J. D., 103; Martha H., 016; Martin, 204; Mary H., 016, 164; Mary, 145, 157; Memory J. D., 026, 117, 171; Nancy A., 134, 186; R.D., 025; R. H., 123; Richard D., 016, 026, 046, 048; Richard O., 043; Robert H., 027, 048, 076;
MOORE: Robert W. B., 053; Robert, 016, 072, 122, 170, 172; Robertur B., 053; Robertus, 016; Robt., 118; S. W.(?), 107; Sarah C., 167; Sarah, 134; Stephen E., 016; Terisa, 176; Thomas Cobb, 016; Thomas, 016, 027, 036, 037, 046, 047, 062, 066, 067, 077, 112, 172, 218; Wells, 130; William C., 017; William W., 172; William, 017, 047; Willie C., 017; Willis, 113, 128, 205; Wm. R., 4th Cpl., 127; Wm., 107; Zip, 039
MOOREHOD: A., Mrs., 090
MORABLE: Wm., 073
MORCOCK: Family, 198
MORE: Abednego, 060; Thomas, 028
MORELAND: Joseph, 047, 136; Mary M., 150; William B., 136; William, 047
MORGAN: Asa, 214; Gazelle P., 175; George B., 172; Georgia A., 151; James, 060; John C., Sgt., 103, 117; John, Ens., 124; Jonathan, 171; Joshua, 115, 209, 211; Joshua, 1st Lt., 127, 205; Joshua, Ens., 125, 203, 204; Joshua, Lt., 125, 206; Joshua, Sgt., 129; Mary, 167; Ruby, 017; Stokely, 052; William W., 037; William, 047
MORRIS: Carrie M., 043; Casper, 017; Cassie, 017; Charles, 017; Charlotte, 178; E.H., Mrs., 047; Garrett, 056, 109, 211; Hannah, Mrs., 071; Israel, 017; James, 047; Joshua, 103, 109, 117, 172; M. M., Mrs., 017; Mary, 176; Robert, 112, 122 170, 203; Robert, 2nd Sgt., 126; Robt., 116; Rosa, 017; Sarah, 183; Soloman A. (chldn. of), 017; Sylvanus, 004, 197
MORRISON: George, 030, 039; William A., 030, 031
MORROW: Thomas, 034
MORTIN: Mary A. J., 164
MORTON (MARTN?): Joseph F., 172
MORTON: C. P., Mrs., 099, 102; Elizabeth, 156; Emily, 097; Frederick S., 017; Jas. F., 113; Jno. R., 113, 116; Joel J., 074, 172; Joel, 017; John R., 130, 205; John, 017, 047, 073, 108, 118, 119; John, Col., 107, 120; Jos. F., 109, 113; Jos. T., 116; Joseph C., 112, 121; Joseph F., 017, 047, 109, 128, 130, 205, 206; Joseph
MORTON: Finch, 196; Joseph, 047; Josiah, 017; Judith, 017, 216; Lizzie, 017; M.B., 017; M.E., Mrs., 017; Margaret J., 017; Martha W., 174; Martha, 221; Mary Ann, 147; Matilda Harison, 162; Polly, 174; Robert, 017; Sarah Louise, 186; Tabitha, 153; Thomas, 113, 121, 207; Thos., 118; William M., 047, 109; William M., Sgt. 210; William, 047; Wm.M., 118, 211; Wm., 109
MOSE: Thomas, 017
MOSEBY: Misses, 134; Thomas Jefferson, 134
MOSELEY: James T., 081; Mathew, 170; Peter, 047, 171; Sally, 047; Thomas (chldn of), 017
MOSELY: Peter, 043, 047; Sally, 043, 047
MOSEMAN: Bessa Leana, 131
MOSES: Aaron J., 047; Henry, 044
MOSS: --, 047, 196; Alford, 126; Alfred, 208; Alfred, Sgt., 207; Amanda M., 164; Daisy, 017; Emma, 017; Frances, 144; John (chldn of), 017; John D., 017, 047; John, 056; Jos., Cpl., 205; Joseph, 047, 052, 113, 116, 171, 206, 210, 211; Joseph, 4th Cpl., 128; Joseph, Cpl., 128; Joseph, Q.M., 129; Julia P., 196; Mary, 183; Milly, 186; Polley, 160; Reuben, 073; Rufus L., 172, 196; Salley, 017; Sally, 178; Susan, 142; Thomas, 017; William, 044, 112, 130; Willis, 017, 171, 210; Willis, 4th, Sgt., 126; Willis, Sgt., 206, 210; Wm., 116
MOTES: Zachariah, 047
MOTON: Nancy, 178
MOTT: Nathaniel, 172
MOULTON: John, 109, 211
MOULTRIE: Briggs B., 047
MOUNCE: John R., 172
MOUNGER: Elizabeth M., 161
MOYNIHAN: Thomas, 017
MOZELEY: James T., Mrs.098
MOZELY: Thomas J., 171
MUCKLE: James, Lt., 126; Needham, 4th, Sgt., 126
MUCKLEHANNON: Francis, 208; Hezekiah, 208; Isaiah, 208
MUFFETT: Gabriel A., Capt., 120
MUFFITT: Peggy, 167
MULLENS: Nancy, 180
MULLIN: Elizabeth, 153
MULLINS: Elizabeth, 093, 099; Robert S., 087
MURDEN: Dora, 017
MURDOCK: Bartlett W., 033, 055; Joseph, 042, 047; Robert, 047
MURF: Samuel, 203
MURPHET: Gabreel, Sgt., 129
MURPHEY: Lewis, 109; Paschal, 047
MURPHY: John W., 056; Paschal, 035, 047
MURR: George, Sgt. 210; Loyd, 208
MURRAY: --, 047; C.W., 220; Cain, 084, 086, 095; Ellen, 085; George, 083, 095; James E., 081; John F., 066, 081; Joseph H., 081; Samuel J., 047; Samuel, 047; Sarah J., 080, 163; William H., 017, 172; William J., 048; William, 047, 048, 062, 108, 119, 205; Wm. H., 220; Wm., 077, 110, 118, 124
MURRELL: Catherine C., 017; Clinton H., 017; George M., 033
MURUBL: Hannah, 084
MUSE (?): George, 210
MUSE: Emely, 090; Emily Antenette, 159; George, 079; George, Sgt., 203
MUSGROVE: William St. L., 170
MYERS: Adrian, 120; Moses, 017; Serenus A., 120
MYGATT: George, 017
MYRICK: David J., 080
NABERS: James B., 048; Mary L., 180; William, 017, 073, 173; Wm., 074, 075
NAIL: Elisha, 017; Joseph, 173
NALL: Eldridge, 206; Eldridge, 3rd, Sgt., 126; Eldridge, Lt., 205; Henry, 182; Lur, 185; Martin, 051; Mary, 182; Richard, 017
NALLS: Eldred, Sgt., 202; Nathan, 173; Phetney, 154
NAMELESS: ?, 084, 095
NANCE: Jno., 113; John, 017, 059, 117, 120, 128, 130, 205; Mary Ann, 175; Reuben, 017, 031; Wesley, 076, 099; William M., 173
NAPIER: Thomas, 053
NASH: Abner, 017
NASON: Hugh M., 136; J.F., 122; James, 136; Richard, 136
NASWORTHY: Henry, 107, 115
NATIONS: William Jasper, 032
NAUNIUS: Joseph T., 081
NEAL: Mayo, 017; R. S., 111; W. N., 017
NEELY: Charles L., 048; David, 052
NEGLE: James, 173
NEGRO?: Creasy, 077; Jerry, 077; Massey, 077; Tilman, 077; William Annie Florence, 077
NEIGHBORS: William, 109
NEILSON: John, 215
NEILSON: John, 215
NEISLER: Anne R., 153; Frances E., 165; Hugh & fam(?), 216; Hugh M., 118; Hugh, 017, 027, 039, 040, 043, 048-050, 054, 117, 217; Susan H., 172
NELMS: F. J., 097; Francis T., Mrs., 091
NELSO: John, 048
NELSON: Nod., 215; Samuel, 048
NESBETT: Miles C., 129
NESBIT: James, 017; John, 048, 196; Mary A., 048; Penelope, 017
NESBITT: Martha D., 017; Mary W., 017
NEVITT: Harry M.,017; John W., 017
NEWBURY: Hopkins, 213
NEWELL: Lott, 048
NEWHALL: George, 048
NEWMAN: --, 031
NEWSON: Elizabeth, 160
NEWTON (?): Welborn, 208
NEWTON: Andrew Jackson, 131; Capt., 202; Catherine, 017; Charlotte, 017, 091; Clary, 017; Cornelia C., 187; E. L., 017, 032, 071; Ebanezer, 048, 060; Ebencar, 213; Ebenezer, 025, 114, 208; Ebenzer, 066; Ebinezar, 048; Eliza L., 035; Elizabeth, 154; Elizar L., 030; Elizar Z., 032; Elizer L., 023, 024, 039, 060; Elizue L., 017; Elizur L., 034, 046, 048;
NEWTON: Isaac, 172; J. H., 048; J., Col., 120; James, 017, 039; John F., 057; John H., 017, 039, 048, 061, 072; John S., 048; John V., 048; John, 198; Josiah, 023, 024, 030, 035, 039, 040, 047, 048, 056, 058, 066, 116, 173, 203; Josiah, Capt., 126, 129, 203; Josiah, Lt. Col., 210; Josiah, Maj., 121, 124, 125, 127, 130, 203-205, 207; Louisa, 155; M. E., 150; Walter J., 017
NIBLACK: Samuel, 052
NIBLETT: Robert L., 048, 057
NICHALS: Emila, 166; G. M., 083
NICHELSON: Robert, 173
NICHOL: Wolsey, 048
NICHOLS: Barak T., 062; Barak, 062; Basak, 063; Caroline L., 146; Eliza A., 145; Emma, 017, 092; G.W., 098; Henry M., 017; James C., 017; John R., 017; John, Mrs., 098; Lilly, 017; Mary A. (chldn. of), 017; Mary

A., 093; Mary C., 092; Milner, 027; O., Mrs., 099, 101; Obediah, 027; R., 109, 115; Ransom, 028, 039, 048, 076, 121, 218; Ransome, 017; Ranson, 026; Roberta, 017; Wolsey, 048
NICHOLSON: Grady, 040; H.B., 018; James M., 018; James S., 048; James, 173; James, 3rd, Sgt., 126; John B., 048; John W., 018, 040, 173; Martha M., 018
NICKAS (?): James, Mrs., 091
NIESLER: Hugh, 036, 042
NILES: Henry, 173
NINSON: Obadiah, 027
NISBER: John, 048; Thomas C., 048
NISBET: Harriett, 169; John, 034, 036, 048, 049; Sarah A., 168; Thomas C., 049
NISLER: Mary J., 163
NIX: Elizabeth, 083, 187; Jesse, 072; Mary, 083, 091, 093; May, 090
NIXON: Edward P., 054, 173; Edward, Ens., 117; Henry, 018, 173; James, 173, 208, 210; Jas., 209; John, 018; Mary, 156; N., 057; Nahun, 057; Rhoda (chldn of), 018; William, 036
NIXSON: James, 027; William, Sgt., 207
NOBLE: Augustus Hill, 028; William G., 028
NOBLES: Jonathan, 042, 215; Stephen, 115, 213; William, 214, 215
NOELL: Carlton, 018; James R. (chldn of), 018; Thomas, 018; Upson C., 018
NOLAN: Littilia, 086
NOLAND: Thomas, 173
NOPPS: Thomas, 074
NORHAM: Alexander, 036; Jeremiah, M.M.E.C., 145
NORRIS: Benjamin, 107, 117; John Q. A., 018; Julia Ann, 187; Kiddy, 154; Mary, 158; W. J., 220; William J., 018; William, 120; William, Sgt., 203; Willis C., Rev., 142
NORTH: John R., 018; Thomas, 018
NORTHAN: Silas, 113
NORTHINGTON: Samuel, 049
NORTON: John A., 030; John, 110, 111; Salley, 149; Silas M., 173; Silas, 128, 130, 205; Thomas, 173; William, 018, 173
NORWOOD: Caleb M., 049; James, 044
NOTH (NORTH?): Elizabeth, 156
NOTT: John, 4th Sgt., 127; John, Sgt., 202
NOTTEY: ?--, 201
NOWLAN: Richard, 109; Thomas, 109
NOWLAND: Richard, 211
NUMALLY: Aaron F., 027, 041; William, Cpl., 206
NUNELLY: Josiah, 121
NUNNALLY: Aaron F., 037, 041, 049, 054; Aaron, 049; Emily H., 177; J. C., 018; John A., 037, 041, 054, 073; John C., 073, 173; John, 018, 049, 173; M. S. D., 018; Martha A., 150; Mary E., 162; Matilda Adeline, 188; Sarah F., 176; Susan A., 179; Virginia B., 162; William B., 051; William, Sgt. Maj., 210
NUNNALY: John A., 046
NURON: Eley, (ch. of), 213; Eley, 213; Eley, Mrs., 213
NUTT: Agnes, 171; Jane, 149; John, 131, 172; John, Sgt., 130; William B., 173; William, 018, 068, 206; Wm., 113, 129
NUTTING: Benjn., 123
O'CONNER: Henry, 134; John, 134; Juriah, 134
O'DILLON: Sarah, 089
O'FARRELL: Charles, 018
O'NEILL: Hugh, 041
OAKES: Jonathan, 173; Jonathan, 1st Sgt., 125; Jonathan, 3rd, Sgt., 126; Jonathan, Sgt., 203; Susannah, 161
OATES: James S., 018; James, 041, 053, 203, 211; James, Capt., 125, 203, 204; James, Maj., 204, 207, 210; Jas., Capt., 127; Richard W., 041, 077, 079
OATS: James, 041; James, Capt., 130; Richard W., 041, 049; Salley, 181
OBARR: Charity, 176
ODGEN: Joseph H., 052
ODUM: Jordan, 054, 109, 119; Jourdan, 054
OGDEN: Joseph H., 018; Joseph, 173
OGLESBEY: S. H., Mrs., 097
OGLESBY: Anna, 018; George S., 046, 049
OGLETREE: Family, 198
OLDHAM: W. D., 018
OLICER: John, Capt., 120
OLIGSBY: Allen, 036
OLIVER: Amelia G., 188; Francis H. (chldn. of), 018; Francis H., 023, 024, 027, 032, 037, 043, 048, 053, 059, 173; Francis W., 058; James, 035, 202; Jno. L., Rev., 142; John L., 037, 048, 058, 059; John, 027, 059; John, Capt., 124, 127, 202; John, Cpl., 205; John, Sr., 037, 048, 058; Whiting, 173; Whiton, 112, 122, 124; William, 173
OMBERG: N. J., 173
ONAR: Benj. (chldn. of), 018
ONSTEAD: John, 039
OQUILBY: Peter F., 029
ORAER: Meriam, 166
ORMAND: James, 129
ORMOND: James, 026, 034, 046, 057, 112, 201, 202; John, 034, 057
ORR: Christopher, 049; Phillip, 049; Robert, 125, 209; Robert, 3rd, Sgt., 127; Robert, Sgt., 125, 205, 210
ORSBORN: A. C., 088; Barbery H., 088; Elizabeth, 154
OSBERN: A. C., Mrs., 099; Sharlott, 173
OSBORN: Ann, 082; Augustus A.C., 173; Eliza, 145; Florida, 101; Francis W., 173; Francis, 018; J. N., 018; John, 018, 173; John, Lt., 119; Nancy, 018; Nicholas, 018, 056; Sallie C., 018; Thomas, 086, 096
OSBORNE: John F., 082
OSBOURN: John N., 087; John, 173; Sarah C., 087
OSBURN: Barbara A., 101; Eveline O., 087; John, 049, 173; Martha, 144; Matilda V., 159; Nicholas, 073; Nicks, 075; Sarah Ann, 153
OSGOOD: Daniel, 049
OVERBY: Artealeer, 142; Basil H., 173; Elanor, 168; J. B. E., 111; James L., 018; Thomas, 018, 173; William G., 075
OWEN: Alfred, 038, 062; David, 173; Edward, 173; Emily, 172; Henry, 077; Jeremiah, 028; Martha Ann, 163; Milly, 077; Thomas, Lt., 201
OWENS: Henrietta, 077; John, 110, 173; Lethia A., 172; Milly, 077; Sarah Ann, 222; Sarah M., 163; Thomas, 4th Cpl., 126
OWINS: Brecy M., 132; Coleman P., 132; Sarah J., 132
PACE (PARR?): John, 123
PACE: Drury, 049, 217; Isaac, 173; James, 074; Jeremiah, 173; Jeremiah, Sgt., 130; Jno., 113; John, 113, 116, 125, 128, 130, 174, 206; John, Sgt., 202; Malinda, 158; Patsey, 173
PACKLETT(?): Lucy S., 169
PAGE: Rebecca, 097; Robert, 175
PAIN: Thomas Jefferson, 175
PAINE: Cornelia J., 164; Courtney, 054; Ed, 128; Edward C., 018, 025, 035, 049, 057, 175; Edward, 018, 035, 044, 049, 060, 108, 113, 116, 124, 126, 173, 205-208; Edward, PayMr., 210; Emely E., 169; Floyd, 018; George D., 018, 049, 118, 119, 128; George M., 042, 051, 066, 175; Seaborn, 018; Sidney B., 175; Sidney, 028
PALMER: Benjamin H., 080; Edmond, 018; Edmund, 048, 050; Elizabeth, 175; H. F., Mrs., 090; John T., 175; John, 116
PANION: Annie, 077; William, 077
PARIN (PAIN?): G. M., 122
PARIS: Wm., 120
PARISH: --, 092; Ana, 091; Anna, 093; Daniel, 061; Henry, 061; James, 174, 208, 209, 210; John, 201; Mary, 159; Nancy, 181; Samuel J., 176; Samuel, 122; Thomas, 061
PARK: John, 174; Nancy P., 187; Robert C., 175; Sarah A., 172
PARKER: Aaron, 174, 213; Arminda E., 142; Benjamin B., 176; Eliza Ann, 158; Elizabeth J., 163; Elizabeth, 161; Frances B., 089; Francis, 220; Frank, 089; Harvey, 089, 220; J. W., 032; James A., 089; James W., 175; James, 174; Jane, Mrs., 221; John, 053, 072, 173, 174; John, Capt., 120, 124, 126, 202, 203; Littleberry, 175; Margaret W., 085; Margaret, 084, 102; Marth J., 187; Mary, 152; Miss, 101; Nancy, 162, 178; Payton, 209;
PARKER; Penina, 089; Peyton, 174; Rachel, 148; Robert L., 089; Rosanna, 180; Rufus H., 089; Sarah, 154, 219; Sarena F., 150; Sheffield, 089; Wesley P., 089; West W., 089, 175; West., Cpl., 206; William H., 018, 174, 206; William, 174, 219; Wm., Lt., 205, 206
PARKERSON: Margarett, 170
PARKS: A.M., Mrs., 090, 093, 094; Elisabeth, 094; Elizabeth & (4 Chldn.), 083; Elizabeth, 090; Garet W., 074; Howell C., 092; Jno. Wm. H., 092; John J., 093; John T., 091; Marshall W., 091; Marshel W., 093; Moses, 175; Robert, 077; Sarah A., 092; Willis, 018; Wilson L., 092
PARKSON: John, 049
PARMALEE: Alberto, 023; Thomas J., 049, 060
PARMELLE: Albert G., 023
PARMER: John, 112, 123
PARMETEE: Thomas, 049
PARMOR: John, 124
PARNELL: Nathan C., 041
PARR (?): Charles, Lt., 120
PARR: B. J., 018, 074; Ben (3), 135; Benjamin J., 031, 042, 175; Benjamin, 038; Bob, 213; Charles D., 209; Charles D., Lt., 210; Charles, 035; Daniel W., 026; John C., 018, 112, 128, 129, 204, 206; John, 205; Leonard, 175; Lewis J., 175; Miss, 071; Patsy, 141; Samuel, 175; V.J., 057; William L., 176; William L., Capt., 124, 125, 202-204, 207; Wm. L., 121; Wm. L., Capt., 125, 127, 205, 206
PARRISH: --, 092; Charles, 018; Eliza, 157; Jas., 114; Jonathan, 176; Jos., 115; Marth, 090

PARSONS: H. H., 147; Jacob N., 175; Rock, 027
PARTAIN: Charlotte, 150
PASCHAL: Caroline, 134; Eliza, 134; Emilia H., 171; Emily, 134; Harriott, 134; John H., 112, 121, 134, 210; Jre. E., 123, 124; Jrie, 116; Virginia C., 153
PASCHALL: Jno. H., 113; John H., 113, 121, 205, 206, 211; Jre E., 112
PASCHEL: John H., 128
PASCOE: John, 049
PASS: Dicy A., 030; Frances, 176; John J., 038, 112, 174, 204, 207; John J., Lt., 207; John, 1st Lt., 125; Thomas W., 030
PATAT: Elizabeth, 094; Francis, 094; J. A., 025; Joseph, 094; Sarah, 094
PATE: John N., 175
PATILLO: John, 175; Leroy, 209
PATILLO?: Leroy, 207
PATMAN: A.C., Mrs., 099; Augustus, 175; John, Mrs., 099; Louisa, 146; Martha, 088, 102; T. H., Mrs., 099; Thomas H., 018, 088, 175; William A., 018, 047; William, 018, 049
PATMON: James B., 174
PATRICH: Ezekiel, 066
PATRICK: Benj., 213; Fich, Mrs., 090; J. E., Mrs., 097; Jane, 099; John N., 055, 174; Robert P., 097; William, 049
PATTAN: Susan, 083
PATTEN: Jonathan, 055; M.B., 112, 129; Susan, 083
PATTERSON: David (Daniel?), Sgt. 210; David, 209; Douglas, 068; Douglas, 2nd Cpl., 127; Eleanor S., 142; Gideon, 046; James M., 175; James, 174; Littleton, 175; Nancy, 167; William, 174
PATTON: Arthur, 058; J. B., 048; James W., 049; Jane, 018; John, 117
PATTS: Susan, 091
PAULETT: Henry, 030, 076, 121; Jesse C., 025, 027, 029, 032, 053, 063; Lewis M., 049, 208; Lewis, 030; Richard, 030, 036, 054
PAULETTE: Jesse C., 026; Richard, 035
PAULLAIN: Felix, 049
PAULLETT: David, 018; Jesse C., 027
PAXTON: Joseph G., 176
PAYNE: Howard, 059
PEALER: Hiram S., 091; Joseph A., 091; Robert B.,091; Susan J., 093
PEALOR: Elisha M., 175
PEANEY: Prudence, 178
PEARCE: Allen, 175
PEARMAN: Frances, 166; Francis A., 100, 102; Mariam, 080; Nancy W., 166; Whitmill, 174
PEARSON: Jno. C., 113, 115; John C., 174, 211; William, 115
PEASMAN: Miriam, Mrs., 102
PEAVY: Peter, 061
PECK: David, 043, 049; George M., 049; Jonathan H., 210; Jonathan M., 115, 208, 209; Marshall, 114, 208; Orin M., 046
PEDEGREW: Ebenezer, 114, 208
PEDGEON: Wm. C., 091
PEDIGREW: Bennett, 114, 208; Ebenezer, 208
PEELER: Amtenet, 100; Benj., 084; Benjamine, Mrs., 221; Cader, 081; Edward S., 081; Henry, 175; Jacob, 175; James B., 081; Mac, Mrs., 101; Margaret, 187; Mariah, & 7 chldn., 087; Mariah, 086, 090, 091; Martha, 086, 101; Mary, Mrs., & 2 chldn., 087; Nancy, 187; Susan J., & (5 chldn.), 083; Susan, 099; Wiley, 175; William C., 081
PEEPLES: Hanry, 043
PEIRCE: Delilah, 182
PEMBERTON: Selum H., 073
PENDAGRASS: Mrs., 094
PENDER: Benj., 085
PENDERGRASS: Hiram, 203; Martha W. Durham, 102; Martha, 178; Mrs., 085; Nathaniel, 174, 203; Rebecca, 170; Sarah H., 181
PENDIGRASS: Hiram, 203
PENDLETON: John B., 054
PENETCOST: John W., Capt., 130
PENNELL: John, Ens., 126
PENNER: John, 113, 130
PENNINGTON: A., 116; Abraham, 112, 123
PENSON: Thomas, 130
PENTECOST: J.W., 204; John W., 049
PENTECOUST: J. W., Capt., 203
PENTICOST: Jno. W., Capt., 203; John W., Capt., 128
PENUR: John, 208
PEOPLES: Harvy, 043
PEPPERS: Samuel, 174
PERKINS: Abraham, 114, 174, 209; Abram, 116, 123, 208, 209; Mary, 162; Robert, 018; Sarah B., 018; Sarah, 093; William R., 201
PERNDLE: Banister, Sgt., 205
PERRY: A. B., 175; Alonzo, 018; Burwell, 036, 118, 119; Dwight, 060; James, 213; Jeptha V., 176; John C., 018; Nancy, 180; Peter, 018; Richard, 071; Sarah Ann O., 142; William H., 049
PERRYMAN: David E., 087, 088; Harriett, 087, 088; R. D., 088; Sarah T., 100; Sarah W., 098, 101; Sarah, 088, 099
PETERS: William M., 174
PETTARD: Humphree, 072; John, 072
PETTEFILS: Andrew, 173
PETTEY: Henry, 051; John, 051
PETTIFROD: Lows, 018
PETTIS: Alford, 018; John, 117
PETTY: Henry, 052, 062; John, 052, 062
PHARR: Benjamin, 069
PHELPS: Aquilah, 173; Glen, Sgt. 205; Glenn, 049
PHILIPS: Elizabeth E., 158; John, 049; Joseph, 049
PHILLIPS: --, 040; B., 049; C., 049; David, 175; Delilah, 147; George, 049; Henry, 174; Joel, 018; John, 049, 174; Jonathan, 049; Joseph, 049; Virginia, 160; William H., Dr., 175
PHINIZY: -- , 050; Ferdinand Bowdle, 018; Ferdinand, 049; Fredinand, 018, 049; Harry Hall, 018; Jacob, 018, 049; John F., 050; Marco, 018; Sarah M., 147
PHINNEY: Elihu, 050
PICKERELL: Andrew J., 081; Mrs., 085
PICKERING: Joseph, 174
PICKRELL: Andrew J., 173
PIDORE: Old Man, 221
PIERCALL: John, 174
PIERCE: Sarah, 100
PIKE: Jacob, 209; James, 133; Lucinda, 133; Sion, 133
PIMER (PINNER?): John, 206
PINCKARD: James, 109, 117
PINCKERTON: David, 052
PINKARD: --, 117
PINKERTON: David, 052
PINNER: Cintha, 134; Jno., 128, 209; John, 134, 202, 205, 208; John, Ens., 205; Lucinda, 134, 184; Thomas J., 175
PINSON: Azariah M., 174; Jane E., 141; Joseph, 018; Lucy, 162; Thomas, 018, 205; Thos., 113; William, 174
PITARD: Humphrey, 073; T. F., Mrs., 090
PITMAN: Lucinda, 163; William, 214
PITNER: Albert G., 175; John C., 018, 175
PITRIER: J. C., 050
PITTARD: America, 018; Edward, 131; Ginnery, 069; Humphrey, 018, 209; James D., 018, 050; John F., 175; John, 072; Mary L. (2 ch), 096; Oreno Susan, 163; Samuel, 050; Samuel, Sgt., 206, 207; William, 018, 175
PITTMAN: James, 203
PITTS: Illender, 149
PLAT: George, 018
PLEDGER: Alvira, 093; Elizabeth, & 2 chldn., 087; Elizabeth, 086; Elvira, & 3 chldn., 087; Elvira, 086, 090, 099; James P., 091; Jane Y., 091; John A., 175; Lerana J., 091; Lorina, 159; Marga, 090; Mary A., 093; Mary, 091; May, 091
PLIDGER: Elisha A., 175
PLUMMER: Samuel, 208
PLUNGER: A., 099
POARCH: Hearty, 160
POGUE: James, 108
POLK: William, 213, 215
POLLEY: Robert, 174
PONDER: Amos, 123; Jamimi, 171; John H., 174; John L., 111, 123; John, 018; Mrs., 221
POOL: Jackson, 018
POORE: Benjamin P., 031, 057, 060; Benjamin, 042
POPE: --, 028, 050, 196; Burwell, 018, 050; Cordelia Ann, 184; Eliza S., 018; Henry J., 050; Henry N., 174; Henry, 026, 050, 125, 207; Henry, Ens., 125, 128; Henry, Sgt., 203; John C., 044, 109; John H., 050; Julia A.T., 180; LeRoy, 039; Mary, 018; Robert, 026, 050; Sarah H., 150; Sarah K., 018, 050; Wiley, Lt., 210; Wilie, 062; Wylie H., 174; Zachary, 050
PORCH: Sherrod, 174; Sherwood, 124; William, 216
PORTER: Anthony, 024; Elizabeth, & 2 chldn., 087; Elizabeth, 086, 099; James H., 050; John W., 050; Oliver M., 050, 174; William, 050
PORTER:(?): Hezekiah D., 050
POSEY: Humphrey, 061, 113, 204, 206
POSS: Humphrey, 112; John, 1st Lt., 125, 128; Marth, 090; Thomas J., 080; Uriah, Mrs., 099, 101
POTMAN: Nod, 077
POTTER: Pleasant, 050; William R., 175
POTTS: John, 052; Napoleon, 175
POULLAIN: Antoine, 031; Felix, 050; Thomas N., 031, 050
POULNON: Susan Jane, 089
POULNOT: Mary Frances, 089
POULOT: Susan J., 101
POUNDS: John, 203, 217; John, Sgt., 129; Patsey, 185; Richard, 018, 029; William, Sr., 018
POWEL: John, 174; Robert, 116, 123; Starling, 050; William, 173
POWELL: Asa, Ens., 126; Burchry, 168; Campbell, 058, 204; Campbell, Sgt., 203, 205; Catherine, 178; Dempsey, 018; Elisha, 174; Elisha, Sgt., 203; Gracy, 174; H., Sgt., 129; Henry, 018; Isaac, 3rd, Sgt., 126; John, 050; Levi, 174; Nancy, 185; Polly, 149; Robert, 112, 124; Sarah, 144; Seymore R., 042; Silvey, 161; William, 050
POWER: John, 118
POWERS: George, 175; Will, 018
PRATER: Elisha, 081;

Francis P., 175
PRATHER: Evan P., 080; William, 080
PRATT: Lemuel, 197; William, 175; William, Capt., 119
PRESSLEY: Elizabeth Antonett, 147; Jane, 050; Samuel P., Rev., 018
PRESTON: Almira, 148; Thomas, 018, 174
PRETCHET: --, 122
PRICE: Elizabeth, 018, 141; H. W. William, 050; James, 018, 111, 122; John, 050; Sarah, 174; Thomas J., 175; W. H. W., 175; William H. W., 111; William N. W., 059; William, 018, 056, 109, 174; William, 4th Sgt., 127; William, Sgt., 120; Wm. H. W. W., Capt., 110; Wm. H. W., Capt., 110; Wm., 109, 211
PRIDGEON: F. J., Mrs., 091; Lantha L., 151; Sophian E., 166
PRIGEN: Ruel K., 175
PRIGEON: Francis J., 093
PRIGGEON: Nathaniel, 174
PRINCE: Ann F., 155; G. W., 079; Garland W., 050; Noah F., 028, 039, 057, 079; Noah, 050; Olliver H., 018
PRINDLE: Coleman, 174
PRINGLE: Banester J., 109; Bannaster, 1st Sgt., 127; George, 018; Rosa J., 179; Sarah A., 183
PRIOR: Allen, 067, 174
PRITCHARD: Elias B., 176; Elias B., Capt., 111; Mary L., 043; Wm., 211
PRITCHETT: William G., 134
PROCTOR: William, 112, 123, 124, 203; Wm., 202
PROKINS: Abraham, 208
PROPHET: James, 174
PRUET: James, 173
PRYANT?: Josiah, 174
PRYER: Allen, 026, 112, 203; Obadiah, 031; Oley, 057
PRYOR: Philip, 113, 130; Phillip, 121, 205; Robert A., 174
PUERMAN: Frances A., 098
PULNATT(?): William, 081
PUNCHARD: Elizabeth W., 184
PURYEAR: Dennis R., 176; Elizabeth J., 176; J., 103; John, 018, 033, 045, 050, 054, 119, 173; John, 4th, Sgt., 126; Judith M., 018; Lucy A., 050; Lucy Jane, 186; Martha H., 165; Mary Ann, 050, 159; Peter, 018, 033, 050, 067, 174; Rebecca W., 173; Sarah S., 170; William H., 018, 050, 073, 109, 121, 207; William H., Sgt., 120; William, 018, 174, 221; Wm. H., 072, 112-114, 121, 205, 207, 208, 211; Wm. P., 073
PUTELLER: Leroy, 207
PUTMAN: Damarius E., 151
PYE: William, 027
PYRON: Emily, 171
QAUVAIN: M. A., 024
QUARTERMAN: Minnie, 018
QUARTERUS: Mary, 141
QUESENBERY: Alexander, Sgt., 130
QUIN: Edward, 048
QUINN: Edward, 038, 047
RACKETT: George, 029
RADCLIFFE: John, 032
RADFORD: Henry, 018; Silas, 018
RAGAN: Josa, 176
RAGLAND: James O., 123, 208; Jas. C., 115; Jas. O., 114; Thomas, 028
RAINES: Mary, 145
RAINS: William, 112
RAINY (RAMY?): John, 206
RAKERSTRAW: Gainham L., 055
RAKESHAW: Robert, 201
RAKESTRAW: Galjham L., 043, 055, 059; Gainhain L., 025; Gainham, 025, 045; Robert D., 050; Robert G., 040, 050; Robert, 050, 052
RALLS: James F., 045, 059, 067, 177; James S., 177
RAMEY: Absalom, 023, 027, 044, 107; Daniel, 076, 118, 174, 216; Daniel, Sgt., 206, 207; David, 050; Edmund, 116, 176; Elizabeth, 018; John Jr., 040; John, 027, 029, 030, 038, 039, 042-044, 049-051, 055-058, 076, 121, 206, 214; John, Jr., 035, 049, 077; Julia Ann, 186; S.L., 061; Sandford L., 176; Sandford, 043; Sanford L., 030, 051, 054, 057, 059; Seaborn J., 177; Seaborn, 051; Stanford L., 061; Stanford, 038; Susannah, 173; Talitha E., 018; William, 018, 031, 036, 050, 215, 216
RAMMY: Sanford L., 030
RAMSEY: Ann, 169; Elizabeth, 152; Gracy, 219; Lucinda, 168; Martha N., 166; Seaborn J., 075; Seaborn, 045; Seaborn, Lt., 117
RAMSON: Sarah, 083
RANDOLPH: Carvey M., 018; James B., 051; James E., 051; James H. L., 018; Peter, 018, 032, 051, 056, 058; Richd. H., 129; Robert, 177
RANEY: Woodson, 118
RANFIELD: Loyd K., 051
RANKIN: Andrew, 051
RANSOM: Reuben R., 177; Reuben, 176
RANSON: Reuben, 018
RASBERRY: James, 176; Jas., 124, 205; Joseph, 051, 176
RASBERY: James, 211
RASBUN: Joseph, 116
RASBURY: James 109; Jas., 130; Jos., 113
RASSON: J., Mrs., 091
RATCHFORD: Joseph, 177
RATHBONE: Jacob B., 029; William P., 051
RAWSEN: Sarah, 083
RAWSON (RANSOM?): Eugenius, 177
RAWSON: Francis, 177; Sarah, 098, 100
RAY: Anderson, 177; Andrew, 177; Betsy, 165; Izable, 149; John, 051, 112, 122; Joseph, 214; Joseph, Sgt., 202; Margaret, 018; Margarett, 133; Margret, 165; Mary, 018, 071, 083, 097; Peggy, 084, 085, 221; Solomon, 051; Temperance, 161; Tolerson, 177; Toleson, 133; Tollison, 109, 110; William, 018
RAYLOR: Roland, 121
RAYMON: Watkins, 148
RAYMOND: Allen H., 043
REA: Melindy, 149
READ: Charles, Capt., 117; Isaac D., 057, 072, 176; Nancy, 147
REAN: Whitehead, 120
REAVES: Anna E., 018; Edward A., 018; Ethel, 018; James A., 043; John (chldn. of), 018; John W., 018; Marzee, 098, 100
REDD: Charles A., 027, 035, 037, 051, 054, 062, 176, 201; William, 051
REECE: Nancy, 051; William M., 050
REED: Daniel, 122; Isaac D., 048; Luke, 051; Mary, 085, 102; Samuel A., 039
REES: John, 051; Thad B., 051; Thaddeus B., 051
REESE (RUSE?): Wmson. C., 207
REESE: Charles M., 018, 051, 062, 177; Charles S., 018; Cuthbert, 052; Elizabeth W.G., 018; G., 051; Henry, 176; John C., 051; Joseph C., 052; Sarah, 181; Sidney C., 018; Sydney C., 177; W.C., 051; Williamson C., 051, 079, 113, 207; Williamson C., Sgt., 121; Williamson, 051, 052; Wmson. C., 207; Wmson. C., Sgt., 206, 207
REEVES: Catherine, 173; James A., 110; James A., Capt., 110; James, 122
REID: Adline, 018; Ann, 155; Frances W., 004; Samuel, 034; Thomas, 061
REMSHART: William, 048
REVELL: S. E., 096
REVIERE: Georges A. (chldn. of), 019
REYNOLD: Thomas, 044
REYNOLDS: Benj., 081; Coleman, 051; Elizabeth, 098; Galland, 204; Gallant, 051, 112; Garland, 204; Greenberry, 111; Greenbury, 123; John A., 177; John, 023, 027, 035, 054, 063, 118; M.W., 018; Mary Ann S., 146; Mary C., Mrs., 032; Matildah, 152; Purmedus, 176; Reuben, 031; Robert (?) Martin, 177; Sarah Ann, 150; Spencer, 117, 214, 215; Thomas, 027, 050, 176; W. N., 018; William, 112
RHOADES: James, 177
RHOADS: J. M., Mrs., 099; Rebecca, 172
RHODES: J. M., Mrs., 102; James M., 080; James, 019; Mathew, 122; Penelope, 147; Zachariah, 109, 211
RIAN: Phillip, Sgt. 206
RIBESON: Saml., Ensgn, 201
RICE: Benjamin (chldn of), 019; Benjamin, 019; Nancy, 028; W. C., 069
RICH: William C., 026, 041
RICHARD: Bessie M., 019
RICHARDS: Elizabeth J., 165; F. S., 059; J. C., 059; Rebecca, 051; Richard, 019; Royal, 051; Sarah, 090; Thomas, 051; Willis, 176
RICHARDSON: Alford, 019; David, 019, 177, 218; Duke, 118, 177; George, 095; Henry H., 177; Hillery A., 019; Hiram, 122; Jackson, 122; James G., 051; James M., 019; James, 019, 051, 176; Jane D., 099; Jane G., 019; John H., 051, 052, 074, 079, 109, 115; John H., Cpl., 206, 207; John M., 023, 120, 218; John W., 051, 177; John, 051, 112, 118, 121, 123, 177;
RICHARDSON: Littleton J., 153; Martha C., 147; N.B., Mrs., 099; Nathaniel, 122; O., 220; Orlando F., 019; R., 116; Richard D., 051; Richard, 019, 035, 043, 048, 051, 067, 112, 122, 176, 221; Richd., 118; Robert, 051; Sarah Ann, 167; Thomas, Fifer, 129
RICHEE: James F., 210
RICHEY: James F., 034, 210
RICHEY: James F., Lt., 126
RICHISON: John, 129
RICKS: Johnanon, 213
RIDDLE: John, 019, 206
RIDEN: Allsey, 093; C.D., Mrs., 091; John S., 032; Nancy C., 155; Rufus, 092; Wiley, 092
RIDGEWAY: Drury, 037, 048, 210; Eliza Ann, 164; Elizabeth T., 180; James M., 177; John N., 081; Lucy B., 165; Nancy H., 080, 170; Nelson, 019, 051, 176
RIDGWAY: Drury, 053, 114
RIDLING: Alsa F., 019
RIED: Louiza, 158
RIEVES: Martin, Ensgn, 210
RIGGS: Aaron, 033
RIGSBY: Allen, 036
RIGWAY: John N., 177
RILEY: John, 103, 118
RING: William, 216
RIPLEY: Obedience B., 048; Samuel

P., 046; Sylvanus, 048, 176
RIPPY: Jesse, 176
RISLEY: Hubbell W., 038; Hubbell, 037
RITCH: --, 053; Jerry, Mrs., 097
RITCHEE: James F., 208, 209
RITCHEY: James F., 054, 123, 208, 209
RITCHIE: J. F., 116; Jas. F., 114; Jos. F., 114
RIVERS: Jones, 041
ROADES: Mary, 181
ROBBINS: Allen, 028, 051; George, 051; Samuel W., 051
ROBERDS: Amy, 095; Grant, 176; Noel F., 176; William, Sgt., 126
ROBERSON: Betsey, 170; Rebecca, 171; Thomas, 176; William T., 177; William, 046, 057
ROBERTS: --, 051; Amy, 085; Anna, 019; Charles, 177; D. A., 019; Deasey Ann, 019; Edward W., 110; Edwin, 051; Jesse, 051; John G., 176; John, 019; Kessiah, 076; Martha, 086, 099, 183; Nancy Jane, 086; Nancy, 152; S., Mrs., 090; Thomas, 019, 176; White, 046; Willie, 051, 214; William(chldn of), 019; William, 028, 176, 205, 207; William, 4th Sgt., 127; Wm., 206, 208; Wm., Sgt., 205
ROBERTSON: Ann, 093; David, Ens., 126, 202; Dock, 019; Elizabeth, 167; Frances, 166; Fredinand, 019; Fryar, 019; Fryer, 176; James A., 019, 050; James S., 058; James, 134; Jeremiah, 176; Jesse M., 019; Jesse, 209; John J., 176; John L.M., 019; John, 134; Katherine, 134; Leml. B., 119; Lemuel B., 109; Lemuel, 103, 109, 118; Lemuel, Ens., 120; Sally, 071, 134; Sarah T., 174; Thomas, 080; Thos., 1st Sgt., 127; Thos., Sgt., 206; W.V., Dr., 019; William T., 177; William, 107; Wm., 134
ROBESON: James, 176; William, 057
ROBINSON: Amanda, 077; David, Ens., 129; Gertrude, 019; Isham, Sgt., 130; James, 176; James, Cpl., 207; James, Lt.129; Jepe, 031; Jesse, 023, 024, 032, 042, 046, 050, 051, 061; John P., 074, 177; John, 019; Lousia Jane, 019; Lucinda, 164; Milly, 161; Patrick L., 044; Sally, 019; Saml., Ens., 129; Sarah, 141; Senith, 019; William, 019
ROBISON: Alexander L., 051; Alexander S., 051; David, 047; Eliza Ann, 019; Isabella, 180; James (chldn. of), 019; James, Lt., 201; Jesse, 177; John L., 051; John S., 037, 081, 177; Pleasant, 057; Saml., Ens., 201; Sarah, 158; William, 044, 046
ROBSON: John, 051, 052
ROBY: Matthew, 052
ROCHFORT: George, 052
ROCKFORD: George, 019
ROCKFORT: George, 033, 217
ROCKWELL: Charles W., 045
RODES: Mrs. (2 chldn), 071
RODGERS: John, 052; Lily S., 019; Osburn, 176
ROE: John, 052
ROGERS: Augustin C., 134; Charlotte P., 134; Edwin G., 038; Edwin G., 1st Lt., 121; Edwin G., Lt., 206, 207; Edwin, Lt., 206; Eliza Ann, 134; James H., 134; Mary E., 157; Moses, 052; Right, 025, 030, 038, 048, 050, 058, 059, 176; Silas. 055; Thomas J., 134
ROLASON: Penina, 213
ROLIN: John, 111
ROLL: Luther, 052
ROMAN: Abraham, 019
ROOSEVELT: Henry L., 052
ROOTES: Serena R., 168
ROSE: S. C., 177
ROSENBERG: H., 019
ROSETT: Nelson, 019
ROSITER: White, 062
ROSS: Absalom B., 176; Candis A., 167; David, 052; Rice F., 033; Richard, 109; William, 052
ROSSEN: Sarah, 086, 093
ROSSER: Sarah, Mrs.,& 3 chldn, 087
ROSSETER: W. 116; White, 019, 023, 027, 031, 047, 052, 066, 112; White, Capt., 129; Wilhilmina, 156
ROSSITER: White, 202
ROSSON: Emeline, 091; Lieucinda, 091; Thomas, 091
ROUGH: Thos., 114
ROULAND: --, 122
ROUNDTREE: George R., 052
ROUNSEVALL: Elizabeth D., 151
ROUSSEAU: Hiram, 052
ROWAN: Abraham, 071, 074; Jane, 082
ROWE: Adna, 052; Chauncy, 052
ROWLAN: Polley, 177
ROWLAND: Andrew, 048, 050; William W., 019
ROWLING (BOWLING): Alexander, 146
ROYAL: E. D., 028; Ed, 032; Elizabeth A., 183; F. E. L., Mrs., 090; F., 102; F., Mrs., 099; Frances (chldn. of), 019; J. H., 019; James M., 019, 177, 213; James, 025; John E., 019; Martha A., 172; Mary A., 153; William H., 055
ROYESTER: Elamus, 087; Elizabeth, 087; Oris, 087; Susan, 087
ROYSTER: Charles, 206; David, 177; John, 019; Robert, 019
ROYSTON: Robertus, 019
RUCKER: Oliver, 019; Tinsley W. (chldn. of), 019; Tinsley, Mrs., 099
RUELL(?): S. E., 097
RUMBLEY: Levin, 215
RUMNEY: Frances E., 177; Mary, 147
RUNNELLS: Annis, 019; Dudley, 019; Edward, 176; Edward, Cpl., 210; Patrick M., 019; Preston, 031, 043; Reuben, 042; Sophia, 052; Wm., 1st, Cpl., 127; Wm., Cpl., 205
RUNNELS: Annis, 052; Coleman, 181; Elijah, 214; Green, 176; Hardin, 052; Harman, 052; Johnson, 214, 215; Lereisa, 174; Preston, 023, 031, 033, 037, 038, 040, 051, 052, 057, 176, 215; Rodey, 174
RUNYAN: Lafayette, 177
RUPERT: John, 052
RUSHIN: Bryant, 052
RUSHING: Briant, 042, 176; Bryant, 042
RUSO: Thadeus B., 027
RUSSEL: Sarah L., 093
RUSSELL: Alexander, 052; Edward B., 019; Hariette, 019; S.L., Mrs., 090; W. O., 052
RUST: Harriett T., 159; R. A., Miss, 187
RUTHERFORD: John G., 207, 208; John G., Capt., 110; John, 109, 211; Thacker V., 043
RUTHLEDGE: Alred, Ensgn, 127
RUTLEDGE: Alna, Ensgn, 205, 206; Catherine, 098; Charles, 2nd Sgt., 127; Charles, Sgt. 205; Elizabeth C., 163; Elizabeth, 177; George, 122; James S., 052; James, 136; John (chldn of), 019; John, 019, 136; Jos., 114; Mary F., 161; Mrs., 094; Nancy Ann, 177; Thomas, 121, 208, 209; Thomas, Lt., 210; Widow, 136; William O., 176;
Wm., Mrs., 102
RYAN: Berry, 059; Julia Ann M., 181; Phillip, 114, 120, 205; Phillip, 201, 208; Phillip, Sgt. 207; Whitehead, Sgt., 126; Whitehead, 112, 119, 120, 201; Whitehead, 1st Sgt., 202
RYLE: James, 052
SADLER: Stanhope, 033
SAFFOLD: William, 052
SAFFORD: Henry, Rev.142
SAGE: Martha J., 019; William F., 052; William P., 019, 052
SAILOR: Nancy, 097
SAILORS: Jeffie, 019; Susan, 098
SALE: F. A., 039
SALESBERY: James , 090
SALMON: James H., 081
SALMONS: Lewis S., 052, 181
SALMS: Kirby, 052
SALTER: Caswell A., 019; James S., 019; John, 133; Julia E., 153; Richard R., 180; Simeon, 133; Susan O., 080; Thomas W., 019; Thomas W., Mrs., 098
SAMS: Joseph, 027
SANDERS: --, 119; Emily Martha Ann, 159; John L., 052; John, 201; Joseph, 178; Julius, 029, 052, 067; Silas, 097; W. A., Mrs., 100; Wiggins, 109; William, 180; Wm., 180
SANFORD: Adolphus M., 052; Epsey T., 179
SANPFORD: Bezabel, 058
SANSEN: (chldn. of), 019
SANSOM (LANSUM?): Clementine, 175
SANSOM: Amanda J., 169; James, 025, 028, 045, 052, 058, 119; John, 045, 177; Martha F., 183; Nancy E., 183; Thomas, 025, 029, 046-048, 052, 072, 074, 075; Thos., 119; William, 028, 111, 122
SANSON: Delilah P., 019; James T. (chldn of), 019; James T., 019; James, 3rd Sgt., 127; John, 019; Robert, 019; Thomas, 019; Virginia, 019
SAPP: Edward (chldn. of), 019; Edward, 019
SATTERWHITE: Mary, 171; Paul, 178; Paul, Capt., 202
SAULTER: Martha, 052; R.R., 051; Richard R., 052; Wesley, 052
SAUNDERS: Julius, 029, 052; Mary Ann E., 175; Peter, 052; Petter, 052; Wiley O., 180; William, 177
SAVAGE: Susan B., 019
SAWERS: Charles, 177
SAWTELL: John W., 031
SAWTELLE: John W., 019
SAWYERS: Sena, 152
SAY: Eliza C., 093; Elizabeth, 091; Joseph A., 091; Margaret A., 099; R. W., Mrs., 090
SAYE: A.H., 061; Agnes A., 092; James W., 019; James, 052; John N., 092; M. E., 097; Margaret A., 093; Mary E., 092; Nancy C., 092; R. W., 061; Richard A., 180; Richard W., 036, 044, 048, 061; Robert A., 092; Sarah F., 092; Wm. J., 092
SAYERS: Peggy, 157
SAYRE: Milton, 180
SCATES: Zedekiah, 113
SCENTER: Louisa, 169
SCHACKELFORD: H. T., 019
SCHELL: Jessie B., 019
SCHENENELL: L., 036
SCHERENELL: L., 052
SCHEVENELL: --, 055; Harman, 180; L., 043; Leonard, 028, 034, 055; Yancy, , 055
SCHINKEL: Peter E., 004
SCHLEY: George, 035
SCHOONMAKER: Lodowick, 052; Lodwick, 043
SCHRODER: Mathilda, 052

SCIPLE: --, 047
SCOGGIN: James J., 179; Martha H., 150; Mary, 179
SCOGGINS: Robinson, 119
SCOGIN: Elizabeth, 149; Lucenda, 161; Millington, 178; Robenson H., 181
SCOTT: A. H., 053; Alfred, 208; Archibald H., 040, 043, 053, 059; Edward, 052; George, 052; James, 039; James, Jr., 043; James, Sr., 052; Jim, 034; John, Ens., 110; M., 208; Mary, 152; Simeon, 061; Taply, 121; Thomas W., 026; William, 032, 052
SCOUVALL: Hezekiah W., Maj., 207
SCOVALL: Hezekiah W., Capt. 205; Hezekiah W., Col., 210
SCOVELL: H. W., 052, 207; H. W., Capt., 128, 130; Hesekiah, 204; Hezekiah W., 052, 053, 205; Hezekiah, 052
SCOWELL: H. W., Capt., 127
SCRANTON: Philmon A., 053
SCRIVNER: Thomas, 216
SCROGGIN: Chatten D., 060; Chattin D., 107; Chattin, 024; Sanders J., 178
SCUTCHIN: --, 045
SEAGLAR: Joseph, 107, 124
SEALE: John, 053
SEAMAN: John B., 053
SEAMANS: William, 056
SEARS: Abner, 053; Albert, 025, 053, 072; Jason G., 024; Marcus A., 019, 027, 053, 118, 119; Marcus A., 2nd Lt., 110
SEATES: Thomas, 178
SEAY (SEARS?): John, Jr., 180
SEGRAVES: Nancy, 098; Rebecca, 097
SEISLER: Hugh, 033, 047
SELERETS(STEWART?): Nancy, 149
SELF: Joseph, 178
SELMAN (?): John, Col., 125
SELMAN: Benjamin, 178; James J., 027, 034, 038, 046, 052, 057, 059, 075, 111, 180, 181; Jas. J., 074; Jno., Col., 127; John W. (cont.), 019; John W., 049, 053, 059, 179; John, 054, 132; John, Col., 130, 204; John, Lt. Col., 124, 126; John, Maj., 129, 201; Simon, 034; Susan V., 038; Susan, 034
SELMON: James J., 023; John, 178
SEMMES: --, 042; Paul J., 181; Sarah H., 151
SEMMS: Mary A., 172
SEOGIN: Joshok H., 072; Robsen H., 072
SERRIT: Jas., 116
SERWNER: Jesse, Ensgn, 117
SESSON: Rodman, 109
SETTLEMOIR: Able, 019
SEWALL: Lewis, 050
SEWART: Robert, 206
SEWELL: H. W., 053; Jonathan, 053; Lewis, 051
SEXTEN: Marion T., 180
SEYMOUR: Bralbon, 053; Henry C., 074
SHACKELFORD: Edwin, 023; Mary A., 150; Lloyd, 024; Rich D., 027; Richard, 027, 178
SHADWICK: Philania, 156
SHAKELFORD: Edmund, 025; Edmund C., 042
SHAKLEFORD: Loyd W., 042
SHALL: George, 214
SHANKLE: Emily A., 148
SHANNON: James, Rev., 145; John, 181; Thomas, 053, 077, 107, 115
SHARARD(?): Polly, 176
SHARK: William H., 053
SHARP: Lewis, 019
SHAVERS: Geo., 079
SHAW: Elizabeth, 053; Geo. W., 028, 119; George E., 029; George M., 060; George W., 024, 048, 049, 051, 053, 060, 061, 109, 179; Henry C., 080; James, 037, 111, 179, 181; Jincy, 157; John William, 180; John, 178; Joseph, 061, 178; Margaret, 019, 032, 056, 058; Martha, 184; Nancy, 179; Nathan, Sgt., 207; Oliver P., 029, 048, 049, 050, 053; Osborne D., 180; William (chldn. of), 019; William, 019, 030-032, 037, 044, 049, 052, 056-059, 074-076, 214; William, Jr., 178, 221; Wm., 074, 075
SHAY: David, 076, 121, 213; Dennis, 073, 181
SHEAR: William, 055
SHEARLEY: Francis, 076; Robert, 076
SHEARLY: Robert, 076
SHEATS: Benajah L., 053; Benajah S., 053, 077; Benejah S., 026; Benjamin J., 053; Eliza B. 154; John L. (chldn. of), 019; Joseph, 019; Lindsey, 179; Linsey, 062; M.M., 074; Malinda, 073; Marshall M., 026, 034, 053, 060, 074; Martha R., 182; Minerva L., 179; Nicholad, 058; Nicholas (chldn. of), 019; Nicholas, 019, 058, 181; Squire, 019
SHED: William, 019
SHEETS: B. S., 222; Celia, 085; Nicholas, 053
SHELTON: Vardy H., 180
SHENALT: Stephen, 053
SHEPARD: Augusta, 019; John, Ens., 202; Russell, 181
SHEPHARD: Laban, 178
SHEPHERD: Carter, 028; James M., 181; James, 053, 178, 181; John Ens., 202, 203; John, 044, 121, 201, 210; Ruthey, 165; Thomas, 057; Thomas, 3rd Sgt., 125; Thomson, 032, 056; Wm., Sgt., 207
SHERIL: Joseph D., 047
SHERLEY: Jane, 179
SHERLING: John, 178; Richmond, 052
SHERLY: Clark, Mrs., 090; Hariett, 099
SHERMAN: Eagan, 063; Elgar, 062
SHERRILL: J. D., 180
SHERROD: Frederic A., 029; Frederic O. A., 029
SHERWOOD: George, 181
SHEWELL: George S. (chldn of), 019; George S., 019
SHIELDS: --, 050, 053, 054; Frank C., 092; Jas. B., 092; Joseph J., 092; Josiah, 053; Nancy E., 092; Nancy, 093; Octavia, 092; Samuel B., 054; Samuel, 043, 044, 049, 053, 054; Stephen, 091; Susan, 092; William, 054; Willie, 077
SHILMAN: John, 054
SHIPLEY: George, 178
SHIRLEY: Jackson, 180; Thomas, 054
SHITTON: William, 185
SHORES: Daniel, 179
SHORT: Augustus D., 181; Sarah, 093; Tapely, 210; Tapley, 112, 113, 115, 121, 205-208, 210; Tarpley, 113, 114
SHORTER: Eli S., 054; James, 054
SHURLEY: Alexander, 092; Harriett, 093
SHYE: Mary, 165
SIBBALD: Jane, 019
SIGON: Joseph, 054
SIKES: Amanda, 088, 098, 100; John R., 019; John, 180; Joseph B.C., 088; Loty A., 088; Mandy (2 chldn.), 095; Mathew, 035; Prudence, 019; Richard, 088, 095; Zachariah, 019; Zachriah, 073
SILLIMAN: Gold S., 055
SILMAN: James J., 072; John, 110; John, Col., 202, 203, 207; John, Lt. Col., 204
SILMON: Fanny, 160
SILVEY: (chldn. of), 019; A. Branham, 071; Abraham, 033, 072, 075, 208; Abraham, 3rd Sgt. 127; Abraham, Sgt. 206; Ann, 145; Barsheba, 071; Cintha, 162; G.F., 019; Henry O., 181; Louisiana, 188; Susan, 172; William, 181
SILVY: Solita Ann, 142
SIMMES: --, 042
SIMMONS: Asa, 150; David, Sgt. 210; James, 178; John, 019; Sarah, 019; Thomas, 112
SIMMS(?): John F., 210
SIMMS: A.L., Capt., 120; A.L., Maj., 117; Albert G., 054; Arther L., 054; Arther T., 054; Arthur L., 028, 046, 049; Arthur, 044; Capt., 079; Davd., 107; Elizabeth, 150; Garling, 113; Richard L., 054; William, 122, 181
SIMON: William, 177
SIMONS: John, 177
SIMONTON: Elizabeth, 179; Frances R., 150; Jean, 019; Margaret, 176; Robert, Sgt., 129; Saml., 101, 119; Samuel, 045, 179, 222; Theophilus (chldn. of), 019; Theophilus, 019; Thomas, 054, 074, 075, 179; Thomas, 4th, Sgt., 126; Thomas, Sgt., 203; Thos., 074, 119
SIMPSON: George Washington, 077; Jemima, 188; John, 042, 112, 124, 202; William, 112, 120, 124; William, Sgt., 202; Wm., 116
SIMS: --, 025; A.L., 109; Amelia, 177; Annie Nobles, 196; Arthur L., 026; Arthur L., Maj., 118; Arthur S., 054; Augustus F., 035; Benj., Sgt. 206; Benjamin L., 179; Benjamin, 025; Benjamin, Sgt. 207; Bennet, 181; Betsey Ann, 162; Betsy, 184; Charly, 019; David E., 080, 082; David, 054, 057, 068, 117, 216; E. Sanford, 180; Garland, 109, 115, 211; Garling, 207;
SIMS: Garlland, 206; George W., 088, 181; Hattie P., 019; James Glen, 041; James, 025, 027, 030, 054, 072, 111, 112, 127, 201; James, Capt., 126, 203, 204; James, Ens., 124, 127, 202; James, Sgt., 130; John H., 030, 031, 034, 042, 051, 052, 054, 057, 179; John Hughes, 054; Loree, 179; Loroner, 054; Mariah, 185; Martha B.,172; Nancy, 150; Ramon?, 026; Robert, 019; S.J., Mrs., 099, 101; Sandford, 122; Sarah J., 088; Walker, 180; William Isaih, 019; William, 033, 054, 180; Zach, 116; Zachariah, 026, 027, 031, 046, 047, 054, 059, 112, 122, 129, 203
SINCLEAR: Joseph, 186
SINGLETON: Almis M., 179
SISON: Sarah C., 175
SISSON: Ann Eliza, 135; Charlotte, 173; Elizabeth, 135; Evelina, 187; Merinda, 135; Rhodman, 060; Rodman, 035; William, 135
SISSONS: Rodman, 019
SIUON: Robert, 072
SIZER: R. W., 019
SKATES: Zed, 128; Zedekiah, 121, 130, 205
SKEATS (SHEATS?): Malinda, 177
SKEEN: John, 177
SKINNER: Ebenezer, 054
SLATER: L. D., 020
SLAVE: Elijah, 055
SLEDGE: Anna C., 142; Charles M., 024, 032, 058, 061; Isham, 034; James A. (chldn. of), 020; Mary

E., 020; Samuel S., 122; Wile, 048; Wiley, 025, 048, 054; Willie, 057, 060, 061
SLOAN: --, 028; Alexander, 033
SLOMAN: S. J., 054
SMALL: William J., 180
SMEDE: Abraham K., 055; George M., 055
SMELLINGS: Sarah, 150
SMITH: Abram, 180; Agnes, 178; Alexr., 134; Alla, 160; Alpha, 098; Amanda, 077; Ambrose, 207; Ammos Young, 020; Anderson V., 034; Anderson W., 059, 181; Anderson, Mrs.,100; Andrew, 040; Ann (Polly), 055; Ann, 186; Anthony S., 180; Araminta, 020; Armind, 167; Arthur, 020, 118; Augustin, Cpl., 207; Bailey, 077; Benajah, 054; Billy, 020; Burey, 180; Catherine, 181; Charles A., 179; Charles, 046, 054, 201; Clayton Augustus, 040; Dan, 054; Daniel S., 179; David, 040, 054, 109, 179, 211; Edith, 152; Edward L., 209; Edwin F., 115; Edwin S., 114, 209, 211;
SMITH: Elem W., 181; Elisha, 077; Eliza (5 ch), 096; Elizabeth Mariah, 020; Elizabeth, 150, 154, 160, 164, 184; Emily, 093; Esther, 148; F.A., Mrs., 180; Family, 198; Fielding M., 179; Francis Alice, 020; Frank, 020; George L., 033; George M., 054; Gilly, 179; H.L., 020; Hardaway, 075; Hardeway, 122; Harknus, 020; Henry M., 020; Henry, 103; Herman (chldn of), 020; Herman, 020; Hill, 054;
SMITH; Horace G., 020; Howard, 037; Hugh, 054; Isaac, 208; Iverson, 036; Jackson, 1st Cpl., 127; Jackson, 206; Jackson, 2nd Lt., 121, 205; Jackson, Lt., 206, 207; James H., 061; James M., Gov., 054; James R., 179; James, 047, 107, 109, 112, 115, 116, 124, 177, 178, 211; James, Ens., 124, 127, 202; James, Lt., 116; Jane G., 181; Jane, 174; Jno. W., 118; Jno., 184; Job, 178; Joher, 180;
SMITH: John B., 181; John H., 180; John M., 080; John N., 103; John S., 054; John W. (chldn. of), , 020; John W., 020, 110, 115, 210, 211; John W., Lt., 210; John, 029, 054, 109, 119, 121, 178; John, Cpl., 206; Joseph, 082, 179; Joseph, Jr., 075; Joseph, Sr., 020, 054; Joshua, 103, 118, 179; L.J., 020; L.K. (chldn. of), 020; Leven, 054; Levin, 020, 219; Lucy, 020, 142, 173; Lula V., 020; Marta, 114; Martain, 178
SMITH: Martha, 170; Martin L., 020; Martin, 120, 128, 206, 210; Martin, Sgt., 206, 207; Mary (chldn. of), 020; Mary Ann Arabella, 020; Mary Ann C., 174; Mary Ann Jennings, 172; Mary Ann L., 186; Mary B., 020; Mary J., 163; Mary M., 157; Mary W., 020; Mary, 020, 097, 099, 165, 185; Miles, Ens., 201; Milse, Ens., 201; Milton B., 196; Nancy, 020, 141, 185;
SMITH: Nathan, 115; Nathaniel, 054; Nellie, 020; Nicholas, 178; Nimrod, 177; Pacience, 178; Patrick, 020; Patsey, 152; Peter, 020; Peyton, 054; Philip, 041; Philo, 202; Poley, 143; Polly, 020; Rachel Emeline, 180; Radford, 024; Ralph, 178; Rebecca B., 182; Robert F., 128; Robert F., Cpl., 210; Robert F., Sgt., 103; Robert M., 020, 179;
SMITH: Robert Ousley, 198; Robert W., 059; Robert, 118, 179; Robt. F., Capt., 129; Rosanna J., 020; Ruby (chldn. of), 020; Sally, 020, 170, 222; Samuel H.(chldn of), 020; Samuel H., 080, 180; Sarah E. (chldn. of), 020; Sarah E., 020; Sarah Frances, 020; Sarah Jane, 180; Sarah, 020, 169, 170; Seaborn J., 181; Sherman J., 180; Sion, 048;
SMITH: Sultana, 151; Susan, 162; Susanna, 169; Synthia, 036; Theodoric L., 181; Thomas, 054, 082, 178, 205, 210; Thompson L., Rev., 147; Thos., 124; Tolbert G., 179; Vines, 055; Wales, 020; Wiley, 128, 205; William E., 055; William P., 180; William, 020, 109, 134, 178, 214; Willie Burch, 020; Winney, 155; Wm. J., 179; Wm., 211; Yelverton P., 055
SMITHWICK: John, 109
SNEAD: Meridith, 041; Patrick H., 055; Roy N., 020; William, Sr., 181
SNEED: Meridith, 026
SNOW: Cassey, 156; John P., 076
SNOWDEN(?): Anderson, 077
SNOWDEN: Gilbert T., 055
SOLOMAN: S. J., 055
SON (SUVIVOR): Andrew, 055
SONDHEIM: Lissan, 055
SONNON: Widow, 084
SORRELL: Capt., 132; Elizabeth T., 152; Ethelred, Capt., 210; Nancy, 020; Needham, 112, 203
SORRELLS: James, 020
SPAIN: Jno., 107; John, 055
SPALDING: Frank E., 020
SPARKS: Hardy, Lt., 117; Henaretta, 152; Martin P., 055; Martin T., 029; Thomas H., 020
SPEAR: Alva, 055
SPEARS: George C., 020; John, 020; Rollins B., 055
SPEER: Annie E., 020; Emory, 027; John, 020
SPEERS: Thomas, 119
SPENCE: Margarett, 155
SPENCER: Mary, 084; Paul (chldn of), 020; R. A., Mrs., 090; Sallie C., 020; William, 025, 055
SPENDER: Mary, 085
SPENKS(?): John C., 081
SPENKS: Allen, 089; Cicero, 089; Eliza E., 089; Henry, 089; John C., 089; Salley, 178
SPERRY: F. L., 055
SPILLAS: Warrington, 033
SPILLER: Charles, 179
SPILLERS: Peggy, 176; Warrington, 112
SPINKS: Bradford H., 180; Bradford, 221; Charles B., 020; Eliza, 101; Elizabeth, 151; Enoch (chldn. of), 020; Enoch, 062, 206, 208, 219; John C., 089; John Cicero, 180; John E., 089; L. L., 084; M. L., 084; Mary, 160; Sarah & (6 chldn), 084; Sarah C., 164; Sarah, 096, 101; V. B., 084; William, 178
SPIRIR: Thos., 201
SPIUR: Thomas, 112
SPIVEY: Abraham, 071, 072
SPPS(?): Susan E., 142
SPRAULDING: Frank, 020
SPRAWLING: Frank, 032
SPRINGER: Job, 214, 215
SPULLOCK: Drury, 020; James (chldn. of), 020; James, 020; Morning, 020; Owen, 020, 207; Winiford, 020
SPURLOCK: Benjamin M., 180; Betsey, 184; Elizabeth, 020, 164; Matilda F., 146; Owen, Capt. 205; Sarah Ann, 167
SQUIRE: Charles, 055, 061
ST. JOHN: David W., 024; Isaac R., 024
STAFFER: Espy, 093
STAFFORD: Epsy, 020; Malcolm, 020; Malcom, Mrs., 090
STALLINGS: John E., 055
STAMPS: Charles, 1st, Sgt., 126; Thomas, 124, 202; Timothy, 055
STANFORD: John R., 168
STANLEY: Charity M., 052; Ezekiel, 178; H. D. (chldn. of), 020; H. D., 020; Julia P., 020; Marcellus, 180
STANLY: Nancy, 152
STANTON: James, 055
STAPLES: Henry P., 180
STARK (?): Benteen (?), 107
STARK: Bowling W., 055; John W., 055; Jones, 181; Jones, Capt., 119; Louisa, 165; Washington F., 180; William, 055
STARKS: Benton, 032, 131; Jones (chldn. of), 020; Mary E., 181; Philip J., Capt., 110
STARN: William, 025, 044; William, Capt., 202, 203; William, Lt., 117
STARNES(STONE?): B. Lucretia, 180
STARNES: Presley B., 180; Sarah, 146; William P., 020; William, Capt., 124, 125, 202; Wm., Capt., 201
STARNS: William, 050; William, Capt., 202, 204; Wm., 091, 107, 121
STATEHAUR: Elizabeth, 153
STATHAM: (chldn. of), 020; Daniel, 180
STATOM: Anderson, 178
STATUM: Anderson, 113, 121, 205; Anderson, Sgt., 125, 206; David, 179
STATUND: Anderson, Sgt., 125
STATURN: Anderson, 4th Sgt., 127
STEADLEY: William, 027, 028
STEAVY: William, 062
STEDMAN: James, 055, 057; Saml., 077
STEEDLEY: William A., 181
STEEDLY: Georgetta, 055
STEEL: George W., 049; James C., 055; John, 055
STEELE: Elizabeth, 171; John H., 055
STEGEMEN: John F., 004
STEPHENS: Alexander, 055; Brankey, 042; Cyntha, & 1 ch., 087; Cyntha, 086; Daniel R., 181; David (chldn. of), 020; David, 020, 027, 041, 042, 048, 051, 055, 059, 077, 135, 181, 217; David, Sgt., 205; Elizabeth, 091, 148, 151, 171; Frankey, 166; Gillis, 148; Harris, 023, 036, 049, 055, 059, 179; Henry Thomas, 181; Henry, 074, 220; James Ens., 202; James, 204;
STEPHENS: Jno. F., 114; John F., 115; John W. H., 020; John, 020, 214; John, Ens., 127; Joseph, 097; Joshua, 028, 037, 042, 045, 055, 059; Joshua, Jr., 179; Lucenda, 097; M.A.E. 168; Mahala, 097, 148; Mariah, 160; Martha, 162; Matha Ann, 097; Michael, 048, 057; Mrs., 097; Nancy, 141; Overon, 122; Overton, 042, 181; Polly, 157; Prince, 020; Rutha, 156; Sally, 158; Susannah, 161; Thomas H., 020; Thomas, 181; William, 178; Young J. W. H., 181; Young John William, 020
STEPHENSON: Martha J., 020; Robert M., 180; Thomas W., 020, 180; Thomas, 073, 075
STERET(?): James, 112
STERET: James, 123, 203
STERN: Charles, 020, 056

STERNS: William, 056; Wm., 107
STETTMAN: George, 179
STEVENS: Cynthia, 091; Gray, 135; James, 178; James, Sgt., 203; John F., 178, 210, 211; John, 178; John, Ens., 203, 204; Mary Emma, 020; Maryann, 184; Minerva, 135; Oliver, 020; Thomas, 055; William B., 049
STEWART: --, 056; ? (chldn. of), 020; Aletha C., 089; Alexander T., 056; Alford W., 089; Alford, 178; Alford, Capt., 129; Alfred J., 075; Alfred, 046, 047, 056, 084, 085, 100, 180; Alfred, Capt., 201; Alvin, 091; Charles D., 056; Charles E., Ens., 203; Charles E., Sgt., 202; Charles H., 056; Charles P., 056; Charles, 020, 056, 113, 130, 205; Charles, Ens., 124; Chas., 128; Clarecy, 172; Elizabeth, 136, 174; Frances, 149; Frederick (chldn of), 020; George R., 202;
STEWART: Hannah R., 183; Isaac, 020; James, 073, 214, 217; James, Capt., 120, 126, 127, 202-204; James, Ens., 201, 202; James, Jr., 209; Jeptha, 202, 214, 216; John, 037; Ketty Elizabeth, 187; Lazarous, 063; Lazarus, 062; Lethia E., 101; Levi, (ch. Of), 079; Levi, 079, 118; Levy, 179; Mariah, 155; Martha Ann, 151; Martha, 214; Mary Cobb, 164; Mary F., 089; Permelia Angelina, 177;
STEWART: Reuben, 062, 109, 115, 178, 205-207, 210, 211; Reuben, Capt., 207; Reuben, Ens., 204, 205; Reuben, Lt., 125, 129; Reuben, Sgt. 210; Reubin, 109; Richard, 020, 177; Robert, 049; Ruben, Ens., 127; Salley, 168; Samuel, 029, 040; Sarah A., 098, 100, 187; Sarah E., 093; Silas C., 180; Thomas, 056, 074, 178, 179; Thos., 136; William B., 180; William, 056; Wm., 136
STEWELL: James, 129
STEWORTE: Thomas, 074
STIDMAN: Charlotte, 143; Elizabeth, 160; James, 055; Patsy, 149
STILWELL: Richard, 033, 061
STINCHCOMB: William A. C., 180; Wm. A. C., 080
STOKES: Archibald, 056; Henry, 052; Joseph T., 179; Joseph T., Sgt., 119; M., 071; Montford, 178; Tabitha, 165; Thomas, 056; William M., 025, 056; William, 025, 056; Wm. M., 178
STONE: Betsey, 077; D. M., 056; Elizabeth, 160 186; James, 020; Joel, 204; John M., 180; John W.N., 020; John, 097; Margarett, 172; Mary, 097; Milley, 171; Nancy, 097; Polly, 157, 173; Sarah Jane, 187; Susan B., 153; Thornton, Sgt., 201; Uriah, 020; Wyturoy, 077
STONEHAM: Henry, 057, 113, 120; Joseph, 056; Henry, 205
STONEURN: Henry, 130
STORY: (chldn. of), 020
STOVALL: --, 053, 056; Alex, 050; Augustine, 056; B.A., 020, 050; Bolling, 050; Charles, 056; Harvey G., 020; Jennie, 050; John (chldn of), 020; John, 056; Littleberry, 031, 111; Lizzie, 050; M. W., 050; Maria, 020; Mary, 183; Nelly, 050; Pleasant, 020, 056; William L., 026; William W., 041
STOVER: Wm., 124
STRACHAN: Alexander, 020
STRAFFORD: Malcom, 180
STRAHAM: Charles M., 004
STRAHAN: Charles Morton, 197
STRAND: John, 056
STRANGER (STRAUN?): Francis, 178
STRATEHAM: David, 110
STRATHAM: Anderson, 028; Nelson, 028
STRAUGHAN: Nancy, 178; Tapley, 178
STRAUGHN: James, Ens., 126; Travis, Capt., 123, 201
STRAUS: Joseph, 056
STRAWN: Sary, 170
STREAT: George S., 178
STRECKFUSS: C. F. (chldn. of), 020; C. F., 020; John F., 020
STREET: George, 3rd Sgt. 127
STRICKLAND: A., (Orphs.) 097; Ansel B., 179; Ansil, (Orph.) 097; Burton, 040; Geo. Washington, 088; Hardy, 179; James Hanon, 088; John A., 020, 119, 179; John J. (chldn of), 020; Mary & ch., 085; Mary, 080, 089, 096, 097; Monroe, 088; Mrs. & ch., 084; Mrs., 098, 100; Noah, 179; Thomas, 208; Washington, 178
STRICKLIN: Mary, 166
STRINGER: James, 020, 030, 035, 043, 054, 056, 214; Leonard, 036
STRONG: Charles, 023, 056, 109; Charles, Sr., 056; Charly, 056; Elijah, 020, 025, 026, 030, 034, 177, 203; Elisha, 046, 050, 056; Elizabeth, 026; Fanney, 174; George J., 038, 039; Harriet, 020; Isham, 020; James M., 020, 051, 058, 118, 179; John, 020, 023, 045, 050, 056, 179; John, Sr., 020; Johnson, 029, 050, 052, 214; Mariah, 158; Marten Luther, 179;
STRONG: Montford, 021; Peggy, 021; Pinina, 049; Polly, 160; Robert, Sgt., 129; Salley, 149, 160; Sally, 149; Samuel J., 040; Sherwood (chldn. of), 021; Sherwood, 021, 025-027, 056; Susanah, 143; Temple, 049; Washington, 027; William (chldn. of), 021; William E., 027, 056, 119; William J., 021, 179; William M., 069; William, 021, 023, 025, 026, 029, 042, 056, 057; William, Jr., 050, 077; William, Sr., 056; Wm. E., 118
STROTHER: John, 213
STROUC: William, 221
STROUD: Eli, 177; Eliza V., 148; James, Jr., 209; John W., 081; John, 021, 179; Leroy, 209; Levi, 114, 115, 177; Levy, 123, 209; Mark, 021, 081, 221; Martha E., 169; Martha, 021; Mary, 146; Orin, 178; Polly, 160; Salley, 160; Sarah B., 157; Susan J., 169; Tensey, 179; William, 021, 057, 075, 121, 178, 205; William, Sgt., 129; William, Sr., 021; Wm., 071, 128, 211
STUART: James, 023; James, Capt., 124; M., 090; Nancy, 160; Robert, 039, 045, 049, 055, 057, 079, 177; Salley, 182; Sarah, 090
STUDIVANT: Jesse, 040
STUDIVEN: Edwin, 178
STURDIVANT: J. Jesse, 035; Jesse, 021, 040; John, 057, 179
STURGES: John, 074, 111; William, 111
STURGIS: Andrew, 021; Henry (chldn. of), 021; Josiah, 025
STURGUS: James Miner, 177
SUBER: E. M., 021
SUIRLING: John, 032
SULER(?): John B., Sgt. 210
SULEY: John, 208
SULLIVAN: Thomas, 208
SULVEY: John B., 211
SUMMERFORD: William, 057
SUMMERGILL: James, 180
SUMMERLAND: Lazarus, 115
SUMMERLIN: Joseph, 113, 206; Lazarus, 112; Nancy, 170
SUMMERS: Daniel, 178, 181; Dewel, 178, 205; Dewell, 208; Duel, 037, 124; Elizabeth, 155, 157, 166; Emeline, 186; Francis, 135; Harden, 135; Mary, 185; Nancy Ann, 182; Nancy, 157; Rachael, 148; Seaborn, 113, 130, 205; Seabourn, 179; Sebron, 124; William, 135
SUMMERY: Peter A., 057
SUMMEY: John S., 057; Peter A., 057
SUMMY: Peter R., 061
SUMNERS: Daniel, 114
SUMNEY: Cupid, 095
SUMTER: James Mc, 122
SUNDERLAND: Martha & ch., 084, 085; Martha, 096, 097; William, 057, 180
SUNDERLIN: William, 181
SUSSDROFF: Gustamus, 052
SUTHERLAND: Edmd., 071; Edmund, 071
SUTTLE: Jane L., 165; Jesse, 028, 053
SUTTLES: --, 057; Isaac, 029; Jesse, 202; Jessie, 057; William, 057
SUTTON: Joel, 057; Williams, 057
SUWENCES: Duel, 116
SWAN: C. C., 097; L., 074; Mary E., 097; Robert, 122, 181
SWANN: Christopher C., 082; Lemuel, 021, 073
SWANSON: John, 057; Lemuel, 112, 114, 115, 121, 208-210; Lemuel, Cpl., 210; Lemuel, Sgt., 202; S., 057; Samuel, 057
SWEART: Lucinda, 083
SWEENY: Miles, 038
SWIFT: Jno. D., 115; John D., 179, 209, 211; Susan Y., 153; William A., 057; Wm. A., 110
SWINNEY: Mark E., 038, 050, 051, 061, 110; Mark, 062; Marke E., 036; Samuel H., 178; Seno D. E., Cpl., 110; Timothy, 179
SYKES: Amanda & 2 chldn., 085
SYKIE: Amanda & 2 chldn., 085
TAIDE: Jency, 143
TAIT: Alexander S., 182
TALBERT: Ann, 086; Caroline, 083; James, 183; James, Ens., 129; Martha J., 146
TALBOT: Arthur, 024; Elizabeth, 053, 057; Emma C., 092; Frances, 092; Geo. J., 092; Henry L., 092; James, 061; John, 183; M. C., Mrs., 093; Mary A., 093; Mary J., 092; Sarah L., 092; Sucky, 143; William, 182; Wm., 092
TALBOTT: James, Ensgn, 201; Westly, Sgt., 202; William, Ens., 117
TALLEY: E., 208; Eleanah, 209; Eleaner, 208; Eleanor, 208; Eleazer, 114; Joseph, 115, 210
TALLY: Elkaner, Capt., 210
TALMADGE: --, 057; C. G., 021; E. A., Mrs., 057; E. W., Mrs., 057; John, 021, 031, 057, 062, 069, 076, 131; M.A.,057; Stephen C., 131; W.A., 057; W.P., 057; William A., 057; William K., 021; William P., 021, 057, 075, 183; Wm. P., 075; Wm. R., 072
TALMAGE: John, 030, 045, 057; Lewis T., 057
TANEER: Martin, 182
TANKERSLEY: Sarah, 149; Whinney, 149; William, Sgt. 210; Wm., Sgt., 207
TANNER: John, 057; Julia, 168; Thomas, 182
TANNING: L. J., 057

TAPPAN: John H., 021; Theodore, 021
TARPLEY: Augustine(chldn of), 021; Augustine, 034; Augustus A., 052; Augustus, 110; Easlena S., 183; Jennett L., 021; Joel (chldn of), 021; Joseph (chldn of), 021; Joseph, 021; Richard, 021
TATE: Caroline, 021; James C., 028
TAYLOR: Benjamin, 026, 057; Catherine, 142; Daniel, 057; Edmond W., 182; Edward W., 027; F. P., Col., 119; Henry, 202; Hugh, 042; James H., 031; James J., 030; James J., Sgt., 110; James Jones, 024, 029, 030, 037, 050, 062; James, 048, 057, 181;
TAYLOR: John H., 027, 041, 043, 059; John, 027, 182, 216; John, Sgt., 206, 207; Josiah, 182; Mary Jane, 162; Mary M., 170; Mary, 150; Nicy, 181; Nimrod, 214; Peter B., 057; Peter, 057; R.J., Jr., 004, 196; Richard D. B. (chldn of), 021; Richard D.B., 021; Richard D., 183; Robert G. T., 021, 183; Roland, 024, 027, 029, 039, 041, 050, 059, 063, 214-216; Rolin, 067; Rowland, 035; Sarah Ann, 021; Thos., Sgt., 202; William B., 028, 033, 037, 046, 048, 057, 066; William, 109; Wm. B., 109; Wm., 103, 119
TEAMAN: William, 057
TEAT: Newton, 097
TEGNER: Hope H., 114; William, 181
TEKLE: John, Sgt., 124
TEMPLE(?): Lea, 058
TEMPLE: Lea, 057; Lee, 026
TENNELL: Francis, 057
TENNEY: Henry B., 184; Shubael, 029, 057, 182; Shubnel, 047
TENNY (TURNER?): Eliza J., 150
TENNY: S., 119
TERRELL: David, 057; James D., 057; John D., 057; William, 042
TERREY: Shubel, 043
TERRY: Alexander, 2nd Sgt., 126; Alexr., Sgt., 129; S., 103
THACKER: Elizabeth, 144; Garrett, 132; James, 132; Katherine, 135; Lucetea, 132; Lucinda, 135; Ostin H., 132; Rebecca, 144; William H., 081
THARASHER: Isaac, Lt., 202
THEATS: Charles, 057
THIMES: Martin, 208
THOMAS(?): Micajah, 182
THOMAS: --, 041; Alla, 177; Almira Catharine, 089; Ann M., 164; Ben, 057; Benjamin F., 057; Delana, 173; Doctor Hook, 089; Drury, 182; Ed L., 114; Edward L., 112, 121, 203, 208; Edward T., 208; Edwd. L., 079; Elizabeth Ann, 165; Elizabeth C., 175; Frances E., 153; Frankey, 143; Frederick S., 051; George, 135; Giles, 043; H. P., 057; Hartwell J., 082, 183; Hartwell, Mrs., 101; Henry, 057, 058; Hershal, 117; J., 058;
THOMAS: James (?), 206; James D., 184; James Henry, 077; James L., 025, 029, 036, 038, 040, 045, 055, 206; James, 111; James, Jr., 044; Jas. L., 113; Jet, 184; Jett, 040, 058; John G., 183; John J., 021; John W., 058; John, 058, 062, 077, 182; Joseph, 055; L.P., 072, 074; Lawrence, 058; Leuis W., 028; Levan W., 120; Levi, 135; Levie P., 075; Levin W., Capt., 117; Levin, 119; Lloyd, 206; Lovick P., 057;
THOMAS: Lovick P., Maj.,110; Lovick Pierce, 183; Loyd, 128; Lucenda, 150; Malind Caroline, 089; Mariah W., 185; Mary Emer, 089; Matilda A., 080; Matilda, 176; Merrill, 058; Miles, 039; Milison D., 182; Penina W., 058; Peninah W., 058; Ralf, 058; Randall, 039, 040; Ruida, 059; S., 058; Samuel, 182; Sarah Ann, 158; Sarah, 142, 213; Stephen, 058, 182, 203; Stephens, 058; Steven, 058; Stevens, 028, 058, 066, 073, 112, 116, 122, 203, 208; Stevens, Jr., 183; Susan Jett, 163; Theophilus, 182; Washington, 184; William R., 027, 052; William, 021, 183; William, III, 183; William, Jr., 183, 219; William, Sr., 021; Wm., 122
THOMASON: James, 117; William, 058
THOMPSON (?): 1st Lt., 205
THOMPSON: Aaron, 183; Allen E., 182; Allen, 107, 117; Ann T., 156; Asbury, 183; Atven Lee, 088; B. C., 213; Benajah S., 081; Betsey, 170; Charles, 058; Elenor, 173; Elizabeth, 156; Emeline E., 081; F. B., 083; Fanny, 173; Frances, 076, 152; Frederick, 182; G. G., 183; George N., 183; Harriett Stan, 089; Hartwell, Mrs., 101; Hugh, 133; J. H., Mrs., 099; James H., 080, 183; James R., 082; James, 182, 183; Joel, 073; John N., 021; John Park, 088; John, 056, 072, 077; Lenora, 133; Lucy, 071; M., 085; Malinda A., 163; Manerva E., 177
THOMPSON: Martha F., 177; Martin, 122; Mary June, 155; Mary W., 183; Mary, 168, 170; Matilda, 153; Middleton, 073, 075, 077, 081, 182; Musette Kate, 131; Payton G., 077; Philamon, 182; Pressie, 186; Ransom, 077; Richard M., 075, 183; Richard, 110, 182; Richard, Lt., 120, 125, 206, 210; Richd., 1st Lt., 121, 127; Richd., 1st, Sgt., 126; Richd., Lt., 130; Robert C., 058; Robert, 044, 055, 058, 182; Ruth, 069, 076, 077; Rutha, 185; S. H., 075; Samuel, 110;
THOMPSON: Sarah, 160; Serena, 101, 102; Susan Amanda, 131; Susan, 185; Swan, 214, 215; Teresea, 133; Thomas B., 040, 058, 059; Thomas, 062, 181, 182; Thos., 125; Wiley, 183; William, 079, 112, 116, 123, 133, 181, 183, 204, 216, 217; William, 1st Sgt., 202; William, 2nd Sgt., 126; William, Sgt., 126; William, Sr., 058; Willis, 122; Wm., 079, 120, 204
THOMSON: James R., 082
THORNE: Mary, 176
THORNTON: Allen, 182; Benjamin, Rev., 147; Beverly A., 183; Eliza, 088; Eluiza, 099; Frances, 113; Frances, Ens., 127, 130; Francis, 043, 204, 205; Francis, Ens., 125, 126, 205, 206; Homer, 040; Isaac N., 021; J.N., 088; James A., 182; James A., Lt., 210; James, 208; John, 095; Louisa, 085, 101; Luiza, 095; Mary Lou, 221; Moland H., 183; Newton N., 095; Sally, 174; Wiley A., 081, 183; William T., 183
THORTON: Charles, 058
THOUMOND: Harris, 103
THRASHER: --, 085; America, 086; Asenath C., 173; Bailey Hilliard, 077; Barber, 058; Bartlow, 058; Barton C., 081, 183; Barton, 021, 058, 059, 103, 108, 109, 113, 114, 118, 121, 128, 130, 205, 208; Big John, 095; Caleb, 095; Carolin, 175; Celestia A., 080; Flora, 077; Frances, 156; Francis, 142; Harbert, 021; Herbert, 021; Isaac (chldn of), 021; Isaac, 021, 074, 079, 109;
THRASHER: Isaac, Ens., 202; Isaac, Lt., 127, 202; Isaac, Sgt., 129; Jackson M., 021, 111; Jackson M., Sgt., 110; James Warren Hill, 077; John F., 021; John O., 077, 080; John, 128, 205, 207; John, Cpl., 210; John, Lt., 206; Joseph C., 021; Josephine V., 021; Martha B., 173
THRASHER: Mary, 083, 171; Marzer, 077; Nancy, 083, 085, 095, 156; Orange, 095; Peter, 096; Phoebe, 083, 086; Pinckney B., 041; Pinckney, 114, 209, 210; Pincknye, 209; Pinkney, 208; Primus, 096; Rhoda, 083, 086; Richard, 096; Ruth, 181; Susan, 142, 161, 188; Tabitha C., 149; Vara, 077; William H., 028, 034, 044, 080
THREATT: Tavner, 183; Thomas C., 183
THRELKEED: Thomas, 221
THRELKELD: J. J., 059; T. D., Mrs., 099; Thomas D., 021; William B., 021
THRELKILD: Thomas D., 080
THURMAN: Anne, 021; Ansan, 025; Benjamin, 031, 039, 049; Evaline S., 021; Harris (chldn. of), 021; Harris, 021, 128, 205; James, 059; John C., 183; John F. (chldn of), 021; John F., 021, 183; John, 039; Lynch M., 059; Mary, 021; Micajah, 059; Philip, 059; Phillip, 059; Richard O., 183; Richard, 060; Richd. D., Mrs., 101; William, 021, 035, 045
THURMAND: John, 021; Margareta (2 chldn), 095; Philip, 095
THURMON: Oliver N., 021
THURMOND: Benjamin (chldn. of), 021; Benjamin, 021, 181; Elizabeth A., 021; Elizabeth, 163; Emily C., 155; Harris, 059, 113, 118, 130, 183; Henry, 059; James R., 183; John, 037, 053; Margaret & 2 chldn., 085; Mary, 188; Nancy, 055; Philip, 067, 072, 074; Phillip, 072; Robert, 201; S.P., 059; Sallie, 021; William H., 080, 183; William, 059
THWEATT: Daniel, 021; Micajah W., Lt., 210; Peterson, 055
TIBERNE: Joseph B., 044
TIDWELL: Roderick, 026
TIFFENS: Elizabeth, 090
TIGNER: Elizabeth, 160; Hope H., 208; Innicence, 156; Nancy, 154; Phil(l)ip, 021, 214, 215; Phillip (chldn. of), 021
TIGNOR: Permelia, 154
TILEYRY: Joshua, 181
TILLER: Amanda, 087; Elisha, 021, 095; Elizabeth, 088; J. R., 099; James A., 087; James R., 088; Jas. R., 098; John, 087; Levisa, 095; Louisa, 084, 085; Margrate, 087; Richard, Mrs., 101; Richd., 102; V., 102; V., Mrs., 099
TILLMAN: Gold, 055
TILLY: John M., 183
TILMAN: Dickson, 059; James, 059
TIMMS: Mary, 187; Rachel, 155; Robert, 183
TINDAL: Bowlegs, 095; Mary, 086, 095
TINDALL: Allathia W., 167; Caroline E., 183; Frances, 077; Frank, 077; Laurana, 021; Louisa, 077; Luckey, 077; Marshall, 077; Walter, 182; William (chldn. of), 021
TINSLEY: James, 024, 050, 109, 114, 119, 120, 208, 211, 218
TIPPANS: Elerar A., 091

TIPPENS: Elizabeth, & 1 ch., 087; Elizabeth, 083
TIPPER: Elizabeth Ann, 171
TIPPINS: Elizabeth, 086, 093
TISSANS (TIPPANS?): Elizabeth, 099
TOBBERT: Albert F., Mrs., 090; Joel T., 091; T.C., Mrs., 090
TODD: Henry Waring, 183; M.L., Mrs. (chldn. of), 021; T. B. F., 021
TOLBERT: Ana, 097; Ann, 182; Carolen, 083; Caroline, 093, 097; James, 072; Jesse, 097; John, 098; John, Sgt., 111; Leanah, 146; Miles, 182; Osburn, 072; Sarah, 182; Tapley B., 182; William, 032
TOMLINSON: Humphrey, 059; Robert, 030
TOMMASON: James, 182
TOMPKINS: Nathaniel U., 059
TONEY: Anthony, 184
TORRENCE: William H., 059
TORRY: Alexander, 040, 217; Alexander, Sgt., 202
TORY: Alexander, 059
TOTHERAW: Isaiah, 072
TOTHERON: Isaiah, 075
TOTHERROW: Isaiah, 184; Isiah, 059; Martha, 059
TOTTEY: John, 042
TOTTY: John, 027-029, 034, 037, 046, 051, 059
TOWNS: Alfred, 021; Amelia Frances, 183; Benj., 119; Benjamin, 024, 029, 058, 059, 109; Daniel, 030; Elizabeth D., 021; James H., 091, 093, 183; John M., 183; Margaret A., 091; Nancy M., 147; Nancy Mary, 180; Susan J., 094; Susan, 090, 091, 093; Wm. H., 091
TOWNSEND: Andrew, 182; Thomas, 181
TRAEDWAY: Elijah, Lt., 125
TRAMELL: H. F., Maj., 202
TRAMMALL: Drakeford L., 208; Milcah, 178
TRAMMEL: Daniel, 049, 059, 063; David, 181; F.H., Maj., 124; Fannie, 051; Francis M., 051; Francis M., Lt., 127; Francis W., Lt., 124; Francis, Lt.129; John, 182
TRAMMELL(?): Harrison, Capt., 201
TRAMMELL: Daniel (chldn. of), 021; Daniel, 021, 031, 051, 054; Elisha, 079; Fanny, 051; Farr H., 110; Farr H., Capt., 201; Farr H., Maj., 126, 202, 203; Ferr K., 123; Frances M., 204; Francis M., 051; Francis M., Sgt., 203; Francis, 041, 043, 051, 059, 182; Francis, Lt., 202; Harris, 182; John, 041, 051, 059, 182, 206; Martha, 097; Robert(chldn of), 021; Robert, 021, 183; Sarah A. A., 151
TRAMMILL: Daniel, 030; John, 128
TRANSWELL: Caswell G., 183
TRAWEEK: Burwell, 112
TRAWICK: Allen, 181; Burwell, 123, 203; Lunsford, 023; Robert, 182; Spencer, 040, 046
TRAYLOR: Francis, 021; Reuben, Sgt., 202; Salley, 185
TRAYWICK: Burrwell, 021; Burwell, 116; Easther, 156; Lunsford (chldn. of), 021; Lunsford, 021
TREADWAY: Elijah, 023, 055, 060, 125; Elijah, Jr., 205; Elijah, Lt., 130, 205; George, 059
TREADWELL: Harney, Sgt, 205; Harrill E. E., 089; Isaac, 021, 073, 080, 182, 183; Jacob, Lt., 124, 202; James, 125; James, Capt., 130, 203, 204; Jas., Capt., 113; Lucy J., 148; Mary, 181; Missouri L., 089; Sarah Alexander, 089; Stephen, 179; Steven, 089
TREDWAY: Elijah, 2nd Lt., 127
TREDWEK: Jacob, Lt., 202
TREDWELL: Isaac, 107; Jacob, 182; Jacob, Lt., 126, 127; James, Capt., 125, 128; Stephen, 115
TRELKELD: T. D., Mrs., 102
TREMBLE: Robert, 181
TRIBBLE: Dicey, 168; Mary E., 021
TROUT: Nathaniel, 059; Sarah, 059
TROUTMAN: M. L., 021
TRUELLE: John, 034
TRUET: Riley, 059
TRUETT: Riley, 059
TRUMMELL: John, 059
TUCK: Boyd, 118; Doctor, 073; Eli B., 119; Elizabeth, 175; Joseph, 118; Margaret E., 173; Martha A. S., 169; Nancy, 219; Richard, 059; Richardson, 182; Robert W., 181; Sarah, 090; Susan Ann, 147; Thoas. A., 073; Thomas A., 037, 073, 075, 182; Thomas G., 059
TUCKER: Benj.F., 182; Coalman, 183; H. H., 059; Marth A., 100; Richard O., 041, 053
TUGGLE: Henry, 183
TUKLE: John, Sgt., 203
TUNNEL: N. E., 084
TUNNELL: George, 072, 073, 074
TURNELL: Ashley D., 080; Eliza A., 146; George, 075, 080, 183; James W., 080; John T., 081; John, 021; Mary V., 163; Robert (chldn. of), 021; Robert, 183; Robert, Mrs., 099; Salena Scott, 021; Susan, 169
TURNER: A. G., 099; Belsey, 132; Eliza, 182; Henry, 132; J.B., Mrs., 102; James G., 059; James, 035, 036, 040, 041, 043, 045, 047, 049-051, 054, 057, 059, 061, 182; John C., 037; John, 135, 182; Mary, 098; Nancy, 132; Polly, 132; Rebecca, 149; Reuben, 132, 182; Richard, 107; Susannah, 178; William P., 023, 037
TURNEY: Shubael, 103
TURNNER: J. B., Mrs., 099
TURPIN: William H., 032, 059
TWEDEWELL: Sarah (1), 135
TWEEDLE: John, 108
TWEEDWELL: John, 117
TWEEDY: J. K. (chldn. of), 021; J. K., 021
TWEINING: Sarah, Mrs., 079
TWINENG: Arianna N., 174
TWINING: Nathaniel, 182; S., Mrs., 079
TWITTY: Thomas, 061, 109; Thomas, Cpl., 207
TYE(?): Thomas, 182
TYE: James, 026; Job, 059; John, 026, 111, 123; Patsy, 148; Saml., 4th, Sgt., 126; Thomas T., 079; Thomas, 113, 130, 205; Thomas, 2nd Sgt., 127
TYNER: John, 182
TYRRELL: Isham, 095
TYSON: E., 1st Lt., 205; Ejune H., Lt., 130; Eugene H., 026, 059, 113, 119, 204, 207; Eugene H., Ens., 206L Eugene H., Lt., 207; Eugene S., 109; Eugine H., 1st Lt., 127; Uje, Lt., 203, 204; Wm. T., 122
ULMER: John P., Capt., 202
UPSHAW: Ben, 021; Martha R., 164
UPSON: Hannah, 045; Stephen, 045, 059
URNHART: John, 184
VAN ANTWERP: Edwin, 063
VAN HOUTEN: Daniel, 052, 164
VANANTWERP: Edwin, 060
VANBIBBER: George, 060
VANDEFORD: Charlotte, 179; John, 207; Richard, 028; Wm., 117
VANDERFORD: Allen C., 184; Augustus, 073; Thomas, 126; William, 030, 107
VANDIFER: Richard, 060
VANDIFORD: A. C., 054; R., 054; Richard, 051; William, 184; Wm., Cpl., 205
VANDIVERE: Artemicia R. A. S., 187
VANIDFORD: John, Sgt. 205
VANNEY: Jasper, 043
VARNER: Eli, 134; John, 134, 206, 207; John, Sgt. 210; Mary H., 134; Mary, 181; Matthew, 071
VARNUM (?): John, 210
VARNUM: G.W., 073; John, Sgt. 210
VASON: David A., 184
VAUGHN: James, 135; John, 184; Rebecca, 163; Reuben, 041
VEAL: Alexander, 184; George W., 081; Jerritt A., 081; Lucy Ann, 163; Martha E., 183; William F. M., 184
VELVIN: Ceiley, 134; Jethro, 134; Mary, 134; Nancy, 134; Robert, 134; Susannah, 134; Tempy, 134
VENABLE: B. F., 184
VENSON: Moses, Capt., 110
VERONE: William, 050
VERONEE: William, 046
VERSTILL: Tristram, 060
VERVNEE: William, 052
VESEY: Caroline, 158
VICARS: Frances, Mrs., 095; Gresham, 117; Martha, Mrs. (4 ch) , 095
VICHERY: Anna, 066
VICKERS: Absalom, 048, 066, 074, 184; Absalom, Mrs., 101; Absalum, 021; Anna, 184; Elias H., 048; Ferdinand, 184; Frances, 101; Graham, 112; Gresham, 043, 112, 114, 208; James, 184; Jane, 153; Joshua, Mrs., 101; Martin, 023, 025, 027, 052, 059, 184; Mary, 181; Silas W., 080; Young, 024, 060, 113, 184; Young, 3rd Sgt. 127
VICKERY: David, Mrs., 100; Gresham, 208; Rebecca, 090
VICKORS: Cathern, 171
VIKUS: Hollensworth, 133; Pollyann, 133; Silas, 133
VINCENT: Capt., 079; D. A., 097; Isaac C., 072; Isaac H., 060; Isaac L., 035, 048; Isaac S., 041, 051, 060, 062, 072, 122, 184; Isaw S., Capt., 118; Issac S., 037; J.S. (Isaac S.?), 220; J. S., 119, 123; J. S., Capt., 118; John F., 092; John, 095; Julia, 092; Lucy A., 092; Martha, 093; Mary E., 094; Moses, 184; Obadiah, Lt., 118; Sarah J., 172
VINSON: Allis, 091; Finny, 091; Isaac V., 184; Isaack, 097; James, Sgt., 207; John T., 091; July, 091; Lucy A., 091; Martha H., 096; Martha, 093; Mary V., 096; Mary, 187; Moses, 062; Moses, Lt., 119; Mrs., 090; O., Mrs., 090; Obadiah, 072, 079, 184; Obediah, 034, 048; Sarah A., 093
VOSS: Alexander, (Wife & ch.), 213; Alexander, 107
WADDEL: Elizabeth P., 165; James F., 208; James P., 026, 048, 052, 057, 185; M., D. D., 144; Wm. W., 079
WADDELL: Charles, 021, 044; William Henry, 021
WADDLE: Jas. F., 114; John, 060
WADE: Ann R., 179; Clementine, 084, 086, 095; John, 186; Martha, 082, 179; Matilda, 162; Robert, 060; Thomas B., 021, 082; Thomas, 047; Thomas, 3rd Sgt. 127;Thos., Sgt. 206
WADKINS: Charles A., 136; Moses, 136; Robert, 209; William J.,187
WADLEY: Ann, 146

WADSWORTH: Archibald H., 110; Francis, 034
WAGES Andrew J., 098; James, 051, 060; Lular, 092
WAGGENER: Seaborn, 081; David, 187; George, 039; Sarah, 153
WAGGONMAN: Susannah, 021
WAGNON: Harriett H., 169; John, 211
WAGONER: Mary S., 155
WAITER(MCCALLAR?): W. H. M., 213
WAKEMAN: Adams, 060; Mark H., 060
WAKER: Vilant, 093
WALDEN: Nancy, 149; William Henry, 184
WALKER: Abraham, 095; Abram, 060; Darcus, 166; Dicken, Lt., 207; Edwin A., 021, 073; Elder J.W., 221; Elizabeth, 133; Emily E., 097; James R., 185; James, 060; Jesse, 133; Jessee, 133; John C., 080; John W., Mrs., 102; John, 023; Joseph, 021, 060, 066; Josiah, 133; Julia (?), 090; Julia M., 069; Mariah M., 141; Martha, 172; Robert, 114, 208; Samuel, 186; Susan V., 023; Susan, 180; Taylor, 031; Thomas W., 187; V., Mrs., 091; Vilia A., 090; Viola, 098, 100; W.M., 097; William F., 023, 033, 034; William T., 080; Willy W., 091
WALKINS: Matthew G., 081
WALL: Amanda, 088, 099, 101, 102; Arthur, Sgt.,129; James E.,088
WALLACE: Charles W., 187; J.J., Rev., 146; James, 026, 060; John, 099; Joseph, 045; Margaret, 170; Samuel, 052, 184; Sarah, 021; William L., 112; William, 111
WALLARD: William, 123
WALLER: William, 185
WALLICE: Frances, 175; Mildred, 184
WALLIS: Amanda, 077; John F., 060; Josiah, 186; Nicholas, 030, 045; Reuben, 188; William B.A., 036; William B., 036
WALLRAVEN: Mary C., 090
WALLS: Arter, 111; Aster, 123; Elizabeth, 169
WALRAVEN: M. C., 100
WALSH: Eliza, 060
WALTALL: E. G., 055
WALTHALL: Adelaide, 048
WALTON: --, 196; George, 040, 060, 120, 208; James W.Y., 060; John C., 040, 054, 060; John, 060; Richard, 131; Robert, 060
WAMALING: Adolphus D., 187; Edward B., 092; George Ann, 093; Julia L., 092; Sarah F., 092
WAMER (WARNER?): William, 213
WAMMELL: Causuell G., 057
WANSLEY: T. A., Mrs., 021
WARD: Capt., 132; Creducy, 094; Edward, 207; Elam, 021; Elizabeth, 180; Emma, 094; Francis W., 165; Gabrielle, 150; Ithamer, 021; James A. (chldn of), 021; James A., 021, 187; John B., 187, 222; John D., 128, 205; John E., 122; John L. D., 074; John L., 111; John, 021, 185; Jonathan, 185, 208; Leonard, 025, 029, 030, 054, 056, 059, 060, 108, 115, 185; Leonard, Capt., 117; Martha Ann, 181;
WARD: Martha, 094, 098, 100; Mary, 180; Matthus A., 021; Mirian, 174; Nathan, 185; Nicy, 174; Obediah, 184; Sarah Ann, 147; Sidney R., 082; Susan, 094; Wiley, Cpl., 206; William T., 187; William W., 185
WARDEN: Robert R., 048
WARE (WARD?): Benjamin, 185
WARE (WIER): Priscilla, 148
WARE: Arquilla, 150; Bennet M., 060; Brittain, 021; E. H., 051; Edward E., 051; Edward R., 021, 060; Edward Rowell, 186; Edward, 109, 118, 119; Margaret E., 021; Mary L., 175; Nicholas, 187; Sally, 021; Thomas, 060
WARREN: Abraham C., 187; Jacob L., 082; John, 112, 203; John, 2nd Sgt., 126; Mary B., 004; Mary Bondurant, 137; Mary, 004; Susannah, 185
WASHAM (WORSHAM?): Thomas, 184
WASHHAUN: Thos., 117
WATERS: Collins, 185; J.P., 021; R. C., 042
WATKINS: --, 050, 060; Edward, 060; Elizabeth, 093; Emily E., 183; Henry M., 060; John, 060; Julia, 055; Lizzie, 021; Mary, 141; Moses, 184; Permilia A., 155; Phillip, Cpl., 206, 207; Rebecca, 055; Rebeckah, 175; Robert J., 021; Robert, 026, 060, 208; Susan, 153; Susie, 077; V., 113; Venson, 130; Vincent, 208; Vincent, Lt., 114; Vinsan, 124; Vinson, 205; William H., 082; Wm., 201
WATKNS(?): Betsey, Mrs., 090
WATLEY: Willis, 206, 221
WATSON: --, 060; Anderson, 060; Ann, 161; Catherine, 150; Columbus, 035; David, 111; John, 079, 112, 122; L.J., Miss, 022; Margarett, 162; Marion, 099; Sarah Ann, 150; Thomas L., 022; Vincent, 184; William, 185
WATTERS: Bash, Mrs., 090; Joseph, 071; Sally, 174
WATTS: Jacobus, 025; James, 030, 034, 060; Jeremiah, 060; John H., 184; L. B., 060; Littleberry, 185
WAYMAN: William, 060
WCELHANNON: Frances, 114
WEAL: Robert, 091; Theadore, 091
WEARING: --, 119
WEATERLY: William S., 045
WEATHERBY: William S., 034; William, 184
WEATHERFORD: Emily, & 4 chldn., 087; Emily, 101; James C., 080; William James, 186
WEATHERLY: Joseph I., 042; Joseph, 059; Josiah, 220; Sarah F., 177; Statery E., 173; William S., 028, 059, 062; William, 046, 054, 060, 112, 123; William, Ens., 207; William, Sr., 062
WEAVER: --, 135; Aaron N., 080; David, 046, 051, 110, 186; Elizabeth, 145; Jacob M., 187; Sofrona Ann, 188; T.A.D., 060
WEBB: John, 184; M. K., 055
WEBSTER: A. H., 208; Alexander, 114, 208; Edwin B., 060; Hosea, 023, 060; Joseph, 045; Robert, 022; William I., 111
WEED: Henry D., 060; Nathaniel B., 060
WEIL(?): Charlotte, 091
WEIL: Charlotte, 093; Peter, 022
WEIR: Charlotte Ann, 142; John N., 060, 069; John, 046; Lucinda, 141; Martha E., 147; Samuel, 112, 203; Sarah C., 175
WEIRE (WARE?): Emily, 142
WELBORN: Jack, 184
WELBOURN: William, 115
WELBURN: Wm. J., Lt., 130
WELCH: Clark W., 187; Elizabeth, 083; James, 034, 037, 040, 045, 046, 060, 109; Jenette, 155; Joshua, Lt., 129; Louisa A., 022; Narcissa L., 022; Saml., Ens., 129; Sarah Ann T., 183; Sophiah E., 180; W. P., 022
WELKINS: Wm., 116
WELLBORN: Abner, 060
WELLBOURN: Mary, 168
WELLER: John, 028
WELLOUGHBY: David, 081
WELLS: Abner, Ensgn, 207; Capt., 079; Elizabeth, 071; Joseph, 185; Mary, 022, 152; Paschal M., 058; Randolph, 075; Sophia A., 155; Thomas, 022, 061, 069, 103, 207; Thomas, Capt., 120; Thomas, Sgt. 206, 207; Thos., 210; W. B., 060; William B., 028, 060; William, 208
WELSEY: Charles, 116
WELSH: James, 039
WELTER: Andrew J., 080; Nicholas, 188
WENSTON: Joseph B., 074
WEST: Daniel, 184
WESTER: Alexander, 208
WESTLY: Sally, 157
WESTMORELAND: Freeman, 187; Mary, 099
WETHEFORD: Emely, 091
WETHERFORD: Emily, 083, 086
WETHERLY: T., Mrs., 090
WETTON (WILTON?): Rebecca, 149
WHALE(?): Joel, Lt., 119
WHALEY: James A., Lt., 110; James, Lt., 117
WHALY: James, 025
WHARTON: Benjamin, 022
WHATLES: Mr., 084
WHATLEY: Betsy, 177; Caty, 084; Eatey, 084; J.P., Mrs. (1 ch), 095; J.P., Mrs., 221; John W., 081, 082; Judge, 134; Judge, Mrs., 098, 100; Lucy, 095; Margaret W., 174; Margaret, 095; Mrs., 095; Nancy, 095; Old Lady, 221; Paschal J., 186; Penina, 134; Walton, 184; Willia, 134; Willie, 084; Willis, 054, 098, 134, 206; Wilson O. B., 186
WHEELE(?): Marth, 091
WHEELER: --, 060; Adam, Mrs., 098, 100; Benjamin, 112; Cathern, 090; Delilah, 160; Isham, 185; James, 022, 115, 184, 208, 209, 210; Jas., 114; Joseph, 039, 057, 061; Lucian R., 186; Mary, 159; Nancy, 165; Sallie, 082; Thomas, 027, 057, 217; William Augustus, 022
WHELER: Ann, 184
WHETEN (?): John L., Cpl., 210
WHIT: B., 103
WHITACUR: Nancy A., 083
WHITAKER: Anna Jane, 142; Annie E., 163; Jared J., 098; Nancy, 090, 094; William S., 092
WHITE: Andrew, 185; Ben, 040; Caraoline E., 097; Caroline A., 147; Cary, 022; Charles F., 022; Christopher, Sgt. 206, 207; Edward, 036; Elisha, 112; Elizabeth A., 187; Elizabeth M., 158; Elizabeth, 083, 090, 147; Frederick, 036; Henry, 114, 120, 208; Hugh, 067; I. R., 022; Jack, Sgt., 202; James W., Mrs., 091; James, 074; Jane, 187; Jno., 1st Lt., 205; John R., 022; John, 022, 060, 072, 075, 185, 187, 206; John, 1st Lt., 127; John, Lt., 125, 203, 204; Lavinah R., 163;
WHITE: Mary A., 101; Mary, 096; Naomi, 158; Palley, Mrs., 100; Polly, 178; Prudy, 090; Rebecca B., 022; Robert, 072; Saml. H., 096; Samuel L. (chldn of), 022; Samuel, 187; Sarah, 147; Thomas W., 096; Thomas, 060; Ulary, 057; Wade, 109, 185; Wade, Lt., 124, 126, 202; William B., 109; William F., 080; William H.H., 060, 188; William N., 022; William N., Mrs., 022; William, 055, 186; Willie F., 096; Wm. B., 119
WHITEHEAD: Aaron, 220; Amos, 084, 085; Arron, 022; Berry, 132;

Boy, 221; Caleb, 132, 186; Elizabeth, 022, 054, 132; Emma J., 089; George, 060, 077, 209; George, 3rd Sgt., 128; George, Lt., 210; George, Sgt., 205; Henry C., 089; Hiram R., 089; Jain, 096; Jame, 084; James T., 109; James, 185; Jane, 085; Jas., 113; Jesse, 187; Jno, 117; John P., 022, 060; John, 117, 132; Julia & 3 chldn., 085;
WHITEHEAD: Julia A., 096, 097; Julia Ann & 3 chldn., 084; Julia, 098, 100; Juliann, 089; Leutisha, 132; Lewis, 089, 187; Martha A. E., 142; Martha, 144; Mary Ann, 150; Mary, 220; Mrs., 221; Peter, 2nd Sgt., 128; Peter, Sgt., 205; Rachel, 026, 153; Ransom A., 048, 060, 109, 186; Ransom A., Cpl., 103, 117; Ranson A., 041; Rawson, 132; Reason, 022, 117, 132, 184, 220; Rebecca, 132, 141; Renchy, 167; Rezon ?, 103;
WHITEHEAD: Richard M., 186; Richard, 022, 026, 132; Richard, Mrs., 221; Richard, Sgt., 202; Rutha M., 144; Samuel, 208; Sandford, 048; Sanford, 060, 061, 132, 186; Sarah, 132, 221; Sophronia A., 089; Thomas, 032, 040; William S., 022; Williamson R., 074; Williamson, 132, 186
WHITFIELD: James, 032; Jim, 024; Joe E., 186; Louisa, 134; Nice, 134; Priscilla, 150; Robert, 186; Thomas, 022, 186; Tucker, 115, 184, 209, 210
WHITING: Benjamin C., 022; Dicey, 097
WHITLAW: John, 081; Mary Ann, 183
WHITLOW: Archibald B., 188; Green, 077; Jesse, 186; John J., 111; John, 051, 060, 079; Martha, 177; Nancy, 179; Warren, 051; William A., 188; William, 186
WHITMAN: Elizabeth, 181; Inman, 205; Jno. W., 119; John W., 109; N.C., 113; Nathan W., 057, 114, 186, 208, 210; Nathan, 208; Nathaniel W., 121; Nathaniel, 112, 121
WHITMON: M. D., Mrs., 090
WHITMORE: Robert C., 060
WHITNER: John C., 187
WHITTAMORE: Thos.,086
WHITTAN: John, 043
WHITTEN: Elizabeth, 157; Inman, 208; John, 115; Lucinda H., 164; Robert, 185; Sophia, 158; William, 130, 208; Wm., 118
WHITTENDON: Clavin, 045
WHITTER: James, 046
WHITTING: Mary, 084
WHITTON: Cassinda, 162; Eliza, 153; Elizabeth, 022; Frances, 182; George, 186; Inman, 114, 121, 128, 185; James, 022; John (chldn of), 022; John, 022, 054; John, Sr., 022; Mary Ann, 162; Millison, 171; Robert, 110, 119; William, 022, 109, 114, 185, 205, 209; Wm., 113, 128
WIDE: Patterson, Sgt., 206
WIER (ERIN?): Hinchy, 206
WIER: Isaac, 203; John N., 075; John, Sr., 022; Lousa, 167; Nathan Hoyt, 022; Robert W., 187; Samuel, 022, 061, 184; Sarah J., 022; William C., 022
WIGGINS: Elizabeth, 179; Frances, 156; Greene, 186; Henry D., 187; John, 109, 211; Mariah, 162; Sanders, 109; Sgt., 117; Wildey, 177
WIGINS: Wm. W., 103
WIGLEY: Jane Camelia, 142
WILBANKS: Stephen, 187
WILBERN: Wm. J., 2nd Lt., 127
WILBORN: Wm. J., Lt., 205
WILBORNE: William, Lt., 206
WILBOURN: William, 107
WILBUN: Wm. J., 185
WILBURN: --, 056; Abner, 061; Wm. J., 206; Wm.J., 2nd Lt.,125, 126
WILEY: L. M., 061; Leroy M., 061; Osborne, 111; Thomas H.S., 188
WILHITE: John R., 061; John, 061; Meshack, 061; Phillip, 061
WILKERSON: Calvin, Cpl., 206; Daniel, 061; Elizabeth, 186; Isaac, 022; Rachel, 156; Richard L., 185; Robert B., 031; Sarah, 145
WILKES: Mary, 135; Samuel, 186
WILKESON: Elijah, 184
WILKEY: Job, 185
WILKINS: Fredric, 132; James C., 045; James, 124, 125, 185, 205; Job, 124, 128, 185, 211; John, 124, 125, 185, 205; Jole, 205; Joseph C., 034, 186; Mary, 158; Mrs., 132; Robert, 185; Robert, Cpl., 206; Susanna, 132; Thomas, 107; William, 061, 107, 112, 123; William, Lt., 109
WILKINSON: Calvin, Cpl., 207; James, 055; Robert B., 049, 050
WILL: Waine, 071
WILLBORN: William, 188
WILLCOXON: Samuel J., 022
WILLEBY: David, 202; Robert, Sgt., 203; Salley, 157; Thomas, Sgt., 203
WILLES: Randoiph, 073
WILLEY: Charles, 123
WILLIAM: Clark P., 186; Mrs., 134; Peggy, 134; William, 134
WILLIAMS: --, 061; A., Mrs., 090; Albert, 061; Alfred W., 082; Ann J., 022; Ann, 093, 158; Austin, 022; Benjamin, 087, 185; Benjamin, Capt., 202, 203; Briant, 134; Bryant, 115, 211; Bryant, Sgt. 210; Burdy O., 187; Christina, Mrs., 071; Clarissa, 080, 096, 102; Clark T., 033; Clarke T., Ens., 120; Dawson, 032, 187; Ebenezer, 033, 061; Edward, 033, 056, 061, 186; Elen P., 147; Elisabeth, 093;
WILLIAMS: Elizabeth S., 162; Elizabeth, 090, 099; Emeline, 093, 099; Eph., 096; Family, 198; Frances E., 083; Francina, 100; G., 099; Geo W., 092; George (chldn of), 022; George K., 188; George W., 061; George, 061, 062, 072, 074, 075, 088, 186; Harriett, 090, 093; Henry F., 092; Henry, 215; Hester Ann, 101; Isaac, 061; Jacob, 039; James M., 074; James, 022, 039, 090, 122, 186; James, 2nd Cpl., 127; James, 2nd Sgt., 127;
WILLIAMS: James, Cpl., 210; Jane, 022, 061, 161, 172; Jas. D., 094; Joe (chldn of), 022; Joel, 022, 025, 059, 185; John A.C., 186; John A., 061; John T., 186; John, 022, 049, 061, 134; John, Cpl., 210; John, Lt., 201-202; John, Sr., 022, 072, 075; Joseph T., 187; Lady J., 092; Laura, 032, 099; Leana, 170; Lewelling, 061; Lewis, 022; Lida J., 187; Lilly A., 166; Malida, 093; Malita, 099;
WILLIAMS: Margaret A., 174; Martha, 148; Mary E., 092; Mary M., 159; Mary, 022, 088, 186; Matilda, 092; Midleton M., 187; Milly, 093, 099; Narcisa, 147; Narcissa, 170; Nathan C., 185; Nathaniel, 042, 061; Paul, 061; Pressey, 154; R.C., 080; R.S., 186; Rebecca M., 096; Rebecca, 132; Robert G. (chldn of), 022; Robert L., 061; Robert T., 187; Robert, 184; Salley, 132; Sarah A., 097; Sarah, 096, 100, 147, 176; Scepio, 095;
WILLIAMS: Scip, 084, 086, 095; Selina Ann, 155; Simen, 096; Sims, 061; Stephen, 113, 116, 206; Steven, 206; Sutton, 061; Tabitha J., 175; Temple C., 061; Thomas A., 184; Thomas, 061; Timothy, 067, 132, 204, 208, 209; Timothy, Ens., 210; Timothy, Sgt., 203; Virginia, 087; Wesley, 110; Wiley, 022; William D., 025; William Leonidas, 022; William, 022, 061, 082, 182, 186, 188, 214; William, Capt., 111; Winney F., 159; Wm., 071; Zachariah, 061
WILLIAMSON: Andrew J., 187; Ann E., 022; Charles, 061; Emma, 077; James C., 187; John D., 081; Micajah, 079; Micajah, 3rd Sgt. 127; Micajah, Sgt., 202; Mr., 184; Peter, 025, 029, 054; Petter, 184; Thomas E., 073, 074, 076; Thomas S., 187; Thomas, Sgt. 205; Thos. E., 074; Thos., 3rd Sgt. 127; William, 028, 077, 121; Wm., 112, 113
WILLIBEY: David, Ens., 127
WILLIBY: David, Ens., 202; Elizabeth, 174, 186; Ellis, 108, 109, 186; Mary, 164; Polly, 163, 174; Robert, 185
WILLICH: Ernest C., 061
WILLIMAN: Gold S., 061
WILLINGHAM: Henderson, 022, 051, 061; Malinda, 153
WILLIS: Banjamin, 061
WILLOUGHBE: Thomas, 184
WILLOUGHBEY: David, 074
WILLOUGHBY: Ann, 173; David, 061; David, Ens., 124; Elijah, 022; Elizabeth, 157; Ellis (chldn of), 022; James M., 081, 186; Martha, 173; Mary, 164; Robert, 022; Sarah, 098, 100, 164; William B., 022; William D., 022; William R. (chldn of), 022; William R., 022; Wm. R., Mrs., (2 orphs.), 094
WILLS: Benjamin, 061, 202; Edward, 022; Elizabeth, 071; Jacob V., 061; Mastin, 120; Randolph, 074, 120; Thomas, 119; Thomas, Capt., 210; Thos., 2nd Sgt., 127
WILLSON: Margarett, Mrs., 071; Martha E., 151; Mary A., 177; Mary Ann E., 180; Westly W., 187
WILOBY: David, 209
WILSEY: Charles, 112
WILSON: --, 060; Albert, 134; Ann, 083; Benjamin, 117; Charles, 185; Debby, 156; Elizabeth J., 164; Elizabeth, 160; Francis, 097; Isabella, 143; J.F., 061; J.R., 187; J.S., 022; James C., 046, 187, 188; James F., 061, 080; James P., 188; James W., 187; James, 036, 134, 209, 210; James, Lt., 210; James, Sgt., 203; Jas., 097; Jesse M., 186; John, 209, 210; John, Cpl., 207;
WILSON: John, Lt., 210; John, Sgt. 205; Lucinda, 174; Martha S., 080; Milton, 134; Moses M., 187; Moses, 036, 073; Nancy, 134; Patsey, 182; Polly, 160; R.S., 061; Richard J., 081; Richard, 022, 047, 134, 208; Richard, Sgt. 210; Richry, 074; Robert C., 022, 074, 075; Robert C., Capt., 110; Sally, 134; Sarah, 143; Silas A., 188; Wesley W., 098; William, 061, 081; Wm. W., 187
WIMBERLY: John, 187
WIMPHEY: Virginia, 094; Walter, 094
WINDSWORTH: Archibald H., 036
WINFHRY: Robert, 091; Sally, 091; Wesly, 091

WINFIELD: Armanda L., 175; Joel, 034, 041, 043, 045, 046, 054, 056, 204; Joel, Lt., 203, 204
WINFREY: Rebun, Sgt., 125; Reuben, Sgt., 205; Reubun, Sgt., 125; Rulew, 4th Sgt., 127
WINGFIELD: Augustin S., 061; Joel, Lt., 126; John, 061, 062; Marcellus A., 061, 062; Marcellus, 062; S. B., 197
WINN: C. J., Mrs., 101; Charles J., 067, 186, 187; David H., 067, 081; Elizabeth M., 179; Henry F., 081; Hinchey, 030, 079, 120, 206; Hinchley, 217; Isaac, 203; Samuel, 203; Susan, 101
WINSTEAD: Elizabeth P., 148; Minerva J., 180; Sarah, 062
WINSTED: Sarah, 213
WINSTON: Joseph B., 027, 049; Joseph, 040; Thomas, 062
WINTER: Henry A., 022; John G., 024; John, 044; Mary Carter, 198
WISDOM: Jesey, 029; Jesse, 029
WISE: Abijah, 185; Elmira, 186; Henry, 187; Jacob E., Capt., 110, 119; Jacob E., Lt., 110; James, 220; Joseph, 187; Louisa, 145; Mary Ann, 158; Mary E., 080; Mary, 220; Melinda, 219; Patterson, 022; Patterson, 1st Sgt., 125; Patterson, Sgt., 205; Rutha, 185; Sarah Ann, 153; Sherwood, 097, 187; Walden, 022; Walden, Lt., 117; Wayne, 185; Wayne, Capt., 110; Wayne, Lt., 117; Williamson P., 022
WITHERFORD: Emily & 4 chldn, 083
WITHERSPOON: Cicero N., 032; Cicero V., 022; Elizabeth, 022, 032; James A.,022; Robert L., 022
WITTER: James, 032, 038, 048, 053, 061, 062
WITTON(?): James, 115
WODDAIL: John C., 034; John G., 188; Thomas, 034
WOFFORD: John B., Capt., 118
WOLBRIGHT: Jacob, 048
WOLFE: Christopher, 062
WOLHOL: Adolso, 213
WOMACK: John W., 109, 211
WOMERLERLING: A. D., 097
WOOD: --, 062; Abner, 188; Ann, 168; C., Ens., 201; Cary, Ens., 129; Delila, 147; Elias, 062; Elisha, Ens., 202; Elizabeth, 086, 154; Elizer, 062; Elizur, 062; Faith, 022; Frances, 167; Henry L., 074; J.L., 072; Jno., 114; John L., 038, 048, 056, 071-075, 077, 080; John W., 187; John, 050, 062, 072, 074, 082, 094, 101, 111-114, 122, 123, 185, 186, 188, 207-209; Jones, 062; Lucinda, 179; Lucy Jane, 159; Lucy, 136, 154; Marrit, 114;
WOOD: Martha, 147; Mary, & 4 chldn., 087; Mary, 086, 099, 085; Merit, 208; Merret, 114; Merrit, 055, 185, 209, 210; Merritt, 185; Mertis Ann, 177; Nancy, 141; Oliver, 038; Oreen, 062; Owen, 109, 158; Owen, 1st Lt., 111; Owen, Lt., 117; Parmelia, 136; Polley, 177; Pucket(t), 041, 185, 208; Puckett, Lt., 210; Richard, 022; Sarah Ann, 151; Sidney Ann, 142; Tabitha, 030, 062, 144, 214; Thomas B., 080; Thomas, 030, 037, 038, 045, 047, 066, 109; Thomas, Jr., 025, 185; Thomas, Sr., 055, 072; Wiley, 187; William B., 036, 186; William P., 022; William, 022, 038, 056, 074, 112, 123, 184, 186, 187; Wm., 075
WOODDARD: Caleb, 059
WOODIS: Cary, 101; Wm. A., 187
WOODLEY: Agustus, 022; Littleberry, 208; Littlebury, 114; Phelep, 130; Philip, 113; Phillip, 119, 206; Phillip, 1st Sgt., 127; William, 114, 208
WOODLIFF: George, 062; Phil, Sgt., 205; Phillip, 206
WOODLY: Phillip, 205; Phillip, Sgt., 126
WOODROUGH: William B., 062
WOODS: B. F. (chldn. of), 022; Elizabeth, 160; James R., 187; Josiah, 022; Middleton, 062; Oliver P., 022; Oreen, 062; S. F., 022; Sarah C., 022
WOODSON: Alexander, 022, 080; Ann Eliza, 080
WOODWARD: John Hartwell, 198
WOOLBRIGHT: Jacob, 058; Jacob, Cpl., 210
WOOLDRIDGE: --, 062; A.D., 186; Caroline Pamelia, 177; Isma W., 026, 033, 035, 036, 038-040, 045, 049, 051, 053, 055, 060, 062, 118, 119, 185; Isma, 066, 067; J.W., 071; Susan J.H., 186
WOOLRIDGE: --, 062; Isma W., 025, 029
WOOTEM: Lemuel, 216; Bartley, 046; Gilly, 046; John, 042, 112; Unisey, 174
WOOTON: Nancy, 185
WOOTTEN: Bartley, 214, 215
WORD: Samuel, 053; T. J., 033
WORRILL: Ransom, 062
WORSHAM: Thomas, Lt., 202
WORTHA: Thomas, Lt., 112
WORTHAM: ?--, 201; Alethia, 168; Notle, 187; Susan, 166; Thomas, 185; Thomas, Lt., 126, 202; William, 062; Zachariah T., Ens., 206, 207; Zachariah T., 205; Zachariah, Ens., 121, 125, 127, 130; Zachariah, Ens., 203-205
WORTHARM: William, 111
WOZENCRAFT: Harriett N., 187; James L., 051; Thomas, 022, 032, 041, 053; William J., 041; William T., 188
WOZENCROFT: James L., 074; Thomas, 058, 059; W. F., 074
WRAY: Frankey, 084, 095; Frankie, 085; Phillip, 062; Thomas, 022; William T., 080
WRIGHT: A. W., 185; Albert, 062; Alfred W., 022; Benjamin, 062; Biddy, 178; C. K., Mrs., 090; Capt., 132; E., Mrs., 091; Elisabeth, 093; James A., 044, 047, 052; James, 072, 204, 210, 211; James, Capt., 124, 127, 202, 203; Jas., 204; Jehu L., 208; Jett T., 188; Jett, 209; Jno. L., 113, 114, 116; John B., 208; John C., 032, 037, 048, 050, 053, 055, 058, 059;
WRIGHT: John C., Sgt. 210; John G., 022; John L., 025, 034, 037, 044, 052, 057, 058, 067, 072, 109, 112, 121, 122, 130, 203, 205, 211; John L., Capt., 123, 126, 129, 201; John L., Lt., 129 201; John, 056, 186; John, Sr., 022; Malissa, 162; Matilda, 178; Moses T., 072; Richard, 043; Robert T., 188; Thomas A., 026, 034, 037, 038, 052, 060, 206, 210; Thomas A., Capt., 210; Thomas A., Lt., 205, 207; Thomas R., 037;
WRIGHT: Thomas S., 043; Thos. A., 052, 211; Thos. G., Capt., 110; W. J., Capt., 120; William G., 031, 036, 040, 050, 072, 112, 121, 128-130, 186, 201, 203, 205, 206; William G., 2nd Sgt., 125; William, 022, 035, 043, 046, 053, 056, 058, 060, 062, 063, 184-186, 204, 208; William, Ens., 202; William, Lt., 117; William, Sr., 060; Winfield (?) J. M., 071; Winfield J., 022, 033, 207, 208; Winfried J., Capt., 210; Wingfield Jett, 033; Wm. G., 112, 113, 114, 117, 208; Wm. J., 113; Wm., 204; Wm., Sgt., 206
WWITHERSPOON: Isaac, 040
WYATT: Edmund, 063; Nathaniel, 063
WYLEY: James R., 063
WYLLIE: Hugh, 063
WYNN: A. M., Rev., 146
YANCEY: Benj. C., Capt., 110; Goodloe H., 028, 034; Goodloe Harper, 198; Lucy D., 022; Lucy Grattan, 022; Sarah P., 022
YANCY: Goodbee H.L., 055; Goodloe H. (chldn. of), 022
YARBOROUGH: Jno., Mrs., 084; Job, 031; John, 022, 029, 030, 037, 045, 046; Lannie Allie, 022; Nancy, 157; Thomas H., 030, 031; William, 036, 063; Wm., Sgt., 129
YARBROUGH: John, 039, 041, 042; Thomas H., 030; William, 046, 048
YATES: James, 3rd Sgt., 125; John, Sgt., 203; Mathew, 079; William, 022; Wm., 2nd Cpl., 127; Wm., Cpl., 205
YEARBORO: William, 220
YEARBY: Berell, 123; Burrel, 112; Burril, 111; Eliza Ann, 165; Laticia, 148; William, 073
YEARLY: Everett, 072
YEARNEST: Sarah, 148
YERBEY: E., 072; Everett, 073
YERBY: Burrel, Mrs., 090; Burwell, 022; Everett (chldn. of), 022; Everett, 022; Frances A., 187; Mary J., 022; Mary Ophellz, 022; Sarah H., 022
YERLY: S. H., Mrs., 090
YOAKIN: Washington C., 034
YORKUM: Washington C., 031
YOUNG: Agnes, 022; Benjamin, 028, 045, 052, 057; Daniel, 022; Gresham, 042; J.D., Mrs., 100; Jane D., 022 099; Martha Jane, 150; Ophelia, 022; Rebeckah, 186; Sanford W., 063; Thomas H., 022 073; Washington, 112
YOUNGBLOOD: John W., 022
YOUNGKIN: E. H., 022; Jesse (chldn. of), 022
ZACKRY: Clemencha R., 063
ZEBENNE: Joseph B., 034; Joseph D., 034
ZUBER: Abraham, 063
ZWOLL: Francis, 046

www.ingramcontent.com/pod-product-compliance
Lightning Source LLC
Chambersburg PA
CBHW021140030426
R18078200001B/R180782PG42334CBX00004B/7
9780893084851